SUGAR & RAILROADS

Oscar Zanetti
Alejandro García

SUGAR & RAILROADS

A CUBAN HISTORY, 1837–1959

Translated by
Franklin W. Knight
& Mary Todd

THE UNIVERSITY OF NORTH CAROLINA PRESS

Chapel Hill and London

Originally published as *Caminos para el Azúcar* by Editorial de
Ciencias Sociales, 1987
© 1987 Oscar Zanetti and Alejandro García

The translation and publication of this book were made possible
through a generous grant from The Andrew W. Mellon
Foundation to the Association of Caribbean Historians and the
Johns Hopkins University.

Designed by Heidi Perov
Set in Electra with Compacta Display
by Keystone Typesetting, Inc.
Manufactured in the United States of America

Library of Congress Cataloging-in-Publication Data
Zanetti Lecuona, Oscar, 1946–
    [Caminos para el azúcar. English]
    Sugar and railroads : a Cuban history, 1837–1959 / by Oscar
Zanetti and Alejandro García; translated by Franklin W. Knight
and Mary Todd.
        p. cm.
    Includes bibliographical references (p.   ) and index.
ISBN 0-8078-2385-6 (cloth: alk. paper)
ISBN 0-8078-4692-9 (pbk.: alk. paper)
    Railroads—Cuba—History. I. García Alvarez, Alejandro.
II. Title.
HE2868.Z3613   1998
385'.097291—dc21   97-40299
                                                    CIP

02 01 00 99 98   5 4 3 2 1

Contents

Tables

Figures and Maps

Illustrations

Foreword

The Association of Caribbean Historians is delighted to welcome this English translation of the important work by Oscar Zanetti and Alejandro García, *Caminos para el azúcar*. This book was awarded the Elsa Goveia Book Prize by the Association in 1989, as the best work on Caribbean history published between 1986 and 1989. Up to now, however, it has been very hard to obtain outside Cuba; and language barriers made it even more inaccessible for those unable to read Spanish. This English version will, for the first time, allow scholars and general readers access to an original and significant contribution to Caribbean, and Cuban, history.

The Association is deeply grateful to the Andrew W. Mellon Foundation for its generous grant, which supported the initial phase of the project to publish English translations of those Elsa Goveia Prize–winning books not originally published in that language. We are also very grateful to our long-standing and very active member, Professor Franklin W. Knight of the Johns Hopkins University, who initiated the project, and saw it through to the publication of the present edition, as well as contributing an introduction. The University of North Carolina Press deserves our thanks, too, for undertaking the publication of the translation.

The Association looks forward to more translations of Elsa Goveia Prize–winning books appearing in the future. In particular, an English translation of the 1992 (joint) winner, G. A. Baralt's *La Buena Vista*, has already been completed. This translation and publication project, in fact, can only further the aims of the Association of Caribbean Historians and help to break down the linguistic and other barriers between those of us who research and study the history of the Caribbean.

Bridget Brereton
President, Association of
Caribbean Historians
April 1998

Introduction

Once in a while a remarkable book appears in the historical literature of the Caribbean that demands international scholarly attention, and even strongly resonates beyond the region, as well as across time. These books are not simply brilliant confirmations of the historian's craft. They are, by any reasonable measure, exceptional intellectual productions. They mark a clear turning point in local perception and local consciousness, an unmistakable break with the past. Caribbean historiography has a number of these brilliant contributions.

C. L. R. James's *Black Jacobins*, first published in 1938, was one such book. Eric Williams's *Capitalism and Slavery*, published in 1944, was another. Manuel Moreno Fraginals's *El ingenio*—first published in 1964 but only widely recognized after a second edition came out in 1978—certainly falls within that distinguished group. Elsa Goveia's *Slave Society in the British Leeward Islands at the End of the Eighteenth Century*, a clear trendsetter, appeared in 1965. And B. W. Higman's *Slave Population and Economy in Jamaica, 1807–1834* came out in 1976 and has been agitating the discipline since then.

These extraordinary books have many commendable qualities in common. They are all brilliantly researched, elegantly written, passionately argued, and address important issues that reach down to the very bedrock of the Caribbean historical experience. They deal, each in its individual way, with the basic experience of slavery and the sugar plantation society. That is more than a coincidence, of course. The issues they address, whether at a local, specific, or regional plane move beyond the parochial and narrowly defined to reach toward the global significance of the event or the experience. Their themes as well as their audiences are therefore universal. They are all books of monumental wisdom and profound insight.

For this reason, and many others, these books are not merely publications of a given year, or a particular decade. They are books for all time, for the ages. Their intellectual value increases as they stimulate the field, forcing all other scholars to rethink conventional positions, rephrase the accustomed questions, and revise the inherited wisdoms. They not only reflect the enormous intellectual vitality of the historical tradition in the Caribbean, but they advance it in all sorts of subtle ways.

These books have come along, at the surprisingly rapid rate of about one every decade. Given the limited intellectual constituency and challenging academic conditions of the Caribbean, this is truly an amazing rate of production of works of such singular distinction. If *The Black Jacobins* was the work of the 1930s, *Capitalism and Slavery* that of the 1940s, *Slave Society in the British Leeward Islands* of the 1960s, and *El ingenio* and *Slave Population and Economy* of the 1970s, then there can be little doubt that *Caminos para el azúcar* by Oscar Zanetti and Alejandro García was *the* publication of the 1980s, and its appearance in English as *Sugar and Railroads: A Cuban History, 1837–1959* constitutes a welcome introduction to a deserving wider audience.

This book is a wonderfully stimulating study: enormously rich in archival sources; sensitively insightful of the seamless links between Cuba and the wider world; brilliantly graphical in its portrayal of the complex interrelationship between social, political, economic, and technological transformations; and majestically sweeping in its scope. Yet it is written with such superb clarity and commendable skill that it is readily accessible to the average reader.

Sugar and Railroads is both a simple and a complicated history. At one level it is the detailed reconstruction of the history of the introduction, establishment, and expansion of the railroad system in Cuba, beginning in 1837 and continuing—in a conclusion—to the contemporary period. All the esoterically technical and general economic information on capital accumulation, technical construction, and geographical routing of the railroads is narrated here—more than enough to satisfy the most fastidious railroad buff. The initial expansion of the late 1830s and 1840s, at an annual rate of approximately fifty kilometers of new track per year, accompanied some profound technical and physical changes of the Cuban sugar estate as the island attained the position of premier cane-sugar producer in the world. The introduction of this new technology revealed not only an index of Cuban economic importance—the first railroads were financed from local sources— but also an index of a new intellectual attitude by the Cuban elites. By the 1850s this first phase of railroad construction (and the third sugar revolution in Cuba) had been accomplished. The pace of new construction slowed considerably. The nature of railroad incorporation and construction also changed.

The importance of this technological development lies not merely in the fact that Cuba was the first sate in the Americas after the United States to adopt the then modern technological system of steam-powered railroads—and the third anywhere in the world—but, as the authors admit in their opening pages, "in contrast to those other countries, the railroad was not developed in Cuba in order to satisfy and stimulate the demands of an internal market but to facilitate the bonds between local producers and their external markets."

An inescapable observation stems from the profound economic ramifications of the railroad. At their simplest, the railroads telescoped the distance between factory and port, reducing dramatically transportation costs and enormously increasing productivity. But the railroads also altered irrevocably the physical nature of production, rupturing the physical concept of the sugar estate, destroying the conventional geographical limits as it progressively eroded what Geoffrey Blainey has called "the tyranny of distance," and eventually leading to the effective separation of agricultural and industrial processes in the production of sugar.[1] The railroads, Zanetti and García convincingly illustrate, were highly instrumental in the establishment of the central sugar *factory*, called in Spanish *La Central*. Without railroads the separation of the agricultural and industrial aspects of this complex agro-manufacturing process would have been quite difficult, and economies of scale could not have been realized at that time.

Another important aspect of the study lies in the unforeseen, complex implications for the work force, for the significance of work, and for the complicated social and labor relations throughout the island as a result of the introduction of a mechanism that was initially viewed simply as a convenient device for breaking a bothersome transportation bottleneck. The railroads became a metaphor for economic development, for industrial progress, and for technological modernity. Yet, the authors contend, the history of the railroads, despite the achievement of linking the island more effectively than the earlier road or water transport systems, provided a clear case of form divorced from function.

Railroads made Cuba neither modern nor developed. Introduced primarily for the sugar interests and the plantations, they served those interests initially irrespective of the general welfare. Railroads facilitated the penetration of the island by foreign capitalists, and reinforced Cuban dependence on sugar, on the plantation, and on the international capitalist economy. Not surprising, the railroads mirrored wider developments in the society: the monopolist behavior of capitalists, the exploitative tendency of employers, and the long-suffering exploitation of laborers. Railroad workers in Cuba were in the forefront of political activity, forming some of the earliest unions to agitate for improved working conditions for all workers. Cuban railroad workers—like the functionaries of the new Cuban state of the twentieth century—were subordinate to an external power that dictated domestic political and economic matters.

Cuban railroads were a conduit for the accumulation of private, often foreign, wealth, and even the attempts to impose Cuban control over them was a long struggle that ended more in greater appearance than greater substance. The "Cubanization" of the railroads—that is, the subordination of the railroads to the priorities of the Cuban state and the Cuban people—did not become a reality until the success of the Cuban Revolution in 1959.

Sugar and Railroads uses the study of one basic organizational structure in the society—the railroads—to explore wider issues that have made Cuban society, culture, and politics what they are today. This study is replete with intelligently provocative observations about individuals, groups, and historical circumstances. But, more important, it raises some important questions about economic development and social change in the Caribbean, and especially in Cuba.

In most Caribbean societies, railroads did not perform an important function, either economically or technically. The Cuban case study, therefore, would seem to have little comparative relevance. Yet this is not so. The history of the railroads is more than the history of a single institution, of a lonesome technical innovation. It is the history of the struggle of a people to achieve their own concept of dignity, respect, and self-awareness. It is a history of the struggle to be fully free, and the difficult constraints of the pervasive legacy of slavery and the indelible plantation socioeconomic structure. Because the history of these Cuban railroads is in large measure the history of the Cuban people, it is also, in part, the history of the Caribbean people. With or without railroads, the forces of external constraint have been common, and the sad social and economic neglects all too familiar and all too frequent throughout the region. Therein lies the wider significance of *Sugar and Railroads*. The railroad is, in many ways, a melancholy metaphor for Caribbean life and times.

Franklin W. Knight
Johns Hopkins University

Preface

Cuba was the seventh country in the world to have railroad transportation, but, for a long time, it lacked a history of its railroads. Except for small monographs and some articles, most of which were on the introduction of railroads in the island in the mid-nineteenth century, very little was published about the development of that means of transportation of such crucial importance in the evolution of the Cuban economy.

That historiographical gap was even more lamentable because, since railroads were one of the oldest organized services in Cuba, the study of their development could contribute considerable information, not only in the field of economic history but also on various sociopolitical processes. The history of the railroads was closely linked to the development of capitalism in Cuba. Through its vicissitudes, some of the specific characteristics and most important problems of that historic phenomenon could be known.

In the interest of filling that vacuum, the Escuela de Historia (School of History—now a part of the Facultad de Filosofía e Historia [Faculty of Philosophy and History]) of the Universidad de La Habana (University of Havana) presented the Ferrocarriles de Cuba (Cuban Railroads) company of the Ministerio del Transporte (Ministry of Transportation) with a research project, which, while solving an important scientific problem, would also meet some of its needs. The agreement then reached laid the bases for this history of Cuban railroads.

The Problem and the Hypotheses

But, what kind of a history? Railroad histories cover a broad range, running from purely descriptive monographs to profound, detailed analyses of the railroad companies' functioning or of the general economic effects of railroad transportation. The absence of any precedents in Cuba—not only of a general history of the railroads but even of historical monographs about the companies—meant that any study of Cuba's railroads would, necessarily, have to be descriptive. But Cuba's railroads, which lacked a history for so long, constitute too complex a phenomenon to be adequately reflected in a mere chronicle. Limiting our history to that sphere would have failed to reflect the full purpose of the research and the development achieved by historical studies in Cuba.

Up to a point, railroad history is the history of a technology, but because of its implications and content, it goes far beyond the technological sphere. As Marx commented in a note to chapter 15 of the first volume of *Capital*, "Technology discloses man's mode of dealing with Nature, the process of production by which he sustains his life, and thereby also lays bare the mode of formation of his social relations, and of the mental conceptions that flow from them." To constrain our analysis to the railroads' technical-economic evolution would mean running the risk of only half understanding that vast historical phenomenon.

The problem should be stated in broader terms, which could capture its full scientific meaning. This was doubly important in the case of Cuba's railroads. Cuba was the first of what are now called the "underdeveloped" countries to use railroads, even before some of the countries that are now developed. The Cuban case thus offered an exceptional opportunity for analyzing railroad technology— which many have considered the revolutionary technological means par excellence of the nineteenth century—in conditions very different from those in which it has generally been studied. This circumstance is very important, for it has been drummed into us that the technological factor, alone, can introduce substantial changes in the life of society. Examined from that perspective, the experience of Cuba's railroads should present very eloquent testimony about the real possibilities of technology and the dialectical relationship between technology and the social conditions for its utilization.

On tackling the history of Cuba's railroads with an all-encompassing approach, we considered it necessary to take up the following aspects.

FACTORS DETERMINING THE USE OF THE RAILROADS

The economic needs that the railroads had to meet—which determined both their early introduction and the later extension of their use—constitute an essential aspect of the historical phenomenon of the railroads. Unlike the railroads in other countries, those in Cuba were developed to promote links between producers on the island and their foreign markets, rather than to meet the needs of a domestic market and stimulate its growth.

Within the framework of Cuba's single-export economy, the use of railroads was determined by the needs of its main—practically only—export product: sugar. The relations between sugar production and the railroads are so close and evident that it would be puerile to make any hypotheses about them. Rather than merely establish the sugar sector's determining role in the evolution of railroad transportation, we would seek to weigh the intensity of that determination and analyze the specific forms it took. In that sphere, it was possible to proffer a hypothesis: the influence of the sugar industry on the railroads was so intensive and absorbing that it minimized and invalidated practically every other incentive to their development, which in some circumstances resulted in the underutilization of their possibilities.

Because economic needs are historically expressed through the interests of classes and social groups, our examination of the factors that determined the utilization of the railroads could only acquire a concrete dimension by defining and analyzing those who promoted railroad development, whose interests took the form of a certain use of that means of transportation. Cuba's railroad history was of particular interest in this regard, because the initiative and control within the railroad sector, which initially corresponded to the same local interests that promoted the growth of the sugar industry, changed as the mode of capitalist production evolved toward its imperialist phase and ended up in the hands of foreign capital.

CHARACTERISTICS OF THE DEVELOPMENT AND FUNCTIONING OF THE RAILROADS

This aspect sums up the descriptive elements that occupied a large part of the investigation, but it would consist of more than simply tracing the evolution of railroad growth and the railroad companies' economic situation and organizational trends. It also involved defining the functional model that Cuba's railroads adopted and its implications for the economies of the companies in the sector. As part of that issue, we should examine the relations between railroad growth and the economic situation, the technological evolution of the railroads, government regulations governing the functioning of railroad service, and other matters that constitute most of the factual basis of every railroad history.

THE ECONOMIC EFFECTS OF THE RAILROADS

The impact that railroad transportation had on the economy is of vital importance for establishing the effective historical meaning of that means of transportation. Most of the considerations that are presented concerning that problem turn on two main issues: the importance of the reduction of transportation costs brought about by the greater productivity of railroads, and the repercussions that the development of the railroads had on other sectors of the economy.

For a long time—and in a nearly axiomatic way—the railroads have been assigned a quasi-magical role in promoting economic progress. Now, however, historical works on the subject seem to have come to a turning point, and a trend to establish more precise criteria in this sphere has developed. Much of that effort has been concentrated on drawing up analytical categories for estimating the amount of the savings in resources that the railroads brought to those societies using them, so as to determine the importance of those savings, relating them to some macroeconomic indexes.

Without ignoring the positive aspects of that effort in terms of the creation of a more precise tool of analysis, we must point to its unilateral nature, which has limited the scope of such investigations. The "original sin" of those studies has been that they reduce the complex, many-sided phenomenon of economic development to the growth rate of certain indexes, such as the gross national product or per capita income.

Any historical assessment of the economic effects of the railroads, therefore, requires a clear definition of the concept of development, one that cannot be restricted to the behavior of certain indexes—which more properly is called "growth." Even though development encompasses that phenomenon, its contents are much richer and include such important aspects as the degree to which a country makes rational use of its natural and human resources and the effects that economic activities have on the people's standard of living. Therefore, it is at least as important to know the "social use" saved resources as it is to determine the magnitude of the "social savings" provided by the railroads. This aspect of social use is conditioned by the class relations of the society in question and by the characteristics of its economic structure.

Viewed from this perspective, the economic effects of the railroads would reveal all their wealth and complexity. We assessed the specific use made of railroad transportation in Cuba, not just its abstract economic impact. We began our analysis with the reduction of transportation costs that stemmed from the use of the railroads, computing its importance not only in general terms but also by productive sector. Thus, we determined how the benefits of the railroads were distributed and what consequences this had for the country's productive structure. The hypothesis we tried to confirm on this point was that the sugar sector constituted the main beneficiary of the railroads, for its comparative profitability was further increased by the new means of transportation, a circumstance that favored the development of a single-crop economy.

The railroads' repercussions should also be examined in terms of the collateral activities that their functioning promoted. Some authors call this aspect the "links" or the "multiplying effect" of railroad investments, which is so overvalued in other regions, where railroads are considered to be veritable promoters of the development of the iron and steel industry and other branches of the economy. In Cuba, because most of the inputs and railroad equipment were imported, it may be supposed that those repercussions were of very little economic importance.

We should note the economic effects that railroad transportation had in other spheres. For example, new regions of the country were incorporated in production thanks to railroad communication. This helped to explain the effect the railroads had on the country's production dynamics and on the regional distribution of economic activity. Likewise, the role of railroad transportation in mobilizing the work force, settling the country, and developing urban centers should also be considered. Along with these key aspects, we should not ignore others, such as the railroads' influence on the evolution of agrarian ownership and their contribution to the development of business forms, which are also part of the generic definition of economic effects.

SOCIAL ASPECTS OF RAILROAD HISTORY

The history of the railroads developed within a framework of specific social relations, and reference to them is indispensable for understanding some key aspects of that process. That need became obvious when we outlined the first aspect to be considered in the railroad sphere, noting the importance of studying the interests that promoted the railroads and imposed a certain operational model on them. But also, from the social point of view, the basic characteristics of the structure of society, with all of its contradictions and conflicts, were reproduced on a given scale in the human collective linked to the railroads, making the railroad sector an active theater of the class struggle. No railroad history would be complete if it ignored that decisive aspect of the problem.

The social history of the railroads is, in essence, the history of the thousands of men who built and operated that system of transportation. The railroad workers also constituted one of the oldest, most militant, and best-organized sectors of the Cuban proletariat. In this investigation, we analyzed them in two regards: first, as the basic factor in the history of the railroads and, second, as an integral part of the Cuban labor movement. In spite of the specific nature of the labor problem, it is preferable from all points of view to examine it in close relation with the evolution of the railroads. In that framework, the dialectics of the class struggle become more clear, bringing out the play of action and reaction between the business interests and proletarian activity.

The Sources

The relative centralization of railroad transportation and the continuity of its organizational forms helped to preserve the extensive documentation generated by Cuba's railroads throughout their history. Though not exempt from the destructive effects of time, the historical sources on the railroads have come down to the present in an acceptable state of preservation and, in some cases, with a degree of organization seldom seen in this kind of material. The process of centralization of railroad property, which led to the creation of two large monopolies, one based in Havana—Ferrocarriles Unidos—and the other, in Camagüey—Ferrocarriles Consolidados—resulted in a concentration of sources at those two points, which made the work of consultation much easier.

The Havana documentation is richer for its antiquity, since Ferrocarriles Unidos de La Habana absorbed most of the railroad companies that had been founded in the nineteenth century. Many of those documents were transferred in recent years to the Archivo Nacional de Cuba (National Archives of Cuba), where they were collected in the Fondo Ferrocarriles.

Even though the documentation was, generally speaking, well preserved, its original organization was lost and the control books were not complete, which made it almost impossible to find individual documents. As a result, we agreed with the head of the Archivo to give priority to making an inventory of the Fondo Ferrocarriles. Not only the students on the research team but also other history students took part in that task. Guided by personnel of the Archivo, they managed to inventory the nearly three thousand legajos of the Fondo in just a little over four months, making it possible to use that material.

The Fondo Ferrocarriles of the Archivo Nacional is valuable but heterogeneous. It contains the minutes of the boards of directors of a large number of railroad companies (including some in the eastern provinces), annual reports, agreements between companies, information on labor and wage aspects, accounts and other economic documentation, service contracts, reports on rates, itineraries, and an enormous amount of material on other aspects of railroad operations. Complementing that material is a small collection of legal documents, retained by Ferrocarriles de Cuba and kept in Havana's main train station. Those documents—and the materials on ownership, concessions, and certain relations with the government—were absolutely necessary for following the organizational process of the railroad companies (foundings, mergers, etc.).

In Camagüey, most of the sources are concentrated in the archives of the División Camagüey (Camagüey Division, now División Centro-Este, or Central-Eastern Division) of Ferrocarriles de Cuba. The documents, which are well preserved and admirably organized, are grouped in two basic collections: the Permanente, or active archives, and the Fondo General de Paquetería, or passive archives. Practically all of the information one could desire for a historical investigation of the railroads is grouped in those two collections, and it is only to be regretted that that wealth of material does not include the first two decades of the century, whose documentation, it seems, was largely destroyed by the railroad companies themselves.

Together with the groups of documents already noted, the payrolls and personnel records were preserved, as were some small collections corresponding to the archives of some departments of Ferrocarriles Consolidados, such as Tesorería (Treasury) and Administración (Administration). Some of the Camagüeyan railroad documents, covering the 1920–30 period, and some documents from the old Ferrocarril Puerto Príncipe a Nuevitas company were transferred to the Archivo Histórico Provincial de Camagüey (Camagüeyan Provincial Historic Archives), where they are now kept.

The public service nature of the railroad companies studied meant that there was more or less strict (depending on the era) government supervision of them, which also left a considerable trail of documents. The oldest of those papers are in the Fondos of the Archivo Nacional corresponding to the agencies of the colonial administration which, in one way or another, handled railroad matters, especially the Real Junta de Fomento (Royal Development Board) and the Gobierno Superior Civil (Higher Civil Government).

The documentation of the agencies that supervised the railroads during the neocolonial period—the Comisión de Ferrocarriles (Railroad Commission) and Comisión Nacional de Transportes (National Transportation Commission)— could be consulted only in a very limited way because, even though some of their collections are deposited in the Archivo Nacional, they have yet to be cataloged. That situation did not pose a great difficulty for the investigation, however, because the government agencies related to the railroad sector published memoirs fairly regularly, and we used the valuable information contained in them.

For the colonial period, the Dirección o Subdirección de Obras Públicas (Public Works Department and/or Section) of the colonial government put out three memoirs that cover all the information of the 1860–82 period without interruption. The U.S. military government put out a last memoir in 1900 which contains information on some aspects of the 1882–98 period.

The reports of the republican period that were published on a yearly basis, are organized in two series. The first, covering the 1901–38 period, was put out by the Comisión de Ferrocarriles. The second, on the 1939–50 period, was prepared by the Comisión Nacional de Transportes. Within that group of government publications, a compilation that the Comisión de Ferrocarriles issued under the title *Concesiones de ferrocarriles de servicio público* (Havana: Imprenta Xiqués, 1902) deserves special mention, for it presents documentation on the concessions granted by the Spanish colonial government.

The statistics contained in the government agencies' reports are one of their most important aspects. Extensive, homogeneous, and relatively constant, the railroad statistics are almost a rarity in Cuban quantitative sources. Their continuity has made it possible to reconstruct general series for nearly an entire century (there is a small gap, covering the 1883–97 period) and for even more complete periods for some of the companies, since the gaps in the government sources can be filled from the data contained in other published documentation of basic importance for research: the *memorias* or annual reports put out by the boards of directors of the railroad companies. Those documents, so typical of capitalist business methods, run from the middle of the nineteenth century up to the present. When we subjected them to a critical examination—some changes had been made in statistical groupings—we were able to draw up quite complete series and make rapid syntheses of the companies' activities in the corresponding years.

The bibliography on Cuba's railroads is lamentably scanty. There are no general historical works and but few monographs. Among those that do exist, Violeta Serrano's detailed monograph, *Crónicas del primer ferrocarril de Cuba* (Havana: DOR, 1973), is an exhaustive synthesis of the information available on this subject. Even though they are not historical works, A. Ximeno's *Origen y construcción de los ferrocarriles de Cuba* (Havana: Rambla y Bouza, 1912) and Luis V. de Abad's *Problemas de los transportes cubanos* (Havana: Editorial Mercantil Cubana, 1944) and *Los ferrocarriles de Cuba* (Havana: Imprenta La Habanera, 1940) contribute detailed analyses of brief but important periods in the history of railroad transportation. These are practically all of the specific bibliographic works available to researchers making studies of the railroads.

Local and regional histories, which were quite frequent in the latter half of the nineteenth century, usually contain abundant references to the construction of the railroads in their respective areas, for those projects revolutionized placid provincial life. Ramón de La Sagra's and Jacobo de la Pezuela's mammoth "historic-geographic-statistical" works dating from the mid-nineteenth century synthesized a considerable amount of information about the first steps taken in Cuba's railroad service, information that was especially valuable as it included a stage not covered by the Spanish government's publications.

Apart from the already mentioned reports put out by government agencies and the railroad companies' annual reports, Cuba's railroads generated practically no sectoral periodic publications. The few specimens of that genre were limited to the *Gaceta de los Ferrocarriles de la isla de Cuba*, a tardy offspring of the Spanish *Gaceta de los Caminos de Hierro*, which came out fairly regularly in the final years of the nineteenth century, and to some publications which appeared sporadically, such as the *Revista de Ferrocarriles*.

Some specialized economic publications, such as the *Revista Económica* and *Revista de Agricultura*, in the nineteenth century, and *El Economista* and *Cuba Económica y Financiera*, during various eras of the twentieth century, proved much more useful for our research. In addition to those materials, we had to consult other periodicals of a general nature, which we did more or less systematically, depending on the nature of the topic.

The sources for studying the labor movement in the railroad sector deserve special mention. In spite of the early organization of the railroad workers and the historic continuity of their labor unions, the sources generated by the railroad labor movement have not been preserved in an organized way. The archives of the Hermandad Ferroviaria and of other labor organizations in the sector have disappeared or have become mixed in with other collections of documents to such an extent that they cannot be located.

We managed to consult some of that documentation, both because we found some materials scattered in various archives and because some old participants in the labor struggles in the sector had carefully preserved small private archives, which they kindly allowed us to consult. However, that material was fragmentary, so an appreciable part of the information on the labor struggles had to be extracted from company documents and by combing through the press—from *La Discusión* and *La Lucha*, dailies published at the end of the nineteenth century, to *El Heraldo de Cuba*, *La Noche*, *Diario de la Marina*, *El Mundo*, and *Hoy* and such magazines as *Bohemia*, *Carteles*, and *Fundamentos*, all twentieth-century publications.

As may be appreciated, both the company documents and the newspapers and magazines—except for *Hoy* and *Fundamentos*, which were organs of the Partido Socialista Popular (People's Socialist Party)—expressed the views of the ruling class, and their use has required scrupulous application of the principles of historic criticism. We managed to counteract the slant of most of the available sources with the oral testimony of a large group of former activists in the railroad labor struggle who, with tremendous patience and, occasionally, serious efforts to recall details, provided us with the information we needed.

The long historic period encompassed in this investigation and the weight of factual material in it have made it advisable to adopt a chronological presentation. The descriptive and interpretive elements are, therefore, presented in close relationship, though we took care to give sufficient importance to the latter, devoting entire sections or chapters to them. For example, Chapters 5 and 6 analyze several of the main socioeconomic aspects of the railroads in the colonial period.

For the reasons set forth, we considered it preferable not to isolate issues related to the development of the labor movement in the railroad sector from the railroads' historic evolution proper. However, we dedicated special chapters or sections to that topic, so readers who are particularly interested in it can follow its sequence of events independently.

In general, the English edition of the book faithfully reflects the structure and contents of the original Spanish version, though we decided to eliminate some unimportant details in the interests of slightly reducing the size of the book. On a very limited scale, as well, some formulations have been modified and others introduced, based on new information provided by works that have appeared recently.

Because of the conditions which the meager bibliographic base—especially the absence of partial monographic studies—imposed on this investigation, the results obtained cannot be considered more than a preliminary synthesis. Cuba's railroad history still contains much material of interest to researchers, both on the plane of regional and company studies and in the analysis of some specific problems, such as the question of rates, which are barely outlined in this work. Far from exhausting this vast field of study, this book seeks to present it with all the wealth of its possibilities, with a view to offering guidelines for future investigations.

A research project of this scope would have been very difficult to carry out without the help of many people. First of all, we would like to thank the history seniors at the Universidad de La Habana who, in 1974, did their research practice by organizing the sources, putting information on cards, doing interviews, and summarizing the data. The richness of the informational base of this book is largely due to that fruitful combination of work and study. The support given the research team by the officials of Ferrocarriles de Cuba and by the political and administrative authorities of Camagüey Province—especially Octavio Louit Venzant, who was in charge of coordinating material support for the investigation on behalf of the Ministerio del Transporte—was also of decisive importance.

We are particularly indebted to the dozens of old railroad workers who told us about the labor struggle and other aspects of railroad activities. We would also like to acknowledge the excellent work of Jorge Oller, who was in charge of reproducing a large part of the graphic material contained in this book. Likewise, the observations which comrades in the Departamento de Historia de Cuba (Cuban History Department) of the Universidad de La Habana and other colleagues made on various parts of the text were extremely useful. Naturally, they are not responsible for any of the defects it may contain.

Lastly, we would like to express our appreciation to the Association of Caribbean Historians, which awarded its Elsa Goveia Prize to this book in 1989. Though possibly undeserved, it opened the doors to this English edition. Certainly, that editorial threshold would never have been crossed without the almost obsessive dedication with which Professor Franklin W. Knight carried out the Association's commission to get the book translated and published—a feat made possible thanks to the generosity of the Mellon Foundation and the book's acceptance by the University of North Carolina Press.

SUGAR & RAILROADS

The Problems of Transportation

In the last decades of the eighteenth century Cuba experienced an enormous demographic and economic transformation. After centuries of slow evolution, the local economy began a rapid change that would, a few years later, convert the largest of the Greater Antilles into "the world's sugar bowl." Such a spectacular modification resulted from the progressive elimination of several inhibiting factors that eventually led to an ever rising rate of sugar production. Overland transportation proved to be one of the most troublesome factors in getting the fledgling sugar industry off the ground.

The increasing sugar production in Cuba resulted from a combination of fortuitous circumstances: ample, fertile lands in the interior of the island; capital amassed over the previous years; and, above all, imported labor exploited under the most inhumane conditions. Equally important were the coincidence of favorable political circumstances and an exceptionally attractive economic climate initiated by the independence of the thirteen British North American colonies. After 1783, the United States of America began to import from the island tropical products formerly supplied by the British West Indian colonies. This unexpected commercial opportunity expanded the economic possibilities created shortly before by Spain by the adoption of the Reglamento para el comercio libre de España a Indias (Regulation of Free Trade between Spain and the Indies) in 1776. Thanks to this new regulation, ports like Santiago de Cuba, Trinidad (Casilda), and Batabanó were included in the category of "minor ports" and authorized to conduct free trade directly with Spain and, on certain occasions, with neutral and allied countries. As a consequence of the slave revolt in French Saint-Domingue in 1791, Cuba's capacity to supply Europe's demand for tropical products on a large scale slowly became a reality. Cuban exports to Europe, sometimes carried out directly, and sometimes through the American "neutrals," greatly increased. This situation became relatively stable during the wars of the French Revolution and the Napoleonic Empire. Cuba took advantage of the rising prices of products in great demand such as sugar and coffee.[1]

At the same time the metropolitan government applied favorable measures to boost commerce, such as the elimination of some export taxes, as well as others applied regularly to the importation of goods and equipment for the sugar industry. These measures culminated in the enactment of free trade with foreigners, although certain restrictions were retained through customs procedures. After a short period, the authorization to conduct international commerce was extended to additional new ports like Matanzas, Manzanillo, Guantánamo, Santa Cruz del Sur, and Mariel.

The economic development of the sugar industry that started around the decade of the 1790s stimulated the process of transformation of the agricultural regime. Land was granted by the municipal governments (*cabildos*), and the new tenants formed a very close-knit oligarchy. The impact of commercial agriculture on the great estates was noticeable in the western part of the island. Lands previously destined for tobacco fields gave way to the construction of sugar mills, coffee plantations, and pasture grounds. This process also promoted the exploitation of potentially productive but previously uninhabited lands. Nevertheless, the rural properties in the central and eastern parts of the island, with some local exceptions, continued to suffer from underpopulation and remained virtually untouched.

The new conditions prevailing in industry and agriculture required the strong support of the Spanish imperial legislation. On this occasion, the support manifested itself through two fundamental measures: the royal order of August 30, 1815, granting the free use of woods and land cultivation, and the act of the Ministerio de Hacienda (Ministry of Finance and Treasury), dated July 19, 1819, that gave complete powers over the land grants received before 1729.[2] These acts allowed full control and rights over those lands held by the traditional oligarchic landowners, to the detriment of the small tobacco or foodstuff producers whose cultivation fell within the boundaries of the estates. The measures also made those oligarchic families linked to the Havana town council powerful instruments in the growth of the sugar industry by creating a compact group of Creole plantation owners who assumed the direction of the economic and political life of the colony. The role played by these plantation owners in the sugar industry boom at the end of the eighteenth century was complemented by two other human and social factors: the critical slave labor force violently uprooted from the African continent, and the new merchant community partly stemming from the oligarchic families and partly from public officials and Spanish immigrants already settled in the country.

Although both plantation owners and traders benefited from the exploitation of slaves, there were obviously some clear differences between them. The plantation owners were the proprietors of the land, the sugar mills, and the slaves, the basic elements in the production of that society. The merchants were also a potentially powerful group. In their hands were the export of sugar and the import of slaves— legally or illegally—as well as machines and equipment such as boilers, packing crates, and other articles for use the on the plantations. The influence of the merchants increased with the capital they amassed through commercial transactions, as well as the banking functions destined to finance the sugar plantation owners. The port warehouses rounded out the financing power of the merchants in a country that began to depend almost completely on foreign trade. The complementary relationship existing between merchants and plantation owners created conflicting interests between the two social groups. Nevertheless, some merchants later became landowners and vice versa so that in some cases a single individual or entity came to control the functions of producing, financing, and exporting sugar.

The organization of large-scale production and international commerce required increased institutionalization of the operations in the colony with the corresponding involvement in administration. The Spanish colonial structure had only two economic institutions that could satisfy the requirements of the moment: the local patriotic societies and the consulados or chambers of commerce. Both had ancient precedence, but, influenced by the "enlightened despotism" of the eighteenth century and the demands of the Creole plantation owners, their functions were expanded considerably.

In 1793, the Sociedad Económica del Amigos del País (Royal Economic Society of Havana) was founded. This society had a weak precedent on the island in a similar society previously founded in Santiago de Cuba. The petition for the foundation was presented with the connivance of Governor Luis de las Casas and a significant group of members of the Havana oligarchy that included the counts of Casa Montalvo, Casa Bayona, and Jibacoa, the marquises of San Felipe y Santiago and of Casa Calvo y de Arcos, as well as Juan Manuel, and José Ricardo O'Farrill, Nicolás Calvo, and other Creoles equally famous for their sugar wealth as for their extensive landowning. Controlled by the Creole producers and supported by outstanding intellectuals, this society took part in almost all the activities that could contribute to the development of the plantation economy and provided useful counsel for colonial officials. The principal role of the society, however, was the introduction and fostering of economic ideas, technology, public administration, and education.

Two plantation owners, Francisco de Arango y Parreño and the count of Casa Montalvo, endeavored to create a department for the promotion of agriculture. These efforts paralleled a measure taken by the metropolitan government to establish a chamber of commerce on the island similar to those already created in other cities throughout Spanish America. The result of this duality of purposes, both of which involved the control of the most important factors of the country's economy, was the creation on April 10, 1795, of a new organization that resulted in an institutional union between merchants and plantation owners: The Royal Havana Chamber of Agriculture and Commerce (Real Consulado de Agricultura y Comercio de la Habana). Its main objectives were supposed to benefit both social groups, and were predicated on the improvement of agricultural production by means of an increase in population, the opening and improvement of ports, and the construction of roads, navigation canals, and irrigation. The first council included the owners of twenty-six sugar mills, including the count of Casa Montalvo, Francisco de Arango y Parreño, and the marquis of Casa Peñalver.[3] The conflict of interests between merchants and plantation owners was systematically manifested in the council. Nevertheless, from the time of its founding under Governor Luis de las Casas to the time of Francisco Dionisio Vives in 1832, the governors of the island were often receptive to the aspirations of the sugar plantation owners and generally endorsed their goals.

The wonderful opportunities opened to the Cuban plantation owners and merchants by the expanding European and North American markets were complemented by the interest of the metropolitan government in fostering the colonial economy and, in a certain way, by the particular geographical location of the largest of the Greater Antilles. Due to its strategic geographical position, Cuba was considered the crossroads of the Spanish Caribbean for centuries and an almost unavoidable stopover for transport and communications between America and Europe. Such strategic and commercial importance made Havana a port of exceptional significance for maritime transport between the island and ports of Europe and America, either continental or insular. Nevertheless, as the port of Havana had the exclusive privilege to conduct the foreign commerce for the entire Cuban colony, the other coastal cities were forced to decide between a legal commerce through Havana up to the middle of the eighteenth century and an illicit trade called "ransom" (de rescate). The first type of commercial activity— the legal one—involved the use of cabotage or, in its place, the opening of new roads through the then thick subtropical forest of the island.

The long and narrow shape of the island of Cuba presented an excellent solution to some inland communications, either by the construction of an arterial highway capable of linking the various regions throughout the island or by the use of cabotage. Cuba is 1,250 kilometers long, with 5,736 kilometers of coastline and a maximum width of 191 kilometers. As its average width is 110 kilometers, there is no point within the island more than 100 kilometers from the coast. This geographical shape enhanced the construction of a central road with short lateral feeder roads. Together the overland transport and cabotage were propitious to the development of an export economy and an efficient supply system for the interior island markets. The Cuban shoreline has over two hundred bays, ports, and coves, many of which are considered among the widest and most protected in the world. Nevertheless, not all its coastal stretches can be easily navigated by large vessels due to the long stretches of shallow waters and abundant keys.

The northern coast has the most favorable areas for navigation, especially the stretches between Bahía Honda and the Hicacos Peninsula in the west, and between Nuevitas and Maisí, in the east. Along these stretches of coast are wonderful bays suitable for ports and wharves such as Cabañas, Mariel, Havana, Matanzas, Nuevitas, Banes, Nipe, and Sagua de Tánamo. In a central region north of Las Villas and Camagüey, which is characterized by marine terraced plains and shallow waters strewn with keys and small islands, the imperative need of sugar exports forced the dredging of the ports of Cárdenas, La Isabela, and Caibarién. The southern coast has less ports and wharves than the northern. In the east, the bays of Guantánamo and Santiago de Cuba have very deep waters, but to the west navigation becomes difficult except in the area between María Aguilar in Trinidad, and Cienfuegos. Artificial modifications of certain shore features made ports like Manzanillo, Santa Cruz del Sur, Júcaro, and Tunas del Zaza accessible to vessels of considerable draft. Also in this area, Surgidero de Batabanó became important, as the natural obstacles to navigation were removed. The proximity of this last port to Havana—fifty-eight kilometers across the plains—encouraged its development as a strategic cabotage point. Batabanó linked the capital to the southern ports and Isla de Pinos (Isle of Pines) until the twentieth century.

Set along two well-defined slopes—the northern with 236 rivers and the southern with 327—the Cuban river system with its generally narrow basins does not present important obstacles for communications between the north and south of the island. But it presents obstructions for the east-west movements in areas not far from the coast. The water levels of Cuban rivers vary considerably during the year. The rivers change from raging torrents during the rainy season from May to November when 80 percent of the rainfall occurs, to small streams during the dry season from December to April. These variations, together with the deep canyons frequently found near the shores, make the Cuban rivers inadequate for satisfactory communication, providing transit for only small crafts for a few kilometers inland.

Although the rainy period prevailing in the country allows the cultivation of yearly crops that can be harvested in the dry season, freight transportation was difficult and hazardous since the wide plains became swampy from the rains and the frequent flooding of nearby rivers. The fertile plains were broken intermittently by gentle hills throughout the island. In the west almost grouped together, are Guaniguanico hills and the slate hills of the south and north. Another lower series of hills runs between Havana and Matanzas on the north and center (the Bejucal-Madruga-Coliseo hills), surrounding the great red southern plains that extend from Artemisa to the outskirts of Cienfuegos. Swamp lands to the south of these plains, mainly in the Zapata Peninsula, inhibit transportation of crops to the south. In the center of the island, the productive lands of the former province of Las Villas fall between the Santa Clara hills to the north and the Guamuhaya Mountains and the Sierra de Trinidad on the south, while the Najasa and Cubitas virtually surround the plains of Camagüey.

The highest mountains in the country are in the eastern region. The hills of Maniabón, Nipe, and Cristal, and the Moa and Toa Cliffs, practically block the east and northeast of the eastern provinces. Toward the south, the Sierra Maestra forms a long coastal ridge hindering overland transportation.

Originally the wild subtropical vegetation of the island was a temporary obstacle to overland transport and communication. Hardwood like *caoba* (mahogany), *ácana*, and different species of *júcaro* were very useful for the construction of ships, docks, and wharves; but the development of commercial cultivation in the second half of the eighteenth century began the process of deforestation of Cuba, which continued to the twentieth century. The abundance of woods also constituted a valuable resource for buildings in general, and a source of fuel for the furnaces and steam boilers of the sugar mills.

The expansion of the sugar industry changed the rural landscape enormously. Sugar estates decimated the forests and even replaced the tobacco fields and coffee plantations. The concentration of sugar estates established around Havana, Guanabacoa, Guanabo, Rio Blanco, Jibacoa, and Canasí was considerable, and it extended eastward in a series of small productive centers including Cangrejeras, Guatao, El Cano, Rincón, Santiago, San Antonio, Managua, and Santa María del Rosario. An almost immediate shift towards the lands west of the Mariel Bay occurred between Guanajay and Quiebra Hacha. This area was considered the most important sugar production center of the country during the first years of the nineteenth century. Although the highest number of sugar mills was located near the coasts, cultivation moved to the southern plains, growing vigorously in the valley of Güines. From four sugar mills existing in 1784, twenty-two more were built in the next twenty years, and by 1827, this number again doubled. Taking advantage of the rich lands of the great southern plains, new concentrations of sugar mills sprang up to the west, toward Artemisa, and to the east toward Palos and Nueva Paz, near the production areas of Matanzas.

In Matanzas the demands of sugar production created a similar situation. The impressive growth of this area took place between 1800 and 1820, covering the space between Corral Nuevo to the west of Matanzas Bay, down to Alacranes and Sabanilla del Encomendador to the south, and all along the Guanábana-Coliseo road to the southeast. The proliferation of sugar production zones in almost all the region made it necessary to create new administrative divisions. A new productive zone developed in the outskirts of the Cárdenas Bay and extended simultaneously toward Bemba and Recreo (now called Jovellanos and Máximo Gómez respectively). The total production of Matanzas Province reached 25 percent of the total Cuban sugar output as early as 1827; and its continuous growth rate propelled the province to 55 percent of insular production by the middle of the nineteenth century.

The saturation of the convenient coastal lands from Pinar del Río to Matanzas drove new sugar production areas to the outskirts of ports located more to the east like Sagua la Grande on the northern coast and Cienfuegos on the southern. Both areas began to produce almost simultaneously between 1820 and 1830. As in other areas, the Havana capitalists had a lot to do with the development of the new concentration in Sagua; in Cienfuegos, however, most of the new investment came from the plantation owners of nearby Trinidad.

Trinidad and Puerto Príncipe were, like Havana, old sugar production zones. By mid-eighteenth century the importance of both areas was considerable, but their isolation from the grouped centers in the western region allowed them a certain independence within the insular economy. Apparently, even though there were fifty-five small sugar mills in Puerto Príncipe in 1795, the later development of the region did not immediately follow the pattern of large sugar plantations. Still, by the middle of the nineteenth century the zone had clearly begun its dependence on sugar. By contrast, sugar production in the eastern provinces, due to its scale and technological backwardness, had little economic significance in the country's production before the early twentieth century.

Driven by rising sugar prices on the European market, the Cuban export volume increased from 13,222 metric tons in 1789 to 32,586 metric tons in 1799. This rate of growth continued throughout the following decades, reaching 104,971 metric tons in 1830, despite a relative decrease in the prices.[4] The territorial expansion of this industry was based on productive centers in which an undetermined number of units were frequently grouped around ports or wharves, both maritime and fluvial, that facilitated the shipping of products either through cabotage or through direct export. The number of sugar mills in such groupings grew astronomically between 1774 and 1827, increasing from 481 units to 1,000.

Both the colonial authorities and local sugar interests acting through the economic society and the royal consulate placed great importance on the condition of roads since these were linked eventually to estate profits. A considerable number of papers and memoirs about roads were written and published beginning in

The Güines Valley seen from La Candela hill, one of the main obstacles between that sugar zone and the port of Havana. (F. Mialhe, *Isla de Cuba pintoresca*. Havana: Imprenta de la Sociedad Patriotica, n.d.)

1795. The memoirs published by Juan T. de Jáuregui and Nicolás Calvo and the unpublished ones by Esteban La Faye, Julián de Campos, Alonso B. Muñoz, Juan A. Morejón, and the marquis of Arcos express a concern for the physical conditions of roads and their excessive vulnerability to the weather owing to poor construction. In one of these memoirs its author lamented:

> All the roads that need to be opened are subjected to the weather and are impassable during the rainy season, or interrupted by extraordinary obstacles. No person ignores the excessive degree of deterioration of the roads that, even after 3 or 4 months of drought, continue to have dangerous crossings that cannot be avoided. . . . In the rainy season, the utter necessity to transport the most essential goods forces the traveler to open paths across cultivated fields or woods with the ax or machete in hand with no respect for crops, or stone, or wood fences that he is forced to destroy by necessity. This solution is useful only for the beasts of burden, as carts must remain in a forced standstill during this season.[5]

Numerous undertakings, as well as suggestions and ideas, sought solutions to the road problem. These generally brought about an official response in which the contribution of the plantation owners would consist of taxes on the land owned, or a poll tax per slave—the two main indexes of wealth of these owners. Nevertheless, the producers were generally reluctant to contribute economically to the construction and maintenance of roads if these were not directly linked to their individual estates.

Initiatives from the Real Consulado and Sociedad Económica to improve the inland communication system paralleled the steps taken by the Spanish king through a series of commissions and grants to the brigadier count of Mopox and Jaruco in 1796. These commissions included the construction of the navigation canal of Güines and the building of a number of roads necessary for the economic development of the colony. To that end, the engineers Francisco and Félix Lemaur, builders of the Guadarrama-Rozas canal (one of the few that the peninsula had), were contracted.

The construction of canals, as a solution to inland navigation problems had successful antecedents in Europe in the seventeenth and eighteenth-centuries. This type of engineering work, specially in countries like Germany, France, England, and the Netherlands, had successfully established true inland communication systems. The English experience on the Bridgewater and Grand trunk canals and the growth of the French canal network were both very recent. In North America, however, in spite of the efforts of George Washington, only the so-called Dismal Swamp Canal was built during this time.

The project for the navigation canal from Güines to Havana had been submitted to Governor Antonio M. Bucarely by the commander of the navy yard, the count of Macuriges, from as early as 1765. Its original purpose had been the creation of an artificial route to guarantee the transport of timber from the southern forests to the Royal Dockyards in Havana Bay. The interested plantation owners considered the building of an efficient and inexpensive route for the transport of their products to Havana as the cornerstone of their prosperity. They revived the project and requested the Lemaur brothers to investigate its possibilities. They rejected the modest original project due to its insufficient water supply and substituted a fantastic canal system with floodgates that should be filled by the rains and the surplus waters of the Güines River.[6] It was precisely the lack of water that made the attempt fail technically. Besides, it required so much money that neither the crown nor the plantation owners could afford it.

Since the dawn of capitalism, roads had been, before and after the opening of canals, of extraordinary importance to the development of internal and foreign markets in European countries. They had contributed in great measure to the economic balance and the consolidation of national states. For these reasons, the enlightened ideas of King Charles III had fostered the construction of a radial system of roads on the Iberian peninsula since 1761. Such a system was designed to enable Madrid to use the surplus coming from the provinces and, in that way, stimulate the development of a national market. Along with these ideas came the establishment of regulations for the wheel base of carts and stage wagons and limitations for timber transport, all of which were intended to arrest the rapid deterioration of the roads. However, at the end of the reign of this monarch, the roads in Spain were still in terrible condition, so it was necessary to enact new regulations to finance the repair of damaged passes and roads.[7]

The conditions of the roads in Cuba were no better than those of the metropolis, as neither the enlightened road improvements of the deceased Charles III, or his successor, Charles IV, had yet reached the Caribbean. The Cuban Real Consulado, using the few resources at its disposal, planned the building of an appropriate cart road, eighty leagues long and seven rods wide, to link Havana with Güines, Batabanó, and Matanzas.[8] The collecting of tolls, first applied in Cuba in 1791, was devised to finance the construction and repairs of the new roads.[9] The low quality of the materials, poor engineering, and the erosive action of tropical rainstorms rapidly destroyed the new roads. Frequently some plantation owners used their influence in the Real Consulado to build roads directly to some particular sugar mill, abandoning other roads of more general interest previously begun, thereby creating chaos in the road building scheme.

Not all attempts at road construction were failures. A few small successes remained in works of relative permanence, such as those that removed the main obstacles to a free passage of sugar from San Julián de los Güines (the formal full name for Güines) to Havana. Creative financing assisted in the removal of some difficult obstacles, such as the grading of the slope on the outskirts of La Candela hill. In this case, a fee was imposed on the supposedly benefiting landholders, prorated according to the number of slaves they possessed. Besides a transit toll financed the maintenance of the rest of the road.[10] Similar procedures were used to solve the problems with the Laguna de Curbelo (Curbelo's Pond) and the Ganuza bridge. The repairs carried out in these areas by the Consulado were completed in 1802, and the plan for the collection of tolls was assigned to a Havana plantation owner, Pedro Diago, in 1800. The success achieved in such cases encouraged other groups of plantation owners to demand similar solutions from the Real Consulado, for example, construction of the road to Güines in the neighborhood of the La Corredera and Nazareno hills. In this case, the contribution of the plantation owners was three slaves each—for a total of thirty—who worked during the dead season under the command of a contracted overseer.[11]

The novelty of the turnpike system in Cuba generated some resistance on the part of the travelers, maybe not as violent as those of England in 1753, but surely more picturesque.[12] The tribulations of Blas Vidal, a toll collector on the road of Güines as told to Pedro Diago, the originator of the toll plan, illustrate the poignant realism of toll collection:

> All the muleteers, or most of them, take the old road to San José that runs between this turnpike and the tavern of the Portuguese to avoid paying the toll. This Tuesday more than 100 beasts of burden took the other road, and every day the coal merchants take other roads openly. On their way to the countryside they go through this turnpike but, so far, they haven't returned yet. . . . It seems very convenient to move the turnpike to Jamayca, placing the toll collection next to the Tavern of Molina, which closes the way used by many sugar carts that come from Güines and its surroundings on their way to Catalina, leaving Jamayca, because this crossing is unavoidable and no one can escape it.[13]

Despite difficulties like these, most turnpikes generated enough income to finance the works initially carried out.

Neither the publicity of the Sociedad Económica nor the coordinating action of the Real Consulado achieved the results that would allow a permanent solution for the problems of overland transportation in Cuba. After relative successes in the most difficult stretches of the Güines road, there followed a long period characterized by slowness and anarchy in the construction of roads, and local government could not resolve even the most elementary annual repairs needed on the main roads—those going to Güines, Batabanó, Guanajay, and Matanzas. Even along such important roads, only a few leagues were kept in adequate

The mule train, the principal means of transport in areas of difficult terrain. (F. Miahle, *Isla de Cuba pintoresca.* Havana: Imprenta de la Sociedad Patriótica, n.d.)

Carts at the Havana wharves. Carts provided the basic means of transporting sugar to the ports. (F. Miahle, *Isla de Cuba pintoresca*. Havana: Imprenta de la Sociedad Patriotica, n.d.)

repair. Moreover, the use of an annual labor force of up to four hundred men contrasted sharply with the poor results obtained. Overall, between 1796 and 1832, more than 3.6 million pesos were invested in the construction and continuous repairs of roads, representing an expenditure of around 100,000 pesos a year.[14]

All the memoirs presented by José Antonio Saco (1830) and Rafael de Quesada y Arango (1832) pointed out the main causes of the poor results, despite large investments. The first factor of blame was the low quality of the materials used, particularly the weak national limestone, combined with technical deficiencies

in the plotting and building of the roads.[15] Second, great importance was attributed to the results of the weather on poorly built roads. Yet another factor, hardly less important, was the increasing volume of cargo carried annually on such roads. Curiously, the chaos created by the construction of secondary roads between sugar mills of the same owner was not considered a contributory factor to the poor results.

Through the long periods during which sugar prices peaked (especially between the years 1791–98 and 1804–18), the Cuban plantation owners covered their production costs with relative ease without bothering themselves about the enormous number of carts, oxen, and drivers involved in the transportation of their products. Influenced by the stimulating price increases and defying risks of foreign market fluctuations, many new sugar mills were built far from the coasts, demanding a constant extension of roads to their brand-new *bateyes* (sugar factories).

In 1826, the first group of big beet sugar factories appeared in France, producing 2,400 metric tons, which rapidly increased to 30,000 metric tons in 1834. The result was a rapid fall in sugar prices between 1829 and 1833 by almost 50 percent of the prices prevailing in the first decade of the century.[16] In addition, the conditions that favored the acquisition of slaves for the estates for several decades changed negatively since Spain was forced in 1817 to sign under the pressures from England, a cessation of the Spanish slave trade beginning in 1820. The repulsion against slavery also reached some of the young Latin American republics, which in addition to England and France, were not only banning the slave trade but also taking steps toward the total emancipation of the captives. The international rejection of slave trading made the commerce of Africans illegal, but for the Cuban traders it only meant the continuation of the business on a similar scale with the addition of a bounty to bribe the authorities. The logical result of these new conditions was an increase in price for every new slave. This increase in slave prices, together with the competition created by the production of beet sugar, forced the Cuban plantation owners to seek a reduction in the production costs on their plantations and in their sugar mills. They were also forced to use extraordinary resources for transportation and to place a surcharge on each exported sugar crate averaging between 10 to 20 percent of its cost.[17]

The persistent challenges to slavery affected institutions such as the Real Consulado and the Sociedad Económica that defended the interests of the ruling class. The alarmed sugar proprietors, faced with increasing competition from European industrial capitalism, whose productive potential and social progress began to affect the anachronistic slave plantation system, complained of the lack of an adequate transportation system that would at least allow a more efficient exploitation of their natural resources.

The problem of transportation evidenced the imperative need to take measures to save, at any cost, the levels of profit that the Creole plantation owners needed. The problem of increasing the rate of production was no longer simply of building and extending roads, no matter how rudimentary they were, but the improvement of the roads in a way that would not only reduce the loss of products but also reduce transportation expenses and thereby increase profits. The plantation owners in Matanzas laid before the Real Consulado their grievous situation: "Carts broken into pieces, destroyed sugar crates, worn out animals, lost days that drag on and cause incalculable losses to the laborious farmer: this is the picture presented by the roads of our city."[18]

Rafael de Quesada described in his report even more bluntly the reasons that motivated the urgent petitions of the producers: "With good roads, the molasses and rums of distant plantation owners, now thrown away, could be sold at regular prices, as transportation now costs as much as their selling price in the capital."[19]

Estates situated near the coast were affected less by transportation difficulties. They sent their products directly to the ports or abroad without the familiar inconveniences caused by absolute dependency on inland roads. The conditions of the roads spurred the increase in cabotage in Cuba between the years 1799 and 1814, and everything indicates that further intensification took place in later years, especially between the ports of Havana, Mariel, and Matanzas.[20]

In view of the incapacity of the authorities to solve the problem of inland transportation, José Antonio Saco and Rafael de Quesada suggested in their respective reports the creation of private enterprises with shareholder capital, which would take care of the building, maintenance, and operations of all paved roads with a well-organized toll system. The results obtained by similar enterprises in the operation of the English and North American turnpikes suggested to the authors the possibility to move some of the capital of the plantation owners into the field of overland transportation. The writings of Saco and Quesada coincided with the interests of the sugar producers, for in 1832 a group of them, including Pedro Diago, Rafael O'Farrill, Gonzalo Alfonso, Antonio M. Escovedo, and Ignacio de Herrera, sent a petition to the Real Consulado asking for the authorization to build a road that would link San Julián de los Güines with Havana. This road would be operated through a group of shareholders: "The chosen road is that of Güines, because, it being the only one in the direction of those rich territories, and consequently the most frequented, it should necessarily be the most productive to the shareholders."[21]

The matter of roads was not only a critical problem to be solved, but it offered a new perspective for a lucrative investment. This duality of purpose would obviously open horizons for the future of transportation in the island, but it would no longer deal exclusively with roads and dirt tracks, but would now include the most modern system of overland transportation that the technological development of that time had conceived: the railroad.

The Güines Railroad

Overland transportation was a nightmare for Cuban Creole sugar producers. A Real Consulado repeatedly rebuilding the same few leagues of cart roads was not a solution. Not even the use of the new technique of crushed stone, an invention of the Scotsman Mac Adam, seemed efficacious, although it had very good results on the neighboring island of Jamaica. Moreover, the situation of the market and its future evolution demanded an urgent solution. Fortunately for the plantation owners, their needs coincided with the first successful tests of a means of transportation that was going to revolutionize profoundly the conditions of overland transportation.

The railroad, more than a great invention, was the result of a prolonged effort of collective creation within a revolutionary process of scientific and technical development. This revolution lead the productive and financing systems of capitalism to an industrial phase. The railroad, a modern solution to overland transportation, went through different phases of development before attaining its final form during the third decade of the nineteenth century. One of its basic principles, transportation on parallel rails, was in use in Germany and England as far back as the sixteenth century. The movement of miner's wagons on rails decreased friction greatly, thereby offering a cheaper and more efficient system of transportation than the cart. The expansion of mining promoted changes in this type of transportation: the primitive wooden rails used initially were first strengthened with iron plates and then later replaced by solid iron rails. The form of these rails was constantly improved to allow better locomotion and reduce accidents. All the mines of England had rail systems by the end of the eighteenth century and some were almost twenty miles long.[1] However, transportation on rails pulled by human or animal force could not be an earthshaking innovation in communications. Its use was restricted to short distances and generally supplemented with other means of communication such as canals and roads. New forms of traction were necessary for long distances. The invention of the steam engine by James Watt in 1775 opened a new possibility to satisfy the needs of overland transportation.

The first attempt to apply steam power to transportation was not on the rail system but on conventional carts. Even though it was not successful, the interest in steam locomotion did not decrease. Those most interested were the proprietors of mines and foundries already using rail systems to move heavy loads in complex conditions. It was for a foundry in 1804—the Penny-Darren factory in Wales—that Richard Trevithick built the first model of what would become the locomotive. Trevithick's machine was able to pull ten tons of ore and, although it was not a success, these results were encouraging enough to motivate many inventors. Most of the inventions ended in failure but some contributed with small innovations that helped in the building of a better machine each time. In 1814, George Stephenson built a locomotive capable of pulling thirty tons at a speed of four miles per hour, proving the effectiveness of the new machine.

In spite of these first successes, the locomotive remained in an experimental phase for some years, limited only to partial jobs in mines and factories. In 1821, the English Parliament passed a bill for the construction of a railroad between Stockton and the iron-making center of Darlington, in Durham. There was some distrust regarding the use of the locomotive as it foresaw that a railroad could be powered by "men, horses, or any other means." Stephenson worked directly in the construction of the tracks, and during inauguration day—September 27, 1825— pulled the first train with freight and passengers with one of his locomotives. The final test came later with the construction of the Liverpool-Manchester railroad. The new track, conceived entirely for steam traction, connected England's main industrial center with its most important port. As both cities were linked by three canals and one road, the railroad could demonstrate not only its operational effectiveness but also its competitive possibilities. The railroad company, wanting to get the best equipment, organized a contest to select the best locomotive in 1829. One of Stephenson's engines, the "Rocket," won the contest, amazing the spectators with a speed of nearly fifty kilometers per hour. Stephenson had introduced important advances into his new machine: the multitubular boiler, invented by the Frenchman Seguin, augmented the boiling surfaces with a notable increase in steam production; the direct connection between the cylinder and the piston of the drive wheel; better inlet steam valves, and some other details that made possible increased traction capacity.[2] The rocket represented the ultimate triumph of the railroad in overland transportation. Although it would still encounter some problems, the railroad had firmly established itself in England.

The new invention spread rapidly throughout Europe. France had its first railroad in the Loire region, with a line between Saint Etienne and Andrezieux. The small line began with animal power but quickly adopted locomotives and shortly thereafter reached the industrial center of Lyon. The first railroad in Austria also began in 1828 with a line connecting the cities of Linz and Budweis. In Austria the state demonstrated great interest in the building of railroads since it foresaw the unbeatable possibility of an effective way to integrate the various nationalities of the empire. The new kingdom of Belgium produced the most important variation in the development of the railroad. There the Belgian Parliament approved a plan that permitted the state to build and operate railroads. Two years later, Brussels and Amberes were connected by the initial links of what would eventually become the most rational and best-organized network of railroads in Europe.[3] Among the many small states of Germany the railroad became a source of prestige and competition among princes and rulers. Almost simultaneously Bavaria and Saxony inaugurated railroads and thereby claimed merit for what would later become the cornerstone of the future German railroad network.

Across the Atlantic the era of the railroad also began early. Beginning with Fulton the Americans were the first to apply steam power to maritime transportation, and soon thereafter introduced it to the railroads. In the early 1820s, some technicians worked on the design of locomotives, and in 1828, the first railroad for public service began operation for the Baltimore & Ohio Railroad. However, this line operated using horsepower. In 1830, the first line designed for steam power ran from Charleston to Hamburg, in South Carolina.

With the opening of these lines, the construction of locomotives began. The first locomotive to run in the United States was the "Lion," built by the British firm Stourbridge, but soon the American factories began to produce machines that followed the principles of Stephenson's "Rocket."[4] The need to adapt the locomotives to rudimentary tracks, built at the beginning with wood covered with iron plates, forced the American builders to sacrifice the pulling power of their machines by using lighter engines. These technical variations made the American locomotives easier to run in curves and slopes. One important variation was the introduction of the "bogie"—a small nontraction cart—placed under the boiler, thus making the locomotive more stable while allowing an increase in weight. The technical differences between the English and American locomotives increased through the years and eventually led to separate railroad technologies.

By the beginning of the 1830s the railroads had proved their efficiency on both sides of the Atlantic. The final success came when the railroad demonstrated its superiority not only in freight transportation but also in hauling passengers. Even those reluctant to accept the noisy locomotive as capable of doubling the speed of a stagecoach, began to take a train when they needed a swift trip. The successive opening of lines along the traditional routes of roads and canals emphasized the final triumph of this new means of transportation. The lack of transportation thereafter would no longer be an obstacle to the development of industry.

In early 1830, the governor of Cuba, Francisco Dionisio Vives, received a letter from the Spanish inventor and publicist, Marcelino Calero, requesting help for a railroad project. Calero asked Vives and the rich Havana proprietors to join with him in building a railroad between Jerez de la Frontera, one of the richest wine-growing areas of the south of Spain, and the port of Santa María. In the letter, as well as in the two subsequent ones, the wise Andalusian offered his services for any similar project in Cuba.[5]

Calero's letters—sent from London, the center of railroad experimentation—received unusual interest from the governor, and were forwarded immediately to the Real Sociedad Económica for careful study. The Sociedad Económica accepted the idea with enthusiasm. A few days later, a commission was created to gather information about railroads. Two of its members, José Agustín Ferrety and Juan Tirry y Lacy, marquis of La Cañada, delivered a report containing detailed narration on the use of railroads in England and the United States.[6] At a meeting of the society, Vives introduced a motion to appoint Calero a corresponding member and to maintain permanent communication with the Andalusian. Convinced of the importance of the project, the Sociedad Económica asked the Real Consulado and the Havana municipal government to participate in a joint commission to arrive at a final decision on the railroad project.

On August 8, 1830, the new commission, called the Junta de Caminos de Hierro (The Railroad Commission), held its first meeting presided over by the highest colonial authorities, the governor, Vives, and the Havana intendant, Claudio Martínez de Pinillos. The members of the junta were the marquis of La Cañada and José A. Ferrety from the Sociedad Económica; Francisco Romero and Carlos Pedroso from the Real Consulado; and Andrés de Zayas and Domingo Herrera from the Havana City Council.[7] The engineers' captain Manuel Pastor and Francisco Lemaur (the unsuccessful builder of the old Güines canal) were asked to be "technical advisors." Vives began the meeting by reading Calero's letters. After pointing out the relevance of the railroad project, he stated that "the present circumstances made it more valuable because as a result of the reduced prices for the products that are the wealth of the country, due to the excessive foreign production that competes in the European markets, we are forced to discuss any means that might lower the costs and improve transportation."[8] Finally, Vives submitted to the junta the possibility of building the railroad between Havana and Güines with later extensions to Matanzas, Lagunillas, and other localities.

From this first meeting, the work of the Junta de Caminos de Hierro focused on three main concerns: the evaluation of the technical characteristics of the railroad and its success in other countries; the plotting of future railways, as well as an examination of location and costs; and the study of the profit potential of the railroad as determined by the economic characteristics of the areas in which it would operate.

The first of these objectives advanced rapidly. The junta's studies concentrated on the already mentioned Tirry and Ferrety report and some other documents among which was a report presented by the American, John L. Sullivan, on the practical principles of the railroad. He had recently arrived in Havana attracted by the news that Cuba contemplated building a railroad. Sullivan delivered a letter to Governor Vives, signed by the president of the United States, John Quincy Adams, in which Sullivan was recommended as an experienced engineer. Although the main interest of the American was to sell a new model of coach to the promoters of the railroad, he took advantage of his condition of "expert" to get involved in the work of the junta.[9]

The matter of plotting the railroad route was more troublesome. The idea that the railway should follow the existing road to Güines was abandoned after Manuel Pastor pointed out that the hills of Camoa would probably be an insurmountable obstacle. The route suggested by Vives along Managua, Guara, and Melena had the advantage of connections with various roads, but that involved a low productive region, which was a serious economic disadvantage. Without admitting it openly, the Junta favored the route suggested by Felix Lemaur, which ran from Havana through Rincón and Buenaventura and ended in Güines. This route would permit transport of products from San Antonio de los Baños and Batabanó, with the possibility of building future branches to those localities.[10]

When the work of the Junta de Caminos de Hierro focused on the evaluation of probable costs, rivalries developed that sometimes obscured opposition to the project. Members of the junta, lacking experience in the railroad business, faced a smorgasbord of contradictory opinions that made any consensus extremely difficult. The construction cost originally calculated by Calero, at about 7,500 pesos per mile, turned out to be without foundation and with self-promotion uppermost. It was harshly criticized. The first objection to Calero's estimates came from Don Francisco Lemaur. Basing his figures on comparisons with English construction costs, the old engineer suggested a Cuban construction figure of no less than 60,000 pesos per mile. Compared with the most optimistic estimates of revenue, such a high cost made the railroad economically unfeasible. The idea of Don Francisco suggested opposition to the project. But fearful of deflating the optimism of the commission, Lemaur proposed some discouraging alternatives. The first one was the building of a system of wooden rails with animal drawn carts, but even then the cost—at approximately 11,000 pesos per mile—was still too high. The other proposal, a sort of monorail along which a sort of bicycle cart traversed, only showed that however the mind of the old Don Francisco rejected modern techniques, it remained full of fantasy.

The Junta de Caminos de Hierro studied several other reports, among them one done by the American, Sullivan, who suggested a change from the high-cost British system of railways to the more economic strap-iron wooden patterns used by some American railroad companies. Felix Lemaur sent a report to the junta that was more honest and sensible than that of his brother. After praising the usefulness of the railroad, Felix Lemaur offered a series of practical considerations about the most economic way to build it. Finally, after analyzing all the reports and opinions, the junta wrote a very optimistic report that put the total cost of building the railroad at 700,000 pesos.

This budget, compared with the estimated income from the railroad, would ensure a handsome profit margin for its investors. To calculate the probable income, the junta asked the treasury official in Havana, Martínez de Pinillos, to gather information about the economic possibilities of all regions served by the railroads. The reports from the jurisdictions of Jesús del Monte, Santiago de las Vegas, and Güines could not be better. In Jesús del Monte 30,985 pesos had been spent in 1830 on freight transportation. In Santiago, 562,227 pesos were spent, but the administrator warned that because of the distance involved, a great amount of this load would not go over the railroad. Undoubtedly the most important freight would come from the Güines Valley. This area alone sent 649,976 arrobas of sugar, 90,992 arrobas of coffee, and 3,541 barrels of rum, as well as considerable amounts of corn, rice, and other minor produce, to Havana in 1830, paying the amount of 364,166 pesos for transport costs.[11] The potential value of the valley was even greater since many of the products, such as rice, were not sent from Güines to Havana because of the high costs of transportation. Of a production of 100,000 arrobas of rice, only 15,000 went to Havana. The economic success of the railroad seemed assured. The Junta de Caminos de Hierra considered that the railroad would be profitable even if rates were reduced to one-half of the current suggestions. Its construction depended, therefore, on the trust of the people. The realization of the scheme would require the creation of a joint-stock company with 7,000 shares valued at 100 pesos with the understanding that it would not be difficult to sell stock entirely in the Havana jurisdiction. With this report the junta ended its task. It was dissolved on January 22, 1831, after agreeing to publish an edition of its report.

After the termination of the Junta de Caminos de Hierro a year went by without any effort to carry out the railroad project. No company charged with the construction of the railroad appeared. The junta members had been too optimistic and in their enthusiasm they did not listen to their colleague the marquis of La Cañada, who warned that "despite its advanced enlightenment, the public spirit of this city, was not clearly demonstrated, and its advantages would require patience and active promotion."[12]

In 1832 a restructuring of the colonial administration in Cuba revived the railroad project. The Spanish commercial code of 1829 restricted the functions of the Real Consulado narrowly to trade matters while those pertaining to population, agriculture, roads, and the like were placed with a newly created Junta de Fomento (Development Board). In Cuba, the code became effective three years after its initial promulgation, and the responsibility of presiding over the new Junta de Fomento rested with the intendant, Claudio Martínez de Pinillos, count of Villanueva, a Creole who had served since 1825.[13] In the Junta de Fomento equal numbers of merchants and plantation owners were represented, and Pinillos managed to nominate as representatives individuals with intelligence and initiative to secure the results of the new institution. The construction and repairs of roads were matters of great urgency to these new institutions. The count of Villanueva, already familiar with the experience of the Real Consulado, would not allow the same old errors to occur again. As soon as he assumed his position as president of the Junta de Fomento, he requested the report of the old Junta de Caminos de Hierro—in which he had participated—with the intention of reviving the railroad project.

When the result of a study on road repairs commissioned by Rafael de Quesada, the deputy superintendent of public works, was released, the railroad project was definitely back on track. According to this report, the repairs and construction of the four roads leaving Havana would cost no less than 142,000 pesos for every one of the next six years. Under these circumstances, the decision of the Junta de Fomento was to repair only the road of Jesús del Monte and seriously to consider building of the railroad to Güines.[14]

With this in mind, the count of Villanueva decided to accelerate his efforts. At the same time he was asking for reports on the American railroads, he instructed Nicolás Campos to prepare a budget for the railroad. Campos, who had previously worked for the Junta de Caminos de Hierro, quickly completed his task, arriving at a budget of 1,220,000 pesos. With this information, the secretary of the Junta de Fomento, Wenceslao de Villaurrutia, and the trustee, Antonio M. de Escovedo—both men supporters of Villanueva—presented a motion in the meeting held on May 9, 1833, that explained "the difficult situation in which we find ourselves as a result of the severe shortage of manpower and the low quality of the materials available to extend our road system beyond the present limit . . . make imperative the construction of a railroad leading to the town of Güines."[15]

Villanueva "accepted the idea favorably" and immediately analyzed the problem of financing the project. As the cost of undertaking the building of the railroad would be around 1.2 million pesos, the count considered it necessary to seek a loan in London. For such a loan—and here was the problem—a royal approval was necessary. Five months later, the Junta de Fomento invested the intendant with full powers to contract the loan. He immediately assigned the subintendant, Joaquín de Uriarte, the task of going to Europe with absolute power to contract such a loan.

With the finance on the way, Villanueva decided to begin determining a right of way and a definite construction cost. For that purpose, American engineer Benjamin H. Wright came to Havana and, together with the land surveyor Alejo H. Lanier and the military engineer Manuel Pastor, studied the Havana-Rincón railroad section. Wright estimated the cost of this part of the line to be 484,000 pesos, which was in keeping with the separate report done by Pastor.[16] According to these studies, the initial estimated budget rose to 1.5 million pesos, without taking into consideration compensation for lands and other minor expenses. The new data and reports were collected in a file that the Junta de Fomento sent to the government of Madrid together with an official request for the queen to approve the loan.

While the steps for the royal authorization were underway, Villanueva contacted some banks in London, assisted by George Villiers, British minister in Madrid. Joaquín de Uriarte, in charge of the negotiations in Madrid, received precise instructions from the Junta de Fomento to negotiate at not less than 75 percent, that is, at 2 million pesos, to get a loan for the amount of 1.5 million, with an interest rate no higher than 6 percent per year. Uriarte was also instructed to ask the queen about the possibility of using part of the revenues of the junta as collateral.[17]

An English banker, Alexander Robertson, agreed to the junta's conditions and, together with Uriarte, began to work out the details. The queen finally authorized the loan through a Real Decreto dated October 12, 1834. Six days later, Uriarte and Robertson signed the contract.

According to the agreed terms, the nominal sum of £400,000 would be reduced to £360,360 after placing bills due on the market at 80 percent of their value, and the Junta de Fomento would receive that last amount in four installments.[18] As a guarantee, there was a collateral consisting of a 1 percent levy on all imports and exports from the port of Havana and a 0.75 percent levy on the rest of the ports of the island. The bills due would accrue a 6 percent yearly interest to be paid twice a year until full amortization on January 1, 1860.

The members of the Junta de Fomento were not entirely satisfied with the contract, particularly with some of its operative terms and the high commissions to be collected by Robertson. Criticisms of the terms of the contract had already appeared in some social circles of Havana, especially those of José Antonio Saco. Saco later explained that while the negotiations were underway in Europe, some Havana businessmen, supported by him through his reports in the *Revista Bimestre* (Forthnightly Review), were trying to gather funds for the railroad project.

The count of Villanueva—according to Saco—paid no attention to these efforts, fearing to lose control over the railroad. In fact, no true evidence supports Saco's claims, and in any case that private initiative seemed quite incomprehensible in light of the two years in which the project remained in abeyance.[19]

The loan might have seemed burdensome but was in accordance with the general conditions of credit at that time. Those years were not characterized by trust and low interest rates—even less in the case of Spain, which was given little credit and whose obligations were negotiated from 45 to 40 percent of their face value. It would also be a mistake to consider the first Cuban railroad as a foreign investment. According to the terms of the credit, the holders received no control over the railroad or any other rights apart from the conditions they were granted as creditors for a debt that, as will be seen later, was punctually paid. The Junta de Fomento was always in control of all initiatives and all railroad operations.

With the financial problem solved, the Junta de Fomento concentrated on the technical matters and manual labor. The junta commissioned Francisco Stoughton, Spanish consul in New York, under the supervision of Francisco Tacón, the Spanish minister in the United States, to contract the manager-engineer for the railroad along with his auxiliary personnel. He was also commissioned to buy the necessary equipment and some of the materials required for the construction of the line. Stoughton contracted one Benjamin Wright, whose son had recently worked for the junta, as general manager of the railroad enterprise. As he could not personally go to Havana, he appointed Alfred Cruger as first engineer and Benjamin Wright Jr. as second engineer in charge of the project. Later on, the junta would engage salaried and daily paid workers to build the line.

Cruger, Wright Jr., and their assistants arrived in Havana on April 1835 with the necessary equipment to measure the route for the first line. The Junta de Fomento commissioned three of its members—Escovedo, Villaurrutia, and Miguel A. Herrera—to administer the project and to make any additional contracts necessary for the work. A few days after his arrival, Cruger started surveying the line, helped by a crew and its overseers. The junta asked for the cooperation of the local authorities to guard the stakes that marked the way in their specific territories. In the plotting, the engineer paid great attention to what was one of the most delicate aspects of the project: the point of departure and exits of the line from Havana. Cruger gave various options for the initial section of the line to the junta: "one from Cerro, beginning in Factoría, one from Cerería, starting at Chávez's Bridge, beginning at Puerta de Tierra, one leaving La Punta, and exiting through Monserrate."[20] After considering the advantages and disadvantages of each case, the junta decided in favor of Monserrate.

In this variant, the railroad would start in the meadows of the Botanical Garden, located in front of the city wall between Puerta de Tierra and Puerta de

Monserrate. From there it would go west along the Zanja Real to follow the Military Promenade or Paseo de Carlos III—then still under construction—passing to the south at a point near the Castillo del Príncipe fort. Since the tracks would cross the works of the Military Promenade being built under the auspices of the Captain General Miguel Tacón, the Junta decided to inform him of the project. Tacón accepted the plans and reports of the road and returned them without immediately expressing any reservations. Nevertheless, a few days later, he asked the Junta de Fomento to modify the route so that it would pass between the promenade and the castle, rather than traverse the works. The junta agreed and sent the new plans to the governor, making clear that such changes would increase the construction costs of the project.

Surprisingly, on May 14, Tacón ordered a halt to the railroad until permission was granted to build in areas near the Castillo del Príncipe fort. Some days later, the governor informed the Junta de Fomento that the projected railroad route violated the defense regulations of the city as it went less than fifteen hundred rods from the castle. As a consequence, the tracks could not be laid in that direction.[21] Tacón's alleged reasons for halting the works were malicious. In the reply to the governor, the junta demonstrated how these regulations had been violated on multiple occasions, even by buildings ordered by the governor himself. The subterfuge was, however, important enough to take the matter directly to the Spanish metropolitan government, resulting in another expensive delay.

Among the difficult obstacles to the railroad project, the latest was the authoritarian and egocentric personality of the governor. Tacón was appointed captain general of the island on May 31, 1834. Coming from a group of military officers defeated in South America, he manifested great distrust toward Creoles, whom he considered covert enemies of the colonial power. He moved the influential Creole families away from the Government Palace and surrounded himself with a clique of peninsular merchants who became wealthy from secretly dealing in the illegal slave trade. During his first months in office, Tacón was on good terms with the count of Villanueva, but conflicts between the two strong personalities soon emerged. The railroad conflict was the first public disagreement between the governor and the intendant. At first some thought that Tacón shut down the works from simple vanity and the belief that the railroad line would obscure the splendor of "his" military promenade.[22] Actually the motivations of the captain general's attitude were considerably more serious. Fourteen days before he ordered a halt to the works on the railroad, Tacón had sent a confidential letter to the Ministry of the Interior in Madrid requesting the right to preside over the Junta de Fomento. The governor pledged that, with the administration reforms, the captain general was deprived of the presidency of the principal economic instrument in the island and that undermined effective local administration. When listing the difficulties of that situation, he mentioned directly the construction of the railroad, alleging that he did not know where it would lead—even though this was of public knowledge—and at the same time insinuated the dangers of foreign engineers drawing plans of Havana.[23]

The railroad became involved in an administrative power struggle. Tacón lusted for a centralization of all colonial administrative instruments under his absolute control. The controversy over the railroad was merely a convenient ruse to undermine the position held by Intendant Villanueva and eventually force him to resign. The royal decision took a year and when it finally arrived it resolved nothing. The royal order prescribed the creation of an Extraordinary Commission formed by officers of the Corps of Engineers and the Junta de Fomento to decide the final location of the railroad line. When the commission was formed, Tacón's supporters constituted a majority. After several months of resistance and evasions, the junta had to yield to a new route. According to this, the new line would enter the city south of the Military Promenade and would run along it, terminating at the Garcini fields, a considerable distance from the city and the port.

With the personnel and the materials already contracted, the Junta de Fomento could not wait for a final solution to the problem of where the first section of the line should run. Even without building this first section, which would ease the transportation of the materials by using the railroad itself, the junta began the leveling of the ground and other works in the sections beyond the Castillo del Príncipe on October 9, 1835.

For the constructions, the Junta de Fomento used the contract system. Once the chief engineer defined the job to be done, the junta signed agreements with private contractors for its execution. The contracts covered all the works but also carts for transportation and several other needs. Most of these contractors, mainly those in charge of the construction, were Americans who moved to the island to work on the railroad.[24]

The most complex part of the road was the section between Havana and Bejucal. The slope from Havana to Bejucal was 320 feet in 16 miles, which made it difficult to obtain 30-foot gradients.[25] The uneven ground demanded complicated infrastructure grading works, leveling hills or even opening paths through them as done in Vento where the American contractor John Pascoe built a 320-foot-long tunnel. The project also included the building of several bridges. An especially difficult job was bridging the Almendares River, a task requiring the use of 200 masonry support pillars imported from the United States. The line was even more expensive because, foreseeing traffic complications, it was designed to have two way lines.

The works also suffered from an inadequate local labor supply. The Junta de Fomento had arranged to contract some local journeymen and mainly rented

The Vento Tunnel with its picturesque entrance in the Moorish style. (*Paseo pintoresco de la isla de Cuba*. Vol. 1. Havana: Imprenta Soler & Co., 1841)

slaves and freedmen.[26] The junta expected strong support from Spain, especially the defeated and exiled Carlist prisoners from the Spanish Civil War, but Tacón reduced the number to 140 at first, and some months later to only 30. The junta, in order to resolve its labor shortage, resorted to the importation of daily paid workers. It signed agreements with some captains of ships to bring contract workers from the Canary Islands. At the same time, Benjamin Wright went to the United States with the same purpose hoping to contract between 800 and 1,200 men who would work in qualified and semiqualified positions.

The construction of the railroad concentrated the biggest salaried force on the island. The Junta de Fomento knew the potential dangers of such a situation. As soon as the first group arrived from the Canary Islands, the junta asked the authorities to see that it was "forbidden to persuade or help any Canary workers to desert by imposing any penalty they might require," as the Junta had "found sound reasons to fear that they might desert, favored by the multitude of persons of the same origin who were well established on the island."[27] Salaried workers, however, could not prosper in a slave system. White journeymen—particularly the Canary Islanders who faced no cultural differences—could easily find other ways to earn their living, often abandoning work that they considered too difficult, or work that had traditionally been assigned to slaves.

The arrival of workers from the United States of America—who were generically called Irish—and those from the Canary Islands provided an ample con-

Bridge over the Almendares River, one of the basic construction projects of the railroad to Güines. (F. Miahle, *Isla de Cuba pintoresca*. Havana: Imprenta de la Sociedad Patriotica, n.d.)

struction crew. The solution was, nevertheless, temporary, because the white journeymen were decimated by epidemics and desertions. The work force was gradually increased by using slaves, despite the fact that they died in great numbers during the construction of the railroad. In the parish of Cerro, 340 railroad slaves were buried between 1835 and 1841.[28] Nevertheless, the works advanced rapidly enough to begin the installment of the superstructure in some sections. The lines were built on six inches layer of gravel to guarantee an adequate drainage. Originally the rails were placed on wooden crossties but the bankruptcy of the lumber dealers forced them to replace these by hewing stones. These stone crossties were 7.5 feet long, 2 feet wide, and 1.5 feet thick and were placed at a distance of 12 feet from one another, supported by smaller stone crossties. The iron rails, imported from England, were "T" shaped and weighed 50 pounds per yard and could be classified as the best of their kind then.[29] The chief engineer for the railroad, Alfred Cruger, considered the quality of the tracks as superior to any needed for the future requirements of equipment and materials that would run on them.

In April 1837, the first shipment of locomotives sent by Robertson arrived from England. These were four Braithwaite locomotives—of a model similar to Stephenson's "Rocket"—and several freight and passenger cars, plus machines and tools for the railroad's service station. As a result of the inconvenience produced by the lack of the first section of tracks and the dispute over the location of the station and warehouses, the equipment and materials remained piled up on the docks and could not be used or kept under proper storage.

Of all the difficulties faced, the worst came just before completing the Havana-Bejucal section. The project ran out of money. Even though the budget was properly calculated, the difficulties that Tacón created, the additional cost of hewing stone crossties due to the bankruptcy of the lumber dealers, the higher price of iron, and the payment of land compensations, plus a host of unforeseen factors, simply overwhelmed the financial resources. The Junta de Fomento was also responsible since despite its promise of an extra yearly 70,000 pesos supplementary help, after three years the Comisión de Ferrocarriles had only received a mere 40,000 pesos. To solve the situation, the junta asked Robertson for an additional 500,000 pesos extension of the loan, in conformity with the agreement on signing the contract. With this extension and some other resources devised by the junta, the construction of the railroad was finally completed.

By mid-1837, only the construction of the initial section of the line, the station, the warehouses, and the service station remained. The Junta de Fomento had no other choice than to accept Tacón's demands or face an indefinite delay in the completion of the railroad. The Garcini lands were bought to build the station, even with the disadvantage of being far from the port and having a gradient of forty-five feet per mile—much steeper than the rest of the tracks—all of which would force an increase in the price of transportation and reduce the number of cars that the locomotives could pull. The warehouses and service station were built on a lot of land from a farm called La Ciénaga (The Marsh) purchased by the commission near the junction of the Cerro and Puentes Grandes roads.

The initial section was built rapidly. On the eve of its conclusion, the Comisión de Ferrocarriles delivered the tariffs for freight and fares to the captain general and these were approved and published a few days later. For the trip from Havana to Bejucal passengers paid fares of 2 pesos and 4 reales in first class cars, 1 peso and 2 reales in second class, and 5 reales in third. Sugar packing crates cost 6 reales each; a sack of seven arrobas of coffee, 2 reales; and animals, 1 peso. At the same time the company contracted the personnel to operate the railroad, Robertson sent eight English engine drivers and some other operators who had recently arrived in Havana to operate the equipment. The Junta de Fomento completed

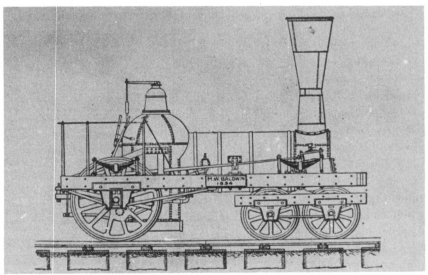

Examples of the first locomotives used in Cuba: the "Rocket" (top) by the English maker, R. Stephenson; and the "Miller" with its bogie by the American, M. Baldwin.

the personnel with section watchmen, warehouse guards, conductors, and other minor laborers.

To commemorate the Saint's Day of Queen Isabel II, the Real Junta de Fomento solemnly inaugurated the railroad on November 19, 1837. In spite of the weather—it rained throughout the previous night—a crowd gathered to watch the noisy locomotives move along newly laid tracks. At eight o'clock that morning, the first train departed to Bejucal. With this departure, Cuba became the seventh country in the world with a railroad, thus anticipating that its mother country Spain by more than a decade.[30]

The exploitation of the Havana-Bejucal section was not an economic success. In the last two months of the year 1837, only 10,778 pesos were collected, and in the first months of the following year, the results were no better. This did not surprise the Junta de Fomento. The territory where the first sixteen miles of railroad ran was not very productive. Only the regions south of Bejucal could provide enough freight to produce profit for the railroad. Also, the income of the enterprise was lower due to the location of the station in Garcini. Even though a contract for the transportation of the freight from Garcini to the port had been sold at auction, no transporter would accept less than 3 reales for each sugar crate. This was exactly half of the fare charged by the railroad for transport between Bejucal and Havana. Under these conditions there were no possibilities for profit.

To counteract this difficulty, the Junta de Fomento had asked Cruger for the study of a railroad branch to Batabanó. This possibility, foreseen by the old Junta de Caminos de Hierro, was revived because "communication with the southern coast promised abundant products . . . new incomes will replace the present losses."[31] The Batabanó branch, representing a railroad connection between the two coasts of the island, allowed the railroad to take over all the southern maritime transportation and connect it directly with Havana. The ships could unload in Batabanó and avoid the long, risky trip around Cape San Antonio.

Aside from the construction of branch tracks, the main need of the railroad was still the termination of the projected line to Güines. No other source of income could compete with the economic injection that the arrival of the railroad to Güines represented. The Junta de Fomento therefore concentrated all its efforts on this task, accelerating the construction of the road.

The track between Güines and Bejucal doubled the distance already built, but it was technically easier. The track went south from Bejucal and along the towns of Buenaventura and Quivicán. After crossing the Quivicán River and making a wide curve, the railroad avoided the Bejucal Heights, which, although not very high, represented a major obstacle. The level land where the railroad ran facilitated the construction of the infrastructure and accelerated the completion of the works. The different sections were put into service as soon as they were finished.

The full line opened to traffic on November 19, 1838, on the first anniversary of the railroad, when the first trains arrived in the prosperous town on the Mayabeque River.

With the opening of the thirty-mile block between Bejucal and Güines, the economic situation of the railroad changed radically. In 1838, revenues amounted to around 100,000 pesos, but the year after, with the railroad at full capacity, income tripled to 171,792 pesos from fares and 136,484 pesos from freight.[32] With revenues approaching 1,000 pesos a day, the railroad was a success. As often happens, the former detractors changed their minds. The Junta de Fomento began to receive requests for the construction of branches, stations, and warehouses from several interested landowners. These competed in generosity, offering land free of charge for the railroad facilities. The landowners of the jurisdiction of San Antonio de los Baños wrote an extensive report to persuade the junta to build the southern branch between Bejucal and the Guanímar cove, and not between San Felipe and Batabanó as the "illustrious corporation" had planned.[33]

The railroad construction was completed three years ahead of schedule. Its cost appears to have been 2,005,479 pesos, but the documents that stated this amount are not very clear. Ramón de la Sagra affirms that, from the total cost, 1,753,590 pesos were spent on the construction, and the rest was spent on warehouses and other works.[34] It is also not clear if the Junta de Fomento included as costs the amounts paid to Robertson to cover up the first installments of the loan.[35] In any case, the relative cost of 40,000 to 45,000 pesos per mile compared favorably with the average cost of similar railroads.

Even though the revenues were high, the Junta de Fomento was not fully exploiting the potential of the railroad. Only two trains a day ran: one for freight with thirty cars and another for passengers with seven cars. Jacinto Salas Quiroga, a Spanish traveler who used the train to Güines in 1839, complained that the cars were too hot and heavy and that the train was very slow.[36]

The operation of the railroad was not without some difficulties. The English locomotives were not very efficient and the engine drivers did not follow the regulations enforced by Cruger. This inefficiency brought about accidents, one of which—caused when the locomotive "Villanueva" hit a bull—gave Tacón the opportunity to launch his last attack against the Junta de Fomento. In 1838, when the Bejucal-Güines section was still incomplete, four out of the eight English locomotives were considered as virtually useless. Cruger, the director, went to the United States and bought two locomotives and contracted three engine drivers. Observing the good results of these engines, he suggested to the junta the complete substitution of American locomotives. Cruger claimed that two American locomotives could do a better job than eight English ones because owing to the size and position of the wheels and the height of the boilers, they were less likely to restrict free movement or damage either their engines or the tracks.[37]

The Junta de Fomento accepted Cruger's suggestions and sent the chief of engines, E. K. Dodd, to the United States to buy two new locomotives.[38] At the same time, the junta decided to return to England the locomotives originally sent by Robertson. This created a fierce argument with the English businessman, who disagreed with the decision. In spite of Robertson's objection to their return, the locomotives were shipped to England and sold at auction. Although the inefficiencies of the English locomotives seem to be undeniable, there is a possibility that Cruger took advantage of the opportunity to open the Cuban market to American manufacturers. In this sense, Cruger scored a success since thereafter all locomotives used by most of the Cuban railroads were American made.

The other problem for the Junta de Fomento was the inconvenience caused by the Garcini station. The junta was not resigned to having the station so far from the port, and the count of Villanueva continued to ask the authorities in Madrid to have it moved. This became possible on April 15, 1838, when one of Tacón's feigned attempts to resign was unexpectedly accepted. Villanueva won a battle in which he had to use all his power and influence. The day after the departure of Tacón from Havana, on April 23, 1838, Madrid accepted the relocation of the station to the grounds of the Botanical Garden. As the approval came some days before the end of the construction of the line to Güines, the junta decided to postpone the move temporarily. In February 1839, with the road to Güines finished, Cruger presented to the junta 148,844 pesos, the estimated budget for the track, and on April 1, 1840, trains began to depart from the Botanical Garden, now converted into the brand new Villanueva Station.

Fostered, built, and operated by the Real Junta de Fomento, the first Cuban railroad could be considered a government enterprise. Cuba, along with Belgium, represented the first countries in which the railroad resulted from direct government policy. In the case of Cuba, however, the government administration did not last long. The junta, following a liberal economic trend, began to take steps to sell the railroad as soon as it was completed.

As soon as the Bejucal-Güines section was finished, there was an attempt to rent the railroad. On October 23, 1838, the Junta de Fomento published an advertisement in the *Diario de la Habana* (Havana Daily) announcing the rental conditions of the railroad. The rental period would be five years and the renter would pay the junta the amount of 130,000 pesos for the first year, increasing progressively by 10,000 pesos every year thereafter.[39] Apparently, this idea was not accepted. Instead, several businessmen inquired about the possibility of an outright purchase of the railroad.

The Villanueva Station.

The Junta de Fomento contemplated the prospect of selling the railroad and also considered that the functions assigned to this institution by the crown were those of fostering and improving the development of enterprises, not that of running one or profiting from it. The lack of resources and the various responsibilities of the junta would not allow its members to face the planned extension of the road. Finally, red tape and the complex and delayed procedures of public administration would limit the indispensable dynamics that an enterprise such as the railroad needed. As a result of this analysis, in April 1839, the junta decided to "ask the Supreme Government for the permission to sell the railroad, or parts of it, convinced that the administration of this enterprise [was] not adequate to our corporation."[40]

Granted the permission by Real Cédula on June 28, 1839, the Junta de Fomento announced the selling of the railroad at public auction. The price settled upon, including all facilities was 3 million pesos, with a 6 percent interest. The sale of the railroad immediately became a public event. The newspapers that hardly mentioned the progress of the railroad during its construction began to publish full page editorials to comment on the news. Describing the atmosphere of the moment, Domingo del Monte wrote to his brother-in-law, José Luis Alfonso, that "in these days nobody thinks of anything but the railroad. You simply cannot imagine the excitement resulting from the announcement of the selling of the one to Güines."[41]

As soon as the Junta de Fomento's decision had been made public, a group of important individuals, lead by the former secretary of the institution, Wenceslao Villaurrutia, created a corporation to buy the railroad. The 258 shareholders of this corporation included the most conspicuous representatives of the Havana aristocracy such as the counts of Fernandina and Peñalver, and the most outstanding Spanish merchants in Havana such as Viada, Cagigal, and Joaquín Gómez who had also been prominent member of Tacón's clique. Meeting at Gómez's house, the members of this corporation—known as "Corporation A"—wrote a proposal to the junta that offered to pay the junta's price if the junta would agree to take over the outstanding balance on the English loan. They also offered to build an eight-league-long branch between Rincón and Guanímar as well as other possible branches, although no formal commitments were made.

The possibilities of Corporation A changed with the creation of a competitor— Corporation B—comprising between twenty and twenty-five wealthy Havana proprietors. In this select group were men like Domingo Aldama, Gonzalo Alfonso, Carlos Drake, Pedro Diago, and Miguel Herrera, the elite of the sugar oligarchy. Its president was Antonio María Escovedo who, as a member of the Comisión de Ferrocarriles of the Junta de Fomento, had considerable railroad experience. The proposal of Corporation B surpassed that of Corporation A in several aspects. It offered to pay 500,000 pesos more, plus a commitment to build twenty leagues of branch tracks—twelve more than Corporation A—as well as a reduction in general fares. It also agreed to recognize the junta's outstanding debt arising from the purchase of the Botanical Garden and the construction of the station.

The rivalry between the two corporations became public and virulent. It served as an exhaust valve to the contradictions that existed among different economic groups of the ruling class. The members of the two corporations paid for supplements to be distributed free in the local newspapers in which they promoted their own offers. Even the philosopher José de la Luz y Caballero felt the need to defend his friends of the Corporation B and wrote a series of articles under the pen name, "The Other."

When the period for the offers closed without any new competitors, the offers went to a selection committee. The members of Corporation A, knowing they were at a disadvantage, fostered the idea of combining both offers. Captain General Don Joaquín de Ezpeleta agreed to this idea. On December 3, 1839, the selection committee rendered its decision to the Junta de Fomento. As was to be expected, Corporation B won, and Villaurrutia, in the name of Corporation A, again proposed the merging of both groups. Escovedo immediately attacked this proposal, generating passionate exchanges between the members present. The junta decided to postpone the final vote. Finally, the junta confirmed the victory of Corporation B, but this victory was voided by Ezpeleta, using the argument of lack of consensus. He decided to send the files of both groups to Madrid so that the metropolitan government could render the ultimate decision.

Ezpeleta's strategy resulted in a two-year delay in passing the railroad over to private hands. Finally, in June 1841, the metropolitan decision arrived. Apparently, the gist of the Spanish decisions was not to decide anything. The government ordered the creation of a new commission that would write another set of conditions for the selling of the railroad. The new conditions were written on the basis of the offer of Corporation B, but they included some new and important stipulations. The purchasers were required to establish an anonymous company with a backing capital of 1 million pesos. As a guarantee, it should mortgage city and rural lands for the amount of 300,000 and 500,000 pesos respectively. It also had to promise to build branch lines to Batabanó, San Antonio de los Baños, and Palos within a stipulated time. The new contract strictly forbade selling the railroad to any foreigners.[42] In return for these conditions, the government granted certain concessions: Batabanó would be officially declared as both a local as well as an international port with the purchasing company granted an exemption from import and export taxes for two years, and with it the right—granted for the first time in Cuba—to enforce expropriation of lands required for railroad construction.

The new conditions were, notwithstanding the concessions, too strong. The members of Corporation B withdrew their offer and dissolved the enterprise. On March 1, 1842, the railroad was offered at auction under the new terms. Juan Poey, a rich landowner, representing a group composed of many of the former members of Corporation B accepted the offer. The Spanish merchants made a last attempt to buy the railroad.[43] Don Francisco Ventosa, in the name of a company that only accepted Spaniards as shareholders offered 100,000 pesos over Poey's offer of 3.5 million pesos. This forced Poey to raise his bid, thereby winning the auction. The Caminos de Hierro de la Habana Company, represented by Poey, finally acquired the railroad.

With the sale of the railroad the circle closed. Intended to solve the needs of the planters, the building of the railroad was a result of the efforts of the main institution of the colony that defended the interests of that group. With the construction completed and its profitability demonstrated, the planters assumed the ownership of the railroad and took over its operations.

3

The Initial Expansion, 1838–1852

The construction of the railroad from Havana to San Julián de Güines instantly changed the traditional concepts of overland transportation of sugar from slow, ponderous carts to a swifter and more economical system. Even before the ultimate success of the railroads could be demonstrated, others were interested in building similar railroads in places more distant from Havana, such as Cárdenas and Puerto Príncipe.

The low, swampy plains surrounding Cárdenas Bay retarded its commercial development at the beginning of the nineteenth century. In spite of these conditions, the first landowners made their slaves move great amounts of dirt, stones, and hardwood to build docks and warehouses near the anchoring grounds of the bay. In various places, including the location that became the port of Cárdenas on the southern side of the bay, local planters built wharves to ship sugar, molasses, and rum during the first decades of the nineteenth century.[1] From these simple wharves cargoes of sugar and other products were loaded into lighters steered by long poles in the shallow waters and ferried to ships anchored in deeper waters.[2]

In spite of its natural difficulties, the port provided the best location from which to ship the products coming from the localities of Lagunillas and Cimarrones, on the south side of the bay, and the new sugar mills of the former *hato* (ranch) of Macuriges to the southeast. The port was also the natural exit for the products of plantations in the plains to the east and southeast in the localities of San Antón de la Anegada and Guamutas. The lack of mountains made this area ideal for sugar production and conducive for the construction of an efficient system of transportation.

Since many of the landowners of the area were well established in Havana and some were also senior officers in the army and the militia, they immediately began to use their influence to promote the development of the area in which they had their estates. On July 30, 1836, a group of these men, mostly landowners in Lagunillas district, met in the house of Brigadier Juan Montalvo O'Farril and wrote what could be properly considered their regional demands to the highest authorities of the colonial government.[3] The principal request involved moving the seat of local government from Lagunillas to the newly founded town of Cárdenas and authorization to open the port direct to foreign commerce. A third consideration, not yet fully expressed as a demand, was the analysis of the "advantages that the construction of a railroad from Cárdenas to Bemba would exert on the agricultural development of the area."[4] Bemba—presently called Jovellanos— was a growing sugar producing area, twenty-eight kilometers to the south of the port of Cárdenas. The first of the petitions to move the authorities to Cárdenas was granted in 1839, including the creation of a compound for runaway slaves.[5] The request to open the port, in spite of the pressures of Montalvo and the enactment of the royal order of February 3, 1838, was delayed until 1843, when other ports were also authorized to conduct international commerce.[6]

By that time an engineer, Manuel de J. Carrera, had already drawn up a project for the construction of a railroad from Cárdenas to Bemba. Antonio Gutiérrez, a Havana businessman linked to the promoters, delivered it to Captain General Miguel Tacón in 1836. The new enterprise, in the form of a joint-stock company, was created on May 23, 1837.[7] The construction of a southeast branch leading to the estates of the Montalvo family in Macuriges was added to the concession three weeks later.[8]

The first stockholders meeting of the Compañía del Ferrocarril de Cárdenas a Soledad de Bemba (Railroad Company from Cárdenas to Soledad de Bemba) took place on April 26, 1837. Montalvo was elected president and the secretary was Domingo del Monte, who was responsible for the management of the corporation within the bureaucratic judicial system of the colonial administration.[9] In this enterprise, Domingo del Monte represented the interests of one of the wealthiest sugar-producing families of the island, the Aldama-Alfonso family.[10] The company began with a capital of 1 million pesos divided into 10,000 shares of 100 pesos each. Montalvo held 40 percent of these shares while the family of Domingo del Monte owned 24 percent. The rest was distributed among the landowners of Lagunillas and Cimarrones.[11]

Construction of tracks began on April 17, 1838. More than two hundred men began to build embankments and tracks, struggling against incessant rains that, within a few months, forced the cessation of all activity.[12] In one year and five months, the first part of the road was finished, and the opening of the section between Cárdenas and Contreras took place on May 25, 1840. The rest of the line to Bemba was finished in December of that year, and the extension to the freight station of Montalvo (nowadays Navajas) to the southeast was completed three years later in January 1844.[13]

The construction of the railroad of Cárdenas created unease among the merchants and landowners of the neighboring city of Matanzas, who had controlled the sugar trade of the region until that moment. In January 1839, the engineer Carrera informed Domingo del Monte that "the businessmen of Matanzas are rising against our project, asking the Junta that we should abandon our line and take it from Bemba to Canímar."[14] Domingo del Monte said something similar to Antonio Gutiérrez, the promoter of the enterprise: "You might have heard about the revolution in Matanzas to change the line of our railroad taking it from Soledad [Bemba] to Canímar. . . . I can imagine our friend Cristóbal Madan [landowner of Matanzas and proprietor of the Canímar estate] representing the main role on that stage; if you happen to see him, be so kind to tell him that the line cannot be changed."[15]

From the point of view of the Matanzas merchants, the situation was quite different. The existence of a nearby railroad could cause the deviation to other ports of part of the freight that had been the basis of their operations of storage and transportation. Only the judicial limitations to engage in international commerce affecting Cárdenas Bay gave competitive stability to Matanzas, so the merchants in Cárdenas requested a similar free-trade permission for their port. Either the Matanzas merchants were relatively successful in their protest, or the request fell victim of the habitual delays of the Spanish administration. In any case free-port permission was granted to Cárdenas only on January 1, 1843, the same year that a train departed from the port of Matanzas for the first time.[16]

The construction of the railroad to Cárdenas was soon followed by initiatives proposed by other landowners within the region of Cárdenas, particularly by some rich Havana proprietors interested in fostering sugar production in the former estate of Managüises. These landowners, whose estates were located east of the Cárdenas Railroad, knew that the railway would only satisfy the needs of the landowners of the western regions and decided to solve their transportation problems on their own. The landowners Pedro Diago, Manuel Castillo, Tomás de Juara, Joaquín de Arrieta, and the count of Peñalver asked the government for permission to build a railroad connecting the haciendas Sabanilla de Palma, Laguna Grande, and Managüises with the Júcaro wharf on the shore of the Cárdenas Bay. With the authorization granted in September 1841, the promoters created a railroad company.[17] The new company had a capitalization of 1 million pesos, divided into 2,000 shares of 500 pesos each. Within a few days of its creation, more than half of its shares were fully subscribed.[18]

The plotting and construction of the new Ferrocarril de Júcaro were assigned to Alfred Cruger, who had recently finished the railroad to Güines. According to the interests of the promoters, the railroad would follow a curve to the south to serve the numerous landowners of San Antón, where the regular transportation of between twelve thousand and fifteen thousand crates of sugar could be expected.[19] After about thirty kilometers, the lines would end in Banagüises to transport the freight from the sugar mills Tinguaro and Ponina belonging to the Diago family, Flor de Cuba belonging to Arrieta, El Narciso belonging to Peñalver, and Conchita of Juara—all the sugar mills belonging to the promoters of the company. The budget estimated for the railroad was 744,804 pesos, but Cruger's calculations were extremely optimistic and, by the time the first section was finished, the company had spent 1,120,000 pesos. The financial difficulties were solved through a £26,200 sterling loan from Alexander Robertson and Brothers, the same firm that previously made the loan for the Güines Railroad.[20] Thanks to this financial backing, the railroad was finished in 1844.

As a business, the Ferrocarril de Júcaro was a "risky speculation." Different from the previous railroad investments and from the following ones, this line ran along a territory that was insufficiently developed to guarantee enough load volume to make it profitable. The venture of the investors caused certain problems as the administration of the railroad had troubles paying the initial installments of Robertson's loan. Fortunately, the investment soon showed promising results as Banagüises and the other region served by the railroad saw an increase in production, especially from a number of large sugar mills such as Progreso belonging to Ignacio de Peñalver. Gradually sugar crates began to pile up in the Ferrocarril de Júcaro's stations and the railroad company began to profit from the economic development fostered by its creation.[21]

By 1846 the two Cárdenas railroads were profitable businesses, and the town, already a minor government seat, experienced a fabulous productive and demographic growth. The production of the 119 sugar mills in the jurisdiction exceeded sixty thousand tons of sugar. The town, which was being called "city" of Cárdenas, quadrupled its population in a decade, to more than thirty-four hundred "souls." The railroads were largely responsible for this growth.[22]

From the perspective of the sugar producer, the railroad was the ideal means of transportation for export products. The invention was also of great interest to the sugar trade merchants who imported all kinds of products and equipment for the plantations. This double interest notably benefited those merchants who controlled the operations of the port of Matanzas in the nineteenth century and they rose to be among the most solid commercial firms of that time on the island.[23]

The success of the landowners of Cárdenas in building a railroad to transport their products to their port soon moved their neighbors in Matanzas to build a line to take advantage of the free-port status they enjoyed. On December 28, 1839, a representative of the sugar production interests of the already mentioned Aldama-Alfonso family in the city of Matanzas, Gonzalo Alfonso Soler, obtained a concession from the captain general, Joaquín Ezpeleta, to build a railroad from that city to the estate called Las Piedras of Manuel Alvarez, passing along one called Sabanilla del Encomendador.[24] Almost directly to the south, in the municipality of Sabanilla del Encomendador, were four of the Alfonso family sugar mills: San Gonzalo, Acana, Triunvirato and Concepción. In the same vicinity the Aldama family already owned the sugar mills Santo Domingo, Santa Rosa, and San José and later built the Armonía and the Concepción. It was, therefore a matter of first priority for that family group, as well as for other local landowners and merchants, to build a railroad in that direction. From the original terms in which the petition presented by Alfonso was written, one could infer that the new enterprise would be a personal matter, or in any case a family business. The colonial authorities, suspicious of the haughtiness of the powerful Creole family, agreed to the petition, but "with the slight modification that the subscription must be open and extended to voluntary subscription among the neighbors, establishing convenient guarantees or securities."[25] The Alfonso family had no other choice than to satisfy these suggestions, and the Compañía del Ferrocarril de Matanzas was constituted with the participation of some other personalities. The president was Francisco de la O García, proprietor of the Jesús María sugar mill in Sabanilla, and a group of landowners settled in Matanzas as merchants, like Simón Ximeno and Francisco de la Torriente, would hold directive seats.[26]

The capital of the enterprise was 1,400 shares of 500 pesos each—a total of 700,000 pesos—and its subscription was a success from the very beginning. Its president said so to the secretary of the Cárdenas Railroad on February 3, 1840: "We have already some money to begin the railroad enterprise from this city to Sabana del Encomendador and Manuel Alvarez or Las Piedras, and, consequently, I have called for the first shareholders' meeting."[27] To show its support for the new project, the Junta de Fomento bought shares in the amount of 146,500 pesos.

The construction of the railroad was assigned to Alfred Cruger, who began the work in September 1841.[28] The line included a deviation to the village of La Guanábana, which had a yearly production of over twenty-five hundred tons of sugar. There, some twelve kilometers from Matanzas, the construction of a warehouse was planned to store the sugar and molasses of the nearby sugar mills. When the 1843 sugar crop was about to start (November 1), the whistles of the locomotive "La Junta" broke the silence of La Guanábana, marking the beginning of railroad transportation with the port of Matanzas.[29] The second section of the track, to Sabanilla, was inaugurated two years later, in 1845, with the horrors of the slave revolt of 1844 still fresh in everyone's mind. That year steps were taken to extend the lines to Taberna de Reyes—Unión de Reyes—eight kilometers to the south, where the Aldama-Alfonso family continued to develop sugar mills. The new concession was granted provisionally on January 4, 1844, and the road in that direction was completed on October 15, 1849.[30]

"La Junta," the oldest locomotive currently in Cuba.

Among the plans of the Matanzas Company was the idea to build a branch of about fifty kilometers running west to east, from a place known as La Cidra in the direction of Matanzas, Sabanilla, and Taberna de Coliseo. The concession was granted to Francisco la O García, as president of the railroad, on August 25, 1842; and this concession for the first time included a specification stating that "the transport of troops will be free in the case of a foreign invasion or a slave revolt."[31] The document also indicated that a new stock offering would have to be floated to carry out the work. Construction of this branch was postponed during the year 1843, apparently because of the fear produced by the slave revolts that took place that year; something similar happened with the Cárdenas Railroad that had planned a branch from its station in Bemba to Coliseo.[32] Under such circumstances, the railroad shareholders were not interested in investing in the midst of a turbulent sugar production area surrounded by mountains conducive for marronage. Details of this situation were set down by the director of the Cárdenas Railroad to the secretary, Domingo del Monte, on October 23, 1843: "We should not even think of the branch to Coliseo; the slaughter in March has given the company bad luck and the people have become lukewarm to the idea of a new track. They say that they want early dividends in cash, so we will probably build only up to Navajas."[33]

The Matanzas to Sabanilla railroad station in Matanzas City. (S. Hazard, *Cuba with Pen and Pencil*. Hartford, Conn.: Hartford Publishing, 1870)

The elimination of the project to Coliseo by both enterprises forced the supposed beneficiaries of that branch—among them the shareholders of the Matanzas Railroad, Simón Ximeno and Cosme de la Torriente—to join the former Matanzas governor, Brigadier Antonio García Oña (also a landowner in the region), to undertake the construction of a branch from Guanábana to Coliseo.[34] The Junta de Fomento showed special interest in the construction of this line and bought 102,000 pesos in shares for the small railroad. The official inauguration of the line on June 1, 1848, did not solve all the needs of the landowners in the region of the shareholders, as many of the sugar mills located east of Coliseo still lacked the needed means of transportation and had no immediate hopes to get them.[35] The particular circumstances of a small twelve-kilometers-long railroad, submitted to the Matanzas Railroad to carry its load to the port, placed it in a subordinate situation to the former. On the other hand, the withdrawal of some of the shareholders with properties east of Coliseo, claiming the need for a branch to Bemba, found constant opposition from the Cárdenas Company, which feared the strong competition of the west. Under such a situation, this was a railroad destined to be assimilated by another.

The copper mines of Santiago del Prado, near the little town of El Cobre, west of the Bay of Santiago de Cuba, were known and exploited with varying intensity since the sixteenth century. The best place of shipping the production of this

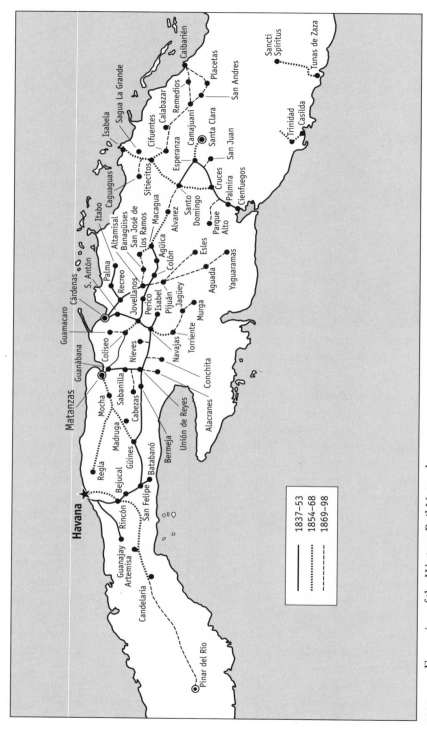

MAP 3.1. Expansion of the Western Rail Network

Havana

Matanzas
Guanábana
Guamacaro
Cárdenas
S. Antón

Regla
Bejucal
Rincón
San Felipe
Batabanó
Güines
Madruga
Mocha
Sabanilla
Cabezas
Bermeja
Unión de Reyes
Alacranes
Conchita
Nieves
Coliseo
Torriente
Murga
Navajas
Jagüey
Pijuán
Isabel
Perico
Jovellanos
Recreo
Palma
Itabo
Altamisal
Banagüises
San José de los Ramos
Macagua
Agüica
Colón
Aguada
Yaguaramas
Esles
Alvarez
Santo Domingo
Parque Alto
Palmira
Cienfuegos
Cruces
San Juan
Santa Clara
Camajuaní
Esperanza
Cifuentes
Sitiecitos
Caguaguas
Sagua La Grande
Isabela
Calabazar
Remedios
Placetas
San Andres
Caibarién
Trinidad
Casilda
Tunas de Zaza
Sancti Spíritus

Guanabana
Guanajay
Artemisa
Candelaria
Pinar del Río

1837–53
1854–68
1869–98

mine was a landing along the bay called, indifferently, Salt Point or Salt Cove. The rough road that led to the wharf required a day's trip during the dry season, or two when it rained, using primitive means of transportation such as mule trains and carts.[36] In 1837 these copper mines belonged to the Sociedad Minera del Cobre. The most important members of this company were John Hardy, then British consul in Santiago de Cuba, and the Havana businessman, landowner, and sponsor of the Ferrocarril de Júcaro, Joaquín de Arrieta.[37] Both the British consul and the Creole landowner thought that a railroad would make the transport of ores from the mine to the port cheaper. Arrieta assured everyone that his properties alone were security enough to obtain a loan in London to finance the construction.[38]

The location of the wharf, far from the city and next to the bay's entrance, aroused suspicion on the part of the colonial authorities that the facilities would be used for illegal trade. This produced constant objections and delays in granting the concession.[39] Arrieta first requested permission in 1837, and repeated his petition between 1839 and 1842, until it was finally granted by a royal order issued on December 20, 1842.

The skillful French engineer, Julio Sagebién, was put in charge of the construction, and successfully overcame the challenging topography of the region by taking advantage of the slopes. The movement of the trains from the mine to the ports was assisted by gravity, thanks to the slopes of the hills and mountains. The weight of the loaded ore cars hauled the returning empty ones, or those carrying coal, up the incline using a system of wires and pulley wheels. Only along the intermediate and final section of the line was power provided by "blood engines," a euphemistic description for the poor mules used in the operation. People at the time called the ingenious design a "self-propelled" railroad.[40] Once finished, the lines were 14.56 kilometers long, including 1.56 kilometers of double track. The total cost of the railroad was 605,056 pesos, and it was financed without any government support and without the usual subsidy from the Junta de Fomento. The rapid completion of the fully equipped lines allowed the operations to begin on November 1, 1844.[41] This railroad was the most profitable of the island. During its first five years of existence it carried 145,010 English tons of ore, of which 119,048 were copper. The revenues obtained in that period of time amounted to 900,118 pesos, producing a total profit of 531,784 pesos—87 percent of the 605,056 pesos invested in its construction. The high profits obtained by this unique Cuban railroad were confirmed by several historians, including Jacobo de Pezuela and Mariano Torriente, who estimated that the annual benefits of the Ferrocarril del Cobre were between 20 and 30 percent of the capital invested.[42]

Even though Santa María de Puerto Príncipe—nowadays Camagüey—was not a coastal city, its high population made it the third urban area of importance on the island. The existence of the wharves of San Fernando de Nuevitas on the northern coast and, to some extent, that of Santa Cruz del Sur on the southern facilitated imports and exports. Nuevitas became a free port in 1784, and Santa Cruz in 1826. Besides cattle, the main bases of the economy of Camagüey were the traditional crops of the country—sugar and coffee—but the small sugar mills of this region were insignificant compared with the powerfully productive machinery of the west.

In 1836, almost at the same time as the petition for a railroad made by the landowners of Cárdenas, the delegation from the Economic Society of the municipality of Puerto Príncipe stated the need of a railroad to drag them out of their commercial isolation. A personality of great prestige in the city, due to his literary talent and his initiatives, Gaspar Betancourt Cisneros, "El Lugareño," had become the crusader of the Camagüey Railroad.[43] On January 10, 1837, together with the landowners Luis Loret de Mola and Tomás Pío Betancourt, El Lugareño requested and obtained a concession from Governor Miguel Tacón to build a railroad from the city of Puerto Príncipe to the port of Nuevitas.[44]

The construction of the railroad was assigned to the American engineer Benjamin H. Wright, who designed a project for a sixty-nine-kilometer line linking both localities. Due to the absence of natural obstacles in the area, there was almost no need for bridges and tunnels. The only additional requirement was an embankment to prevent flooding during the rainy season. Wright's budget for the construction was 340,981 pesos. The track, designed with a width of 1.60 meters between the rails, was unique in Cuba. The designer underestimated the expenses of the excessive width as he counted on a considerable saving from using local timber from the nearby woods for the crossties.[45]

Despite expecting the concession, tracks were not laid until after 1840, apparently because the subscribers failed to pay their shares on time.[46] As the sugar production of Puerto Príncipe alone was insufficient to fill the service of a railroad, the investment was not very tempting to the possible subscribers. In spite of this, Wright completed the tracks for the first twenty miles in February, 1841. Later, on March 30, 1841, an anonymous company was created with 10,000 shares valued at 100 pesos each.[47]

The difficulties with the colonial officials paled against the economic problems of the enterprise. El Lugareño tried to solve them by attracting investors from Havana and asking for help from the Junta de Fomento. The help of the intendant, Claudio Martínez de Pinillos, was not as strong as it could be expected, and when he left his post in 1841, the possibilities for the financing of the railroad became even more limited.[48] In October, 1843, the sixty-one kilometers between Nuevitas and Sabana Nueva, the first step in the construction, remained incomplete. Betancourt went to Havana to try to find solutions. "El Lugareño is in

Havana pressuring on the Junta de Fomento for 50,000 duros for his railroad, but the junta, niggardly as ever, is shunning him. . . . although I know his firmness and constancy for his railroad and his land, I am afraid that, this time, he might get nothing from them."[49]

Restlessly, El Lugareño continued his maneuvers in support of the railroad. With that purpose he wrote to Domingo del Monte: "What is left now is that every one of the friends of Camagüey and of this island insists and intercedes for us; all use their relationships with any person who might have influence with the president and spokesmen of the Junta. . . . There are six miles built, and altogether about eighteen and a half embanked. What remains is just a matter of a month's work with no more than fifty men to complete some fourteen miles of track."[50]

But the help from the Junta de Fomento was reduced to a series of small subsidies, which in 1846 hardly amounted to 50,000 pesos. Betancourt was not discouraged and on April 5, 1846, the first section of railroad, some sixty-one kilometers between Nuevitas and the O'Donnell Station in Sabana Nueva, was finally inaugurated.[51]. That year, 1846, El Lugareño's political position against the colonial government forced him to leave the country, and he did not return until 1861. Nevertheless, the railroad was able to extend its lines to Puerto Príncipe five years later on December 25, 1851, finally completing the seventy-three kilometers planned in 1837.[52]

By the first half of the decade of the 1840s, sugar plantation development had reached the central region of Cuba, known as the Five Towns district—Las cinco villas. There, a rather uneven rate of production took place in scattered and dissimilar areas. The most intensive development took place in the old Trinidad Valley with smaller centers like Remedios, Villa Clara, and especially Cienfuegos, the most rapidly expanding of all. The relative isolation of these areas brought about different initiatives for the construction of small, individual railroads, all of them more or less simultaneously.

Since 1841, the inhabitants of Cienfuegos, a town founded two decades before on the shores of the Bay of Jagua, planned the construction of a railroad to link their port with Santa Clara, a small city in the center of the island. They assigned the job of designing the future line to Alejo Lanier and the French engineer Julio Sagebién.[53] As soon as the project was designed, it was made public in Havana in an attempt to attract financing for the new enterprise. The new project was economically attractive, because between Cienfuegos and Santa Clara were fertile lands of black soil with immense possibilities for sugar plantations. The producers could also count on a wonderful port—Cienfuegos—to export their crops. Finally, and unlike the Puerto Príncipe–Nuevitas Railway, this railroad would not only link an important inland city with the coast, linking Cienfuegos and Santa Clara, but would establish communication with a series of small towns in between. In

1841, the municipality of Villa Clara had a population of 44,366 inhabitants, and its capital, Santa Clara, had a population of 6,132 inhabitants. There were eighty-one sugar mills and one coffee estate in the region. Cienfuegos, less populated, had 23,313 inhabitants—2,437 of whom lived in the city—sixty-eight sugar mills and two coffee estates.[54] Besides, there were a number of smaller, intermediate towns, with an approximate total of 24,000 inhabitants, and the railroad would have revenues from the transport of abundant crops, merchandise, and passengers. The inhabitants of Villa Clara and other localities could easily travel to Cienfuegos and from there to Batabanó by steamboats, and later by railroad to Havana, shortening the existing long trip through the country over cart roads. This would make both traveling and commerce cheaper, and communications between the two areas could be intensified. The conditions and the beneficial effects of the railroad to Villa Clara were stated by the designers Lanier and Sagebién in a report published in 1847: "Isolated in the middle of that large territory, its inhabitants could benefit from their coastal neighbors as a result of short communications, the growth of commercial transactions and maritime commerce."[55]

The reasoning about the benefits that Villa Clara would receive were comprehensible. The drive to build a railroad from Cienfuegos to Villa Clara was based on the economic interests of a group of landowners with properties in the region of Cienfuegos, mainly around the towns of Palmira and Cruces. They saw a railroad as a cheaper way to transport their sugar to the port than in the traditional oxcart. In practice, therefore, the same scheme followed in Havana, Matanzas, and Cárdenas was being repeated in Cienfuegos.

The promoters obtained the government's authorization in 1842 to open the selling of shares for the funds to construct the railroad. The initiative was paralyzed for some years probably due to the economic and political difficulties of the 1844–46 period. In 1847, with a renewal of the original authorization, the neighbors of Cienfuegos held a meeting in which a provisional board of directors was elected for the promotion of the project.[56] Initial sales were disappointing, and the amount obtained, 189,000 pesos fell far short of the requirement for the planned project.[57]

In a new meeting, held on May 24, 1847, new elements were incorporated. Antonio Gutiérrez from Havana, known for his promotion of the Cárdenas Railroad, and Joaquín Santos Suárez, from Villa Clara, who had strong links with the Junta de Fomento and the Sociedad Económica Amigos del País, took charge of getting support from the junta in Havana to obtain the necessary approval of the new enterprise by the colonial government. Simultaneously, agents were sent to Havana, Sancti Spíritus, and Santiago de Cuba to find more subscribers for the company.[58]

The results of their promotion were very successful. The government granted a fifteen-year exemption from duty for all the equipment to be imported for the construction of the railroad.[59] The Junta de Fomento granted an interest free loan of 70,000 pesos.[60] Subscriptions were made in the amount of 402,500 pesos, half of the total share capital authorized for the enterprise, of which 49 percent came from Havana, 23 percent from Villa Clara, 20 percent from Cienfuegos, and the remaining 8 percent from Sancti Spíritus and Trinidad.[61] This varied contribution in capital removed control of the enterprise from the Cienfuegos landowners. The first elected board of directors reflected these new interests. The first president was the count of Fernandina.[62] Other directors included Joaquín Santos Suárez, one of the promoters, and the Havana slave traders Rafael Rodríguez Torices and Manuel Pastor.[63]

The budget calculated by Lanier and Sagebién was 1,205,989 pesos, but the one authorized by the treasury intendant was lower (907,000 pesos), and both exceeded the original capital raised.[64] The total extension of the line would be sixty-eight kilometers, curving to the northeast toward Palmira and Sabana de las Cruces, where most of sugar mills of the region were located.[65] The town of Palmira, first step in the construction of the railroad, not only had a large number of sugar mills but also, owing to its location in the Ciego Abajo plains, was an important intersection of the main road between Villa Clara and Matanzas—a location through which flowed not only the general products from distant municipalities but also the mail for most of the interior of the island.

Construction of the Cienfuegos to Villa Clara Railroad began in 1847 despite the decreasing sugar prices that year. The first section, from Cienfuegos to Palmira, began operation on October 21, 1851. Apart from the necessary excavations made along this section—sometimes twenty-two feet deep—in the outskirts of Caunao, the capricious route seemed conveniently designed to carry the fifteen hundred crates of refined sugar produced by the Candelaria sugar mill belonging to Antonia Guerrero de Santa Cruz (the only sugar mill that produced that kind of sugar) and the fourteen hundred barrels of muscovado from the Regla mill of Juan Bautista Sarría and the Delicias mill of the Rivas heirs.[66]

Two years after the inauguration of the first section on November 15, 1853, the railroad reached the sugar production zone of Cruces, thus serving the sugar mills Recurso of Juan Bautista Estensa, Majagua of Agustín Cerice, and Hormiguero of the Gorozabel heirs. The owners of these sugar mills, as well as all those having business located near the lines, all participated in the railroad company.[67] The real reason for building the Ferrocarril de Cienfuegos a Villa Clara was clearly to transport the sugar of the Cienfuegos's landowners, and it worked well during the company's first four years. The long-term goal to connect the tracks to Villa Clara would take a few more years and the addition of new supporters.

Six months before the inauguration of the first sector of the Cienfuegos Railroad a locomotive ran for the first time on the northern coast of that central region opening service along a nine-kilometer stretch between the town of Remedios and the port of Caibarién. The old Villa of Remedios was the center of a small sugar production area with thirty-seven sugar mills that produced 3,870 tons of sugar and 2,479 barrels of molasses in 1846.[68] That year, a group of twenty-one landowners in the jurisdiction agreed to build a railroad that could connect their town with the wharf to facilitate the export of their products.[69] Their small company, with a capital of 90,000 pesos, was authorized to build the railroad in October 1847.[70] They employed engineer Simon Wright, the brother of the builder of the Puerto Príncipe Railroad. Even though the construction costs of the line were low due to its short extension and simple technical requirements, the total cost amounted to 132,392 pesos, exceeding by more than 40,000 pesos the company's small capital. The deficit was covered by the personal fortunes of Colonel Manuel J. de Rojas and his son-in-law Estratón Bausá, both wealthy landowners of the region who had been the main promoters and shareholders of the railroad.[71]

The small railroad investment soon showed results as a stimulus to the local Remedios economy. In 1851, the jurisdiction of Remedios had fifty-one sugar mills—fourteen more than in 1846—and the export assets of Caibarién would grow by almost 300 percent to reach to an average of 438,336 pesos in the 1851–55 period.[72]

The fortunate situation of the sugar market during the first decade of the railroad development in Cuba allowed the landowners to finance the initial railway expansion. Although there was a gradual decline in sugar prices after 1841, prices remained over 7.7 cents per pound on the London market until 1847.[73] Since 73 percent of Cuban sugar production was sold in the United States and England, and in both countries there was a considerable increase in consumption per capita between 1841 and 1851—17 to 27 pounds in England and 13.5 to 30 pounds in America—the decreasing prices did not bring about a reduction in sugar production and consequently in the railroad construction. Although the rhythm of construction varied, it showed a slight decrease at the beginning of the 1850s.[74] The strategy of the Cuban producers was to increase production and reduce transport costs with the help of the railroad. For that reason, the growth of the railroad in Cuba followed the direction of the sugar industry and expanded geographically toward the center of the island. From the establishment of sugar mills near the coasts, the landowners began to build sugar mills inland and, supported by the new means of transportation, began to link all the productive areas of the country with the ports. This situation created the peculiar distribution of the railway system in Cuba. Different from most of the European and American railway networks with a definite radial system departing from the capital cities to other important ones, the growth of the Cuban railways followed an isolated pattern.[75] Since every sugar production center shipped directly abroad, Havana could not be the only port to control foreign commerce due to the long shape of the island. Every production area exported through the nearest bay or cove, reducing transportation costs. The triad formed by the plantation, the railroad and the port developed coastal cities like Matanzas, Cárdenas, Cienfuegos, and others, and produced a railroad pattern that was to be repeated all along the island.

All the railroad companies established in Cuba during the nineteenth century, and most of the subsequent ones, followed the original tendency to provide an exit to the main sugar production areas of the country. This was the principle that caused the construction of the railroad to Güines, and it continued to hold for the rest of the railroad enterprises. The construction policy of the Havana Railroad Company was followed when the company took over the Havana-Güines Railroad in 1842. Its lines ran to the south, the southwest, and the southeast, covering all the main areas south of Havana. The first branch had the objective to link the line with the port of Batabanó. It was fulfilled with the construction of a 15.5-kilometer branch line departing from San Felipe, a station on the main line. The port of Batabanó was the center of the southern coastal commerce, linking Havana with Vueltabajo, Cienfuegos, the Isle of Pines, Trinidad, and Santiago de Cuba, eliminating the risky sea voyage around Cape of San Antonio. This branch produced immense revenues to the railroad company, earning 60,000 pesos in its first year of operation.[76]

In December 1844, another twelve-kilometer branch opened between Rincón and San Antonio de los Baños to the west.[77] As part of the agreement on buying the Güines Railroad, the San Antonio branch was built with much more thought. The new line went directly toward Guanajay, one of the oldest and most important sugar production areas of the west, where only five years later the Caminos de Hierro de la Habana would extend its route. With this extension of more than twenty-two kilometers, the lines were at the threshold of the westernmost region of Cuba. At the same time, in the opposite direction, the company extended the lines across the red southern plains east of Güines. This important branch, fifty-two kilometers long, extended to the sugar mills of the areas of San Nicolás, Palos, Nueva Paz, and Alacranes to link the railway finally with the Matanzas Railroad at Taberna de Reyes in November 1848, a point in the east that, due to the railway junction, began to be called "Union."[78]

A decade after the inauguration of the first railroad, the present territory of Havana Province was criss-crossed in different directions by railways, bringing service to the districts of Havana, Güines, Bejucal, Santiago de las Vegas, San Antonio, and Guanajay. In 1846 the zone served by the parallel railroads from Havana had 169 sugar mills with an annual production of more than forty thousand tons of sugar and forty-five thousand barrels of molasses, which amounted to

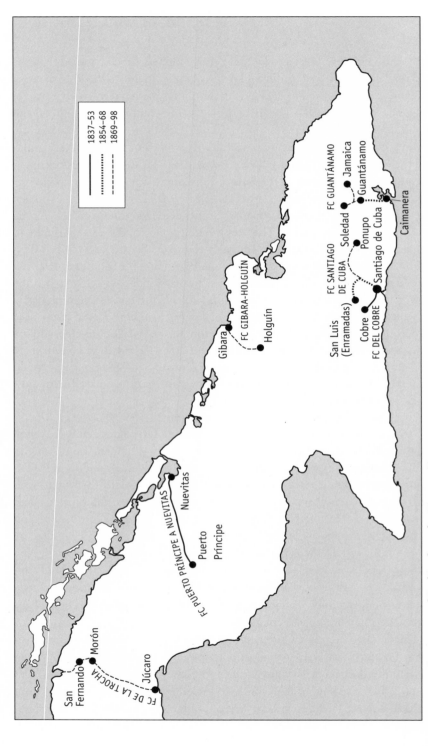

MAP 3.2. Expansion of Railroads in the Eastern Zone

approximately four hundred tons of sugar per kilometer of track, more than enough to assure the profitability of the railroad company.[79]

After taking its parallel tracks to Unión de Reyes where the link with the Caminos de Hierro de la Habana took place, the Ferrocarril de Matanzas began a rapid expansion to the east to reach a junction with the end of the Cárdenas Railroad lines at Montalvo (Navajas). This junction was not the objective of Ferrocarril de Matanzas. By extending its lines to the east, the Matanzas railroad wanted to transport the sugar produced in the area of Bolondrón, Güira de Macuriges, and Corral Falso (nowadays Pedro Betancourt), pilfering part of the freight of the Ferrocarril de Cárdenas. This competitive effort became more evident when the Matanzas Railroad extended the lines to Isabel by the end of 1848. With this strategic expansion, the Ferrocarril de Matanzas ran from east to west cutting through the former hato of Macuriges, placing their lines nearer to most of the sugar mills than the ones of the Cárdenas Railroad. This competitive "appetite" fostered the construction within a year of an extra thirty-seven kilometers of lines to their originally small network.[80]

At the time these things were happening, the center of interest of the Cárdenas railroads had also begun to move eastward. In the beginning, the two railway enterprises operating in Cárdenas, although at times having their port terminals quite near to each other, nevertheless served distinctly different clients among the interior sugar mills of the region. The Cárdenas Railroad Company expanded to the southwest toward Bemba and Navajas; the Ferrocarril de Júcaro went to the southeast toward Altamisal and Banagüises. The constant proliferation of sugar mills in the plain called Nueva Bermeja or Colón became a strong area of interest that would create a brutally competitive instinct between the two companies. The Ferrocarril de Cárdenas began to expand to the east from Bemba, reaching the town of Perico in December 1850, the newly founded town of Nueva Bermeja (nowadays Colón) three months later, and Agüica in December 1851.[81] In this way, the Ferrocarril de Cárdenas used against the Júcaro Company the same strategy that the Ferrocarril de Matanzas used against it three years before in the area of Macuriges. The tense relations between the two enterprises lead to a furious competition for the products of the plains of Colón.

Moved by necessity or ambition, the western railroad companies grew enough to theoretically allow traveling by train across most of the western sugar zone by about 1850. However, as the railroads were built with the exclusive goal of transporting sugar, the connections between lines remained inconvenient, discouraging the traveler by frequent changes and long hours of waiting. For these reasons, the use of stage coaches and *volantas* (two-wheeled coaches) across the northern hills or the use of steamships between Havana, Matanzas, and Cárdenas continued to be the preferred means of transport for travelers long after the three cities were interconnected by railway lines.[82] In the case of freight, each company tried to monopolize the production of the areas covered by its networks, a process that from the very beginning was inherently competitive.

During the fifteen years after the inauguration of the first railroad between Havana and Bejucal, nine railroad companies began to operate in Cuba.[83] The average growth of railway lines was 37.2 kilometers per year, with a total of 558 kilometers of lines in full service by 1851. This primitive railroad development followed the anarchic pattern of every capitalist growth. Of the 558 kilometers in operation in 1851, 80 percent was in the western part of the island, while the vast region east of Sancti Spíritus had the remaining 108.5 kilometers controlled by two railway companies. The railroads did nothing but duplicate the regional distribution of sugar production and clearly reflected the interests that created them.

The Years of the Railroad Boom

The construction of new railway lines expanded at a rate of almost fifty miles per year during most of the 1840s, but by the end of this decade it began to decrease noticeably to reach a poor annual average of about twenty miles between 1850 and 1854. The intensity of the initial railroad expansion halted. Caminos de Hierro de la Habana, the most powerful company at the time practically ceased expanding after the Palos-Unión extension was completed in 1848. The Ferrocarril de Cienfuegos a Villa Clara, a latecomer to the railroad expansion boom, built sixty-eight kilometers so slowly that it contrasted sharply with the rhythm characterizing the first period of railroad construction on the island.

Railroad construction reflected the contemporary economic problems. Sugar production, after experiencing unfavorable weather conditions between 1844 and 1846, stagnated between 1847 and 1850, with production varying between 200,000 and 250,000 tons. This situation became worse with the constant decrease of world sugar prices, which fell on the London market from 11.4 cents per pound in 1840 to 4.7 in 1852.[1] Although lower prices increased consumption in the receiving countries, the Cuban industry faced serious problems in taking advantage of the situation. The sugar plantation system, based on slave work, required the importation of great numbers of slaves in order to boost production. And to make matters worse, a Spanish law of 1845 established severe penalties for participants in the slave trade, which was made illegal by an agreement signed with England and the United States. These measures resulted in a marked decrease in the importation of what were called "ebony pieces," and according to some estimates, in the five years between 1845 and 1859 inclusive, only 27,000 slaves were imported compared with the clandestine importation of 100,000 slaves during the previous five years.[2]

To the parlous situation in the sugar industry should be added the crisis in coffee production. There, exports were constantly declining as a result of the very factors that boosted sugar production and gave initial impetus to railroad expansion. As a result of this expansion, the existing five hundred kilometers of lines was a considerable achievement if compared to the population and dimensions of the island. Yet, it was far from being considered an integral railroad network because of the six or seven isolated companies in operation. Only the Havana, Matanzas, and Cárdenas Railroads were interconnected.

In 1852, sugar production began to show signs of recovery, and, to illustrate the increase, production surpassed 300,000 tons the following year. This change immediately influenced railroad development and soon the government began to receive requests for new concessions. Interestingly enough, the requests sought not only the extension of existing lines, but also the creation of a number of new companies. The number of requests overburdened the colonial officials, who in 1857 alone had to deal with seven requests, three from entirely new companies. The concentration of legal work was accompanied by a feverish construction activity, and between 1855 and 1860 the new lines were laid down at a rate of eighty kilometers a year, about four times the average of the previous five years.

Cuba was suffering from the railroad fever that had afflicted countries in other latitudes during the first years of the 1850s. Around the middle of the nineteenth century, only Great Britain, Belgium, and part of Germany had railway networks, while there were countries in Europe—like Spain—that did not even have one railroad. Between 1850 and 1870, the nations of western Europe equipped themselves with railway networks that went beyond their frontiers to form a continental system. Spain, a latecomer to this development, tried to catch up by building a national network at a rate of 340 kilometers a year between 1855 and 1868. The United States began the building of the transcontinental railroad that, motivated by generous land concessions, linked the two distant coasts. Railroads began to appear in different regions. Asia (India), Africa (Egypt), and South America (Chile, Paraguay, Argentina, and Brazil) joined the railroad era.

The locomotives then in operation were incomparably superior to the old "Rocket." Placing the pulling wheels behind the boilers, using the bogie, and many other technical innovations permitted the hauling of loads in excess of 150 tons, and trains could ascend mountains, where they could not venture before. Standardization of many technical elements and mass production lowered the cost of building railroads and attracted new investors. Financing procedures, more sophisticated and deceptive, lured investors with a system of low-entry-price shares and soon became an object of the most shameless speculation. The European bourgeoisie, solidly in power after the revolutions of 1848, blindly trusted in the railroad, which, in the excessive optimism of the time, was considered the magic wand of progress.

This unlimited trust in the possibilities of the railroad was also present in the

Cuban railroad development. Nevertheless, the real determining factors were quite deeper than optimism. The productive growth that began in 1853 maintained itself throughout the decade, surpassing 500,000 tons of sugar in 1859. Cuba took advantage of the increase in consumption in the European and American markets, resulting from the elimination of tariffs and the opening of free trade.[3] The sugar industry not only expanded, it modernized itself. Between 1851 and 1859 Cuba imported 5,343,137 pesos' worth of equipment for its sugar mills.[4] The lack of work hands was temporarily relieved by the importation of tens of thousands of Chinese workers under conditions not far removed from slavery.[5]

The timely outbreak of the Crimean War (1854–56) further stimulated sugar expansion based on the reversal in the downward price spiral. This went up from the 4.8 cents per pound in 1854 to 7.9 in 1857.[6] The immediate consequence of the price increase was an economic boom in Cuba. Merchants and great landowners found themselves almost overnight, with unexpectedly huge sums available for investment. "The plethora of cash brought about the creation of numerous credit institutions . . . with the objective of widening the credit activity, promoting all kinds of enterprises without meditation or control."[7] Interest rates, usually very high, fell to between 5 and 3 percent. A great part of the available capital found its way into the new railroad companies giving rise to a new building boom. Another part of the investment capital moved to the field of sugar production, marketing, and distribution, promoting the constitution of the first great limited-liability companies—La Gran Azucarera (The Great Sugar Production Company) and the Compañía Territorial Cubana (Cuban Land Company)—dedicated to the operation of sugar mills.[8] The availability of capital surpassed the real and immediate investment need. The narrow basis for investment offered by the monoproductive economy and mainly by the lack of a solid financial experience brought about a speculative fever. The public squares of Havana became improvised stock markets where shares of the most imaginative joint-stock companies were offered. The colonial government received formal requests for the constitution of 263 companies whose total capital reached the then astronomical figure of 584 million pesos.[9] The objectives of these companies were curiously diverse and in some cases simply implausible—the promotion of cock fighting or the protection of helpless old persons. The predictable outcome came in July 1857 with the problems of some commercial institutions and the rise of the discount rates in the Spanish Bank, closely followed by panic and numerous bankruptcies. The 1857 crisis, however, did not reach the disastrous proportions that the existing financial speculation would have supposed. Even though the price of sugar fell in 1858, it remained steady at a relatively high price, allowing a recovery and the normal functioning of the economy in the following two years. But this fact made a lot of companies delay liquidation in the hope of being able to recover part of their investments, thereby contributing to an atmosphere of distrust on the part of the investors. The new blow came in 1861—together with a new fall in the price of sugar—and this time the proportions were bigger than the panic of 1857. Bankruptcies amounted to 28 million pesos, and the financing structure of the island was profoundly shaken.

The impact of the continuous economic commotion influenced railroad development. A clear sign of this was the fact that in the 1860s no new companies were founded. The effects of the crisis were particularly evident in the financial aspects of the railroad business. The monopolization of credits and the high interest rates following the 1857, 1861, and 1866 crises forced the railroad companies to look for foreign capital in an amount and under conditions that deserve separate considerations. Nevertheless, these problems did not totally undermine the railroad boom. The almost forty kilometers of new lines placed in use each year during the 1860s was far from paralysis. This is partly explained by the true nature of railroad investment, which is usually long term, but also by the characteristics of the economic phenomena mentioned. The crises of this period were mainly in the field of financing, not in the productive growth. In 1861 there were signs of an alarming economic decay, but the outbreak of the United States Civil War that year created conditions that mitigated the impending disaster. The expansive tendency of sugar production continued, reaching 749,000 tons in 1868, despite the 1866 crisis. This tripling of production in less than two decades—and the physical expansion involved by the plantation system—offered a firm basis for the constructive apogee of the railroad.

The development experienced by the railroad system during those years retained and accentuated the basic features of the Cuban railway system begun in the 1840s. Nevertheless, the improvement of the Cuban railroad business as well as the influence of concepts and procedures derived from the maturity of the capitalist way of production on a worldwide scale molded the Cuban railroad system in ways that can be examined more fully.

The regional pattern characterizing railroad construction in the 1840s was retained by most companies after 1853. The particular interests of different localities to have an easy and economic means of transportation continued to play the main role in the creation of railroad projects. In some cases, old sugar production areas were able to satisfy their transportation needs during this period; in others, newly developed areas found their solution in the railroad expansion. The case of the railroad to Trinidad exemplifies the first of these cases.

Founded in the center of a valley near the southern coast of the central region of Cuba, Trinidad was not only limited because of its particular geographical location, but also because of the greed of the neighboring cabildo of Sancti Spíritus, which appropriated most of the surrounding lands. However the Trini-

dadians took advantage of their fertile valley and some other circumstantial resources to develop sugar plantations independently by the end of the eighteenth
century.[10] Around 1825 the production of the area of Trinidad amounted to 10
percent of total Cuban sugar production, offering a stable economic situation to
the proud landowners and merchants of the area.[11]

Given the strong regional economy, it was not surprising that Trinidad was one
of the first localities promoting a railroad project. In 1833, two American merchants —and presumed slave traders—settled in the town. Frederick Freeman and
James Tate asked for the privilege to build a railroad between Trinidad and the
nearby port of Casilda where they already had their warehouses.[12] Despite official
support, this early project foundered until 1837 when it was revived by a group of
landowners from Trinidad led by the count of Casa Brunet. This time the project
progressed as far as engaging the American engineer John Easton to make some
preliminary studies and prepare a budget. But seven years passed without action.
In 1844, three well-known personalities, Joaquín de Arrieta, Manuel Pastor, and
Antonio Parejo, attempted to build the Trinidad-Casilda Railroad, but their initiative—maybe a simple speculative maneuver—did not go farther than some brief
approaches to some offices of the colonial government.[13] The relentless frustra-
tion surrounding the Trinidadian project contrasted sharply with the success
obtained by localities with weaker economies like Remedios. The characteristics
of the Trinidad plantations, relatively concentrated and close to the coast, seemed
to explain the reasons for this curious phenomenon, for they did not have serious
transportation problems. The Trinidadian landowners could also count on the
Agabama and Guaurabo Rivers, through which they transported their products in
barges to the coast where they loaded the ships directly.

While the Trinidad railroad project went from hand to hand without solution,
the economic situation of the valley underwent considerable changes. Even
though the sugar production of Trinidad continued to increase to about 70,000
arrobas in 1846, the productive potential of the jurisdiction was surpassed by
others like Cienfuegos, which had started plantations some years before. In fact,
the growth of exports from Trinidad (Casilda) between 1835 and 1845 (25 percent)
compares favorably with any of the exporting ports in the western part of central
Cuba.[14] Yet such data obscure the fact that the Trinidad economy had peaked. By
midcentury, sugar plantations covered all the lands of the valley and some, worn
out by decades of uninterrupted cultivation, were already offering diminishing
returns. Moreover, the sedimentation of the Agabama and Guaurabo Rivers
threatened to interrupt the fluvial communication system used to export the
production.[15]

These were the conditions prevailing when Justo G. Cantero—one of the
wealthiest local landowners—revived the railroad project in 1852. The idea of the

railroad was not then the proud expression of the Trinidadian landowners at the summit of power, but the possible solution to their increasing problems facilitated by the prosperity of the 1850s. Cantero got the concession in February 1853, and in September he passed it on to a joint-stock company constituted by local proprietors in charge of executing the project.[16] The task was more difficult than that of previous projects, as it intended to run the tracks to the town of Sancti Spíritus, almost seventy kilometers from Trinidad. This extension was highly rational. During the first decades of the nineteenth century the Sancti Spíritus economy—basically cattle breeding—had become a satellite of the Trinidad plantation system, subordinated to it from the mercantile point of view. By midcentury, the economic development of Sancti Spíritus began to move to the rhythm of its sugar mill bells, many of them created by folk from Trinidad, and the export production of the region increased notably. By extending their railroad to Sancti Spiritus, the Trinidadians hoped to ensured the flow of that production to Casilda and retain their control over the commerce of Sancti Spíritus. Nevertheless, the plotting of the tracks was set in a most absurd manner. The line would start in Casilda and after crossing Trinidad, would continue north bypassing the mountains in a long curve to reach Sancti Spíritus. Apparently, the personal interests of some of the shareholders imposed the illogical route, which, by the way, left aside some of the most productive areas of the valley of Trinidad.

The execution of the the center of the project was fraught with problems, not only those technically related to the chosen route, but also the ones related to manual labor and the repeated bankruptcy of construction contractors. Besides, the real cost of the work constantly exceeded budget, causing a progressive increase in the indebtedness of the railroad. In 1862, seven years after the work began, only twenty kilometers of the tracks between Casilda and Trinidad-Fernández were finished.[17] This represented less than a third of the project. Above all, precious time was lost in the meantime and the people from Sancti Spíritus had begun to build their own railroad, which would liberate them from Trinidad-imposed transport costs.

Not enthusiastic about a railroad that would link them to Casilda, the people from Sancti Spíritus began to take independent steps to build a railroad between Sancti Spíritus and Tunas, the port within their jurisdiction located at the mouth of the Zaza River.[18] In 1859, Antonio M. Del Valle and Roque Fernández de Lara—the principal promoters of the project—were granted a concession to build a railway covering the thirty-nine kilometers between Sancti Spíritus and Tunas.[19] The work began the next year at a slow but constant pace and was finished in 1865. So while work on the Trinidad Railroad ceased for the lack of capital, the group from Sancti Spíritus repeated the railroad pattern of a local track for local needs.

Sugar was undoubtedly the only appropriate motor of the Cuban railroad development. While a decadent Trinidad plantation system could hardly build itself a railroad, the young sugar production center of Sagua built its own at a rate of twenty-five kilometers per year. In 1830, when Trinidad produced one-tenth of the Cuban sugar production, Sagua was practically a wild territory with no other mercantile activity but the movement of carts from Villa Clara to a small wharf located on the mouth of the Sagua la Grande River. The expansion of the western sugar plantation economy soon transformed the Sagua Valley. By the end of the 1830s, Havana sugar promoters, after building some sugar mills in the coastal plains between Sierra Morena and the sea, went into the Sagua Valley to promote, together with some local interests and proprietors of Villa Clara, a vigorous plantation development.[20] A decade later, Sagua, already officially turned into a jurisdiction of almost seventeen thousand inhabitants, and had fifty-nine sugar mills which produced altogether more than a million arrobas a year.[21] The plantations of Sagua expanded along the Sagua la Grande River, and by midcentury its sugar mills extended into the territory of the Amaro estate, forty kilometers from the mouth of the river. As in other regions, the progressive inland development of plantations created transportation difficulties for sugar export.

By the end of 1852, a group of Sagua proprietors undertook steps to build a railroad to solve its local transportation needs. Even though the initiative was praised by the Havana local press and by influential individuals, the promoters could not gather the necessary capital within their own jurisdiction. For that reason, the promoters sent commissions to Villa Clara and Havana to recruit more shareholders. The future Sagua railroad was very attractive to investors. According to estimates of the *Diario de la Marina*, the new railroad could transport between 20,000 and 25,000 passengers a year, 24,600 sugar barrels, and 11,170 barrels of molasses, which, together with another 40,000 loads of assorted produce, could generate an income of 300,000 pesos a year.[22] With the necessary investors, the governing board met in Havana in May 1854. It brought together Antonio Parejo, merchant and slave trader, José Morales Lemus, presumably representing the Alfonso-Aldama family, Urbano Feijoo Sotomayor, merchant and representative of the of Galician labor suppliers, José E. Moré, a rich Havana merchant and owner of the La Merced sugar mill in Sagua, and Tomás Rivalta, Edmundo Depestre, and Fernando Eguilior, all landowners of Sagua la Grande.[23] It is clear that the control of the enterprise moved from the hands of the original Sagua group—represented only by three members on the Board—into the control of the powerful economic interests of Havana. The president was José E. Moré who— together with Rafael Rodríguez Torices, a merchant soon to be rich from the trade of coolies—made the request for a concession to the government.

The initial idea of building a section to Villa Clara was almost immediately abandoned in favor of a longer branch toward Santa Isabel de las Lajas, which was

Sagua La Grande Railroad Station from an anonymous painting of the period.

more advantageous because it crossed along a potentially superior productive area. The access to Villa Clara would be possible through the Ferrocarril de Cienfuegos, with a common rail junction for both lines at the town of Cruces. This would also allow a connection between the southern and northern coasts, a system that had given excellent results to the Caminos de Hierro de la Habana.

The projected first track of 18.5 miles would depart from Boca (Isabela) and pass along Sagua and its surroundings, ending in Sitiecitos, and would cost approximately 484,605 pesos. The second section, 32 miles between Sitiecitos and Cruces would be built at a cost of 940,357 pesos. The project would also include a 19-mile branch at a cost of 102,185 pesos to link Sitiecitos with the town of Cifuentes running along an area with numerous sugar mills.[24]

By the end of 1855, with the concession granted, work began under the direction of engineer Joaquín de las Cuevas. In January 1858, the first section was solemnly inaugurated and before the year finished the important branch to Cifuentes was opened. Even though the path of the line had basically followed general economic considerations, it could not avoid the familiar curves and deviations caused by the personal interests of the principal shareholders of the company. In January 1860, the last track opened linking Sagua with Cruces and the Cienfuegos line, and the wealthiest families of both cities paid each other a visit to celebrate the opening. In less than four years the Sagua Railroad had built the longest system in the central region of Cuba, some 102 kilometers.

Almost two decades after the inauguration of the first Cuban railroad, the extensive Departamento Oriental virtually did not know the benefits derived from the new means of transportation. Except for the mines of El Cobre with a small railway, the eastern producers continued to transport their merchandise on mule trains or carts, as they had done for centuries. The complicated topography and the scarce and unequal agricultural development combined to delay the progress of their communications. Oriente, a territory with marked regional differences in production and level of economic development, constituted a mosaic of local economies. The jurisdiction of Cuba, headquarters of the city of Santiago— capital of the entire department and second largest city in the island in terms of population—was the most prominent local zone. That jurisdiction was the scene of an active economic life with agricultural conditions for a railroad far before many other regions of Cuba. The city, however, had been founded on a small coastal valley surrounded to the east and north by the Sierra Maestra and to the west by the Gran Piedra Mountains, which made communications difficult with the rest of the country. Indeed, an important part of the hinterland of Santiago was on the other side of the mountains, in the plains surrounding the Guaninicún and the Maroto Valleys. The products of these regions were transported to Santiago by mule trains and carts through some passes between mountains, the only routes of communication to the city. Such topographic obstacles, salvable by beasts, placed the region out of the technical possibilities of the early railroads. Notwithstanding, the geographical complications were only part of the explanation for the delay in building a railroad in Santiago. The region was prosperous at the beginning of the 1840s. The local population comprised more than ninety thousand inhabitants—half of whom were slaves. The production of its 123 sugar mills and 604 coffee estates allowed the port of Santiago to export goods valued at an annual average of 7,619,612 pesos, a figure only surpassed by Havana.[25] These years of prosperity were followed by a crisis produced by the commercial problems of coffee. Exports for this product fell from 541,302 arrobas in 1840 to 367,347 arrobas in 1845 and remained at the same level, or even lower, during the following five years. The fall in the price of sugar and the stagnation of its production caused a reduction in exports of some 30 to 40 percent in relation to the average of the first years of the 1840s. The economic downturn produced the progressive disappearance of 100 coffee estates whose proprietors sold their slaves to the western landowners as a way to cope with the situation.[26] Under such circumstances, a railroad promoter would have found very few investors in that region.

By the middle of the decade of the 1850s favorable conditions permitted the construction of a railroad in Santiago. On the one hand, the revival of the general economic situation began to be felt at the local level, and on the other hand, improvements in railroad technology eliminated obstacles that existed only a few years before. In October 1855, three Santiago landowners, Antonio Vinent, Manuel del Castillo, and Pedro Griñan, asked the government for a concession to build "a railroad between Santiago and Santo Cristo, dividing at this point into two branches, one leading to Sabanilla and the other through the valley of Maroto to Enramadas."[27] The three petitioners acted in concert with a group of local proprietors motivated by the economic prospects of a regional railroad project. Most of the members of this group were landowners with sugar mills located on the far side of the mountains, who had long suffered from difficulties in transporting their sugar to the city.[28]

Notwithstanding, Santiago would not be the first locality in Oriente to have a public service railroad. Eight months before the request from Santiago, a commission of proprietors from the region of Guantánamo traveled to Havana to ask for the necessary authorization to build a railroad in that district. Their interest was based on the fact that Guantánamo was one of the few regions in Oriente in which there was an appreciable volume of exports. Fostered at the beginning of the nineteenth century by a group of French immigrants coming from Haiti, the Guantánamo plantations were, during the first decades of the century, basically coffee producers.[29] By midcentury, the coffee crisis produced a radical reorientation. The facts are illustrative enough. In 1846 Guantánamo had eleven old sugar mills producing raw sugar and their production was practically consumed locally. In 1852, 28,544 arrobas of sugar were exported, a small amount, but it was doubled in three years.[30] Before the end of the 1850s, Guantánamo was exporting 250,000 arrobas of sugar. New products required new transport needs. The heavy crates, and the even heavier barrels, could not be transported as easily as coffee had been on mules. The proprietors sought to create an infrastructure that would fit their new merchandise. In 1854 they opened a port in Cerro Guayabo, on the coast of the Guantánamo Bay, but the ten kilometers separating it from the town of Santa Catalina (nowadays Guantánamo City) was flat and clayey and impossible to cross in the rainy season. The solution was a railroad, and they immediately sought a concession.[31] The leading individual in the group, however, was not a landowner, but an English merchant called Thomas Brook, who was the owner of the largest exporting firm in the area with branches in Havana and Santiago and with the most important business connection in the United States.[32] While the red tape procedures were underway, the promoters engaged an experienced engineer, the Frenchman Julio Sagebién, who had built the Cienfuegos and El Cobre Railroads, to do the project. When the concession was granted on August 24, 1855, everything was already in place to begin the construction. The favorable topography allowed a simple, straight line without curves or slopes and the construction was completed in less than a year.[33] The efficient railroad service immediately transformed the region economically. The Cerro Guayabo wharf, low and unhealthy, and earlier chosen because of its nearness to the town of Santa Catalina, was then replaced, after the railroad eliminated the distance factor, by a better location in Caimanera. The railroad extended the tracks to the new port in 1858, increasing the total length of the small regional railroad to twenty kilometers.

In Santiago, things were not proceeding as fast. In spite of the granting of a concession in 1855, almost two months after the request was made, the economic and technical problems of this railroad project required a slower pace. The project was in the hands of engineer Rafael de Carrera, brother of the builder of the Cárdenas Railroad, who faced the most complex route done in Cuba until then. The toughest section was the one connecting Santiago de Cuba with the sugar mill Santo Cristo. This track, beside crossing several rivers and streams, had to climb a steep slope rising 50 feet per mile, and, one of its gradients, a stretch of 204 feet, required a stationary steam engine with a winch that would help the locomotives to overcome the obstacle.[34] From Santo Cristo the line parted, with one track running the fourteen kilometers to Enramadas (now San Luis) and the other, twenty-four kilometers to Sabanilla. Both branches were easier to build and were located in the main operational area of the railroad and allowed easy future extension to Bayamo and Guantánamo.[35] The total cost of the work was estimated at 1,640,077 pesos, an investment that would be quickly recovered by the estimated 300,000 pesos a year revenue expected from the railroad.[36]

In March 1856, work to grade the track bed began. The setting of the rails was guaranteed four months later by a contract with the British firm of Robinson and Dalton, which offered do the job at a cost of 1,100 pesos per mile.[37] Again financial problems worried the promoters. They had asked for a government subsidy of 10,000 pesos per mile due to the technical complexity of the work and the government transferred the request to the metropolis to decide the matter together with the final concession.[38] Given this uncertainty, the promoters took advantage of the financial optimism prevailing in the spring of 1857 to formally constitute a joint-stock company: the Compañía del Ferrocarril y Almacenes de Depósito de Santiago de Cuba (Santiago Railroad and Warehouse Company), with a nominal capital of 1 million pesos, divided into shares of 100 pesos each. Among the main shareholders were the promoters Vinent, Griñán, and Castillo, as well as other landowners like Juan Kindelán, Francisco Boudet, and Juan Vaillant. The group also included representatives of important firms established in the city like Siegler, Beola and Company, Brook, Miguel Bon and Company, and Valiente and Company.[39] The financial situation of the new railroad was backed later by a government loan of 360,000 pesos excluding interest. Even though the accustomed niggardliness of the metropolis had converted the subsidy into a loan, the promoters were happy to be beneficiaries of the greatest economic aid ever given by the government to a railroad enterprise in Cuba. The liquidation terms were not bad either, as they had to complete the payment of the loan in seventeen years, with seven years of grace.[40]

In March 1859, three years after work began, the company inaugurated the first section of track leading to Santiago-Boniato.[41] This completed the technically most difficult part of the railroad, and the company could begin to earn profits from the investment. From that moment on, the work proceeded at a swifter pace. In December 1860, the nine-kilometer section between Boniato and Santo Cristo was opened, finishing the main trunk of the railway. Simultaneously, the Maroto branch progressed, completing the eight kilometers from El Cristo to Dos Caminos in July 1861. This rapid rhythm of construction was amazing when one considers that the section from Santiago to that point, included nineteen bridges, one of them—the Vargas—was 16 meters high and 225 meters long.[42]

Unfortunately, the rhythm of construction was affected by financial difficulties. In 1862, the finished tracks had consumed almost all the company's capital and all the government's loan, with only half of the project completed. Although the income earned by the operating tracks was high, the final investment proved inadequate to complete the work. The completion of the Maroto branch was in danger. To prevent this, the company asked for an additional loan to the Banco de Cuba, a local bank. They agreed on a loan of 100,000 pesos to finance the section to Vega Botada.[43] With this loan, the directors of the company even began to finish the Sabanilla section, but the rapid depletion of the funds forced a recess in the works. An extension of credit in the amount of 50,000 pesos allowed the completion of the branch to Enramadas in 1865. The funds ran out, however, and the branch to Sabanilla was delayed for many years. Looking at the unfinished project, some complained that the 1857 boom fostered the irrational investment of many people from Santiago in unnecessary works such as the Caney Railroad and undermined resources for the main regional railway project.[44]

The construction of the railroads of Guantánamo and Santiago helped to overcome, to some extent, the great differences in railroad transportation existing between the western and eastern regions of the island. Nevertheless, the operations of these small enterprises were far from solving the transportation needs of the entire territory of the Departamento Oriental. The effects of the railroads were felt only in the two most developed zones in the east.

All the railroad companies so far described repeated the formula prevailing since the 1830s, with their own particular peculiarities: the landowners and merchants of a region promoted a railroad line to facilitate the export of their products from the interior to the coast. The railroad company was seen primarily as a means to accelerate the movement of merchandise and only secondarily as a profitable investment. This was the general concept of the business, and even though it remained as such in most of the country, in Havana new methods and ideas had already started to develop. The constant and direct contact with the world market allowed the businessmen in Havana a faster assimilation of advanced techniques in capitalist organization and their more sophisticated economic perspectives.

The 1856–57 boom allowed investors to turn the western region of the island into a large laboratory for financial experimentation. The railroad was a safe business that provided a good return on any investment. The plantations between Guanajay and Villa Clara had a railway system that allowed the commercialization of the production in an acceptable manner. The new railroad projects could not count, then, on the monopoly of whole regions that favored the first lines. In fact, any new line in the western region was forced to be competitive to survive.

Havana, during the exciting year of 1857, created the scenario for three new railroad projects that broke the traditional pattern established by the earliest railroads. The first and most important was the Ferrocarril de la Bahía de la Habana a Matanzas (The Havana-Matanzas Railroad). The name itself suggests the new idea: it was not a railroad built to link a production area with a port, but a link between the two most important ports of the island. Its promoter, Eduardo Fesser, was known for the creation of the first limited joint-stock company dedicated to large-scale storage of sugar: the Almacenes de Regla (Regla Warehouses). Founded in 1843, with the limited capital of 150,000 pesos, this society had, ten years later, facilities that would allow storage of half of all Cuban sugar production, and had ten times its original capital.[45] The success of the company had attracted to Fesser a number of important associates from a variety of fields. This group, which had gone into a collateral storage business, was one of the most active during the speculative fever of 1857. Its first step was the consolidation of the credit functions of the enterprise by the creation of a specialized entity and later the Banco de Comercio—which sold shares valued at 2 million pesos in the greedy and improvised stock market in Havana. With the backing of the bank and with wide resources for investment, Fesser decided to invest in the railroad business. The convenience of running a railroad branch to the Almacenes de Regla was conceived years before, but it was planned in the form of a small branch linked to Caminos de Hierro de la Habana.[46] Then, with the new economic conditions, the project grew into an independent business supporting the storage interests.

The concession was requested in February 1857. The line would run parallel and relatively near to the north coast from Regla to Matanzas. As the region crossed—maybe with the exception of Aguacate and Ceiba Mocha—would not yield enough volume of freight, the objective of the line was evidently to attract to Havana, literally to the Regla Warehouses, part of the sugar that was stored and exported through Matanzas. Another purpose was to use the line to communicate rapidly and easily between the two cities, as the existing link based on the combination of Caminos de Hierro de la Habana and Ferrocarril de Matanzas forced the

The Regla Warehouses, one of the main depots for sugar to be exported, was directly on the line of the Ferrocarril de la Bahía de La Habana.

travelers to take a long roundabout course to the south. With these objectives in mind, it was evident that the enterprise had a calculatedly competitive character.

With a capital of 2 million pesos the Ferrocarril de la Bahía de la Habana a Matanzas found subscribers easily, but the control of the company remained in the hands of Fesser and his group. This was not only because of their personal investments, but also because of the participation of the Banco de Comercio, which became the main shareholder with a participation of 365,000 pesos.[47] The capital was less than the projected budget for the eighty-seven kilometers of line between Regla and Matanzas, estimated by the engineers at 2.3 million pesos. This small difference did not worry the investors, and the work began by the end of 1857. Due to the expected competition, the construction was to be done with the most modern equipment to ensure a service of optimal quality. During 1858, the first section between Regla and Minas was finished as well as a small branch to Guanabacoa, with service starting on April 4, 1859. The news, communicated to the investors, was accompanied by another less encouraging report: the construction of the branch to Guanabacoa and the acquisition of the steamship enterprise of the bay had increased the budget by some extra 250,000 pesos. The deficit was covered by the Banco de Comercio, with a loan of 500,000 pesos. In 1861, the lines of the company ran to Aguacate and the trains could reach Matanzas but only by using the lines of Caminos de Hierro de la Habana, a need that limited the competitive possibilities of the enterprise. Under such circumstances, the enterprise reported that the capital, as well as the loans given by the Banco de Comercio, had been exhausted and that there were numerous outstanding debts with contractors and suppliers.[48] The situation was critical since finance from the Banco de Comercio had reached a limit and, with the credit conditions in Cuba after the 1857 crisis, it was impossible to get further loans at an acceptable interest rate. To overcome the difficulty the management of the company agreed to a £250,000 loan with the London firm J. Henry Schröder and Company in 1861. Principal and interest became due in fourteen years, and, as a guarantee, all properties of the railroad company were mortgaged in favor of the Schröder firm.[49] That loan provided the resources to complete the construction of the final section from Aguacate to Matanzas in 1863. The final effort left the company with multiple debts and obligations. Under such conditions, a new £100,000 loan was agreed with Schröder, this time on behalf of the Banco de Comercio and the company. After all this hard experience the railroad finally reached Matanzas burdened with debts.

In spite of the financing problems, the operations of the railroad were not bad. In the period between 1860 and 1864, revenues were 976,304 pesos, quite a respectable sum considering that the line was not yet fully in operation. The Regla Warehouses had also benefited from the railroad operations, increasing their storage capacity from 579,137 crates in 1857 to 827,403 in 1865—63 percent of all the sugar stored in Havana that year.[50] Nevertheless, these achievements were overcome by the financial obligations of the railroad company. Besides, the commercial results of the Matanzas terminal did not satisfy the expectations of the investors. The multiple alternatives opened to transportation in this city created a strong competitive situation that could only be solved by reaching the production areas directly. The first intention of the management of the Ferrocarril de la Bahía de la Habana was to establish agreements with all regional railroad companies—Matanzas and Coliseo—to combine their operation. The failure of these attempts opened the way to a new financial maneuver, the purchase of the Coliseo Railroad.

With the acquisition of the Coliseo line, from Matanzas to Bemba (Jovellanos), the Ferrocarril de la Bahía de la Habana could penetrate into the heart of the sugar production area of Matanzas. This possibility, in the words of the management, would improve the situation of the company and would make exploitation of the railroad more economical. Buying the railroad was not difficult, as among the proprietors was, just by chance, the Fesser family.[51] The offer of 1,950,000 pesos, was good enough to clear the way. In this way the Ferrocarril de la Bahía de la Habana secured its future, and the Fesser family pocketed a nice sum. As was to be expected, the money came again from London through a £400,000 loan—2 million pesos—at 7 percent interest, agreed with the Schröder house. With this final loan, the debts of the company reached the sum of 4 million pesos, a load too heavy for the future existence of the railroad.

The Ferrocarril del Oeste, the second of the railroad companies founded in 1857 in Havana, also had a history plagued by financial difficulties. The concession for this line was requested in August 1857, when the first signs of the crisis appeared. The concessionaires were the brothers Joaquín and Luis Pedroso Echevarría, the well-known heads of one of the oldest and most powerful oligarchic families of Havana.[52] The selling of some of their sugar mills to the limited liability company, La Gran Azucarera, during the boom left the Pedroso family with a large amount of cash to create a merchant company with a capital of 2.4 million pesos and to begin several businesses, including the trade of Chinese coolies and railroad investments.[53] The railroad project of the Pedrosos was the construction of a line to link the city of Havana with the town of Pinar del Río, capital of the westernmost jurisdiction of Cuba. The economic objective was not that of sugar transportation, but the transportation of the rich tobacco production of Vueltabajo. In the jurisdiction of Pinar del Río alone, more than three thousand *vegas* (tobacco fields) were cultivated, with a yearly production of nearly fifty thousand cargas of the precious leaf. As there were no railways in the area, the producers loaded their products in carts and transported them to the southern wharves to ship them to Havana via Batabanó in a combined service of cabotage boats and the Caminos de Hierro de la Habana.[54] Some interested in this traffic created a plan to build a railroad from Pinar del Río to the southern wharf of La Coloma as a way to facilitate the traditional transportation system. This solution would have followed the traditional production area–port railroad pattern but was replaced by the audacious project of the Ferrocarril del Oeste, which would link Havana directly with Pinar del Río by a 187-kilometer-long line, the longest of any built in Cuba. Even though this railroad company would take the line into an area lacking the modern means of transportation, the first part of the lines would cross areas already controlled by the Caminos de Hierro de la Habana. From Cristina, its terminal in Havana, to Güira de Melena, it would run almost parallel to the lines of Caminos de Hierro de la Habana, even crossing it in Rincón. Knowing this, the directors of Caminos de Hierro de la Habana proposed that the Oeste Company modify its project, placing the terminal of their branch in Guanajay, but the proposal was dropped.[55] After twenty years of monopoly, the old Havana enterprise had to face the simultaneous competition of two new railroad companies—Bahía and Oeste—throughout almost all of its service area.

Around mid-1858, the directors of the Ferrocarril del Oeste began the construction of the first sections of the line near Havana. They used a large number of imported coolies and some Basque contract laborers. The poor results of the first year—only five kilometers of line—convinced the directors of the Ferrocarril del Oeste to take personal care of the construction of the line, which had been assigned to the British contractors Dumbar and Chamberlain.[56] Under the new direction the work went faster, and by the end of 1861, the twenty-two kilometers between Cristina and the town of La Salud were operational. After these technical difficulties came the financial ones. Many of the shareholders did not pay the full value of their shares, so the company only counted on half of its 3,159,500 pesos capital as circulating shares.[57] The directors obtained some small loans from local institutions like the Caja de Ahorros and the Banco de Comercio. With these funds, and some personally advanced by the Pedrosos, the railroad built eighteen more kilometers to Alquízar in 1863 and twenty more the next year. This brought their lines to Artemisa, the approach to the western region. All the territory covered by the lines coincided, more or less, with an area serviced years before by the Caminos de Hierro de la Habana, which forced the Ferrocarril del Oeste to operate competitively by reducing tariffs below a break-even point. The prospects were discouraging. The area that the railroad was to cross now— Artemisa to Consolación—was the least productive of all the lines, and its economic possibilities depended entirely on the impact that the railroad would exert on its economy. In 1866 the section to Candelaria added another twenty-two kilometers to the line. The next nine kilometers of track from Candelaria–San Cristóbal was so simple that the engineers intended to finish it in two and a half months.[58] It took them five years. The financial difficulties of the enterprise seemed to crush the Ferrocarril del Oeste, when more than eighty kilometers of line remained to be built.

The last offspring of the western investing wave was the Ferrocarril de Marianao, which was the most exceptional of the three studied. This new line did not pretend to serve as transportation of any production or to grab part of the business of any other enterprise; its only and limited objective was to facilitate communication and foster development of the territory of Marianao, a suburban town of the capital where the wealthy families of Havana were building their summer manor houses. This railroad, projected late, found time to be its worst enemy. The concession was granted in February 1858, when the investing euphoria of Havana was already reaching its end. The promoters, Joaquín de Porto and Félix Cabello, did not find much support in the business world and passed the concession on to the Sociedad General de Crédito Mobiliario (General Property Credit Company). This firm, with better relations, built a limited liability company with 1.2 million pesos capital in 1859 in which a great number of members of the Spanish commercial clique of Havana, including Salvador Samá and Julián Zulueta, participated.[59] In spite of the wealth of the associates, the company was not able to build the line effectively. The unstable economic situation of the first months of 1860 caused a number of associates to withdraw and, after a reorganization of the company, Salvador Samá became president and leading shareholder of the railroad.[60] The new directors negotiated a £60,000 sterling loan in February 1862 from the British firm William Gibson.

Although the funds failed to cover the necessary budget, the directors ordered the beginning of work under the direction of the engineer Julio Sagebién. The short extension of the line allowed it to be finished in a little more than a year, on July 19, 1863. The opening generated some desperately needed incomes, as the construction left a debt of 260,000 pesos, and there were still facilities to be built worth some 200,000 additional pesos. In 1865 the situation was stable and allowed a balance in the operations. The revenues of that year were 35,533 pesos, which was not bad for such a short line, but made it clear that transportation of passengers, the main resource of the company, would only offer a low profit insufficient to pay off the growing obligations. According to studies made in 1866, the railroad could only earn 65,000 pesos and was forced to pay more than 200,000 pesos.[61] The alternatives were clear: to proceed to liquidation or to be ready to suffer a more or less long agony with the risks of discredit and the grief of judicial processes. The shareholders, hoping for a better general economic situation in the near future, decided on the latter.

The three Havana railroad projects of 1857 broke the pattern of the established system and paid the price. No doubt, the economic circumstances of the moment were not favorable for success. Most of the economic difficulties that they suffered were the result of the crisis, but from the point of view of their future economic perspectives they did not have the guaranties of the other railroads. There were no rich agricultural regions waiting for their transport services. The service operations of these railroads were limited to competition. With their difficulties, these three railroad companies illustrate the limits imposed on the railway business by the economic situation of the time. (See map 4.1.)

The legacy of the development of railroad transportation in the period 1854–68 was the existence of 700 new kilometers of railway. Most of this growth—around 430 kilometers—was the result of the new enterprises already described. Nevertheless, an important part of this growth (40 percent) was due to the extension of the lines of the old companies, founded during the 1840s.

The same factors that promoted the construction of the new railroads favorably influenced the old ones. This fact resulted in the conclusion of those projects, like that of Cienfuegos, that were unfinished with the arrival of the decade of the 1850s. In 1854, the Cienfuegos–Villa Clara line only reached Cruces, almost forty kilometers from its final destination. With the boom, the directors of the company decided to finish the project and to cover the debts existing before 1862. With this renewed spirit, the company took the lines to Ranchuelo (1856), Esperanza (1859), and finally to Villa Clara (1860). The extension of the service tripled the

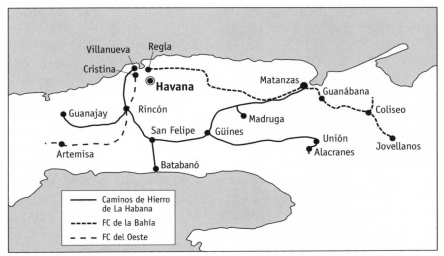

MAP 4.1. Competitive Position of the Western Railroads, 1860–1870

revenues of the railroad, leaving an average profit of 150,000 pesos that allowed it to pay the debts contracted during its construction.

The small line Remedios-Caibarién was soon inadequate for the region. Wanting to consolidate their commercial position with the railroad, the directors asked the experienced engineer Alejo H. Lanier to extend the lines toward the inland tobacco production territories of Camajuaní and San Andrés.[62] In spite of the well-designed project, work began only in 1859. The concession of the Sancti Spíritus–Tunas line that year was also encouraging, because the junction of the two lines could open the possibility of having in the center of the island the same north-south link that was so successful in the Havana-Batabanó line. With that purpose, in 1860, the Remedians began the extension of the twelve kilometers from Remedios to Taguayabón, finished in 1863. Three years later they opened the next ten kilometers to Camajuaní, a town that offered an easy communication to the nearby city of Villa Clara. The opening of the last section between Camajuaní and San Andrés took longer, and was finished only in 1871. By that time, the link with Sancti Spíritus was already forgotten.[63]

Aside from unfinished projects and utopian ambitions, the expansion of sugar plantations was the true stimulus for the extension of the railway network. This was especially true in the region of Matanzas and Cárdenas, where more than half of the extensions took place. The railroad consolidated the commercial situation of the plantations in Matanzas, and it soon became the vehicle of its expansion. Areas far from the ports of Matanzas and Cárdenas, tens of kilometers away, like Bolondrón, Corral Falso, and Macuriges started to increase the number of sugar mills with the presence of the new transportation system offered by Cárdenas after 1844 and Matanzas after 1849. The landowners were no longer afraid to settle far from the coasts, and expanded their business to the south until the water-logged lands of the Zapata swamp stopped them. As they moved, so did the Ferrocarril de Matanzas, building a twenty-two-kilometer branch from Navajas to Claudio to offer the Pedrosos, Montalvo, and Torriente economic transportation to their crops.[64] The southern direction reached its limit, so the Ferrocarril de Matanzas started to expand to the east to Cuevitas (1864), Caobillas (1865), Santa Rita de Baró (1866), and Guareiras (1869), crossing to the rich lands of Colón, which it reached in 1872.

That same route was previously taken by the Cárdenas Railroad. Its trains reached Nueva Bermeja (Colón) in 1851. The surprising arrival of the Ferrocarril de Cárdenas in Colón—the thirty kilometer line between Bemba and Colón was built in around a year—created a wild competition with the Ferrocarril del Júcaro, which previously controlled and developed the area. Each company reduced its fares by pirating the load of its competitor. The competition took the form of a rate war and was quite disastrous because of the lack of official regulations. The continuous reduction of fares condemned the two companies to ruin, but the Cárdenas Railroad took the hardest blow. The competitors then sat down at the negotiation table. A gentlemen's agreement was reached in 1853, stabilizing the fare system and allowing common transit at common fares.[65] In pursuit of a more complete integration, the companies linked their lines by a small branch surrounding the Bay of Cárdenas, allowing the Júcaro Railroad to use the port. After long negotiations, the directors of both enterprises signed the merger agreement in 1857. The new enterprise was called Empresa Unida del Ferrocarril de Cárdenas & Júcaro, with a capital of 4,500,000 pesos, distributed in 2,511,628 pesos to the old shareholders of the Cárdenas Company, and 1,988,362 to the Júcaro Company.[66] Merged, they resumed the expansion planned by the old companies. To the north, the branch from Recreo to Sabanilla de la Palma was extended with a new sixteen-kilometer line to Itabo which was concluded in 1867. To the center, the extraordinary productive branch toward the sugar production area of Banagüises followed the expansion of the sugar mills and reached San José de los Ramos and Palmilla in 1855. And finally to the south, with the extension of the old Bemba-Colón-Macagua branch, more to the east, the extension reached La Esperanza, where they wanted to build a junction with the Cienfuegos line and thereby enter into Villa Clara. In 1869, with the first eighteen kilometers of this branch built and in operation, it was possible to have, although inconvenient, a railroad network between Havana, Villa Clara, Cienfuegos, and Sagua.[67]

Competition was an important factor in the growth of the old railroad enterprises. Its effects, perceptible in the three railroads of Matanzas, are clearly evident in the case of the Caminos de Hierro de la Habana. At the beginning of 1857, the possibility of a railroad communication between Havana and Matanzas—the mentioned Ferrocarril de la Bahía de la Habana—caused alarm among the directors of the Caminos de Hierro de la Habana. Any route followed by this line would have great advantages compared with the existing 158 kilometers covered by the old line between the two cities formed by the combination of the Havana and Matanzas Railroads. As an emergency solution, the main shareholders of the railroad, Gonzalo Alfonso and Domingo Aldama, requested a concession to build a direct branch from Güines to Matanzas. The decision of the colonial government took nine months, and the concession was granted only on March 18, 1857, the same day the Ferrocarril de la Bahía de la Habana was authorized—and after the request was made.[68] With the concession in hand, the promoters tried to persuade the promoters of the Bahía to accept an agreement that would eliminate the competition. After the refusal from the Bahía Railroad, they began the construction of the branch. The fifty-eight kilometers of the new line would start at Güines, pass through Catalina, Ceiba Mocha, and other small towns, and arrive in Matanzas. This branch represented a saving of thirty kilometers compared with the former Havana-Matanzas route. Even though this line would be forty kilometers longer than the Bahía line, it was enough to place the Caminos de Hierro de la Habana in a competitive position.

The Güines branch was built amazingly fast. It opened on October 14, 1860, and among the passengers the first train took Captain General Francisco Serrano and the president of the company, Gonzalo Alfonso, as well as a company committee.[69] Shortly after, in its annual report to the shareholders, the directors informed them that "the works of the new line [the Güines-Matanzas branch] can compete with the best of its class allowing the trains to run at speeds of 60 kilometer per hour."[70]

To strengthen its position, Caminos de Hierro de la Habana built some small branches—between Robles and Madruga, for example—and started to build ten miles of double lines leading to the entrance to Havana. This project, originally conceived in Alfred Cruger's planning, would make the operations faster and would help to compete against the parallel line that the Ferrocarril del Oeste was building. Through fear of competition, Caminos de Hierro de la Habana built sixty-five new kilometers of tracks.

The fifteen years of the railroad apogee that ended in 1868 was characterized by a dynamic development of the railways and the maturity of the railroad business. The growth of this business was marked by anarchy and competition, resulting in an uneven development of the country, by which some regions had, and others lacked completely, the possibilities offered by this modern means of transportation.

The Island Railroad Network

With the railway expansion that took place between 1853 and 1868, the Cuban colonial railroad system reached its fullest extension. There were railroads in practically all areas of agricultural development, and railroads became the most preferred means of transportation. At the same time, the railroad companies, either from the operational or the economic point of view, reached maturity in their management techniques. All of this permits an analysis of the basic characteristics of the railway system as a whole, characteristics that remain valid not only for the period under review but also for the rest of the nineteenth century.

By the end of the 1860s the railways in Cuba could be considered a complete system—the only functional one—of inland transportation. The 1,262 kilometers of lines in operation were distributed irregularly among twenty-one railroad companies, each having between 4 and 238 kilometers of lines. Based on the relatively small population of the island at that time (1,359,238 inhabitants), Cuba was ahead of the world in kilometers of track per inhabitant—0.749 kilometer per 1,000 inhabitants—followed by England, the railroad country par excellence with 0.736 per 1,000 inhabitants. The physical proportion—kilometers of track per square kilometers of surface—was not so significant, and in this respect the island lagged far behind most of the European countries.[1]

The distribution and characteristics of the system were a different matter. The distribution of the first lines in Cuba, in common with other countries, resulted not from any global plan, but rather from the will of a group of promoters who made decisions based on the narrow needs of local economies. The common economic motivations produced the repetition of a basic scheme by different railroad companies. The monoexport economy of Cuba demanded from the railroad a cheap and efficient means of transportation to carry sugar from the inland plantations to the ports and to replace the increasingly inefficient traditional cart transportation. The railroad was not intended to conquer virgin lands but to follow the old cart roads replacing the existing system of transportation by a qualitatively more efficient one. Consequently, the plotting of the lines resembled the river systems of the island, going from the center to the coasts of some bays, collecting the sweet merchandise produced by the plantations along its way.

The long, narrow shape of the island, as well as the abundance of natural ports gradually authorized for international commerce, influenced deeply the pattern of the Cuban railway system. This system did not spread as the long tentacles of any one dominant port, but as successively small regional lines linked to a number of independent ports. Havana, Matanzas, Cárdenas, Cienfuegos, Remedios, Sagua, Trinidad, Sancti Spíritus, Santiago de Cuba, and Guantánamo all had the triple combination of plantation-railroad-port. This combination enabled each region to perform the same economic activity autonomously.

The first Cuban railways were therefore designed to facilitate the transportation of export products, and only secondarily in the minds of the promoters did the possibility arise of establishing an integrated system of communication between different regions and cities of the island. For a long time the various enterprises extended their lines side by side without establishing any connections. Even in some cases, such as the junction between the Matanzas and Cárdenas Railroads in Navajas, the connections were the result of the desire of one of the involved enterprises to control the area serviced by the other. Then, as a result of the expansion rather than the desire of any individual company, a small railway network began to take shape in the western region of the island. Before the end of the 1840s this system connected the cities of Havana, Matanzas, and Cárdenas. The connections were neither convenient nor efficient. The line between Havana and Matanzas—90 kilometers apart—followed a long southern arch necessitating 180 kilometers of tracks. In the Matanzas-Cárdenas case the communication was even more irrational, taking a long and complex angle to the south, 120 kilometers long. This situation demonstrated that the network was more a juxtaposition of small regional lines than a railway system as such.

The boom of the 1850s helped to rationalize communications by completing and improving the western railway network. Competition among companies created new lines between some important cities (Havana-Matanzas) and shortened the itineraries. The improvements were not only in the network, but also in the services offered, such as a better itinerary and coordination among companies. In 1864, a traveler could go from Havana to Macagua (Los Arabos), the easternmost limit of the network, in eight hours and forty minutes.[2] The west, the emporium of the Cuban plantation system that covered the area from Artemisa to Macagua, was virtually covered with railroad lines. In 1868, there was no point in this region farther than twenty kilometers from a railroad line.

Interior of the lounge coach of the Matanzas Railroad, the highest grade of comfort offered by the Cuban railroads during the last third of the nineteenth century.

Besides the previously mentioned geographical area, there was no other railroad system that went beyond a local area. The global distribution of the lines built up to 1868 was highly disproportional. While the area west to Sancti Spíritus had 1,128.41 kilometers of tracks, east of it there were only three companies having, altogether, a total of 133.59 kilometers of tracks. This represented an average of 0.023 kilometers of track per square kilometer in the western region against 0.002 in the eastern one. The cause of this disproportion is obvious: the railroad grew because of and for the sugar plantation; therefore, it occurred only in the region of the plantations. Because of this, railroad services were limited to the immediate needs of the plantations, and their technical and economic possibilities did not often go beyond those needs.

The railroad development of the first decades lacked the long-term perspective that would permit the growth of a national grid. The basic idea of the time was the connection of the northern and southern coasts of Cuba. This solution, performed first by Caminos de Hierro de la Habana with the branch to Batabanó, and later with the combination of the Sagua and Esperanza railroad lines, was a result of the traditional scheme of Cuban communications. In that scheme, the railroad helped to avoid long unnecessary trips by boat, especially around the

Publicity for the first express service in Cuba. (ANC. Fondo de fotos y grabados. Caja 632, No.2)

western region of the island, and made the transportation of passengers and merchandise easy. Therefore it did not imply a radical modification in the island's communications. Still, there were some bold projects. Around the middle of the 1850s, ideas about using the railroad for a general system of transportation for Cuba began to appear. The shape of the island suggested the basic idea of a longitudinal railroad line running from east to west. Due to the narrowness of the island, no locality would be more than fifty kilometers away from this master line. In 1853, the Junta de Fomento mentioned for the first time the Ferrocarril Central as part of a general plan of communications.[3] The Spanish government was interested in the project because of its obvious strategic importance and ordered the first field studies. In spite of the official interest and the favorable opinions of some prestigious engineers, the idea of the Ferrocarril Central had little acceptance in the circles of economic power.[4] In 1868, only the section between Macagua and Cienfuegos was being built. The only section with an immediate economic interest, it linked the western railroads to the Cienfuegos and Sagua Railroads, establishing continuous transit between Havana and Villa Clara. The difficulties of the railroad as an essential means of communication and integration at an islandwide level contrasted with its absolute success as a local instrument of the sugar export economy. This dominant economic function not only determined the shape and amplitude of the railway system, but also some basic characteristics of its services and internal economic dynamics.

The circumstances surrounding the establishment of the railroads in Cuba are quite different from those of Spain. In Spain, where the development of the railroad came late, the initial attitude of the government was a mixture of hostile indifference and poorly directed attempts.[5] In Cuba, on the contrary, there was tacit recognition on the part of the colonial authorities of the vital need of the railroad for the sugar industry, the main resource of the colony. Such recognition determined that the successive colonial governors' position toward railroads (except for Miguel Tacón) was characterized by a clear laissez-faire, the effects of which could be seen in the construction of the first lines.

The railroad matters, as every official proceeding, had to undergo all the complicated steps of the Spanish public administration, even though the railroads were able to move easily through the proverbial bureaucratic labyrinth. In Cuba, by contrast, all matters related to the railroads went under the jurisdiction of the Real Junta de Fomento until 1854. From then on this institution only functioned as a consultative body, and administrative decisions on railroad matters remained in the hands of the Dirección de Obras Públicas (Department of Public Works), later changed into a *subdirección* (bureau) directly responsible to the Gobierno Superior Civil (senior civilian governor).[6] With the creation of the Consejo de Administración in 1861, the consultative functions of the Junta de Fomento were transferred to jurisdictional boards of agriculture, industry, and commerce. These small institutions simply transferred the railroad requests to the captain general, the most senior government authority of the island.

Since 1836, the captains general of the island had the authority to grant provisional railroad concessions, which were later confirmed by the government of the metropolis. In these matters, the colonial administration exceeded the 1844 legal regulations of Spain by granting concessions for eighteen months. Four years later, a Spanish public company law tried to centralize such decisions in the Cortes.[7] Needless to say, neither the 1844 regulation nor the 1848 law was enforced in Cuba where the captains general continued to grant provisional concessions that were renewed or extended at the request of the concessionaires. As the regulations for the private company law were not effective in Cuba, the creation of such companies was not needed to build railroads. Until 1857, the concessions were granted to individuals without any other formal process or guarantee. The paradox was that the metropolis had laws without railroads while the colony had railroads without laws.

That weak regulation was the major contribution of the colonial government to the Cuban railroad development, as well as some privileges granted to the railroad promoters, such as the right to alienate lands by force in case of public utility (facilitating the plotting of the lines), the right of perpetual property of the lands, and certain exemptions for the importation of materials and equipment. By offering such advantages, the colonial government gave to the promoters full responsibility for the expensive construction of the roads, a problem of great importance that created a constant demand on the colonial government from the sugar producers. These grants were a sort of compensation for the lack of subsidy or direct help from the Spanish government, miserable and miserly, as always. In this game, the government lost its regulating authority over the plotting of the lines and some other aspects of the economic functions of the enterprises, giving arbitrary control on the part of the promoters over the development of this vital communication infrastructure.

Nevertheless, the Junta de Fomento, the institution representing the sugar interests and economically autonomous in relation to the Real Hacienda, worked as a stimulant to the railroads not only in the administrative and informative aspects but also in the economic field. The Junta de Fomento was responsible for the initiative and construction of the first line between Havana and Güines, the decisive first step for the following railway development. Afterward, the Junta gave economic support to many of the successive railroad constructions by buying a number of shares. The magnitude and distribution of this help can be seen in Table 5.1.

The help provided by the Junta de Fomento was not substantial—only 14

Copy of the first credit letters against the loan for the construction of the first railroad.

percent of the 3.2 million pesos constituting the total initial investment of the enterprises mentioned—but more than once its timely help prevented the fledgling companies from severe financial difficulties.

The government's policy looked better after the 1850s when Spain started its own railroad development. In 1854, a Progresista government, strongly linked with the interests of the metropolitan financial bourgeoisie, came to power and supported measures favorable to railroad development. These were included in the Railroad Law of 1855 (Ley de Ferrocarriles), which freed the railroad companies from the legal obstacles derived from the public incorporation law of 1848. The new legislation facilitated the granting of concessions and authorized the government to subsidize the enterprises by paying a certain amount for each kilometer of track built. At the same time, it established technical and economical regulations for the operation of railroad companies as well as for the government support.[8] Extended to Cuba through a *real decreto* of December 1858, the Spanish railroad legislation had contradictory effects in the island. As the Cuban railroads were not affected by the previous regulations, this liberalization of the

TABLE 5.1. Shares in Cuban National Railroad Companies Purchased by the Junta de Fomento, 1840–1854 (in pesos fuertes)

Company	Year	Shares
FC de Matanzas a Sabanilla	1840–41	146,550
FC de Júcaro	1842	35,000
FC Nuevitas–Puerto Príncipe	1844	50,000
FC de Coliseo	1846	102,000
FC de Caibarién	1846	20,000
FC de Cienfuegos y Villa Clara	1851–54	90,000
Total		443,550

new law made no sense in the prevailing Cuban environment. On the contrary, the attempt to regulate the development and operations of railroads disrupted the paradise of anarchy in which the Cubans operated. So, against the perpetual private property that the Cuban railroads enjoyed, the new regulation established that the railroad rights of way were public domain and of general utility, thereby granting controlling rights to the government. Based on this principle, the government assumed that it had the authority to reduce rates and forced the companies to build an electric telegraph system to guarantee traffic safety.[9] Even though the enterprises constituted before 1857 could continue to enjoy part of their privileges, the enforcement of the *real decreto* of 1858 raised a storm of protest. The enterprises complained of the obligations imposed by the new law and opposed the government's control. Some authors blamed this law for the stagnation of the following years, but the truth is that in the period between 1858 and 1868, 579 kilometers of new tracks were built. In fact, most of the regulations established in 1858 became dead letters, as happened with the model kilometric rate that caused so much disagreement among entrepreneurs. But even with the laws, the government's inefficiency undermined any attempt to exercise effective control over the railroad enterprises.

The Cuban railroads of that period had an amazing technological similarity, if one considers the operational liberty they enjoyed due to the lack of regulations on that matter. This was a result of the American origin of most of the constructing engineers and technical personnel, some of whom worked with several companies, using the same technological criteria. Another important unifying factor was the identity in economic motivations, that influenced the system of roads. The few intersections were made to provide a choice of port or company to the sugar producers, rather than to facilitate transportation. The lines were normally single tracks, with short stretches of double tracks being the exception. The lack of

double lines was the cause of serious traffic problems, until the use of the telegraph made circulation of trains easier and safer. In the opinion of the company
officials, the telegraph was equivalent to a double line. For this reason, in 1853, the
Caminos de Hierro de la Habana began to set telegraph lines along all its stations,
from Garcini to Unión, Batabanó, and Guanajay.[10] Immediately after, the other
railroad companies installed their telegraphs, except for the Puerto Príncipe line
owing to its limited resources and small amount of traffic.

During the first twenty years of railroad construction, the lines were set on what
was called the "road bed," a graded dirt road, twenty to twenty-one feet wide.
usually paved with the dirt and stones coming from the construction excavations.
Ballast was used at the end of the 1850s by the Caminos de Hierro de la Habana to
renew its line from the Almendares River to Aguada del Cura. The new Ferrocarril de la Bahía de la Habana also began to use it on its lines.[11]

Until the 1860s the use of the very hard Cuban lumber for crossties was not
generalized, even though there were still abundant hardwood forests throughout
the country. The location of the sawmills and the transportation of the logs over
difficult roads made their supply difficult and irregular for the consistent demand
created by the railroads. However, American merchants offered all the white pine
and oak that Cuba needed at a very low price.[12] As the railroad moved inland, the
use of nearby timber became available. Imported lumber showed low resistance
to humidity and heat so the railroad companies decided to use the local forest resources, mainly *quiebra hacha*, *jiquí*, and certain varieties of *júcaro*.

Almost all the Cuban railroad companies used a standard width of 1.45 meters
for their lines. Small, short tracks like the Ferrocarril de Carahatas, the El Cobre,
and some other private branches employing animal power used narrower gauges.[13]
The notable exception was the Ferrocarril de Puerto Príncipe a Nuevitas. It used a
wider standard—1.60 meters—which would later be the standard of the Spanish
railway network.[14]

The companies paid no attention to the regulations and recommendations
enacted by the colonial government to set fences to isolate the lines, especially in
the stations. Consequently, the trains continued to mix with the life of the country
and the towns, scaring the beasts of carts, hitting loose animals, and setting fire to
cane fields with the sparks of their locomotives.

The Cuban railroads did not go through the classical phases of wooden rails,
animal force, and its later substitution by iron rails and steam power, as occurred
in England and the United States. As the invention was already effective and fully
tested in industrialized countries, and the needs of the plantation owners demanded a radical solution to the export of sugar, the railroad was introduced in
Cuba with the latest technology. This included iron rails and steam locomotives,

usually with six wheels. Jacobo Pezuela, used to seeing the wide Spanish lines, remarked that "its particular distribution and short distance between the axes allows them to run without difficulty along curves of smaller ratio than the Europeans."[15]

From the first "Rocket" model of the Havana-Güines and its American substitutes, the "Colon" and "Cervantes," almost all the locomotives of the Cuban companies came from Philadelphia, Boston, or New York.[16] In 1868, Cuba had 176 locomotives and 179 tenders, or auxiliary cars, for fuel.[17] This number of engines was excessive in relation to the distances of the lines, as the proportion was approximately one locomotive for every 7.3 kilometers of line. This was the result of the abundance of small enterprises, which increased the number of engines every time a small branch opened service and did not allow a rational use of the equipment existing in the country.

At first, the fuel used was firewood and, to a much lesser degree, American and English coal. The forests of the western plains, Jagua and Guantánamo, and the sabana woods of Puerto Príncipe began to disappear to be used for the construction of crossties and as fuel for the trains and sugar mills. Coal soon became more economical, especially since it had a regular supply and distribution system. Caminos de Hierro de la Habana was forced to modify its use of wood and substitute coal in areas where the forests had disappeared. This reduction of wood went from being 98 percent of the total fuel used in 1858 to 30 percent in 1866.[18]

As with the locomotives, the railway cars were first brought from England and later from the United States, even though some continued to come from England. The first cars had only four wheels and were built to carry 2.5 tons of freight. At the end of the 1850s, eight-wheel cars were used, enabling the hauling of four times more load than the previous ones.[19] Although the normal procedure was to buy the cars already finished, kits were also bought to be finished in Cuba. In 1868 the total number of cars was 2,295—264 for passengers and 2,031 for freight. The passenger cars were classified as first, second, and third class. The American R. H. Dana, who traveled to Limonar on the Ferrocarril de Coliseo in 1859, referred to these classes in the following way: "There are three classes of cars, all after the American model, the first of about the conditions of our first-class cars when on the point of being condemned as worn out; the second, a little plainer; and the third only covered wagons with benches. . . . The freight cars responded to the needs of the freight, changing from cells to platforms or to covered cars depending if they were going to transport sugar, cattle, or general freight."[20]

The complementary equipment necessary to any railroad network of branches included huge freight platforms and ample warehouses in every economically important place. There the sugar crates, barrels of molasses or muscovado, and pipes of rum that composed the freight for the trains were accepted. The large warehouses and maritime wharves at the terminal ports completed the export system linked to the railroad. The operations that took place in such places were controlled directly by the railroad company or a related enterprise usually controlled by the same sugar producing interests that promoted the railroad.

As the railroad was basically created and expanded to transport sugar from the inland sugar mills, by the 1860s railroads transported almost 80 percent of the 500,000 or 600,000 tons of sugar produced in the island. Of the twenty-nine administrative jurisdictions of the island, railroads traversed twenty.[21] However, nearly ten years before, in areas of great production like Cárdenas, Matanzas, Güines, or Cienfuegos, the proportion of sugar carried by the railroad varied from 41 to 58 percent of the total produced by the sugar mills. It was only at the end of the 1860s that companies like those in Cárdenas and Matanzas, in their successful foray into the plains of Colón, carried a greater volume of freight than they collected within their local areas.

Something similar happened with the new competitor, the Ferrocarril de la Bahía de la Habana a Matanzas, which signed contracts with the plantations on the northern strip between Havana and Matanzas and with the sugar mills of the Coliseo-Bemba branch. It transported freights traditionally carried by the Cárdenas, Matanzas, and the Caminos de Hierro de la Habana companies taking the freight toward its warehouses at Regla.

The lack of an important production volume of sugar or any other kind in the area of Puerto Príncipe and Nuevitas negatively influenced the operations of the railroad that linked these two cities of Camagüey. By 1854, this company could only move two trains a week, and sometimes an additional one when a ship arrived or left the port of Nuevitas. This situation got better after 1867, because service increased to four trains a week.

The passenger waiting rooms of the main stations, as well as small rudimentary buildings at the minor stops completed the service network of the railroad. Nevertheless, as the railroads were built for the transportation of sugar, transportation of passengers was a secondary business. Besides, the population of the country was small, nearly 12 inhabitants per square kilometer. Cuba had a total 1,359,238 inhabitants in 1862, distributed between the two main departments. The Eastern (Oriental) had 255,919 inhabitants, while the Western (Occidental) had 1,103,319 inhabitants. This total was not large enough to maintain a viable passenger service since the total is deceptive. With the existing slave system in Cuba not all the population enjoyed freedom of movement. Only the white and the colored freemen—747,388 in the West and 203,986 in the East—could be considered as potential passengers. The rest of the population, 407,864 persons, included slaves, a small number of *emancipados* (freedmen), and some Chinese *colonos*. None of these groups could be considered regular passengers.

Again the observation of the traveler R. H. Dana is valuable to confirm this situation: "The railroad is intended for the carriage of sugar and other produce, and gets its support almost entirely in that way; for it runs through a sparse, rural population, where there are no towns; yet so large and valuable is the sugar crop that I believe the road is well supported."[22]

The subordination of passenger trains to freight was quite common in Cuba before 1853. Five years after the junction between Caminos de Hierro de la Habana and the Ferrocarril de Matanzas at Unión, the government was forced to intervene on behalf of passengers who had to change trains there. Because of the competition among companies for the transportation of sugar, passengers were abandoned for a whole day in that place before they were able to continue their trip to Havana, Matanzas, or Navajas.[23] Even in 1862, there were persons who claimed that the Ferrocarril de la Habana a Matanzas took longer than a steamboat between the two ports.[24] The useful connection of the Sagua and Cienfuegos Railroads in the center of the island was also not very efficient since in 1868 the passengers from Sagua had to wait more than three hours in Cruces before taking the train to Cienfuegos.[25]

The irrationality of a railroad service lacking efficient connections and the arbitrary regulations of railroad administrations reached a climax during the 1860s as a result of the strong competition that took place among the companies. As the competition began to reflect negatively, not only on the passengers, but also on the economic interests of the companies involved, some sort of rationality gradually appeared. Facing the possibility of total disaster, the railroad companies decided to establish agreements on traffic and even mergers that would integrate their service, such as in the case of the Cárdenas and Júcaro Railroads. Possible mergers were studied between the Sagua and Cienfuegos Railroads and Caminos de Hierro de la Habana and Ferrocarril de la Bahía de la Habana.[26] There was even an audacious project of monopoly fostered by Miguel Aldama, who planned the merger of all the railroad enterprises operating in Havana, Matanzas, and Cárdenas.[27] Although these mergers did not all take place, the agreements among companies spread and did facilitate the transportation of freight and passengers. The agreements were quite precarious, but they contributed to a reduction of the inconveniences of the anarchic railroad transportation services.

The Cuban railroads, built to serve the needs of the sugar industry, increased their revenues commensurate with the expansion of sugar production. Figure 5.1 illustrates how the railroad revenues from freight reflected the increase in production. A different situation, however, arose in the case of "fares, mail and express" as these depended on different factors, particularly the population density and

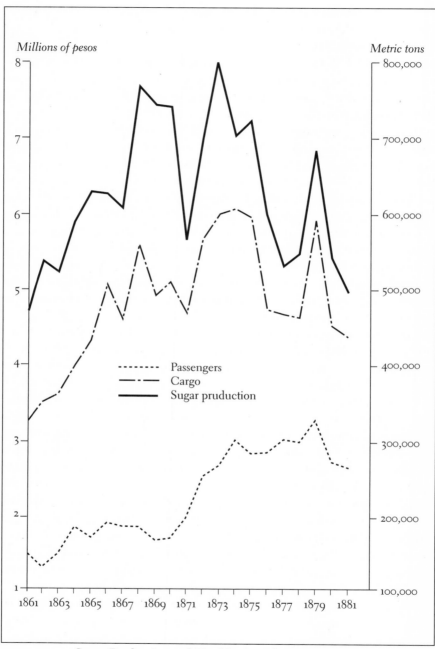

FIGURE 5.1. Sugar Production and Total Income for Cargo and Passengers on Cuban Public Railroads, 1861–1881

grouping. Considering that fares contributed only 25–30 percent of the total revenues of the railroad, its impact did not have much effect on the overall increase in income derived from the sugar business.

In 1862, when the Cuban railroads entered a phase of maturity, the total revenues of all the railroad companies approximated some 5 million pesos, or about 6 percent of the global value of Cuba's three main products—sugar, tobacco, and coffee—estimated that year at around 80 million pesos. The proportion is significant considering the weight of the railroad business within the island's economy, but a more precise picture of the meaning of these figures can be established when seen in an international perspective. In 1862, operating revenue per kilometer from operating of the Cuban railroads was 4,782 pesos. This figure was significantly lower than that of European countries with bigger railroad development—Great Britain, France, Austria, and Belgium—which had revenues that varied from 5,600 to 8,600 pesos. It was roughly similar to the Italians—4,949 pesos per kilometer of line—but higher than the Spanish, with revenues of only 3,703 pesos per kilometer.[28] The Cuban railroads held an intermediate revenue position.

The revenue situation derived from the nature of railroad traffic, especially the volume and intensity of merchandise moving in the areas served by the railroad. In European capitalist countries, with well-structured internal markets, the railroad had a huge, regular, and continuous flow of freight. In Cuba, merchandise circulation was not diversified and was oriented to export, so the railroad enterprises could not exploit optimally their facilities and equipment. The freight did not circulate regularly—the flow of freight from inland to the ports was not backed by a similar return flow. The trains that went inland for their freight usually ran with most of the cars empty. The virtual lack of an internal merchandise traffic and the low proportion of the imported goods that went to the regions inland—most of this merchandise was destined to the port cities—affected the rationality of the railroad economies, and these enterprises tried to compensate by imposing high tariffs on export goods. The specific characteristics of every Cuban railroad enterprise were influenced by its region of operation as well as for the length of its lines.

Table 5.2 shows that revenues for the four big western companies—Caminos de Hierro de la Habana, Ferrocarril de la Bahía de la Habana, Ferrocarril de Matanzas, and Ferrocarril de Cárdenas y Júcaro—were ahead of the group and could compare advantageously with the Europeans. This was the result of a combined effect of relatively long systems and service in highly productive regions. By contrast, Ferrocarril de Trinidad, Ferrocarril del Oeste, and Ferrocarril de Nuevitas–Puerto Príncipe were all affected by different factors such as low merchandise flow, unfinished lines, an area of low productivity, and other factors that adversely affected their revenue yields. Even though it is impossible to make a detailed analysis of each company here, the Ferrocarril de Santiago de Cuba and the

TABLE 5.2. Annual Income per Kilometer for the Fourteen Largest Railroad
Companies in Cuba, 1861–1868 (in pesos fuertes)

Company	1861	1862	1863	1864	1865	1866	1867	1868
FC del Oeste	2,254	2,292	2,988	2,525	3,514	3,976	3,066	3,072
FC de la Bahía	4,961	4,185	5,125	8,762	4,233	7,046	6,206	7,607
Caminos de Hierro de La Habana	6,700	5,875	5,834	5,691	5,704	5,838	5,636	6,581
FC de Cárdenas y Júcaro	6,085	5,764	6,525	6,007	6,749	7,471	6,230	7,834
FC de Matanzas	6,607	7,224	2,350	6,975	7,243	7,660	6,538	8,045
FC de Cienfuegos y Villa Clara	4,166	4,585	4,246	4,610	4,985	5,610	4,839	5,772
FC de Sagua	2,655	2,527	2,491	3,381	3,424	3,723	3,561	4,842
FC Nuevitas–Puerto Príncipe	2,392	2,280	2,287	2,842	2,943	3,654	3,053	2,815
FC Santiago de Cuba	3,610	5,057	5,646	5,695	5,223	6,610	6,213	6,766
FC de Guantánamo	3,426	3,646	4,062	3,841	3,625	4,358	4,193	4,366
FC de Coliseo	4,961	5,446	6,086	6,748	–	–	–	–
FC Tunas–Sancti Spríritus	–	–	866	1,889	1,715	2,382	2,103	2,360
FC de Caibarién	5,062	5,492	5,149	4,762	4,432	2,810	4,850	5,687
FC de Trinidad	1,857	1,915	2,553	2,281	–	–	–	–

Sources: Cuba, Subdirección de Obras Públicas, Memoria sobre el progreso de las obras
públicas en la isla de Cuba, 1859–65 (Havana, 1866); and J. Jáudenes, Memoria sobre las
obras públicas de la isla de Cuba, 1865– 1873 (Havana, 1873).

Ferrocarril del Oeste deserve attention because of the progressive increase in
their revenues following every newly opened branch.

This analysis of the revenues cannot address the real economy of the railroad
companies since figures for operating expense are unfortunately lacking in most
cases. However, the series of expenditures per kilometer of the eleven main railroad companies of the island shown in Table 5.3 offers a small basis for analysis.

In spite of the rudimentary systems of control and the classification of expenses
at that time, the expense rates per kilometer constitute an acceptable index to
detect certain problems.[29] In the first place, expenses were obviously related to

TABLE 5.3. Annual Expenditures per Kilometer for Eleven Cuban Railroads, 1865–1868 (in pesos fuertes)

Company	1865	1866	1867	1868
FC del Oeste	2,812	4,159	3,001	3,007
FC de la Bahía	3,203	4,808	4,561	5,301
Caminos de Hierro de La Habana	3,813	3,995	3,844	4,234
FC de Cárdenas y Júcaro	2,660	2,947	2,767	3,294
FC de Matanzas	3,140	2,709	3,703	3,476
FC de Cienfuegos y Villa Clara	2,126	3,481	2,700	2,601
FC de Sagua	1,942	2,120	2,104	2,130
FC Nuevitas–Puerto Príncipe	1,446	1,449	1,727	1,137
FC Santiago de Cuba	3,719	3,809	3,776	3,851
FC de Guantánamo	1,261	1,657	2,024	1,797
FC Tunas–Sancti Spíritus	1,015	859	924	1,285

Source: J. Jáudenes, Memoria sobre las obras públicas de la isla de Cuba, 1865–1873 (Havana, 1873).

the size of the company, so the smallest ones such as Tunas, Puerto Principe, and Guantánamo have the lowest expense rates. However, the expense differences per kilometer among companies with more or less similar services may reflect the existence of poor administration, the route structure, or the influence of competitors. Significantly, low expenses were shown by Ferrocarril de Cárdenas y Júcaro, one of the biggest companies, when compared with similar ones like Caminos de Hierro de la Habana and Ferrocarril de Matanzas. In this case the influence of an extraordinarily advantageous route, with no steeps at all, was significant because it resulted in great savings on fuel and locomotive wear and tear. The Ferrocarril de Santiago de Cuba, operating in mountain lands, had results that were exactly opposite. The expenses of Caminos de Hierro de la Habana and particularly of Ferrocarril de la Bahía de la Habana were good examples of the negative effects of competition, which forced both to maintain frequent service, resulting in high costs for fuel, equipment replacement, and wages.

The most interesting information is the direct comparison of revenues and expenses. The best instrument is an old formula of the railroad economy called razón de operación (operating ratio). It is a simple arithmetic division of expenses (E) over revenues (R) by which E/R indicates what part of the revenues is used by the operation expenses and, therefore, if the enterprise was profitable. By this ratio, any approximation to parity represented a sliding scale of profitability. If the

TABLE 5.4. Operating Ratio for Thirteen Cuban Railway Companies, 1865–1868

Company	1865	1866	1867	1868
FC del Oeste	0.80	0.95	0.98	0.97
FC de la Bahía	0.75	0.68	0.73	0.69
Caminos de Hierro de la Habana	0.66	0.68	0.68	0.64
FC de Cárdenas y Júcaro	0.39	0.39	0.44	0.42
FC de Matanzas	0.43	0.48	0.56	0.43
FC de Cienfuegos y Villa Clara	0.43	0.44	0.55	0.45
FC de Sagua	0.56	0.56	0.59	0.44
FC Nuevitas–Puerto Príncipe	0.49	0.40	0.56	0.38
FC de Santiago de Cuba	0.63	0.57	0.60	0.56
FC de Guantánamo	0.34	0.38	0.48	0.41
FC Tunas–Sancti Spíritus	0.59	0.39	0.45	0.59
FC de Caibarién	0.47	0.36	0.35	0.39
FC de Trinidad	—	1.01	0.96	0.92

Source: Calculated from data in J. Jáudenes, *Memoria sobre las obras públicas de la isla de Cuba, 1865–1873* (Havana, 1873).

result of the ratio was equal or above the unit, the economic conditions would indeed be precarious. Table 5.4 reflects the operation coefficient of the most representative Cuban railroad societies between 1865 and 1868.

Cuban railroads were, in general, reasonably profitable. Except for the Oeste and Trinidad Railroads, the revenues obtained by the companies easily covered the operational expenses, by varying amounts from the profitable Ferrocarril de Cárdenas y Júcaro to less profitable ones like Ferrocarril de la Bahía de la Habana, Ferrocarril de Santiago de Cuba, and Caminos de Hierro de la Habana. But the profits at first sight suggested by basic differences between revenues and expenses are somewhat misleading. These profits were not necessarily indicative of net income. The expenses considered so far only included wages, fuel, material, and maintenance of equipment. Those were just part of the total expenses of the companies. To those should be added some other expenses, such as the payment of taxes, insurance, depreciation, and, above all, the payments of the obligations contracted by loans. Together these narrow considerably the difference between the gross totals of income and expenditures. The burden that those various overlooked obligations represented for the profitability of a great number of railroad companies deserves special attention.

The first railroad investments were done under an atmosphere of general prosperity that favored the railway projects. The success of the well-planned railroad between Havana and Güines gave confidence to the capitalists linked to the sugar business. Landowners and merchants opened their wallets for the fantastic prospect of rail transportation of sugar products. That would allow them to regain rapidly the investments made on railroad construction and later to dedicate themselves to profiting from the sugar interests that gave them life. But the financial resources of the railroad promoters, apparently unlimited, just allowed the construction of the first kilometers of the main line planned. The lack of precise budgets that could estimate the real cost of the railways became a problem to the capitalists of some enterprises, unable to cope with the costs of construction of their projects.[30]

The need for money by the companies, together with the lack of a real banking organization in the main commercial centers of the island, led to the repetition of the financial procedure used in the construction of the Havana-Güines project: a resort to foreign loans. These loans—mortgage loans—were contracted with British firms, especially with Alexander Robertson & Bros., which was responsible for the financing of almost all the first railroad projects in Cuba. However, until the middle of the nineteenth century foreign financing had little importance in railroad investments,. Before 1857 foreign capital amounted to no more than 3.7 million pesos, of which, 2.5 million belonged to the initial loan for the construction of the Ferrocarril Habana-Güines. During that first period, the general favorable economic climate allowed the railroad companies to find solutions by increasing the number of shareholders, or resorting to aid from the Junta de Fomento. After 1857, the progressive decline of the Cuban economy and, even worse, the devastating effects of successive crises on such a weak financial infrastructure, increased the dependency on foreign sources of financing. In the short span between 1860 and 1865, the loans contracted by the Cuban railroads doubled the capital contracted for these concerns during the preceding twenty years. A detailed sample of such situation is shown in Table 5.5.

These loans were all contracted with London firms, dominated by J. Henry Schröder and Company, an Anglo-German bank that started to operate in Cuba in 1853 with a loan of £200,000 for the Ferrocarril de Matanzas.[31] The total amount of the financial resources contributed by English banks to Cuban railroads up to 1868 was 12,701,000 pesos, a figure that represented around 25 percent of the total capitalization of the Cuban railroads as a whole.[32]

The credit companies already in Cuba were less significant in the financing of the railroads compared with English bankers. Few and small, the Cuban banking enterprises only offered small loans, always at high interest rates and with short mortgage terms. The local loans to railroad companies were always motivated by the common identity of interests that controlled the banks and the railroads.

TABLE 5.5. Loans Contracted by Cuban Railroads, 1860–1865 (in pesos fuertes)

Year	Company	Lender	Amount
1860	FC de Cienfuegos y Villa Clara	Robertson & Bros.	450,000
1861	FC de la Bahía	J. H. Schröder & Co.	1,250,000
1862	FC de Marianao	William Gibson	300,000
1862	FC de Matanzas	J. H. Schröder & Co.	1,500,000
1863	FC de la Bahía	J. H. Schröder	500,000
1863	FC de Sagua	Cavan, Lulilak, & Co.	1,500,000
1865	FC de Sagua	Unknown	800,000
1865	FC de Caibarién	Unknown	500,000
1865	FC de la Bahía	J. H. Schröder & Co.	2,000,000
1865	FC de la Bahía	J. H. Schröder & Co.	170,000

Sources: Constructed from data in Copia simple de la escritura de contrato para el empréstito de los FC de Sagua, in ANC, Fondo Ferrocarriles (Cuban Central Railroads), legajo 279, expediente 15; for Sagua, Memoria (1870), pp. 1, 12; Escritura de préstamo del FC de Marianao, in AFC (ETH), anaquel 26, caja 5; FC de Matanzas, Informe de la Junta Directiva a la general de accionistas (1863), p. 5, in ANC, Fondo Gobierno Superior Civil, legajo 1010, expediente 35138; Banco de Comercio y Almacenes de Regla, Antecedentes y contratos referentes a los negocios con el FC de la Bahía (Havana, 1882), pp. 3, 16, 18.

Nowhere is this connection better illustrated than in the loan of 700,000 pesos granted by Crédito Territorial—under the influence of the Aldama-Alfonso clan—to Caminos de Hierro de la Habana, the loan of 292,000 pesos granted by Banco de Cuba to the Ferrocarril de Santiago de Cuba, and the loans of almost 2 million pesos by the Banco de Comercio to the Ferrocarril de la Bahía de la Habana, the highest local grant ever made to a Cuban railroad.[33] Adding to these some loans made by firms like Banco Español de la Isla de Cuba and Caja de Ahorros, it is probable that the total financial amount to the railroad provided by local credit institutions might have been 5 million pesos by the end of the 1860s.

The magnitude of the contracted debts represented a heavy fiscal burden for more than one railroad company. The loans contracted before 1857 were smaller and more infrequent and could be liquidated without serious problems, but the larger loans made afterward constituted too high a burden for many companies. In 1865, the Ferrocarril de Marianao, with revenues of 40,000 pesos a year, had to face the first installment of its English debt and some other minor loans, which totaled almost a quarter of a million pesos. This was, no doubt, an extreme case, but not unusual. The Ferrocarril de la Bahía de la Habana with its debt with Schröder of almost 4 million pesos and the 2 million pesos owed to the Banco de

Comercio was in no better shape. Debt service used all the revenues and was not enough to free the companies from the constant demands of the creditors. Other railroad enterprises created in the 1850s such as Oeste, Santiago de Cuba, and Trinidad experienced the same difficulties. This does not mean that the railroad business in Cuba was not profitable as a whole. The most important companies, which were also the oldest, operated with profits and covered their obligations. The railroads of Cárdenas and Júcaro, once merged, paid dividends regularly that represented 7.5 to 13 percent of the nominal value of their shares. The credit granted by the Sociedad de Crédito Industrial in 1857 was liquidated five years later and from that moment on, the company was free from debts.[34] In spite of the amount of the loan contracted by the Ferrocarril de Matanzas with Schröder, the enterprise was able to keep a solid net income and pay regular dividends of 5 to 10 percent of its capital.[35]

The oldest railroad company, Caminos de Hierro de la Habana, had a solid credit from the sugar tycoons Domingo and Miguel Aldama, and Gonzalo Alfonso from whom it also contracted frequent internal loans.[36] Its solvency allowed it to liquidate the 2.5-million-peso English loan in 1865 contracted by the Junta de Fomento with Alexander Robertson.[37] The growth of this company, as many others, was based on an intelligent capitalization of the profits, from which a lot of resources were used to extend lines and modernize the equipment. In the period of 1861–63 alone, Caminos de Hierro de la Habana made a capital of 754,748 pesos while paying the shareholders' dividends of 8 percent of their shares.[38] Even during the critical economic year of 1866–67, the directors of Caminos de Hierro de la Habana expressed optimism to the shareholders about the future of the company:

There has been a reduction in the transportation of products this year due to the economic crisis that our island has been facing for several months. The chickenpox epidemic in Matanzas in the first three months of the year reduced considerably passenger traffic with this city. Despite the decrease of crops and the competition that others exert on us, our revenues compare quite favorably with that of other companies.[39]

The first thirty years of railroad service in Cuba, although without ostentatious results, did not dampen the hopes of the promoters and investors, despite their uneven fortunes. It is difficult to find a more concise or precise summary of this period than the one written by the Subdirección de Obras Públicas of the colonial government in 1866: "In spite of the different financial crises that have left so many disappointed, and the small profits generated by the railway companies compared with other speculations, there has been a real advance in its development."[40] One can now explore the economic implications of this development.

The inauguration of railroad service reduced the costs of transportation considerably. The magnitude of this phenomenon is difficult to measure, however, as there are no official data on this matter, nor the existence of a public source of specific rates to offer some basis for comparison. Nevertheless the testimonies of some contemporaries offer an approximate idea of the reduction of transportation costs produced by the railroad. According to Ramón de la Sagra, around 1830 the transportation of a sugar crate—between sixteen and twenty arrobas—from Güines to Havana cost 4 pesos, which was approximately 20 percent of the price of the product at dockside in Havana.[41] José Antonio Saco, who confirms Sagra's estimate, stated that with the introduction of the railroad the costs were reduced by 70 percent.[42] The initial cost of the railroad, 6 reales—0.30 pesos—per crate from Bejucal to Havana was reduced even more when the line was transferred to the Compañía de Caminos de Hierro de la Habana. The charge between Güines and Havana for a sugar crate was set at 16 reales—0.65 pesos—and reduced to 8.5 reales in 1839. As railroad transportation increased, different regions slowly benefited from the progressive reduction of costs. In 1847 the cost of the Ferrocarril de Júcaro to transport sugar from Banagüises to Cárdenas, a distance of forty-nine kilometers, was 8 reales per crate, a price very similar to the one that the first railroad charged ten years before in the shorter stretch (twenty-seven kilometers) from Bejucal to Havana.[43]

The economic importance of the reduction of the costs of transportation produced by the railroad had other implications. As the world sugar market expanded, it became much more competitive. Any reduction of costs in transportation on the island increased the competitiveness of Cuban sugar. A modest estimate allows an evaluation suggesting the reduction between 10 to 20 percent of the total cost of production for the sugar-producing landowners due to the railroad. Although neither the statistical basis nor the tariff system of the Cuban railroads allows one to estimate with precision the amount of the resources saved by the railroad, a rudimentary calculation about this magnitude in a specific region—Güines—may offer an idea of its importance. In 1862, the jurisdiction of Güines produced approximately 170,000 sugar crates, whose shipment, if transported at the prices of the cart system of 1830, would have cost about 680,000 pesos. The transportation of these products by railroad represented a saving of more than 500,000 pesos, the equivalent of 13.5 percent of the total value of the product at the then current price. Even if we consider that, because of the region chosen and the assumptions of the calculation, these figures may be above the average, everything indicates that the savings contributed by the railroad to the Cuban economy were great, since the geographical conditions of the island (stated in Chapter 1) reduced considerably the possibilities of having a means of

TABLE 5.6. Principal Products of the Jurisdiction of Güines (in arrobas)

Year	Sugar	Coffee	Rice	Corn	Tobacco
1827	640,000	91,500	84,265	89,988	2,522
1862	3,061,268	15,263	194,048	134,990	2,866

Sources: *Cuadro estadístico de la siempre fiel isla de Cuba* (Havana, 1827); Conde de Armildes de Toledo, *Noticias estadísticas de la isla de Cuba en 1862* (Havana, 1864).

transportation with the economic efficiency equivalent or even approximate to that offered by the railroad.

The reduction of transportation costs not only strengthened the competitive position of Cuban sugar on the international market, but also increased the availability of investment capital. "The railroad, and not the introduction of steam engines in the sugar mills"—Manuel Moreno Fraginals correctly points out—"is the first element of the industrial revolution that completely altered the productive conditions of Cuba."[44] It may be an exaggeration to state that the railroad saved the slave-run sugar plantation from ruin, but it is certain that without this new means of transportation, it would not have expanded as it did in the middle of the nineteenth century. It is not only a matter of reducing the costs; the possibility of a better way to transport the delicate or heavy equipment safely allowed the sudden increase in productivity and the progressive mechanization of the industrial operations. Besides, the reduction of transport costs offset the continual increase in the cost of slave labor. The paradox is that the railroad contributed to the delay for some decades of the expected end of slavery.

Even though, theoretically, the benefits of the railroad would reach every product of the regions it served, the truth is that sugar production, because of the volume and weight of its freight, remained the main beneficiary of the railroad. Consequently, the relative profit of the dominant culture of the Cuban economy increased to the detriment of other products. The productive evolution of the jurisdiction of Güines, as shown in Table 5.6, is a clear example of this.

Between 1827 and 1862, sugar production increased by 465 percent. Rice increased by 230 percent. The growth of rice is not surprising, considering that the population doubled in the same period; but the increase registered by other products is poor, notwithstanding the commercial crisis that coffee suffered. Cuban railroads also affected internal marketing, although the impact was quite different—opposite in fact—to the effects that the railroad had in other countries, particularly in Europe. The common assertion in many railroad histories that the railroad, by closing the distance between consumers and producers, consolidated national markets, favoring regional specialization.[45] In Cuba, the railway lines were not set to link the different regions of the country, but to give each region a faster road for the export of its products through the nearest port, and this had quite distinct consequences. The reduction of transportation costs destroyed the barriers that protected certain local crafts and agricultural productions, which were substituted by imported products that arrived at low prices to the consumers. The same road that opened the door to produced exports opened the door to consumer imports. By increasing the relative profit of the sugar production and reducing the costs of import goods in the internal market, the railroad helped to accentuate the characteristics of the Cuban export economy. This economy approximated the theoretical model of the plantation, which satisfied all its needs with imported goods, acquired with the resources of a single export product.

Needless to say, in the Cuban case, the railroad did not cause the "multiplier effect" that is generally attributed to it, particularly in the iron and steel industry. Its identity as an imported technology identified closely with the railroad remained unchanged in the following years, in the rolling stock and the material for the lines, but also in some important products like fuel.

As a system of transportation, the railroad had an "economic structuring strength" superior to any other traditional means of transportation, due to its higher speed, load capacity, and operational advantages.[46] Therefore, its influence in the geographic distribution of the economic activity is not surprising. The railroad changed deeply the characteristics and rhythm of sugar expansion. Since the eighteenth century, the plantations had expanded discontinuously, coordinating the quality of the land with the nearness to the coasts. In 1840, this expansion had its western limits in Quiebra Hacha and Guanajay, and its eastern in Sagua and Cienfuegos. More to the east, some important nuclei like Santiago de Cuba, Guantánamo, and Trinidad had developed, but were geographically isolated. Between 1840 and 1870, sugar production increased five times, from 160,000 tons in 1840 to 772,000 in 1872, without altering the territorial limits of the plantation. With the railroad, the direction of the expansion changed as plantations moved inland. The discontinuity disappeared. From Artemisa to Colón there was a uniform and monotonous sea of sugarcanes covering the red plains. Surrounding the plains of Manacas in a thin coastal line in the north and the wide Calimete-Amarillas-Yaguaramas path in the south, the cane fields extended continuously to cover the fertile lands of Sagua and Cienfuegos.[47] The railroads made this expansion possible, liberating land for new plantations, and telescoping the distance between productive center and port. There was no need for large pastures for the oxen that pulled the carts. There was also no need to reserve lands for rice and other products that could be easily imported at low cost and brought inland by the railroad. These forms of agriculture disappeared, or in some cases, only remained as marginal activities on lands that barely supported their development. Coffee, which suffered a crisis, yielded its lands without opposition. The railroad also facilitated reallocation. The cane fields abandoned unproductive, exhausted lands surrounding Havana for fresher but farther territories. The growing city, then, widened the land dedicated to the cultivation of provisions.

An important factor in the infrastructure is that the railroad attracted investments. In Cuba this had a curious effect. Since the railroad companies had no subsidy, the plotting of the lines during the first three decades only reached those regions that could guarantee an adequate volume of freight for the railroad. Consequently, the economic stimulus that the railroad produced operated in favor of the regions having more relative development, emphasizing regional differences. In 1827, the eastern part of the island produced 7 percent of Cuban sugar production. Twenty years later, when the western region began to enjoy the advantages of the railroad, the proportion was reduced to 4.8 percent. There was only a small increase during the 1860s. In 1862 the proportion reached 15 percent, with three-quarters of it supplied by the jurisdictions of Santiago, Guantánamo, and Sancti Spíritus—recently supplied with railroads—with the rest of this wide territory relatively unaffected by the new developments.[48]

The modifying effect of the railroad not only affected the economy but also the geographical distribution of the population. For three decades one could properly talk about a railroad settlement, even though in Cuba this phenomenon was different from other regions. By midcentury, the Cuban territory was incompletely settled or farmed. A rapidly growing population with a considerable contribution of immigrants and abundant space to be occupied, created a settlement pattern of moving frontiers, characterized by the founding of new towns and villages. However, these settlements were not of the magnitude that was to be expected. In 1841, the urban distribution was very poor. The capital and its the suburbs had 14 percent of the population of the country. Seven cities had more than five thousand inhabitants each and accounted for another 10 percent; and twenty towns had populations between one thousand and five thousand inhabitants. The rest of the urban areas were simply small villages with less than fifty houses each.[49] This situation was the result of a combination of factors. In the first place, many of those subjected to slavery lacked the liberty to settle where they wished and lived concentrated in the barracks of the sugar mill. On the other hand, the basically export orientation of the economy gave life to some important ports, but made regional markets unnecessary. No less important was the fact that the colonial administration, excessively centralized, concentrated most of its services in a small number of cities, and particularly in the capital, Havana. Thus the poverty of the urban centers of development was not only a demographic phenomenon but also a functional attribute. The majority of these inland towns did not constitute attractive centers for the surrounding regional life, but simple stopover points on the way to the capital or some other important city. The original nucleus of a large number of towns derived from their function of being simply a sales center or post that offered some services to the travelers, around which some other services, like a smith's shop, slowly established themselves.

The new railroad towns were no exception of this rule. At the railway junctions where passenger and load transfers were made, some small groups of living quarters appeared around the station, followed by a warehouse and a tavern or a general store available to travelers, the homes of the railroad personnel, and some other installations. That is the original history of quite a number of towns: Rincón, founded in 1841, at the junction of the San Antonio de los Baños branch with the main line of Caminos de Hierro de la Habana; Unión de Reyes, the origin of which was a small tavern, which profited from the connection of the lines of Caminos de Hierro de la Habana and Ferrocarril de Matanzas; Navajas, at the junction of the Cárdenas and Matanzas lines; Recreo (nowadays Máximo Gómez), at the junction of the branch to Itabo of the Ferrocarril de Júcaro; and Cruces, at the connection of the Sagua and Cienfuegos lines. The stopovers where loading of merchandise for a region was concentrated became attractive urbanization points. From this function originated such towns as Las Vegas, Bermeja, and Palos, on the main line of Caminos de Hierro de la Habana; Cidra, Guanábana, and Bolondrón on that of Matanzas; Santa Isabel de las Lajas on the Ferrocarril de Sagua; Ranchuelo on the line of Cienfuegos; Camajuaní on the Ferrocarril de Remedios; Enramadas (San Luis) and El Cristo on the Ferrocarril de Santiago de Cuba; and many other such centers.

Other towns, whose origins were unrelated to the railroad, nevertheless received a vital impulse from it. This is the case of Batabanó, founded at the beginning of the eighteenth century, but which in 1840 was no more than an unimportant and sad hamlet until the railroad—Caminos de Hierro de la Habana—converted it into its connecting terminal with the coastal shipping lines of the southern coast. The railroad constituted a reordering factor that favored some localities—or created them—to the detriment of other older ones. Thus Sabanilla progressively lost its importance in favor of its new neighbor Unión de Reyes. The old hamlets of La Jagua and El Roque, which were on the margins of the railroad lines, witnessed the birth of two new towns: Palos (close to La Jagua) and Perico (at two leagues from El Roque), which, through their close association with the "arteries of progress," grew rapidly in the face of an ostensible stagnation and retrogression on the part of their older neighbors.

In spite of the extensive list of railroad towns mentioned, the Cuban railroad populating stimulus was weak compared with other countries where the railroad contributed to populating whole regions. It is worth reiterating something mentioned before: the Cuban railroad of that period did not constitute a means of penetration to colonize virgin territories. The lines were projected in regions relatively populated, and therefore, although the railroad became a powerful magnet for population, it was not exploited conscientiously as a force in the increase of population, with a possible exceptional case in the region of Cárdenas. When the Cárdenas railroad projects were promoted, that region had hardly begun to be exploited. It had only a few sugar mills in areas to the east and west in cattle ranches like Guamutas, Macurijes, and Guareiras, and *corrales* like Managüises, Nueva Bermeja, and La Managua. The countryside was practically virgin. In 1836 Cárdenas was a small wharf for coastal trade with a population of 926, which did not even attain the classification of center of a petty partido. The railroad tracks, which began to be laid in 1840, especially those of Ferrocarril de Júcaro, played an important part in the development of the region. By 1846 Cárdenas was a jurisdiction with 199 sugar mills, and this figure, already quite significant, would be tripled in the following twelve years. The Ferrocarril de Júcaro brought the plantation to the area of Banagüises, converting it into the sugar bowl of Cuba, with the largest and most modern sugar mills of the island.[50] The Cárdenas wharf, converted into a railroad terminal, acquired the position of a port qualified for international commerce. In 1844, 165 ships loaded with sugar sailed from that port. In 1858, the number was 449. The demographic increase of Cárdenas was the most surprising in Cuba during the nineteenth century: 926 inhabitants in 1836, 3,200 a decade later, and 10,885 in 1862.[51] The average rate of increase in this period was 4.1 percent a year. The urban network grew and became strong thanks to the railroad. Some stopovers remained insignificant, but many grew into important towns such as Bemba (Jovellanos), Banagüises, San José de los Ramos, Corral Falso (Pedro Betancourt), Recreo (Máximo Gómez), Perico, Colón, Itabo. The railroad may well claim to be the father of the fabulous Cárdenas population growth.

The case of Cárdenas underscores the possibilities of the railroad as a factor in development. In 1862 Cárdenas had almost 10 percent of the Cuban population, but more than half of its inhabitants were slaves. Its most important production was sugar and its by-products. In Cárdenas and, in general, in Cuba, the railroad played a decisive role as a catalyst for expansion. Between 1837 (year of the inauguration of the first railroad) and 1868, the value of the Cuban sugar crop increased fourfold, exceeding 80 million pesos, despite the fact that the price of sugar was 37 percent lower than in the latter year. However, this was a unilateral growth, a deformed one. The railroad favored the productive increase without being able to change the essential characteristics of the Cuban economy. The conditions that determined the use of the railroad in Cuba restricted at the same time the economic possibilities of this technological innovation. In the Cuban socioeconomic context of the period, the railroad did not produce many of the beneficial effects generally attributed to it elsewhere. In Cuba it was a factor of growth, but not a factor of development.

Human Dimensions of Cuban Railroads

The development of the Cuban railroad service required the participation of an ever increasing number of specialized individuals. Their diverse position and social situation in the complex railroad world was not so much a manifestation of the specific organizational requirements of that business, as it was an expression at this particular level of the complicated social structure of the time.

Promoters and Contractors

The railroad constituted in Cuba an inseparable link with the sugar industry, and, therefore, its promoters were found among the leaders of the sugar industry. The task of unraveling the individual relationships that characterized those social groups is not an easy one. The social class that established its economical power based on sugar production, constituted a strange historical subject. Stimulated by the development of the capitalist world market, this social class could only find its place by appealing to some atavistic slave modes of production, which converted it, from the very beginning, into an anomalous case within the world in which it tried to insert itself.[1] This anomalous "bourgeoisie," which did not obtain its riches from the exploitation of wage labor but from the direct possession of a slave labor force, was hardly a bourgeoisie at all. It had "of the revolutionizing bourgeoisie of that time only the intellectual spirit, the merchandise and the market."[2] The structure of such an economy complicates the task of any social analysis of the activities of this class. The situation is complicated even further by the fact that Spaniards and Creoles exploited equally slave labor in a process of growing differentiation and opposing aspirations. So it should not be surprising that an analysis of this social class is still very far from yielding any definite conclusions.[3]

Cuban historiography in general, and at times with a certain conceptual confusion, finds it convenient to differentiate between two groups of this "slave bourgeoisie," relying on certain economic and political criteria. In the first place, the sugar business relied on two groups: plantation owners, associated with sugar production; and merchants, devoted, as the name implies, to the marketing aspects of the business, but also tangentially involved in a fairly usurious financing of the production sector. The political distinction was much simpler since they broke down into *peninsulares* (those from the Iberian peninsula) or *criollos* (Creoles, those born in Cuba), or more properly, Spaniards and Cubans. Sometimes the distinction resolved itself easily into Cuban landholders and Spanish merchants. This concept, although more or less adequate for explaining some aspects of the society at the beginning of the nineteenth century, is hardly relevant for an examination of the problems of Cuban railroads with which this book deals. The landholder-merchant dichotomy within the so-called "slavist bourgeoisie" has very clearly defined limits within the middle and lower layers of this class where the landholder with one or two sugar mills or boiler houses, or the relatively small merchant firm appears. Owing to their limited economical resources, these social sectors played an insignificant part in railroad investments. The railroad business attracted members of the economically more productive and more dominant classes. At that level, not surprisingly, commercial and productive functions tended to bond together, so that big landholders operated in commerce and important merchants tended to own sugar mills.[4] This higher strata of the bourgeoisie, however, did not constitute a homogenous group. Indeed, participants in the railroads indicated a series of distinctive circles or groups. In the early years of railroad construction in Cuba (1835–45), three groups can de distinguished within the upper levels of this class.[5]

The Havana municipal oligarchy. This group included the true patriarchs of the plantation system with their vast grants of land, obtained through the generosity of the Havana town council, that they controlled during the sixteenth and seventeenth centuries. These oligarchs also amassed considerable capital through the lucrative contracts for supplying the imperial navy, and later through the monopolistic privileges enjoyed through the exercise of Bourbon mercantilism. Since they controlled both land and money, this group became the principal promoter of the accelerated "takeoff" of the sugar plantation during the last decades of the eighteenth century. A little more than a dozen family names, some of them conveniently enhanced by titles from Castille and others with "Spanish Grandees," made up this interlocking oligarchy. The names Peñalver, Pedroso, Herrera, Cárdenas, Montalvo, Calvo, O'Reilly, and a few more appear repeatedly and, buttressed by successive endogamous marriages, they reify the social existence of this group.[6] The Havana municipal oligarchy that surrounded Francisco Arango y Parreño and represented the economic, technical, and political vanguard of the plantation seemed by the 1840s to have lost much of its initial vigor and to have slipped appreciably toward being demonstrably investor oriented.

The plantation newly rich. This group was made up largely of immigrants and their offspring who had come to Cuba during the last quarter of the eighteenth century or the first years of the nineteenth. These individuals, attracted by the economic promises of the first phase of the plantation development, generally made their way from commerce—of goods as well as people—or some other secondary activity. They invested their fortunes progressively in sugar mills without abandoning completely their original mercantile interests. Some of these names were quite well known: Alfonso, Aldama, Drake, Poey, Diago, Escobedo, Villaurrutia, Arrieta, and, of course, Martínez de Pinillos.[7]

The great Spanish merchants. Although this designation is both a little restrictive and misleading, it is worth retaining. This group is most representative of those that the historiography has traditionally used to illustrate the community of "Spanish merchants." Similar to the second group, it was largely composed of immigrants from the Spanish peninsula who arrived in Cuba around 1820. The economic and social evolution of this group also paralleled the second group.[8] The newly arrived first built a strong position in commerce and then slowly expanded their operations into sugar production. The years between 1820 and 1840 were marked by deeply significant economic and political events. The stabilization of the sugar market at the end of the Napoleonic Wars and the later tendency of prices to fall, combined with the proscription of the slave trade, which became more expensive as it became unlawful, pushed the profits of the sugar business toward the side of the merchants. The merchant, the provider of both slave and credit, began to get hold of more and more of the surplus produced by the slave, thus leaving less and less for the owner-planter. That is why merchants, although investing heavily in sugar production—and by the 1850s some of the largest sugar mills belonged to merchants—firmly retained their commercial base. The political changes were no less important. After the loss of the Spanish colonial empire on the American continent, the prolonged "honeymoon" between the colonial government and the Creole slave-based bourgeoisie came to an end. Spain persisted in retaining its last possessions by designing a colonial policy that was equally rapacious and exclusivist. From then on every colonial subject was considered to be potentially unreliable and had to be strictly excluded from holding public office. Beginning with the administration of Tacón (1834–38), to be Spanish born almost became a profession in Cuba. The richest Spaniards in the colony formed a clique surrounding each successive captain general. The names of Gómez, Samá, Marty, Pastor, Rodríguez Torices, Parejo, Zulueta, Moré, and others frequently figured among the most assiduous visitors to the governor's palace. There, between games of *tresillo* (a card game) and hot choco-

late, the indispensable complicity of the authorities could be obtained to facilitate
the conduct of the illegal slave trade, which was the main source of the group's
riches. This explains why, in contrast to the earlier immigrants, the members of
this group could, more or less adapt themselves, without really becoming Creole
in thought or conduct. The qualification of being a native Spaniard was indispensable for retaining status within the group.

When the histories of the members of these groups are placed against the
background of railroad development in Cuba, it is clear that almost all of them
took part in one or another railroad venture. The roles, however, were not indiscriminately distributed. Almost all the promoters of the first railroad projects
between 1835 and 1845 came from the second category, the "plantation newly
rich." Two of the three members of the commission constituted by the Junta de
Fomento to carry out the building of the Güines Railroad—Villaurrutia and
Escobedo—as well as the very president of the junta, Claudio Martínez de Pinillos, came from that group. From that group also came the entire governing board
of the Camino de Hierros de La Habana; and the names Alfonso, Aldama, Domingo del Monte, Poey, Diago, and Arrieta appear among the investors in the
Matanzas, Cárdenas, Júcaro, and El Cobre railroads. These parvenus of the 1820s
and 1830 demonstrated all the vigor that the old oligarchy was slowly losing, and
supplanted it completely as a technical-economical vanguard of the plantation
system. Nor is it only a matter of the railroads. Almost all technical innovations in
the method of sugar production between 1830 and 1860 came from that group.
Wenceslao de Villaurrutia was the first to introduce the Derosne process, the
most important advance in sugar manufacture at that time, to his sugar mill; and
that initiative was shortly followed by Joaquín de Arrieta in his sugar mill, Flor de
Cuba. Juan Poey boasted for thirty years that his sugar mill, Las Cañas, was the
best-equipped sugar mill in Cuba. The Diago family for years conducted the most
important experiments with labor and machines.

Members of the old oligarchy also appeared in the list of railroad investors, but
they never seem to initiate the idea. Their role seemed to be that of financial
supporters. R. T. Ely is mistaken when he supposes that the presence of some of
these individuals among the first group of railroad directorial boards was merely
to lend prestige and reliability to the companies.[9] Surely there were not many
Cubans who could purchase hundreds of railroad company shares at one time as
did Brigadier Juan Montalvo, or the count of Peñalver, to name just two of the
most conspicuous investors. A similar role was performed by some of the old
Spanish bureaucrats, equally rich and ennobled, such as Cecilio Ayllón, the
marquis of Villalba, and first president of the Júcaro Railroad, and the marquis of
Cañada (Tirry), and of Esteva de las Delicias. In each case these aristocrats
contributed capital to schemes developed by others, moved by a common busi-

Claudio Martínez de Pinillos, count of Villanueva, from his office as president of the Junta de Fomento, was one of the principal supporters of the development of the railroad in Cuba. (Picture by Amérigo. BNC, Colección Cubana)

ness interest in sugar estates in the area to be served by the railroad, or by family ties to some of the promoters. The only exception is the Pedroso family. Among the oldest in Havana, this family took a special interest in the Ferrocarril del Oeste, which came about because of its sponsorship.

The action of the Spanish commercial clique exhibits some peculiar characteristics. After the failed effort of Joaquín Gómez, Pancho Marty, Samá, and a few others to take over the Güines railroad during the auction sale of 1839–41, the group kept itself away from railroad activities. Only at the end of the 1840s does it reappear when Manuel Pastor, Antonio Parejo, and Rafael Rodríguez bought a significant number of shares in the Cienfuegos Railroad. After that, the activity of the group increased in concert with their increase in economic power in Cuba. In general, however, the group did not form active sponsors of ventures except in the cases of the Marianao and Bahía Railroads. Rather their method seemed to be the slow acquisition of working enterprises by gradually increasing the number of shares held. Such seemed to be the case with the Sagua Railroad, promoted by local interests and controlled by José E. Moré and Antonio Parejo; or the Coliseo Railroad boldly acquired by Salvador Samá, Rodríguez Torices, Eduardo Fesser, and the marquis of Esteva. A similar process appears with the Remedios Railroad, and can be deduced later in the 1870s with the Cienfuegos, Cárdenas, and Júcaro Railroads.

For all those groups the railroad constituted—logically to varying degrees—an important entrepreneurial academy. Cuban landowners and merchants, with the collaboration of French immigrants and from contact with North American merchants, educated themselves in the methods of the current financial techniques. They were, however, inexperienced in corporate organizational enterprises and large, long-term undertakings such as railroad companies were beyond the financial capacity of individuals. The more farsighted were aware of this. In his report to the Junta de Caminos de Hierro in 1831, the marquis of Cañada stressed the importance of the problem: "The system of public association, so new to us, but so useful and general everywhere, naturally causes momentary distrust since it clashes with our customs."[10] The observation could not be more precise. The first railroad could only be built with the decisive financial assistance of the Junta de Fomento. Only when this example had proved successful did the general distrust fade and joint-stock companies for building railroads become common.[11] These joint-stock companies, evidently copied from foreign models, developed in a milieu of inexperienced owners and inadequate Spanish corporate legislation. The first railroad promoters counted on the active collaboration of the wisest Creole at that time, Domingo del Monte. From his position as secretary of the Cárdenas Railroad Company, he not only guided the initial experiment in company operation but also acted as an advisor to many other companies. His colleagues in the other companies were more or less men of the same background: Felipe Poey, later to become a famous naturalist, was the secretary of Caminos de Hierro de la Habana, and the poet José Jacinto Milanés advised the Matanzas railroad. The latter, in particular, felt very inadequate in his position and frequently consulted with Domingo del Monte, often about extremely minute problems. The following excerpt from a letter is quite illustrative of the general inexperience:

> Last night we discussed, at the board meeting, the way to elect a manager for the concern, and it was decided by majority vote to call a meeting of all shareholders to see who would take charge of this matter in the most intelligent and expert way. But not knowing how to proceed, and being aware of your intelligence and expertise in this matter, Don Francisco García [president of the Matanzas Railroad] asked me to inquire of you what those requirements should be.[12]

Apart from their inexperience, the new railroad managers also had to confront the conservatism of many of their shareholders. If the initial resistance to investment could be overcome, the distrust in handling capital entrusted to new railroad companies did not disappear. The misgiving arose in the form of constant pressure on the board of directors to authorize payment of dividends, even at the expense of needed expansion in service. Such a situation ruined the projected branch to Coliseo of the Cárdenas Railroad in 1843. That same year El Lugareño had to resort to the Junta de Fomento and struggle to find the resources to continue work on the Puerto Príncipe line. His bitter complaint reached Domingo del Monte: "If the Junta does not help us in time, here we will lose everything, because the shareholders are not willing to risk anything and only God may soften their hearts."[13] The Camagüey Railroad suffered most from the weakness of its investors. As the project needed to be complete to be productive, many of those who had initially patronized the idea lost heart and left many shares unpaid. The lack of funds caused an early bankruptcy and delayed the effective exploitation of that line for a decade. It took years and experience before the line could generate support by steadily increasing its dividends.

By the time the 1850s arrived the railroad business was mature. A fairly large proportion of the accumulated money, thanks to the high sugar prices, was invested in the railroad sector. If the first railroad investors did not see that as an independent business, the development of railroad activities, drawing on the infusion of new resources, generated a logic of its own. This new conjuncture turned into an appropriate framework for the blossoming of typically entrepreneurial attitudes. Competition turned into a direct motivation for investment. In the plains around Colón, three railroad companies extended their lines to try to get the biggest slice of the rich sugar production there. Farther to the west,

Caminos de Hierro de La Habana rapidly constructed a line between Güines and Matanzas to block the operations of the Ferrocarril de la Bahía, a line built strictly to compete with it. The crassly competitive nature of the companies was reflected in their annual reports, and quite a few company presidents proposed to their shareholders line extensions so that "not a single atom of the production of the region escapes, thereby eliminating the possibility of competition by any other enterprise."[14] The competitive aggressiveness was mixed with the necessary caution and negotiating ability when reduced fares imperiled company revenues. Under such conditions rivalry gave way to common fares and mergers that would create a monopoly of some regional transport. While the Cuban railroad impresarios spoke a modern language, their actions often belied their thoughts, and Miguel de Aldama could still exchange thirty slaves for an equal number of the Matanzas Railroad Company shares.[15]

In the dense financial atmosphere of the 1850s it is possible to detect some interests operating on a large scale within the railroad sector. Generally they stemmed from powerful economic groups that extended their interests in many directions. Foremost was the Alfonso-Aldama family clan that owned no less than thirteen sugar mills, warehouses in the port city of Matanzas, as well as minor businesses in which they participated or controlled, such as the first Compañía de Vapores de la Bahía (the Bay Steamship Company), Compañía de Seguros Marítimos y Descuentos (Maritime Insurance and Discount Company), Préstamos y Descuentos San José (San José Loan and Discounts), and later the Almacenes de Depósitos de Hacendados (Land Owners Deposit Warehouses) and the Crédito Territorial Cubano (Cuban Land Credit).[16] The family's early interest in railroads gave it total control over the Caminos de Hierro de La Habana (Havana Railroad) at the same time that it was among the most influential shareholders in the Matanzas and Cárdenas Railroads. In the decade of the 1850s its influence spread to the central region with varying numbers of shares in the Cienfuegos, Sagua, and Remedios Railroads. In this respect the Pedroso family was no less important. In 1857 while Joaquín Pedroso Echevarría promoted the Ferrocarril del Oeste (Western Railroad), his brother, Julio, was elected president of the recently merged Cárdenas and Júcaro companies; and both brothers were among the major shareholders of the new Ferrocarril de la Bahía (Bay Railroad). The family ranked for a very long time among the old Havana oligarchy. Its economic position was solid. At the time of his death in 1800, the grandfather of Joaquín and Luis Pedroso left the fabulous amount of 2 million pesos fuertes in cash, beside considerably property—at least ten sugar mills and extensive real estate holdings. Their enthusiasm for profit led them into commerce where they were not reluctant to enter such complicated business as the coolie trade between Canton and Havana. Although they were not essentially linked by kinship ties, the members of the Spanish commercial elite acted together in intimate business associations. In 1868, this business group controlled the Marianao, Bahía, and Sagua Railroads and was an influential investor in those of Cárdenas and Júcaro, Cienfuegos, and Remedios.

The Cuban railroads already had, by their maturity phase, a certain number of businessmen. Nevertheless, it would be unwise to rush to the conclusion that Cuba had any equivalent to the Vanderbilts. The figure of the railroad baron that appeared in the enthusiastic capitalism of the nineteenth century did not flourish among the sugarcane fields of the tropics, with their slaves costing a thousand pesos each. Inserted in the sugar cycle, the Cuban railroads would, for many years, lack a distinctive entrepreneurial stature. The major promoters of the railroads would be first and foremost engaged in productive and commercial ventures in sugar and only secondarily were they railroad men.

Technicians, Bankers, and Suppliers

The introduction of the railroads required the presence of able personnel for its construction and operation. As the railroad represented imported technology, the details of which were almost completely unknown in Cuba, this technical personnel had to be foreign for quite some time. This palpable reality constituted a clearly differentiated foreign sector within the railroad community, which included, beside technicians, financial agents and suppliers.

Chronologically speaking, the first foreigners to be involved in a stable manner in the Cuban railroad business were the financial agents, especially the British banker, Alexander Robertson. The circumstances surrounding the birth of the first railroad led its promoters to seek external financing.[17] These were found in London, then the financial capital of the world, and the loans were made on the basis of the personal credit of the Cuban secretary of the treasury, Intendant Martínez de Pinillos. The operation, the first foreign loan in Cuban history, was contracted with the banking firm of Alexander Robertson who not only took care of the issue and placement of the bonds but also acted as agent for the Junta de Fomento (Development Board) in purchasing running equipment and other railroad material. This first contract marked the beginning of a close relationship between Robertson and Cuban railroad companies that would extend itself over two decades. The permanent attention that Robertson had to pay in connection with the payment of debentures for the Güines railroad—the debt was not amortized until 1865—was soon increased by new business. When the new railroad ventures of Matanzas and Júcaro needed financial assistance, nothing was easier for them than to follow the path already taken by the Junta de Fomento and contract two loans with the Robertson bank. Although these new contracts involved smaller amounts than the initial loans and their amortization terms were shorter, the interest of London bankers in Cuban railroads increased considerably. After that Robertson was always on the lookout for new business, focusing his attention on the ever increasing needs of the Cuban railroads not only in the financial field but also in matters of equipment purchase and construction contracts. On many occasions Robertson supervised his Cuban business personally, and therefore it was no surprise to the people of Sagua to see him appear, at the beginning of his first contracts for the Sagua Railroad, at the docks of that town in his "beautiful, sail-studded yacht."[18] The English banker, attracted by the promising business, had taken advantage on one of his frequent cruises in Cuban waters to consider directly the Sagua Railroad project and to encourage its promoters. On that occasion Robertson could not sink his teeth in the company since the Sagua Railroad was built without his services. After a modest participation in the Santiago de Cuba Railroad in 1857–58, the figure of Robertson began to fade, replaced by other British banking firms. The 1860s brought new names to the business, especially the Anglo-German banking firm of J. Henry Schröder, which negotiated the large loans for the Bay Railroad.

If the British dominated the financial scene, they were far less successful in the technical sphere where they faced energetic North American competition. From the very beginning, the Cuban railroad promoters entrusted the execution of their projects to American engineers. The first engineer to be contracted in 1834 was the American Benjamin Wright, the builder of the Erie Canal. Although only three years before Wright had been against railroads, he did not hesitate when the Junta de Fomento approached him.[19] However, old Wright's activities and indispositions prevented his traveling to Cuba personally and the effective work fell to the German-American engineer Alfred Cruger.

In all fairness, Cruger should be considered the first railroad builder in Cuba. His achievements included the Güines Railroad, considered at the time a major feat in railroad engineering, as well as the Júcaro Railroad, and the first stretch of the Matanzas line. Two other Americans, sons of Benjamin Wright, also participated in the first railroad projects. Benjamin H. Wright, who arrived as second in command to Cruger on the Güines Railroad, soon clashed with him and resigned his contract. In spite of his annoyance, Benjamin H. Wright did not leave Cuba altogether, and a few years later signed a contract with El Lugareño for the execution of the hazardous Puerto Príncipe to Nuevitas project. Despite the confusion surrounding the similarity of surnames, it seems that Simon Wright, Benjamin's brother, also participated in the Güines work, and engineered the small Remedios Railroad.

Owing to the absence of qualified labor in Cuba, the American presence was not confined to the higher technical positions. Cruger arrived in 1835 surrounded by a technical staff designed to help him survey the line and supervise the construction works. This initial group was followed by various contractors who were responsible for different aspects of the construction.[20] At first the American participation seemed limited to merely building the lines, since Robertson's contract stipulated that the equipment that he purchased would be delivered with the technical personnel needed for its operation. However, the less than satisfactory service of the British-built locomotives, combined with a few accidents imputed to their machinists, gave Cruger a reason to propose to the Junta de Fomento that they contract American-built locomotives and their engineers. This change sealed the Yankee predominance among the technicians on the railroads. After that the operators, stokers, machinists, and qualified shop workers were all Americans.

Some of the personnel contracted for the first railroad went on to work for other railroad projects. This happened not only in the cases of Cruger and the Wright brothers, but also with minor functionaries such as Ezra K. Dodd, head of the Güines Railroad workshop, who after working with Cruger on the construction of the Júcaro Railroad was appointed administrator general of the company in 1842. However, Dodd's case must be considered exceptional, since technical-administrative posts were usually reserved for Cubans or Spaniards because of the trust demanded by the positions. Possibly the clearest illustration of this sort of functionary was José A. Echevarría, closely bound to the Alfonso-Aldama family, who for more than two decades served as general manager for the Caminos de Hierro de La Habana.

Contrary to general belief, it was not an American but a Frenchman, Julio Sagebién, who was the most active engineer during the first phase of railroad construction. Sagebién was credited with managing six companies. The Frenchman started his activities by surveying the El Cobre Railroad line and also managed the construction of the Cienfuegos–Villa Clara line in 1846. Two years later he supervised the extension of the Júcaro line, and immediately thereafter constructed the Guantánamo Railroad. At the other end of the island Sagebién busied himself with surveying and building the first stretch of the Western Railroad, and later he became general engineer for the Marianao Railroad—but not before doing some small jobs with the Santiago de Cuba Railroad.

With only a few exceptions, Cuban participation was not entirely absent in the first phase of railroad construction. Manuel de J. Carrera, an engineer with sugar interests in the region, planned and supervised the building of the Cárdenas Railroad. During the 1850s Cuban-Spanish technical input became more frequent. The Sagua, Las Tunas-Sancti Spíritus, Trinidad, El Caney, and Santiago de Cuba Railroads all employed Cuban-Spanish engineers. Rafael de Carrera, the brother of the Cárdenas Railroad's engineer, built the highly complex Santiago de Cuba Railroad. The substitution of the foreign technical staffs that took place in the 1850s and 1860s was even more pronounced among the qualified middle-level positions. Progressively the lists of Cuban and peninsular machinists and workshop employees increased as they acquired the necessary experience and practical skills.

Suppliers composed another group of foreigners connected with Cuban railroads. In the beginning there was no direct connection between Cuban companies and foreign firms supplying the material for the railroads. Contacts were normally made through the intermediaries related to the railroads, such as Robertson or Cruger. Otherwise the promoters availed themselves of their connections with some foreign merchants—mainly Americans—to have them act as purchasing agents. Such was the case of Moses Taylor, who, for quite some time, handled the purchase of equipment and material for several companies, including the Havana, Júcaro, and Cienfuegos–Villa Clara Railroads.[21] With the progressive development of their operations, some companies established direct ties with certain American firms producing rolling stock, such as the Baldwin Locomotive Company of Philadelphia, or the West Point Foundry, as well as Eaton, Gilbert and Company, manufacturers of coaches and cars. Some of these firms, along with others that made rails, crossties, and other smaller parts, sent agents to Cuba to attend the auctions held by the local railroad companies for the supply of material and equipment.

Workers

Regardless of the skill of the technicians or the degree of audacity of the investors, the railroad was definitely the work of those who toiled under the burning tropical sun, who laid the rails and later ran the engines: the railroad workers. The main characteristic of that vast conglomerate may be defined by a single word: heterogeneity. The railroads represented a diversity of races and cultures, a diversity in the recruiting mechanisms, and finally a diversity in the forms of exploitation. In its labor relations the phenomenon of the railroads cut across the contradictions and imbalances of the existing social structure.

The importation of a means of transport, which, like the railroad was an archetypal product of a powerful industrial capitalism, brought with it the rapid assimilation of organizational schemes, especially the joint-stock company, and a conspicuous modus operandi that constituted a notable contribution to modern business techniques in Cuba. Nevertheless, this propagation of characteristic elements of capitalist production modes encountered powerful resistance within the field of labor. The first railroad promoters were well aware of this situation. As sugar producers they knew perfectly well the old story of the Cuban labor problem. On an island with an extremely low demographic density and still very far from full economic exploitation, the sudden increase in sugar production could only be achieved on the basis of an increase in African slavery. The white people, whether natives or immigrants, were generally exempt from extraeconomic coercion, and found innumerable possibilities for work in the city or the rural areas, avoiding the rigors of the climate and the brutalizing demands of manual labor. And if they were disposed to accept such, it was only in exchange for wages that made them incomparably more expensive than slave labor.

The construction of the railroads had to mobilize hundreds of unskilled laborers. What kind of workers would they be? That question presented a quandary for the Junta de Fomento. To send its employees to recruit among the markets for clandestinely imported Africans was not exactly convenient for the entity of a state that had signed a treaty agreeing to abolish the slave trade. Besides, the corporation had just negotiated a loan in London where abolitionism was at its peak. The solution to the problem was easily found in the importation of white workers. By virtue of this circumstance, the railroads introduced an idea that would become an obsession in the following decades: white immigration or colonization. "Soon there arrived in our port [Havana] two 'colonies': one of Irishmen and the other from the Canary Islands, both quite expensive, but they assured the construction of the railroad tracks."[22]

It is worthwhile to pause for a moment to see what the Junta de Fomento did with these "colonies." The "Irish"—actually a conglomerate of workers of diverse nationalities brought from the United States by engineer Wright—were subjected, without any previous acclimatization, to the rigors of the outdoor work, often under adverse conditions during the rainy season. Badly sheltered and fed, they soon succumbed to the effects of tropical diseases. Some of them (old victims of another "slavery," that of wage labor) were hardened drunks and turbulent individuals who quickly found their way into the colonial jails, where a number died. Some survived, and after completing their contract, sauntered through the Havana streets where they died awaiting the promised repatriation that the Junta postponed indefinitely.

The arrivals from the Canary Islands did not fare much better. Fearing desertions given their Spanish language and possible family connections, the Junta subjected them to what approximated a military regime (see Chapter 2) and once secured, forced them to work for between fourteen and sixteen hours per day. Many died along with their Irish colleagues, compared with whom the Canary Islanders had the risky advantage of flight. With the completion of their contracts, the decimated contingent spread out in many directions, seeking work as far away from the railroads as possible.

Railroads and immigrants! That was the magic combination that had turned the United States prairies into a grain-producing country, that had aided a complex Argentine unity, and populated extensive zones of Canada, but which in Cuba was of scant historical consequence. In the United States and in some other countries the governments gave the railroads extensive quantities of land, which the companies were interested in populating, since only successful homesteading could produce the freight to support the transport business. The Cuban railroads received only narrow strips of land alongside the tracks, but their trains were guaranteed freight from the sugar business. Railroads did not go anywhere that sugar was not produced. Sugar production also rapidly and desperately needed manpower. But the sugar plantation, predecessor of industrial organization in agriculture, required individuals who were disposed to cut the sugarcane of others with the instruments provided by others. As such, those workers did not come willingly but were brought forcefully as slaves. Colonization, therefore, confronted the dynamics of the sugar plantation. Individuals transferred in those decades under the euphemistic concept of "colonists" were actually no better than journeymen semienslaved under contracts. In that sense, the first railroads did carry out a vanguard experiment indeed. They ruthlessly exploited their daily paid workers during the legal period of their contracts. After that, the unskilled railroad construction, in common with other unskilled labor, remained "a matter for Negroes." During the 1840s, railroad construction was confined to those who had no choice: slaves and convicts.

The railroads got slaves in two basic ways, either by purchase or by rental. Rental was the more widespread of the two, and started during the construction of the first line. The Junta de Fomento, like an ambidextrous gambler, combined the negotiation of the importation of white daily-paid laborers with an announcement in the Havana newspapers of its decision to rent any available surplus slaves.[23] The rental of slaves was conventionally used in the construction of highways and was easily adapted for the railroads. Although the amount paid for a rented slave was almost as high as the wage of a free worker, the slave was easier to obtain and regiment. More expensive than an outright purchase, the use of a rented slave freed the contracting company from obligations such as clothing and, above all, it did not incur a loss through death or flight. Slaves were rented from failing agricultural enterprises, or from households where the additional income offset any temporary domestic inconvenience.[24] This does not take into account individuals who made a living by renting slaves.

The rental system did not prevent railroad companies from owning a variable number of slaves. The most extreme case was the Cárdenas and Júcaro Railroads, which acquired a large number of slaves as the only way to secure a pool of labor in an area where the expansion of the plantation system had resulted in an acute shortage of slaves.[25] Slaves, owned or rented, were used by the railroads for the most exhausting nonskilled tasks. The majority of slaves worked on construction and maintenance, and the few lucky enough to find themselves at other chores were usually in the stores and warehouses. Railroad companies that became slave owners could not avoid the risks inherent in the position. Runaways were such a problem that the reference became commonplace in the annual reports of the companies.[26] Railroad slaves also participated in one of the most notorious uprisings in the history of Cuban slavery. In 1843, on learning of the slave revolt among slaves on the Alcancia, La Luisa, and other sugar mills of the Bemba region, the supervisor of the Cárdenas Railroad immediately ordered the transfer of all company slaves working on the Bemba-Navajas branch to Cárdenas.

> In spite of having taken all measures to isolate the Negroes from information about the conspiracy, the gathering in Cárdenas Province [sic] of almost all the white families of the region, the evident fear they showed regarding the Negro uprising, gave those belonging to the company the idea of a total and definite triumph, and as a result, part of the company crew, 136 Negroes, rebelled imitating those of the Bemba region.[27]

The Cárdenas fugitives started an audacious march toward Bemba with the aim of joining the local rebels, but they were intercepted by a company of lancers and massacred before they reached their destination.

Owing to the chronic scarcity of slave labor, the use of *emancipados* (emancipated slaves) constituted a welcome relief to the railroad companies. *Emancipados* were Africans captured before their clandestine introduction to the island. According to the Anglo-Spanish treaty of 1817, captured Africans were immediately declared to be free and handed over by their captors—almost always cruisers of the British navy—to the Spanish colonial government, under whose custody they would remain until their return to Africa, or declared competent to live in Cuba. With repatriation out of the question, the Cuban government complied with its part of the agreement by offering the *emancipados* to any individual or institution that would support and instruct the African in return for the usufruct of his labor for a period of five years. As public utilities, the railroads benefited from the generous use of these individuals, and regarded their acquisition to be an indication of public support. The first railroad was a state project and from the start had 150 *emancipados* on its work force. The generosity of the government with *emancipados* gradually reached out to other companies and the numbers obtained reflected the influence of the promoters with the highest colonial administrators. The precarious legal situation of the emancipated made them victims of various vile tricks on the part of the government and individuals who seldom failed to take advantage of the opportunity to convert them to slaves.

Although the term of service was limited, in practice their condition was worse than slaves since the concessionaires exploited them ruthlessly during the period in which they enjoyed usufruct.

Like the emancipated, convicts were also used as a form of government assistance to the building of railroads. Although less frequent, this type of help was normally given in cases where some official interest existed. Recipient companies paid a certain amount to the government in return for the convicts, took care of their general maintenance, and paid the salaries of the guards. On some occasions a small wage was paid to the convicts or an equal amount was sent to the official agency in charge of the prisons.

Therefore the railroad companies supplied their labor needs during the first phase of their expansion with real or de facto slaves. In the early 1850s the renewed increase in sugar production accentuated the labor crisis adversely affecting both plantations and railroad companies. This situation was more favorable for discussion of new colonization projects. In 1853 a Spaniard connected with the Havana commercial elites, Urbano Feijoó Sotomayor, presented the captain general, Juan de la Pezuela, a plan for the importation of Galician settlers through a company called the Sociedad Patriótica Mercantíl (Patriotic Mercantile Company).[28] Feijoó was a representative to the Cortes for Orense and thought that he would use his political connections to recruit daily paid laborers in his impoverished Galicia, transport them to Cuba, where after a short period of acclimatization, they would be contracted to planters and merchants. The condition of the contract, in accordance with the terms made with the Puerto Príncipe Railroad, stipulated the payment of 5 pesos per month to the laborer and 10 pesos to the foreman. In addition, each worker would be given two outfits, three pairs of shoes, and three pairs of hemp sandals in each of the five years of the contract. For each contractee delivered, the company received 150 pesos.[29]

Within the railroad sector, the unfortunate Trinidad Railroad fell for the attractive colonizing scheme of Feijoó Sotomayor, who took advantage of the urgent needs of the people from Trinidad to begin their railroad. They made their offer through the firm of Noriega, Olmo and Company, which promised to cover all railroad work with their contract. The first contingent of Galicians to arrive in Havana was sent on to Trinidad without the benefit of acclimatization. That decision clearly violated the terms of their contract and created much uneasiness among the Galicians, a situation not helped when Feijoó Sotomayor refused to compensate them for the first days of work. The Galicians reacted worse than expected, abandoning their work, and marching through the streets of Trinidad creating disturbances and "spewing insults against Sotomayor."[30] Only the intervention of the infantry stationed nearby succeeded in restoring order among the furious workers. Once the precedent was established, things progressively became worse. New conflicts arose over working hours, living conditions, and other factors, causing such frequent work stoppages that the company decided to look for more "manageable" workers among the slaves of the locality. The experience of the small group of Galicians contracted by the Puerto Príncipe Railroad was hardly more encouraging. After only two years the "colonists" requested that their contracts be rescinded.[31] Once more the white "colonists" did not submit meekly to the rigorous working conditions imposed by local plantation owners in Cuba.

The failure to promote white colonization contrasted sharply with the success in the hazardous business of importing Chinese workers. After the abolition of slavery in the British West Indies, the owners of plantations resorted to the importation of East Indians to replace the ex-slaves, who were reluctant to return to their former places of exploitation. The satisfactory result of this new type of labor converted the coasts of Asia into the launching pads for a new type of trade not much different from the former African slave trade. Encouraged by the desirable results of their British neighbors, the Cuban landholders and merchants also turned their eyes toward Asia and found a new source of diligent workers from the southern provinces of China. There on the small island of Amoy, some British and American traders repeated the hesitant forays of the "Mongo" slave traders of Guinea by establishing bases for the massive export of unfortunate Chinese peasants.[32] The first shipment of 571 Chinese workers arrived in Havana in 1847. In July of that year, the board of directors of the Caminos de Hierro de La Habana resolved "to take on a trial basis 20 Asians to work on the railroad."[33] Thus from the very beginning the Asians contributed to the heterogeneity of the railroad workers. Nevertheless, the Chinese trade was not established in Havana until 1852–53 when the first firms, Villoldo, Wardrop and Company, and Machado, Pereda and Company, dedicated themselves exclusively to the business, using contacts made with some North American suppliers. Shortly afterward, the firm La Cololonizadora of Rafael Rodríguez Torices became the first to control the entire scandalous operation, from contracting in China to delivery in Cuba.[34] From 1854—the year in which 1,711 Chinese arrived—the number gradually increased until it reached a figure of 13,385 men in 1858, at which time the rate was comparable with that of the previous African slave trade.[35]

From an economical point of view, the Chinese became the first viable alternative to the African slaves. For a total expenditure of no more than 600 pesos the landholder could get an excellent worker for eight years. The railroads did not take long to note that advantage. Caminos de Hierro de La Habana pioneered the effort, using 98 Chinese in 1856, and increasing the number until, in October 1861, it had 322 on its list. That same year the Cienfuegos Railroad used 150 Asians and both the Ferrocarril de la Bahía and the Coliseo Railroad each used 200. A somewhat later report (1866) mentions 128 Chinese in the service of the Sagua

Railroad, and smaller groups are recorded with both the Guantánamo and Santiago Railroads. The unquestioned record for the exploitation of the new "colonists" was held by the Ferrocarril del Oeste, an enterprise that held 751 Chinese in 1859. Such a high figure can be explained easily since its promoters, the Pedrosos, were directly involved in the yellow slave trade.[36]

The introduction of Asians was a timely solution to the nagging problem of labor for the railroads and facilitated the expansion during the period between 1853 and 1868. Yet the importance of the Asians lay not only in their availability but also in their greater versatility. In 1859 the American traveler, R. H. Dana was surprised to see Chinese working as brakemen on the Coliseo Railroad.[37] That, however, was not unusual. Had Dana stayed a bit longer he would have seen Chinese working as furnace attendants, brakemen, and a wide range of railroad jobs. The Chinese supplied manual labor and replaced the rented slaves and free wage laborers, thereby boosting company profits.[38] An analysis by the directors of the Matanzas Railroad indicated that the monthly salary for the Chinese worker was 4.65 pesos, compared with 20.25 pesos for the hired slave and 21.30 for the free daily paid laborer. Even with some allowance for contracting fees, the Chinese worker seemed to be around 70 percent of the cost of the other two categories of workers.[39] According to the calculation of the Ferrocarril del Oeste, its contingent of Asians—deducting the daily wages lost on account of flights, illnesses, and deaths—probably produced a profit of 68 percent of their costs at the end of eight years of service.[40]

The economical advantage of the Chinese derived from his exploitation. Taking advantage of the extremely low living standards in their native country, the Cuban contractors subjected them to working conditions that white workers refused to accept. Besides, the Asian was deliberately isolated from the rest of the population, a factor made easier by the existing cultural barriers. Although colonial legislation established legal distinctions between the Chinese worker and the slave, the treatment meted out to both indicated no substantial difference. Nor should it be surprising that the demographic profile of Chinese "colonists" and African slaves manifested great similarities, as illustrated in Table 6.1.

The data indicate an average mortality rate over the five years of 51.8 per 1,000, an exceptionally high figure considering the absence of any infant mortality figures, since that was an adult male population. On the other hand, during the acclimatization phase the mortality rate could shoot up to nearly 80 per 1,000 as occurred in 1862, a year when 50 percent of the work force of the Caminos de Hierro consisted of recently imported Asians. The high incidence of escapees and the elevated mortality figures resulting from suicides show that Chinese laborers did not meekly accept their working conditions in Cuba.

The work force of the railroads were a sort of demographic "babel" consisting

TABLE 6.1. Status of Asian Day Laborers for the Caminos de Hierro de La Habana

	1862	1863	1864	1865	1866
Employed	287	255	216	257	279
Died	22	20	8	8	9
Escaped	5	12	8	8	16

Source: Caminos de Hierro de La Habana, Informe de la Junta Directiva a la general de accionistas (1862–66).

of the most varied mixtures of races, conditions, and cultures. The employees of the Ferrocarril de La Bahía (Bay Railroad) at the start of its construction in 1859 graphically illustrates the variety. They consisted of 197 convicts, 42 emancipados, 526 slaves (both owned and rented), 273 Chinese contract workers, 15 free blacks, and 20 white daily paid laborers.[41] It would be hard to imagine a company anywhere else assembling such a varied work force. In such circumstances, it is indeed difficult to speak of the railroad workers as a clearly defined category. And the many cultural, racial, and legal barriers made integration virtually impossible.

The case of the Ferrocarril de La Bahía with its preponderance of slaves in the workforce—almost 50 percent of the personnel—contradicted the pattern of railroad employment. That was a special situation in which a new line was being constructed with a large number of rented slaves. In the majority of established companies, slavery as a source of labor diminished gradually throughout the decade of the 1860s. By the time the Ferrocarril de La Bahía completed the line in 1865, the work force had only one slave—but its labor force consisted of 446 Chinese.[42] Caminos de Hierro de La Habana had a small slave gang of 8 in 1865, and allowed the number to decline without replacement until it had only 2 in 1867. By that time, the Sagua Railroad used no slaves, and its neighbor, the Cienfuegos Railroad, had only 11 slaves.

The records of the Cárdenas and Júcaro Railroad show the labor tendencies clearly. Always strongly relying on slaves, the company bought 44 in 1862 at the remarkable price of 1,130 pesos each. What worried the administration then was less the high price than the fact that "to this date it has not been possible to get even one-half the workers that the company needs at this time."[43] Three years later, when explaining the increase in expenditures for wages to its shareholders, the board of directors lamented about "the large number of white daily paid laborers it had to acquire."[44] At the opposite end of the island in that very year, the administration of the Santiago Railroad echoed the complaint, pointing out that the average cost of a worker had increased to 2.19 pesos per month because of the hiring of "a greater number of free laborers as the number of useful slaves for hire had been inadequate and the number of Asians on which they counted had diminished."[45] The crisis of slavery, foreseeable since the initial formal prohibition of the trade, was already an undeniable fact. The intermediate options available through the use of a semienslaved group such as the Chinese exposed the inadequacy of measures that were destined to disappear in an era based on a free, mobile, labor force. The railroad companies—and all the landholders on the island—noticed how the wage labor situation lurched from one series of crises to another. The most serious deficiency was the absence of a reserve army of industrial workers who would constitute a reserve of cheap labor and at the same time be an efficient and economical substitute for slavery. The wage of an unskilled Cuban railroad worker was about 20 percent higher than his European counterpart.[46] Nevertheless, the inevitable transformation could not be achieved easily. It would require profound political and economic changes to break the stubborn resistance to free labor.

7

Relative Stagnation

After decades of practically uninterrupted growth, the public railroads entered a stage of relative stagnation, which, with some ups and downs, continued throughout the last third of the nineteenth century. The sustained effort of laying track that had begun with Ferrocarril de Güines resulted in 1,220 kilometers of track in use by 1868. That movement of expansion had reached its peak in the 1856–60 period, when an average of 80 kilometers of track was brought into service each year. In the next five years, the rate of construction fell off sharply, with an average of only 35.6 kilometers of new track per year. Even though that average was still high, it was an undeniable symptom of decline when compared with the figure for the previous five years, and the results in subsequent years fully confirmed that trend. (See Table 7.1.)

In all, 532 kilometers of track—a little less than half the amount laid in the three preceding decades—was added in the 1868–98 period. Table 7.1 clearly shows the decline in such activity at the time. It began in 1866 and was most acute in the 1876–85 period. In fact, the clearest manifestations of the paralysis had appeared a little earlier, in 1873, when, for the first time since the introduction of trains in Cuba, a whole year went by without a single kilometer of track being added to the lines serving the public. That significant situation was repeated in 1877 and again in 1881, 1882, 1892, and the 1896–98 period.[1]

While the growth in track summed up the relative stagnation of the public railroads most clearly in numerical terms, other aspects also testified eloquently to that phenomenon. A qualitative analysis of the growth in track for those years shows a high proportion of kilometers laid in branches of secondary importance, to be used to improve the service offered by some companies. In contrast, relatively few branches of track were laid to take trains to regions that lacked that means of transportation. The situation in the business sector was even more expressive: between 1868 and 1898, only one new railroad company, Ferrocarril

TABLE 7.1. Cuban Railway Expansion, 1861–1900 (in kilometers)

Years	Annual Average
1861–65	35.6
1866–70	22.6
1871–75	20.0
1876–80	10.4
1881–85	16.0
1886–90	29.8
1891–95	21.0
1896–1900	8.0

Sources: A. M. Jáudenes, Memoria sobre las obras públicas de la isla de Cuba, 1865–1873 (Havana: La Propaganda Literaria, 1875); L. Tejada, Memoria sobre las obras públicas en la isla de Cuba, 1873–1882 (Havana: Imprenta del Gobierno, 1887); Cuba, Secretaría de Obras Públicas, Memoria sobre los ferrocarriles de la isla de Cuba in los años económicos de 1882–1883 hasta 1897–1898 (Havana: Imprenta Universal, 1902).

de Holguín a Gibara, was founded, and it did no more than build and operate a small narrow-gauge line.[2]

The causes of that prolonged contraction in the growth of Cuba's railroads should be examined from a broader perspective than that of the railroads themselves. In previous chapters, we showed how closely the development of the railroads had been linked to the needs of the island economy and especially to those of sugar production. Therefore, an analysis of those general circumstances is necessary as a starting point for explaining the disturbances noted in the railroad sector.

Cuban history in the last third of the nineteenth century was that of a convulsive transitional stage filled with conflicts and transformations that affected all aspects of life on the island. None of the changes in that period were free of violent disturbances. The most visible of them, the fall of the Spanish colonial regime, was the result of a bitter struggle that wreaked havoc with the island's economy. For at least half of that thirty-year period, Cuba's struggle for independence was waged with all the violence and destructive capacity of a war without quarter. The structural changes that were effected in those years took place against a backdrop of severe economic crises, from which it sometimes appeared the island would be unable to recover. The railroads, naturally, were hard hit by those events, which were of tremendous importance and which occurred quite close together—to such an extent that it is nearly impossible to isolate their specific effects.

The latent conflict contained in Cuba's colonial subjugation to Spain broke out violently in late 1868. One sector of the Cuban bourgeois slavocracy, which had been radicalized by economic difficulties and by the conviction that Cuba's problems could not be solved within the colonial structure, threw aside the timid, prudent attitude that had characterized the political manifestations of its class until then and headed a broad insurrectional movement. Within a few months of the proclamation of independence at La Demajagua, the insurrection had spread through the Departamento Oriental, Camagüey, and several jurisdictions of Las Cinco Villas. Time and again, the Havana regional leadership of the conspirators in the western part of the island put off the uprising, and these vacillations gave the colonial government an opportunity to consolidate its positions in the richest region in the island.[3] The military effort of the pro-independence forces, therefore, was limited to the eastern half of Cuba, where the devastating war raged for an entire decade.

The confinement of the war to the central and eastern regions left most of the railroad lines outside the theater of operations. Only three railroad companies (the ones whose trains linked Puerto Príncipe and Nuevitas and served Santiago de Cuba and Guantánamo) were permanently harmed by the military operations, and five others (the ones in Las Cinco Villas) suffered from sporadic damage as a result of the war. Even so, no matter how far its tracks were from the scene of the fighting, no railroad company escaped from the multiple (and very expensive) consequences of the war. Both in the zone of operations and in the rear guard, trains were of key importance to the colonialist military apparatus. Because of the general conditions of land transportation in Cuba, trains were the most effective means the Spanish command had for transporting and provisioning its troops. This meant that the trains and their collateral resources, such as the telegraph and repair shops, were immediately placed at the service of the military.

The military transports adversely affected the service of nearly all the railroad companies in the country. Caminos de Hierro de La Habana was in charge of handling the heavy traffic of soldiers and war matériel between Havana and Batabanó, from which point they were shipped on coastal vessels to Santa Cruz del Sur, Manzanillo, and Santiago de Cuba. Sometimes the transfer of troops to the front was even more complicated for the railroad companies. Between 1869 and 1871 and then in the 1875–77 period, when the Mambí forces fighting for Cuba's independence remained active in the region of Las Cinco Villas, the Spanish command moved its forces by land from Havana, which meant that the services of several companies had to be combined. The railroad companies involved in that work had to set aside their old rivalries in view of the express demands of the highest Spanish military authorities, who required coordination that would guarantee "the regularity and exactitude of military transportation."[4]

Logically, the Spanish staff used the lines that were close to the zone of operations much more intensively. In the first three years of the war alone, Ferrocarril de Cienfuegos y Villa Clara transported 78,000 men and 650 tons of war matériel, not counting horses, prisoners, and an enormous amount of food.[5]

Trains were a decisive factor in the colonial army's logistics on the strategic plane, but the lines that functioned in the areas of the fighting were also used for tactical purposes. In Puerto Príncipe, for example, the Spanish command asked the railroad company to armor its cars and use its reserve locomotives to guard the track and take troops quickly to any intermediate point. The train was of particular importance in the case of Puerto Príncipe, an inland city surrounded by territory controlled by the Mambí army. The railroad line was the only means of escape in conditions of a virtual siege.[6] Not only in Puerto Príncipe but also on the Santiago-Enramadas, Guantánamo, Cienfuegos–Villa Clara, and other railroad lines, the Spanish army organized flying units which, using special trains that gave them great mobility, could cover large sectors of territory whose protection would otherwise have required much larger forces. The same role was assigned to the trains in the complex defense plan for La Trocha, a line of fortifications stretching between Júcaro and Morón, from coast to coast, that split the island in two in an effort to isolate the rebel forces and limit their operations to the Camagüey and Oriente regions.

Turned into tools of the colonial army, the trains became subject to attack by the liberation forces. The Cubans didn't have the means required to halt the train service permanently, but they did burn bridges, pull up rails, block the track, cut telegraph lines, and engage in other actions that interrupted train service so frequently that they temporarily limited the enemy's use of the trains. For the Mambís, the trains were not always weapons of the enemy, however; at times, especially during the first few months of the war, small shipments of weapons, other war matériel, and medicine were smuggled to the liberation forces by political activists in the cities who were helped by railroad workers who sympathized with the cause of independence. In August 1869, Captain General Antonio Caballero de Rodas warned in a circular to the managers of the railroad companies that "confidential information of the greatest reliability states that the rebels are receiving resources over the Ferrocarril Central, which leaves this city, goes through Macagua and winds up in Cascajal."[7] As a result, the military chief took severe measures to control all packages sent by rail and sent police officers to inspect all activities in the railroad warehouses.

A small but important group of railroad stockholders and officials who were linked more or less closely to the activities of the pro-independence conspirators in Havana and other cities were arrested or went into exile in 1869. Taking reprisals, the Spanish government issued an embargo on their property, which included railroad stock, a large number of sugar mills, and other holdings. Some of those hit by the embargo measures held important positions in the railroad companies. This was so in the cases of Francisco Fesser and José Morales Lemus, presidents of Ferrocarril de la Bahía and of the Cienfuegos and Caibarién Railroads, respectively. Others hurt by the measures included Miguel and Domingo Aldama, the main stockholders in Caminos de Hierro de La Habana; Manuel J. de Rojas and R. Fernández Criado, important individual stockholders in Ferrocarril de Caibarién and in Cárdenas y Júcaro, respectively; Miguel de Embil, Antonio Fernández Bramosio, José Angarica, José R. Simoni, Carlos del Castillo, and other important members of various railroad boards. The Spanish repression also touched some officials who were accused of being conspirators; they included José A. Echevarría, manager of Caminos de Hierro, and Joaquín Fortún, manager of the Cienfuegos Company, who was arrested soon after the war began.[8] After the embargo was decreed, around 10 percent of the railroads' issued stock was controlled by the colonial government's Administración de Bienes Embargados (Department of Goods Placed under Embargo), and the Spanish and other procolonialist elements' positions on the boards of the railroad companies were strengthened.

The boards of many companies were terrified by the possibility that some of their members' attitudes would lead them to be suspected of disloyalty. The board of Ferrocarril de Cienfuegos y Villa Clara, which Morales Lemus headed until 1869, stated this baldly in its annual report for 1870:

> As soon as the board heard of the uprising in Las Cinco Villas and learned that it coincided with the arrest of D. Joaquín Fortún, manager of the line, . . . it begged Exmo. Sr. Don Tomás Terry, a wealthy landowner of Cienfuegos who holds more than an eighth of the capital stock in this company, to accept appointment as inspector of the line and the commission entrusted to him, investing him with all the powers necessary for carrying out those duties, with full preference and without being held back by costs; all of the ordinary and extraordinary services that the government requested were provided.[9]

The railroad companies' boards, which were then controlled by the pro-Spanish faction, went on to outdo one another in servility. Most of the railroad franchises set forth the companies' obligations to the state, and most of the boards fell all over themselves offering every possible facility for military transportation. A few months after the war broke out, the companies stopped charging for the transportation of troops, and they even set lower rates for carrying provisions and other equipment for the colonial army. But the "patriotic vocation" of the railroad magnates did not stop there; they then took up subscriptions to buy weapons for

TABLE 7.2. Investment by Two Railroad Companies, 1868–1878 (in pesos)

Year	FC Santiago de Cuba	FC Nuevitas–Puerto Príncipe
1868	253,989	208,320
1869	111,684	63,858
1870	138,706	137,219
1871	127,652	192,083
1872	121,364	240,834
1873	264,121	134,544
1874	164,005	97,983
1875	180,068	68,628
1876	160,080	84,532
1877	217,733	150,894
1878	203,987	154,915

Sources: A. M. Jáudenes, *Memoria sobre las obras públicas de la isla de Cuba, 1865–1873* (Havana: La Propaganda Literaria, 1875); L. Tejada, *Memoria sobre las obras públicas en la isla de Cuba, 1873–1882* (Havana: Imprenta del Gobierno, 1887).

the Volunteers' corps and made donations for the wounded. The companies paid for the construction of garrisons, and they even underwrote the expenses of the forces of the Guardia Civil for a time.[10]

A more specialized contribution, of materials and equipment for Ferrocarril de la Trocha de Júcaro a Morón, was borne equally among the various railroad companies in the country, which underwrote a substantial part of the costs of building that strategic line. In 1875, when the forces of Máximo Gómez entered Las Villas, the railroad companies once again came to the rescue of the depleted colonial Hacienda (Treasury), advancing funds for bringing twelve thousand reinforcements from Spain.[11] That attitude of unconditional support for Spain was not without its benefits, of course. The colonial government expressed its gratitude by providing special protection for the railroad installations and, even more important, by applying a liberal policy with regard to railroad rates, which enabled the companies to pass a considerable portion of the economic costs of the war on to their passengers and others who used their services.

The Ten Years' War hurt the railroad companies economically in various ways. In addition to its more direct effects, such as the material damage the rebels did to the tracks and cars and the enormous costs the companies assumed in providing military transportation, the war hurt the railroads by harming the country's economy.

First of all, there was the effect that military operations had on the productive levels of some regions. Starting with General Valmaseda's offensive in the Cauto Valley in 1869, the Spanish forces destroyed all the property of the rebels and those who were thought to be collaborating with them. In addition, they destroyed all crops to make it harder for the Mambí army to get supplies. The Cubans' reply came immediately: from then on, no chief hesitated to put all of the installations and crops that might contribute to the economy of the colonial regime to the torch. With that systematic destruction by both sides, economic life was paralyzed in entire regions. Even when railroads in the areas affected by that situation managed to keep operational, they had no freight to carry. The effects of the situation on two railroad companies in different regions affected by the war are shown in Table 7.2.

Both of the companies suffered from the war, though to different extents. In Santiago de Cuba, the effects were immediate. In 1869, a Mambí offensive in the mountain valleys north of the city destroyed twenty-three sugar mills and fifteen coffee plantations. This initiated a period of hard times for the railroad company, which its board of directors recalled years later as follows:

> Since this railroad was built for the main purpose of carrying the large amounts of rich products from the coffee and sugar estates that lie along the track and in the Sabanilla and Maroto Valleys, it is clear that, when those products disappeared, the railroad had to die. . . . In that critical period, when there wasn't even a hope of making a profit from passenger fares, because, in such a calamitous era, the only ones who used the trains were government troops and a few individuals . . ., the stockholders considered their capital lost, so they sold their stock for even less than four pesos.[12]

In Puerto Príncipe, the war was even more devastating: of the one hundred sugar mills that had been in operation in the area in 1868, only one remained standing ten years later. The first year of the war cut the railroad company's income to a third of what it had been, and the railroad was able to survive at all only because it was the only way to supply the city with provisions.

In spite of the fierce fighting, the war did not break any of the railroad companies. It is true that one of them, Ferrocarril de Trinidad, went under during the war years, but it had always been sickly; the war simply dealt it a coup de grace. The situation of the Trinidad Railroad Company had been critical for years before the war began. In 1867, a group of stockholders had suggested that the company be liquidated, but the project was abandoned in hopes that administrative measures would improve the company's finances. In the case of Trinidad, the destruction caused by the war coincided with the practical failure of the measures proposed, and, in 1872, when all hope had been abandoned, the definitive liquidation of the company was agreed upon.[13]

The regions served by the large railroad companies in the western part of the country were untouched by the war, so those companies were able to maintain and even raise their former income levels, but this in no way implied that the western companies escaped unscathed from the devastating effects of the war. While it is true that their income developed normally, their expenditures sky-rocketed, due to increases in some items and the appearance of other, new ones. In addition to the tremendous expenditures involved in military transportation, there were many other services that were "difficult to measure, such as the need to work at night in the repair shops, paying double wages; that of having more workers in the stations, to provide unforeseen services; continual delays in the trains, which, in addition to the disturbance they cause, require more fuel; the need to improvise stables on the cars for transporting horses, which causes considerable material deterioration; and the telegraph services, lodging, and other items, which, in the final analysis, always cause extraordinary expenditures."[14] Those expenses reached an impressive level, as shown by the fact that Caminos de Hierro de La Habana spent the respectable sum of 235,000 pesos on services provided free of charge to the state in the 1875–77 period alone.

In addition to those extraordinary expenses of the service, there were taxes, imposed to obtain funds for waging the war, which proved to be equally extraordinary. In its customary indigence, the Spanish Hacienda Pública was unable to come up with the funds needed for the military budget. The fairest solution, in the view of the metropolitan power, was to extract the resources needed for the war from the Cuban colony itself. The colonial authorities' fiscal rapacity reached unprecedented heights when countless new taxes were levied on the Cubans. The railroad companies were particularly hard hit by a 5 percent tax on net profits and by a 2.5 percent tax on capital. On more than one occasion, the railroad boards tried to use their collaboration with the colonialist military effort to obtain exemptions from payment of the new taxes, but the government generally proved inflexible. Moreover, with manifest distrust, it ordered a semiannual examination of the companies' books to prevent any evasive accounting shenanigans.

In spite of all those fiscal measures, the money obtained was insufficient to cover the growing expenses of the war. The colonial Hacienda had to "resort to various measures, such as loans, suspensions of some payments so as to give priority to military expenditures, and the issuance of nonconvertible bills by the authorized bank: the Español de La Habana. The result of this was a process of inflation and unlimited speculation."[15] During the first five years of the war, the bank issued 74 million pesos in nonconvertible bills, which quickly depreciated. In May 1873, the rate of exchange was 28 pesos and 37 centavos per ounce of gold; barely a year later, it was 163 pesos per ounce.

The monetary disorder caused serious problems in the railroads' economy.

When the fiduciary currency was virtually devaluated, the companies were faced with the situation of having their services paid for with bills whose real value in terms of gold was far inferior to the established rates. However, when they had to purchase materials and equipment, especially imported goods, they had to make their payments in gold. Thus, their balance between income and expenditures was totally upset.

In December 1873, a group of railroad companies addressed the Gobierno Superior Político (Higher Political Government), requesting that the railroads be allowed to demand payment in gold for their services. After much delay, in April 1874, the railroads were finally authorized to be paid in bills with the application of a discount rate based on the gold quotations in Havana. Even so, the authorized rate of exchange was lower than the one established by the reigning speculation. This led to some alarming situations involving deficits, about which the dismayed boards of directors informed their stockholders periodically. Monetary disorder therefore became an added source of difficulties for the already beleaguered railroad economies, especially in view of the fact that monetary circulation was not stabilized in Cuba until many years after the war was over.[16]

The diverse and complex economic upsets occasioned by the war nearly always caused increases in the railroad companies' expenditures. With clear capitalist logic, those companies fought to reduce their expenses in order to maintain a satisfactory profit margin. Their investment funds for expanding and improving the service were the first victims of this policy of enforced cutbacks. To economize, expenditures on maintenance and the replacement of track and equipment, which were susceptible to greater control, were also reduced. The measures drawn up for that purpose, which were applied just when the increase in the service, the circulation of special trains, and the transportation of cargoes that were heavier than usual caused greater deterioration in the equipment and materials, led to the progressive deterioration of the companies' technical equipment and to the deplorable state to which their installations were reduced by the end of the war.

Just when the war was having a ruinous effect, the Cuban economy was also faced with the adverse turn taken by the international economic scene. Closely linked to the world market, Cuba had always suffered from the cyclical phenomena characteristic of the capitalist system. The 1857 and 1866 crises upset its economic life, wrecking the island's nascent financial apparatus.

Although the crises brought out the structural weakness of the economy, they did not eliminate its expansion possibilities. Even in the midst of the war, sugar production continued to grow vigorously, especially with the large sugarcane harvests of the 1868–70 period, each of which amounted to over 700,000 tons. The high prices paid for sugar in 1871 and 1872 (the quotations, which were close to 6 cents a pound, were the highest since the "crazy year" of 1857) were such an incentive that 775,000 tons of sugar was produced in 1873, the highest figure obtained by the island's industry.

That same year, the world was shaken by a violent crisis, perhaps the worst in its history prior to the one that hit in 1929.[17] The price of sugar plummeted, to 4.5 cents a pound in 1875. The Cuban producers, who were accustomed to the ups and downs of the world market, prepared to weather the storm and wait for another boom. Their hopes seemed justified in 1877 when the price once more rose to over 5 cents a pound, but it didn't last long; the price dropped yet again and, after another crisis, in 1883–84, settled at around 3 cents a pound.[18]

In fact, a new era had begun. With the crisis of 1873, the economic cycle entered a depressive phase, with a steady drop in prices, that lasted until nearly the end of the nineteenth century. That decline appeared as the logical result of the development of the productive forces, which, both in industry and in agriculture, gave rise to an ever greater volume of consumer products. Moreover, the advance in transportation technology (trains, propeller-driven ships, etc.) helped to link distant regions with the world market—and, therefore, with new producers. The increase in demand was thus surpassed by the growth in supply, which led to decreases in the prices of a large number of articles.

Within that context, the sugar situation was especially serious. Since the beginning of the nineteenth century, European markets had seen the appearance of a new saccharine product, beet sugar, which, with a slow but steady growth in production, was supplying 20 percent of the sugar consumed in the world in 1860. It had an effect on the market, but its competition was still a local phenomenon in that period, one that particularly affected western Europe, where French beet sugar, which was given considerable protection by the state, dominated the market. Starting in 1860, however, the development of new, powerful sugar beet producers (Germany, Austria-Hungary, and Russia, among others) gave that product an unprecedented boost. Between 1864 and 1871, beet sugar production doubled, amounting to a million tons. Ten years later, with a world production of 1,831,847 tons, beet sugar production surpassed that of cane sugar for the first time in history.[19] Competition between the two was keen, with world production of sugar rising from 3 million tons in 1874 to 8 million tons in 1894. That sharp increase in the supply caused a precipitous drop in the price: from 6 cents a pound in 1872 to 4.4 cents a pound in 1884 and to barely 2.3 cents a pound in 1895.

Beets, which had less sucrose content and whose industrial processing was more expensive, did not have natural advantages for competing against sugarcane. In their favor, they were excellent as a crop to be rotated with grains and as feed for cattle, but the main factor in that era was the application of an improved technology that made it possible to extract more sugar from them than could be obtained from sugarcane. However, the main advantage of beets lay not in agricultural or technical factors but in a device of trade policy: state subsidies. The European governments (especially those of France and Germany) protected their production of beet sugar with a system of subsidies for exports that made it possible for that sugar to be sold at prices that were lower than its production costs. Thus, in 1884, for example, 100 kilograms of German beet sugar, which cost $10.32 to produce, could, with a subsidy of $4.50, be sold on the New York market for $7.12, while 100 kilograms of Cuban sugar, which cost $8.78 to produce, was placed for sale on that same market for $11.38.[20] In the face of such unfair competition, cane sugar was bound to lose ground. In 1876, 69 percent of the sugar consumed in Great Britain had been made from sugarcane; in 1890, cane sugar accounted for only 19 percent of the sugar consumed there.[21]

Cuba suffered more than any other country from that turn in the world market. In the 1860s, somewhat more than half of its exports went to the European market (including Spain), with England its main purchaser. A few years later, in 1877, around 80 percent of Cuba's exports went to the U.S. market, and only 6.7 percent to the English market.[22] Its loss of markets and the growing concentration of its exports placed Cuba in a dangerous state of dependence, whose tragic consequences became evident very quickly. In those difficult circumstances, not even the U.S. market was assured for Cuba, and its share of U.S. sugar purchases dropped by 20 percent between 1865 and 1885.[23]

The Cuban industry was faced with a life-or-death alternative: to produce at a cost that would ensure survival, even with the drop in the price of the finished product, or to stop producing sugar. More than mere technological modernization, it was a matter of radically transforming the productive structure in the sugar sector and jettisoning the concepts that had ruled its development up until then.

Based on slavery, the Cuban sugar industry had, for a long time, depended on a trade advantage that assumed the exhaustive use of cheap labor. But slavery was a serious obstacle to progress and, by clinging to it, the estate owners were sacrificing the future of the industry for an immediate advantage. Attempts to use machines in the industrial process on slave plantations achieved only partial success; in the middle of the nineteenth century, Cuba's production was still essentially manufacturing, and it was clear that not much more progress could be made in that field within the framework of slave relations.[24] From then on, sugar techniques stagnated or became involuted: the gap separating Cuba from the more advanced exponents of the world sugar industry grew wider. It would require a tremendous effort to bridge that growing distance. At that decisive moment, Cuba's industry was faced with extremely adverse circumstances: the fall in the price of sugar, the lack of Cuban banking institutions that could finance the modernization process, and the economic bankruptcy caused by the war.

The main issue in the transformation of the productive structure was a change in the regimen of work. The ideologues of the bourgeois slavocracy had conceived of that process as one of gradual transition in the course of which the state would indemnify the owners for their slaves as they were manumitted. The facts did not follow that "happy" scheme of things. In 1869, at Guáimaro, the pro-independence forces proclaimed a constitution that abolished slavery without stipulating compensation of any kind for the slave owners. The next year, the Spanish government, which had been forced to cede, decreed that all slaves' children who were born after September 1868 would be born free. No matter what the political alternatives were, the end of the opprobrious institution was decided upon. Definitive abolition came in 1886, with a law that the Spanish crown had promulgated six years earlier; it provided no indemnification.

With the end of slavery, a new factor was added to the crisis of the Cuban economy: lack of manpower. This lack had begun to appear some years before abolition, thanks to the definitive extinction of the clandestine slave trade and the Chinese empire's cancellation in 1873 of the agreement that had authorized the traffic in coolies. Because of this last action, which was of tremendous importance, the Cuban estate owners were left with neither slaves nor indentured Chinese, who had been the most effective substitutes that had been found for them.

Attacked from such diverse angles, Cuba's sugar production fell off abruptly. The record of 775,000 tons of sugar obtained in the sugarcane harvest of 1873 remained an unalterable production ceiling for nearly twenty years. In fact, production was unable to maintain that level; in the midst of sharp ups and downs, it held to a downward trend, with harvests averaging somewhat less than 600,000 tons throughout the decade of the 1880s. Not until the next decade did it recover from that fall, and then only at the cost of fateful dependence on the U.S. refining trust.

The old sugar-railroad equation recurred then in adversity. It wasn't by chance that the lowest average growth in track—13.8 kilometers per year—in that period coincided exactly with the critical decade of 1876–85, whose sugarcane harvests averaged only 558,795 tons. The contraction in production adversely affected the railroad companies, the volume of whose main cargo declined. Moreover, paralysis of the plantations' physical expansion removed the incentive for extending the tracks. That work was slowed and reduced to a very limited scale, largely conditioned by the structural transformations by means of which the sugar industry tried to emerge from the crisis.

Between 1868 and 1898, rather than growing or expanding, Cuba's railroad network was improved within its old, relatively narrow limits in an effort to adjust to the new economic circumstances. Only around 15 percent of the 532 kilometers of track that was laid in those years pertained to the rail systems of new companies created in the period. The bulk of the construction effort was in prolongations and branches of the tracks belonging to companies that had been founded prior to the war. Three of them, Matanzas, Cárdenas y Júcaro, and Ferrocarril del Oeste, accounted for more than 65 percent of the track built and were the only ones that experienced any process of expansion.

In the case of Ferrocarril del Oeste, the explanation was simple. That company's ambitious project of having a 176-kilometer-long line linking Havana and Pinar del Río was still far from having been completed when the stage now being analyzed began. In 1868, Oeste's tracks had only reached the town of Candelaria, more than 80 kilometers short of its goal. In financial straits since its founding, the westernmost of Cuba's railroad companies carried on with its project with a tenacity that can be explained only by its hope of reversing its economic situation when the line should reach the rich tobacco region of Vueltabajo. Spasmodically, every three or four years, Ferrocarril del Oeste added on a dozen kilometers to its interminable line. Finally, after reorganization and the company's transfer to new owners in 1892, the last stretch of track—the 14 kilometers between Puerta de Golpe and Pinar del Río—was finished and opened to service in 1894.[25]

Ferrocarril de Matanzas and Ferrocarril de Cárdenas y Júcaro, two of the country's first railroad companies, had completed their original plans years before. Since then, they had continued growing to meet the needs of the expanding Matanzas plantations. They competed with each other, each striving to be the first to extend its tracks to every region where the burning of undergrowth announced the forthcoming founding of a new sugar mill.

By 1868, the Matanzas plantations seemed to have reached the limit of their expansion possibilities, but there was still a strip of fertile red earth south of Colón which, after crossing the Hanábana River, headed southeast to Aguada de Pasajeros and Yaguaramas, towns near the Cienfuegos plantation area.[26] That promising region proved to be the new scene for competition between the rival companies.

Ferrocarril de Cárdenas y Júcaro, encroaching on Ferrocarril de Matanzas's turf, inaugurated a branch line twenty-four kilometers long between Retamal and Calimete in 1871, seeking to absorb the cargo from the Triunfana, Indarra, and Godínez sugar mills, to which the Araujo and Porfuerza (the main sugar mills in the region) were soon added. That branch was slowly extended southward: to Amarillas in 1875, to Aguada in 1885, and finally to Yaguaramas in 1888. That last stretch contributed to the development of the Perseverancia sugar mill.

In 1886, Ferrocarril de Matanzas laid a parallel track starting from Guareiras that was very close to the other one—at no point farther than fifteen kilometers away—to facilitate transportation of sugar from Carrillo's Mercedes sugar mill and to compete with Cárdenas y Júcaro for the sugar from the Porfuerza sugar mill. That new line also crossed the Hanábana River and headed toward the

Cienfuegos plantations, but it ended at Esles, a small hamlet some ten kilometers from Rodas, which would prove to be the eastern terminus of the Matanzas railroad system.

Outside that region for which the two Matanzas railroad companies were contending, they continued developing their old areas of expansion. Thus, Cárdenas y Júcaro extended its main track from Macagua to Esperanza, the first section of the projected Ferrocarril Central, that would provide direct access by rail to the city of Santa Clara. Once the concession was obtained in 1867, the company set about the work with tremendous energy and completed the first two sections (from Macagua to Alvarez and from Alvarez to Santo Domingo) in 1871. At Santo Domingo, Cárdenas y Júcaro linked up with Ferrocarril de Sagua. Once this intermediary goal had been met, the Cárdenas Railroad apparently lost interest in the project, which wasn't finished until fourteen years later.[27]

For its part, Ferrocarril de Matanzas continued to extend its important branch line from Navajas, first with a fourteen-kilometer stretch to Jagüey Grande in 1878 and then with an eleven-kilometer section in 1893. With this last section, the company offered direct service to the Australia sugar mill, which had been founded in 1882. Direct service to sugar mills became the main characteristic of Ferrocarril de Matanzas's development, which largely explains why that company had the largest growth in the 1868–98 period. In those thirty years, Ferrocarril de Matanzas built a total of eighty-four kilometers of branch lines to serve such important sugar mills as the Conchita, Atrevido, and Desquite. The increase in the sugar mills' milling capacity and the sending of larger volumes of sugarcane from ever more distant points, by virtue of the process of industrial concentration, made that new kind of service profitable, expressing an even closer relationship between the public railroads and sugar production.

The old and powerful Caminos de Hierro de La Habana and Ferrocarril de la Bahía, which were hemmed in by the tracks of the three companies mentioned earlier, experienced no substantial growth in that period. Ferrocarril de la Bahía put out a small, narrow-gauge branch line from Coliseo to Guamacaro, an important sugar center whose freight it sought to control, but its hopes were dashed by Guamacaro's utter decline when the sugar crisis hit.[28]

Caminos de Hierro de La Habana's growth was also limited to a small branch line ten kilometers long, from Unión to Alacranes, which was then called Alfonso XII, to transport sugar from the Las Cañas sugar mill, which was owned by Juan Poey, an intractable stockholder in the company.

In the regions of Las Cinco Villas, what scanty railroad development there was didn't deviate from the models already examined. Near the end of the 1880s, Ferrocarril de Cienfuegos decided to build two branch lines: one twenty-three kilometers long, toward the Parque Alto sugar mill, and the other, only eight kilometers long, to the town of San Juan de los Yeras, which would also benefit the Pastora sugar mill.

Ferrocarril de Sagua also expanded its network with two branch lines to share in the sugar transportation business: the first was fifteen kilometers long, toward Caguaguas, extending the company's track close to the sugarcane area of Quemado de Güines; the second, more important one, extended the old Sitiecitos-Cienfuentes branch through Encrucijada to link up with Ferrocarril de Caibarién's line at Camajuaní. In addition to connecting Ferrocarril de Caibarién with the western railroad network, that branch, which was completed in 1890, served the important sugarcane district of Calabazar, which had over twenty sugar mills, some of which—the Purio, Santa Lutgarda, Macagua, and Constancia—were engaged in an accelerated process of centralization.

Lack of negotiating ability by the board of directors of Ferrocarril Remedios-Caibarién led to the most important railroad construction in Las Villas in that period. Sugar magnate Julián Zulueta, who had begun to develop the Zaza sugar mill, near Placetas, in the mid-1870s, began talks with the Remedios Company, trying to get it to meet his transportation needs. When the company did not offer favorable conditions, Zulueta chose to build his own narrow-gauge line, connecting the Zaza directly with the port of Caibarién. That new railroad line, which was inaugurated as a private railroad in 1878, was authorized to serve the public shortly thereafter, which created a situation of competition that was disastrous to Ferrocarril Remedios-Caibarién and was overcome only through the subsequent merger of the two lines, forming the Empresa Unida de los Ferrocarriles de Caibarién.

The slow railroad growth of those years was even more obvious in the eastern half of Cuba. Between 1868 and 1883, not a single kilometer of track was laid in all the territory east of the Jatibonico River (except the railroad at La Trocha, for exclusively military purposes).[29] Even so, there was no dearth of attractive projects.[30]

In 1880, as soon as the last echoes of the war had died away, the idea of building a railroad to link Puerto Príncipe with the port of Santa Cruz del Sur began to be batted around in Puerto Príncipe. The Camagüeyan project, whose antecedents went back to the era of El Lugareño, was to be a kind of southern prolongation of the Nuevitas line, that would make it possible to reproduce in Camagüey the north-south "master plan" of Cuban railroad communication. Even though the project was kept alive throughout the 1880s, its subscribers in Camagüey never contributed enough capital to carry it through.

In contrast, construction in the eastern part of the country was renewed at the eastern tip of the island. In 1883, Ferrocarril de Guantánamo decided to extend its tracks ten kilometers to the town of Jamaica, to take them even closer to the heart of the coffee plantations in the region. The following year, a small branch line was built to the Soledad sugar mill, owned by the Brook family (which just so happened to be the main stockholders in the Guantánamo Railroad). First through the operations of their commercial firm and then as the virtual owners of the railroad, the Brooks had become the most powerful estate owners in Guantánamo, where, in addition to the Soledad, they also owned the important Romelie and Isabel sugar mills. Those circumstances favored the growing subordination of Ferrocarril de Guantánamo to the sugar interests of the family.

Santiago de Cuba's Ferrocarril de Sabanilla a Maroto should really have left Sabanilla out of its name, for the projected branch line from El Cristo to Sabanilla, which had been planned in the 1860s, never got beyond the drawing board stage. However, the exploitation of the Ponupo manganese mines, near La Maya, constituted a new and powerful incentive for pushing through the forgotten Sabanilla branch. In 1894, Ferrocarril de Santiago de Cuba, which was already controlled by the same U.S. interests that owned the mines, began construction of the twenty-four-kilometer branch line between El Cristo and La Maya, and it went into service the following year.[31]

The only new public railroad company created in that stage, Ferrocarril de Gibara-Holguín, was also founded in the eastern part of the country. Even though the first studies on that line date from the years prior to the Ten Years' War, the project did not take shape until 1883. Its main promoters were the owners of the most important businesses in Gibara: Longoria, Beola, and others. They considered the railroad ideal for their dual purpose of giving trade a boost in the agricultural regions near Gibara and extending their commercial control to the important settlement of Holguín, economic hub of that vast and rich northeastern region. The concession was obtained in 1884, and the first section of the narrow-gauge line (ten kilometers long, linking Gibara and Cantimplora) was inaugurated the following year. Contradictions between the commercial interests of the residents of Gibara and Holguín, however, placed so many obstacles in the way of that simple railroad project only a little over thirty kilometers long that it was not completed until 1894, when the eight-kilometer section between Aguas Claras and Holguín was inaugurated.[32]

Even though, strictly speaking, it was not a public railroad, another line that appeared in that stage should be mentioned here, for it had approximately the same economic importance as the Gibara Railroad. This was the narrow-gauge railroad which was built between Viñales and San Cayetano, in the westernmost part of Cuba. The creation of that line linked the development of Viñales as a tobacco-growing center to the transformation of that area into the axis with the most spectacular economic and demographic growth in that period of Cuban history.[33] The purpose of the twenty-four-kilometer-long narrow-gauge line was to carry the region's growing tobacco crop to the tiny landing stage of San

Cayetano—Puerto Esperanza—and it carried out that function profitably until 1895, when a hurricane did serious damage to most of the track, which couldn't be rebuilt, because the military operations of the War of Independence were extended to the region.

In those three critical decades, the Viñales and Gibara Railroads echoed what had been the classical model of Cuba's railroad growth during its initial phase of expansion, but there was little else that was reminiscent of those times. Competition still acted as a spur to growth—note the case of Cárdenas and Matanzas—but, in that difficult era, small investments with assured profits became the norm. Such investments necessarily implied a closer relationship between the railroads and the new needs of sugar production. Meanwhile, the country still lacked a railroad network that would link all of its regions.

Conceived of as a veritable axis of all the tracks in the island, Ferrocarril Central had become the immediate "historic task" required for the development of Cuba's railroads. The plan, which had been outlined as early as 1853, embodied the first integral concept of a modern system of communications for the island.[34] The construction of the great central track implied surmounting the limited use of trains on short lines running from the center of the island to the coasts or from the northern to the southern coast (as occurred in some cases) and adopting a long longitudinal line that would traverse the island from east to west. That plan was nothing new. Cuba's shape called for a longitudinal axis as the main direction of travel linking its various cities. That was the direction adopted by the impractical Camino Real de Cuba and, later, by the diverse lines of coastal shipping, which, in their constant going and coming along the northern and southern coasts, kept the various regions of the country in contact with one another.

Even though the great railroad project had been studied on the spot since 1854, it was not until 1862 that an acceptable, well-defined draft plan was presented, the work of the engineer Manuel Fernández de Castro.[35] That plan linked the main cities in the interior of the country: Villa Clara, Sancti Spíritus, Puerto Príncipe, Tunas, Bayamo, Jiguaní, and others, centers which, up until then, could be reached only by combining several means of transportation (vessels used in coastal shipping, [sometimes] local railroads, and uncomfortable covered wagons), all of which implied a high cost and enormous loss of time. Apart from that intrinsic advantage in favor of the important project, there was the fact that the railroad would go through the most backward and undeveloped regions of the country, and it could be a powerful factor in promoting their development. No less important were the considerations of a strategic order, the facilities that Ferrocarril Central would offer for taking troops to any point in the island, substantially improving the conditions for its defense.

This last argument seems to have been particularly attractive to the Spanish authorities, who expressed their interest in the project very early in the game. Already in August 1862, a royal order urged the civil governor of Cuba to offer all possible and preferential support to the project of the Ferrocarril Central. Two years later, a royal decree authorized a special credit for studying the important railroad project. Along with that measure, government engineers made economic studies and surveys of the various stretches of the track, for use in granting future concessions.

Right from the outset, the Spanish government's interest contrasted sharply with the extreme caution with which the colonial government considered the first offers for construction of the line.[36] As a result of that policy, although the government possessed quite detailed studies on the project by 1868, it had authorized work to proceed on only the first, eighty-kilometer-long section, between Macagua (Los Arabos) and La Esperanza, which it assigned to the Cárdenas y Júcaro Company.

The Ten Years' War initiated a long hiatus in the efforts to build the Ferrocarril Central, but, at the end of the war, the harsh experience that the colonialist forces had derived from it was turned into overwhelming arguments in favor of the project. In 1880, after the discussion of reforms in the colonial administration of Cuba had been opened by Martínez Campos's government, the question of the Ferrocarril Central came up as one of the main topics under review. Some of the old chiefs of the colonial forces, such as General Armiñán, whom Máximo Gómez had defeated at Las Guásimas, spoke out hotly in favor of the project, emphasizing the importance of the railroads during the recently concluded war.[37]

The usefulness of railroads for military purposes, which had been brought out by the circumstances, appeared as the most telling argument, but the participants in the discussions paid equal attention to other factors, especially immigration and the settling of depopulated areas, a matter of pressing concern at a time when the abolition of slavery had made the growing lack of manpower in Cuba a key issue. The rich potential of the land which the railroad would make accessible was emphasized, and it was suggested that "a system of colonization could be combined with the work on the Ferrocarril Central, so that the workers, while always retaining the right to withdraw from the work and even to return to their own countries, could purchase land, houses, and other means of living in towns that would be built alongside the railroad."[38] Thus, efforts were made to assimilate the experience of the great U.S. and Canadian transcontinental railroads and of the Argentinian railroads, whose success in combining colonization with the onward thrust of the tracks caused a sensation in their time.

As a result of the 1882 discussions, it was announced that bids for the concession of the Ferrocarril Central would be considered, but nobody took up the offer.

This led to a new discussion of the matter in the Spanish Cortes and the election of a commission from among its members to once more study the railroad project and present it in terms that would be more attractive to investors. At the end of that process, a law was passed that made the concession more advantageous, for it stated that it would be awarded through a contest. However, that new procedure was no more successful than its predecessor had been: nobody submitted any entries.

From that point on, the history of the Ferrocarril Central split into two parallel and apparently contradictory processes. First of all, there were all the steps the Spanish government took and all the efforts it made to seek someone to implement the project. Its lack of results presents a picture of absolute indifference on the part of investors. But, at the same time, between 1880 and 1884, the colonial government received no less than six offers by syndicates and other groups that were interested in the project, proposals that the authorities systematically turned down.[39]

A first explanation of the curious dialogue of the deaf that surrounded the railroad project was put forth in an article by José de Armas y Céspedes, which appeared in 1885.[40] De Armas considered that the crux of the matter lay in the position assumed by the engineers of the Ministerio de Ultramar (Overseas Ministry) and especially by Leonardo de Tejada, director of public works. De Armas noted that, in addition to introducing absurd modifications in the plan, Tejada set a ridiculous budget of between 25,000 and 30,000 pesos a kilometer for the concession, when even the most conservative assessments made previously had called for 57,000 pesos per kilometer. A modification of such importance was enough to make the concession unacceptable to any businessman in full command of his faculties.

The obstacles that the engineers of Ultramar placed in the way of the project seem undeniable, yet it is hard to believe that those second-rank functionaries, by themselves, were able to derail a project that was important enough to hold the attention of the Cortes and the ministers of the government in Madrid.

The Ferrocarril Central also faced covert but much more powerful opposition by the Spanish interests linked to coastal shipping. They transported nearly all the merchandise and passengers that traveled along the length of Cuba, and the Ferrocarril Central would spell disaster for them. Those numerous influential coastal shipping companies had coexisted with and even complemented their services with those of several railroad companies, especially the ones like Caminos de Hierro de La Habana that owned transversal lines linking the island's northern and southern coasts.[41] However, the companies or tracks that ran longitudinally, such as Ferrocarril del Oeste and Ferrocarril de la Bahía de La Habana a Matanzas, had caused furious competition by the shipping concerns.[42] In the case of the projected Ferrocarril Central, it was only to be expected that that situation would be reproduced on an even higher plane. The interests linked to coastal shipping rose up to keep the project from being implemented, doing everything they could to block the official channels through which the project had to pass, for the existence of the railroad would mean serious competition that every investor contemplated with apprehension.

From the narrow business point of view, it must be admitted that investing in the Ferrocarril Central raised more than one question. First of all, there was a substantial difference between the projected railway and the lines that had been built in Cuba prior to then. The overwhelming majority of Cuba's railroad investments (see Chapters 3, 4, and 5) had been built as "sure things," that is, to facilitate transportation in regions whose volume of cargo guaranteed that the service would be profitable. Ferrocarril Central, however, would have to prove itself. Nobody doubted the tremendous fertility of the land that the new railroad would open to the world of mercantile relations, but the economic circumstances of the time and those of the foreseeable future didn't offer any certainty concerning their possible use. This time, sugarcane didn't mark the route to be taken by the rails, nor was it to be expected that the sugarcane growers would follow on the heels of the men laying the track. Without sugarcane and sugar, there would be no assured cargo for a large railroad in Cuba. In a letter to the civil governor, the board of directors of the Compañía de Cárdenas y Júcaro noted that "the Camino Central will bring advantages of a political, administrative, and economic nature, . . . but, for purposes of speculation, it must be admitted that they are very few. . . . The benefits which the Ferrocarril Central may bring will depend solely on the movement of passengers and small and miscellaneous cargo, so, on undertaking its construction, we must accept some probabilities against its success as a profitable speculation."[43] Placed in that context, the Ferrocarril Central project couldn't prosper in the conditions in which Cuba's railroad projects had traditionally been carried out. Exceptional measures were required, but none were taken.

The Spanish railroad legislation in effect in Cuba wasn't precisely a factor to stimulate investment, but neither did it constitute an insurmountable obstacle for a flexible and interested government. What the circumstances required was the granting of a subsidy, an assured rate of interest, or some other substantial stimulus to investment that would improve the prospects of the project, but the Spanish government, which had handed over hundreds of millions of pesetas to the railroads in Spain, had never demonstrated any willingness to make outlays for its "esteemed colony" in the Antilles. The function of the colonial Hacienda was to drain off resources, not grant them. The Ferrocarril Central forced Spanish colonial policy to choose between the needs (and even security) of the colony and the rapacious fiscal habits of the metropolitan center. Thus, the circumstances were propitious for the interests opposed to the railroad project to tip the balance their way. The century in which Cuba had built one of the first railroads in the world ended, leaving the island without a true railroad system.

The Impact of Structural Changes

The thoroughgoing transformations noted in Cuba's economy and social structure in the last third of the nineteenth century had several repercussions in the railroad sector. Both in the organization of production and in the labor system, the changes wrought implied overcoming the contradictions that had led to the definitive crisis of the slave plantations, taking the only possible way out: that of consolidating capitalist relations of production. In Cuba, however, that substantial modification didn't change the structural characteristics of its single-export economy. To the contrary, it created the conditions for accentuating that distortion within the framework of the new relations of dependence on imperialism, which began to develop precisely in that stage.

The challenge posed by beet sugar and the subsequent drop in the world price of sugar could only be met by reducing the production costs of the cane sugar producers. In essence, it was a matter of productivity, of achieving a substantial increase both in milling capacity and in the yield of the cane. Sugarcane processing had to be readied for a definitive leap from small-scale manufacturing to large-scale industrial production. In that regard, the development of the production of beet sugar made an involuntary contribution to the industrialization of sugarcane processing, which assimilated important aspects of the advanced beet sugar technology. And, since France probably had the most developed sugar technology in that era, it should come as no surprise that the French colonies pioneered in the great sugarcane industry in the Antilles.[1]

Work in this direction had begun in Cuba in 1840 with the introduction of "Derosne trains," a French technology that was a considerable advance in technifying the manufacturing process. In the 1860s, Cuba already had some large sugar mills, such as the Alava, Flor de Cuba, Progreso, and San Martín, which could produce up to 1,250 tons of sugar per harvest, but there were few of those units, and some of them were far from an economic success. Large-scale industry didn't mesh well with the traditional structure of the Cuban sugarcane cycle. The enlargement of industrial capacity required a considerable extension of the area planted to sugarcane and the incorporation of a prohibitive number of new slaves on the plantations. Therefore, the investment required for industrial development was beyond the possibilities of nearly all of Cuba's estate owners.

Quite a lot of argument and discussion centered around this problem, and many theoretical solutions were proposed over the years, but industrialization in the sugar sector remained bogged down until economic pressure made change an absolute necessity. That was when the way was opened to the only practicable solution: to separate the agricultural and industrial aspects of the sugar cycle into two basic phases once and for all.

Beginning in the 1870s, there was talk of large sugar mills that would multiply several times over the production levels of the old roller mills. The owners of the new units had to employ their resources exclusively in industrial investments and leave the supply of their raw material in the hands of independent sugarcane growers. In 1880, conde Francisco F. Ibáñez became a fervent propagandist for the system of large sugar mills. As a powerful estate owner, he put his theories into practice by installing the new system in his San Joaquín sugar mill, in Matanzas Province. After complete remodeling, it became a modern industrial plant with tremendous production capacity.[2]

Others followed up that initiative, and large sugar mills were created first in Matanzas and, shortly afterward, in the other sugarcane regions in the country, thoroughly transforming the structure of the sugar sector. The new fall in the price of sugar following the crisis of 1884 greatly speeded that process. For example, eleven sugar mills were developed or enlarged between 1884 and 1890 whose combined production in 1891 was estimated at 100,000 tons of sugar.[3]

With the implacable logic of capitalism, the appearance of sugar mills with high levels of efficiency and profitability inevitably meant that many small producers disappeared, for their deteriorated steam-powered machinery and obsolete "Jamaican trains" didn't enable them to produce sugar of a high enough quality at a low enough cost to meet the market requirements.

Since, generally, the large sugar mills could extract twice as much sugar from their raw material as normally obtained by the old mills, it proved feasible to pay the sugarcane growers the equivalent of a proportion of sugar very similar to what they would have been able to get if they had milled the cane in their antiquated mills. This fact turned the large sugar mills into receivers of nearly all the sugarcane planted near them. Ceding to the laws of economics, many estate owners abandoned their old status as sugar mill owners, of which they had been so proud, and became colonos, or small-scale sugarcane growers. Many farmers who had never grown sugarcane before also joined the ranks of the colonos, for the new system of large sugar mills offered them that possibility. In other cases, the large sugar mills rented the land of nearby farmers to ensure their supply of raw material.

The old sugar structure, in which agriculture and industry were integrated on the basis of single ownership and single management gave way to an organization with two clearly differentiated phases that were linked by mercantile relations. It was a new productive reality with new transportation demands, as shown by this wise testimony from the era: "Moreover, the railroads are just as necessary to the sugar mills now as are the mills themselves. With the area planted to sugarcane extending for thousands of hectares, primitive carts, which move slowly and lazily, don't meet production needs, for, by the end of the harvest, hundreds of thousands of tons of cane have passed along their conveyor belts."[4]

As in the past, when the railroads solved the problem of how to market the finished product, they once again came to the rescue of the sugar business, this time to solve the problem of the reception of raw material. The question arose as soon as the construction of the first large sugar mill was undertaken. Immediately after the project for the centralization of the San Joaquín was drawn up, conde Ibáñez went to the managers of Ferrocarril de Matanzas and asked them to assign a number of railroad cars for transporting sugarcane.[5] Even though the Matanzas Company entered into the business with some reservations, it carried 39,658 tons of sugarcane the following year, which brought it 15,098 pesos in income. In the 1882 sugarcane harvest, Ferrocarril de Matanzas transported only half as much sugarcane because two other companies broke into the new business: Bahía and Cárdenas y Júcaro.

In 1885, over 125,000 tons of sugarcane was carried by rail. The three companies just mentioned were the only ones offering this service, which shows that, in general, centralization had not reached beyond the bounds of Matanzas Province. The process attained its greatest strength between 1886 and 1894, sweeping through the main sugarcane-growing regions in the island. In 1895, all of the railroad companies in the western part of Cuba reported the movement of large volumes of sugarcane over their tracks. Table 8.1 shows the magnitude of that new line of cargo.

Since the companies listed here include neither Ferrocarril de Oeste nor Ferrocarril de Sagua, which (especially the latter) usually transported large quantities of sugarcane, it is perfectly reasonable to estimate that a fourth of the sugarcane milled in the great harvest of 1895 was carried by public service railroads.

However, it cannot be said that the railroad companies were particularly ecstatic about this new task. Some of them didn't even bother to hide their annoyance. In 1882, the board of directors of Ferrocarril de Cárdenas y Júcaro informed its stockholders that "the transportation of sugarcane to be milled in the central sugar mills has been begun on a large scale. This innovation, which is

TABLE 8.1. Volume of Cane Transported by Rail during the Harvest of 1895

Company	Volume of Cane in Arrobas	Income	Percent of Total Cargo
FC Unidos de La Habana	69,114,400	252,876	14
FC de Matanzas	48,350,000	172,196	16
FC de Cienfuegos y Villa Clara	17,226,084	28,659	7
FC de Cárdenas y Júcaro	51,119,631	114,929	11

Sources: Ferrocarriles Unidos de La Habana, Memoria (1894), pp. 41, 95, ANC, Fondo Ferrocarriles (Ferrocarril de Matanzas), legajo 23, expediente 1, estado 4; Ferrocarril de Cárdenas y Júcaro, Memoria (1894–95), p. 6; Ferrocarril de Cienfuegos y Villa Clara, Memorias (1894–95), p. 30.

more harmful than beneficial to the railroad companies, is imposed by force of circumstances."[6]

While the transportation of sugarcane became a new source of income for the railroad companies, the business was not very profitable when you consider the large volume of freight and low price that were involved. Since they couldn't impose high rates for hauling cane, which was a low-price item, the public railroads tried to compensate for that negative aspect of the business by using loads of cane as a means of ensuring that they would transport the sugar, whose handling did bring a good profit. A clause that committed the contracting estate owner to use the services of the railroad company to haul the sugar and its byproducts became an obligatory part of all the contracts the railroad companies entered into for transporting sugarcane.[7]

Transporting cane meant that the public service railroads had to acquire and maintain a tremendous amount of rolling stock that was used for only four or five months a year. In addition, they had to make enormous investments in branch lines, sidings, and other work related to the tracks to facilitate taking the sugarcane from the plantations to the sugar mills. Naturally, the railroad companies managed things so as to pass a large part of those expenses on to the estate owners, who owned most of the branch lines and sugarcane sidings. The railroad companies built them for an agreed price, which they nearly always added as a surcharge to the normal transportation rates.

The companies also adopted a policy of reducing the rates in those cases in which the cane was transported in cars belonging to the estate owners, as an inducement to them to acquire rolling stock, generally from the companies themselves. If any thrifty estate owners dug in their heels about making those purchases, delays in the railroad company's making its cars available to the estate owners during the harvest and other difficulties in the service provided powerful arguments in favor of their getting their own cars.

The many initiatives that the railroad companies adopted to keep the transportation of sugarcane within economically advantageous bounds were not enough to prevent other difficulties in the service, however. By 1885, the managers of Ferrocarril de Cárdenas y Júcaro were already complaining that the twenty-seven branch lines and forty-one sidings with which the company operated constituted a nuisance for the organization of traffic.[8] And this was when centralization had barely begun. Five years later, when the invention of the sugarcane transshipper revolutionized loading by making it possible to multiply the number of loading points and, therefore, of sidings, the traffic situation became even more tense, though the greater speed which the new apparatus gave to loading and unloading the cars allowed for better use of the rolling stock.

The conditions in transporting sugarcane grew considerably worse starting in 1890, when, after prolonged stagnation, sugar production began to increase rapidly. Then, the proliferation of branch lines and sidings and the tremendous circulation of trains created veritable chaos in railroad traffic that not only reduced the efficiency of the service but also caused unaccustomed wear and tear on the tracks and breakdowns for trains.

The Revista de Agricultura described the transportation situation in the 1890 sugarcane harvest as follows: "During the last harvest, there was a generalized outcry by our estate owners over the lack of rolling stock, not only for transporting the cane but also for carrying the processed sugar, which remained piled at the packing plants for nearly two months, until it could be taken to the warehouses and ports of embarkation."[9]

Echoing the feelings of the estate owners, the magazine called for an increase in the rolling stock and in the operating efficiency of the railroad companies, plus reductions in several rates. In the 1891 sugarcane harvest, with a sudden growth in production of nearly 200,000 tons of sugar, the transportation situation became critical. The amount of cane proved too great for the public service railroads to' handle. Stable service was provided for taking sugar to the ports, using relatively concentrated loading points, but the haulage of the cane implied the public railroads' complete subordination to the needs of sugar production, turning them into bridges between the unstable, complex sphere of agriculture and the systematic demands of the sugar industry.

It became obvious to everyone that the public railroads could not assume the formidable task that the foreseeable increase in sugar production would place on their shoulders. The estate owners and railroad companies, therefore, took the steps required to enable the sugar mills to assume autonomous operation of the small railroad networks that connected them with the plantations. The construction of private branch lines and the railroad companies' sale of cars to the estate owners was then completed with sales of locomotives and the granting of authorization for the private sugarcane trains to use the public service tracks during the sugarcane harvests.[10] Prodded by the demands of a service that they could not continue to provide, the public railroads contributed to the development of the private railroads, younger brothers that weren't always friendly.

The use of railroads as a collateral element in commercial or productive installations dated back to the 1850s in Cuba, when the owners of warehouses, quarries, and other installations began to request the colonial government for authorization to lay short stretches of track (rarely more than five kilometers long) for their own use, to facilitate the movement of cargo in their businesses. Some of the estate owners adopted exactly the same procedure to use trains to alleviate "the great inconveniences incurred in transporting produce in carts along extremely poor roads to the railroads with which they are related."[11]

In general, the cars were pulled along those short tracks by draft animals or the tracks had been laid solely to facilitate circulation of the public railroad's rolling stock, so it could reach the manufacturing installations belonging to the track's owners. The few privately owned tracks that existed in the sugar sector linked the sugar mill communities with the public service railroad lines. In 1873, only one sugar mill (José Barrio's Santa Catalina) was reported to be using a railroad line to connect the sugar mill community with the fields of cane that supplied it.

That situation began to change rapidly, starting in 1875. Progress in the technology of smelting (and especially the development of steel) in that era gradually brought down the price of the tracks' materials and made it possible for larger numbers of people to buy them. Moreover, there was the recent invention of the "portable railroad," which seemed made to order to meet the sugarcane plantations' needs. It consisted of a track composed of sections around ten feet long and thirty or fifty centimeters wide, built of light-weight rails (sixteen or twenty-five pounds) joined by metal crossties. Cars loaded with up to 2.5 tons of sugarcane could circulate on it. Since the system could be taken apart, it could be moved from one field to another as the harvest advanced. The new technique, which offered great efficiency, spread rapidly, and 118 of Cuba's sugar mills used portable railroads in the 1879 harvest.[12] Too much importance shouldn't be placed on that technology, however; portable railroads were never more than an efficient substitute for carts in the conditions typical of the era, in which plantations had from 535 to 670 hectares planted to sugarcane, and the distances the railroad had to cover were relatively short.

The concentration of the sugar industry revolutionized the concept of the private railroads, assigning them a function that would remain the keynote of that transportation system in the subsequent era. Up until the 1880s, the overwhelm-

Temporary Railroad. Such removable equipment was used to transport cane, especially by the private companies of the central factories.

TABLE 8.2. Construction of Private Branch Lines along the Route of
Ferrocarriles Unidos de La Habana, 1880–1890

Year	Number of Branch Lines	Length (in kilometers)
Before 1880	8	25.457
1881	2	6.794
1882	2	1.398
1883	1	—
1884	—	—
1885	—	—
1886	2	9.857
1887	1	6.637
1888	4	8.608
1889	8	20.067
1890	11	20.545
Total	39	99.444

Source: Banco de Comercio, Almacenes de Regla y Ferrocarriles Unidos de La Habana,
Memoria (1889–90), p. 43.

ing majority of the railroads listed as privately owned were, in fact, nothing more
than small branch lines of public railroads, without any operational autonomy.
Most of the private rail development that occurred in the 1880s was also of that
kind, although carried out with such intensity that it gave special significance to
that phenomenon. The construction of the private branches linked to Ferrocarriles Unidos de La Habana is a good example of this (see Table 8.2).[13]

The fact that two-thirds of the branch lines were built in the 1886–90 period,
when centralization was sweeping the country, reflects the concentration of the
sugar industry. The short length of the branch lines (which averaged only two or
three kilometers) shows that, like most of the sugar mill branches, they lacked
autonomy and were, in fact, part of the public railroad systems. Naturally, there
were some exceptions, and they are important because they soon became the
norm. Especially in the area around Cienfuegos, where the public railroad did not
consist of a network in the strict sense of the word (up until 1890, the Cienfuegos–
Villa Clara line had no branches), the estate owners who were involved in the process of centralization realized that they would have to establish important private
lines. Such was the case of the fifty-kilometer-long narrow-gauge system linking
the Lequeitio and San Agustín sugar mills, both owned by Agustín Goytisolo, with
the public railroad's tracks, and also of the ninety-eight-kilometer-long system

Sugarcane train of Central Soledad in Guantánamo. (W. H. Carlson, *Report of the Special Commissioner on Railroads*, p. 192. Havana, 1901)

leading from the public track to the Caracas sugar mill, owned by the Terry family. This last was the most important sugarcane railroad of its time.

The previously small group of sugar mills with real railroads of their own grew quite quickly as the sugarcane transportation crisis became critical. Motivated by the need to guarantee and stabilize their supplies of raw material, the most powerful estate owners took the steps needed to obtain autonomy in transporting sugarcane to their mills. As already pointed out, the public railroads, which wanted to ease the pressure that the transportation of sugarcane created for their other services, helped them to do so. Moreover, whenever it didn't interfere with their main interest of transporting sugar and its by-products, the public companies provided the indispensable service of giving the sugarcane railroads access to their port installations for shipping their products out.[14]

The new trend could be seen everywhere in the growing number of requests that the Oficina de Obras Públicas (Office of Public Works) of the colonial administration began to receive starting in 1888, asking for authorization to introduce steam traction in the private railroads.[15] When they had their own equipment for hauling the cars, the estate owners became completely independent in transporting their sugarcane, turning what had been mere private railway lines into railroads that could carry out all of the functions proper to that means of transportation.

Once they had become an integral part of the sugar production cycle, railroads helped to structure that sector of the economy. Slow and hazardous transportation by cart ceased to be an obstacle holding back the enlargement of the plantations, whose cane fields could now be extended, thanks to the railroads, in consonance with the growth of the sugar mills' industrial capacity. Railroads played a key role in the process of centralizing agricultural ownership, with large latifundist plantations becoming the economic unit typical of the sugar sector.

Moreover, the estate owners immediately became aware of an important additional advantage that would accrue from having their own railroads. Small-scale sugarcane growers who used the services of public railroads could sell their cane to the highest bidder and usually got a fairly good price, but those who had to use a private railroad to take their cane out would have to accept the price set by the estate owner whose railroad they used. In the hands of the estate owners, railroads became powerful tools for monopolizing the raw material, and the sugar mills engaged in fierce competition for the exclusive right to lay their lines in the sugarcane-growing regions. A contemporary described that process clearly:

> New sugar mills were created. The railroads sent their steel tentacles out in search of fertile new plantations, and one day two sugar mills that, some years before, had been separated by extremely thick forests began competing at the ends of their lines for areas that were good for planting sugarcane, and each of the rivals sought to ruin the other, trying to get the owners to give it the exclusive right to run its locomotives through their land.[16]

Stimulated by such diverse circumstances, private railroads grew and gradually acquired their present characteristics. At the end of the century, official records recognized the existence of 107 duly legalized private railroads, 93 of which served sugar mills. Of these sugarcane railroads, 56 had their own locomotives, and some of them (the one serving the Caracas sugar mill, for example) had more locomotives than some of the public service companies. At that time, the private railroads had a total of 1,394 kilometers of track, just 500 kilometers less than all the track in the public service network, which dated from much earlier.[17] The private railroads had come of age as a transportation system.

Industrialization of the sugar sector required essential changes in the prevailing relations of production. The abolition of slavery became absolutely necessary for the Cuban economy, and the abolition movement could no longer be considered motivated by more or less powerful pressures from abroad. The old system, based on the ownership of men, had been denounced by the countries that had adopted the modern mode of capitalist production, for which the work force, now a commodity, should circulate freely in the market. Such ideas had even been echoed by the liberal Spanish government, but the War of Independence that the Cubans began in 1868 was the decisive factor accelerating the end of the slave system in Cuba, for it declared that all the inhabitants of the island were free.[18] Ten years later, the Zanjón peace treaty confirmed the historic validity of that action by ratifying the freedom of all slaves and small-scale Asian sugarcane growers who had fought on the side of the pro-independence forces.

The social and political circumstances created by the war forced the Spanish government in 1870 to decree what became known as the "free bellies" law. That law stated that all slaves' children born on or after September 17, 1868, would be free, though they would be under the guardianship of their mothers' owners until they turned eighteen. The law also freed the slaves who had served in the war under the Spanish flag, those who were owned by the state, and slaves over sixty years old.[19]

In spite of all laws and international conventions, the slave trade continued until 1873, but on a much smaller scale. Together with this, the internal factors that favored the dissolution of the system (such as the war itself, the high mortality rate, and the reduction in the slave trade) caused a decrease in the number of slaves, both men and women. In 1871, there had been 287,653 slaves; in 1878, there were 184,030. That is, the number had dropped by 36 percent.[20]

Chinese and Spanish immigrants who arrived in Cuba as indentured workers replaced the slaves as manpower. Though involving payment of a wage, the indentures maintained nearly the same degree of exploitation as had the system of slavery. The terms which conde Ibáñez, an estate owner, imposed on the immigrants from the Canary Islands whom he imported in 1878 are an eloquent example of the regimen governing free labor in Cuba at that time. The wages paid to Chinese workers shortly before then had been between 4.56 and 4.80 pesos a month, so the conde "generously" paid each worker 8.00 pesos a month plus food (but deducted 2 pesos a month for payment of the worker's passage and to cover other expenses he had incurred). For this amount, each man was expected to work twelve hours a day Monday through Saturday and six hours on Sunday.[21]

The Spanish Cortes considered the need formally to abolish slavery, which had been speeded by the effects of the Ten Years' War, and it expressed that need in its February 1880 law on the abolition of slavery, better known as the Ley del Patronato (Sponsorship Law). The text of that law established an eight-year transition period leading to the definitive abolition of slavery. During that time, each of the "sponsored" would be fed and clothed by his "sponsor"—that is, his former owner—and exploited by him. Each "sponsored" between the ages of eighteen and twenty-five would be paid a wage of two pesos a month, and each "sponsored" over twenty-five years old would receive three pesos a month.[22] Even though it did not, in fact, mean the abolition of slavery, the law provided the mechanisms for replacing one form of exploitation with another when it was in the interests of the sponsors to do so.

By the beginning of the 1880s, before the old forms of work had been totally eliminated but when most of the workers in Cuba were already being paid wages, more than half of the railroad companies were hiring free workers. As a result, the different manifestations of the exploitation of labor that had succeeded each other throughout the century coexisted for some time.

This collection of coexisting forms of the use of manpower caused a lot of uneasiness among the owners of the railroads concerning how to maintain discipline among their slave laborers and other day laborers, who were constantly exposed to the "bad example" of the freedmen.[23]

In spite of that difficulty, 18.5 percent of the day laborers working for Ferrocarril de Cárdenas y Júcaro, which had used slave labor on a massive scale, were still slaves as late as June 1883. Another 27.9 percent of those laborers, who did the hardest work, were indentured Chinese, and the remaining 53.6 percent were free workers. By paying a variable sum in cash to the company, some of the slaves owned by that railroad purchased their freedom; the rest (twenty-eight in all) were freed by the board of directors later on.[24]

In some cases, the conversion of slave labor into free increased the payroll expenses for certain tasks. "More has been spent on the stokers, yard crews, and woodcutters than in 1881–82 because, since the Negroes who remained would soon be freed from sponsorship, it wouldn't be possible to count on any of them."[25]

Even so, ending slavery and sponsorship was to the companies' economic advantage, as shown in the 1885 report issued by the board of directors of Ferrocarril de Cárdenas y Júcaro:

> Complying with the decision of the stockholders' meeting that was held last October 30, twenty-seven of the remaining "sponsored" were emancipated on May 8, which reduced the expenses for day laborers, since they were mainly engaged in cutting wood and, when the contracts for the coming sugarcane harvest were drawn up, it was stipulated that, when the price was raised, the wood would be provided already cut, ready to use. With emancipation, it has been possible to close the infirmary at Cárdenas, which had cost $3,100 in gold a year.[26]

Each case of sponsorship had also cost the company three pesos a month, as established by law. In addition, the end of sponsorship meant that the company was freed of the obligation to feed and clothe the "sponsored," in however rudi-

TABLE 8.3. Ferrocarril de Sagua La Grande Company Expenses, 1865–1880 (in pesos)

Item	1865	1877	1880
Wages of Asians	6,465	1,300	936
Salaries of Emancipados	445	—	—
Rental of Negroes	7,129	600	136
Wages of Daily Workers	11,809	100,100	90,565

Source: Ferrocarril de Sagua La Grande, Memorias de la Junta Directiva (1865, 1878, 1880).

mentary a fashion. Moreover, tasks could then be contracted out for only those months in which they were necessary (during the sugarcane harvest). The savings resulting from closing down the infirmary was also considerable.

Other companies that had been less addicted to the use of slaves had modified the composition of their day laborers much more quickly. The payroll expenses of Ferrocarril de Sagua la Grande between 1865 and 1880 shows this clearly (see Table 8.3).

While the elimination of the slave trade and the abolition of slavery resulted in savings in the amounts allocated for the work force, they made it impossible for the estate owners and the railroad companies to compel their workers to serve their interests. This situation led some contractors to import the number of hands they deemed necessary to guarantee low-priced manpower on their estates and in companies of all kinds.

The number of white immigrants in the era in which slavery prevailed had been small, but this changed after 1880, when white workers were brought in on a much larger scale. In just four expeditions, railroad potentate conde de Casa Moré brought 1,162 immigrants to Cuba from the Canary Islands. Marquises of Sandoval and of Placetas brought in over 1,000 men between 1881 and 1883, through the ports of Bahía Honda and Caibarién.[27]

The end of sponsorship in 1880 put an end to slavery in Cuba, and the day laborers who had been under the absolute control of the owners up until then were placed under a regimen of free contracting of work. That situation led the new proletarians to engage in an ongoing search not only for the highest wages but also for estates on which the "sugar mill stores,"[28] which were generalized, would cheat them less and where, at some point, they might have a little cash in hand at the end of the sugarcane harvests.[29]

That freedom of movement caused the estate owners to lament nostalgically when analyzing the reasons for the higher wages they had to pay their work force at the beginning of the 1891–92 sugarcane harvest:

> A third cause consists of the day laborers' great mobility, which is easier now because of the facilities they have for traveling on the many railroads that cross certain regions, especially our sugarcane-growing areas. Compared with earlier periods, when work was regimented and such movement wasn't possible, there are considerable numbers of those people, who are always passing through, who never stay on the same estate for three days running, and who have already become accustomed to that kind of nomadic life.[30]

The movement of workers from one place to another was not a characteristic exclusive to the recently freed slaves but was rather a generalized phenomenon of those who did physical labor to earn their living. Chinese, Spanish, and white and black Cuban day laborers constantly went from one sugar mill to another to offer their manpower, the only thing they had to sell, still lacking the energy to create a united proletariat. At the beginning, the Cuban proletariat was heterogeneous, not only in terms of its national origins but also in terms of the regimen of exploitation to which its members had been subjected in the past as "sponsored" slaves, indentured laborers whom growers reduced to semislavery, contracted immigrants, and free workers who were contracted directly by their employers.

The men who were contracted by the railroad companies were heterogeneous in their origins, too: Cubans and Spaniards held the better-paying jobs; Spaniards, Chinese, and white and black Cubans served as stokers, brakemen, and day laborers. Their shared work gradually smoothed away their differences, but, at first, they were a negative factor holding back the creation of a homogeneous class awareness.

Except for the occasional hiring of day laborers by a contractor in charge of repair work or construction, the relations between the workers and the railroad companies usually began when a man entered (generally) the railroad workshop as an apprentice. Like the apprentices at the dawn of European capitalism, such a man received no pay until the head of the workshop considered him efficient at some task. In the second stage, such a worker was usually paid no more than two pesos a month.[31]

Once he had gone through the first stages of work and was doing a definite task, the most the railroad worker could aspire to be paid was 100 pesos a month—which, of course, was a high wage in the 1890s—in the posts requiring the greatest skill and trust. Table 8.4 presents some figures on the wages paid by two Cuban railroad companies in 1893–94.

Since the railway employees had to pay for their meals and lodging at the end

TABLE 8.4. Wage Rates of Ferrocarriles Urbanos de La Habana and Ferrocarril de Sancti Spíritus a Tunas, 1893–1894 (in pesos)

Job or position	Salary
Station chief	60–100
Conductor	50–80
Machinist	68–100
Assistant machinist	30–50
Fireman	34–35
Handyman, switchman, brakesman, and others	20–30

Sources: *Gaceta de los Ferrocarriles de la isla de Cuba*, November 30, 1894, p. 303; *Gaceta de los Ferrocarriles de la isla de Cuba*, October 5, 1893, p. 185.
Note: Salary reflects the range of both enterprises.

of the line, their wages, in real terms, were much lower. This situation often led those employees to fall into the clutches of the usurers who abounded in that era, giving rise to claims addressed to their employers that their wages be attached in payment of their debts. In such cases, the owners solved the problem by simply firing the workers.[32]

The engineers, stokers, conductors, and platform personnel usually worked eighteen hours a day, nonstop except for one ten-minute break for lunch and another, also ten minutes long, for dinner. Then they had five or six hours in which to rest before beginning all over again.[33]

Cuban workers at the end of the century had no social security. One of the basic aspirations of the proletariat was protection in case of illness, disability, or death for those who were dependent on the fruits of their labor. When a worker failed to go to work because he was sick, had had an accident, or had personal problems, the railroad company did not pay him for that time, which meant an immediate saving for the company, and it fired the worker if he stayed away too long—no company allowed a worker to stay away for more than two months, and some, less.

Service Order 21 of 1894, issued by one of the largest railroad companies on the island, stated that a substitute worker would be paid a fifth of the wage normally paid for the job during the first month and a quarter of the normal wage the second month. If the regular worker didn't return at the end of that time, he was fired, and his job was given to somebody else.[34]

The case of workers who became too old to do their work or were prevented from working as the result of an accident was even more unfair. Moreover, the widows and children of workers who died were left to fend for themselves, even if the deceased had worked for the railroad company for a long time. In both cases, only occasionally did the owners give the needy any charity.[35]

As was only to be expected, the low wages of the track, construction, and repair shop workers; the poor working conditions of the train crews; and their lack of job and social security led to the first workers' protests in the railroad sector and also to the first solutions of a cooperative nature, forerunners of unity and a system of organized mutual aid. The first halting expressions of the railroad workers' movement were strikes, the most vigorous form of workers' struggle, and the organization of mutual aid societies, which were also a classic phenomenon in the early history of the proletariat as a social class. The former (strikes) were local actions by isolated groups of workers against individual companies or company officials. The latter (mutual aid societies) managed to achieve a (weak) national character in the railroad sector, though, at first, they didn't go beyond the bounds of a single company.

The workers began to use strikes as a weapon in their struggle at the same time the mutual aid societies were created, and, like them, the strikes were strictly local affairs. The first mention of a railroad strike is contained in the records of the Sagua la Grande Railroad Company, in 1885. The strike was called in response to the company's decision to lower the wages of the lowest-paid workers. The day laborers and stokers expressed their opposition to the measure by refusing to work and trying to get the rest of the workers to support them. The strike interfered with the movement of the trains, so the company called in the police, who crushed the protest.[36]

The workers in the Ciénaga and Batabanó repair shops went out on strike on May 6, 1890, demanding higher wages.[37] The fact that, in this case, a group of strikers went to the station and repair shops in Regla to spread the strike and that the strike was called simultaneously in two such distant places as Batabanó and Havana shows that there had been some prior agreement to guarantee participation by a large number of workers, which extended the local nature of the movement.

In July 1892, a conflict broke out in the machine shops of the Matanzas Railroad when the company ordered the head of the shop, J. Valladares, to fire several workers. When Valladares refused to do so and resigned in protest, the company replaced him with an Englishman, Mr. Tynan, and brought in less experienced workers to replace the strikers.[38] The situation was aggravated when the engineers joined the strike and the company made an unsuccessful attempt to replace them with strikebreakers contracted in the capital. In solidarity with their comrades in Matanzas, the Havana engineers refused to work, which led the company to set a deadline before which its workers would have to get back on the job. Thus, it tried to get the key workers to give up their demands and go back to work.[39]

The strike lasted for around twenty days, winding up formally on July 23, 1892, when a compromise was reached and signed by the marquis of Altagracia, on behalf of the company, and Miguel Eiguerra, for the workers. In that document, it was agreed that those of the strikers whose jobs had not been covered by strikebreakers would return to work, and the rest of the workers (the less necessary ones) would wait "for the company to call them." In practice, the agreement enabled the company to teach a lesson to the workers who had supported the strike most firmly.[40]

As noted earlier, the search for some timid solutions for the problems caused by lack of social security led some groups of railroad workers to create mutual aid societies. The first of these societies which functioned in this sector in Cuba included the Caja de Ahorros y Sociedad de Socorros Mutuos de los Empleados de la Compañía de Caminos de Hierro de La Habana, which, even though it sought to unite only the workers of a single company, went beyond the limits of a single place or of a single province, because of that company's size.[41]

The Sociedad de Empleados de los Ferrocarriles, which was founded in a preparatory meeting held in Havana on October 21, 1894, went beyond the limited, local aspirations of that society.[42] Representatives of Ferrocarril de Cienfuegos, Ferrocarriles Unidos de La Habana, Ferrocarril de Caibarién, Ferrocarril de Cárdenas y Júcaro, and other companies attended the meeting. They decided that the institution would be a corporation, with stock that railroad employees would purchase through 2 percent deductions of their monthly wages. It had two main sections: benefits (in case of need) and savings (which would function like a bank, receiving savings as capital and making loans at a low rate of interest).[43]

The corporation was formally constituted in a stockholders' meeting on December 9, 1894, which was attended by twenty-two employees, some of whom were chosen to be its officers. Those employees were also officials of the most powerful railroad companies.[44] A month after its founding, the corporation had 277 members throughout the country, and a branch was established in the important Sagua la Grande Railroad yard in April.[45] The Matanzas, Cienfuegos, and Santa Clara Railroads, however, turned it a deaf ear.[46]

An analysis of the members that was made in mid-1895 shows the Sociedad's lack of importance, especially among the lowest-paid workers. On June 30, 1895, it had a total membership of 357 (around 4 or 5 percent of the active railway workers in the country). Of them, 171 were operating personnel, 56 worked on track maintenance and in construction, 51 worked in the engines, 50 were office workers, and 29 were in the carpentry shops.[47] Their distribution by railroad company was as follows: 292 worked for Ferrocarriles de La Habana; 33, for Ferrocarril de Sagua la Grande; 16, for Ferrocarril Urbano in the capital; 6, for Ferrocarril del Oeste; 3, for Ferrocarril de Cienfuegos; and 2, for Ferrocarril de Cárdenas y Júcaro.[48]

By July 1895, the Sociedad had a capital of 2,500 pesos and had issued loans totaling 2,384 pesos.[49] The close relationship between those two amounts shows that the savings capacity of its members was similar to their need for loans, which indicates that the organization must have been in quite precarious financial straits.

In 1895, the number of members grew slowly, reaching a peak in December of that year with 476 members out of a total of nearly 8,000 railroad workers at the time.[50] Starting the next year, the Sociedad's membership began to decline, as did its funds, when workers were fired in response to the effects of the War of Independence, which had been resumed on February 24, 1895.

The Sociedad's political position was expressed in the guidelines to its members which it issued in January 1896, urging them to abstain from taking out loans and to use their 2 percent wage deductions to purchase railroad company shares, instead, to help the companies in the midst of the war.[51] The attitude taken with regard to nationality was even clearer. "The situation with which the country is faced is no concern of the Sociedad de Empleados y Obreros, for its purposes aren't political and it seeks only to achieve well-being for white- and blue-collar workers."[52] Because of its ineffectiveness and lack of prestige, the Sociedad de Empleados de los Ferrocarriles declined from 1896 on.[53]

The intensity and rapidity with which the war against the Spanish colonial yoke was resumed in February 1895 brought out the real dimensions of the Cuban people's decades-long struggle for national independence. The Mambí forces' goal of destroying the sugar industry in the western provinces in order to cut off the colonial government's main source of income was achieved in less than a year of military operations, thanks to the skill of the great strategists of the war, Generals Máximo Gómez and Antonio Maceo, and the daring of the Cuban forces.

When the countryside was put to the torch, the rural population lost its source of work. In the cities, only a few industries (such as those making cigars and shoes) continued to function, barely providing sustenance for small groups of workers.[54]

The war accentuated the workers' poverty, and the polarization of the forces engaged in the struggle was reflected in the heterogeneous mass of workers, leading them to take different positions. Many of the railroad workers were Spaniards, and the companies frequently gave bonuses for the "patriotic services" rendered by some of their employees. Those services generally consisted of taking military trains to war zones and especially of putting in extremely long hours providing telegraph services or using trains to support military activities.

The situation in the railroad sector was largely determined by the origins of the companies' boards of directors, for most of them were composed of recalcitrant supporters of Integrismo (which sought to keep Cuba under colonial rule so as to preserve Spain's national "integrity"). They often made decisions that lowered

TABLE 8.5. Comparative Data of the "Economies" Obtained by the Ferrocarril de Matanzas a Sabanillas through Wages and Daily Rates, 1895–1896

Salaries of	1895	1896
Employees	68,752	50,317
Telegraphists	11,527	8,470
Total	80,279	58,787
Daily payment for workers in		
Machinery	88,437	36,898
Carpentry	45,422	13,662
Masonry	2,871	530
Peonage (exploitation)	80,852	40,579
Track repair	74,388	22,377
Total	372,249	172,833

Source: *Gaceta de los Ferrocarriles de la isla de Cuba*, February 14, 1897, p. 21.

the workers' wages. For example, the boards of directors of Ferrocarril de Cárdenas y Júcaro, Caibarién, Matanzas, Sagua, and Cienfuegos resolved that each corporation should contribute 0.50 for every 10,000 pesos of its capital stock and 1.5 percent of the workers' assets to help enlarge and improve the navy.[55] Ferrocarriles Unidos de La Habana offered Captain General Valeriano Weyler a contribution of 10 percent of its employees' wages in 1896 when two troop-transport trains collided in Güines.[56]

Starting in mid-1895, the owners' policy of lowering wages and firing workers spread to nearly all of Cuba's railroads, though each company used a different procedure. Some, such as Ferrocarriles Unidos de La Habana in its Ciénaga repair shops, reduced the number of workdays per worker rather than the number of workers.[57] Others, such as Ferrocarril de Puertro Príncipe a Nuevitas, adopted proportional wage reductions, which ranged from 10 to 30 percent of the workers' wages.[58]

For their part, the boards of directors of Ferrocarril de Matanzas and Ferrocarril de Santiago de Cuba arbitrarily combined wage cuts, layoffs, and reductions in work hours to suit their interests.[59] In 1896, Ferrocarriles Unidos de La Habana fired 569 of its 2,167 workers, thus saving 408,701 pesos (41 percent) of its 983,460-peso 1895 payroll.[60]

The "savings" were achieved mainly at the expense of the lowest-paid workers, with white-collar workers' wages cut much less drastically. A comparison of the wages Ferrocarril de Matanzas paid in 1895 and 1896, presented in Table 8.5, illustrates this.

The salaries of the office workers and telegraph operators were cut by nearly 27 percent from one year to the next, while the wages paid for all other work were slashed by over 53 percent. The measures that were taken to fire workers and reduce their wages were applied with a political yardstick. Those who supported Integrismo were kept on, and unconditional servitors of the owners, who were expected to do more than just their jobs, were rewarded with bonuses and wage increases.

When the War of Independence took front stage center and the railroads became willing tools in the Spaniards' military operations, the railroad companies began to discriminate among their workers, which tended to accentuate their differences. Contrary to what might be supposed, however, that policy was not entirely successful, even among the Spanish workers, some of whom were sympathetic to the Cubans' aspirations and took their side against the oppressors of their class brothers.

9

Denationalization

During the years between the Ten Years' War and the War of Independence, transformations were wrought in Cuba that defined technical and organizational aspects of the sugar industry and modified the country's social structure. Important socioeconomic changes took place within a political framework characterized by the crisis of Spanish colonial rule in a series of alternating periods of peace and war.

Just as the technical innovations that were introduced in the sugar industry had substantially changed the organization of production and the social base that underlay the labor system, that industry's decisive weight in the country's economy—and especially in railroad services—meant that it became a matter of pressing importance for them to adapt to the new needs. Since the tracks and rolling stock had been subjected to intensive use during the ten years of the war and had been neither repaired nor replaced, the railway system was not in optimal condition for meeting the needs of the sugar sector in the precarious peace that began in 1878. Moreover, the end of the war meant the restoration of competition among the various companies in the western part of the country to the same level as had existed prior to the war. The outbreak of hostilities on February 24, 1895, involved all the railways in the military campaigns, not only causing the destruction of installations and rolling stock but also speeding the process of transfers to foreign capital, which had begun years earlier.

Starting in 1878, in view of the increased demand for transportation services and competition, the western companies turned all their efforts to carrying as much freight as possible and adopted whatever advantages contemporary technological advances had to offer. The companies in the eastern part of the island, which had been much harder hit by the war—not only directly but also by the destruction of the sugar mills and sugarcane in the areas they served—set about reconstruction with the same aims as the western companies, but at a great disadvantage.

The process of technological change affected Cuba's railroads from 1878 on. This was shown mainly in the improvement of the tracks and in the increased capacity of the locomotives. In the case of the tracks, the change consisted in replacing the iron rails, which had been characteristic of the railroad up until then (and from which the Spanish name, ferrocarril, or iron rail, was derived), with new rails with a steel surface, which were much more resistant to wear and tear. In the case of the locomotives, a series of modifications was introduced that allowed for the construction of much heavier and faster locomotives, which guaranteed greater hauling capacity. When this kind of locomotive was adopted, the bridges had to be either reinforced or rebuilt, using iron girders. Railroad technology was also modified with the application of vacuum brakes in passenger trains—and later, toward the 1890s, in freight trains, as well—and the installation of automatic switches.[1]

The technological norm followed in the construction of tracks in Cuba up to the 1860s had been that of using iron rails that normally weighed no more than sixty pounds a meter, which were laid on a bed that was not always ballasted. Steel rails were probably first introduced in Cuba in 1871; that was when the Ferrocarril de la Bahía Company decided to purchase that kind of rails for its Guanabacoa branch—which, because of its intensive use, had become much more worn than the rest of the company's lines. It was hoped that these rails would last five or six times as long as the iron ones.[2] As it was pointed out that the cost of steel rails was similar to that of iron ones, several companies set about renewing their tracks in this way when they became worn. In other cases, it became necessary to replace old tracks sooner than would ordinarily have been done, due to their general deterioration and to the continued incorporation of heavier locomotives. One of the companies that advanced in this process most quickly was Caminos de Hierro de La Habana, which, by 1887, had replaced 75 percent of its track with steel rails from Germany and the United States. When that company merged with Bahía in 1889, some 87 percent of the track of the new company consisted of steel rails; that figure was raised to 91 percent in 1895.[3] Other companies, such as those of Matanzas, Cienfuegos, and Puerto Príncipe, purchased their rails from French and Belgian companies.[4] The trade agreement that the United States and Spain signed in 1891—the Foster-Cánovas Treaty—reduced tariffs on U.S.-made rails and led to increased rail purchases from the United States.

The new locomotives that were built from 1880 on were perfectly suited to make use of the advantages offered by the steel rails and, in turn, provided tremendous hauling capacity and greater speed, which made it possible for the

TABLE 9.1. Increase in the Number of Freight Cars of Four Railroad
Companies, 1881–1897

Company	1881	1891	1897
FC Unidos de La Habana[a]	1,044	1,402	1,679
FC de Cárdenas y Júcaro	650	885	1,093
FC de Matanzas	551	786	1,031
FC de Cienfuegos y Villa Clara	125	434	468

Source: Reports of the respective companies for the years indicated.
[a]Caminos de Hierro de La Habana and Ferrocarril de la Bahía merged in 1889.

companies to increase freight service without having to increase the number of
trains. Consolidation locomotives, which were made in Philadelphia and had
large-capacity boilers, a new kind of (more efficient) compensated valve, and six
interconnected wheels, with a forward bogie and small wheels at the back, were
among the locomotives that the Cuban companies preferred. "The maximum
effective steam pressure is 9.3 kilograms per square centimeter. Their proportions
are such that, by increasing their weight by only 14 percent and their coal consumption by 35 percent, they can haul an average of 53 percent more than the
most powerful old locomotives."[5]

The intensity with which competition was maintained among the western
companies had led them to seek greater hauling capacity, adding several cars to
the trains and organizing the traffic better—and, therefore, improving operating
conditions. When sturdier locomotives were obtained to meet the railroads' growing needs, it became absolutely necessary to purchase a large number of flats and
boxcars to carry the sugar, and cattle trucks for the sugarcane. Table 9.1 clearly
shows the increase in the number of cars belonging to the four western railroad
companies that owned nearly 65 percent of the tracks in Cuba.

Yet another factor in the panorama of the technological evolution of Cuba's
railroads in the nineteenth century was the trend that was observed starting in the
1850s regarding the use of coal as fuel, which began with Caminos de Hierro de
La Habana and then extended to the rest of the companies as sources of wood
were exhausted. All of the Havana companies switched to coal soon after midcentury, and Ferrocarril de Matanzas used two-thirds coal and only one-third wood in
1880, but the companies that operated in areas where it was still possible to obtain
wood used it as their main fuel.[6] This was true of such companies as Ferrocarril
del Oeste, Guantánamo, and Cárdenas y Júcaro, which even in 1884 stated that
wood was "the only fuel their locomotives used."[7] Even so, they agreed to use coal
in their new rolling stock three years later, so coal constituted 25 percent of their

fuel at that time. Ferrocarril del Oeste also began to burn coal at about that time, using it on 15 percent of the distances its trains covered. In any case, since the use of wood or coal was determined by the availability of forests, it was only a matter of time before coal would replace wood.

In general, the technical innovations that Cuban railroads incorporated before the end of the nineteenth century were adopted mainly in the western provinces, where the sugar industry hadn't been dealt crushing blows in the first armed conflict and where the transformations required by that industry were implemented more thoroughly. The railroads tried to adapt to those transformations because they were faced with the threat of competition and the need to maintain and increase their profits in view of the battering they were given by the turn-of-the-century depression, which resulted in substantial changes in the structure of ownership in a large number of companies.

An economic depression lasted throughout nearly all of the 1873–98 period, and its consequences, which were somewhat confused with those of the war, adversely affected the railroad companies' income. This situation was particularly aggravated in 1880–81 and 1883–84, when sugar production fell far below the levels attained in prior sugarcane harvests, and between 1895 and 1898, mainly because the sugar mills in most of Cuba were destroyed but also because the price of sugar on the world market plummeted starting in 1894. Hard hit by these circumstances, the railroad companies were forced to stabilize their income levels at all costs in order to meet their financial obligations, pay at least a minimal dividend on their stock, and carry out the technological renewal that was urgently required so they could serve the sugar mills, survive in a competitive world, and make needed repairs on and replacements of tracks and rolling stock.

Some companies, especially the ones that operated in the easternmost province and the Nuevitas-Camagüey, suffered directly from the war until 1878. When peace was signed and they set about resuming normal service, they found that their installations had deteriorated greatly. In addition, they didn't have any prospects for immediate recovery, because of the discouraging economic situation in the postwar period. Only a very few of the railroads in the western provinces suffered directly from the war, even though, in general terms, all of those companies had had to place themselves at the service of the war. Nearly all of those companies were involved and adversely affected by military operations in the 1895–98 period, and only in exceptional cases were they able to prevent a sustained drop in their income. Meanwhile, their rolling stock was subjected to intensive use by the Spanish troops and was harassed by the Mambí forces fighting for Cuba's freedom. Both the economic and political situations in the country affected the companies' solvency, which became even more precarious in peacetime. Such was the case of the prosperous Caminos de Hierro de La Habana, whose stock took a beating in 1884 in spite of the company's acknowledged solidity.[8]

The reduction in the volume of freight to be carried and in rates led more than one company—Ferrocarril de Cárdenas y Júcaro and Bahía de La Habana among them—to offer their services at lower rates to attract the business of sugar estates that had traditionally used competing companies and also to keep their own clients from being enticed away.

> The satisfactory results of this company have fallen off in this twenty-eighth fiscal year, due to the crisis now affecting the island, which has had repercussions in the fall in the price of sugar; in view of these circumstances and for the convenience of all, the board of directors has been forced to declare a 20 percent reduction in the rates for sugar and molasses in the 1884–85 sugarcane harvest; as a result, our profits have decreased by 4 percent, compared with those of the last fiscal year.[9]

Figure 9.1, on the income obtained from each kilometer of track, shows how the figures dropped in 1880 and did not return to their former levels until 1892, after which they began to decline again, reaching a critical level when hostilities between Cubans and Spaniards were renewed in 1895. The effects of this long critical period influenced the railroads' stability profoundly, even bringing about the ruin of some companies. The graph shows how the loss of income began to become evident in 1876, and, though it shows a sporadic increase in 1879, the downward trend continued, reaching very low levels between 1883 and 1889. The relative upswing of the curve starting in 1891 reached the same income levels as had been obtained prior to 1875 when sugar production increased, but, with the resumption of the war, the curve dropped again, reaching record lows—less than 2,000 pesos per kilometer—for Cuban railroads. (See Figure 9.1.)

Significantly, the two companies that adopted the desperate policy of reducing their rates between 1883 and 1885—Ferrocarril de Bahía de La Habana and Ferrocarril de Cárdenas y Júcaro—were precisely the ones whose income per kilometer in some of the critical years was the lowest of all. Something similar, though caused by a very different reason starting in 1895, may be observed in Ferrocarril de Matanzas and Ferrocarril de Cárdenas y Júcaro. In those cases, the incredible drop in income per kilometer of track came as a direct result of the Cubans' military operations near the sugar mills on the plains of Colón.

The graph on the main railroad companies' operating costs per kilometer of track (Figure 9.2) presents similar variations, with the companies molding their costs—except during the war—to fit their income. Because costs were somewhat dependent on administrative decisions, however, they reflected greater similarity among the companies and greater stability than income did. It is particularly clear

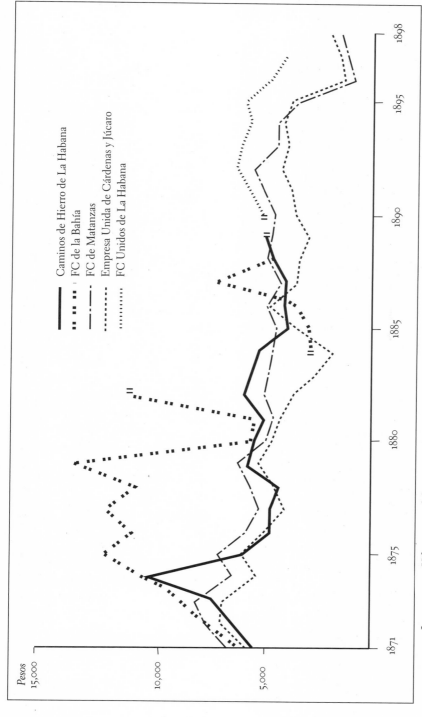

FIGURE 9.1. Income per Kilometer of the Four Main Railroad Companies, 1871–1898

Legend:

Caminos de Hierro de La Habana
FC de la Bahía
FC de Matanzas
Empresa Unida de Cárdenas y Júcaro
FC Unidos de La Habana

Pesos
15,000
10,000
5,000

1871   1875   1880   1885   1890   1895   1898

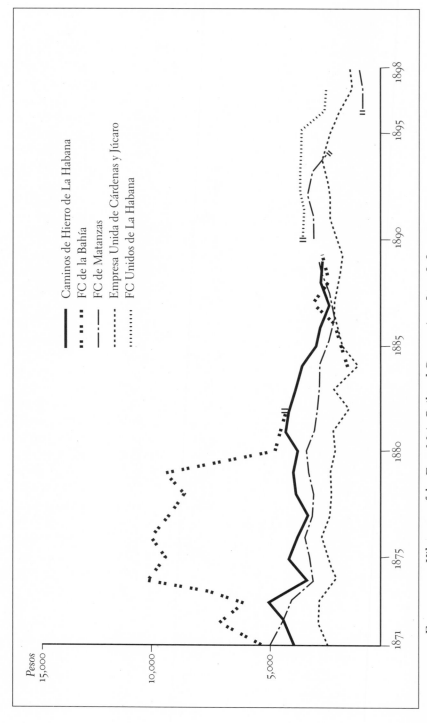

FIGURE 9.2. Expenses per Kilometer of the Four Main Railroad Companies, 1871–1898

Legend:
Caminos de Hierro de La Habana
FC de la Bahía
FC de Matanzas
Empresa Unida de Cárdenas y Júcaro
FC Unidos de La Habana

Pesos
15,000
10,000
5,000

1871 1875 1880 1885 1890 1895 1898

that the Matanzas and Cárdenas y Júcaro Companies reduced their costs to such low levels that they managed to survive during the three years of the war without suffering irreparable ruin, in spite of their meager income. (See Figure 9.2.)

As has been seen, the depression from which the island suffered for more than two decades had serious repercussions in the railroads, breaking the resistance of the ones that were most vulnerable financially. The company that owned the suburban Marianao-Havana Railroad went under during the prolonged crisis; Ferrocarril de la Bahía de La Habana a Matanzas came to the end of its rope; and Ferrocarril del Oeste, which was still trying to thrust westward to the capital of Pinar del Río province, went bankrupt, too. In each of those cases, English capital—which, as the mortgage holder, had previously been limited to the role of banking capital—took over financial control and the direct administration of the railroad in one way or another.

Right from the beginning, the railroad that linked Havana and Marianao had had the least likely prospects for success, not only because of its lack of financial resources but also because of the basis on which its services rested—that is, the transportation of passengers between Havana and the then little-developed town of Marianao, whose population was not large enough to generate sufficient income to repay the original capital outlay for the construction of the line and to meet its financial and operating expenses. Therefore, the company had to be liquidated in 1865. The direct cause for this early decision was the company's inability to make the principal and interest payments due on the 300,000-peso debt it had contracted in 1861 with the firm of William Gibson and Company, of England. As a result of those circumstances, the firm which held the mortgage bonds of Ferrocarril de Marianao filed suit for the company's assets to be auctioned off in 1876. The amount of the debt was 349,746 pesos at the time.[10] Starting with the company's reorganization in 1879, an English name—The Havana-Marianao Railway Company, Limited—appeared for the first time among the Spanish names of Cuba's railroads. Operated directly by foreign interests, this company would be of key importance to absentee English capital in its expansion over Cuba's railroads.

The anarchy that was characteristic of all attempts to lay out Cuban railroads was an early indication of the need for some companies to merge so as to end the competition that constantly threatened their very existence. This trend toward the centralization of services began in the 1850s, when the railroads in Cárdenas merged with those serving the docks at Júcaro; a second merger, between Ferrocarril de la Bahía de La Habana a Matanzas and Caminos de Hierro de La Habana, was effected thirty years later but under conditions that, at the same time, implied the progressive sale of both companies to foreign capital.

Ever since shortly after its founding, Ferrocarril de la Bahía de La Habana had

had so many economic problems that they had become the norm. Even though its tracks were laid out to offer a shorter, faster way to get from Havana to Matanzas and some of the main sugarcane areas in that province, its main competitor, Caminos de Hierro de La Habana, had partially repeated its main trunk line with the construction of a branch from Güines to Matanzas. As a result, the two companies entered into competition with each other—a situation that they tried to solve in 1868 with a merger of the two companies.[11] The attempt failed, however, and the situation could only be alleviated temporarily, between 1878 and 1881, by means of annual agreements. When most of the sugar mills served by the branch to Guamacaro were demolished, it stopped showing a profit, and this, too, conspired against the profitability of the Bahía Company. Moreover, because the branch built between Guanabacoa and Havana was practically an urban line, it required a high frequency of trains, which made it uneconomical. In spite of these problems, Ferrocarril de la Bahía did the best of all the Cuban companies in both absolute and relative terms—as shown by total expenses and income per kilometer—and made the highest profits; at the same time, however, its costs were also the highest in the country. (See Figures 9.1 and 9.2.)

Because of its very liberal policy on obtaining and using credit—and, as was learned later, its bad management—Ferrocarril de la Bahía had to submit its books to a representative of the Schröder bank of London, which held its mortgage bonds, starting in 1870. In 1876, the railroad's debt to Schröder amounted to more than 5 million pesos, and its debt to the Banco del Comercio, to 3.6 million. The English firm's threats to foreclose its mortgage on this railroad date from that time. That situation gradually worsened throughout the 1880s, until both Ferrocarril de la Bahía and Almacenes de Regla had pledged all of their assets to that banking house. Failure to pay the yearly amounts set forth in the contract with the English led to the inevitable denouement, and R. Allan McLean, Schröder's agent representing the Compañía Limitada de Tenedores de Bonos del Ferrocarril de la Bahía de La Habana, formally demanded of Antonio G. Bustamante Piélago, director of the Sociedad de Almacenes de Regla y Banco del Comercio, payment of the overdue debts—which action determined the transfer of Ferrocarril de la Bahía to English hands.[12]

At almost the same time that Ferrocarril de la Bahía was having to cede to the demands of its English mortgage holders, thus reducing its Spanish and Cuban stockholders to the status of minor partners, a process of similar origin—which was, however, different in form—took place in Caminos de Hierro de La Habana, the company traditionally considered Bahía's rival. The transfer of power in that company took the form of replacing the group of Cuban estate owners—mainly the successors of Domingo Aldama and Gonzalo Alfonso, who had controlled the company for four decades—with a group of Spanish interests headed by Ramón Argüelles Alonso, of Asturias, who later became known as "Cuba's railroad king."[13]

Two main factors must have influenced the criollo magnates' decision to withdraw from the railroad business: the first was the drop in its operating profits, and the second, the impossibility of uniting the western railroads under the Aldama-Alfonso clan—an impossibility that had been shown time and time again. With regard to the first factor, it may be said that the value of the company's stock had steadily declined ever since 1883, with a consequent reduction in dividends, which hovered between 10 and 12 percent.[14]

The resignations of José Luis Alfonso, marquis of Montelo, as president of the company and of Gonzalo Alfonso Aldama as a director—plus those of other directors—meant a radical displacement of the interests of the Cuban group and increased control by the Spaniards, but it also gave Shröder a firm foothold in this railroad, which had been considered free of debt to that banking house up until 1881. The pledge that was made to Schröder in exchange for a 1,502,800-peso loan had been entered into to pay for an investment that Domingo Aldama and Gonzalo Alfonso made to build the branch line from Güines to Matanzas, which amount had been acknowledged as a liability in the company's books; thus, the criollos' departure also meant Schröder's entry in Caminos de Hierro de La Habana.[15]

Reflecting the common interests that prevailed in Ferrocarril de la Bahía de La Habana a Matanzas and Caminos de Hierro de La Habana—that is, between the group of Spaniards living in Cuba and the English absentee owners—the two companies agreed on June 8, 1889, to initiate the legal proceedings for a merger, and the merger itself was signed on July 1 of the same year.[16] The firm's name was changed to Banco del Comercio, Ferrocarriles Unidos de La Habana y Almacenes de Regla, and Ramón Argüelles was named president.[17]

Just three months after the merger, the president of the new company and Arturo Amblard, its secretary, set off for London to seek refinancing of the earlier loans arranged by Ferrocarril de la Bahía and Caminos de Hierro de La Habana and to obtain more credit for the new company so it could buy out another Cuban company and thus achieve the monopoly aims of the alliance between the interests of Schröder's and Spanish capital in Havana.[18]

The monopoly aim of making larger profits than the two railroad companies had managed to obtain separately in the past became evident even before the ink had dried on the merger. In August 1889, Ferrocarriles Unidos de La Habana informed the board of Ferrocarril de Cárdenas y Júcaro that, because of the merger, the competition between Ferrocarril de la Bahía and Caminos de Hierro had ended, and passenger fares for combined transportation and freight rates would be raised immediately in all areas outside the sphere of action of competing companies.[19]

In addition to cutting back on administrative personnel, tracks, and stations in the company's branches in its efforts to reduce costs, the new management also lowered the wages and stepped up the exploitation of its workers.[20] The merger of the two most important railroad companies in Havana was an economic success and ended competition in transportation between Havana and Matanzas after more than twenty years of conflict, temporary arrangements, and contradictions, in which the workers could do nothing but were dragged into the senseless conflict between the owners.

Ferrocarril del Oeste's slow advance toward the city of Pinar del Río was carried out at the cost of the assumption of enormous debts, which made the company's economic situation desperate by the beginning of the 1880s. Unlike other railroad companies on the island, Oeste had not been dependent on foreign credit when it laid out its lines but had obtained its financing from its promoters, the Pedroso brothers, who drew on their own funds and what they could obtain in Havana's financial market. This circumstance shaped the debt in such a way that around 2 million pesos of the company's 3-million-peso debt in 1881 were owed to the Pedroso family. Another large chunk of it—540,000 pesos—was owed to the heirs of the marquis of Esteva, a well-known investor. At the height of its administrative inefficiency and class abuse, the company also owed back wages to its workers.[21]

During that same year, the company had been forced to suspend the special train that ran between the Cristina Station in Havana and the town of Artemisa because it had been running at a loss. Several reports stated that the company "was overwhelmed with debt and unable to find any sources of credit."[22] Also in 1881, it had to halt construction of the line between San Cristóbal and Soledad "because, otherwise, it would have had to continue not paying the workers' wages and putting off repairs to the rolling stock."[23]

When the situation was aggravated in 1882, some of the creditors initiated attachment proceedings against the company's assets, but the bankruptcy law that had gone into effect that same year served to keep matters from coming to a head, at least for a while.[24] An agreement that declared a moratorium on the debt was finally signed by representatives of the company and its creditors.[25] It alleviated the situation, but the income obtained during those years was insufficient to rebuild and extend the tracks. Meanwhile, the search for a banker who would lend the money to pay the debts the company had already incurred proved fruitless, both in Cuba and in Europe and the United States.[26]

This was the situation throughout the decade: new debts for materials, equipment, and wages were added to the old ones that had been postponed, and economic disaster loomed. Thus, the stage was set for foreign capital to move in.

Tiburcio Pérez Castañeda, a Cuban who served two masters—English capital and the Spanish crown—stepped forward to propose a "saving formula."[27] This consisted of conveying the railroad's assets to a new company and obtaining a small loan with which to finish laying new track and repair the existing one. Since that figurehead had acquired three-fifths of Ferrocarril del Oeste's outstanding loan, he filed suit against the company to force it to sign an agreement with him as its creditor. The project that the intermediary presented consisted of reorganizing the firm and issuing shares in the new company in exchange for the old ones, which were assessed at 36 percent of their face value. This new loan would be for 1,050,000 pesos and would be used not only for repairs and construction but also for payment of the remainder of the company's old debts.[28]

The creditors brought pressure to bear and managed to push the agreement through. Thus, the English got hold of Ferrocarril del Oeste. The Western Railway of Havana, Limited, was the new name adopted for that railroad in 1892. Marquis Julio Apezteguía, a large Cuban stockholder in the old Ferrocarril del Oeste and a supporter of Integrismo was named chairman of the firm's local board, serving as a front for the foreign interests managed by Joseph White Todd, an English promoter.[29]

Fifteen years after the so-called Little War, which lasted from August 1879 to April 1880, the most illustrious fighters in the struggle for independence, united by the persevering efforts of José Martí, initiated new military campaigns to free Cuba from the Spanish yoke. In 1895, in an impressive feat, the war was extended from the eastern part of the country to the west; thus, that war involved a larger area of the country than had the preceding one. After successfully waging the battle of Mal Tiempo on December 15, 1895, the troops headed by General Máximo Gómez and Antonio Maceo, second in command of the Liberation Army, advanced into Matanzas Province to burn the fields of sugarcane prior to that year's sugarcane harvest, which was about to start.

The fact that, this time, the struggle affected the entire country meant the nearly complete paralysis of the sugar industry, since its sources of raw material were systematically eliminated. The success of the westward push was demonstrated in January 1896; the burned canefields and General Maceo's arrival in Mantua, in the extreme western part of the island, proclaimed it. One of General Máximo Gómez's orders called for the destruction of the industrial installations on the sugarcane estates where efforts were being made to bring in the harvest in spite of everything. The Cubans' tactic had immediate effects on the colony's economy, which had already been tottering toward ruin as a result of the depression under which it had been laboring for more than two decades. Table 9.2, comparing the amount of sugar produced in those years, the average price of sugar on the world market, and the total value of Cuba's sugarcane harvests

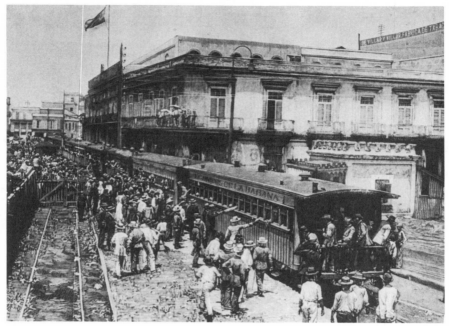

Spanish volunteers depart from Villanueva Station to fight the *mambises*, toward the end of 1895. (*La Ilustración Española y Americana*, Madrid September 15, 1895)

between 1894 and 1898, presents a clear picture of the effects the war had on this key sector of the island's economy. To understand just how ruinous the situation was during those years, consider also that sugar brought only 3.52 centavos a pound in 1893.

Since control of the railroads and the sugar industry had shifted in the period between the outbreak of the Ten Years' War and the resumption of hostilities in 1895, the correlation between politics and class interests more clearly defined the role each class would take in the conflict. The managers of the railroad companies were committed to the colonial government, both because of the role the companies played in society and because of the social composition of their boards of directors, so it was only logical to suppose that they would cast their lot with the Spaniards in a war in which Spanish rule in Cuba was at stake.

The rebels fell on the railroads, powerful strategic ally of the Spaniards, in an unstoppable wave, paralyzing their commercial operations. After harassing Ferrocarril de Puerto Príncipe a Nuevitas throughout nearly all of the second half of 1895, the Mambís turned their attentions to the railroads in the western part of the country.[30] Starting on November 10, 1895, attacks on trains, together with the

TABLE 9.2. Cuban Sugar Production and the Price and Value of Harvests, 1894–1898

Year	Production (in metric tons)	Average price (in cents/pound)	Total Value
1894	1,086,262	2.63	62,105,853
1895	1,034,794	2.02	43,440,932
1896	232,068	2.52	13,066,421
1897	218,497	2.17	10,307,375
1898	314,632	2.19	14,988,717

Sources: Ramiro Guerra, *Azúcar y población en las Antillas* (Havana: Editorial Lex, 1961); Rafael Pedrosa Puertas, *Cinco siglos de industria azucarera cubana* (Havana: Ministry of Sugar, n.d.).

burning of bridges and other actions, coincided with Gómez's and Maceo's operations in the Cienfuegos area, and the rebels reached the tracks of Ferrocarril de Matanzas on December 22.[31] That company's report for the year described the first Mambí attack as follows: "Five boxcars were burned at the Diana switch, and locomotive number 46 was sent off along the Atrevido branch with its valve open, heading downhill toward Navajas with two boxcars and a flatbed car; the locomotive and cars overturned, sustaining considerable damage."[32]

The Cuban troops engaged in many actions after that, reaching the tracks of Ferrocarriles Unidos de La Habana immediately and attacking its installations many times. The report of that company, too, described the situation: "In the last decade of the year, we have experienced at first hand the horrors of the war that is scourging this island. Rebel groups reached our tracks near Jovellanos and burned down the Madan, Tosca, Coliseo, and Sumidero stations; several small bridges were also destroyed, as was the telegraph."[33] The Cárdenas y Júcaro Company also reported the burning of its stations at Manacas, Altamisal, Hato Nuevo, Retamal, Sabanilla, Gispert, Contreras, and Medina.[34]

Such actions took place repeatedly as the Cuban troops advanced westward and the state of war created by their passing was stabilized: "There has rarely been a day on which telegraphic communication—which is more necessary now than ever before—hasn't been cut and a bridge hasn't been destroyed, either by burning or by the explosion of a bomb on the tracks, or a section of track has been destroyed, causing trains to be derailed, or the trains have been attacked."[35]

Like the tracks of Ferrocarril de Matanzas, those of Ferrocarril de Cárdenas were also destroyed: "Today [January 11, 1896], the installations that had been damaged yesterday and were just repaired were burned again; this damage is so

Caibarién Railroad train derailed and burned by Cuban insurgents. Spanish soldiers guard the engine. (*La Ilustración Española y Americana*, Madrid, January 22, 1896)

constant and is effected with such fury that it makes us wonder if all the efforts we can make will suffice to keep the service from being halted."[36]

Doubly hit by the military campaign because of their drop in income and the demands for "special services," which, because of their frequency and size, required tremendous resources, the railroads joined in the war effort on a permanent basis. What in the Ten Years' War had been a sporadic relationship among companies, aimed at solving the need for transporting troops and supplies ("combined transportation"), on this occasion became a system organized and supervised by the quartermaster general of the Spanish army.[37] By means of that department, the railroad companies established a transportation service that pooled and used the tracks and cars of all the companies. Only the locomotives remained on their own sections of track, being replaced where each company's track adjoined that of the next company. In the new campaign, the rates that had been in effect

since 1896 were cut by 50 percent (Military Order 32) for military transportation. This matter had never been clarified previously, since many railroad franchises had been granted with a clause stating that, in case of war, troops would be transported free of charge. In order to maintain direct communication with the various military areas, the colonial government and the railroads also entered into an agreement to link the telegraph circuits of the various companies with the Palace of Government.[38]

The establishment of combined transportation and the linking of all telegraph lines with the office of the Captain General signified more than rendering a service to the government; it meant the militarization of both means of communication. Demands were made day and night for emergency locomotives and cars.[39] The scope and urgency with which that service was demanded may be observed in a telegram that the manager of Ferrocarril de Cienfuegos sent to his

Small fort constructed to protect the tracks of the Tunas to Sancti Spíritus railroad.
(*La Ilustración Española y Americana*, Madrid, November 22, 1895)

counterpart at Ferrocarriles Unidos de La Habana: "Beg Unidos place eight locomotives and personnel for eight trains in Jovellanos earliest possible tomorrow and number of scouts you deem necessary to ensure circulation of our matériel on your lines round trip repeat earliest possible please. Paradela."[40]

One company, that of Matanzas, moved 486 military trains in 1896 alone—more than 1 a day—over a total of 23,255 kilometers, averaging 47 kilometers per train.[41] Thus, the railroads in Matanzas and Cárdenas served as a bridge linking Ferrocarriles Unidos and Ferrocarril de Cienfuegos, which bore the brunt of the military traffic.

The companies also supported the war by building small forts along the tracks to try to protect both the government's system of communication and their own property, but neither the fortifications nor the armored train cars and their escorts achieved the hoped-for results.[42] An important example of this was the Camagüey-Nuevitas track, bristling with small forts throughout its entire length. "A small force of the battalion of volunteers from Madrid garrisons the line so the passenger train from Minas to the city of Nuevitas may advance without any danger. Even so, the rebels have laid ambushes and set off explosions on the track, killing several Spanish soldiers."[43]

To a greater or lesser extent, all of the railroad companies suffered from the Mambí fire, and that harassment, together with the destruction of the material base of their commerical operations—sugar mills and canefields—plus the wear and tear on and destruction of the installations and equipment caused by their use in the war, led the managers of the railroads to take some measures to guarantee their survival.

Soon after the war reached the western part of the country, the railroads economized by cutting down on personnel. One of the first to make a drastic reduction of staff was Banco del Comercio, Ferrocarriles Unidos de La Habana y Almacenes de Regla. On February 1, 1896, that company fired 73 percent of the workers at Almacenes de Regla and left only three of the thirteen employees in the Banco del Comercio. Referring to the railroad and other workers who were kept on, it reported, "Their wages have been slashed, leaving them with the bare minimum they need to survive and carry out their duties."[44]

The militarization of railroad transportation, however, required increased activity by station, workshop, and track maintenance workers, so soldiers and Spanish workers who supported Integrismo were selected to perform these additional tasks and were given benefits in the form of extra rations and bonuses.[45]

The war that had begun in 1895 reaffirmed—this time, more closely—the bonds between the railroads and the colonial government; the fate of both depended on how well the government did in the conflict. That tacit pact gave rise to a give-and-take relationship between them—the railroads giving and the government taking. Because of the war, the companies had seen their income from the transportation of freight and passengers fall to very low levels; at the same time, the services they rendered the government had to be provided at a 50 percent discount on their usual rates. The government might win or lose the war, but the railroads lost money every day, and the government could hardly compensate them for their losses.

The gravity of the situation led representatives of the Ferrocarriles Unidos, Matanzas, Cárdenas y Júcaro, Sagua, Cienfuegos, Caibarién, and Marianao Railroad Companies to meet in 1896 to petition the government of the island to raise their rates, on which a ceiling had been placed in the preceding decade. The owners' request sought to force the government to choose between increasing the rates by 20 percent as a stopgap measure and facing the prospect of the halting of railroad traffic;[46] their brief summed up the situation exactly: "The considerable losses suffered daily as a result of the iniquitous work of destruction wrought by the rebels, who view the railroads as a powerful ally of the government; . . . the

Cárdenas y Júcaro train wrecked at the Flora bridge in south Matanzas by the *Mambi* troops invading the west.

increased expenses required for the fortification and defense of the tracks; and the excessive reduction in income that has been in effect for a long time, terribly aggravated by the lack of a sugarcane harvest—which, as is known, represents the main source of these companies' income—have placed the signatory companies in extremely difficult straits, which must be remedied without any loss of time."[47]

The result of the companies' plaintive claims was the granting of the 20 percent increase in rates which they had been requesting since November 5, 1896.[48] Barely three weeks later, the companies, in turn, made a new monetary contribution to the lost colonial cause, earmarking it "for enlarging and improving the national navy."[49]

The war period was characterized by the destruction of tracks and equipment and by insufficient income and wound up with a naval blockade that U.S. forces imposed on Cuba. This was how the United States began its war against Spain, in Cuba. The combination of military events implied by the war had devastating effects on Cuba's railroads and created a situation that was propitious for their falling into foreign hands. This situation, which was extremely common, facilitated the sale of Ferrocarriles Unidos de La Habana: "The war destroyed large sections of track, stations, and other assets of the company. The amount of reconstruction that has to be done and the large quantity of materials purchased in the

United States show the magnitude of the damage. The lines were left almost impassable; it became necessary to use several trains for reconstruction purposes; and many sections had to be closed to traffic because of the imminence of accidents, due to the state of the tracks."[50] Similar situations didn't have the same repercussions in all of the companies, however. Some of them, such as Ferrocarril de Sagua, Cárdenas y Júcaro, and Matanzas, managed to remain solvent throughout the conflict and to repair the damage done to their installations relatively quickly and efficiently. None of those companies—except Ferrocarril de Matanzas, which had a residual debt of 97,000 pesos to the Schröder bank—was pressured by financial commitments that conspired against its economic stability.

The case of Ferrocarril de Matanzas deserves a more extensive explanation, because special factors of a diverse nature converged in it. For many years, that company had underwritten the extension of its lines and the construction of new branch lines by means of new stock issues. By proceeding in this way, it not only avoided the systematic assumption of new debts but also enlarged the social base of its issued stock. Moreover, the shares that were issued were usually placed among small- and medium-sized merchants and the owners of estates who were nearly always linked to the company's services. Unlike the boards of directors of Ferrocarril de Sagua and Cárdenas y Júcaro, the members of the board of directors of the Matanzas Railroad—including its chairman, Tirso Mesa Hernández— were all Cubans.[51]

When the rebel forces entered that province and the railroads were pressed into the endless task of moving troops, mules, and munitions, which resulted in a great dispersion of locomotives and cars, the managers of the company decided to be more organized about providing the services the government required and, at the same time, took the measure of protecting their locomotives and freight cars by concentrating them on the extensive railroad sidings in the city of Matanzas.[52] More with a view to economy than in resistance to the bullheaded orders of the military commander of the town concerning the indiscriminate use of locomotives for scouting and the construction of small forts at every switch, small bridge, and wayside station, the Matanzas Company built only eight small forts and reduced the use of its locomotives for scouting purposes to passenger trains only. The manager of the company stated in 1898 that to do otherwise would be ineffective and would constitute a heavy burden in terms of the railroads' operating costs.[53]

Nevertheless, the circumstance that seems to have helped that railroad and also those of Cárdenas and Sagua la Grande the most was related to sugar production in the areas served by their tracks. Neither the Cubans' torches nor Captain General Valeriano Weyler's edict ordering the reconcentration of the rural population could keep the estate owners, merchants, and railroad functionaries from achieving their commercial aims, using Spanish bayonets to do so. As the Matanzas Railroad Company's report for 1897 stated, "Enjoying more tranquillity in the province of Matanzas during the past year than in the preceding one, either because the forces operating in it are more numerous or because harassment of the rebel groups crushed them to a large extent, the work of the sugarcane harvest was begun with real determination . . . and, struggling against enormous difficulties, some of which were nearly insurmountable, twice as much sugar was made as in the other harvest; after it was in, the estate owners and colonos dedicated themselves to tending the fields."[54]

In this regard, the company's cooperation was manifest in the assistance it provided by transporting farmers who had been reconcentrated to the production areas:

> It is true that the third class is the one that provides the largest contingent to the company's passenger trains; and, since most of the members of that class are day laborers who have been reconcentrated in the towns and cities without even the essentials for their survival, they could hardly have the wherewithal for traveling from one place to another . . .; and this is so true that, the authorities of this locality having wished that many thousands of those who used to be here would return to their old towns, either so they could work in the fields . . . or so as to get them out of the city, where they could live only by begging, the company granted all of them free tickets during the months of April and May 1897 and, thanks to this, transported 2,325 people. Recently, last December, the same concession had to be repeated to enable all of the farmers who had been reconcentrated and lived here to go in search of work to the sugar mills and the sugarcane plantations that were preparing for the work of the sugar harvest, and another 2,781 were transported.[55]

This company was so adept at handling the situation that, in the course of 1897, in spite of the seriousness of events in the country, it managed to give its stockholders a 2 percent dividend, "which, at least, has shown that it is developing smoothly now and that the capital represented by the company's shares can and should be considered well placed."[56]

Of all the western railroad companies, Ferrocarriles Unidos de La Habana was the one most closely bound up with the Spanish military campaigns. It was indispensable for the military apparatus of the colony, both because of the length of its lines and because its installations and tracks were placed strategically, striking out from the capital of the island to the west, south, and east. Since the company had large warehouses on the shore of the Bay of Havana and the island's political, military, and administrative decisions were made in Havana, the opera-

TABLE 9.3. Troops Lodged in the Regla Warehouses, 1896

Month	Number of men
January	600
February	1,200
May	522
June	210
August	1,224
September	22,076
November	8,000
December	10,500
Total	44,322

Source: ANC, Fondo Ferrocarriles, legajo 795, expediente 53, p. 19.

tions of receiving, dispatching, and provisioning troops could be directed from its central office in the capital, using the "combined" tracks as far east as Las Villas province and the Batabanó branch—the main axis of north-south communication—to reach any point on the southern coast of Cuba through coastal shipping. The war turned Almacenes de Regla into a garrison and military hospital in September 1895; for that purpose, initially, the warehouses of the sixth building were made ready to house two thousand men, "giving them also abundant water, which the trains provide in their magnificent tank cars."[57]

The use of the warehouses as a military barracks was inversely related to the storage of sacks of sugar. In 1895, some 1,043,550 sacks of sugar and 11,148 barrels of molasses had been stored there; in 1896, the amount of sugar was reduced to 163,126 sacks, and the molasses, to 1840 barrels.[58] The absence of stored products made it possible to increase the warehouses' capacity for quartering troops by means of the use of other buildings, so, in 1896, the numbers of soldiers shown in Table 9.3 were quartered there.

Their troop capacity was enlarged even more in 1897. The sugar business declined and was replaced by that of war, but its remuneration at "reduced rates" did not entirely compensate for the drop in regular income.[59] Nevertheless, the company boasted that "nearly all of the reinforcements that have arrived from Spain have landed at Almacenes de Regla and have been moved from there on our trains."[60]

The transportation of soldiers and matériel produced compensatory income of some size—which would have been greater if the government had paid for those services punctually, but it let its debts to Ferrocarriles Unidos y Almacenes de Regla slide until they amounted to more than 300,000 pesos a year.[61] But it wasn't only the services Ferrocarriles Unidos provided for the government that upset its financial equilibrium. Since the safety of land transportation, especially that by rail, had been very precarious ever since the outbreak of the war, the company had to resort to a reduction in rates that was even more drastic than any it had applied in the worst days of competition. The company did this to try to retain what little there was of freight and passenger traffic between the cities of Havana and Matanzas. Therefore, in practice, the 20 percent increase in freight rates authorized by the government did not have the effect that had been hoped for in terms of improving the company's financial situation, for the rate increase that was adopted resulted in a 21 percent drop in income in 1896–97, compared with that in the previous year.[62]

In spite of the reduction in operating income and the government's delay in paying what it owed, the military services provided by Ferrocarriles Unidos—and this was also true of Ferrocarril de Cienfuegos, to some extent—enabled the company to maintain an income per kilometer that was far higher than that of the Matanzas and Cárdenas y Júcaro Companies. (See Figure 9.1.) Even so, insufficient operating income in the early years of the war prevented the company from making its payments to Schröder and Company when they fell due every six months. The delay in the payment due in July 1896 and the certainty that the company would not be able to make the payments that would fall due in January and July 1897 led Ramón Argüelles to go to London to enter into new negotiations with the English.[63] Those negotiations wound up with an agreement that Argüelles and Schröder signed on October 30, 1897. It created a new entity, this time an international one, that would assume control of Ferrocarriles Unidos and Almacenes de Regla,[64] the Banco del Comercio remaining outside the new company.[65] On March 26, 1898, five months after the agreement was signed, it was ratified by means of a contract registered with an official notary.[66]

The assets transferred to the new company included both the railroad and the warehouses and the valuable urban properties of Tallapiedra and Villanueva.[67] The contract stated a commitment to issue stock to pay the main debts of the old company—that is, the ones Schröder had granted a moratorium on and the 100,000 pesos Argüelles had advanced at a critical moment. One hundred fifty-four thousand shares with a face value of ten pounds sterling each—50 pesos— would replace the 35,000 shares with a face value of 200 pesos each that corresponded to the capital stock of the old company.[68] The value assigned to the total assets for their transfer was 2.1 million pesos, which was considered more than what the stock of the old company would bring on the market.[69] This assessment was equivalent to 27 percent of the company's capital stock, which was the portion of the new company to which stockholders in Cuba were reduced.

To meet the requirements of Spanish law, the head office of the company was established in Cuba, following the same procedure that had been used by the Marianao and Oeste Railroad Companies when they were taken over by foreign concerns. That procedure consisted of creating two boards of directors: one in London—the real decision-making center—and the other in Havana. Enmanuel McGuire Underdown headed the former, all of whose members—except for Antonio G. Bustamante Piélago, marquis of Solar and former director of the Banco del Comercio—were English. The board of directors in Havana consisted of Ramón Argüelles, as the largest stockholder in the Cuban company; Luciano Ruiz and Arturo Amblard, who had been directors of the old company; and R. Allan McLean, representing Schröder.[70]

In the final year of the War of Independence, the creation of United Railways of Havana and Regla Warehouse, Limited, completed the English takeover of Cuba's three westernmost railroads, laying the bases for a process of monopolization that would extend past the creation of the republic.

At the end of 1897, Spanish colonialism in Cuba was faced with imminent military and political defeat; threats that U.S. imperialism, then taking its first steps, would intervene in Cuba's War of Independence further dimmed the outlook for Spanish capital's control of Cuba's railroads—which control had already been considerably reduced. The by no means farfetched possibility that the United States would take control of Cuban businesses must have been a factor speeding the process of monopolization of the railroads in the western part of the country, a matter in which the English had been engaged since the 1870s. Both the difficult economic conditions created by the war and the existing uncertainty about the future made it possible to transfer ownership of Ferrocarriles Unidos de La Habana and Almacenes de Regla to a British company and, at the same time, spurred a rapid deployment of "the City'''s financial resources in Cuba, aimed at gaining absolute control of the railroads that operated in sugar-rich Las Villas province—before it was too late.

The main railroad companies serving that province—not counting Ferrocarril de Trinidad, which was paralyzed—were Ferrocarril de Cienfuegos y Villa Clara, Compañía Unida de los Ferrocarriles de Caibarién, and Ferrocarril de Tunas a Sancti Spíritus.[71] Ferrocarril de Sagua had a total of 157.6 kilometers of track, 51.4 of which corresponded to the main trunk line that linked Sagua la Grande with the sugarcane area of Cruces. With 3 million pesos' worth of issued stock and an insignificant 8,000-peso residual debt, it was considered to be financially sound. Firmly controlled by Spanish capitalists, the company had been presided over since 1890 by Leopoldo Carvajal Zaldua, marquis of Pinar del Río, an intransigent member of the Spanish cause.[72]

The Caibarién and Cienfuegos Companies confronted a very different situation. The former had 53 kilometers of broad-gauge track (that didn't reach its supposed destination, the settlement of Sancti Spíritus) and 37.5 kilometers of narrow-gauge track (that went to Placetas). The company's mortgage amounted to 276,000 pesos on an original loan of 300,000 pesos that had been obtained in 1892. Dr. Francisco Cabrera Saavedra, a Spaniard, was its president.[73]

The main trunk line of Ferrocarril de Cienfuegos y Villa Clara covered the 68.5 kilometers that separated the two cities, and the company had over 100 kilometers of railroad sidings. The company's business had been so hard hit by the war that its net operating revenue had dropped from 287,263 pesos in 1894 to 13,795 in 1897 and 33,384 in 1898. These circumstances were aggravated in 1898 when its warehouses and offices in Cienfuegos were burned.[74] Debts contracted in Cuba to the value of 770,000 pesos weakened the financial situation of this company, whose only support was the credit of its president, Ramón Argüelles, who was at the same time a stockholder in and creditor of the Sagua and Caibarién Railroad Companies.

Contacts were made between the owners of these companies and British capital through the professional zeal of Tiburcio Pérez Castañeda—who also served as procurer in the transfer of Ferrocarril de Oeste—to whom, as in the case of the westernmost railroad in Cuba, the English magnate Joseph White Todd granted the powers needed to carry out the monopoly operation. Rumors that the English were going to purchase shares sent the stock of the Las Villas companies up,[75] so the solicitous Pérez Castañeda had to employ his greatest powers of persuasion.[76]

The first formal proposal for purchasing the Sagua Company was made in January 1899; the heart of the offer lay in exchanging its shares, with a face value of 200 pesos each, for 180-peso fractional shares, which implied purchasing them at 90 percent of their value. Two other options were proposed to the stockholders: one was to turn their stock into mortgage bonds bearing 5 percent in the same proportion just cited, and the other was simply to buy the stock at its par value for cash. The purchasers' proposals stimulated sales. A proposal similar to the one that was made to Ferrocarril de Sagua was presented to Ferrocarril de Caibarién, but, in that case, the proportion was different: 400 pesos' worth of new stock would be given for every 500 pesos' worth of the old—which meant that only 80 percent of the value of the old stock would be honored. Of course, the offer to purchase the stock at its par value for cash remained in effect. Once the number of shares required for approving the merger of the two companies was obtained in each of them, the Sagua and Caibarién Railroad Companies were merged on April 30, 1899, and the new company was named Cuban Central Railways, Limited, with its main office in London. Its capital was stated at 9 million pesos, and an issue of mortgage bonds with a total value of 3.5 million pesos was approved, plus another issue worth 978,200 pesos, to meet the obligations of Ferrocarril de Caibarién and of Ferrocarril de Cienfuegos (which had not yet been included in the merger).[77]

The procedure of including Ferrocarril de Cienfuegos was formalized a few days later (on May 5), and, in spite of the company's debts, it benefited from a better purchase offer—230 pesos' worth of new stock for every 250 pesos' worth of the old, which meant that 92 percent of the face value of the old stock would be honored.[78] By late May, the merger of the three companies had been completed. Reporting on this, *Gaceta de los Ferrocarriles de la isla de Cuba* commented that "Most of the old stockholders of the Caibarién, Cienfuegos, and Sagua Companies have been paid for their shares, and a large first-class company has been created."[79] In exchange for disbursing something over 5 million pesos—not counting the acknowledged mortgage debt—the interests represented by Joseph White Todd and Tiburcio Pérez Castañeda got a monopoly on the railroads in Las Villas province. The tiny Ferrocarril de Tunas a Sancti Spíritus line, only 39 kilometers long, was the only company to escape the monopoly grab—a rather insignificant omission when contrasted to the 339.1 kilometers of track then held by Cuban Central, which the merger had made strong enough to rival Cárdenas y Júcaro and United Railways of Havana in importance. (See Map 9.1.)

For a quarter of a century, Cuba's railroads were subjected to a process in which, one after another, they were sold to foreign interests. The first case of such a transfer was the nearly complete replacement of the powerful Cuban group by the influential homogeneous conglomerate of Spanish owners living in Cuba. In no way could it be considered an isolated manifestation in the general situation of the 1860s and 1870s; rather, it was part of a much more all-encompassing phenomenon that was not limited to the sphere of economic activity but also extended to other important aspects of the colony's life. The features of this distinguishing situation were accentuated during the Ten Years' War, which polarized the general interests of Cubans and Spaniards. The Spanish functionaries and owners reached the height of their power in or around the 1880s, but their position in the heart of the railroad companies was, in many cases, undermined by the penetration of British banking capital, which held the mortgages of those companies. This situation forced the absentee English creditors and the Spanish stockholders living in Cuba to enter into an alliance, which created an intermediary stage that was propitious for the second group's retaining its supremacy for some time in the sector of land transportation, even though the weakest railroad companies had begun to cave in to their foreign creditors starting in 1879.

The War of Independence that began in 1895 accelerated the process of transfers of ownership of the railroads, both because of the severe economic losses caused by the destruction wrought by the war and because of the Spanish stock-

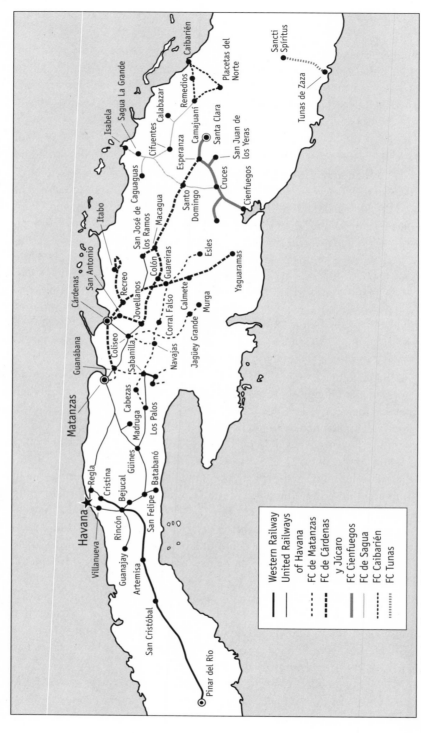

MAP 9.1. Cuban Railroads by Company Lines, 1899

Legend:
Western Railway
United Railways of Havana
FC de Matanzas
FC de Cárdenas y Júcaro
FC Cienfuegos
FC de Sagua
FC Caibarién
FC Tunas

Place names (west to east):
Pinar del Río, San Cristóbal, Artemisa, Guanajay, Villanueva, Rincón, Bejucal, Cristina, Regla, Havana, San Felipe, Batabanó, San Felipe, Güines, Madruga, Cabezas, Los Palos, Navajas, Jagüey Grande, Sabanilla, Coliseo, Guanábana, Matanzas, Cárdenas, San Antonio, Recreo, Jovellanos, Corral Falso, Calmete, Murga, Colón, Guareiras, Esles, Yaguaramas, Macagua, San José de los Ramos, San José de Caguaguas, Itabo, Isabela, Sagua La Grande, Cifuentes, Calabazar, Esperanza, Santo Domingo, Cruces, Cienfuegos, Camajuaní, Remedios, Caibarién, Placetas del Norte, Santa Clara, San Juan de los Yeras, San Juan de los Yeras, Tunas de Zaza, Sancti Spíritus

holders' insecurity in view of the possible loss of the colony and the English investors' haste to get a foothold in Cuba's railroads before they might be forestalled by U.S. investors. As a result of these factors, Cuba's railroads lost nearly all of their national character during the final decades of the nineteenth century. Their promoters and original owners had been criollos closely linked to the sugar interests; those who replaced them—the Spaniards living in Cuba—cannot be described in a cut-and-dried way as foreigners, for, even though they were aligned with the government of the metropolitan center in the political sphere, they represented foreign capital only to the extent that it supported them as a ruling group. As long as the decision-making centers of the companies represented by the Spaniards remained in Cuba, those companies could still be considered Cuban, though to a much lesser extent than the companies that had been founded in the first half of the nineteenth century. Once British capital changed its role of mortgage-holding creditor and began to operate the railroads directly, reporting back to a decision-making center in London, the situation changed drastically. From that moment on, the property could be considered as totally foreign, even though some stock in the companies was still held by Spaniards and Cubans. In view of this, it may be said that, basically and with but few exceptions, the process of denationalization of Cuba's railroads had been completed by the end of the nineteenth century.

U.S. Intervention

Cuba's thirty-year struggle for independence ended practically with the close of the nineteenth century—but without achieving its goal. Far from it: the economic and political characteristics that had been shaped in the course of centuries proved a negative influence on the path that the battered Cuban archipelago took in its efforts as a new republic seeking to become an independent nation.

The Spanish empire, once so powerful, reached the end of the nineteenth century without having been transformed into a modern state. Weighed down by its insufficient capitalist development and unable to tackle both colonial wars and political unrest at home at the same time, Spain, challenged by the Cubans' courageous determination to win their freedom, was also forced to defend itself against the United States, whose expansionist aims threatened its last colonial bastions in the Americas. At a time when Spain was still basing its existence as a declining power on its waning colonial empire and throwing its last material resources into the struggle for an unjust and lost cause, the modern world was witness to the advent of a new phenomenon—imperialism—whose inherent nature would lead it to upset constantly the course of international relations. The changes which that economic and political phenomenon implied had operated in a specific way in the more developed capitalist countries, building on a previous colonial system in some cases and, in others, having free access to a broad national market with prospects for development.

Based on the development of science and technology and nearly always aided by protective tariffs, it grew apace in such European countries as England, France, and Germany and in the United States. This facilitated rapid development of the process of concentration of production and the centralization of capital. The new, developed form of capitalism promoted combinations and mergers among production and service companies, which used different integrating procedures to control markets and production itself, thus giving rise to the formation of monopoly capital.

In his classic work on this phenomenon, *Imperialism, the Highest Stage of Capitalism*, Vladimir Ilyich Lenin described the history of monopolies as follows: "1) 1860–70, the highest stage, the apex of development of free competition; monopoly is in the barely discernible, embryonic stage. 2) After the crisis of 1873, a wide zone of development of cartels; but they are still the exception. They are not yet durable. They are still a transitory phenomenon. 3) The boom at the end of the nineteenth century and the crisis of 1900–1903: Cartels become one of the foundations of the whole of economic life. Capitalism has been transformed into imperialism."[1]

Through the formation of monopoly capitalism, the banks stopped being mere depositories of money and became investment entities capable of reinforcing the power of the industrial and service monopolies, serving, with them, as the basis for very close links between banks, industry, and transportation. This led to the appearance of a new kind of capital: finance capital. That concentrated form of capital retained by minority power groups facilitated the establishment of a financial oligarchy, an agent of decisive weight in the state apparatus. Referring to this, Lenin stated, "The 'personal union' between the banks and industry is completed by the 'personal union' between both and the state."[2]

The search for areas of investment for finance capital was generalized at the beginning from the large financial centers of Europe, first in the form of loans and then by means of direct investments. In view of the role those financial centers played in the exploitation of foreign markets, their investments in railroads were especially important for the expansion of the new phase of capitalism.

Only through them [the railroads] was it possible for Europe to use the products of those countries in such colossal proportions and for the market to be extended so rapidly, to become a world market. Nevertheless, the fact that exports of capital should become necessary now for the construction of those railroads—which were built almost exclusively with European (especially English) capital—was even more important.[3]

When monopoly capitalism appeared in Germany and the United States, those countries began to compete economically with England and France; thus, it became necessary to divide the world into spheres of influence among the nine capital-exporting countries and the ones that had maintained their predominance in the past. That historic situation was extremely unfavorable to the Cubans' desire to obtain complete self-determination. At that time, Spain was declining rapidly as a world power; England had interests in Cuba, but they were limited almost exclusively to the railroad sector. The United States, however, was ready to test its military and naval power to achieve its goal of dominating the largest island in the Antilles.

For nearly all of the nineteenth century, England had been the largest exporter of capital in the world; its historic role in financing railroads hadn't been limited to its colonies but had also extended to other parts of the Americas, including the United States and Canada.[4] During the years of Spanish rule in Cuba, the English had also made investments in Cuban railroads in a more or less direct way. With the passage of time, "the City" became the creditor of nearly all the Cuban railroad companies, and, at the end of the nineteenth century, it took direct control of over half of the island's means of public transportation. Even so, once the United States had become a power seeking to extend its sphere of influence to Latin America (especially the Caribbean), it may be supposed that the situation wasn't propitious for England's attempting to shore up Spanish rule in Cuba or stepping into Spain's shoes. The English sought only to gain possession of the railroads in the western part of the country as a means of protecting their earlier investments in that sector.

This was not so in the case of incipient U.S. imperialism. It clashed with the tottering lion of Castile, at the end of Cuba's War of Independence, to prevent the birth of an independent state in the territory on which it had been casting a covetous eye for so many years. U.S. intervention in the Spanish-Cuban War, as later historic experience would show, was mainly aimed at seizing the Cuban archipelago as a neocolonial enclave and replacing Spain as the main power not only in the Caribbean but also in the rest of its insular possessions.

By the time it intervened in Cuba's War of Independence, the United States had already gone through the first phases of imperialist development. Starting in the 1880s, with the help of a protective tariff in its foreign trade and almost absolute freedom for private enterprise within the country, the formation of combinations that joined several companies together into units that had capital on a scale never even dreamed of up until then had been intensified.

That was the era which saw the birth of such enormous corporations as the Standard Oil Company, the American Sugar Refining Company, and the Bethlehem Iron Works. Mergers also took place in the important railroad sector, giving control of thousands of kilometers of track to Vanderbilt, Morgan, Hill, and Harriman.[5] By 1897, the United States had invested 684 million dollars in five continents. Over $300 million of that amount was invested in Latin America, with almost $50 million—7.2 percent of the total—in Cuba.[6] U.S. investments in the island at that time were mainly concentrated in the mining of iron, manganese, and nickel, through the Juraguá Iron and Transportation Company, the Spanish American Iron Company, the Cuban Steel Ore Company, the Sigua Iron Company, and the Ponupo Manganese Company, all of them linked to a greater or lesser extent to Pennsylvania's Bethlehem monopoly. The American Tobacco Company made monopoly investments in the tobacco sector, and three sugar mills that were linked in one way or another to the American Sugar Refining Company formed the vanguard of direct investments in the production of sugar, which the U.S. sugar trust had already penetrated commercially.

Even granting that certain U.S. circles linked to the sale of sugar or to the mineral-metallurgical exploitation of Cuba did not welcome the United States's intervention in the Spanish-Cuban War at the time, it is a fact that, shortly afterward, criteria favorable to the war prevailed, stimulated by the possibilities it opened up for expansion of the U.S. market and for the formation of an advantageous sphere for the investment of U.S. capital. The yellow press mobilized support for the war among the people of the United States, ostensibly defending the Cubans' right to be free—and thus creating the subjective conditions in public opinion for carrying out a large-scale military action against Spain. By means of that political-military action, the old expansionist idea that U.S. statesmen from Thomas Jefferson to William McKinley had cherished was turned into reality. With the U.S. intervention in Cuba's War of Independence, the bases were laid that guaranteed U.S. finance capital's control of the island's resources.

After the U.S. battleship Maine was blown up in Havana's harbor, the U.S. government engaged in diplomatic maneuverings in Madrid in an effort to get the Spanish government to cede its most important Caribbean colony. When those efforts failed, the U.S. Congress passed a joint resolution authorizing McKinley to end the war in Cuba.[7] The U.S. military command on the island employed a treacherous tactic centered on denying the status of belligerents to the Cuban forces; drawing on their local chiefs for assistance; and, after the Spaniards had been defeated, refusing to let the Cuban fighters enter the main cities, to keep the Spanish army from capitulating to the patriots. The last act of hostility in the struggle was carried out by the U.S. troops against the Cubans, excluding them from the signing of the protocol that set forth Spain's surrender. Thus, the island's sovereignty passed from the hands of Spanish colonialism to those of U.S. imperialism. The Treaty of Paris, which was formally inspired by humanitarian principles and a high sense of social and moral duty, covered up what was, in fact, the United States military occupation of Cuba for an indefinite time and its acquisition of Spain's Caribbean and Pacific colonies as the spoils of war.[8]

The United States military intervention in Cuba officially began on January 1, 1899, a terrible time for Cuba, which had just emerged from a devastating war that had destroyed the main means of production and decimated the population. Sugar production had dropped by 67 percent compared with the rate in 1895, and income from the sugar sector fell from 45 million pesos in 1895 to only 19 million in 1900. It has been estimated that the war took a toll of around 200,000 human lives and also adversely affected the normal growth of the population.[9] The reports of the U.S. officers who were appointed to govern Cuba's provinces contain some particulars in this regard. The following excerpts are from testimony by General Fitzhugh Lee, governor of Pinar del Río and Havana Provinces:

> Agricultural operations had ceased; large sugar estates with their enormous and expensive machinery were destroyed; houses burned; stock driven on for consumption by the Spanish troops or killed. There was scarcely an ox left to pull a plow, had there been a plow left. Not a pig have [sic] been left in the pen, or a hen to lay an egg for the poor destitute people who still held on to life most of them sick, weary and weak. Miles and miles of country unhabited [sic] by either the human race or domestic animals were visible to the eye on every side. The great fertile Island of Cuba in some places resembled an ash pile, in others, the dreary desert. . . . Chaos, confusion, doubt, and uncertainty filled with apprehension the minds of Cubans.[10]

Matanzas and Santa Clara Provinces, which normally produced 80 percent of Cuba's sugar, had suffered heavy losses in their processing capacity: of the 267 sugar mills that had been in operation in those territories in 1894 and 1895, only 83 were still standing in 1899. The livestock of all kinds had been reduced from over 1.5 million head to a little over 60,000 by that same year. Referring to the condition of the roads in the two provinces, Brigadier General James H. Wilson, commander of Matanzas and Las Villas Provinces reported, "The roads have been so long neglected that they are nearly useless. In the rural districts they are generally nothing more than bridle paths, the stones, vegetation, and mud holes making them impassable for all wheeled vehicles."[11]

The situation in Camagüey and Oriente Provinces was even worse, for industry had made less progress there than in the western part of the country. Most of the few people in those provinces lived in towns near the coast or were scattered throughout the large forests or on the vast plains. The military operations of the War of Independence had reached the fields and populations of those provinces on two occasions without any real period of recovery during the truce of earlier years. General Leonard Wood reported to his superior on the state in which he found that extensive region:

> On the sea-board and near some of the large towns, large sugar estates were dragging on a painful existence, producing from one-third to one-tenth their normal crop. They considered themselves fortunate to have saved their machinery and buildings from destruction. . . . Those individuals who were engaged in the raising of cattle had lost everything and it was difficult

to find a cow or an ox. Horses were few and in wretched condition. Mining had ceased; all industries were practically dead. . . . Such railroads as existed in this province were largely crippled by destruction of bridges and rolling stock and greatly in need of repairs, which had not been attended during the war.[12]

United States citizens found more than just ruin and poverty in Cuba, however; they also contemplated the possibility of obtaining more complete control of the Cuban market, an important source of minerals and raw sugar, and an excellent place in which to invest their capital profitably. On arriving in Cuba, they also cast their assessing and rapacious eyes on everything that might be exploited easily to make them rich quick. The previously mentioned reports that the governors of the districts sent to the general governors, J. Brooke and L. Wood, periodically; the detailed census of resources and population that had been taken in 1899; and the report that Robert Percival Porter, special envoy of the U.S. government, had made proved extremely useful in this regard. With the help of those exhaustive reports, the intervenors made a veritable inventory of Cuba's human and natural resources, chattels, and real estate as a starting point for exploiting their recently acquired colony. The most promising area proved to be the eastern part of the country, because the large extents of land there still had their original vegetation, the population density was low, and the area was linked to the rest of the country only by coastal shipping, all of which made the region ideal for the creation of neocolonial enclaves.

Cuba's natural conditions for recovering its former levels of production and improving its domestic situation were relatively propitious; all that was needed was a work force and loans for purchasing the required means of production, but the men of working age had been decimated by the war, and capital was scarce. The recommendations that envoy Robert P. Porter made concerning Cuba's "industrial rehabilitation" did not consider the United States as a source of labor. The U.S. technician viewed his compatriots' role in this task not as that of pioneers founding farming settlements such as Gloria City,[13] but rather as that of business promoters and executives.[14] The English capitalists—such as Joseph White Todd, the representative of Western Railways of Havana and of Cuban Central—expressed similar views. In giving his opinion on the country's reconstruction, the railroad magnate recommended that workers be brought in from underdeveloped parts of Europe, such as southern Italy and Spain, and put to work raising sugarcane for the sugar mills.[15] Porter suggested spheres in which U.S. investors would have the greatest probabilities of success; they were related to services and public works, most of which would be underwritten by the Cuban Treasury. Porter referred specifically to the aqueducts, sewer system, electric lights, ports, communications, public roads, and—of course—railroads.[16] Cuba's so-called industrial rehabilitation was conceived of only on the basis of capital from the United States, which, rather than guaranteeing the country's development, would ensure its dependence and foreign exploitation, which would be accentuated later on as market demands and the terms offering that capital permitted.

When the U.S. army took over in Cuba, there were no important ties between U.S. capital and Cuba's railroads. The $150,000 worth of mortgage bonds in the Empresa del Ferrocarril y Almacenes de Depósito de Santiago de Cuba that the Ponupo Mining and Transportation Company, a U.S. firm, had held since October 1895 were an exception to this general rule. The relationship between the two companies had become quite close because the private railroad belonging to Ponupo was practically a branch of Ferrocarril de Santiago, over whose main trunk line the mines' products were transported to the company's docks.[17] When Cuba's sovereignty was transferred to the U.S. government, the latter took over the military railroad from Júcaro to San Fernando as spoils of war; even though the railroad had been built to defend the line of forts between Júcaro and Morón, it had a public freight and passenger service. The tracks of Ferrocarril de Trinidad, which had been abandoned since the Ten Years' War, were also placed under the military government in much the same way. The intervenors also built a short railroad (9 kilometers long) for military purposes between the Triscornia dock on the Bay of Havana and the lines of Ferrocarriles Unidos,[18] charging it to the public purse. As a result of all this, the U.S. administration directly controlled over 100 kilometers of track.

Practically from the beginning of United States intervention in Cuba, U.S. private capital moved into the two companies that operated urban railroads in Havana. The transfers of both companies were effected between January and June of 1899, placing the capital's mule-drawn streetcars and the old Ferrocarril de Regla a Guanabacoa, known as "La Prueba," in the hands of a syndicate of U.S. capitalists. The newly created companies stated that they would adopt electric power for rail transportation within the city and, therefore, were constituted as electric power companies, under the names Havana Electric Railway Company and Cuban Electric Company.[19]

In 1900, halfway through the period of U.S. intervention, the total extent of the railroads serving the public was 1,960 kilometers, including the urban railroads in Havana. Sixteen companies were registered in this sector of transportation, representing capital from several countries. A similar number of lines, most of them of narrower gauge, had a combined length of 1,384 kilometers, owned by 107 private—sugar- and mining-related—railroad companies, which operated on small circuits, usually connecting with lines serving the public. Table 10.1 shows

TABLE 10.1. Kilometer Distribution and Capital Sources of Cuban Public
Service Railroads, 1900

Company	Spanish-Cuban Capitalists	Occupying Government	Yanqui Capital	English Capital
Western RR of Havana	—	—	—	177.7
Cuban Central RR	—	—	—	344.5
United RR of Havana	—	—	—	417.6
Marianao y Havana RR	—	—	—	13.0
FC de Guantánamo	36.4	—	—	—
FC de Matanzas	284.0	—	—	—
FC de Matanzas y Júcaro	338.9	—	—	—
FC de Santiago de Cuba	50.9	—	—	—
FC de Puerto Príncipe	73.0	—	—	—
FC de Gibara-Holguín	31.4	—	—	—
FC Tunas-Sancti Spíritus	39.0	—	—	—
FC S, Cayetano-Viñales	24.0	—	—	—
FC Júcaro–San Fernando	—	67.0	—	—
FC de Triscornia	—	9.4	—	—
FC de Trinidad	—	29.4	—	—
Havana Electric RR	—	—	20.2	—
Cuban Electric Co.	—	—	4.2	—
Total	877.6	105.8	24.4	952.8

Source: William H. Carlson, "Report of the Special Commissioner of Railroads to the
Military Governor," Leonard Wood, Civil Report of the Military Governor (Havana, 1901),
pp. 273–75.

the public service railroads in Cuba at the beginning of the century and the
source of financing of each.

Almost all the tracks were what was known as standard gauge (1.435 meters
wide), but there were also some exceptionally wide-gauge tracks, such as those of
the Puerto Príncipe–Nuevitas line (1.524 meters wide), and narrow-gauge tracks,
such as those of the San Cayetano–Viñales and Gibara-Holguín railroads (0.76
and 0.94 meters wide, respectively).

In all, the companies' capital stock amounted to around 65 million pesos, as
follows: the acknowledged capital of the English companies, 29,759,000 pesos;
the stock of the companies then controlled by the U.S. government, 1,715,000
pesos; the stock that Wall Street–based imperialist companies were authorized to
issue, $15 million; and what might be considered Cuban capital—that is, the

TABLE 10.2. Yield per Kilometer of the Main Public Service Railroad
Companies, 1900 (in dollars)

Company	Yield
United RR of Havana	46,795
Cuban Central RR	41,739
Marianao and Havana RR	36,472
Western RR of Havana	30,096
FC de Guantánamo	27,027
FC de Santiago de Cuba	24,829
FC de Cárdenas y Júcaro	23,247
FC de Matanzas	20,966
FC de Puerto Príncipe	13,513
FC Gibara-Holguín	12,859

Source: William H. Carson, "Report of the Special Commissioner of Railroads to the
Military Governor," in Leonard Wood, *Civil Report of the Military Governor* (Havana,
1901), pp. 273–75.

capital of those companies whose decision-making centers were located in the
country—18,601,000 pesos. It should be noted that the proportion of English
capital was much higher than the rest, largely because of the high capitalization
of the English companies' assets. See Table 10.2.

Not all of the companies listed in these tables were operating; both Ferrocarril
de Trinidad, which had been abandoned in practice twenty-six years earlier, and
Ferrocarril de San Cayetano a Viñales, which had been considerably damaged
during the last war, were paralyzed and had little hope of being reactivated.[20] The
rest of the companies were more or less in a state to continue offering their
services to the same extent as usual, so the western part of the country offered little
scope for incursions by U.S. capital in the sphere of railroad transportation.

As was pointed out in earlier chapters, Cuba's railroads were conceived of as a
means for transporting products from inland areas to the ports. That was how the
simple networks of rails were created in Cuba; fed by their respective sugar
branches, they led to terminals located at the main shipping ports. Built by the
sugar producers and port merchants, whose interests were interlocked, the tracks
ran in a north-south direction to the sea, just like Cuba's rivers. The lines that
went in an east-west direction, lengthwise through the country, had been built
mainly to bring in freight from areas far from the axes that had been laid out
originally, and not primarily to connect with the north-south lines.

Within a framework of so well-defined regional interests, the companies that were founded prior to 1858 had obtained letters patent from the Spanish government, each of which plainly authorized the organization of the stock company and the construction of tracks without even mentioning the conditions, restrictions, prerogatives, or rates under or with which the railroad thus created should operate. The first laws and regulations of a general nature that were applied to Cuba's railroads were issued in 1859. They reproduced the ones in the same sphere that had been promulgated shortly before in Spain and called for the establishment of a standard rate (which was never actually applied).

Years later, in 1880, a budget law was issued whose Articles 7 and 27 facilitated the construction of Ferrocarril Central and introduced in Cuba the laws and regulations that had been in effect in Spain since 1877. Those new provisions also contemplated the establishment of a general rate based on the distance covered.

A group of royal writs issued in 1888 and between 1895 and 1897 added new elements of confusion to the until then fragmentary railroad legislation in Cuba. The combined railroad laws of a general nature and royal writs issued for specific cases, both before and after 1858, in no way contributed to the linking up of services but rather maintained and accentuated the anarchy that reigned in the railroad sphere. This is why, even though regulatory laws existed that could have been applied to that important activity, the colonial government had nearly always limited itself to handling (approving or turning down) requests for concessions, approving the itineraries that the companies presented for transporting passengers, and making an occasional (negligent) inspection of the tracks and rolling stock.

As for rates, even though the principle of linking rates to distance was formally in effect, the companies had steadily refused to accept it, with different rates per kilometer charged by different companies and also for different stretches of track owned by the same company, depending on whether there was any competition from other companies. This meant that rates were very high in areas served by only one company and nearly always lower and generally subject to individual agreements with the estate owners in areas where there were competing services. In no case were the rates directly related to the distance covered, even though this was one of the factors to be considered in establishing prices for transportation. The other element to be considered in rates—the weight or volume of freight— rested on units of measurement hallowed by tradition, which sometimes reflected regional conventions: sacks, boxes, and barrels of sugar (which were of different weights in different regions); casks of high wine; "thirds" of tobacco; and "loads" of wood, also of different volumes and weights in different areas.

The differences in the interests of the various companies led Cuban railroads to operate independently of one another during the nineteenth century, for the companies did not feel a need to establish true connections at the railway junctions, much less establish common rates for passengers or freight. In general, each company classified merchandise differently, using a different method for calculating shipments. The combined transportation that had been established in response to the needs of war, when the Spanish government took charge of moving troops and supplies to where the fighting was going on, had been practically the only exception. This situation contributed to a boom in coastal shipping, not only for communication between the eastern and western parts of the country, which lacked adequate land communication, but also between the western ports and Havana, Cárdenas, and Sagua, even though the provinces where those cities were located had many railroad lines. At the beginning of the twentieth century, according to reports by the U.S. intervention officials, this situation had not been straightened out yet. Direct connection between lines is unknown. A shipper has to change and start all over at each intersection. Each company controls the traffic along its route, not allowing rival transit, and the railroad and merchants at the ports served by such lines jealously support and defend this unfortunate state of affairs.[21] The problem of rates and railroad connections, to which the colonial government had not paid enough attention, remained for the intervenors to solve, and they had nothing to do with the interests that had given rise to the situation.

When representatives of the United States took over the government of the island, the country's main problem centered around the need to get sugar production back up to the levels it had reached in the years prior to the war. This, of necessity, implied the reconstruction of sugar mills and plantations—and, of course, the revitalization of the railroads, which were an important element in the infrastructure. At the beginning, the U.S. interests gave priority to the production of raw sugar for their refining industry and to mining and sales of tobacco, so their railroad policy during the first two years was aimed at maintaining the balance between the interests of the estate owners and the railroads and of trying to reform the rates—an effort that had been unsuccessful under Spanish rule. However, as the construction in Cuba of Ferrocarril Central by a group of U.S. capitalists became imminent,[22] the intervenors incorporated protection of the new investment—come hell or high water—in their activities. In general terms, the policy that was followed in the sector from then on was vigorously aimed at establishing a single system of rates that would facilitate the transportation of passengers and merchandise from the lines of one company to those of others in order to speed combined transportation and make railroad transportation in the western provinces, extending as far east as the city of Villa Clara, both faster and more efficient.[23]

A single system of rates, complemented by efficient railroad combinations, could not only eliminate the slow, annoying aspects of the railroads, which held back the dynamics of trade, but also help speed traffic to and from the area that became a focal point of U.S. interests: Camagüey and Oriente Provinces. When the supervisory government laid down this railroad policy, it also helped to equalize the prices of the service offered to the sugar industry, thus furthering the process of "standardizing" the work in that sector of production.

The establishment of a strict order entirely controlled by the intervenors cannot have been unaffected by such subjective concepts as the U.S. rulers' absolute faith in the "civilizing" role assigned to them in the hemisphere and, of course, the superiority of U.S. railroad legislation, compared with Spanish legislation in this sphere. To achieve operational control of the railroads and design his strategy in the sector, President McKinley sent William H. Carlson, a technician, to Cuba as his railroad commissioner. Carlson drew up the famous "inventory" on the general state of the Cuban railroad companies and their equipment, obtaining information by means of a military order issued on May 16, 1899, which stated that an archives should be created containing full details on Cuba's railroads.

In 1899 and 1900, the government of occupation continued to intervene in the railroad sphere within a conciliating framework, trying to get the railroad companies to adopt a uniform rate that would be proportional to the distance covered and would, at the same time, mean a reduction in freight charges. J. R. Villalón, secretary of public works, made the first of the government's demands in this regard when, in February 1900, he filed suit against the companies, demanding that they reduce their rates and adopt a single system of classifying merchandise. The railroad executives replied by presenting an appeal that contested the powers with which the Secretariat of Public Works claimed to be invested for implementing the regulation on railroad rates, which had for such a long time been subject to the discretion of the companies. Therefore, as set forth in the railroads' report of those years, "a circular was sent to the companies on June 19, 1900, inviting them to reform and unify their rates in the sense of establishing transportation prices that would be applicable to well-defined units and would be related to the distance to be covered and to a uniform classification of the merchandise, abandoning any idea of a reduction."[24]

Thus, the government contented itself with adopting a uniform rate and gave up its demands for reducing freight charges. The railroad companies' protest continued to have positive effects for them, for it forced the intervenors to issue a military order that eliminated the 3 and 10 percent taxes on the transportation of passengers and freight and to reduce the customs duties on materials that were imported for use by the railroads.[25] Even though the railroads benefited from these measures at first, the situation began to change in 1901, when the government took more decisive action to achieve the goals that were the axis of its railroad policy—that is, the unification and reduction of railroad rates and control of their services through a state organization created for that purpose. Those goals also constituted part of the minimum guarantees sought by large U.S. capital, which had just established itself in the country's railroad sector through the Cuba Company, which planned to build a railroad between Santa Clara and San Luis. In December 1900, the supervisory government had begun to pressure the established companies to achieve its aims. Several military orders and circulars were issued for this purpose in May and June 1901. They called for rates to be unified and regulated other aspects of combined transportation. Military Order 149, of June 5, 1901, created an agency to regulate railroad activity in Cuba: the Inspección de Ferrocarriles, with the powers of a court and inspection functions.[26] Because of the resistance that the companies had put up against the government's measures and also because of the small time margin that the provisional nature of the government allowed it for achieving its aims, the U.S. intervenors set about reaching those goals in the railroad sphere by means of force and tried to guarantee that they would remain in effect even after the neocolonial republic was installed. The new series of measures began with Military Order 246, of November 25, 1901, which revoked Article 49 of the Railroad Law of 1877 and allowed the government to modify rates without the prior consent of the companies.[27]

Starting in January 1902, the government stepped up its pressure on the railroads to force them to reduce their rates; Military Order 1, of January 3 of that year, was issued for that purpose. The existence of a large number of individual contracts between estate owners and the railroad companies made the measure ineffective, however. Therefore, a new military order, number 16, was issued in that same month annulling the former one. In view of this situation and the reiterated failure of the measures taken, the U.S. government decided to replace all the railroad legislation then in effect on the island and, together with the U.S. railroad capitalists who had just begun their penetration in Cuba, to adopt a brand-new general law that would benefit capitalism on the island and particularly favor those promoters.

William Van Horne, the top man at the Cuba Company, headed the work of preparing and drawing up the new railroad law. A New York lawyer, E. R. Olcott, was in charge of the technical aspects, assisted by Edward A. Moseley and Martin A. Decker, secretary and undersecretary, respectively, of the Interstate Commerce Commission of the United States, the agency in charge of regulating railroad services in that country. U.S. Secretary of War Elihu Root and Leonard Wood, governor of Cuba, had invited them to participate in the project.[28] Even though the new law was clearly drawn up with Van Horne's interests in mind, its general content was inspired by similar laws in effect in Canada and the state of Texas. Some details on how the text was drafted are contained in Wood's report for 1902. He stated that he had obtained the services of a well-known New York lawyer, E. R. Ollcott, who had been assisted by Fernando Vidal and Frank Steinhart. They eventually overcame the strong reservations of the directors and the president. He also noted that Sir William Van Horne and General Grenville Dodge had used their vast experience to rectify some defects in the original draft of the law and that the local directors of the Cuban railroads, Pearson, Liversey and Woolf had also made some input. He stated that along with Edward A. Moseley and Martin Decker, members of the Interstate Commerce Commission, he had personally examined the draft, and that Moseley even made a second visit to the island to participate in the preparation of rates with the new railroad commission.[29]

This description might make you think it was a group project, but Wood acknowledged the main role played by the personal envoy of the U.S. secretary of war, who acted as legal adviser. Wood pointed out that Olcott directed the operation from the initial drafting of the original bill to the very end, with the rest of the committee merely important collaborators.[30]

The new railroad law was implemented through Military Order 34, of February 7, 1902. It revoked all prior legislation and established the norms that were to govern the relations between the railroads, those who used them, and the government. At the same time, the Comisión de Ferrocarriles was created, an agency that would be in charge of regulating all activities by the railroads, including those that had, up until then, been the province of the Inspección de Ferrocarriles. To give the comisión more weight, the law also stated that, as set forth in Canada's railroad law, it would be composed of three members of the Council of Ministers. Military Order 34 established the rules governing everything related to railroad transportation, from the most elementary procedures to those applicable in cases of bankruptcy, but most of its articles seem to have been aimed at ratifying the steps the Cuba Company had taken in building the line between Santa Clara and San Luis and at paving the way for its subsequent expansion.[31]

The real essence of the railroad law didn't escape those affected by it. They interpreted both its form and its true aims accurately. As an article by José M. Gálvez that appeared in El Economista the next year stated:

> That casuistical, hazy, and disorderly law has not followed a rational, methodical plan, and, even though it has much that is good and usable, it suffers from defects which must be corrected. Among them, its involved and improper language; lack of guarantees; and invasion of the field of civil, commercial, and criminal law, and even that of the administration of justice, are the most serious. Its provisions include some that seem to have been drawn up to serve interests of the moment exclusively, and the Empresa Constructora del Gran Ferrocarril Central, which has already brought rapid, direct communication to nearly all the towns and cities

on the island, has taken advantage of them. Supported by this Military Order, that company has forced its way all over, either with or without the consent of the owners of the land through which it has built its tracks.[32]

Even so, Military Order 34 did not lead the railroad companies to raise an immediate hue and cry. That came nearly four weeks later, when Military Order 61 was published on March 3, 1902, establishing an official classification for rates and standardizing the procedures the companies were to follow in their dealings with the Comisión de Ferrocarriles. That order proved to be the opening shot in a pitched battle between the railroad companies and the comisión.[33] The old companies expressed their opposition to the order by means of meetings, documents, protests, and the like and followed manifestly dilatory tactics, trying to stave off change until the end of the U.S. military intervention, which had been announced for May 20 of that year, hoping that, later on, they would be able to modify the situation imposed by the occupiers.

In defense of their assumed right not to submit to the decisions of the Comisión de Ferrocarriles and to the military orders concerning the railroads, the companies—especially the ones in the western part of the country—clung to the unencumbered royal writs that had originated their respective privileges. With complete disdain for the lawsuits initiated by the companies and, at the same time, pressured by the announced end of the military intervention, the military government decided to establish ceilings for Cuba's railroad rates once and for all. They were published as Military Order 117, of April 28, 1902.[34] To preserve the laws and norms imposed on the railroads and make them binding in the future, the U.S. officials issued an unequivocal new order that same day: Military Order 118. Its text stated that the rates contained in Military Order 117 could not be suspended or invalidated by any appeal. Therefore, Military Order 118 challenged the powers of the Supreme Court, for it declared that the highest legal authority in the land was not competent to discuss the validity of the orders issued or to rule on the verdicts and decisions of the Comisión de Ferrocarriles.[35]

The supervisory government's stratagem as regards Cuban railroad legislation was completed with Military Order 119, issued on May 12, 1902, barely a week before the United States formally pulled out of the government of the island. That order tried to temper the incursion the former military orders had made in the Cuban Supreme Court's powers, recognizing that court's exclusive right to hear appeals against the established rates and laws.[36] In short, the legal conclusion of the "civilizing control" which the U.S. government imposed on Cuba's railroads was similar to the laws it applied in other matters of similar importance. This function was carried out in masterly fashion by Article IV of the Platt Amendment, which stated, "All the acts of the United States in Cuba during the military occupancy of said island shall be ratified and held as valid, and all rights legally acquired by virtue of said acts shall be maintained and protected."[37]

The supervisory government's laws on railroads protected the investments that U.S. companies had made in the eastern part of the country and, at the same time, cleared the way for rail communication between the eastern and western provinces, benefiting trade by promoting the transportation of freight and passengers between the capital and the eastern part of the island. Even though the railroad laws of 1902 did not benefit the Spanish-Cuban companies, they did help to destroy the regional limitations under which they had been operating. The obligatory establishment of combinations between companies and the unification of their rates, based on the distance covered and favoring long-distance transportation, would be of undeniable value in promoting the integration of Cuba's domestic trade. The increase in internal circulation and the lowering of costs for transporting sugar must be acknowledged as elements that promoted the extension of capitalist relations in Cuba, both domestically and in its international trade relations.

Military Order 34 was extremely generous with regard to private railroads. Under it, any person or company was empowered to build and exploit railroads of this kind freely and without restriction and could also dispose of them as he or it saw fit. The only prerequisite for their construction was that the Comisión de Ferrocarriles would have to agree in those cases in which the line would go through land that was in the public domain.[38] Even though the private railroads created under that order sometimes used their autonomy as a cover for providing public services, the most important aspect of the order was that it ensured that the new sugar companies that would be established in the future would be able to build railroads not only to take sugarcane to the mills but also to take the finished product to their own docks. Thus, it opened up advantageous possibilities for creating sugar enclaves in areas far from the railroads serving the public.

Technical advances in the sugar sector and the process of the concentration and centralization of capital, which was typical of the monopoly stage of capitalism, replaced the intimate relations that had existed between the railroads and the estate owners in the nineteenth century with a new reality. The hallmark of the twentieth century would be the polarization of interests between the giants of the Cuban economy: the sugar mills, with their networks of private railroads, on the one hand, and, on the other, the large English and U.S. railroad companies, which tried to monopolize the transportation of sugar in the new developing areas. The classic expression of this phenomenon appeared in the eastern part of the island, where U.S. investments became entrenched in both sectors during the first decade of the twentieth century.

11

The Ferrocarril Central and Imperialist Interests

When the twentieth century was ushered in, Cuba's economy entered a period of reconstruction and growth. More and more of the initiative and capital involved in that process, however, came from the United States, as U.S. capital penetrated the various branches of production and services, taking over old businesses and starting up new ones in an all-encompassing, sweeping movement that placed the mainstays of the country's economy in U.S. hands.

The condition in which Cuba had emerged from the War of Independence was particularly favorable to imperialist penetration. Exhausted and ruined, the island was not able to exploit its resources. Those businesses that hadn't already gone bankrupt were on the brink; land was being sold for a song; and the people, famished and jobless, constituted a cheap source of labor. In addition to those economic advantages, the political conditions on the island were favorable as well. Spanish sovereignty had given way to a "provisional" U.S. military occupation, whose real duration nobody could foretell. Suddenly, U.S. investors could feel just as safe as at home—or more so, since the U.S. military authorities ruling the island permitted a greater margin of freedom for private enterprise than did any governor of a duly constituted state. Though uncertain, the future was in no way a depressing unknown. No matter what the destiny of the island might be, even if it should manage to become an independent republic, nobody doubted that it would remain attached to the United States "by ties of singular intimacy and strength,"[1] which would offer U.S. capitalists sufficient guarantees for their investments.

Within the framework of that pleasing prospect for investors, the eastern provinces of Cuba were a particularly tempting morsel. Less developed than the western half of the country, the provinces of Camagüey and Oriente had abundant resources, a good part of which had yet to be exploited. They contained extensive territories still displaying the exuberance of the original vegetation on the island, with thick forests of precious wood and virgin soil. Oriente, in particular, had rich mineral deposits that had been attracting the nascent U.S. metallurgical monopolies since the last decade of the nineteenth century. Ownership of the territory in those regions also reflected their backwardness. The boundaries of many large landholdings were inexact, and they provided their owners with no effective return save for the products sent them occasionally by sharecroppers and tenant farmers. Most of the estates were preserved intact with the same legal status in which they had been turned over to their owners centuries before, and the property rights of their occupants were bedecked with complicated formulas of little legal force.[2] In such circumstances, aggravated by the prevailing poverty, that land would fall easy prey to foreign capitalists.

The birds of prey soon flocked to the easy pickings. Following the forces of occupation, a wave of adventurers and speculators invaded the country, anxious to make the most of the situation. Within two years, more than a hundred claims to mineral deposits had been lodged—more than the number of concessions granted by the Spanish government over the course of decades. Land speculators bought up enormous tracts of land, subdivided them, and sold them to farmers from various parts of the United States, whom they dazzled with promises that they would be opening up a new "frontier." But, in spite of their vast numbers, those activities were no more than light cavalry operations compared with the cautious advance of the monopolies. In 1899, U.S. capital penetrated Cuba's tobacco industry. That laid the bases for the creation of the American Cigar Company, a subsidiary of the American Tobacco Company, which swallowed up more than twenty cigar and cigarette factories. By the next year, after defeating the British interests in that sector, the trust controlled 90 percent of Cuba's exports of processed tobacco.[3]

United States investments in the sugar industry, which had begun two decades earlier, were given a tremendous boost with the United States's occupation of the island. Manuel Rionda, of Spanish-U.S. descent, bought the Tuinicú sugar mill in 1893 and, in association with other U.S. interests, obtained title to more than 26,800 hectares of land in southern Camagüey in 1899 to build the Francisco sugar mill. At the same time, the United Fruit Company was building another sugar mill in the old banana-growing area around Banes and, by engaging in some pretty shady maneuvers, got hold of nearly 80,400 hectares of land in Nipe for the amazing price of $189,000.[4] R. B. Hawley made a similar investment near Puerto Padre, where he built the Chaparra sugar mill, which, together with the Tinguaro and Mercedes sugar mills in Matanzas, would soon form the industrial base of the Cuban American Sugar Company. Frequent press reports about the formation of capitalist syndicates in New York, Boston, and other cities in the United States for the purpose of investing in Cuba added to this flurry of financial activity, enveloping the country in a dense atmosphere of speculation, which, many said, would lift only when nothing Cuban was left in Cuba.

As was only to be expected, the public service sector was one of the areas that drew the most astute capitalists from the north. The street lights in Havana and other cities, the aqueducts and sewage systems, transportation, and some other services quickly figured in the designs of more than one group of investors, but business did not move ahead so quickly in this field. In March 1899, some U.S. political sectors whose interests were opposed to the annexation of Cuba managed to get the U.S. Senate to pass an amendment presented by Senator J. B. Foraker, which stated that the U.S. government and its military authorities in Cuba could not grant any concessions as long as the island was occupied. With affected Puritanism, the Foraker Act tried to guard the military administration of Cuba against the enticements of capitalists and speculators, to keep it from being involved in any of the scandals that periodically rocked the branches of the federal government. Even though nobody doubted that the application of the law would be less strict than its wording, investors in public services were forced to direct their first steps toward gaining control of the old companies in that branch, which held concessions granted by the Spanish colonial government. The preceding idea was not an original one, at least as regards the railroad sector, since British capital, which had been linked to Cuba's railroads for a long time and was the creditor of many of them, had taken a lead and, by early 1899, controlled nearly all of the important railroads in western Cuba. The only railroads that were still in Spanish-Cuban hands were the Matanzas and the Cárdenas y Júcaro, whose financial situation was quite solid, and Ferrocarril Urbano de La Habana. This last company, which had been founded in 1857, provided public transportation in the capital, using an outdated system of animal-drawn streetcars. Its proprietors had obtained authorization to install electric power for the lines in 1897, but the company's disastrous financial straits led it to postpone that improvement until after the war.[5] Ferrocarril Urbano de La Habana was not what might be called a good business at the time, but its possible development with an injection of capital augured a brilliant future. Some English capitalists (probably Schröder's, the group that had obtained control of Ferrocarriles Unidos in early 1898) became aware of this and decided to make the board of directors of Ferrocarril Urbano a purchase offer in March 1898.[6] The stockholders in the streetcar company discussed the offer, but the negotiations were never completed, probably due to the situation created by United States intervention in Cuba's War of Independence.

When the U.S. authorities took over the Cuban government in January 1899, Ferrocarril Urbano de La Habana was still in the hands of its old owners. The presence of that weak company in such a strategic position immediately caught the eye of would-be investors. In March 1899, a powerful New York syndicate whose members included T. F. Ryan, P. A. B. Widener, E. L. Elkins, George Harvey, Percival Farquhar, H. M. Whitney, and others who controlled the street-car business in New York and other large cities in the United States began to compete with the company's callow British "suitors." Several other groups, in-cluding one of Canadian capitalists who operated several streetcar companies in that country, joined the ranks of the competitors. By mid-1899, no fewer than six syndicates were engaged in the battle for control of Havana's streetcar company. The New York group emerged the victor and rechristened Ferrocarril Urbano, calling it the Havana Electric Railway Company, the name under which Ha-vana's streetcars were operated from then on.[7] Since the capitalists were willing to squabble over a few kilometers of track, it was only logical that the most important railroad project of the time—the Ferrocarril Central—should be resuscitated. Drawn up in the nineteenth century, the Ferrocarril Central plan had been the object of many studies and evaluations, but its implementation was hindered by a series of adverse factors and interests. This time, however, it wasn't private entre-preneurs who dug up the old project. The strategic importance of the central railroad didn't escape Robert P. Porter, the U.S. agent President McKinley had commissioned to make a study of the situation in Cuba at the conclusion of the hostilities against Spain. In his report, Porter recommended the immediate con-struction of a railroad "from one end of the Island to the other." His illustrative arguments in favor of this enterprise deserve to be cited at greater length:

> No revolution could have existed in Cuba if such a railroad had been com-pleted by the former Government, and nothing will so rapidly tend to the revival of commercial and general business as the facility for quick passage from one end of the Island to the other. . . .
>
> All political turbulence will be quieted thereby and prevented in the future. The entire country will be open to commerce; lands now of prac-tically no value, and unproductive, will be worked; the seaport towns will become active and commerce between the Island and the United States will soon be restored to the former figures.[8]

Divested of all rhetoric, two aspects remain very clear in Porter's view: the Ferrocarril Central would be a key component for achieving political-military control of Cuba, and its construction would strengthen the island's economic ties with the United States, facilitating the entry of imperialist capital. The impor-tance that Washington gave this matter was expressed shortly afterward, when the topic of the Ferrocarril Central occupied a prominent place in Secretary of War Russell A. Alger's annual report.[9]

With such a favorable atmosphere, no time was wasted before proposals for building the new railroad began to be made. As on former occasions, several groups of capitalists sought the Ferrocarril Central concession, though it should be noted that, in this case, newspaper reports were not precise in clearly identifying the groups and projects. Everything indicates that the English syndicate that had acquired three railroads in Las Villas Province and consolidated them under the name of Cuban Central Railways was one of the first groups to express an interest, but this went up in smoke with the passage of the Foraker Act, since it couldn't be hoped that the Washington government would break the law to hand over control of the Cuban railroad system to an English company.

Undoubtedly, the most active promoters were some capitalists in the group that controlled Havana's streetcars, headed by Percival Farquhar. In June 1899, his representative, General Guyon F. Greenwood, manager and chief engineer of the Havana Electric Company, presented the Secretaría de Obras Públicas (Secretariat of Public Works) of the supervisory government with a formal request for permission to build the Ferrocarril Central. The following month, the press reported that Greenwood had begun negotiations with Lille Constructions, a French company which had bid for Ferrocarril Central in 1885 and, it was said, had the most complete available studies on the projected line.[10] This spate of activity wound up by catching the public's attention. The matter even reached the stage of a Havana theater (the Lara), where the play *El Ferrocarril Central* premiered in November 1899. Interest didn't ensure success, however. General Greenwood's project failed to elicit a warm enough response among the authorities in Havana and Washington, and it began to languish by the end of the year. It seemed that the construction of the Ferrocarril Central would be frustrated yet again, this time by the Foraker Act, unless someone with the prestige and connections needed to smooth its way were found. That man arrived in Havana in January 1900: William Van Horne.

Cuban and foreign historians have woven an attractive myth around the personality of Sir William Van Horne, stating that, more than a common businessman, Van Horne was a creative, intrepid, tenacious entrepreneur who kept in mind the needs of the countries in which he operated. Like every myth, this one, too, collapsed when confronted with a detailed analysis of the facts.

Born in Illinois, the United States, to a family of Dutch immigrants, William C. Van Horne typified the railroad builders who filled an entire chapter of U.S. economic history. He began his career at the age of fourteen by working as a telegraph operator for the Illinois Central Railway and, thanks to a mixture of energy, ability, and luck, managed to rise quite rapidly to executive positions in the management of several railroad companies in the northwestern part of the United States.

In 1881, he resigned his post as general manager of the Chicago, Milwaukee and St. Paul Railway Company to take charge of the construction of the Canadian Pacific, the transcontinental railroad that was planned for Canada. Under his direction, the work progressed rapidly, and the Canadian Pacific attained its cherished goal of linking the country's two coasts. The achievement made Van Horne famous; he had built what many considered the most important railroad of the century.

Three years later, he was made president of Canadian Pacific, and shortly afterward the British crown rewarded him with a knighthood. Sir William had become an institution in the business world. An important stockholder in Canadian Pacific and other railroad companies, he did not limit his activities to that sphere but ventured far afield. He bought land and flour mills; founded a salt-extracting company; and invested in mining, streetcar companies, and other branches of production and services. From all this, he made some important friends. Here, we will note just three: Russell A. Alger, who was secretary of war in McKinley's cabinet, with whom Van Horne founded two important pulp paper companies in Canada; William MacKenzie, his partner in controlling the city streetcars in Toronto, St. John, and other Canadian cities; and H. M. Whitney, with whom Sir William collaborated in developing mining and metallurgical companies in Cape Breton. After long years of service, Van Horne resigned as the president of Canadian Pacific in 1899, retaining only the honorary position of chairman of the board. Freed from those responsibilities, he was ready to embark on his Cuban "adventure."[11]

It had begun some months earlier when, together with MacKenzie and some other partners in his Canadian streetcar businesses, Van Horne founded one of the syndicates that fought for control of Ferrocarril Urbano de La Habana. As has been seen, that business was finally controlled by a powerful group from New York, but, after some talks, its members considered it wise to include Van Horne and MacKenzie on the board of directors of Havana Electric. The first few days of the twentieth century found Sir William en route to Havana. At some point on the trip, he met with Alger and Elihu Root, his successor as U.S. secretary of war. "Van Horne heard them discuss the desirability, on strategical grounds, of building a railway through the eastern provinces, and also the apparently insurmountable obstacle which the Foraker Act had placed in the way of such a project."[12] In Havana, Percival Farquhar, of Havana Electric, met Sir William and lost no time in speaking to him about streetcars and inviting him to join a party that was about to leave for Las Villas Province on a special train. Van Horne returned from that trip determined to build the Ferrocarril Central. There are too many coincidences here. What was William Van Horne doing, taking a trip to the unhealthful tropics to visit the property of a small company he didn't even control? Was his meeting with Alger and Root coincidental? If, at least, Farquhar and Greenwood, of Havana Electric, hadn't spent months arranging the Ferrocarril Central concession . . . When the various threads are tied together, the myth must yield. Van Horne was not the only one responsible for the Ferrocarril Central, and sole paternity cannot be ascribed to him, but he unquestionably was the man indicated for carrying it out—or, as his colleagues would have described him, the right man in the right place. With excellent connections in the highest spheres of the Washington government, Van Horne also had sufficient prestige as a railroad builder to convince investors of the success of the enterprise, whose legal ramifications were so uncertain. Moreover, that creative personality, a knight of His Britannic Majesty, could hardly be presented as an adventurous speculator by any U.S. congressman who didn't like the way the Foraker Act was being applied.

The act was the main obstacle to carrying out the project. As soon as he returned to New York, Van Horne consulted with Howard Mansfield, an expert railroad lawyer, on what to do about it. His idea was to buy land in Cuba and build the railroad as a private venture of a Cuban company. Mansfield considered that in that case, as long as no official concession was required, the Foraker Act wouldn't be applicable. But Van Horne needed more security. Together with Grenville Dodge,[13] who had built the Union Pacific, the first U.S. transcontinental railroad, Sir William visited Washington and presented his plans personally to President McKinley. "The President expressed approval of the project and promised to do what he properly could to have it protected in law before the Occupation ended."[14] With that guarantee, Van Horne set about founding the company that would undertake the work of building the railroad. It was not hard to do, since a large number of its future stockholders already supported it. Such was the case of Percival Farquhar, W. L. Bull, P. A. B. Widener and W. L. Elkins (his brother-in-law), Anthony Brady, and Thomas F. Ryan, of the Havana Electric Company.[15] Ryan's inclusion was particularly important, for he would bring the new company the financial backing of the Morton Trust Company, which he controlled. Morton's president, Levi P. Morton, was a former governor of New York and vice-president of the United States. Others who purchased stock in the new company included Henry P. and William C. Whitney, capitalists from the mining and railroad sector; G. G. Haven, a railroad man connected with the house of Morgan; and some old buddies of Van Horne's, such as R. B. Angus, former manager of the Bank of Montreal, and C. R. Hosmer, both members of the board of directors of Canadian Pacific; Thomas C. Shaughnessy, president of that company; and James J. Hill, president of several important railroad companies in the northwestern part of the United States. E. J. Berwind, a coal magnate linked to the house of Morgan; Henry M. Flagler, a railroad man from Florida; J. W. Mackay, founder of Commercial Cable and of Postal Telegraph; Samuel Thomas, a railroad man and a key figure in the Chase National Bank;

and General Grenville Dodge, who had collaborated with Van Horne in the preliminaries for founding the company, also put a lot of money into the company. With that list of associates, whose aggregate wealth amounted to several hundred million dollars, Van Horne founded the Cuba Company in April 1900. Incorporated under the laws of the state of New Jersey, it had an authorized capital of $8 million but issued only 160 stock certificates, each worth $50,000. This indicated both the financial standing of its stockholders and the closed concentration of capital in the company, which was unquestionably the most powerful of all those which invested in Cuba during the first neocolonial decade.

Van Horne's first action after the Cuba Company's New York office was opened was to send a party of engineers to Cuba to make an on-the-spot, definitive decision concerning what route the railroad would take. L. A. Hamilton, land commissioner for Canadian Pacific, accompanied them to assess the natural resources of the regions crossed by the projected line and to conciliate economic interests with technical criteria in the details of the design. The route that was finally approved was not much different (see Map 11.1) from the plan that had been drawn up for the railroad in the 1880s. The railroad that would link the cities of Santa Clara and Santiago de Cuba would run through the center of the island, following the watershed whenever possible, so as to keep the construction of bridges to a minimum and to simplify the infrastructure work. That design would link the main cities outside the capital, and small, single-track branch lines would provide access to those cities which, for technical reasons, could not be included on the main line—for example, Sancti Spíritus and Holguín would be left out. The project was favored by the topographical characteristics of most of the territory the railroad was to serve, which had few high mountains. The only critical point in that regard would have been the entry to Santiago de Cuba, but that obstacle had, fortunately, been overcome half a century before by the tiny railroad line between Santiago de Cuba and Sabanilla and Maroto. At the end of the nineteenth century, the Santiago de Cuba company had been virtually in the hands of U.S. capital, represented in that case by the Ponupo Mining Company.[16] After some brief negotiations with the mining company, Van Horne obtained control of Ferrocarril de Santiago de Cuba, in what may be considered his first important operation in Cuba.[17]

Without greater technical or economic difficulties, the main problem confronting the Cuba Company's project was of a legal nature. Because of the Foraker Act, the company would have to obtain the right of way without any official concessions and without the possibility of exercising the useful privilege of forcible expropriation. The land to be crossed by the railroad would have to be purchased from its owners on a voluntary basis, without resorting to any kind of

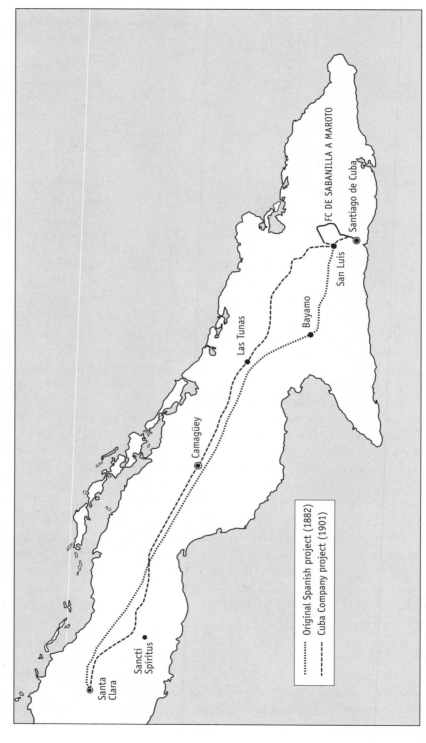

MAP 11.1. The Central Railroad

Original Spanish project (1882)
Cuba Company project (1901)

Santa Clara

Sancti Spíritus

Camagüey

Las Tunas

Bayamo

San Luis

FC DE SABANILLA A MAROTO

Santiago de Cuba

Forests cleared in Oriente for construction of the Central Railroad. (W. H. Carlson, *Report of the Special Commission on Railroads*. Havana, 1901)

legal pressure. That situation called for a line of conduct that Van Horne defined to the officials of his company without any beating about the bush:

> Deal with them throughout with politeness, . . . for we cannot afford to antagonize even the humblest individual if it can be avoided. Our engineers will give the first impression of the Cuba Company to the people in the districts where they are operating, and they should seek in every way to create among these people a pleasant impression. . . . Anyone unable to control his temper and who violates the rule which should be made in this regard should be promptly got rid of. I am anxious that the people throughout the country should become impressed as quickly as possible with the desire of the Cuba Company to treat everybody with the greatest consideration and to deal with them in all matters with perfect fairness.[18]

In a population accustomed to see foreigners behave like masters, the conduct Van Horne defined naturally came as a pleasant surprise. This was an important element in the myth. The purchase of land was preceded by a heavy barrage of propaganda. The officials of the company provided the newspapers with plentiful information about the benefits the new railroad would bring, painting the company as a quasi-philanthropic entity.[19] For the same purpose, Van Horne wrote personally to the civil governors of the eastern provinces and even to the various municipal authorities in the region. Lastly, the Cuba Company contracted the services of some prestigious Cuban lawyers who would act as the vanguard of the agents who would buy the land, explaining the company's intentions and good-will to the people.[20] This tactic promptly bore fruit. In October 1900, a large group of landowners from Santa Clara, who had been called together by Mayor Gerardo Machado, decided to cede the strips of land needed for the railroad to cross through that region. The land was contributed free of charge in many cases and for a minimal charge in others.[21] The same thing was repeated in other places, and the municipal authorities even took a hand in convincing those owners who opposed the land transfers. The land thus acquired guaranteed that the Cuba Company would have long strips of land on which to lay its tracks, plus plots on which to build new towns and even to develop extensive agricultural areas. However, that land lacked the continuity required to carry out the railroad project in full. Here and there, the land the company had obtained was cut by rivers, public roads, and state land, which it could not cross without official authorization. Therefore, even though Van Horne had begun the work of expla-nation, stating that his purpose was to clear everything up and then request the concessions after the sections had been completed, that was nothing but hot air.[22] The various sections could not be laid in fragments, and, as the work advanced, it became absolutely necessary to obtain official authorization to cross state prop-erty. The position that the supervisory government took on this matter would be decisive for the success of the project.

Leonard Wood, military governor of Cuba, had known and approved of Van Horne's railroad project right from the start, but now official decisions had to be made with regard to it, a matter that involved considerable risk. As the highest-ranking U.S. authority in Cuba, Wood was in charge of seeing to it that the Foraker Act was complied with, and, even though he was an ardent partisan of the construction of the Ferrocarril Central, he was not ready to compromise his promising political career by taking responsibility for a scandalous violation of the law. The crafty governor decided to pass the buck to Secretary of War Elihu Root and did so in a letter dated December 22, 1900: "I do not think that it is contrary to the letter or spirit of the Foraker resolution since the State is not making any concessions. . . . I think, nevertheless, that this business deserves to be thought through and definitely concluded. If there are objections it is better to have them now than later. I think that the work is of vital importance and should be properly done. . . . It is my wish to avoid any embarrassment either to the President or to you. . . . I think that the matter is of great importance to the island and I would like to finish the work if at all possible."[23] Wood was evidently anxious to boost the work on the railroad but didn't want to take full responsibility for the matter and, while wanting to "avoid an embarrassment" for Root and McKinley, he protected himself by reporting the situation to them.

While the governor of Cuba was consulting with his superiors, Van Horne moved quickly in Washington's official circles, calling on President McKinley; Root; and Senators Aldrich, Foraker, and Platt, among others. From those consultations and clandestine meetings, there emerged the magic formula of a "revocable license." Governor Wood could grant "revocable licenses" authorizing the Cuba Company to cross public property. Since those licenses were granted provisionally, investing the beneficiary with no permanent rights, neither the Washington government nor its authorities in Cuba could be accused of giving public land to private individuals. Even so, Wood did not put the handy solution into practice until he had gotten the go-ahead from the secretary of war. In spite of everything, the licenses were generally granted in the midst of a show Van Horne put on to give Governor Wood added protection. When the track came close to a river, road, or other property in the public domain, the officials of the Cuba Company halted the work and laid the workers off, claiming that the company was not authorized to continue. Telegrams from the town halls, workers, merchants, and other groups adversely affected by the work stoppage would then pour in and begin piling up on Wood's desk, requesting him to grant the company the license it needed to continue the work. The governor, a "soft touch," would then agree to grant the licenses in response to the people's will.

By means of the timely stratagem of "revocable licenses," the Cuba Company overcame all of the obstacles in its path in the early months of 1901, and it continued to benefit from that procedure until the end of the U.S. military occupation of Cuba.[24] Van Horne, however, took every opportunity to bring out the weak legality of the licenses and the risk the Cuba Company was running by building under conditions that left it "entirely at the mercy of the people of Cuba." He said that he was willing to do this only because of his "faith in the honour and justice of the Cuban people."[25] He was working on his myth. Sir William was perfectly aware that, along with the formulation of "revocable licenses," the U.S. government was trying to impose a legal instrument—the Platt Amendment—on Cuba that would govern Cuban-U.S. relations and reduce the sovereignty of the future republic to pure fiction. Article 4 of the amendment was made to order for the Cuba Company. When, after putting up tenacious resistance, Cuba's Constitutional Convention was forced to accept the amendment, the Cuba Company's "revocable licenses" were shored up solidly.[26]

The shady dealings surrounding the construction of the Ferrocarril Central did not pass unnoticed by Cuban public opinion. In a letter to the editor of the influential Havana daily La Lucha, José Lacret Morlot, a general in the Liberation Army and a delegate to the Constitutional Convention, denounced the fact that "a company seeking the concession of a railroad from east to west says and assures, hiding the truth, that the line is private, suggesting that the enterprise is of an almost philanthropic nature . . ., but its mask slipped, and the line crosses streets, roads, and rivers." With acute perception, Lacret foresaw the outcome of the matter: "The companies that are not legitimate will be legitimized by the Platt Amendment, which tramples on legality."[27]

Not satisfied with the legal position attained, Van Horne took an active part in reshaping Cuba's railroad legislation. For that purpose, he presented Governor Wood with a draft modeled on Canada's railway regulations. After some experts of the U.S. Interstate Commerce Commission studied and amended it, it was adopted as the railroad law for the island of Cuba.[28]

Logically, Military Order 34 was of a vast and general scope, but some of its articles reflected the situation of the Cuba Company so exactly that they seemed to have been drawn up for its exclusive benefit. Such was the case of Article 3 of Chapter XI, which facilitated the rapid conversion of private into public railroads; the facilities granted in Chapter V for acquiring all kinds of property and modifying rivers, roads, and the like in any way; and the possibilities for registering all of the territory that had been acquired, no matter what its extent and characteristics, as a single farm in the pertinent land registration office.[29] The problem of land ownership was another of Sir William's worries, one that he shared with all other U.S. businessmen who had acquired land in eastern Cuba. The complicated forms of land ownership in the eastern provinces made it difficult to legalize its transfer, leaving the owners of recently acquired land in a shaky position and limiting them in the full exercise of their "rights." The military occupation solved that problem, too, in a manner favorable to the interests of the U.S. businessmen, with the promulgation of Military Order 62, "on the setting of boundaries and the division of estates," in whose drafting Manuel de Jesús Manduley, Van Horne's and Wood's lawyer, played a considerable part. Once the legal difficulties were overcome, construction of the main track progressed with tremendous speed. The work had been begun in November 1900 in Santa Clara and San Luis—the two ends of the projected line. To speed the progress of the work, intermediate construction points were opened later on in Ciego de Avila and Camagüey, places that had railroad connections with the coast, which facilitated the movement of materials. For that purpose, the Cuba Company rented Ferrocarril de la Trocha (Júcaro-San Fernando) from the U.S. authorities for three years.[30] In Camagüey, where it used the services of Ferrocarril de Nuevitas, the company benefited from a considerable donation of land, which was later used for the construction of the railroad's repair shops and main office. In November 1901, the roadbed extended for a little more than thirty kilometers east of Santa Clara and for about the same distance west of San Luis. Work at the intermediate construction points was also progressing, in spite of the particularly bad rainy season of 1901. When the dry season began, the pace was stepped up, and at one time six thousand men were employed in grading and the laying of track. In March 1902, Van Horne announced that the roadbed had been completed and that 120 kilometers of track had been laid. Most of it was in the sections near Santa Clara and San Luis, which were the most difficult because of the many bridges that had had to be built. Then, with the more complicated sections completed, it was hoped that the railroad would be able to begin operations before the end of 1902.[31]

With the creation of the Republic of Cuba on May 20, 1902, the legal uncertainty that might still surround the work of the Ferrocarril Central was banished once and for all. The Foraker Act was no longer applicable, and Tomás Estrada Palma, the recently inaugurated president of Cuba, had hastened to ratify the validity of "all the acts of the United States in Cuba during the military occupancy" and "all rights legally acquired by virtue of said acts."[32] A few days earlier, on May 1, 1902, a new company, the Cuba Railroad Company, had been founded in New York to build a railroad between Alto Cedro and the Bay of Nipe in Oriente province. That line was simply a branch of the Ferrocarril Central that Van Horne had already planned, so as to establish a rail link between the main line and the port that the Cuba Company wanted to build at Corojal point, on the western shore of the Bay of Nipe.[33] The Cuba Railroad Company was created for two reasons. First, the work on the Ferrocarril Central had gone over its budget, and, by issuing stock in a new company, more of the required capital would be obtained. Second, Cuba Railroad would be registered in Cuba as a public service railroad, so it could take charge of operating the Ferrocarril Central without any great complications.

This ingenious operation wound up in September 1902 with the transfer of all of the Cuba Company's railroad property to Cuba Railroad. The Cuba Company retained ownership of the land and became the holding company of the Cuba Railroad Company, since it owned 60 percent of the new company's common stock.[34] In addition, several million dollars' worth of preferred stock and shares in Cuba Railroad remained, which could be placed on the stock exchange to obtain the capital required for future branches and extensions.

At the time of the transfer, work on the railroad had been practically completed. The last rail was laid in an official ceremony near Sancti Spíritus on November 12, 1902. Less than a month later, on December 1, the Cuba Railroad Company's trains began running between Santa Clara and Santiago de Cuba.

The construction of the central line and circulation of trains throughout the length of the island responded to an old need of Cuba's economy. Even though the part of the country that the new railroad served constituted 70 percent of its national territory, only 35 percent of the Cuban people lived in the area, and their proportional weight in the GNP was even less than 35 percent. The Ferrocarril Central ended the isolation of some of the richest regions of Cuba and opened up the possibility of using those new resources to speed the country's production dynamics. By facilitating the movement of men and products, the new railroad helped to consolidate the structure of a domestic market that was indispensable for the development of the Cuban economy, and it also constituted an important base for the political-administrative unification of the country.

All of those possibilities, which champions of the Ferrocarril Central project had been publicizing for half a century, would now have to be explored under the political and economic dictates implied by Cuba's new neocolonial status. And this was not merely in theory: the Ferrocarril Central was owned by a foreign company, and its actions had to please stockholders living thousands of kilometers away from Cuba, who would assess its results not in terms of the greater or lesser benefits the railroad would contribute to Cuba's economy but rather in terms of the interest they would get on their capital investment. The strategy the Cuba Company drew up for doing business expressed that reality with exceptional clarity.

The Ferrocarril Central had to promote development. Its first trains ran through extensive territories that were virtually untouched and were sparsely populated—and, therefore, did not have the freight and passengers required to pay for the railroad's operations. The company's financial success depended on radically changing that situation. The Cuba Company therefore had to become an indispensable part of the infrastructure underlying all productive activity in the eastern provinces and promote forms of exploiting the territory that would be most beneficial to the railroad.

There was much to be done in the first regard. Ipso facto, the Santa Clara–Santiago de Cuba Railroad would be the main artery of Cuban transportation, even though a network of branch and secondary lines that would bring it passengers and freight would have to be built for each region to ensure its smooth functioning. The general outlines of such a system had been brought out nearly simultaneously with the design of the main line. More than mere indications of possible branches, they included a complex infrastructure of railway lines, stations, warehouses, ports, and other installations.

The initial results of Ferrocarril Central's operation confirmed the need for those new investments. Gross income for 1903–4, the first year in which the railroad was operating at full capacity, amounted to only $524,041, which barely covered its operating costs. The main source of that income was passenger fares, a sphere in which the Cuba Railroad Company had eliminated any possible competition in November 1903 by inaugurating a service of express trains with com-

FERRO-CARRIL DE CUBA.

El lúnes 8 del actual á las 7 a. m. saldrá de esta Estación el PRIMER TREN de pasajeros para OCCIDENTE.

TARIFA DE PASAJES.

de Santiago	1.ª clase		3.ª clase	
á Las Túnas . .	6	10	3	05
„ Puerto Príncipe	9	35	4	70
„ Ciego de Avila	12	10	6	05
„ Placetas	15	30	7	65
„ Santa Clara . .	16	30	8	15
., HABANA . . .	24	00	12	00

Santiago de Cuba, 6 Diciembre 1902

Asher Gruver,

Administrador División del Este.

Imp. M, Morales, Marina baja 16.

Announcement of the beginning of passenger service between Santiago de Cuba and Havana on the completion of the Central Railroad.

fortable Pullman cars, which made the trip between Havana and Santiago de Cuba in just twenty-four hours.[35] But passenger service does not offer a solid base for a large railroad. It needs freight, and there wasn't much for the Cuba Railroad Company, both because of the little development in the regions it served and because some of the population centers had other means (ports) for sending their goods out.

Van Horne and his associates found themselves in the position of a cardplayer whose only possibility of winning lies in upping the stakes. It was absolutely necessary to increase their investment, and they couldn't expect the Ferrocarril Central's operations to contribute much for that purpose in the immediate future. That need had, to some extent, been foreseen; the creation of the Cuba Railroad Company, with several million dollars' worth of marketable stock, seemed an adequate solution, but the situation was not favorable for Van Horne. In 1903, the U.S. stock market was still reeling from the effects of the 1900 world crisis, and the quotations for the Cuba Railroad Company's stocks and bonds were unfortunately low. Some of the stockholders in the Cuba Company (Ryan, Widener, and Elkins's group in particular), perhaps too concerned by the effects of the depression on their other businesses, even refused to increase their capital contributions by the amounts previously agreed upon. That serious situation was alleviated in December 1903 when Robert Fleming, a Scots banker, decided to buy a large block of stock in the railroad company.[36] With that step, English capital made its entry in Ferrocarril Central, though the railroad continued to be dominated by U.S. interests.

Apart from his efforts in international financial circles, Van Horne began trying to get the Cuban government to allocate economic assistance for the railroad, at least enough to enable it to meet its payments for the first mortgage on Cuba Railroad, which had to be met to maintain the company's credit. In a message to Congress on November 7, 1904, President Estrada Palma echoed that view of the situation and asked for authorization to grant the railroad company a subsidy of $798,450, which would cover the first three annual payments of its mortgage.[37] Both houses of Congress considered the proposal and finally approved it in August 1905. One month later, Hacienda (Treasury) Secretary Juan Ríus Rivera handed over the first $266,150 as a noninterest-bearing "refundable advance to be repaid in ten years." Moreover, it could be repaid by providing services to the Cuban government. Van Horne described the passage of the bill as "one of the cleanest transactions of the kind I have ever seen," while ordering that the 13,000 pesos paid to his lawyers for facilitating the procedure be recorded as "development costs."[38]

Even before the government loan was granted, the financial recovery following the 1903 crisis led some stockholders in the Cuba Company to increase their investments by around $2,725,000. Robert Fleming joined them, buying another block of stock for $700,000, considerably increasing British capital's influence in the company. Later on, W. H. Whigham, one of Fleming's men, would have a seat on the board of the Cuba Company.[39] Once those difficulties had been surmounted, the Cuba Company went ahead with its development plans. Prior to December 1904, it had been able to inaugurate only one small, eighteen-kilometer-long branch line, which connected the main line with the city of Sancti Spíritus. The Alto Cedro branch and the Nipe port project, which had been the express purpose of the Cuba Railroad Company's founding in 1902, had had to be put on hold but then received greater attention. While the docks and warehouses of what would be the port of Antilla on Nipe Bay were being built—a port that the Cuba Company hoped would become one of the country's main export centers—work was pushed ahead on grading and laying track for the Alto Cedro branch, which was opened to traffic in April 1905. Two years later, the eighteen-kilometer-long branch between Cacocúm, on the main line, and the city of Holguín was finished, thus completing the Cuba Company's primitive rail plan. Future extensions would be more important and ambitious. The company's engineers had been studying the most advantageous routes for the growth of the railway system for some time. First of all, they emphasized the need to extend rail-road services to the extremely rich valley of the Cauto River, which the main line barely touched in conditions that didn't allow it to handle the transportation of its products. For that purpose, the engineers designed a branch line that would run in a southeasterly direction for 226 kilometers from Martí, a hamlet on the main line at the eastern border of Camagüey, through the city of Bayamo and other towns to the foothills of the Sierra Maestra until it linked up with the Ferrocarril Central again in San Luis.[40] That important line, in turn, would have a fifty-two-kilometer-long branch line between Bayamo and Manzanillo, a port city with inhabitants where the Cuba Company could build docks and warehouses.

In addition to that line, plans called for the construction of a branch in Las Villas province, between Placetas and Fernández, the last station on the un-finished Ferrocarril de Trinidad, which the Cuba Company was thinking about acquiring, together with the port installations at Casilda.[41] Studies were also being made of the possibility of extending the main line to Cienfuegos through the Manicaragua Valley and of building a line between Camagüey and Santa Cruz del Sur, an old railroad dream of the residents of Camagüey Province.

Stimulated by the fruits obtained from his recent negotiations with the Cuban government, Van Horne sent his lawyers to persuade some members of Congress to draw up a law that would permit the government to subsidize the construction of railroads in those regions where it deemed this convenient. A bill was presented and discussed in Congress between April and June 1906 and was finally approved by President Estrada Palma on July 5 that same year.[42] Although the law promoted the construction of a dozen railroads, some of them outside the sphere of the Cuba Company, it gave top priority to the Martí-Bayamo-Manzanillo-San Luis and Placetas-Fernández branches—that is, to the extensions that the Cuba Company proposed to build immediately.

The law empowered the president to subsidize the construction of the routes called for at a rate of up to 6,000 pesos per kilometer, allocating 500,000 pesos of the national budget for that purpose every year. This law gave the government a handy instrument for promoting means of communication in those regions of the country that most needed them. That possibility, however, was made less likely when the proposed lines were defined in accord with the more or less expressed interests of the main railroad companies.

Two months after the law was promulgated, the Cuban government signed its first contract, with the Cuba Railroad Company, to build the Martí-Bayamo-Manzanillo-San Luis branch, for which it granted the maximum subsidy of 6,000 pesos per kilometer. The contract called for the railroad company to begin building the new line the following year. Even though the work was beset by difficulties of various kinds and the contract had to be renegotiated with the administration of José Miguel Gómez, the Bayamo branch was opened for service on January 1, 1911.[43]

At the close of its first decade of operations, the Cuba Company had a railroad network 935.6 kilometers long serving the regions in the eastern provinces that were the most important economically. Those lines offered the only railroad access available to three of the main ports in the area, one of which (Antilla) was owned lock, stock, and barrel by the railroad company. The growth of the rail system was accompanied by a corresponding increase in the company's rolling stock, which, by the end of 1910, consisted of 58 locomotives, 65 passenger cars, and 1,449 freight cars. A large, modern railroad repair shop had been set up in Camagüey to provide maintenance for them, and the company's main office in Cuba was located there as well. In addition to its railroad installations (stations and warehouses), Cuba Railroad had also purchased hotels in the main cities served by the line and had entered into freight agreements with several shipping companies, to facilitate the movement of passengers.

Convinced that prosperity in the railroad business depended on the promotion of freight, the Cuba Company took some decisive steps to promote production, especially in the agricultural sector. Van Horne's initial views on this matter were full of the traditional concepts of railroad development in North America and of his own experience in promoting agricultural development on the Canadian prairies. In synthesis, these involved the classic model of farming colonization, consisting of the sale or leasing of relatively small plots to individual farmers who would settle on them, developing production. That system promoted the simultaneous growth of both production and population, which, in railroad terms, meant freight and passengers. This concept is what led Van Horne to make his famous attack on large landholdings, urging Wood to levy heavy taxes on unproductive land, a stand that liberal historians have praised into the ground.[44] The railroad promoter had no doubts that operating his railroad in the midst of large unproductive landholdings would be like opening a restaurant in the middle of a desert. But Van Horne soon became aware of the distinguishing characteristics of Cuban agriculture and its economy, especially of its real development possibilities within the U.S. imperialist sphere. If he had any misgivings, the Cuban-U.S. "Reciprocal" Trade Agreement of 1903 laid them to rest. From then on, he spoke of sugar mills and plantations, not farms.

Even though the Cuba Company promoted settlements of U.S. farmers in several places in the eastern provinces, including some on its own land (at Bartle and Omaja, for example), early on—as early as 1903—it started concentrating on building sugar mills in the territories served by its railroad.

Years later, William Van Horne himself, who had suggested that drastic measures be taken against the large landholdings, would boast to the stockholders that his company owned around 121,500 hectares of land in Cuba, much of which was lying idle but which he preferred to hang on to because land prices were going up.[45] Some of it consisted of the strips of land that were the railroad's right of way and small plots between thirteen and sixty-seven hectares in size close to the line in towns or at stations, which would be most useful if subdivided into city lots. But, in addition to that land, the Cuba Company had acquired farms and estates of undeniable agricultural value, many of which were large enough to be considered large landholdings. They included a group of farms in Jatibonico that were more than 5,360 hectares in size; the Tana sugarcane plantation at Guáimaro, 3,028 hectares; the Mano Pilón estate, 2,787 hectares, near the port of Antilla; a 10,720-hectare section near the Baraguá estate, near Alto Cedro, which the company renamed the Van Horne sugarcane plantation; and, above all, the Cabaniguán (Jobabo) estate, 40,374 hectares, on the border between Camagüey and Oriente Provinces.

The use the Cuba Company made of its land is very indicative. After making some small initial investments in, for example, lumbering, sawmills, and cattle, it concentrated on sugar. In 1904, the Cuba Company approved a $4 million stock issue to finance the construction of two sugar mills. Almost immediately, it began work on one of them in Jatibonico, in western Camagüey, where the company had acquired a large amount of land when the railroad was being built. The new sugar mill went into operation at the end of the 1906 sugarcane harvest and made its owners a profit of $158,027 in the next harvest.[46] The second sugar mill, which

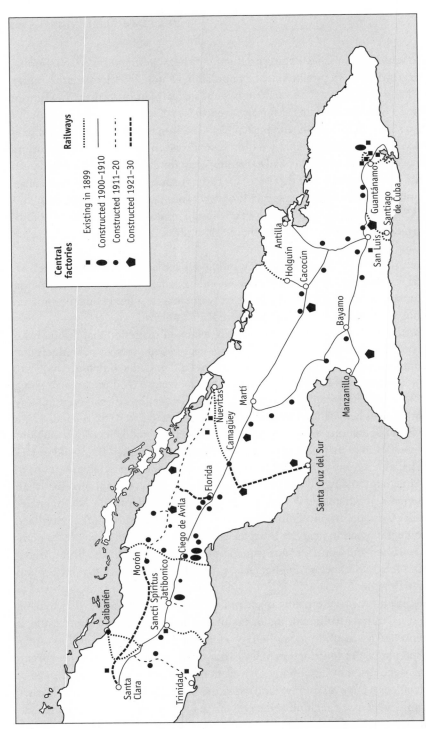

MAP 11.2. Expansion of the Eastern Network and the Development of Central Factories, 1900–1930

was to have been built on the Tana sugarcane plantation, in Camagüey, was finally built in Jobabo, in the center of an estate over 40,200 hectares in size. The Cuba Company thus took the initiative in seeing if large landholdings in the rich territories in eastern Cuba would prove successful if planted to sugarcane.

The results obtained in the first decade were not very satisfactory: only four sugar mills (two of them belonging to the railroad company itself) began to exploit the areas served by the Ferrocarril Central. But, in the next decade, with a favorable economic situation, the Cuba Company was delighted that its railroad system was surrounded by the canefields of thirty-one sugar mills (nineteen of them owned by U.S. interests) whose aggregate agrarian holdings came to over 400,000 hectares of land.[47] (See Map 11.2.)

The Ferrocarril Central brought civilization to the eastern regions of Cuba—only, in this case, "civilization" took the form of a gigantic imperialist plantation. The figures show the nature of the advance. When the Ferrocarril Central was inaugurated, the eastern provinces contributed only 17 percent of the nation's sugar, which was then estimated at 850,151 tons. Twenty years later, those regions provided 50 percent of the nation's sugar, which was five times as great as it had been. Productive inequality had disappeared, and the country was unified—under the aegis of single production.

Demographic inequality wasn't done away with so quickly, however. Even though the population in the eastern provinces had grown at a higher rate than the national average, people did not multiply as quickly as sugar production. The most eloquent case is that of Camagüey.[48] Between 1899 and 1919, Camagüey's population nearly tripled, but its sugar production multiplied 140-fold. That phenomenon cannot be explained by a spectacular increase in the productivity of the Camagüeyans. Rather, it was due to the fact that seasonal workers who were brought in from outside the province did a considerable part of the work. Demographically, the Camagüey plains continued to be a desert, where the sugarcane grew for half the year untouched by human hands.[49]

Growth without population: that is the reality which the large sugarcane estates imposed. And the railroad wasn't divorced from that situation. During the sugarcane harvests, the trains transported thousands of day laborers who went to the vast and alien world of the plantations in search of sustenance. The Ferrocarril Central, of course, was not the determining factor in that situation, but it did play a key role in its existence.

Moreover, the railroad service had another demographic effect that should be brought out. In 1899, there were only ten towns with over one thousand inhabitants along what would be the Cuba Company's main lines. Two decades later, there were nineteen such towns, five of which (Jatibonico, Florida, Martí, Jobabo, and Antilla) owed their very existence to the building of the railroad. Ten years after inaugurating its services, the Ferrocarril Central had achieved unquestionable economic success. In 1912, Van Horne announced with jubilation that the railroad company's gross income amounted to $3,819,253, so that, after meeting its expenses, it could pay 6 percent interest on its preferred stock and 4.5-percent interest on its common stock—quite a respectable rate.[50] The global interests of imperialism had also been satisfied: the riches of the eastern part of Cuba were laid open to the monopolies' voracity. Only the hopes of the Cuban economy were defrauded; once more, the railroad was a factor of growth but not of development.

The Ferrocarril Central, which headed straight east from Santa Clara, dipped southward when it reached Alto Cedro to reach Santiago de Cuba. Thus, it skirted an enormous territory, the easternmost part of Cuba, whose complex topography and numerous mountains in the Sierra de Nipe and Sagua-Baracoa ranges presented serious obstacles to railroad transportation. In that generally mountainous area, there was one important exception: the Guantánamo Valley. The basis of a flourishing economy, the fertile land of Guantánamo had first been settled by coffee growers, who then gave pride of place to sugarcane, which was already the main economic activity in the valley at the end of the nineteenth century.

Commercial operations in the region had, since 1856, used the services of Ferrocarril de Guantánamo, which connected it to the city of the same name, with a landing stage at Caimanera, and which had branch lines to some important sugar mills.[51] The railroad company and a large part of the commercial operations were controlled by the Anglo-Cuban Brook family, which also owned three of the largest sugar mills in the area.

The War of Independence did less damage to Guantánamo than had the Ten Years' War.[52] The local economy recovered rapidly, and its eleven sugar mills contributed around sixteen thousand tons of sugar in the 1899 sugarcane harvest. Even so, the estate owners in the Guantánamo area, like those nearly everywhere else in the country, were faced with a difficult financial situation, because of the combined effects of the war and the low world price of sugar.

The Brook family was no exception. In 1903, when the signing of the "Reciprocal" Trade Agreement ensured the commercial prospects of Cuban sugar, the brothers Ernesto and Teodoro Brook went to U.S. financial circles (where they had old connections) in search of credit and backing. As a result, the Guantánamo Sugar Company was created in 1905, consisting of the Brooks' three sugar mills (the Isabel, Soledad, and Los Caños), the railroad, and the warehouses and port installations at Caimanera. Even though Ernesto was on the board of directors of the new company and Teodoro was vice-president and general manager, the Brooks had become the junior partners of a group of powerful U.S. capitalists, among whom James H. Post was prominent.[53] With the creation of the Guantánamo Sugar Company, the old Ferrocarril de Guantánamo, while theoretically continuing to be a public service railroad, in practice became the private railroad of the sugar company.

Meanwhile, in the same region, other U.S. interests began to develop one of the most fabulous cases of railroad speculation in the history of the neocolony. The Cuban Eastern Railroad Company, promoted by a group of small-scale capitalists grouped around New York's Knickerbocker Trust Company, had been founded in the state of Maine, the United States, on September 19, 1902. According to the request presented to the Comisión de Ferrocarriles de Cuba (Cuban Railroad Commission) a few months later, the company proposed to build and operate a 40.7-kilometer-long railroad between Boquerón, on the eastern shore of Guantánamo Bay, and the town of Sempré, on the northwestern rim of the valley. The railroad's promoters thought that the new railroad could easily assimilate the cargo from some of the sugar mills in the area, whose transportation needs were not met by the old Ferrocarril de Guantánamo. In view of the richness of the valley, it wouldn't be difficult to promote other businesses, which would guarantee the prosperity of the new railroad service.[54]

The plan was completed with the construction of a port in Boquerón, for which the group of investors created a new company in 1904: the Cuban Eastern Terminal Company, which would be in charge of building and operating three docks and warehouses large enough to handle around forty thousand sacks of sugar. Immediately after those investments were completed, the same group created another company, the Northeastern Cuba Railroad, with a capital of $2 million. This third company would be in charge of building another railroad line to link the terminal of the Cuban Eastern Railroad Company, in Sempré, with the Ferrocarril Central line in San Luis. The new line was inaugurated in 1907, but not before the building company had to assume a $2.5 million mortgage, which the Knickerbocker Trust Company held.[55]

Such a proliferation of small companies promoted by a single group of capitalists clearly shows the speculative nature of its investments. That system of supposedly independent bodies was a guarantee against the insecurity of each investment, for, if any of them should fail, the others would not be endangered.[56] Moreover, each new company represented a possibility of placing new stock on the market and, with it, of "fishing" for the capital of small, incautious stockholders. The basis of all these business conglomerates was, moreover, incredibly weak, and each new project expressed a hope of finding, with that business, the wherewithal for putting the earlier ones on a sounder footing. Thus, even though the line had not been completed to San Luis, the promoters of the Cuban Eastern Railroad Company brought out another, more ambitious plan. As always, it involved creating a new company—in this case, the Eastern Railroad Company of

Cuba—which would consolidate all of the earlier ones and build a new line between San Luis and Manzanillo. The second part of the plan was an attempt to snatch the Cuba Company's planned Bayamo—San Luis branch away from it—a branch for which the Cuban government had just approved a subsidy of 6,000 pesos per kilometer. Even though that attempt failed, the Cuban Eastern Railroad Company was still founded in February 1907, with an authorized capital of $4 million.

The Guantánamo investment ruse failed to survive the world crisis of 1907, for the Knickerbocker Trust, its financial underpinning, was the first New York bank to close its doors, triggering the financial panic in October of that year.[57] What followed was one of those complicated processes of judicial complaints, liquidations, and reorganizations that, under the pretext of achieving financial stability, are, in fact, aimed only at eliminating the small stockholders, who are ruined.

A Comité de Tenedores de Bonos (committee of bondholders) from the four companies (Cuban Eastern Railroad, Cuban Eastern Terminal, Northeastern Railroad, and Eastern Railroad) was created in January 1908 to assess the situation and find a way out of it.[58] The prospect could not have been more depressing: the four corporations had slightly more than $15 million worth of stock in circulation. The physical property represented by that enormous sum consisted of 148 kilometers of track, around three hundred railroad cars, the stations, and the terminal at Boquerón. Moreover, the state of the property left a lot to be desired: the poorly ballasted track had drainage problems, and some excavations were so narrow that landslides fell onto the rails. As a result, storms could put large sections of the line out of service, as had happened in the summer of 1908. The bridges and stations were in bad condition, and the condition of the rolling stock showed where management had tried to cut corners.[59] Technicians estimated that it would take another $750,000 to restore all of the service elements to good condition.

Nevertheless, the most important thing in the eyes of the large stockholders was to reduce the amount of the companies' debts and thus enable them to recover their financial balance. The solution required no great stretch of the imagination: capitalism's bag of tricks included some well-established procedures for such cases. The existing companies would be liquidated, and all their property would be consolidated, creating a new entity with an authorized capital in the appropriate proportions. In September 1909, the Guantánamo and Western Railroad Company was created, also under the laws of the state of Maine, the United States. Its board of directors, properly rejuvenated, would be in charge of getting the Guantánamo business back on an even keel.[60]

British Monopoly in the West

In the last few decades of the nineteenth century, one old railroad company after another in the western part of Cuba passed into English hands. With a movement that showed the tremendous changes wrought in the mode of capitalist production, the big British bourgeoisie had given up its disquieting but distant role of creditor and taken direct control of the business, which, years before, it had been content merely to finance.

A British group's early acquisition of the insignificant Ferrocarril de Marianao in 1876 was the first step in that trend. Fifteen years later, after some complicated negotiations, another group of English capitalists managed to take possession of the worn out and unfinished Ferrocarril del Oeste. The next steps came more quickly. In 1898, English capital obtained a new and important company: Ferrocarriles Unidos de La Habana. The damage done by the war and Cuba's nebulous political future induced the owners of that Havana company, most of whom were Spaniards, to transfer control of the railroad to its old creditors in the J. Henry Schröder bank. While the final details of the reorganization of Ferrocarriles Unidos were being worked out in London, agents of the British group that owned Ferrocarril del Oeste (Western Railways of Havana) arranged for the sale and merger of three railroad companies in Las Villas. The operation, which was rushed through during the uncertain spring of 1899, ended with the founding of Cuban Central Railways, a British company that would operate 339 kilometers of track in central Cuba. Thus, when the neocolonial period in Cuba's history was inaugurated, English imperialist capital had managed to take over nearly all of Cuba's western railroads.

The railroads in Matanzas were the only important, though temporary, exception to that massive transfer of property. Ferrocarril de Matanzas and the Empresa Unida de los Ferrocarriles de Cárdenas y Júcaro had, for many years, headed the list of the most profitable businesses on the island. The Cárdenas y Júcaro Company, the Spaniards' favorite investment, survived the war free of debt and kept its old colonial pride solidly buttressed by the coffers of the Banco Español de la Isla de Cuba and the personal fortunes of some prominent figures in the Spanish colony, such as don Ramón Argüelles. Its capital stock of 8 million Spanish pesos, consisting of 16,000 shares worth 500 pesos each, had remained unchanged for a long time, as track extensions and other investments were usually made by charging them to the company's profits without being capitalized.

For its part, Ferrocarril de Matanzas was one of the few railroad companies in the country that was headed by a Cuban—Tirso Mesa, who was also its main stockholder. An exceptional case, the Matanzas Company had remained true to the original property outline of Cuba's railroads. Its long list of stockholders, a high proportion of whom held small and medium-sized blocks of stock, mainly consisted of the estate owners, merchants, and other owners in the region served by the railroad, who benefited both from its profits and from its services.[1] Even though Ferrocarril de Matanzas had taken out loans from English banks on more than one occasion (it had obtained one from Schröder at the end of the nineteenth century), it always made its payments punctually, so its credit standing was excellent. Like the Cárdenas line, the Matanzas company had low capitalization (both were between 20,000 and 25,000 pesos per kilometer of track), constituting one of the rare cases in which the value of the property was similar to or even greater than the company's registered stock.

The singular economic position of the Matanzas railroads wasn't the result of pure chance. In Matanzas, as nowhere else in Cuba, the railroads cooperated with the sugar industry in an optimal way, with resultant benefits in terms of profits for them. On the red dirt of that province, the tracks had been laid only after carefully weighing the benefits of each rail in terms of tons of sugar to be transported, to ensure that each connection or extension would have the traffic to pay its way. In the last decade of the nineteenth century, Matanzas contributed slightly more than 30 percent of the sugar produced in the country, a proportion that had been even higher in the preceding decades. That level of production ensured a considerable volume of freight for the railroads in the province and a lot of income for transporting it. The operating expenses of those railroads were generally less than the average for the large companies in the country, because of the favorable conditions of the routes their tracks covered, where gentle hills meant a considerable saving in material and wear and tear on locomotives. The combination of such propitious factors resulted in the high profits of the two companies, which frequently issued annual dividends of more than 10 percent. Even in the difficult circumstances of the War of Independence, when Matanzas was directly affected by the military operations, the railroads in the province had an advantageous situation. While most of the railroad companies in the country were struggling to keep their heads above water, Cárdenas y Júcaro and Ferro-carril de Matanzas kept on paying annual dividends, which, though reduced to around 2 or 3 percent, were never suspended.[2] At the end of the hostilities, the Matanzas companies worked hard to restore their service and managed to do so relatively quickly. In the first few months of 1899, the two Matanzas railroads had returned to normal or, at least, it would seem so, judging from the sensitive thermometer of Havana's stock exchange, where the stocks of both companies on May 13 were going for 108 percent of their face value.[3]

The high quotations for stock in the Matanzas railroads were something more than an indication that all was going well with those companies. Early in May, Havana learned of the successful conclusion of the negotiations in which the three Las Villas railroads had merged to become the Cuban Central, and not a few people predicted that the Matanzas companies would soon do the same. And they were not mistaken. In fact, British agents headed by their old procurer Tiburcio Pérez Castañeda were already putting out feelers to the directors of the Matanzas railroads to negotiate their purchase, only this time it seems that they were given a cold reception. The matter became public on May 18, 1899, when the Havana daily La Lucha published a letter to its editor from "a stockholder" in the Cárdenas y Júcaro Company. Among other things, it stated the following:

> It is said that the Board of Directors of this company has turned down the offer that a foreign syndicate made to purchase the company for 10 percent more than the value of its stock. It is also said that a group of powerful stockholders wants to get a higher price than the one cited, in view of the desire expressed now in England to purchase our railroads. The former Ferrocarriles del Oeste, de Caibarién, de Sagua, and de Cienfuegos y Villa Clara are already owned by one English company. Ferrocarriles Unidos de La Habana is owned by another. Isn't it risky for the stockholders to think that the Cárdenas y Júcaro Company will hold out alone against such powerful adversaries, who, we have heard, will soon seize the Matanzas-to-Sabanilla railroad, as well? If we hold out for too much, the buyers may withdraw and, instead of try-ing to purchase our company, extend a branch of their own from Jovellanos to Santo Domingo. What will our stock be worth then? And what if, as is also said with apparent certainty, one of the English companies gets the conces-sion for extending a branch line to Cárdenas? What would that mean for us? The right time for successfully opposing the sale was when the English made their first offers to buy the other railroads that they already have. Now, it's too late, and, since the depreciation of our stock in the not too distant future would mean an unequal struggle and perhaps disaster for us, the most pru-dent thing would be to accept the high price we are offered right now."[4]

The signatory stockholder did not identify himself, but it would have been difficult for Tiburcio Pérez Castañeda himself to have been more persuasive. Ten days later, the *Gaceta de los Ferrocarriles de la isla de Cuba* expressed criteria that were very similar to those of the anonymous stockholder and, in an obvious attempt to alarm the Cárdenas company's stockholders, slipped in the "news" that it couldn't declare a dividend of more than 5.5 percent.[5] As the date of the annual stockholders' meeting of Cárdenas y Júcaro approached, certain organs of the press stepped up their barrage of propaganda in a sort of artillery softening-up designed to eliminate all resistance to the sale. In mid-June, on its front page, no less, *La Lucha* openly criticized the Cárdenas board of directors for having turned down the purchase offer and accused it of having "made serious mistakes and taken on great responsibilities by assuming powers or faculties that correspond only to the stockholders."[6] For its part, sowing confusion among its readers, the *Gaceta de los Ferrocarriles de la isla de Cuba* assumed that the two Matanzas companies had been sold to the English. The day before the general stockholders' meeting of Cárdenas y Júcaro was held, *La Lucha* tried to stir things up by reiterating its earlier "suggestions on behalf of the stockholders" and once more railed against the Cárdenas board of directors, which it accused of not providing stockholders with copies of the company's rules and regulations and of not managing its business well.[7] In spite of the propaganda effort, the stockholders of Cárdenas y Júcaro supported the decision their board had made concerning the Cuban Central's offers. The British company had to fall back and wait for a more propitious moment. A few months of the U.S. military occupation had been enough to calm the rich Spanish bourgeois who owned the Cárdenas Company. Now, the masters of the former Spanish colony saw the handwriting on the wall: their future would be increasingly linked to the island's definitive annexation by the power to the north.

There was no dearth of purchase offers from that point on the compass. As soon as the Cuban Central's attempt to buy out the Cárdenas Company failed, three U.S. agents representing Ryan and Whitney's American Indies Syndicate made their appearance, trying to buy and merge the two Matanzas railroads.[8] The boards of the two companies turned down that offer, as well. They probably had a tacit agreement in this regard, for it was clear that the sale of either of them would lead to the isolation and rapid liquidation of the other. However, "Business is business," and, in early 1901, the Havana papers reported that Cuban Central had decided to extend its Parque Alto branch to make an independent connection with Ferrocarril de Matanzas. The project posed a serious threat to Ferrocarril de Cárdenas y Júcaro, for it would limit its possibilities for expansion to the south. Moreover, if the plan were carried out, it would surely mean that the Cárdenas Company would lose its sugar business in the Aguada area, since the sugar mills there would choose to send their products to Cienfuegos, their nearest port, using the services of Cuban Central.

The announcement of those plans was the preamble to a new purchase offer that the persevering Tiburcio Pérez Castañeda presented to the Cárdenas board on behalf of Cuban Central.[9] In spite of the justified alarm that the British plan caused, the Cárdenas y Júcaro board decided to turn the offer down yet again and to take measures for meeting competition in the threatened area. For that purpose, the Cárdenas Company's engineers drew up a project for extending its rails from Yaguaramas to La Sierpe point on the Bay of Cienfuegos. That twenty-five-kilometer stretch of track would offer the sugar mills in the region an alternative of shipping their sugar out through the port of Cienfuegos that would be quicker and cheaper than the one Cuban Central would offer them with its Parque Alto branch.

While the Cárdenas y Júcaro company was locked in struggle with Cuban Central, Ferrocarril de Matanzas had established a kind of modus vivendi with its British neighbor, Ferrocarriles Unidos, which appeared to be less ambitious. In 1902, the Matanzas company managed to pay off its debt to Schröder's and declare 240,000 pesos in dividends, which it distributed to its stockholders.[10] The financial situation of Cárdenas y Júcaro was just as satisfactory—if it hadn't been, why would it have put up so much resistance against being bought out?—and it paid dividends punctually and kept its stock quotations at par, even though its management had been involved in a strange and scandalous case of fraud.[11] Events, however, were unfavorable for the Matanzas companies. After the rapid process of centralization that had swept the railroad sector, the once powerful Matanzas railroads had been reduced to the status of middle-rank companies, as measured by the size of their networks and the amount of their capital. And now the tide turned in favor of the bigger fry. Government officials favored railroad concentration, and the legislation in effect (pushed through at the last minute by the U.S. military government)[12] supported that trend. Thus, when Military Order 117 increased the railroad rates, the big companies, such as Ferrocarriles Unidos and Cuban Central, benefited with 30 and 50 percent increases, respectively, while Cárdenas y Júcaro and Ferrocarril de Matanzas obtained only 20 percent increases.

The position of the Matanzas railroads was also undermined by a much more harmful, though nearly imperceptible, factor: stock transfers. Some stockholders, who were timorous about the future of the business, preferred to sell their stock while it would still bring a high price. As was only to be expected, brokers working for the British companies kept on the lookout for those shares and bought them up. As a result of that procedure, Schröder's managed to control 1,703,000 pesos' worth of stock in the Cárdenas y Júcaro Company by the end of 1905, an amount that made it the principal stockholder.[13] The balance tipped definitively in favor of the English. The October 19, 1905, special stockholders' meeting of Cárdenas y Júcaro resolved to merge with Ferrocarriles Unidos de La Habana, which the Schröder bank already controlled. The stockholders in the Cárdenas company would receive "5 million pesos' worth of mortgage bonds bearing 5 percent interest and 5 million pesos' worth of stock in Ferrocarriles Unidos de La Habana y Almacenes de Regla Limitada in payment and exchange for the stock which constitutes the company's present capital stock, proportional to their respective participation in it."[14] The definitive agreement, which was signed in London a month later, stipulated that the merger would be effective on January 1, 1906, on which date the officials of Ferrocarriles Unidos would take charge of the property of Cárdenas y Júcaro, simultaneously beginning to effect the stock exchange of the company that was being swallowed up.

The balance the two railroads in Matanzas Province had maintained by protecting each other's back in the midst of the British siege had finally been upset by Ferrocarriles Unidos's purchase of the stronger of them. That left Ferrocarril de Matanzas a sitting duck. Operationally and financially, the company's situation was unbeatable: the track was in perfect condition; new locomotives had been purchased to upgrade and increase its stock; and the condition and number of its railroad cars, for both passengers and freight, was just as satisfactory. The reports of its treasurer showed a growing trend toward income and profits, which had enabled it to pay a total of 1,620,000 pesos in dividends between 1903 and 1906.[15] But now, with its system completely surrounded by the track of Unidos, Ferrocarril de Matanzas lost all possibility of being independent. Schröder could wage commercial war on it, invade its territory, take freight away from it, and force it to incur heavy expenses—in short, strangle it—if its board of directors didn't bow to the inevitable. The only survivors of the inexorable denationalizing process, the stockholders of Ferrocarril de Matanzas quickly understood that it was in their individual interests to sell. Some of them, such as Zaldo, Gelats, and Argüelles's heirs, had plenty of experience in sales to the English.

For its part, Schröder seemed to consider the purchase of Cárdenas y Júcaro and Ferrocarril de Matanzas as a single operation. As soon as the merger with Cárdenas had been completed, it began negotiations with Matanzas, using the services of Zaldo y Compañía, which held a large block of stock in the railroad.[16] On June 19, 1906, Zaldo sent the board of directors of Ferrocarril de Matanzas a list of the conditions for the merger. Two days later, Tirso Mesa, president of the company, called a special stockholders' meeting "for the purpose of deliberating and reaching a decision on the company's merger with Ferrocarriles Unidos."[17] The participants in the meeting, which was sparsely attended, voted unanimously for the merger. The terms were very similar to those agreed upon in the case of

Cárdenas y Júcaro: half of the stock would be exchanged for mortgage bonds bearing 5 percent interest, and the other half, for common stock in Ferrocarriles Unidos. In August, a delegation headed by Tirso Mesa went to London and, with Baron Bruno Schröder, signed the definitive merger agreement. From then on, the former president of the Matanzas Company would have an empty but decorative position on the London council of Ferrocarriles Unidos. On November 15, 1906, Robert M. Orr, manager of Ferrocarriles Unidos, took possession of the property of the old Ferrocarril de Matanzas. The operation wound up satisfactorily for Schröder. More patient and skilled than its compatriots at Cuban Central, it ended up with what it had set out to get, making Ferrocarriles Unidos the most powerful railroad company in the country. At the end of that long and complex process of penetration, the nearly two thousand kilometers of track in the extensive western railroad system (the most productive in Cuba at the time) were owned by British imperialist interests.

English capital's monopoly grab of Cuba's western railroads was completed successfully in the first few years of the neocolony, seemingly without the U.S. companies' doing anything to prevent it. Except for the American Indies Company's brief effort to seize the Matanzas railroads, it might be imagined that there was a tacit agreement under which the U.S. companies reserved the development and control of the railroads in the eastern provinces for themselves, giving the British a free hand in the other half of the island.

That division, however, was the result not of any hypothetical agreement but of a series of objective circumstances. The English, whose ties with Cuba's railroad companies went back a long way, had already occupied the key positions in the railroad network of the west when they survived Cuba's military occupation by the United States. The British, therefore, had the advantage of a head start and greater financial agility, since London, not Wall Street, was still the financial heart of world capitalism. After putting out feelers, therefore, the U.S. companies opted for concentrating on the eastern half of the country. Havana Electric Railways, which owned Havana's streetcar company, was the only U.S. transportation company in the west, and it was surrounded by the British lines.

The owners of Havana Electric did not resign themselves to the lack of perspective imposed by that situation. In May 1902, the recently created Comisión de Ferrocarriles de Cuba (Cuban Railroad Commission) received a registration request from a company that planned to develop interurban streetcar lines between the capital and the main towns in Havana Province. The new company, Insular Railways Company, had been founded some months earlier in Trenton, New Jersey, by the stockholders of Havana Electric. The new company's immediate aim was to lay two main lines: one through Managua and San José de las Lajas to

Güines and the other through Hoyo Colorado (Bauta) and Guanajay to Mariel.[18] Even though this was a streetcar plan, it included a connection to Havana's San José docks, and its promoters spoke publicly about the profits to be made from transporting root vegetables, pineapples, and other fruits.

The officials of Ferrocarriles Unidos were not unaware of the implications that a project of that kind might have for their business. In July 1902, the Havana Local Council of Ferrocarriles Unidos heard of a letter that the London board of directors had sent, inquiring about what consequences the concessions obtained by Insular Railway in Havana province might have for the British company.[19] Two weeks later, the managers sent London a detailed report stating that the competition in Güines wasn't to be feared and that, as regards Guanajay, the threat would be considerably reduced if the Ferrocarril de Marianao line (which Unidos controlled) were extended to Hoyo Colorado.

Even though the report had a calming tone, the local board of directors decided to keep an eye on Insular's activities, a task that it assigned to Robert Orr, the manager. But Ferrocarriles Unidos did not limit itself to passive vigilance; from then on, the British company dedicated itself to harassing Insular Railway's projects in the Comisión de Ferrocarriles with greater or lesser vehemence, depending on their importance. Luckily for the English interests, the promoters of Insular Railway either were short of capital or didn't feel sure about the profitability of their plans, so they carried them out only in part, and slowly.

The founding of the Havana Central Railway Company in May 1905 gave a serious aspect to the until-then-latent conflict between U.S. and British interests. Even though Havana Central appeared to be an independent company, its manager, Guyon F. Greenwood, held the same position in Havana Electric and in Insular. In fact, Havana Central was an offshoot of Insular, created for the purpose of getting enough capital to give a boost to some old projects which had been put off, particularly the Havana-Güines line. With its much more aggressive style, Havana Central would prove to be much more of a threat to Ferrocarriles Unidos than its predecessor had been. At first, the new company demanded that the Tallapiedra land (which Ferrocarriles Unidos owned) be forcibly appropriated so its terminal could be built there. Because of its location, the land that was claimed would facilitate Havana Central's access to Havana's port area, whose railroad links were, in practice, a monopoly held by the British company. Two years earlier, the local board of directors of Ferrocarriles Unidos had had to exert all its influence to stop a similar project by Insular Railway in the San José dock area. Now, Havana Central had the nerve to propose the same thing, on land owned by the English company itself. In fact, Ferrocarriles Unidos had not made any use of the Tallapiedra land, and it couldn't keep the Comisión de Ferrocarriles from granting a part of it to Havana Central, but, even though that part of the battle had been lost, the British refused to give up; to the contrary, they set about building warehouses and laying tracks in the area to hinder Havana Central's construction work and make it more expensive.[20]

The conflict between Ferrocarriles Unidos and Havana Central took place at a moment of extreme tension in the relations between the latter and the Cuban Railroad Company, which was also U.S.-owned. The two found it impossible to come to an agreement on the combined traffic of Ferrocarril Central. Negotiations had been begun in 1903 but had come to a standstill.

Hoping to pressure the British, Van Horne announced his decision to extend the Cuba Railroad Company's lines through Cienfuegos and southern Matanzas Province to Havana. Since Van Horne was also a stockholder in Havana Central, he proposed to the board of that company that he use the Havana-Güines line to give Ferrocarril Central access to the capital. Thus, Havana Central's activities took on an unsuspected dimension that was much more dangerous to Ferrocarriles Unidos. Irritated by the U.S. challenge, the English responded with threats that they would invade the Cuba Railroad Company's territory in the eastern provinces. The "entente cordiale" between the two imperialist interests in the railroad sector was blown to smithereens.

At that precise moment, the board of directors of Havana Central decided to take a step that was to prove fatal. Its officials presented the Comisión de Ferrocarriles with a request to extend the Güines line as far as Cienfuegos. Blinded by ambition, the managers of Havana Central tried to wrest a large section of Van Horne's projected extension toward Havana away from him. Incensed by the evident bad faith of his associates, Sir William got rid of all his stock in Havana Central and convinced the Comisión de Ferrocarriles of the Cuba Railroad company's right to the Cienfuegos-Güines connection.[21]

Van Horne's and Ferrocarriles Unidos's dual attack was too much for a small company to withstand. With its competitive outlook seriously weakened, Havana Central was faced with a situation that was entirely unfavorable to its interests. First, the liberal insurrection of August 1906 frightened the investment sectors linked to Cuban business and led them to retrench; then, before the bad feeling created by the insurrection had dissipated, the world crisis of 1907, which hit New York's financial circles particularly hard, came along to put the finishing touches on the disaster. Havana Central, which didn't have an easy financial situation, couldn't come up with the funds it needed for continuing to operate. Some of its stockholders even began dumping their shares at a low price.[22]

The Schröder bank, logically, did not let the opportunity go by. Its skillful agents began buying up Havana Central stock and soon amassed enough of it to

Villanueva Station at the beginning of the twentieth century showing new urban growth.

replace its board of directors.[23] In 1907, just two years after its founding, Havana Central was controlled by English capital, which thus reaffirmed its position as the indisputable lord and master of Cuba's western railroad system.

For a long time, the sharpest conflict between U.S. and British interests in the first republican era was eclipsed by one of the worst scandals in Cuba's neo-colonial politics: the swapping of the Arsenal land for the Villanueva Railroad Station. That important confrontation stemmed from the difficulties Ferrocarriles Unidos had been having with its Havana terminal. Ferrocarriles Unidos had inherited the old Villanueva Station from Caminos de Hierro de La Habana when they merged. Built in 1839 on land belonging to the Botanical Garden, Villanueva had long benefited as a passenger station from its functional location, but Havana's growth wound up reducing its advantages.[24] Surrounded by the city, the station lacked the capacity and efficiency required to handle the increase in its freight. Above all, it wasn't close enough to the port. By the end of the nineteenth century, Villanueva had become an embarrassment in the center of the city.

Even before it passed to British ownership, Ferrocarriles Unidos had been exploring the possibility of moving its terminal to a better location, but the matter, when proposed to the colonial authorities, did not prosper. Soon after the republic was founded, the British board of directors of Ferrocarriles Unidos drew up a project for swapping the Villanueva Station for the state land of Arsenal. The project, which was sent from London to the Havana Council, was shelved because Antonio Sánchez de Bustamante, the company's learned counselor, considered "that, in the present situation, the Government could not dispose of the Arsenal land in the form the company seeks."[25] Certainly, what the London board of directors of Ferrocarriles Unidos sought was no small thing. The Arsenal land, so called because it had pertained to the arsenal of the Spanish Navy, was much larger than the Villanueva plot and also had an excellent location, near the Atarés inlet in the Bay of Havana. The able lawyer, who was also a senator of the republic, had a good eye for the scope of the Platt Amendment and knew that President Estrada Palma was incapable of venturing into any such matter just a few months after his inauguration.

Shelved for several years, the land-exchange project reappeared in the most unexpected way. In one of his first messages to Congress, President José Miguel Gómez recommended that the legislators consider swapping the Arsenal land for the Villanueva Station. Gómez waxed lyrical when describing the many benefits the government would derive from the proposed operation, including Ferrocarriles Unidos's building five docks and a garbage incinerator for the Cuban government and the granting of a 2.5-million-peso loan by the British company so the Cuban government could construct a presidential palace and other public buildings on the Villanueva land. It seems that the Ferrocarriles Unidos board of directors had considered José Miguel Gómez's rise to power in 1909 as a propitious moment for presenting its exchange plan. Its able officials in Havana played on the president's notorious greed with an alluring list of "advantages."[26]

Right from the first, Congress and some newspapers that viewed the operation as an undeniable contribution to the appearance of the capital supported the proposal. However, more detailed consideration of the project soon showed that the Arsenal land (109,474 square meters) was quite a bit larger than the Villanueva plot (43,418 square meters) and that its location and port possibilities made it much more valuable. It was incredible that the government was not aware of the evident imbalance in the swap. Many people smelled a rat, and soon there was talk of the Arsenal "goat," referring to a Jack-and-the-Beanstalk type of trade. The press wasted no time in attacking the government's project.

The plentiful ranks of its critics included just about everyone, from honest journalists who lamented the venality with which the government was administering the nation's assets to members of the opposition party (who were no less corrupt than those in the government), for whom the exchange was a golden opportunity for increasing their lean popularity. A group with an exotic accent—the U.S. newspapers that were published in Havana—was outstanding in the

El canje del Arsenal

DON LUCIANO.— He trabado á Liborio.... ¡Algo se saca!
Ya le cambié la chiva por la vaca.

The transfer of land between the arsenal and the Villanueva Station provided much satirical material at the time. (*La Política Cómica* of July 17, 1910)

amalgam of critics. It seems suspicious that the usually reserved and circumspect U.S. press in Havana was among the most fiery opponents of the swap. Although its arguments centered, as did almost all of them, around the administrative honesty of the government, something more than ethical principles unquestionably lay behind the U.S. attitude.

One Havana newspaper, *La Lucha,* included an argument that offered a good clue to the hidden motivations for the U.S. hostility to the deal. It pointed out that "if such exchange is consummated the republic will sooner or later be exposed to some very serious complications. The United Railways of Havana, being an English company, is under the laws of Great Britain bound to give up its properties to that nation whenever it may demand. Should England ever consider it necessary to occupy the part of Havana harbor where the Arsenal lies for a coaling station or for any other naval or military purpose she would not hesitate to compel the United Railways to withdraw, leaving the premises entirely at the mercy of that nation."[27] While *La Lucha's* servile logic led it to carry its arguments to absurd lengths, the Havana daily was not wrong in considering the port issue the crux of the matter.

With the Arsenal land, Ferrocarriles Unidos would acquire a 14,000-square-meter strip of shoreline at a strategic place in the port of Havana. The English company already owned the port installations of Almacenes de Regla and also, through Havana Central, the de Paula and Luz docks. Acquisition of the Arsenal land would therefore place Ferrocarriles Unidos in a dominant position in the port, and control of the port had been shown to be a particularly sensitive issue in the relations between U.S. and British interests in Cuba. It was precisely the port and shipping concessions that Cuba planned to grant England in the much debated 1905 Cuban-English Treaty of Reciprocity, which caused the greatest displeasure among the U.S. citizens and their local business associates and finally led to failure to sign the agreement.[28] We have already seen how quickly Ferrocarriles Unidos reacted to the attempts the U.S. railroad companies made to get a foothold in the port of Havana. Now, it was the British company that sought to consolidate its position in the port. Moving the railroad terminal to the Arsenal land would make it possible to completely reorganize the port's system of railroad connections, reinforcing Ferrocarriles Unidos's monopoly in that sphere. In the new terminal, the merchandise could be moved straight from the ships to the railroad cars, reducing the time and expenses of that operation. Such attractive advantages would soon give Ferrocarriles Unidos control over most of Havana's port traffic, which already amounted to more than a million tons of cargo a year.

While the press continued to dedicate ample space to the exchange and the Congress of the republic became the scene of heated debates on the bill authorizing it, E. V. Morgan, U.S. minister in Cuba, notified President Gómez of his government's official position on the thorny issue. Washington's objections centered on two of the main conditions of the projected exchange: "One of these was the Government increasing its indebtedness by borrowing money from the railroads for the erection of a palace and other buildings and the other that the invaluable waterfront in the Arsenal should pass under the control of one or more foreign railroad companies."[29]

The Arsenal exchange proved to be an auspicious occasion for premiering the new procedures of the "preventive politics" in which the United States assigned its diplomatic representative in Havana the function of tutor to the Cuban government. The U.S. attitude was not intransigent, however. The minister let Gómez know that his government would not object to the exchange if the loan were eliminated from its bases and if control of the proposed Arsenal terminal remained in the hands of a U.S. company.[30] The U.S. hostility to the exchange was not based on the promptings of demagogic honesty; rather, it was the product of entrenched, well-defined imperialist interests. The United States was not about to cede an inch of its monopoly on the financing of the Cuban government, and it gave a solid foundation to its hegemonistic "rights" in key spheres of the island's economy.

The British quickly became aware of the seriousness of the situation. On previous occasions, Ferrocarriles Unidos had fought successfully with one U.S. company or another, but now it was a matter of a head-on collision with the essential interests of U.S. imperialism. The English realized that, this time, they would have to cede.

On July 1, 1910, the Havana Terminal Railroad Company was founded in Maine, the United States. The new company, with a capital of $5 million, was the solution Schröder contributed to the troublesome conflict of the exchange. Created through the offices of W. E. Ogilvie and the officials of Havana Central, which had been absorbed, Havana Terminal would also be under the control of Ferrocarriles Unidos, but the U.S. government could consider its main demand to have been met: the Arsenal land would remain in the hands of a U.S. company.[31]

Once a satisfactory solution had been achieved, the business of the exchange ran its course without any greater difficulties. On July 10, 1910, three weeks after the founding of Havana Terminal, the Cuban Congress passed the law authorizing the exchange.[32] All reference to Unidos's loan for the construction of Villanueva had prudently been removed from its text, and the English company's obligations were limited to the construction of the five docks and the garbage incinerator. The Washington government should feel perfectly satisfied. Now, the Havana press could go wild accusing the government of fraud. Its uproar would not be echoed in the imperialist Olympus. No matter that the assessing comission had established a difference of 1.5 million pesos between the value of the Arsenal land and that of Villanueva, even when it was generally accepted that the Arsenal land might be worth as much as 4 million pesos more than the land of the old railroad station; no matter that rumor had it that the assessors had been paid a "mere" 114,000 pesos for their "meticulous" work.[33] The exchange would go quickly ahead.

On December 23, 1910, President Gómez tore himself away from his fishing to return quickly to his Havana office. Hours later, in the presence of Jesús M. Barraqué, the president of the Republic of Cuba signed the Escritura de Permuta, Obligaciones y Concesiones (Deed of Exchange, Debentures, and Concessions), by means of which the exchange acquired legal force. As soon as the ink was dry, Robert M. Orr, manager of Ferrocarriles Unidos, who had been empowered to sign the agreement, put the deed in his briefcase and headed for the office of notary Antonio González Solar, where George A. Morson, an old official of Unidos who now legally represented Havana Terminal, was waiting. Without any delay (there was no need to bother the U.S. Legation in Havana), the two officials signed the papers transferring the recently acquired Arsenal land to Havana Terminal, winding up the swap.[34] Only a few, minor details remained pending—and, of course, the construction of the new terminal, the contract for which was given

The Villanueva property finally provided the location for the construction of the
National Capitol (presently the Academy of Sciences of Cuba) during the regime of
Gerardo Machado. The new construction appears behind the old Villanueva Station.

to Snare and Triest, a U.S. building firm. By means of prudent, frank acceptance
of the U.S. hegemony, Ferrocarriles Unidos added an important piece to its growing transportation monopoly in the western part of Cuba. The old link between
trains and ports was already ensured in the case of the Bay of Havana. A year later,
after purchasing Matanzas Terminal, a small company that controlled the railroad connections at the port of Matanzas, Ferrocarriles Unidos would complete
its system and become the most important railroad company in the country.[35]

By 1914, the 2,481 kilometers of track in the western system was owned by four
companies, three of which were British; the last, Havana Central, was nominally
U.S. but had been controlled by English capital since 1907. At first glance, that
distribution did not justify talk of a monopolization of the western system. It is
true that one of the British companies, Ferrocarriles Unidos de La Habana,
operated 1,368 kilometers of track by itself, but that figure constituted only a little
over half of the western system. In spite of that legal appearance of a diversity of
companies, however, all of the western railroad companies in fact were controlled
more or less directly by a single monopoly group: Schröder and Company.

After consolidating its position in the Havana area by controlling Havana

Central, the owners of Ferrocarriles Unidos concentrated on two neighboring British companies: Ferrocarril del Oeste (Western Railway of Havana) and Cuban Central. The group of capitalists headed by Joseph White Todd, who controlled those two companies, had managed to maintain a standoff with Schröder in the early years of the twentieth century. That balance, however, was upset by Ferrocarriles Unidos's purchase of the two Matanzas railroad companies in 1905 and 1906. That merger and Unidos's subsequent control of Havana Central gave Schröder hegemony in the western system. Even before those happenings, the board of directors of Ferrocarriles Unidos had done everything it could to weaken the two other British companies in the region, especially Ferrocarril del Oeste.

Ferrocarriles Unidos employed a procedure against that company which its predecessor, Compañía de Caminos de Hierro de La Habana, had been using successfully since the preceding century. It consisted of making transportation agreements with the coastal shipping companies that operated between Batabanó and the small ports along the southern coast of Pinar del Río province. One agreement of that kind, which Ferrocarriles Unidos and the Vueltabajo Steamship Company maintained for many years, was particularly prejudicial to Ferrocarril del Oeste, whose representatives repeatedly asked the Comisión de Ferrocarriles to halt that "treacherous" competition.[36] The systematic combined activities of Ferrocarriles Unidos and the shipping company wrested a considerable part of its freight from Ferrocarril del Oeste and forced it to offer cut rates, which were also prejudicial to balancing its books. After years of softening up, Schröder proposed an honorable way out to the Ferrocarril del Oeste stockholders: stock in Ferrocarriles Unidos in exchange for their own stock. Convinced that that operation would be beneficial in the long run, the general stockholders' meeting of Ferrocarril del Oeste accepted the offer on November 22, 1911. One month later, the Unidos board of directors took over the property and operations of Ferrocarril del Oeste, though it continued to function as an apparently independent entity for nearly a decade.[37]

Control of Ferrocarril del Oeste cleared the way for taking over Cuban Central, in Las Villas. The situation that had been created in Cuba's railroads did not require many arguments to show that a monopoly on the western system would be more advantageous for the stockholders in Cuban Central if they became stockholders in that monopoly, especially since the Las Villas company was hemmed in by two giants: Ferrocarriles Unidos to the west and Cuban Railroad to the east.

On December 29, 1913, at a special meeting of the stockholders of Cuban Central, representatives of Ferrocarriles Unidos presented a stock exchange plan that was similar to the one presented to Ferrocarril del Oeste two years before. In this case, they offered £7.5 sterling worth of stock in Ferrocarriles Unidos for every £10 sterling worth of Cuban Central stock.[38] In the two months following the

TABLE 12.1. Foreign Capital in Cuba, 1913–1914 (in millions of dollars)

Country	Amount
England	216
United States	215
France	13
Germany	5

Source: Oscar Pino Santos, *El asalto a Cuba por la oligarquía financiera norteamericana* (Havana: Editorial Casa de las Américas, 1973), p. 37.

offer, 87,994 of the 90,000 shares of common stock issued by Cuban Central were exchanged. With that operation, Unidos got effective control of Cuban Central, even though it couldn't exercise absolute control until some years later, as the exchange of 90,000 shares of preferred stock remained pending.

Schröder's British capital had established a monopoly over the western railroad system. What relative weight did it have in all foreign investments? More important, what influence did it probably have on the correlation of imperialist interests in Cuba during that period? An astute expert on the activities of foreign capital in Cuba has called attention to the seldom considered importance of English investments during the early years of the republic and to the probable repercussions they had in other spheres at the time.[39] The approximate state of investments in Cuba in 1913–14 is shown in Table 12.1.

It becomes immediately apparent that British capital, which was even estimated as being somewhat greater than U.S. capital, had considerable proportional weight. This fact leads to questions concerning the probable influence of the English imperialist interests in that period. Within the English capital shown in Table 12.1, the $125.6 million invested in the railroads (58 percent of all English investments in Cuba) played a key role.[40] An analysis of the nature of the English railroad capital is therefore of particular value in any study of the weight and influence British interests had in Cuba.

We have already analyzed the process of English capital's penetration in the railroad sector, mainly from the organizational and operational angle. Now, we will examine the financial aspect. Table 12.2 presents a synthetic view of the process of penetration and monopolization in terms of capital.

The figures given in Table 12.2 for 1913–14 coincide quite closely with those given in the analysis cited, especially if you add the $20 million or so that corresponded to Havana Central and Havana Terminal, which are not included in the table because, nominally, they were U.S. companies. But some aspects should be commented upon. First of all, note that capitalization doubled in the period

TABLE 12.2. Western Railroad Companies' Capitalization and Length of Lines

Company	1899–1900		1913–14	
	Capitalization (in millions of pesos)	Length of Lines (in kilometers)	Capitalization (in millions of pesos)	Length of Lines (in kilometers)
FC Unidos	17.2	417	81.1	1,368
FC de Matanzas	5.8	284	—	—
FC de Cárdenas y Júcaro	8.0	338	—	—
Marianao and Havana RR	0.7	13	—	—
Western RR of Havana	5.0	177	8.1	261
Cuban Central RR	12.2	345	20.7	706
Total	52.3	1,557	109.9	2,335

Sources: William H. Carlson, "Report of the Special Commissioner of Railroads," in Leonard Wood, Civil Report of the Military Governor (Havana, 1901), and Cuba, Comisión de Ferrocarriles, Memoria (1913–14), statistical appendix, Table 2.
Note: Capitalization includes the issued stock and mortgage bonds.

under analysis, while the tracks grew by only 33 percent. This indicates a clear trend toward a higher proportional increase in capital than in the companies' operating capacity. The most glaring example is doubtless that of Ferrocarriles Unidos, whose capital quadrupled in fourteen years. Since Ferrocarriles Unidos was an extreme case and also the main company, which was absorbing or controlling the rest, an examination of the capitalization process in Ferrocarriles Unidos offers some keys for understanding the nature of that phenomenon. Table 12.3 presents that process.

In spite of a lack of data for some years, Table 12.3 shows that capitalization remained relatively stable until 1906; from then on, it grew by considerable leaps in some key years, such as 1907, 1908, 1911, 1912, and 1914. We have already shown the changes that took place in the railroad sector in those years, so it shouldn't prove difficult to associate the changes in capital with those organizational changes: 1907, the merger of Ferrocarril de Matanzas and Cárdenas y Júcaro; 1908, control of Havana Central; 1911, the creation of Havana Terminal; 1912, control of Western Havana (Ferrocarril del Oeste); and 1914, control of Cuban Central.[41] Each increase in capital was linked to a step in the progressive monopolization of the western system. Those increases are deceiving, however, if you look only at the statistics. In terms of the distortions that were produced, the cases can be grouped into two increases.

The 1907 increase. Unquestionably, the greatest. In this case, it provided financ-

TABLE 12.3. Capitalization of Ferrocarriles Unidos de La Habana y Almacenes de Regla Ltda. (United Railways), 1900–1914 (in pesos)

Year	Capital Issued	Debentures	Total
1899–1900	8,239,000	9,583,200	17,822,200
1900–1901	—	—	—
1901–2	—	—	—
1902–3	—	—	—
1903–4	7,453,600	9,583,200	17,036,800
1904–5	7,453,600	9,583,200	17,036,800
1905–6	7,453,600	9,583,200	17,036,800
1906–7	26,765,200	22,494,200	49,259,400
1907–8	29,270,960	28,574,500	57,704,460
1908–9	29,270,189	28,721,656	57,991,845
1909–10	29,272,380	28,273,660	57,996,040
1910–11	34,133,890	33,129,987	67,252,877
1911–12	41,843,327	33,529,987	75,373,207
1912–13	41,876,560	33,534,997	75,401,557
1913–14	47,657,613	33,534,937	81,192,550

Source: Cuba, Comisión de Ferrocarriles, Memorias (1899–1914).

ing for the mergers of the Matanzas and Cárdenas y Júcaro Railroads. As will be recalled, the agreement called for Ferrocarriles Unidos's giving stock in exchange for half of the Matanzas companies' stock and debentures for the other half. To provide the capital for the merged companies (10 million pesos for Cárdenas y Júcaro and 6 million for Ferrocarril de Matanzas), Ferrocarriles Unidos had to increase its capitalization by 16 million pesos, distributed equally between issued capital and debentures. In 1906, the British Parliament authorized it to increase its authorized capital by 50 percent, and Ferrocarriles Unidos issued stock and bonds for something over 32 million pesos, as Table 12.3 clearly shows in the difference between the figures for 1905–6 and 1906–7. The operation was capitalized with no less than double the amount required.[42]

The maneuver has fraud written all over it, but it was a procedure admitted by the questionable ethics of capital finance, in whose argot it figures as "watering the stock." The board of directors of Ferrocarriles Unidos took advantage of the conservative capitalization of the Matanzas companies (between 20,000 and 25,000 pesos per kilometer of track) to pull off a fantastic maneuver that gave them a margin of several million pesos. Once integrated in the Unidos system, the Matanzas and Cárdenas y Júcaro lines saw their capitalization increased to

40,000 pesos per kilometer. The takeover of Havana Central in 1908 and the creation of Havana Terminal in 1911 were also accompanied by stock watering, but on a much smaller scale. The takeover of Western and Cuban Central was accompanied by a watering of stock to the tune of nearly 3.5 million dollars. Such stock watering resulted in overcapitalization of the companies, which, therefore, came to have far greater capital than the real value of their property. This procedure obviously burdened the companies with financial obligations and was a deadweight on their economy, but it was an excellent business for the bankers who issued the stocks and bonds and trafficked with them on the stock exchange. It should be recalled that Ferrocarriles Unidos was owned by a bank, J. Henry Schröder and Company. It would appear that these maneuvers with assets provided more profits for Schröder than the profits obtained from providing the railroad service itself.

The 1912 and 1914 capital increases. They were motivated by the stock exchanges for Western and Cuban Central. To effect each exchange, Ferrocarriles Unidos had to increase its capital by an amount corresponding to the amount represented by the stock to be obtained—that is, 5,330,000 pesos for Western (1912) and 4.5 million pesos for Cuban Central. In the first case (1912), the increase was a little over 7 million pesos; in the second (1914), it was almost 6 million pesos—that is, always more than was required. But those excesses were not as flagrant as the fact that, since both Western and Cuban Central continued to exist legally, their stock, though kept in the Ferrocarriles Unidos safe, remained in effect for statistical purposes, thus producing an artificial duplication of that portion of British railroad capital that was registered both by Western and Cuban Central and by Ferrocarriles Unidos.

In all cases, the analysis leads to the same conclusion: Ferrocarriles Unidos—and, with it, all the British railroad investments—was considerably overcapitalized. For example, in 1914, Ferrocarriles Unidos's capitalization per kilometer of track (59,345 pesos) was double the figure calculated by the U.S.-owned Cuba Railroad Company (29,432 pesos). Therefore, the figures offered in assessments based on the companies' nominal capital would not show the real economic weight and influence of English railroad capital. For a more realistic approximation, we must consider the weight of British railroad capital from the viewpoint of its control over the most important transportation system in the country—most important not only because of its extension but also because it completely covered what was still the most productive region in Cuba. What influence could that have? It made the British an undeniable power in the railroad sector and in the western region. Proof of this is the success they had in fending off all would-be competitors' attempts to challenge them in the west. It would be irresponsible to deduce more than this.

The limits of the English companies' possibilities in the sector where they predominated were shown at the time of the Arsenal-Villanueva land exchange, when the English had to accept the conditions imposed by the United States and seek a compromise. The limits were brought out even more clearly in 1912, when the Cuban government put the concession for a railroad line from Caibarién to Nuevitas up for bids. Cuban Central was one of the bidders, seeking to use the concession to extend into the eastern part of the country. On learning of that intention, the Washington government sent its representative in Cuba the following instructions: "Information received in this office leads us to believe that there is a renewed attempt to place before the Cuban Congress the project of English capitalists for the Nuevitas-Caibarién Railroad concession. You should solemnly alert the president of the convenience of postponing a final decision in order to allow a complete and thorough investigation, pointing out the burden that would accrue to the Cuban Treasury should the award be made to capitalists who are neither North American nor Cuban."[43]

It goes without saying that this note put paid to Cuban Central's hopes. Neither its weight nor its distribution in the various spheres of the Cuban economy made British capital a serious threat to U.S. imperialism's global interests. This was especially so because Cuba's dependence on the United States was solidly based, politically and economically, on the Platt Amendment and the Reciprocal Trade Agreement of 1903. Even so, we should not ignore the presence of the British interests and their probable influence, above all in the years leading up to World War I—years filled with tension, in which interimperialist relations were in a delicate balance.

War, Sugar, and Railroads

Unlike the first few decades of railroad development in Cuba, in which the capital invested in producing sugar and the money used for promoting railroads were all jumbled up in a symbiotic embrace, the twentieth century would see a growing organizational differentiation between the two sectors of the economy. The concentration of sugar production in ever larger manufacturing units and the accelerated monopolization of the public service railroads led to greater business autonomy in both activities and the ostensible loss of the personal nature of their ties. As the end of the nineteenth century approached, the names of the estate owners who, in the past, had filled all the positions on the boards of directors of the railroad societies began to be replaced. In the twentieth century, diluted in the anonymity of corporations, they disappeared altogether.

Carried out under the aegis of imperialist penetration, this process would establish new formulas that were more in line with the needs of monopoly capitalism than the old, close relations between sugar and the railroads. Those relations were not changed in essence or intensity, however. To the contrary, the growth of the Cuban economy in the first few decades of the twentieth century would consolidate the railroads' dependence on sugar, under the inescapable weight of a single-crop economy.

Ever since Cuba became the main supplier of the U.S. sugar-refining industry's raw material, it was increasingly forced into the traditional mold of a country with a single export product. The commercial possibilities of the expanding U.S. sugar market stimulated the creation of new sugar mills on the island and made it possible to reopen some others that had been shut down during the War of Independence.

Transportation needs in the production and export of sugar led to the establishment of new railroads and the extension of the tracks belonging to old companies.

This had also been the reason for railroad development in the nineteenth century. The sugar market had stimulated the Cuban sugar industry, and it did the same for the railroads, in nearly perfect synchrony. Sugar and railroads, dependent on each other, were also dependent on the foreign market—European or U.S.—which was the real source of their growth. The free play of supply and demand prevailing in the market economy through the mechanism of prices was a key factor in the case of sugar, causing a shower of gold over Cuba at some moments and times of penury, bringing ruin to the weakest producers at others.

The demands of the U.S. sugar market caused an almost continuous rise in Cuban sugar production between 1900 and 1913, with increases averaging 166,000 metric tons a year. Prices remained steady, at around 2.5 cents a pound, during those thirteen years, except for 1902, 1903, 1906, and 1913. In that last year, there was a sharp drop, to a low of 1.95 cents a pound.

In the midst of those market conditions, World War I broke out, involving the European sugar-producing countries and causing tremendous changes in sugar production and sales. The war immediately stimulated sugar production in the areas not directly affected by the conflict. Among them, Cuba registered the greatest increase—54 percent between 1913 and 1919—followed by India (with a 19.8 percent increase). The other sugar-producing countries in the Americas and Asia managed to raise their production by only 9 percent or less during those years.[1] The jump in Cuba's sugar production, from 2,441,980 tons in 1913 to 4,011,831 tons in 1919, for an average annual growth of 269,500 metric tons, nearly doubled the rhythm of the years prior to 1913. From 1914 on, prices accompanied the ascending curve of the volume of production, reaching an average of 11.9 cents a pound in 1920[2] and the amazing figure of 20 cents a pound in May of that year.[3]

The high prices led Cuban and foreign capitalists (from the United States) to build new sugar mills and reactivate and modernize old ones that had been shut down during the War of Independence. A total of nearly thirty sugar mills went into production between 1914 and 1920,[4] some of them in traditional sugarcane-growing areas, such as Matanzas and Las Villas, but most of them on the vast uninhabited plains of Camagüey and Oriente. These last provinces became the favorite theater of operations of the U.S. companies, which erected colossal sugar mills that determined the industrial profile characteristic of those regions. In just a few years, the eastern provinces considerably increased their proportional weight in the nation's sugar production, from 29 percent in 1912–13 to 44 percent in 1919–20.[5]

The concentration of sugar shipments in certain port areas also transformed the relative importance of Cuba's ports. During the sugar boom, all ports increased their export activity except Havana—which maintained its natural preeminence as the capital of the country. The export potential of the western ports was surpassed by some in Camagüey and Oriente, which, like Nuevitas and Puerto Padre, had begun the century with little or no exports.[6]

The logical counterpart of the growth in Cuba's exports was registered in the tremendous increase in certain lines of imports, especially foodstuffs, chemical products, and manufactured articles. Cuba's imports in 1913 were worth only 140 million pesos, but they rose to 567 million pesos in 1920.[7] The increase in foreign trade intensified port activities and at the same time increased the demand for railroad services, both for exporting sugar and for distributing the imported merchandise on the domestic market. Pressured by the needs of trade, the links between the railroads and ports were improved. The ferry service between the railroad terminal of the Florida East Coast Railroad, in Key West, Florida, the United States, and the port of Havana was established in that era (in 1915, to be exact). That system allowed for direct connections between Cuban and U.S. railroads, facilitating the rapid transportation of merchandise from one country to the other on railroad cars without any need to unload and reload their contents.[8]

The volume of the sugar and its derivatives that Cuban railroads had to transport nearly doubled in seven years. Most of that cargo was assimilated by the public service railroads, but the private railroads owned by the sugar companies began to carry a not inconsiderable part of that traffic. Either because their industrial units were far from the public railroad networks or for reasons of economic convenience, the large sugar companies began to use their own railroad lines to take their products to the ports and landing stages they used, most of which were privately owned. Thus, in some regions, the private railroads began to assume the export function that had been the exclusive province of the public service railroads up until then.

As in earlier eras of plenty, the sugar expansion in the second decade of the neocolony was also reflected in the growth of the railroad lines. However, the growth in track belonging to the public service railroads—523 kilometers between 1914 and 1920—cannot be considered an absolutely true indicator of the increase in sugar production. On the one hand, track density in Cuban territory was already great enough to handle the transportation of sugar without any need for new extensions; on the other, the process of railroad monopolization, especially in the western part of the country, had led to some rationalization of the system of tracks, with some lines and branches that provided parallel services deactivated, thus reducing the statistics on the growth of the lines.

Nor should it be forgotten that the sugar expansion generated by World War I took place in some organizational patterns that were quite different from those of the nineteenth century. The new production regions in the eastern provinces were placed in exploitation by promoting large sugar mills, most of which could

"Mikado" steam locomotive (top) and Consolidated Steam Locomotive from the United States. Both were used at the beginning of the twentieth century in Cuba.

process over six thousand tons of sugarcane a day and required an extensive area of tributary plantations. The links between those industrial giants and their sugar-cane "colonies" were established by means of vast networks of private railroad lines, which were often more than a hundred kilometers long. As a result, the railroad demands of the sugar boom were expressed, above all, in the growth of the private railroads. Those tracks, which had amounted to little more than a thousand kilometers at the beginning of the century, surpassed nine thousand kilometers by the mid-1920s, twice as long as the public service railroads.[9]

The effects the sugar boom had on the growth of the public service railroads is shown more clearly in the considerable increase in the rolling stock those companies used. Table 13.1 presents the figures for the four largest railroad companies in the country.

The considerable increase registered in the railroad companies' rolling stock shows that the demands of the new leap in sugar production were expressed more in the intensification of traffic on already existing track than in the opening of new lines for service. However, the growth in track in the 1914–20 period—nearly eighty kilometers a year—was important enough to deserve a more detailed examination.

The intensive movement of trade that the anomalous European situation brought about in Cuba led to the construction of new railway lines even in

TABLE 13.1. Freight Cars Owned by Four Railroad Companies

	1913	1920	Increase
United Railways of Havana	5,913	7,129	1,216
Havana Central	291	568	274
Cuban Central	2,378	3,334	966
Cuba Railroad	2,036	5,541	3,505

Sources: Cuba, Comisión de Ferrocarriles, Memorias (1913–14, 1919–20).

regions that appeared to be saturated with them, as in the western part of the island. With but few exceptions, those new lines were built to improve the system of communications in the region, linking some areas that had been left isolated during the period of railroad construction in the nineteenth century.

This was the case of Trinidad, in Las Villas Province, whose tiny railroad had remained unfinished and had been deactivated in 1873. Early on, the possibility of extending railroad service to the Trinidad Valley was considered as part of Cuba Railroad's strategy of railroad development, and the project obtained official support when it was included with high priority in the Railroad Subsidies Law of 1906. Using an undeniably fraudulent procedure of taking bids,[10] the Mario García Menocal administration finally awarded Cuba Railroad the concession for building a railroad to link Trinidad with Placetas, using the tracks of Ferrocarril Central, in 1914. With the construction of the Placetas-Trinidad-Casilda track, which included putting the lines of the old Trinidad Railroad into service, Cuba Railroad was able to handle the production of the sugar mills in the area and extend its control over trade to the port of Casilda, which became its westernmost port.

Motivated by similar aims, Cuban Central built a branch along the northern coast of Las Villas Province to the town of Corralillo to take the sugar from the Rancho Veloz and Quemado de Güines mills to Sagua la Grande, thus taking over the function that the horse-drawn railroads of Sierra Morena and Carahatas had fulfilled in an earlier period. The two most important events that affected the vast and complicated western network, however, turned out to be a little contradictory.

The first of them, of an organizational nature, was the formal and definitive incorporation of Western Railways of Havana (Ferrocarril del Oeste) and Cuban Central in the Ferrocarriles Unidos monopoly, a company that, from then on, owned all of the public railroads in Pinar del Río, Havana, and Matanzas Provinces and most of them in Las Villas. Even though, financially, this process had begun in 1913, it was not completed legally and organizationally until 1920.[11]

The other event worthy of mention was the breaking of the absolute monopoly

Ferrocarriles Unidos (United Railways) had obtained in the west, when a U.S. company set up a small railroad network right in the heart of the region that Schröder and its British partners had patiently monopolized. That new railroad, which was set up for purely sugar purposes, was built in Havana Province in an area of narrow plains and small valleys east of the capital, which had been one of the first centers of the colonial sugar industry. That region, consisting of the old Río Blanco, Santa Cruz, and Jibacoa estates, was practically abandoned when sugar planters moved to the fertile land of the red plains in the south, and some old mills were all that was left there to testify to its past glories.[12]

When the price of raw sugar went up as a result of the war in Europe, some U.S. sugar refining companies and others that used sugar as a raw material in making their products threw themselves into pursuing new sources of supplies. Such was the case of Hires and Company, Armour and Company, and the Hershey Corporation in Cuba.[13] This last chose the old sugarcane area that was languishing northeast of the capital and built a modern sugar mill and refinery there to produce sugar to supply its industrial installations in Pennsylvania, the United States.[14] The company was one of those known in U.S. finances as "independent," since it was not linked to any of the large finance groups. The same degree of independence could be seen in Cuba, since it had no financial ties with any other sugar or railroad company in the country.

The Hershey Corporation established itself in Cuba by buying the land and installations belonging to the Purísima Concepción (later called the Carolina) and San Juan Bautista sugar mills. The then extremely modern Hershey sugar mill, now the Comandante Camilo Cienfuegos, was built close to the site of the former and became the center of operations of the Cuban subsidiary. The sugar mill community was pompously called the company's sugar town in Cuba, just as the town the company had founded in a Pennsylvania valley twenty years earlier had been called its chocolate and cacao town.[15]

Hershey created a railroad company, Ferrocarril Cubano de Hershey, on May 19, 1916, to transport sugarcane to and sugar from its beautiful mill.[16] That company was to build a railroad that would link the sugar mill with the landing stage of Santa Cruz del Norte, the city of Matanzas, and the port of Havana, thus guaranteeing that the sugar could be sent in the company's hermetically sealed cars from the mill to the ferries that would take it to U.S. ports, from which it would be sent on to the corporation's chocolate factories. The first tracks were laid to the landing stage of Santa Cruz, on the north coast, and also southward to link up with the lines of United Railways of Havana, at Bainoa. Those lines were opened to the public in September 1918.[17]

The company's sugar business had been conceived of on a large scale, and the new railroad's aims were of a size to match. More and more sugar mills were added to the original ones: Rosario, Nuestra Señora del Carmen, Jesús María, and San Antonio, all bringing land with them to this new kind of large landholding planted to sugarcane, just outside Havana.[18]

United Railways didn't look kindly on the presence of a railroad in Havana Province that didn't belong to it. As soon as the *Memoria* of the project that Ferrocarril de Hershey presented to the Comisión de Ferrocarriles was approved, Ferrocarriles Unidos presented its claims and formulated its protests before the same comisión, alleging that both the main trunk line and the projected branches would duplicate the English company's authorized route—and, therefore, its services—and would be prejudicial to it. In its petitions, United Railways accused the builders of the new railroad with being spurred by the "evil desire for competition contrary to law." The comisión, however, didn't pay much attention to the English monopoly's claims, and its challenge got nowhere.[19]

Ferrocarril de Hershey continued its construction without interruption and inaugurated its service to Matanzas in October 1921. Early the next year, the section of the main trunk line that ran to Casa Blanca, on the shore of the Bay of Havana, went into operation. Electric locomotives replaced the steam ones that same year.[20]

Hershey's aggressiveness as a sugar and railroad company was shown even after 1921 with the acquisition of new sugar mills, one in Nueva Paz, south of Havana, and another in El Porvenir, with its railroad installation in Santa Ana-Cidra, which enabled Ferrocarril de Hershey to reach the branch line between Aguacate and Madruga.[21] The 1925 crisis was the only thing that stopped the company's expansion,[22] with its tracks limited to a main trunk line 132 kilometers long and 96 kilometers of secondary lines, some of them used only for transporting sugarcane and others used also for general cargo and passenger service.

The most outstanding manifestations of the importance sugar had in the island during World War I and the postwar period appeared on the plains of Camagüey, where sugar became a key crop, increasing that province's share in national sugar production from 7.89 percent in the 1913–14 harvest to 22.6 percent in the 1919–20 one.[23] Therefore, it was only logical that the most important railroad advances in that period should also take place in that vast territory.

Camagüey had large extents of flat land interrupted only briefly by the widely separated Cubitas and Najasa mountain ranges. This made it a very good region for raising large-scale crops and for using railroad transportation. A few sugar mills with relatively high production had been built in the province during the first few years of the century, but the area's enormous agricultural potential was still far from fully exploited.

In or around 1913, three railroad companies operated in Camagüey: Cuba Railroad, whose main track, the Ferrocarril Central, ran through the province on

the concession for building a railroad line between Camagüey and Santa Cruz del Sur.[39]

The offer was very tempting for Cuba Railroad, whose operations in Camagüey province were weak because its lines had no links to ports. The deal Tarafa proposed meant the possibility of immediately acquiring the port terminal of Pastelillo, in Nuevitas, which Ferrocarril Nuevitas y Camagüey owned, and the prospect of building other port installations in Santa Cruz del Sur. As soon as the deal was made, Tarafa sold Cuba Railroad the properties and concessions that had been pledged, receiving 800,000 pesos in cash and recovering the 150,000 he had lent as a bond in 1912.[40]

The favorable changes that began to take place in the sugar market starting in 1914 were of decisive importance in improving Tarafa's situation, helping to put his railroad plans into effect. Efficient new sugar mills, such as the Morón, Patria, and Adelaida, went into operation in the area he hoped to serve with Ferrocarril Nuevitas y Camagüey, and construction began on other, even larger ones, such as the Cunagua. With improved prevailing conditions and promising sugar prospects for the country, the value of the railroad concessions the Cuban government had granted increased tremendously.

In view of those gratifying possibilities, Tarafa told President Mario G. Menocal that he would begin work on the project immediately. At the same time, he asked the executive for the permission he needed to transfer the concession that had been granted to Ferrocarril de la Costa Norte y del Sur to the Júcaro and Morón Railways Company, perhaps to take advantage of the fact that the latter was registered in the United States and, therefore, could be considered more likely to attract U.S. capital. The president authorized the change in Decree 323, of May 6, 1916.[41]

Tarafa then set up a new railroad company in U.S. territory to handle the financing of the enterprise. It was called the Cuba Northern Railroad Company, incorporated under the laws of the state of Delaware in June 1916. Its specific aims were to build Ferrocarril de Nuevitas a Caibarién's tracks and to lease Ferrocarril de Júcaro y San Fernando. In addition, it was to purchase the twenty-kilometer-long railroad that linked the Patria and Adelaida sugar mills with the main trunk line of the Júcaro, which was known simply as Ferrocarril de Morón.[42]

Through the Cuba Northern Railroad Company, Tarafa managed to attract the interest of U.S. and Canadian capital in such firms as the Montreal Trust Company, the Royal Bank of Canada, and the National City Bank of New York. Starting in August 1916, the first of those banks held $10 million worth of first mortgage bonds of Cuba Northern. A few months later, in December, the second provided a $2.5 million loan[43] for covering the main construction expenses. Tarafa assumed

TABLE 13.2. Value of Stock and Cash J. M. Tarafa Received from the Cuba
Northern Railroad Company

	Stock Common and Preferred Stock	Value (in dollars)	Cash (in dollars)
Ferrocarril Nuevitas y			
Caibarién concession	92,000[a]	9,200,000	—
Studies (outlines, plans, etc.)	—	—	500,000
Ferrocarril Júcaro-Morón			
Concession	22,500[a]	—	—
Materials	10,000[b]	3,250,000	2,700,000
Ferrocarril de Morón	19,500[a]	1,950,000	350,000
Total	124,000[a]	13,400,000	3,600,000
	10,000[b]		

Sources: Escritura, 30 (July 17, 1916), and AFC (d.C.), Fondo general de paquetería
paquete 2–1943, expediente 100–30, pp. 67–70.
[a]Common.
[b]Preferred.

control of the corporation's stock by making an exceedingly high assessment of
the concessions he held. With an authorized capital of $15 million (10,000 shares
of preferential stock, worth $100 each, and 140,000 shares of common stock, also
worth $100 each), he used 95 percent of the stock to pay for the assets contributed.
The profits Tarafa made, both in control of the stock and in cash, are shown in
Table 13.2, based on data from the deed of assignment to Cuba Northern.

As a result of this maneuver, Colonel Tarafa received $3.6 million in cash. His
ownership of nearly all the stock gave him complete control of Cuba Northern.[44]
In such favorable conditions for its promoter, the Ferrocarril Nuevitas y Caibarién project got off to a flying start, with work on the infrastructure beginning west
of the city of Morón on October 16, 1916.[45]

Track was laid along the routes set forth in the plan, with work going on
simultaneously to the east and west of the city of Morón, where the company's
repair shops and administrative center were established. Progress was quick and
uninterrupted, with 77 kilometers of track laid in the first year (1917), 40 in 1918,
about 168 in 1919, and 35 in the 1920–21 period. By then, the railroad had 320
kilometers of track, and the line extended westward to the Chambas River, near
the Las Villas border, and eastward to its final goal, the port of Nuevitas, where a
huge sugar terminal called Puerto Tarafa was built on the shore. An important

branch line ran from the tracks in Woodin (Esmeralda) to a point midway between Nuevitas and Morón and headed south to the area around the town of Florida, where many sugar mills had been built. There, the Nuevitas y Caibarién competed with the Cuba Railroad Company for their business.

Another, smaller branch line headed north to handle the sugar produced by the enormous Cunagua sugar mill. Later, in 1921, that line would also be used for transporting the sugar produced in the largest sugar mill in Cuba: the Jaronú. The many services offered to those modern plantations would ensure the company's economic success once and for all.

In 1919, the Comisión de Ferrocarriles approved a change in the proposed plan. Instead of extending toward Caibarién, the line was directed toward Santa Clara, where it would hook up with the main line of the Cuba Railroad Company. The plan was completed in full in 1930.[46]

Right from the beginning of Cuba Northern's operations, Tarafa urged that the company he had founded in the United States be "Cubanized" so it could receive the subsidy of over 3 million pesos that the Cuban government had granted for construction of the railroad without being the target of public criticism because it was foreign. In line with that thinking, Tarafa set up a new company, this time under Cuban law, to which he transferred the other company's stock and concession.

Ferrocarril del Norte de Cuba began its operations in May 1918.[47] The only difference between it and its predecessor, apart from its nationality, was that its name was in Spanish. Colonel Tarafa's daring in the field of business had made it possible to create a "Cuban" company whose services corresponded exactly to the needs of the big U.S. sugar companies that had established themselves in northern Camagüey. By so doing, he had feathered both his own nest and those of the foreigners who invested in the enterprise.

Ferrocarril del Norte de Cuba served the single-crop economy, meeting the needs of large twentieth-century imperialist plantations. Vast uninhabited areas planted to sugarcane became typical of northern Camagüey, proof that advantage was being taken of the opportunity the war had provided for making a killing in sugar.

The effect that the high (but short-lived) price of sugar had on Cuba's railroads was the same as in the productive sector. Greater sugar production was followed by heavier railroad traffic. In the traditional sugar-growing regions, where the railroads had been established for many decades, the building and reactivation of small and medium-sized sugar mills during the war did not create new transportation services of any considerable size, but, in those areas where sugar was being produced under optimal technological conditions and with abundant capital, it became possible to create new railroads: Ferrocarril Cubano de Hershey, in

TABLE 13.3. Passengers and Freight Carried by the Main Railroad Companies in Cuba, 1913–1918

Company	Number of Passengers		Freight (in metric tons)	
	1913	1918	1913	1918
United Railways of Havana	1,873,918	3,390,648	6,810,254	9,494,853
Cuban Central Railways	989,020	1,619,390	3,246,564	4,389,519
Cuba Railroad Company	1,215,690	2,084,018	1,770,174	5,260,151

Sources: Cuba, Comisión de Ferrocarriles, Memorias (1913–18); United Railways of Havana, Reports (1913–18); Cuban Central Railways Company, Reports (1913–18); and Cuba Railroad Company, Annual Reports (1913–18).

Havana, and Ferrocarril del Norte de Cuba, in Camagüey. In addition, some sugar companies, such as the ones that owned the Juraguá, Resulta, Caracas, Perseverancia, and Portugalete sugar mills,[48] in Las Villas, and some of the giants in the eastern part of the country, such as the United Fruit Company's Boston and Preston sugar mills, made some public railroad services possible.

The demand for railroad service grew impressively, placing the railroad companies in an exceptionally good position for doing business. Table 13.3 shows the importance of the 1913–18 period in terms of passengers and volume of freight for three of the main railroad companies in the country.

As the table shows, the increases were of enormous importance, especially in terms of the freight carried by United Railways of Havana and the Cuba Railroad Company. In both cases, transportation of the sugar produced in the sugar mills near the company's lines was just as important as carrying the machinery needed for the new sugar mills, which quite frequently entered Cuba through the ports of Havana and Nuevitas and was taken to its final destination by rail.

The railroad companies' participation in the boom years was not limited to increasing their business operations; through the Comisión de Ferrocarriles, which represented them, they also presented continual demands for higher rail rates. Ceding to the companies' pressure, the government granted increases that set the situation back to what it had been like prior to Military Order 117. The increases granted in 1914, December 1917, and April 1918 amounted to between 20 and 50 percent in the first case, 20 percent in the second, and 20 percent in the third.[49] In all three cases, the base rate for combined transporation was respected, but increases were authorized for each company's networks separately. Since sugar was never carried over long distances, the rate increases had to be paid by the estate owners, especially in the western part of the country, where they were helpless in view of the English monopoly.

Irate protests by sugar growers seem to have upset President Mario García Menocal, who drew up a decree for nationalizing Cuba's railroads.[50] The president's decision was based on the fact that the increase in Cuba's production and trade had resulted in a great demand for moving merchandise, which the railroad companies had been unable to meet. This situation was prejudicial to the estate owners and merchants who depended on that means of transportation.

The decree itself brought out the president's weakness in a debate in which the interests of the estate owners and those of the railroad companies were in conflict. In sharp contrast with the government's approval of the rate increase, the decree stated that rate increases held back the country's industrial development. The impotence of the executive was also shown when the president alleged that, if reductions in the rates were decreed, conflicts with friendly nations might arise, since the resolutions that were adopted might favor Cuban estate owners. The threat of nationalization was manifestly aimed against the English railroads in the western provinces, since they operated in the area which contained the sugar mills owned by Cubans.

The nationalization farce kept cropping up for several years, sometimes through statements made by government officials and at other times through articles in the press. The issue remained pending until May 1920, when a commission of Ferrocarriles Unidos stockholders from London visited the president; the meeting was terminated abruptly with the declaration of nationalization.[51] Subsequent press commentary brought out the fact that a commission had been created in 1916 to study the project but had never met,[52] which made it difficult to take the whole thing seriously.

The rate increases and the intensity of railroad traffic in the war and postwar years added to the railroad companies' funds, increasing the country's railroads' global income from something over 21 million pesos for the period from July 1913 through June 1914 to nearly 55 million pesos in the 1919–20 fiscal year.[53] In 1919–20, United Railways of Havana received 33 percent of the total income from freight, passengers, and parcel post;[54] Cuban Central received around 13 percent; the Cuba Railroad Company, 26 percent; Norte de Cuba's unfinished lines, 4 percent; and the rest of the companies, the remaining 24 percent.

The world war brought ephemeral prosperity for the island; the railroads benefited from that situation, but the outset of the war also coincided with the use of automobiles as public carriers. The old dirt roads in Havana and Matanzas Provinces, which had not been used for passenger transportation for many years, began to have their potholes filled in and uneven surfaces smoothed during the

TABLE 13.4. Income the Main Railroad Companies in Cuba Obtained from Passenger Fares and Freight Charges for Carrying Sugar, Sugarcane, and Molasses, 1920 (in percent)

Company	Passenger Fares	Sugar	Sugarcane	Molasses
United Railways of Havana	28	26	8	3
Western Railways of Havana	37	17	17	—
Havana Central	58	29	—	6
Cuban Central Railways	21	32	15	3
Cuba Railroad Company	30	21	9	3
Ferrocarril Nuevitas-Camagüey	11	46	1	7
Ferrocarril del Norte de Cuba	21	51	4	3
Guantánamo and Western	33	45	15	2
Ferrocarril Cubano de Hershey	7	21	28	3

Source: Cuba, Comisión de Ferrocarriles, Memoria (1919–20). Figures based on income data.

Menocal administration (1913–21), which made them more usable for the shaky vehicles of the era. Cuban railroads charged extremely high passenger rates for going to places as close to the capital as Güines and Madruga,[55] so taxis, which were always ready to go whenever their clients wanted their services, began to take clients away from the railroads, reviving the specter of competition on the Havana-to-Güines and Havana-to-Matanzas-and-Cárdenas lines, including intermediary points.

The fact that each company had become dependent on its income from passenger fares made certain companies more vulnerable than others to competition, though it may be said that, in general, nearly all of the Cuban railroad companies got more than a third of their income from transporting sugar, which temporarily exempted them from the dangers of that kind of competition.

Table 13.4 presents figures on what proportion of the main Cuban railroads' income in 1920 came from transporting passengers, sugar, sugarcane, and molasses. It shows that a company with such extensive control and such a privileged location as United Railways received only 28 percent of its income from passengers, while 58 percent of the income of the upstart Havana Central, whose modern electric trains managed to establish rapid passenger service between Havana and Güines and between Havana and Guanajay, also serving several other towns around the capital, came from passengers.

Passenger service was of little importance for Ferrocarril de Nuevitas a Camagüey and Ferrocarril Cubano de Hershey. The former was governed by the commercial role of the port of Nuevitas, and the latter proved very inconveneient for passengers trying to reach the capital; without access to the main railway station, it couldn't do much to increase the number of passengers using its trains.

Table 13.4 shows an inverse state of affairs when it comes to income from transporting sugar. In this case, Ferrocarril del Norte de Cuba, which was specifically built for the sugar service, obtained the highest proportion of its earnings—51 percent—from that business; it is followed by the old Ferrocarril de Nuevitas a Camagüey, rejuvenated by its new owner, which turned it into the means for transporting the sugar produced along the lines of the Cuba Railroad Company in Camagüey Province. Until the Santa Cruz del Sur branch line was completed in 1923, that seventy-three-kilometer-long stretch was used to solve that company's sugar-exporting problems.

The transportation of sugar was also an important part of Ferrocarril de Guantánamo's income (45 percent), since it was the main public service line that operated in the Guantánamo Valley. Sugar was less important for Western Railways of Havana (17 percent of its income); the main export products it carried were hundredweight bales of leaf tobacco, from Pinar del Río Province to the docks in Havana.

The transportation of sugarcane was particularly important for Ferrocarril de Hershey—28 percent of its income—for the railroad had been built precisely to carry the cane and the sugar produced by the Hershey Corporation's three sugar mills in Havana. Paradoxically, the transportation of sugarcane was also an important source of income for the tobacco-carrying Western Havana (Oeste) railroad—another 17 percent of its total—since that line served several sugar mills in Artemisa and other areas west of Havana and especially the Toledo sugar mill, near the capital, whose sugarcane fields were at a considerable distance from the mill.

Cuban Central, whose lines were linked in several places with the private networks of the sugar mills in Las Villas Province, also obtained a sizable part of its income from transporting sugarcane. However, the sugarcane-related Ferrocarril Norte de Cuba did only a minimal amount of sugarcane hauling, so its income from that source amounted to only 5 percent of its total. That company's operating criterion had been drawn up on the basis of the more remunerative transportation of sugar, so it left nearly all of the more troublesome transportation of sugarcane to the private railroads belonging to the large sugar companies it served. Not surprisingly, that company's expenses as compared to income were the lowest of the most important railroads: its operating ratio was 0.49, while the operating ratios of the other companies were 0.64 or more.[56]

The high market price of sugar helped to entrench and clearly define the functions assigned to railroads in the Cuban economy. The establishment of large monopoly plantations in the western part of the country, such as the one owned by the Hershey Corporation, and the near exclusion of all other activities from some regions, as in the northern part of Camagüey, required that several hundred kilometers of new track be incorporated in the public service railroad system. Together with that, the specific needs of the new organizational plan of the sugar cycle promoted an incomparably greater growth of the private railroads, whose functions also began to include the transportation of sugar and molasses. The two railroad systems continued to grow peacefully side by side as long as the boom continued, but, when the bottom fell out, contradictions between them promptly appeared.

U.S. Monopolies and the Tarafa Bill

The Cuban sugar boom resulting from World War I reached its peak at the end of 1920. By then, plantations had expanded throughout nearly all of the nation's territory, occupying areas of the island that had always been sparsely populated, if at all. During the boom years, countless sugar mills had gone into production. Some of them were new, but others were old ones that had been shut down and were reactivated. With sugar going for exorbitant prices, sugar mills with a wide variety of technological characteristics and financial resources and in a wide range of geographic locations could operate at a profit.

In the western part of the country, nearly all of the sugar mills that were placed in production were reactivated, improved units that did not cause any basic changes in the traditional links between the sugarcane estates and the public service railroads. That link was maintained with few if any changes, for the only difference was that railroad traffic increased.

The new sugar mills in the eastern part of the country, however, were of two kinds. The first consisted of new ones that were built near existing railroad tracks. The second, though few in number, were important because of their size; they were built relatively close to the coast and used private railroads to transport their sugar to the ports. Thus, some of the new giants in Camagüey and Oriente, in addition to greater production capacity and industrial efficiency,[1] had that additional advantage for exporting their products and importing what they needed at a lower cost than the other sugar mills on the island.

As long as the price of sugar remained high, the productive, commercial, and transportation sectors all benefited. During the war, a system of price controls had been in effect; when the armistice was signed, however, those controls were lifted. The result was unlimited sugar production based on equally unlimited credit extended by Cuban banks. That veritable marathon in speculation involved not only the finished product but also the raw material and even the sugar mills themselves. As already pointed out, 25 percent of the sugar mills in Cuba changed hands in that period, and at very high prices.[2]

When the sugar-producing areas that had been kept out of production by the war resumed their normal activity, their sugar plus that produced in other countries whose production had been stimulated by the temporary high prices caused a glut, which inevitably caused the bottom to fall out of the market. The result for Cuba was disastrous; it meant ruin for professional speculators, bankers, and estate owners who had assumed that prices would remain high. Not all were affected to the same degree, however; the ones who had been the most daring in basing their operations on credit without having the financial resources to back them up were hardest hit. Of course, the U.S. companies, which had more liquid assets available to them than the Cuban ones did, not only weathered the storm but benefited from it, thanks to the liquidation of many Cuban sugar and banking concerns.[3]

The railroads had also benefited from the high sugar prices, with steady increases in their rates. Later, as was only to be expected, their income fell off somewhat. Even so, from the financial point of view, since most of their transactions were long-term ones, the railroad companies had not been so dazzled by the short boom years to count on continued prosperity. The main problem with which the railroads were faced at the end of the inflationary period was that of quickly adjusting from large incomes (based on great volumes of freight and passengers at high rates) to reduced income from their operations. Most of the measures they took to remain profitable were the same old standbys they had always resorted to in times of crisis: slashing wages and laying off workers.

In general, the 1920 crisis had only temporary consequences for Cuba's railroads, because most of their property was backed up by U.S. and English capital and had not been put up as security for feverish speculation. The main effects had been in terms of trade. During the first few months of 1921, some optimism had been restored, and the boards of directors of the railroad companies felt that the worst was over: "Fortunately at the time of this writing, the Cuban situation is greatly improved, and it is expected that the recuperative power of that wonderful island will place business in the near future at its regular level, and that production will soon be catching up with normality."[4]

The next year, a spokesman of United Railways of Havana, which was one of the companies that had been hardest hit, made a similar statement. "It is quite true that the outward and visible signs are not very striking: still we believe the position is improving. There is certainly more confidence in the island as to the future, and I think that everything points to better times for us in the years to come."[5]

The economic situation had begun to recover and, by 1923, had returned to its pre-1920 levels. The readjustment of expenses so they would be in line with the levels of income obtained in the railroads' operations had been achieved quite quickly, in large part due to the economies introduced in terms of wages. Figure 14.1 presents figures on the income obtained from operations and the amount that went for expenses of three of the most important railroad companies between 1919 and 1923. In those cases, readjustments made it possible to obtain a greater margin of gross profits during fiscal year 1922–23 than in the preceding years. The income registered that year was nearly up to traditional levels. (See Figure 14.1.)

The country's economy had returned to normal by 1923, and, if it hadn't been for the Cuban property that had passed to U.S. hands as a result of the 1920 crisis, it could be said that the situation began to be good that year. The total value of the 1923 sugarcane harvest—400 million pesos—was only a little less than that of the 1919 harvest, and the price of sugar had risen once again, to 4.9 centavos a pound (it had gone for 2.8 centavos a pound the year before).[6]

Even though the price of sugar had recovered, a new obstacle appeared to hurt Cuban sugar in its main market, the United States. The U.S. government decided to raise the tariff on imported sugar, thus forcing Cuban producers into an ongoing struggle to reduce their production costs so their sugar could enter the U.S. market on a competitive basis. The sugar companies had to make the main effort to cut those costs, but, of course, they tried to pass on a part of their sacrifice to the railroads, either by pressuring them to reduce their rates or by doing without that public service transportation whenever possible.

The sugar companies cut their production costs mainly by reducing the sugar growers' share of the profits and by cutting expenditures for labor and transportation to a bare minimum. As regards this last aspect, that of transportation, the large U.S. companies had an advantageous position, for they could do without the public railroads completely, both for hauling the sugarcane and for transporting, storing, and shipping out the sugar. In those conditions, the privileged sugar companies could appropriate nearly all of the surplus value that the workers in the sugar sector created, without passing any of it on to the railroad companies.

This factor was quite important, because, during the war and postwar years, the Cuban government had systematically promoted the sugar interests by authorizing them to use private ports as terminals for periods of up to twenty or even thirty years, thus violating the Ports Law of 1890.[7] As reported in the Cuban Senate, that policy resulted in the fact that, between 1920 and 1923, a total of forty-seven sugar mills shipped their products out through private ports more or less openly, either with or without permission, and nearly half of the sugar produced in the country was neither transported over public railroads nor exported through any of the ports used for general trade.[8] Even though the figure seems rather exaggerated, everything indicates that, just as a large number of sugar mills passed into the hands of a few U.S. companies—mainly the ones created by the National City

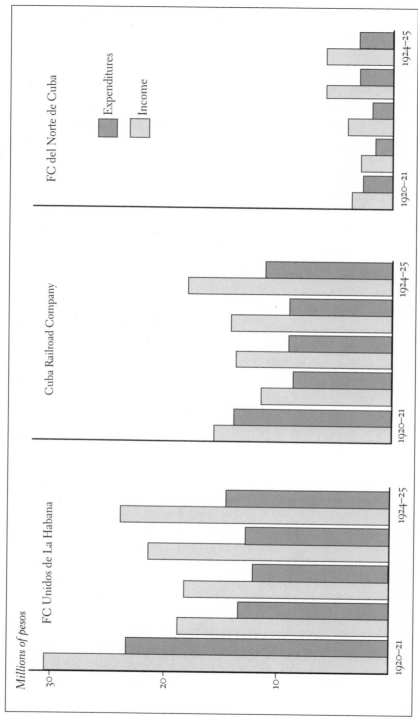

FIGURE 14.1. Income and Expenditures of the Three Main Railroad Companies, 1920–1921 to 1924–1925

Bank—as a result of the 1920 crisis, those companies used the private ports of some of the sugar mills they controlled for shipping out not only the sugar produced by those mills but also that produced by other sugar mills they controlled, which did not have ports of their own.

Another aspect of this same phenomenon was the sugar capitalists' systematic efforts to obtain rate reductions so as to maintain their profit margins in the deflationary situation. In the case of the private ports, a rigid dichotomy arose between the railroads and those ports, with Ferrocarril del Norte de Cuba and the Cuba Railroad Company the ones worst affected. Since that problem was mainly restricted to the eastern part of the island, it was a localized situation. In the case of the tariffs, however, the interests of all the railroad and sugar companies were involved, and this led to the first important contradictions between the two sectors, near the end of 1920. (See Map 14.1.)

During the boom years, the Comisión de Ferrocarriles had authorized reiterated rate increases for railroad services, which mainly benefited interline traffic. At the end of that period, in November 1920, however, it approved Rate 5, which established new increases in transportation rates.[9] They went into effect in December 1920, just when sugar prices were plummeting. The new rates thus came at the worst possible time and were extremely harmful to the sugar growers' interests. Approval of the new rates led the sugar interests to mobilize immediately, and they tried to make the matter a key national issue. Their protest quickly took the form of a bill, which the Senate passed in February 1921 at the request of its president, Senator Aurelio Alvarez, of Camagüey. The so-called Alvarez bill proposed a return to the rates in effect in April 1919,[10] abolishing the ones approved by the Comisión de Ferrocarriles.

The railroad companies also mobilized, through the diplomatic representatives of England and the United States, who pressured President Mario García Menocal,[11] alleging that the progressive rate increase had led to a steady rise in railroad workers' wages and that a reduction in the rates would be sure to cause a nationwide strike. That blackmail forced Menocal to yield to the diplomats' demand; he vetoed the Alvarez bill on February 2, 1921, leaving the rate increase in effect.[12]

Not all the companies held the same views on the matter, however. The situation that prevailed in 1921 and 1922 was not propitious for a rate increase, and the logical thing would have been for the railroad companies to accept their share of the deflation, as they had shared in the benefits of the boom. The Cuba Railroad Company tried to defend the increase, however, claiming that its operating costs had increased considerably. Later on, it changed its tune, adopting a more realistic tone, until its position approximated that of United Railways and Norte de Cuba, which felt that the companies would be forced by circumstances to reduce

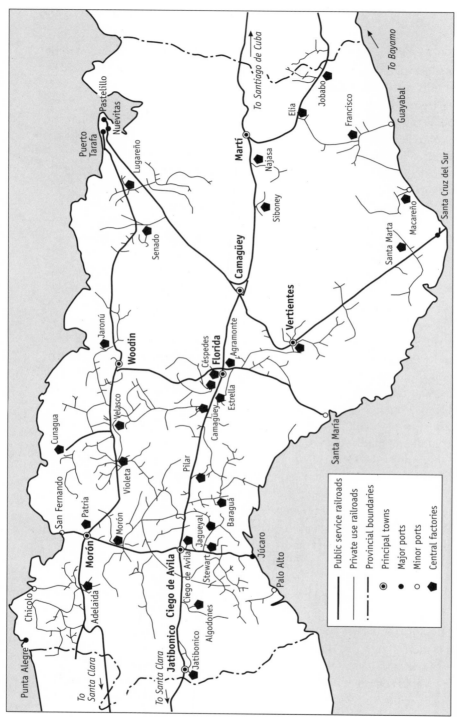

MAP 14.1. Distribution of Public and Private Networks in Camagüey

Public service railroads
Private use railroads
Provincial boundaries
◉ Principal towns
● Major ports
○ Minor ports
⬠ Central factories

To Santiago de Cuba
To Bayamo

Pastelillo
Nuevitas
Puerto Tarafa
Lugareño
Jobabo
Francisco
Elia
Guayabal
Najasa
Senado
Siboney
Martí
Camagüey
Santa Marta
Macareño
Santa Cruz del Sur
Jaronú
Woodin
Céspedes
Florida
Agramonte
Vertientes
Velasco
Estrella
Camagüey
Cunagua
Pilar
Violeta
Santa María
San Fernando
Patria
Morón
Baraguá
Jagüeyal
Júcaro
Palo Alto
Punta Alegre
Chicola
Morón
Adelaida
Ciego de Ávila
Jatibonico
Stewart
Algodones
Jatibonico
To Santa Clara
To Santa Clara

their rates on their own if they wanted to maintain the volume of their services. In general, the companies' attitude reflected the uncertainty of the times.

All of the companies tried to bring pressure of one kind or another to bear on the president, not only concerning their rates but also (and mainly) to obtain guarantees that the government would take a firm stand against the workers when the companies applied the wage cuts and layoffs that they considered indispensable for reducing their operating costs.

A letter that one of the top officials of the Cuba Railroad Company wrote to another clearly illustrates that view. It implied that there was to be an understanding with Tarafa and Jack that they would see President Zayas in order to inform him that they could not continue to pay high salaries and hoping that the government would assist them in lowering wages to the normal levels for Cuban workers. The ruse would be to object to government interference in the bargaining process with the workers, but to welcome it if it led to better worker discipline and lower wages. The only problem they envisaged was that of a powerful workers' union. In any case all blame would be put on the government for both the living conditions of the workers and the high prices charged by the railroads.[13]

The officials of the Cuba Railroad Company were confident that the repressive political apparatus of the Cuban government would help them further their interests. They confidently asserted that as a North American company they had good relations in Washington and that gave them an advantage over local Cuban companies. While Tarafa could get better terms from the Cuban government, that government was in no position to take measures that could hurt the Americans, and that gave them an advantage over Tarafa.[14]

While counting on the protection that their relations with the politicians supposedly gave them, those officials also hoped that the workers' defensive action would give them an opportunity to act against them on their own. "It would not be altogether a bad thing if our men would go out on strike so that we could fire the lot and replace them with new workers at lower wages at the same time that we lowered rates."[15]

The issue of rates had to be settled at the level required by the situation. The need to reduce costs in the sugar industry combined with the no less pressing need of the railroads to maintain their level of operations. The House of Representatives and the Senate supported the solution offered by the Alvarez bill in December 1921 by unanimously overriding President Menocal's veto, which had been irresponsibly dictated by his decision to favor the interests of the Cuba Railroad Company.

The railroads' relative unity with regard to the rates issue was very precarious. The criteria upheld by the three main companies reflected their different situations. United Railways (Ferrocarriles Unidos), for example, had ninety-six sugar mills along its lines, and it carried all of their freight, except for that of the mills owned by the Hershey Corporation. Its sugar mills were relatively small, and most of them were owned by Cubans, who were faced with monetary difficulties. The railroad needed the sugar mills' business to survive, and they had to have an immediate rate reduction to be able to remain in production.

In the eastern part of the country, especially in Camagüey, the situation was different. There, two railroad companies were competing: the powerful Cuba Railroad Company, which was largely dependent on transporting passengers and general freight, and Ferrocarril Norte de Cuba, headed by José M. Tarafa, a Cuban, which was much smaller and was almost exclusively used for carrying sugar. That area had the greatest number of large sugar corporations, each of which owned several sugar mills that were relatively close together and had extensive networks of railroad tracks and private ports. Those corporations' ever more intensive use of those installations had already caused concern among the officials of the railroads operating in the eastern provinces.

In that context, the situation of Ferrocarril del Norte de Cuba was particularly difficult. That company had been created in an era of high sugar prices, drawing on credit based on the size of the sugar business. In spite of Tarafa's skill in getting the largest sugar mills of the time to use its services, it had the disadvantage of being entirely dependent on the transportation of sugar. To survive, it had to compete with the Cuba Railroad Company, whose finances were much stronger. The fact that Norte de Cuba was not connected with Ferrocarril Central, the country's system of passenger and general freight transportation service, was another problem; the only possible places where its lines might link up with it were in Ciego de Avila and Florida, where Norte de Cuba and the Cuba Railroad Company were competing for the sugar transportation business.

It was Norte de Cuba's financial situation, not the general state of business operations, that triggered the most important railroad events of that decade. In fiscal year 1921–22, that company had deferred liabilities of over 18 million pesos, which meant that its capitalization debt amounted to $75,000 per mile of track, whereas that of its competitor, the Cuba Railroad Company, was less than half: $34,500 per mile. In that situation of indebtedness, Norte had to pay nearly a million pesos a year for interest, alone.[16]

Even though Tarafa's company was small compared with the Cuba Railroad Company, the Cuban's initiative, based on his vast stores of influence with government officials, enabled him not only to make certain moves in the "railroad chess game" in Camagüey but also to become the key figure in the relations between the estate owners and the railroad companies of his era. Coordination between sugar mills, railroads, and ports of embarkation was once more the order of the day, but not as just a practical matter; rather, it became an area of conflict that involved all of those two important sectors of the country's economy, in which U.S. finance capital had considerable interests.

In a far from strong financial position but yet with certain competitive advantages,[17] Tarafa, in Norte de Cuba, had become a thorn in the flesh of the directors of the Cuba Railroad Company, making unpredictable decisions. "I don't know what to do with Tarafa," the president of Cuba Railroad, H. C. Lakin, commented. "I wonder if anything can be done. He has his own ideas and goes ahead with them to please himself, not considering anything else."[18]

Tarafa's apparent stubbornness was based on his financial inability to keep his company operating in a deflationary period in which the prospects for increasing the areas planted to sugarcane without limit, as had been done in previous years, were a chimera.[19] In the boom years, Norte de Cuba had obtained authorization to extend its tracks westward from Chambas to Zulueta and, from there, to Santa Clara, thus changing the original plan, which had called for going into an area that United Railways served to some extent. This change would allow Norte de Cuba to hook up with the western railroad system in Santa Clara. Norte de Cuba's expansion eastward had been completed with the construction of a branch line from its main line in Woodin (Esmeralda) to the town of Florida, where a group of modern sugar mills had been built some years earlier. Most of them sent their products out by using the Cuba Railroad Company.[20]

Another of Tarafa's projects had been achieved in May 1920 with the purchase of Ferrocarril de Júcaro a San Fernando. Norte de Cuba's concentration point for the sugar it carried was the same as for the Cuba Railroad Company: the Bay of Nuevitas. A port facility, Puerto Tarafa, had been built there which was larger and more efficient than the Cuba Railroad's installations at Pastelillo.[21]

The fact that Norte de Cuba had a lower operating cost coefficient than any other Cuban railroad enabled it to devise an extremely daring policy as regards rates, even when the railroad companies were trying to defend the increases authorized under the administration of President Menocal. From then on, Norte de Cuba tried to take Cuba Railroad's customers away from it and provide the services requested of it in any part of Camagüey. Therefore, it signed special contracts with the sugar mills that employed its services, such as the Patria, Adelaida, Morón, Cunagua, and Jaronú, setting low enough rates for transporting their sugar to keep those companies from building their own branch lines to the coast. In the case of the sugar mills served by the Cuba Railroad, its policy was the same: to offer transportation services at a lower rate and sign contracts for longer periods of time, to guarantee greater stability in its income.

Such aggressiveness in its business policy, however, didn't improve Norte de Cuba's situation. Tarafa himself was forced to admit in June 1921 that the sugar transport business had declined considerably, and it appeared that the planters were holding back their sugar at the mills while they shipped that which was warehoused already at the ports. As a result that part of the business had been virtually paralyzed, and he surmised that other transport business would also decline, and he proposed a gradual reduction of wages and employees so that a complete shut down of the line could be averted.[22]

Tarafa had played a clearly defined role with the U.S. interests in both sugar mills and railroads, especially as regards the National City Bank's direct interests in Cuba. This was another reason why, even though the Cuba Railroad Company struggled to maintain the rate increase of 1920, Norte benefited from clauses stating that the sugar from certain sugar mills linked to that bank had to be transported over its lines. The National City Bank tried to lower the costs of the sugar mills it managed, especially through the General Sugar States. To do so, it used both the lowest public railroad rates and the private shipping facilities belonging to some of its sugar mills. Within the New York bank's global strategy in Cuba, Ferrocarril del Norte's role was to lower the railroad rates for both passengers and freight.[23]

Even so, Tarafa's strategy didn't solve Norte de Cuba's problems. It allowed him only minimal room for maneuvering.

> Tarafa has ambitious plans to develop a sugarcane zone in the eastern part of the province of Las Villas between Chambas and Zulueta, but it does not seem that he can carry that off at this time; on the other hand he seems to want to set up some deal with our company. . . . following my conversation with Tarafa he seems to want to sell the Norte de Cuba or join us and is maneuvering to get the best possible price. I suppose that he has convinced himself that he cannot get the money to carry out his projected extensions and it is possible that he is having some problems running his railroad. I know that he likes to plan and build railroads, but the running is another matter entirely.[24]

Those steps necessarily led to a rapprochement with Cuba Railroad. In the situation created by competition, it was difficult for a single company to try to monopolize all of the railroad lines in Camagüey, so negotiation was required.

Since 1922, the Cuba Railroad Company had also been studying the possibility of an agreement with Norte de Cuba, to do away with its bothersome and, at the same time, growing competitor. For his part, Tarafa, in his eternal scrabbling after funds, was also trying to find takers for some of his railroad's first-mortgage bonds, so he could extend its lines to Santa Clara. Therefore, he entered into negotiations with a representative of the J. P. Morgan banking house.[25] At the same time, rumors were circulating that J. P. Morgan was buying a part of Ferrocarril del Norte de Cuba's stocks and bonds at a very high price.[26]

While visiting Havana, Morgan's agent, Edward Stettinius, agreed to negotiate without running any risks or making any commitments. He merely proposed as a condition that a group of engineers and accountants appointed by the house of Morgan and paid by Tarafa carry out a careful investigation and that any decisions be based on its report. The group that was formed to carry out that task included an expert named George Hardwood, who, with Tarafa's permission, made double use of his work: he worked for Morgan and, at the same time, for Cuba Railroad, providing it with a copy of the technical and financial study of Norte, so that the competing railroad's officials might make a decision on whether to take over Tarafa's holdings.[27]

In his efforts to sell his railroad to the highest bidder, Tarafa also put out feelers to the National City Bank. In this case, the matter was more serious, and a greater number of interests were involved, since the bank also controlled several sugar mills in Camagüey and had been building two new large private ports in the southern part of the province: one at Baraguá, serving the Baraguá, Pilar, and other sugar mills, and one at Santa María, from which to ship out the sugar from the sugar mills in the Florida region and from the Vertientes sugar mill. If, at that time, the National City Bank had decided to export the sugar from its sugar mills through those ports while Cuban Cane shipped the sugar from the Jagueyal and Stewart sugar mills though Palo Alto and the Rionda firm shipped out the sugar from the Francisco and Elia sugar mills through the private port of Guayabal, the public service railroads and the regular ports would have lost the business of handling most of the sugar produced in that large area in the southern part of the province.

While Tarafa was carrying out his maneuvers and threats, the Cuba Railroad Company maintained a policy of watchful waiting.

> We are on the fringe of the situation here, in part because it is obvious that the House of Morgan, as the backer of this project, will take over the Norte, but fundamentally because it has strongly refused to back the projected route via Chambas to Santa Clara. . . . With greater or lesser goodwill between both railroads in the matter of rates and eliminating the possible danger of an extension by the Norte, I do not see that there is anything to worry about, and even so, the only real point of all this comes from the pending negotiations between Tarafa and the National City Bank with respect to the transport of sugar from the "Estrella" and "Pilar." central factories.[28]

The officials of Cuba Railroad believed that, in its talks with Tarafa, the National City Bank was trying to force Norte de Cuba to reduce its rates even more for the sugar mills that the bank controlled.[29] At that time, the said officials were content because, in a meeting of executives of the Cuba Railroad Company,

Percy Rockefeller, a director of the bank and of Cuba Railroad, had promised them that "finally the Cuba Railroad would be carrying on much more business with the central factories 'Pilar,' 'Vertientes,' and 'Agramonte' than it had ever done before."[30]

In that complicated situation, Tarafa took the initiative to make a proposal that, while solving his own financial problems by guaranteeing Norte de Cuba's expansion westward, would also maintain the volume of sugar carried by the public railroads to some extent. Though not very important in the three westernmost provinces, it was essential in Las Villas, Camagüey, and Oriente, the stronghold of powerful U.S. sugar and railroad interests. At the top of the pyramid was the National City Bank, trying to juggle its various interests and providing the financial backing needed to achieve a harmonious solution for the conflict between the companies. At that time, the National City Bank had a considerable portfolio of businesses in Cuba: it directly controlled General Sugar States, with its Pilar, Estrella, Vertientes, Camagüey, and Agramonte sugar mills, all along the lines of the Cuba Railroad Company. It also had important financial ties with Cuban Cane, which owned the Jagueyal, Lugareño, Stewart, Morón, and Violeta sugar mills, all in Camagüey Province, along Tarafa's lines and very near those of Cuba Railroad. The bank also influenced American Sugar Refining, with its Cunagua and Jaronú sugar mills.[31] At the opposite extreme were the same bank's railroad interests, represented by Percy A. Rockefeller, on the board of the Cuba Railroad Company, whose direct representative was Horatio S. Rubens, "a great friend of Cuba's."[32]

In an interview Tarafa gave to a committee of estate owners in June 1923, he set forth the premises on which he would base his initiative for solving the sugar-railroad confrontation:

Nearly all of the sugar companies controlled by U.S. interests have realized that, by opening ports of their own, they can ship their sugar out at less cost to themselves, ignoring the fact that such practices ruin the national ports, which cannot grow and prosper. To the contrary, if they are deprived of their normal traffic, they will be condemned to inactivity and diminishing importance. . . . Exports and imports are authorized to pass through those private ports, even though they serve only a single interest, and the result is that that single interest, in detriment to the public interest, handles its imports through that single port and the business of [normal] transportation along its own lines. It doesn't pay anything for the business of importing and transportation, so it doesn't contribute anything toward defraying public expenses and, though a sugar mill, has a privilege that is denied to the vast majority of the other sugar mills, which, by paying their freight charges to the public service railroads, help to maintain them. . . . Every time a public railroad doesn't transport the sugar produced in the area it serves, this hurts those sugar mills that continue to send their sugar out by public railroad and through the public ports. . . . In Cuba, because of its topography, the problem is more serious than in any other country. If adequate legislation isn't forthcoming, Cuba's shape will make it unable to maintain its public railroads, because nearly all of the sugar mills will ship their sugar out through private ports.[33]

Tarafa was speaking as both a railroad executive and the owner of an estate served by a public service railroad.[34] His main interest was to halt the growing trend toward exporting sugar products through private ports and to ensure the operability of his railroad by means of legislation that would limit the privilege of the private ports and force the sugar companies to use the public service railroads. Many sugar companies, representing nearly forty sugar mills, were interested in maintaining that privilege. The companies most closely involved in that system of shipping included General Sugar States, the Manatí Sugar Company, Punta Alegre Sugar, the Cuban American Sugar Company, and the United Fruit Company.[35]

In July, the confrontation between the important railroad and sugar interests had become a public matter. The chairman of the committee that the Asociación de Hacendados (Association of Estate Owners) created to solve the problem made some statements, too:

Always, systematically, the public administration has allowed the transportation companies to influence the official agencies in charge of serving the public, rather than vice versa. . . . To say the Comisión de Ferrocarriles is to state that that agency is a dependency of the railroad companies. Personal initiative, which is the only thing manifest in Cuba in the sphere of various private activities, has operated in such a way that the cherished hope of every sugar man plundered by the railroads is to be freed of them by using his own lines and rolling stock to haul his products and have his own export points.[36]

To buttress the defense of his railroad, Tarafa not only threw himself into the role of champion of that transportation sector but also defended the country's ports and port populations. The railroads' cause was much more likely to gain support in public opinion than the hateful exclusiveness of the sugar corporations that used private ports.

At present, most of the sugar mills transport their sugar by public service railroads to public ports. By doing so, they help to maintain the railroads and contribute to the development and prosperity of the towns that have grown up around those ports. They develop and prosper from the exports and imports that pass through them, to such an extent that, if we were to take that traffic away from them by using private landing stages, they would cease to exist. The private ports reduce the volume of traffic through the public ones. Therefore, the cost of transportation will increase for those sugar mills which, with their cargo, contribute to the enhancement of our towns and to the support of the public railroads.[37]

Tarafa's pose of defending the public interest was simply a front for trying to force the big sugar companies to use the services of the public railroads—especially those of "his" railroad—as a means for guaranteeing its income. It was faced with the prospect of a settlement or sale, and its stability and income level would be of key importance in either case.

In the latter half of 1923, Tarafa directed his activities toward coming up with relatively permanent solutions for the problem of sugar shipments and, at the same time, toward giving legal form to a settlement or agreement that would allow Norte de Cuba to survive and even expand. Even though Tarafa was not a legislator, he got both issues incorporated in a body of law that was known from then on as the "Tarafa bill."

The bill called for the consolidation of three railroad companies, two of which should be Cuban and at least 400 kilometers long. Unquestionably, this referred to Norte de Cuba and Ferrocarril de Camagüey a Nuevitas, both of which were registered in Cuba. The third company would be the Cuba Railroad Company, which was U.S.-owned and held stock in the Nuevitas company, so the consolidation was really of just two companies. The consolidation should guarantee a 25 percent reduction in rates for sugar carried for distances of over 125 kilometers, which favored its shipment through the large sugar terminals, especially the one in Nuevitas. The bill tacitly prohibited the construction of new railroads in the areas served by the consolidated ones. The use of ports by private railroads would be authorized only in those cases in which that method had been used prior to the promulgation of the new law and where no public service railroads served the port. It also stated that private railroads could not go public.

Those prohibitions and regulations provided the legal underpinnings for a railroad monopoly in Cuba. Article 9 of the bill set forth the regulations for private ports, using a new classification, based on the ports' economic and demographic importance.[38] The thorniest part of the bill was Article 11, which levied a tax of from 5 to 20 centavos on every hundred pounds of sugar exported through private ports.[39] The tax would increase the costs of the sugar companies that used private ports, making them choose between paying the government the amount stipulated or, however unwillingly, using the services offered by the public railroads with a reduction for long-distance haulage, which would mean abandoning the railroad and port installations the sugar mills had built for exporting their products.

The Trinidad Sugar Company had to choose between closing down its own landing stage and sending its sugar to a public port, which would increase its transportation costs from 43 centavos to 58 centavos a sack, and continuing to use its installations and paying the tax, which would raise its transportation costs to 59 centavos a sack. Other sugar mills, such as the Soledad, were faced with similar situations and had to abandon their river landing stages and use the railroads. The Beattie, Francisco, and Manatí sugar mills calculated that, as a result of the Tarafa bill, their annual expenses would increase by 40,000, 72,000, and 102,000 pesos, respectively.[40]

José M. Tarafa was the most visible champion of the railroads in the conflict, because the two other large companies—Ferrocarriles Unidos and Cuba Railroad—remained formally uninvolved, even though the boards of directors of those companies had already arranged matters to suit their interests. While in London, General Archibald Jack, manager of Ferrocarriles Unidos, had been informed of a possible consolidation in which his company was invited to participate, but his personal opinion of the matter was that the estate owners would thwart the legislation Tarafa had proposed.

H. C. Lakin, president of the Cuba Railroad Company, expressed the old colonialist mentality that underlay the English manager's attitude: "Jack is against this since he thinks that foreign corporations should never make deals with Cubans."[41] Cuba Railroad, accustomed to neocolonial procedures, adopted a hypocritical position, appearing not to participate in the matter so Tarafa would seem to be the only interested party:

> The Cuba Railroad will have nothing official to do with this. Whatever cooperation that we have with Tarafa will depend on the type of deal he can cut without any help from us on the matter of the legislation. The estate owners are not as strong as they seem in this matter. They have made quite a bit of money this year and their position could be based solely on the proposition that they can make much more money for themselves and that the Cubans would make much less because the bigger business of these planters would put them at the margin of the railroads serving the public, for the railroads would probably have to pay lower wages and raise the rates charged to the Cubans in order to offset the loss of business from the foreign sugar producers. . . . You will probably see when you examine the situation that our main opposition are the North American planters. The

Cubans do not have sufficient private resources to build private ports. So all these Cubans will favor the legislation.[42]

The bill on the railroad consolidation and private port regulations was unexpectedly presented in the House of Representatives on the afternoon of August 9, 1923, without having been included on the agenda. It hadn't been submitted for study by any committee in the House or by any members of the commission supposedly appointed for that purpose. Nor were the legislators familiar with the text of the bill that was being pushed through. However, a report that had appeared in the *New York Times* saying that the State Department was opposed to the bill (when those who should vote for or against it in Cuba weren't yet familiar with its contents) was reproduced in Havana. To calm any disquiet that the *New York Times* article might have caused among the legislators, copies of a speech that U.S. President Warren Harding had given the previous June were circulated among them. In it, the U.S. president had stated that he supported the consolidation of railroads in the United States.[43]

The session in the House of Representatives began at three o'clock. At the request of several legislators, it was declared in permanent session until the morning of the following day.[44] In the House's sessions that day and night, representatives who were pledged to each of the sectors involved in the struggle accused the foreign companies that controlled the sugar and railroad sectors of exploiting the country and the Cuban workers and of flouting the law. The exploitative, monopoly nature of both groups in dispute was exposed, but the discussions were ludicrous because of the superficiality with which the legislators treated both the accusations and the defense of the interests they represented. Typically, the Comisión de Ferrocarriles and the U.S. market were blamed for the high rates for railroad service and the high price of sugar sold to the people, absolving the railroad companies of all responsibility.[45]

Representatives Jorge García Montes and Viriato Gutiérrez were two of the most fervent champions of the sugar interests. The former, going straight to the nub of the matter (the reduction in production costs that resulted from the use of private ports), pointed out that "since the production of sugar on land near the coast, where it can be shipped out directly, means cheaper sugar because it avoids the most costly of our means of transportation, which is the railroad, it is clear that every limitation on the use of our outlets to the sea constitutes an attack on that basic interest."[46]

Viriato Gutiérrez, representing the interests of his father-in-law, estate owner Laureano Falla, one of whose sugar mills was near the northern coast of Camagüey, sought to present the issue as one of bourgeois nationalism when he, too, attacked the proclaimed "nationalism" of the Tarafa bill:

To pass laws in the Cuban Congress in favor of the railroad companies under the cloak of protectionism and the defense of national interests is to seek to be deceived, for we all know that no such nationalism is involved. They are trying to protect the interests of Wall Street and the Strand in London—not those of Obispo or any other street in Havana. I sustain that this law is not nationalist and that it is in no way patriotic. Moreover, I think that, in many regards, it seems to have been drawn up by a declared enemy of the republic.[47]

Representative Gutiérrez's allegation was geared to fit the historic moment, for a maturing national awareness had become evident in the early 1920s and was projected in some quite important political movements, such as the Protest of Thirteen, made by a group of intellectuals headed by Rubén Martínez Villena, and the so-called Movement of Veterans and Patriots, which expressly demanded, among other things, that the Tarafa bill not be passed.[48] The opportunistic use of nationalism by the champions and opponents of the Tarafa bill turned the whole process into a ridiculous tragicomedy that served only to bring out the vulnerability of the country's genuine interests in the midst of the degrading neocolonial situation.

The Tarafa bill, as presented to the House of Representatives, said nothing about the confiscation of port installations or about the inequality of rights between Cuban and U.S. interests. Even so, the U.S. press (probably paid by the U.S. sugar interests) kicked up a tremendous ruckus, claiming that U.S. property would be confiscated without compensation of any kind. It also talked of the establishment of "penalties" instead of taxes, and engaged in other distortions and lies,[49] all to confuse the real issue: the proposed taxes on sugar exported through private ports.

The companies that would be adversely affected set their own well-greased apparatus for influencing affairs in motion; the Punta Alegre Sugar Company, Baraguá Sugar Company, Trinidad Sugar Company, and Soledad Sugar Company sent memoranda to the State Department, using the services of Elihu Root's law office—Root, Clark, Buckner, and Howland—to keep the Tarafa bill from going into effect. Cuba Cane, the Manatí Sugar Company, the Francisco Sugar Company, and the Beattie Sugar Company engaged in parallel actions, using the powerful firm of Sullivan and Cromwell.[50] By ignoring the Cuban political levels and appealing directly to the imperialist decision-making center, the sugar companies showed that the key issue in all the hullaballoo surrounding the Tarafa bill was that of the U.S. monopoly interests' carving up Cuban businesses as they pleased.

The real source of power was mobilized; while Sullivan and Cromwell, in New

York, drew up a compromise formula for the interests in conflict, the U.S. president sent a note to Cuban President Alfredo Zayas through the State Department. U.S. property would have to be protected, the note declared, or the U.S. government would take whatever measures it deemed necessary to achieve that aim. At the same time, U.S. Ambassador Enoch Crowder invited Tarafa to meet with U.S. Secretary of State Charles E. Hughes, to reach an agreement that would be acceptable to both parties. Later, Tarafa was told to go to New York to complete the transaction.[51]

After that conciliating act had been carried out in the monopolies' financial capital, the Senate of the republic passed the bill on September 21, 1923,[52] with Wall Street's finishing touches still fresh. Those amendments accommodated the special interests of each of the parties. Among the exceptions listed in Article 8 concerning the opening of new railroads, the new text listed the lines that Ferrocarril Cubano de Hershey and Ferrocarril Terminal de Hershey would build in Havana and Matanzas Provinces and the lines that Ferrocarril de Tunas (which was owned by the Manatí Sugar Company) was planning to build or already had under construction from its hookup with Cuba Railroad in the Tunas Station to the Bay of Manatí and the branch that would run from that line to the town of Nuevitas, a length of no more than sixty-eight kilometers.

Other exceptions included the extension of the lines that the Guantánamo and Western Railroad Company had in Oriente Province and the railroad that would link the isolated settlement of Baracoa with the other public service railroads, if its lines were over 250 kilometers in length.[53] The most important change made in the bill in New York was the elimination of Article 11, which taxed the sugar shipped out through private ports. Therefore, the big U.S. sugar companies retained their advantages. Instead, the secretary of the treasury was empowered to approve use of the private ports that had been active during the 1922–23 fiscal year, after due authorization. The change legalized shipments of the same amounts of sugar through private ports in the future as had been shipped out up until then and excluded only those cases in which sugar had been shipped without permission.

The modified bill also authorized the use of private ports to export and import goods in those places along the coast not served by public railroads and ordered the Comisión de Ferrocarriles to report on the details of each case.[54] So no doubts would remain about the "confiscations" that the imperialist mass media were so up in arms about, the reformed bill established timid penalties that did not go beyond small fines or the seizure of goods in those cases in which the private ports were used for smuggling. With its new text, the bill was accepted by all the litigants as a kind of equitable sharing of the apple of discord between the U.S. sugar interests and the eastern railroads. The strong containing wall which the

Tarafa bill was intended to have been at the beginning became riddled with cracks when the ruling sugar interests on the island brought pressure to bear against it.

In the sphere of business, the so-called consolidation (more correctly, monopolization) of railroad transportation was carried out, bringing the big U.S. sugar and railroad interests that exploited the eastern part of Cuba closer together. Behind them, more or less directly, was the National City Bank of New York, which forced them to settle their differences as in a family quarrel, which led to a compromise between the sugar and railroad interests with the least possible prejudice to both. The solution necessarily implied an end to the competition that Tarafa had unleashed with such daring.

Everything indicates that the man responsible for the monopoly idea was the lawyer Horatio S. Rubens, a member of the board of directors of the Cuba Company and, at the same time, a partner in several of Tarafa's sugar businesses: Cuban Distilling, Flora Sugar, and others. The possibility of monopolizing Cuba's railroads seems to have always been considered by the financial interests—the National City Bank—to which Rubens was linked.[55] Therefore, that operation wasn't just a need of Tarafa but also a decision of U.S. monopoly capital. In October, there were some reservations about how it should be carried out, because of the state of Norte de Cuba's finances.

> Our Executive Committee has examined the situation as a whole and come to the conclusion that no financial readjustment of Norte de Cuba would entirely cover that company's high proportion of indebtedness concerning the total value of its property. The members of the Executive Committee consider it a fact that Norte de Cuba won't be able to obtain enough financing from any New York banking house. They consider that the Cuba Railroad Company could obtain that financing, giving its own guarantee, but they don't think that the amount which could be raised by selling the joint assets of the two railroads would justify the risks the Cuba Railroad Company would incur by arranging and guaranteeing the financing of Norte. Moreover, Tarafa says that, to serve the interests of the small stockholders in his company, Cuba Railroad would have to pay cash for Norte's stock. This would imply that Cuba Railroad would have to pay for the legitimate liabilities of Norte de Cuba and also obtain the money with which to pay for its stock. Tarafa still insists that the common stock of his railroad is worth 6 million, and that price is clearly very high.[56]

The final form adopted for achieving the monopoly was that of a consolidated company, holding the stock of the three companies that were joined together— the Cuba Railroad Company, Norte de Cuba, and Nuevitas-Camagüey—which were to retain their administrative autonomy. Of the three companies, only the Cuba Railroad Company and Norte retained their identity: once the Nuevitas Company was included in the consolidation, it was dissolved on May 14, 1925, and its assets and liabilities were incorporated with those of Cuba Railroad.[57]

Thus, Ferrocarriles Consolidados de Cuba was created and registered in Cuba, as provided for by the Tarafa bill. The product of complicated maneuvers, it was only fitting that its board of directors should reflect that fact. Big names from U.S. financial circles would take their seats on it: J. E. Berwind, a founding member of the Cuba Company, which was linked to the house of Morgan and the coal business; Percy Rockefeller, a bulwark of the National City Bank; W. H. Woodin, president of American Car and Foundry; and H. W. Bull, representing the important railroad firm of Harriman and Company. Its junior members were Richard Van Horne, the son and heir of Sir William, and Colonel José M. Tarafa, the apparent promoter of the monopolizing maneuver.[58] Horatio Rubens was chosen to head the new company; he had prestige in Cuba and was also in the confidence of Percy Rockefeller. Two Cuban functionaries, Domingo Galdós, of Cuba Railroad, and Oscar Alonso, of Ferrocarril del Norte de Cuba, served as his lieutenants.

The capital stock of Ferrocarriles Consolidados consisted of 800,000 shares: 400,000 common and 400,000 preferred. The former had no par value; the latter had a value of 110 pesos each. The Cuba Company received 60 percent of the common stock and 66 percent of the preferred stock, which gave it control over the company. Norte received the remaining 40 and 34 percent. In the following years, the Cuba Company bought 200,000 shares of preferred stock from Tarafa, further strengthening its hand.[59]

A similar process took place with regard to the common stock, which was the foundation of Consolidados's decisive voting trust. As a result of those sales and exchanges of stock, by the end of the 1920s the Cuba Company controlled nearly all of the voting stock in the company, reducing the rest of the stockholders and associates, including Tarafa, to the status of mere bondholders.[60]

Thus, José M. Tarafa, "the great Cuban railroad promoter," ended as he had begun. The colonel had played his role by providing the transportation services needed by the big U.S. sugar companies in the full spate of expansion. Support from Wall Street had enabled him to create Ferrocarril del Norte de Cuba, his novel project of rail communications. When overwhelmed by adverse circumstances, the Cuban threatened to become a factor that the imperialist interests which had supported him would be unable to control, but they pulled strings skillfully and got him to toe the line. The "Tarafa case" thus illustrated a situation which Lenin had defined in masterly fashion some years before: "It so happens that just a few monopolies control the commercial and industrial operations of

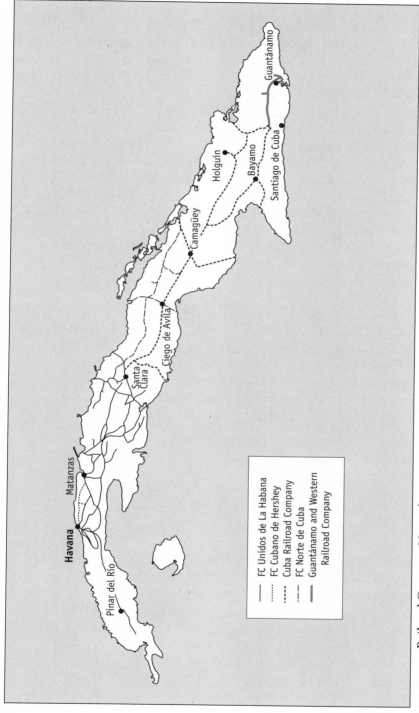

Legend:

——— FC Unidos de La Habana
········· FC Cubano de Hershey
—·—·— Cuba Railroad Company
— — — FC Norte de Cuba
——— Guantánamo and Western
         Railroad Company

Cities labeled on map: Havana, Matanzas, Pinar del Río, Santa Clara, Ciego de Ávila, Camagüey, Holguín, Bayamo, Santiago de Cuba, Guantánamo

MAP 14.2. Railroad Company Networks, 1929

every capitalist society, placing themselves in a position to know the exact situation of different capitalists, after controlling them and exerting influence over them through the arbitrary extending or withholding of credit, and finally in controlling their fate entirely."[61]

The last service Tarafa performed had been precisely that of laying the legal foundations for an absolute monopoly over the public railroads in Cuba. That aim could not be achieved completely, however, because the English railroad company in the west decided to remain apart from the maneuver. In the eastern provinces, monopoly conditions had been well laid with the consolidation of the three main companies in the region and the rapid absorption of some smaller ones. Such was the case of the old Ferrocarril Tunas–Sancti Spíritus, which had been sold by its original owners, the Valle family, to the Tuinicú Sugar Company and then transferred to Ferrocarriles Consolidados in April 1925.[62] Ownership of the railroad that linked the city of Las Tunas, in Oriente Province, with the port of Damañuecos, which was owned by the Manatí Sugar Company, also passed to Consolidados.[63]

Only three small regional companies remained independent of the railroad monopoly in Oriente Province: the narrow-gauge railroad between Holguín and Gibara, Guantánamo and Western, and the public service railroad belonging to Guantánamo Sugar. With nearly all the tracks in the eastern provinces monopolized and with the Tarafa law closing off all chances of other companies' laying new public service tracks in that region, Ferrocarriles Consolidados became the power determining the future of Cuba's railroads. (See Map 14.2.)

Organization of the Railroad Proletariat

During the first quarter of the twentieth century, while railroad ownership was being centralized, creating two large monopoly groups, the railroad workers became quickly organized and created their first national trade union. This improved organizational process included a series of actions—strikes, protests, and others—that were both a spur and a support for the entire movement. Organization and struggle were thus clearly linked in the development of the labor movement.

In 1899, the war had ended and there was a new government. Its strings were pulled by the United States, it is true, but "independence" could be descried on the horizon in spite of dark storm clouds of uncertainty which cast ominous shadows. After three years of a devastating war, life slowly returned to normal. The members of the working class, who, together with the farmers and other low-income sectors, had borne the brunt of the fighting, cherished great hopes. In fact, they had little else. The strict economies that the companies had decreed during the war, with their resultant wage cuts and unemployment, had condemned the workers to hunger. But, once the war was over, they hoped their luck would change. The rusty gears of the economy began to function once again, and, above all, the new authorities represented a nation considered one of the freest and most democratic in the world. Hungry but filled with hope, the workers mobilized to obtain better living conditions.

The railway workers were no exception. Barely two weeks after the U.S. authorities were installed in power, the manager of Ferrocarriles Unidos informed the military governor of Havana that a strike had broken out in the Ciénaga repair shops. The apprentices in the shops, supported by the workers in the coach and car repair shop, were demanding an increase in their daily wage.[1] With government approval, the company proceeded to take rigorous measures against the strikers: temporary suspension of the leaders and orders for the other participants to get back to work by a deadline that didn't leave them much time to think. And the movement was crushed.

It wasn't much of a starting point, but the workers' protest couldn't be silenced that easily. A few days later, strikes broke out in other departments of Ferrocarriles Unidos—tracks and projects, stokers, and others—and also in other railroad companies, such as Cárdenas y Júcaro.[2] To put an end to the continuing protests, the companies whose workers were on strike agreed to some small increases in the daily wages, but the concessions were extremely feeble, a far cry from what the workers had demanded. Persistent disquiet and agitation became generalized among the workers, creating an explosive situation of which the railroad conflicts were only a slight indication.

In that propitious climate, the Liga General de Trabajadores Cubanos (General League of Cuban Workers) was created in September 1899, promoted by the former anarchist leader Enrique Messonier and some other leaders of various ideological leanings. The workers in Havana quickly adopted the Liga General's manifesto-program, which was drawn up on September 14,[3] and they threw themselves into a broad strike movement before the month was out.

Masons began the strike, and workers in other sectors supported it. By September 25, it had spread to the entire city. Carpenters from the Ciénaga repair shops and the railroad warehouse and station workers from Villanueva, Cristina, Marianao, and Fesser (Regla) joined the general movement of Havana's proletariat, as did the employees of the urban railroad. Frightened because its workers were taking part in such a large movement, the management of Ferrocarriles Unidos circulated a call to order among them, which, among other things, said that the railroad workers were different from the rest of the strikers and wouldn't gain anything by becoming involved in a movement of that kind.

The Havana workers' strike was broken not by those diversionary measures but by the drastic repressive measures taken by Military Governor William Ludlow. He ordered that the main leaders of the movement be arrested, after which the police began breaking up the strikers' meetings by systematically beating up the participants. The unexpected brutal repression caught many strikers off guard. Some of the more cowardly and traitorous leaders called for prudence, and that was the final blow. The workers went back to work by the end of September without having obtained any of their demands.

After the failure of the September 1899 movement, class activity by the proletariat declined, though it didn't entirely disappear. During 1900 and 1901, railroad workers continued to be active in various places on the island. In July 1900, the Ferrocarriles Unidos stokers called a strike to oppose the "economies" announced by the company's management.[4] Even though the company arrested some strikers immediately, the movement continued for four days and seriously affected train service.

Shortly afterward, in September, the Cuban Central workers staged a walkout in Sagua la Grande and other towns in Las Villas Province. That movement,[5] which was supported by several sectors in the province, continued until General José Miguel Gómez, civil governor of the province, intervened directly. Using the prestige he had gained as a Mambí general in the War of Independence against Spain, Gómez appealed to the patriotism of the strikers, claiming that the Constitutional Convention, whose members were even then being elected, would bring independence.

In February 1901, the Ferrocarril de Cárdenas y Júcaro workers called a strike that effectively cut the city of Cárdenas off from the rest of the country.

The significant increase in the railroad workers' activities during the 1899–1902 U.S. military occupation was not accompanied by any great rise in their degree of organization. The strikes and protests were still isolated actions which only occasionally managed to involve workers with different skills. They were brief, nearly always spontaneous outbursts supported by bodies created for the purpose which usually disappeared when the movement ended. Since the proletariat's actions lacked stable organizations and effective mechanisms of class solidarity, the companies controlled them easily, sometimes through repression and at other times by the more subtle means of granting partial concessions and fomenting splits.

After the installation of the neocolonial republic in 1902, proletarian activities gradually decreased. To some extent, this reflected an improvement in the economic situation, but it was also a result of the imposition of the Platt Amendment on the Cuban people, which opened Cuba's doors to U.S. intervention. On more than one occasion, the government and the Cuban bourgeoisie used the threat of a new U.S. intervention as an effective tool of moral pressure on the workers.[6] The feared U.S. intervention came about, however, not as a result of legitimate struggle by the working class but because of the political ambitions of various sectors of the bourgeoisie.

In 1907, when Cuba was once more ruled by a U.S. supervisory government, the workers' class activities grew stronger. The cigar makers in Havana began a long strike in February, and it was supported by many sectors, including the railroad workers. The striking workers' main demand—to be paid in U.S. dollars[7]— was in line with U.S. interests, so Governor Magoon gave tacit support to the movement, which contributed to its success. The strikers' victory filled the ranks of workers with enthusiasm. Braced by the prestige of victory, the leaders of the "currency strike" created the Comité Federativo (Federal Committee). In fact, it was a reformist organization for coordinating the actions of the various workers' brotherhoods and other labor organizations as a preliminary step toward the creation of a regional federation of proletarian organizations.

The close to 10,000 railroad workers were one of the largest contingents of the Cuban proletariat. They felt that the time had come to present their own demands. The movement began in Cárdenas on September 14, 1907, stemming from a conflict between the workers of that division and a Ferrocarriles Unidos official. After consultation with the Comité Federativo in Havana, the railroad workers in Cárdenas called a strike, demanding that the problem-causing official be removed, that they be paid in U.S. dollars, and that an eight-hour workday be established.[8]

Supported by the Comité Federativo and the Obreros Unidos de los Ferrocarriles de la Isla de Cuba (United Railroad Workers of the Island of Cuba) group,[9] the strike movement spread quickly. On September 26, the stokers and other workers at the Ciénaga division downed tools, and the Ferrocarril del Oeste workers joined the walkout the next day. Before the end of the month, the strike had spread to the railroad companies in the three eastern provinces, though it wasn't fully supported in all departments. Many engineers, for example, said that they would be willing to work if they were given protection. The unwillingness of some workers to join the strike resulted in clashes between those in favor of the strike and those who did not want to be involved in the conflict.

In spite of those internal divisions, the movement was creating serious problems in the train service by early October, and it even halted the trains on some lines. In view of this, the Ferrocarriles Unidos management announced that it was hiring strikebreakers. After an unsuccessful attempt to use a group of immigrants from Triscornia as scabs, Ferrocarriles Unidos brought in fifty strikebreakers from New York, hired through a U.S. agency of private detectives.[10]

While both the companies and the strikers were maneuvering to strengthen their positions,[11] the authorities (including Governor Magoon himself) sponsored negotiations between the parties to the conflict. The talks, which were officially presided over by Emilio Núñez, mayor of Havana, began to bog down in mid-November, for the concessions the companies were willing to agree to did not meet the strikers' basic demands, and the strikers refused to cede without obtaining a substantial gain.

Because the Ferrocarriles Unidos had managed to normalize its service to some extent by using strikebreakers and some workers had gone back to work, the government decided to end the conflict by means of violence. While banning actions and demonstrations by the strikers, it mobilized all the power of its repressive apparatus. The police raided the headquarters of the Círculo Obrero (Workers' Club) on November 22 and arrested the leaders of the Comité Federativo, the

Strike Committee, and nearly three hundred workers who were in the building.[12] The repression, combined with the financial drain of a walkout that had already lasted for over two months, gave some workers weak knees, and they started going back to work.

Even though the Comité Federativo sought legal redress—without getting any results—and the staunchest workers stood firm, the strike had begun to lose ground. By mid-December, Robert Orr, the manager of Ferrocarriles Unidos, boasted that his company's service had been completely restored, and he refused to negotiate with the strikers. One month later, on January 17, 1908, with their strength exhausted, the last, isolated strikers decided to go back to work, taking up the manager of Unidos's promise of "reemploying, as their services should become necessary, those workers who were left without work as a result of the walkout."[13]

The defeat was painful, but the railroad workers had given the greatest demonstration of strength in their history. For the first time, they managed to unite the workers of various companies and job categories in a broad, cohesive movement, keeping a large-scale strike going for nearly three months. Diverse factors had conspired against their success: the indecision and inexperience of the leaders, underestimation of the power of the owners, and the repressive nature of the government, as a result of the success of the "currency strike" and others. However, it was the splits within the workers that did the most to undermine the strike and bring about its failure. Those splits had deep roots and were based both on the weak organizational links between the workers of different companies and departments and on the different conditions that various categories of workers had. Table 15.1 presents an overall view of the situation as regards wages.

Those wage inequalities were accompanied by differences in treatment and in working conditions. This helps to explain why many engineers, for example, did not feel solidarity with movements promoted by workers in "inferior" categories. Moreover, the strike was not taken up by the workers in the companies in eastern Cuba, with whom they did not have firm relations.

An important organizational experience took place in eastern Cuba shortly afterward. On January 18, 1910, a group of Cuba Railroad Company workers headed by engineer Carlos Loveira—who became very well known some years later for his literary work—created the Liga Cubana de Empleados de Ferrocarril (Cuban League of Railway Workers) in Camagüey. The purposes of the group, as set forth in its constitution, were quite moderate and retained the spirit of the old mutual assistance societies: "To protect and improve the conditions and interests of railway workers, for which purpose it will try to harmonize the interests of its members with those of the railroad, so as to improve service. For that purpose,

TABLE 15.1. Comparative Data on Daily Wage Rates of the Principal Railroad
Companies, 1905–1906 (in pesos)

Category	FC United	Cuban Central	Cuba Railroad
Upper Level Staff	8.09	14.84	8.57
Other Staff	3.38	5.14	5.11
Office Workers	2.43	1.64	2.14
Station Workers	0.82	1.08	0.95
Machinists	3.41	4.10	3.84
Firemen	1.24	1.37	1.54
Conductors	1.90	2.15	2.92
Mechanics	1.76	1.70	2.45
Carpenters	1.59	1.95	1.69
Other Workshop Workers	1.05	0.85	1.18
Switchmen	0.96	0.94	1.00

Source: Cuba, Comisión de Ferrocarriles, Memoria (1905–6).

too, it will work to improve the education and learning of its members. . . . It will
give aid to its members in case of sickness or accident that makes it impossible for
them to work, and to their relatives in case of their death."[14]

The Liga Cubana was not a local or company organization but sought to
represent all railroad workers, no matter what company they worked for. The
terminology of the curious structure adopted for that purpose was more reminiscent of a commercial body than a workers' organization: the leadership was in the
hands of a "head office," whose headquarters was in Camagüey, and it had a series
of "branch offices" in the main railroad centers. It seems that the promoters of the
Liga Cubana achieved some success in its formation, for, a few months after its
founding, it had "branch offices" in Santiago de Cuba, Banes, and Sagua la
Grande.[15] Even though Loveira stated in his memoirs that the Liga Cubana had
fifteen hundred members at one time,[16] the figure seems exaggerated, since the
minimum dues—a peso a month—would entail a serious economic sacrifice for
the workers in the lowest-paid blue-collar categories.

In the first few months of its existence, the Liga Cubana did not engage in any
particularly intensive activities. It put out a newspaper, El Ferrocarrilero; meetings
were held to get new members; and workers made a few denunciations of bad
treatment. However, it seems that that was enough to alarm the management of
Cuba Railroad, which reacted by taking a series of coercive measures against its
members. The employers' pressure, accompanied by some internal disagree-
ments, began to create difficulties within the recently founded group.[17] In May

1910, Cesáreo Migueltorena, president of the Liga Cubana, presented his resignation, saying he was tired and felt "disappointed and helpless, because I don't believe in the goodwill and civic worth of the members."[18] Carlos Loveira, who had already served as president, was then named to that post again. He had to confront the difficulties of the following months, which saw a steady thinning of the ranks. In the face of that critical situation, it was decided in November 1910 to move the Liga Cubana's "head office" to Sagua la Grande, a railroad center with a long proletarian tradition. Loveira moved there, too, but only as an adviser to the organization.

As was to be expected, the Liga's transfer to Sagua la Grande annoyed Cuban Central Railways, the local company. Its management, however, resorted not to coercive measures but to the much more subtle maneuver of creating a Sociedad de Beneficencia e Instrucción (Welfare and Instruction Society), to split the workers. When that attempt failed, the company threw itself directly against the Liga Cubana, firing some of its members and leaders.

The workers' response wasn't long in coming. On May 10, the board (*directiva*) of the Liga Cubana informed the manager of Cuban Central that, if the workers who had been fired were not reinstated and if the company did not publicly declare that it would accept the existence of the workers' organization, the workers would go out on strike the following day.[19] When the employers made no reply, the strike began early on the morning of May 11.

Confrontations between strikers and company supporters turned into disturbances, which the Guardia Rural (Rural Guard) used as a pretext for unleashing all of its repressive brutality. By nightfall, the town had been seized militarily and the main leaders of the Liga had been arrested. In spite of the repression, the striking workers stood firm, and they began to be supported by other brotherhoods in the city. The threat of a conflict of vast proportions led Gerardo Machado, secretary of the interior (*gobernación*), to go to Sagua la Grande. By skillfully combining the use of a carrot and a stick, Machado managed to halt the strike and got the main leaders of the movement to leave Sagua. Thus, the last body of the Liga Cubana was dismantled.[20]

The outbreak of World War I in 1914 caused the price of sugar to rise steadily, which triggered a rapid expansion in Cuba's sugar production. The simultaneous increases in price and volumes of production resulted in unprecedented profits for the U.S. monopolies and the Cuban bourgeoisie. The same factors that led to higher prices for sugar, however, also influenced other articles, especially imports, causing a steady inflationary trend. In 1920, the price indexes of imported food, which constituted a substantial part of the workers' diet, had risen to 150 percent above their 1913 level.[21] In that inflationary situation, the workers' daily wages remained quite stable, with the wages paid in 1917 being essentially the same as those paid four years earlier, but they had less purchasing power, and the general living conditions of the proletariat deteriorated. The generalized discontent caused by the exacerbation of the workers' exploitation created conditions favorable for a broad upsurge in the workers' struggles.

The first manifestations of the new wave of class activity repeated the characteristics of the preceding years. The strikes were still local affairs, affecting only one company or even only certain departments of a single company. But, even though there were no large-scale actions as yet, firmer ties of class solidarity could be seen, such as between the rail workers and other working sectors. The strength of the growing solidarity would be seen in late 1918, when two big strikes were called. Havana dock workers began the first one on November 4. It was militantly supported by diverse sectors, especially the railroad workers, and managed to virtually paralyze the capital of the country, achieving a resounding victory.

A few days later, the railroad workers benefited from class solidarity. On November 18, just after the dock workers' strike had ended, Cuba Railroad workers in Camagüey began a strike for wage increases and other class demands. Within a few days, the strike had spread throughout the railroad system between Santa Clara and Santiago de Cuba, with a daily train for journalists the only thing moving on the tracks.

President Mario García Menocal had refused to have the government arbitrate in the conflict, and he decided to put its repressive apparatus in motion. On November 30, army troops occupied Camagüey militarily, and soldiers on leave were ordered back to their garrisons in Santiago de Cuba. The government's action triggered a broad wave of solidarity with the strikers. Ciego de Avila and Guantánamo were declared "dead cities" by the local brotherhoods, and a general strike in solidarity with the railroad workers was declared in Santiago de Cuba on December 6.

A Comité Circunstancial de Huelga (Circumstantial Strike Committee) was formed in Havana to coordinate actions in support of the railroad workers. The Havana brotherhoods began to walk out on December 9. The government's and owners' position became very compromised; the spreading conflict was affecting the sugarcane harvest to an extent that alarmed the estate owners and companies in that sector.

In view of the strikers' firmness and the extent of the movement of solidarity supporting them, Cuba Railroad was forced to take a conciliatory position. The differences between the workers and owners were bridged. Senator Aurelio Alvarez, a veteran Camagüeyan politician, used all his influence to get the strike leaders to accept the concessions offered by the railroad company, even though they fell far short of what the workers had demanded. On December 11, the workers agreed to go back to work.[22] The real importance of that proletarian victory lay in the magnitude of the movement, not the concessions obtained.

The dynamics of the struggle led the railroad workers to achieve high levels of organization. Strike committees were created, composed of representatives of various brotherhoods and even workers who didn't belong to brotherhoods. Although most of those committees were disbanded at the end of the strikes, the relations they channeled became more firmly rooted and gave rise to a new kind of organization, which grouped the workers of a single company who worked in the same place or railroad center, no matter what their skills or what departments they belonged to. The first of them was La Unión (The Union), of Camagüey, founded in 1916. Its members worked in the repair shop, transportation, track, and other departments of the Cuba Railroad Company. Even though its leaders were essentially reformist, La Unión engaged in militant activities and had directed the November–December 1918 strike.

Also in 1916, Ferrocarril del Norte de Cuba's workers in Morón created the Unión de Empleados (Employees' Union). More radical than its Camagüeyan counterpart—its leaders were clearly influenced by anarchosyndicalist ideas—the Morón Unión had a broader class outlook, for it called for the unity of all Cuban railway workers and extended its influence to collateral sectors, such as the dock workers.[23]

The Federación de Empleados y Obreros (Federation of Employees and Workers) of Ferrocarril de Cuba was founded in Santiago de Cuba in 1918. Its initial nucleus was the Asociación de Retranqueros y Fogoneros (Association of Brakemen and Stokers), which had been created in the same city shortly before.[24] An active participant in the 1918 strike, the Federación de Empleados y Obreros became the unquestionable center of activity for the Santiago de Cuba railway men.

Similar organizational tendencies were manifested in the central region of the island. In 1918, another union was founded in Sagua la Grande to unite the various brotherhoods of workers in that railroad center.[25] The next year, the railway men in Cienfuegos created their Unión de Empleados Ferroviarios (Union of Railroad Employees).[26]

In Havana, whose traditions went back farther, the workers of Ferrocarriles Unidos tried to bring the workers from that company in the three western provinces together in a single organization. The Federación Nacional Ferrocarrilera (National Railroad Federation), founded in the early 1920s, was the result of that effort, but it never really became a nationwide organization.

The organizational process was very complex. Advances were not made at the same speed in all places, and the trend toward unification had its setbacks, too. Camagüey's La Unión was quickly weakened when the workers of the transporta-

tion department formed a splinter group, the Hermandad de Maquinistas y Fogoneros (Brotherhood of Engineers and Stokers). The telegraph operators quickly
followed suit, creating their own brotherhood. Thus, La Unión was reduced to
the smaller scope of the repair shop workers, and its influence was undermined.[27]

The hierarchical and departmental differences in the railroad sector generated
divergent partial interests, which, if they were not overcome by clear class awareness, could constitute a serious threat to proletarian unity. The owners—especially in such a clever, reactionary company as Cuba Railroad—played on those
factors to encourage splits, employing a wide range of methods to break the
proletarian organizations.

In 1920, the economic boom caused by World War I came to an end, leading to
a sudden economic crisis. Many sugar companies and banks went bankrupt, and
the effects of the crisis were also felt in the railroad sector, with a reduction of the
rates then in effect. The railroad companies, which had been so stubbornly
opposed to any wage increases during the "fat" years of the 1916–20 period, now
hastened to pass the brunt of the crisis onto the shoulders of their workers. The
powerful labor struggle in the preceding years had managed to increase railroad
wages by 50 percent over the prewar level,[28] but this was only a modest achievement, since the cost of food had risen by 150 percent during the same period.
However, the railroad companies dictated their economies without taking that
fact into consideration. The railroad workers had to struggle tooth and nail to
hang on to their meager advances.

The movement began in February 1921, with a strike that the Guantánamo and
Western workers called in protest against the layoffs dictated by the company.[29]
The following months saw strikes in several departments and divisions of Ferroca-
rriles Unidos, a company whose economic policy had a particularly serious slant.

In Camagüey, Cuba Railroad refused to pay for overtime and ignored the
agreement it had signed with its workers the year before. On April 26, the labor
organizations declared a strike, paralyzing all the activities of the system and
halting the circulation of trains. The company, which felt confident because a
battalion of U.S. Marines had been stationed in Camagüey since the war years,[30]
responded by firing twelve strikers. At the same time, H. C. Lakin, president of
Cuba Railroad, asked the State Department in Washington to get the Cuban
government to take a tougher stand against the workers, claiming that "the unions
are dominated by Spanish socialist agitators who seek conditions equivalent to the
sovietization [sic] of the railroads."[31]

Since the victorious October Revolution had sown panic among the exploiters,
the government didn't delay in supporting the owners, arresting three of the strike
leaders and banning workers' meetings. Some moves were taken to expel the

foreign workers, and the strikers were threatened with being hauled before the courts, but they refused to cave in. Railway workers all over the country supported them—especially those of Ferrocarriles Unidos, who refused to unload five hundred boxcars of sugar from the region affected by the conflict. The prolongation of the strike was hurting the pockets of the estate owners and merchants in the eastern provinces, and they pressured the government to come up with a quick solution for the situation. Temporizing, Secretary of the Interior Charles Hernández began to mediate between Cuba Railroad and its workers, proposing a formula that, while not constituting a complete victory for the workers, would force the company to grant important concessions. Once their differences were smoothed over, the workers ended the strike on May 8.[32]

Strikes opposing the owners' economies continued to be held in 1921 and 1922. In early January 1922, the manager of Ferrocarriles Unidos announced that wages would be cut by 10 or 15 percent in the various departments of the company. Negotiations concerning that measure lasted until June, when the owners' inflexible position caused the declaration of a strike. After that test of strength, the company agreed to reduce the wage cuts to 5 and 10 percent, but small-scale clashes involving only a few departments at a time continued in Unidos throughout the rest of the year, evidence of the prevailing discontent among the workers.[33]

The strength demonstrated by the railroad proletariat made that sector the object of the first law to be promulgated in the republic on workers' retirement: the Pension Law for railroad, streetcar, and telephone workers and employees. The bill, which was presented by conservative Senator Aurelio Alvarez and was passed into law in November 1921, showed that some sectors of the bourgeoisie understood that it was necessary to employ new methods with the labor movement.

Even though the law implied immediate political benefits for its promoter, Senator Alvarez—the railroad sector had over fifteen thousand potential voters, a figure not to be sneezed at—its class aims were shown in more than one detail of its articles.[34] Thus, for example, only workers who had contributed to the Caja de Jubilaciones (Retirement Fund) for at least ten consecutive years would be entitled to a pension. Since there were no laws to protect workers against being fired, that prerequisite gave the companies an excellent coercive tool, since, if a worker was fired, he would lose his right to a pension and to all the contributions he had already made to the Caja de Jubilaciones.

The workers were not blind to this maneuver. Commenting on the text of the law, *Nueva Luz* magazine stated, "This absurd law we are commenting on wasn't inspired by any humane feelings on the part of the government that approved it. . . . In making their calculations, our guardians have seen to it that those companies won't be adversely affected by strike movements."[35] Moreover, the companies' contribution was considerably lower than the workers'—between 1 and 1.5 percent—and the procedures foreseen for retirement left a wide margin for favoritism by the owners.

The workers' opposition to the terms of the law initiated a period of litigation and negotiations, which several politicians used for drumming up votes demagogically. Senator Alvarez, who was determined not to cede any advantages accruing to him for his paternity of this measure of "social reform," sponsored a bill that modified some aspects of the law, especially by creating a Caja Nacional de Jubilaciones (National Pension Fund) on which a workers' representative would serve. The law was finally modified in line with the Alvarez bill by a presidential decree in January 1924.

Because of the strategic position occupied by the railway workers in an era in which nearly all transportation in the country depended on their services and the strength of their class activities, the exploiters had to adopt a new strategy. Since the organized, active railway workers' movement was already a fact of life, the ruling classes sought to direct it along channels more favorable to their own interests.

The Cuban economy began to recover in 1923. Higher sugar prices and a sustained increase in production showed clearly that the crisis had passed. In line with the new situation, the workers' collectives in the various railroad centers in the country mobilized, demanding wage increases and other improvements that would counter the restrictive measures that the companies had taken during the crisis. This new movement coincided with a generalized atmosphere of social agitation, marked by the appearance of diverse movements—student, intellectual, and women's—on the political scene and the spread of antiimperialist sentiment.

In mid-December 1923, a new conflict broke out in Camagüey between the railway workers and the Cuba Railroad Company. For some time, the brotherhood of workers in the transportation department had been demanding that the company place a limit on the movement of trains that personnel from the sugar mills operated on the public service railroad's tracks.[36] Other demands were added by the workers in the repair shop, track, projects, and other departments, creating a very tense situation.

In the midst of that tension and in a manifest display of arrogance, the management of Cuba Railroad decided to lay off nearly three thousand workers from various departments. On December 19, the Unión de Talleres (Repair Shop Union) and the brotherhood of engineers, stokers, and telegraph operators decreed a stopping of all activities and called on all the workers in the other divisions of the U.S. company to join in the strike. The movement spread quickly through the three eastern provinces, even including Ferrocarril del Norte de Cuba's line, where the workers walked out in response to a call by the Morón Unión.

Cuba Railroad and the Asociación de Hacendados (Estate Owners' Association) joined forces to oppose the strike movement and asked the government for help. That assistance took the form of an infantry battalion's being sent to Camagüey and the imposition of martial law in that city; in addition, some of the strike leaders were arrested. After its show of force, the government decided to send a mediator to Camagüey. That delicate mission was entrusted to Carlos Loveira, who had become a famous writer and government official. Loveira's efforts quickly ended in failure, largely because Cuba Railroad viewed the strike as a test of strength with the workers and expected to obtain substantial advantages from it, making the most of some internal differences between the labor organizations.[37]

The failure of the "Loveira mission" left the way open for an important political maneuver. The governor and Liberal Party honcho of Camagüey, Rogerio Zayas-Bazán—who had maintained a demagogic stand concerning the labor conflict—proposed a new mediator to the workers: General Gerardo Machado.[38] Almost simultaneously, in Havana, the lawyer Viriato Gutiérrez made the same proposal to the Asociación de Hacendados. The railroad strike thus became an ideal proving ground for launching Machado as the probable Liberal Party candidate in the 1924 presidential election.

Cuba Railroad and the other parties involved in the conflict welcomed Machado's mediation. This was especially true of the estate owners, who were confident that he would solve the problem quickly—and a rapid solution was required, in view of the fast-approaching sugarcane harvest, if they were to hold out against the workers.

Before leaving for Camagüey on his mediating mission, Machado held some preliminary talks with the interested parties in Havana. In one of them, a secret meeting with the managers of Cuba Railroad, the details of the masquerade that was staged soon afterward were worked out. Lakin, the president of Cuba Railroad, described to his vice-president in charge of operations in Camagüey that after a meeting it was agreed that there would be an official gathering where the workers' demands would be presented. He claimed that Machado had arranged to be absent for the first part of the meeting, but that some estate owner would propose a solution that would be unanimously accepted asking that Machado negotiate with the workers. He (Machado) would then take a train at around nine that night for Camagüey. It was also arranged that the president would not get any special privileges, and that the special rail passes issued would not be used. On his arrival in Camagüey, Machado would first meet with the workers and indicate that a settlement would not be easy, but he would try his best not to fail. Of course, all would all be carefully arranged ahead of time. He further advised to disregard any rumors and to be candid with Machado since he was a rather delightful individual who was ready to listen to their points of view and sympathize with them.[39]

Before leaving for Camagüey, Machado acted decisively in Havana, getting Abelardo Adán and Juan Arévalo to set aside the demands of the Strike Committee and accept the formula that Machado and the owners' representatives had drawn up.[40]

Machado arrived in Camagüey on January 2 as an "impartial judge" of the conflict and went through the motions of the planned farce meticulously. He advised the workers to change their tune, making them believe that their cause was lost and then proposing a document in which most of their demands were reduced. It was the same one he had prepared ahead of time with the company's representatives.

On January 4, President Zayas jubilantly announced that the conflict had been solved and that trains would soon be back in service in the eastern provinces.[41] Many railroad workers went back to work thinking that the little they had gained was due to the "good offices" of General Machado.

The strike had focused the attention of all railroad workers in the country on Camagüey. It seemed only appropriate that the leaders of the Camagüeyan brotherhood should head a national organization of railroad workers. Therefore, when the Dirección Central de la Hermandad Ferroviaria de Cuba (Central Leadership of the Railroad Brotherhood of Cuba) was founded on February 2, 1924, it functioned simultaneously as the local leadership of the Camagüeyan railroad workers and the national leadership of the entire railroad sector.[42] Andrés Otero Bosch, president of Camagüey's former brotherhood, headed the Dirección Central, and Juan Arévalo, as organizing delegate in Havana, was assigned the important task of bringing the Havana railroad workers into the new organization. Manuel Castellanos, a conservative lawyer and politician, was legal counsel for the new Hermandad Ferroviaria.

As soon as the new organization was officially established, committees were sent to the main railroad centers in the country to set up local branches, or delegations. This was done relatively easily on the basis of the old local groups or unions, which, when they joined the Hermandad Ferroviaria, automatically became delegations.

The first of those delegations was formed in Santa Clara, followed by Havana, Sagua, Caibarién, Cruces, Cárdenas, Cienfuegos, Matanzas, Puerto Padre, the two Guantánamo companies, and Santiago de Cuba. By the end of 1924, the Hermandad Ferroviaria had fourteen delegations throughout the country.[43] Only two important railroad workers' groups did not join Camagüey's Unión de Talleres, which had long-standing, serious differences with the Hermandad's backers, and the Unión de Empleados, of Ferrocarril del Norte de Cuba. One of the most militant organizations in the sector, the Morón Unión had, for several years, had an exceptionally talented leader, Enrique Varona,[44] whose class awareness was too great to allow him to swallow the reformist hook dangled by the Hermandad.

Even though the railroad workers could feel proud of being the first labor sector in the country with a national organization, the new group left a lot to be desired as regards its main line and leaders. U.S. trade unionism influenced the Hermandad Ferroviaria, not only in terms of its name and structure[45] but also in its early membership in the Confederación Obrera Pan-Americana (Pan-American Workers' Confederation), an organization that Cuba's Primer Congreso Obrero Nacional (First National Workers' Congress) had denounced four years earlier as an obvious expression of yellow trade unionism on a continental scale.

A few months after the founding of the Hermandad, Juan Arévalo, one of its main leaders, did not hesitate to state that "the Hermandad Ferroviaria can never be radical. . . . The transportation organization must necessarily be conservative."[46] Moreover, right from its founding, the Hermandad was affected by politicking, partly because of the direct influence that such demagogues as Rogerio Zayas-Bazán, Manuel Castellanos, and Aurelio Alvarez exerted on it but mainly because Otero Bosch and some of its other leaders used their positions to get votes. Unfortunately, the Hermandad had come into being garbed in reformism of the worst kind.

In spite of that, the ranks of the railroad proletariat included workers with a keen class awareness, and the Hermandad's grass-roots organizations and delegations included leaders of proven honesty, who were able to confront the pro-owner elements and political hacks of the Dirección Central.

The railroad workers' tradition of struggle could not be crushed easily. The founding of the Hermandad led to conflicts that were among the best struggles in the sector. In Havana, Archibald Jack, the grim British retired general who was manager of Ferrocarriles Unidos, stubbornly opposed the creation of the local delegation of the Hermandad Ferroviaria. He refused to allow his workers to join the national organization, especially since its headquarters was in Camagüey, which led him to suppose that the Cuba Railroad Company would have the greatest influence on it.[47] He was also irritated because his workers wanted to accompany the creation of the delegation with the signing of a work agreement setting forth their main demands. Jack tried to launch a company-run organization, the Unión Ferroviaria (Railway Union), to take members away from the Hermandad, and he also proceeded to fire some of the Hermandad's members.

In view of the possibility that another strike would break out—it was barely two months since the Camagüey strike had ended—the government intervened in the conflict, attempting to get the manager of Ferrocarriles Unidos to take a more flexible stand, but especially trying to gain time. The workers responded by creating a strike committee that declared staggered railroad strikes throughout the country, and a large number of workers' groups immediately supported that decision.

Faced with this course of events, Jack opted to negotiate with the Hermandad, recognizing it as the workers' representative, and he expressed his willingness to discuss a series of petitions. Shortly afterward, on March 26, the leaders of the Havana delegation of the Hermandad sent the management a document containing twenty-one demands.[48] Little disposed to accede to the petitions, Jack engaged in delaying maneuvers that made the workers indignant. Since a new strike seemed imminent, the government decided once again to intervene, and President Alfredo Zayas himself served as arbiter in the worker-owner dispute. As was only to be expected, the results of the president's mediation favored the interests of the company, reducing the scope of the workers' demands considerably.[49] However, the leaders of the Hermandad, who were nearly as fearful of a strike as was the company itself, hurried to comply with President Zayas's ruling, presenting it as a great workers' victory.[50]

Even though he had benefited from the president's arbitration, Archibald Jack showed little willingness to implement the terms of the agreement; this caused frequent conflicts with workers in the various departments of the company. In mid-May, some of those conflicts led to the declaration of strikes in Matanzas and Sagua, while, in Havana, the Ferrocarriles Unidos management and workers clashed.[51]

Even though Arévalo and other leaders of the Hermandad had not authorized some of the strikes, the intransigent position of the manager, Jack, and the spontaneous mobilization of the workers led the Hermandad to declare a strike on May 28, 1924. It completely paralyzed the Ferrocarriles Unidos system and was immediately supported by the railway workers in the eastern provinces, who threatened to declare a strike in solidarity, and by the dock workers and others.

On May 30, the government issued a statement calling on the parties to the conflict to exercise prudence. It also did its best to discredit the strikers' positions and gave its tacit support to the manager of the English company. Emboldened by the government's support and by that expressed by sectors of the bourgeoisie through the Federación Nacional de Corporaciones Económicas (National Federation of Economic Corporations),[52] Jack dug his heels in, frustrating Senator Aurelio Alvarez's efforts at mediation.

In view of the hardening of the owners' positions, the Hermandad Ferroviaria decreed a work stoppage in the eastern provinces, so the railroad strike spread throughout the country. On June 5, worried by the extension of the conflict and the failure of Alvarez's mediation, the government took a more flexible position and initiated contacts between the company and the strikers. In doing so, it came

Train derailed in Las Villas during the great railroad workers' strike of 1924.

up against the pigheadedness of the British manager, who considered himself a champion of owners' rights. An unexpected action changed the course of events, however.

On June 9, in a desperate, untimely act, a striker tried to kill Jack, managing to wound him seriously. Even though the attacker said that he had acted independently, on his own,[53] the government ordered that the strike leaders be arrested and that the railroad centers be occupied militarily, alleging the existence of a plot.

In view of the repression that was unleashed, many labor sectors declared their support for the strikers,[54] but the leaders of the Hermandad, made fearful by the course of events, decided to enter into rapid negotiations with the management of Ferrocarriles Unidos. This wishy-washy attitude baffled some of the strikers, who decided to go back to work, which further weakened the labor organization's bargaining position. On June 17, the Hermandad signed an agreement that constituted an unquestionable victory for the Unidos management.[55] Thus, the weakness of the Hermandad's leaders caused one of the railroad proletariat's most powerful movements to end in failure.

Outside the Hermandad Ferroviaria, the Ferrocarril del Norte de Cuba workers, led by Enrique Varona, continued to engage in working-class activities. Even though it had no formal ties with the Hermandad, the Morón Unión expressed its support for the railroad strikers' main movements, a stand that on more than one occasion led to Varona's imprisonment. Moreover, the leaders of the Morón

Unión didn't limit their activities to the railroad scene but, with a broad class view, established links with workers in related sectors, such as the stevedores at Puerto Tarafa and the workers in the sugar mills served by Ferrocarril del Norte de Cuba.

At the end of September 1924, the workers in some of those sugar mills declared a strike, demanding strict compliance with the Arteaga Law[56] and the right to join the Morón Unión. The sugar companies refused to accept any of their workers' demands, so the Morón Unión boycotted freight from the sugar mills involved in the conflict. On October 15, acceding to a demand presented by the sugar owners, the military supervisor of Camagüey ordered the arrest of Varona and other leaders. The Morón Unión replied by stating it would call a strike if its leaders were not freed within seventy-two hours. Concerned by the problems that a railroad strike would cause just a few days before the holding of the presidential election, Secretary of the Interior Iturralde and Rogerio Zayas-Bazán, governor of Camagüey, maneuvered to get Varona and his comrades freed.

As soon as he was released, Varona declared that the strike would be called anyway if the repression against the sugar workers, who were being evicted from their homes by members of the army, were not stopped. The strike was declared throughout the Norte system, and, at the same time, the railway workers sent a trainload of strikers' families to Morón to hold a permanent public protest there.[57] The movement came to a brilliant climax with the declaration of a strike by the stevedores and day laborers at Puerto Tarafa. In view of the new course taken by the conflict, the Morón Unión called on its colleagues in the Hermandad Ferroviaria for support. The reply by the top leadership of the Hermandad, which was sent by Arévalo and Dr. Manuel Castellanos, deserves to be quoted: "The Hermandad is not participating in the current strike at the sugar mills in Camagüey province, because this is a strike unrelated to railroad workers. . . . The fact that the workers of Ferrocarril del Norte de Cuba are involved does not give them any right to call on our aid, since this is not a railroad workers' strike but was called by elements at the sugar mills who don't even have an established organization."

Up to this point, it was an expression of shameless opportunism; what followed was outright betrayal: "If, as a result of political agitation or for any other cause, a conflict should arise that might endanger the existence of the republic or provoke intervention by foreigners, the Hermandad would be on the side of the constituted government, because, above all, it is Cuban."[58]

Those declarations triggered a strong response by the Morón Unión and repudiation by broad sectors of the Cuban proletariat, even within the ranks of the Hermandad. Judging those events, *Lucha de Clases*, the organ of Havana's Agrupación Comunista (Communist Group), pointed out, "A shameful exception: the Hermandad Ferroviaria, which not only considered itself to be outside the movement, refusing to help its brothers in struggle to achieve a victory over the bourgeoisie, but also offered itself to the government if the sugar mill strike should breach the [bourgeois] peace. . . . What the Hermandad Ferroviaria has done shows its bourgeois structure, its complicity with the enemies of the working class."[59]

The prolongation of the strike to just a few days before the general election and the negative effects it had on the preparations for the next sugarcane harvest brought out the need for a quick solution. On October 25, U.S. Ambassador Enoch Crowder met with President Zayas and said that the strike in Camagüey should be ended quickly, because it was harmful to U.S. interests.[60] A few hours later, the estate owners supplying the sugar mills involved in the strike declared their acceptance of the bases proposed by the workers. On October 28, after some problems that had been pending with Ferrocarril del Norte de Cuba were solved, the strike was ended.

That situation didn't last long, however. At the beginning of November, the workers at the Florida, Céspedes, Jatibonico, Vertientes, Estrella, and Algodones sugar mills stopped work, demanding the same rights that the sugar mill workers who had taken part in the earlier strike had obtained.[61] This time, solidarity was even broader, because, in addition to the Morón Unión, Camagüey's Unión de Talleres and several trade union organizations in Oriente, including the delegations of the Hermandad Ferroviaria in Guantánamo and Santiago de Cuba, supported the strike movement.

As on previous occasions, the government responded by sending more troops to Camagüey "to keep the peace," though the real purpose of the military presence was to create a reign of terror in the sugar mill communities. The mechanisms of workers' solidarity were better prepared, however. Understanding the strategic importance of the sugar workers' organization, Varona had promoted the creation of the Sindicato Provincial de Trabajadores de Camagüey (Provincial Trade Union of Camagüeyan Workers), which welcomed representatives of the province's sugar mill workers. Moreover, the railroad organizations that supported the sugar strike had declared a boycott on freight from the sugar mills, a situation that led to a clash with the railroad companies themselves, which wound up on December 9 with the declaration of a strike in Ferrocarril del Norte de Cuba, the Oriente division of Cuba Railroad, and the Guantánamo and Western Railroad.

The leaders of the Hermandad Ferroviaria, concerned by the discredit that their attitude in the earlier strike had brought them, decided to act more prudently in the new situation and promised economic support for the strikers.[62] Meanwhile, a Comité Conjunto Obrero (Joint Workers' Committee) was created in Havana to coordinate the activities of a general strike if one should prove necessary.

Alarmed by the prospect of a generalized conflict, the government took a temporizing position, inducing the Asociación de Hacendados y Colonos to consider the sugar workers' demands. The association expressed its willingness to make some concessions—which fell far short of meeting the strikers' demands.[63] However, on December 13, it was learned that the workers at some sugar mills, probably exhausted by the repression and by the economic effects of the strike, had decided to go back to work on the estate owners' terms. That decision weakened the basis of the strike, but the railroad workers decided to maintain it until their specific demands had been met.

The railroad companies said they would agree to the workers' demands if the workers promised not to declare any more strikes in the next two years, a condition the workers' organizations turned down. On December 25, when the sugarcane harvest was about to begin, the railroad companies finally accepted the workers' demands. The strike wound up with a resounding victory for the proletariat.

The growing development of the railroad workers' struggles in 1924 also affected the Hermandad Ferroviaria. The opportunistic, traitorous position that its Dirección Central had taken during the October sugar- and railroad-workers' strike brought on a serious crisis in the organization. After publishing some severe criticism of the Dirección Central, Delegation 2, in Havana, decided to expel Juan Arévalo, the Dirección Central's representative in the capital, removing the organizing delegate from his post. Even though the Dirección Central immediately disallowed Delegation 2's decision, it had to exert all its influence to reinstate Arévalo.[64]

Notwithstanding that temporary victory, the leaders of the Hermandad were unable to curb the masses' growing hostility. At the end of 1924, Andrés Otero Bosch, president of the Hermandad, announced his decision to retire to private life[65] "in view of the attacks that are being made on my beloved organization." The process wound up in early 1925 with an election of members of the Dirección Central, in which most of the opportunistic elements were removed from their posts.

That movement didn't imply any substantial change in the reformist slant of the railroad organization, however. The existence of high-wage categories among the railroad workers favored the formation of an elite, constituting a culture that was always propitious for reformism. But, even within the ideological molds of reformism, Agustín Pérez, the new president of the Hermandad, and the other new members of the Dirección Central were incomparably more advanced and honest than their predecessors.

The year 1925 was one of great achievements for the Cuban proletariat. On February 15, the 2nd Congreso Obrero Nacional (2nd National Workers' Congress) was held, attended by delegations from trade unions in all the provinces, including some representatives of the Unión de Empleados of Ferrocarril del Norte de Cuba. That important meeting, a product of the sustained organizational efforts of Alfredo López, a typesetter and leader of Havana's Federación Obrera, resolved to call quickly a new congress in which the first national trade union organization in Cuba would be officially created. The new congress—the 3rd Congreso Obrero Nacional—was held in Camagüey in August of that same year. The 3rd Congreso, which had even more participants than the previous one in Cienfuegos, resolved to create the Confederación Nacional Obrera de Cuba (National Workers' Confederation of Cuba) as the proletariat's national governing body. Even though anarchosyndicalist thinking prevailed in the new organization, it would represent all the trends and organizations of the working class in a unified way.[66]

At nearly the same time as that important organizational step, a meeting was held in Havana that, though small, was of enormous political and ideological importance. On August 16, the Congreso Nacional (National Congress) of the Agrupaciones Comunistas de Cuba (Communist Groups of Cuba) founded the Partido Comunista de Cuba (Communist Party of Cuba). The Cuban proletariat's struggles were thus crystallized with the near simultaneous founding of its first trade union federation and of its vanguard party.

The labor movement's manifest rise and the growing rebelliousness of other sectors of Cuban society filled the Cuban bourgeoisie and foreign capitalists with justified alarm. Alfredo Zayas's administration had been plagued with events symptomatic of the breakdown of the neocolonial system. The apparatus had to be shored up, and the inauguration of a new president in May 1925 constituted the first step in that direction.

Gerardo Machado, the new incumbent, was a relatively "new" political figure who, during his much-talked-about electoral campaign, had striven to present himself as an efficient, energetic administrator who could put the disorderly state apparatus in order.[67] After taking office, Machado obtained growing support from all of the interests linked to the imperialist system of domination, which managed to form a veritable "united front" around him. The "great responsibilities" that had been entrusted to him required total support.

One of the most important tasks assigned to Machado was unquestionably that of controlling the militant Cuban proletariat. The labor question was a focal point in the Machado administration's platform,[68] and Machado's political history in that sphere—including his "mediation" in the December 1923 railroad strike in Camagüey—indicated that he would be implacable.

The first step was to split and control the trade union organizations by means of a series of repressive actions, which included the deportation or murder of the most outstanding and steadfast labor leaders. Other measures were aimed at stabilizing the economic situation, providing some sources of employment—this was one of the aims of Machado's showy public works plan—and creating mechanisms for containing conflicts between the workers and owners. The final objective was to limit the development of the Cuban labor movement and confine it to the bounds of "yellow" unionism controlled by the government apparatus.

Because of its economic importance and the militance it had demonstrated in the preceding years, the railroad sector was one of the main targets in Machado's antilabor strategy. Within the railroad workers' movement, Enrique Varona's activities had dangerous repercussions in the vital sugar sector. In addition, there was another cause for annoyance: the Hermandad Ferroviaria's original group of docile and corrupt leaders had been replaced with a group who couldn't be maneuvered nearly so easily. That fact became evident in the long conflict between the Hermandad and the Cuba Railroad Company that had begun in March 1925 and was still going strong when Gerardo Machado took office on May 20 of that year.

The Cuba Railroad management's refusal to discuss a new work agreement that the Hermandad had presented in mid-February led the labor organization to begin a "passive strike" on March 6, in which the workers complied strictly with the railroad legislation in effect, thus causing the railroad company considerable losses.[69]

The honorable position taken by the new leaders of the Hermandad led some pretentious nobodies of the old railroad Dirección Central to issue some "calls to order," stating to the press that they were not "entirely in agreement with the actions of the Hermandad, as we think that those who now head this organization should keep in mind the wise policy followed by their predecessors in the Hermandad leadership."[70]

As was only to be expected, the workers paid no attention to those divisive statements, solidly supporting their leaders' positions in the negotiations with the company. The Cuba Railroad Company tried to justify itself to public opinion through statements by its vice-president, Domingo Galdós, while taking repressive measures, such as firing seven hundred workers at the end of March, an attitude that exacerbated the conflict, nearly pushing it into a general strike.

The Hermandad Dirección Central's refusal to give in to the pressures that were brought to bear against it won it the support of Havana's Federación Obrera and Morón's Unión. The latter declared a work stoppage in solidarity with its Camagüeyan comrades. The conflict lasted for over a month without any settlement, until Machado, who had just been inaugurated, decided to intervene personally. The president's mediation achieved a temporary agreement which merely postponed the conflict, making it dependent on a new discussion of the work agreement that would be held some months later.[71] The president needed time to set the mechanisms of his "labor policy" in motion.

In mid-August 1925, Mariano Cibrán, the manager of Cuba Railroad, was visited by Captain Galís, who had been sent by President Machado to become informed about the labor situation in Camagüey. The meeting was short, because the captain had orders to go immediately to Morón and take note of the agitators in the Ferrocarril del Norte de Cuba area, since the president intended to deport the foreigners and imprison the Cubans in La Cabaña. He planned to use harsh tactics to quash the labor movement that had broken out in several places on the island.[72] The haste in going to Morón was understandable; Enrique Varona was a top-priority target in the government's repression.

The plan to eliminate Varona was under way. On August 20, coinciding with Captain Galís's visit to Camagüey, Varona was be to tried, accused of having dynamited a train. The prosecutor was asking for a life sentence. Postponed until September 2, the trial ended with Varona's being found innocent, for lack of proof. Barely ten days later, the railroad leader was arrested again, this time accused of having placed a bomb on the Chambas line. On September 15, in view of the lack of any evidence, Varona was released again. He was convinced that he had been set free so he could be murdered.[73] On September 19, 1925, while going with his wife and daughter to an activity sponsored by the Morón Unión in the local Niza Movie Theater, Enrique Varona was shot down by a hired assassin.[74] With his death, the railroad proletariat lost its most outstanding and courageous leader.

Meanwhile, in Camagüey, the Hermandad Ferroviaria kept its conflict with the Cuba Railroad Company in abeyance. The negotiations on the work agreement, which had begun in July 1925, continued until April 1926 without achieving any positive results. In early November, the company had accepted the agreement proposed by the Hermandad, but then it turned the agreement down, alleging that it could not "uphold commitments that imply an increase in our expenses, since the low price of sugar on the market has caused a difficult economic situation. We have decided to cooperate with General Machado's policy and reduce our railroad rates."[75]

While insolently failing to keep its promises, the railroad company, together with the military authorities in Camagüey, egged on divisionist elements in the Hermandad, using old yellow labor leaders for the purpose. Not letting themselves be provoked, the Hermandad Ferroviaria leaders staunchly defended the rights the workers had obtained through the agreement, in such conditions that even the Congress of the republic was forced to recognize the justice of their position.

At the same time, government officials who were much closer to Machado—such as Rogerio Zayas-Bazán, then secretary of the interior—suggested to the company that it "proceed with your policy, making the workers think that you are really willing to make concessions, even though you don't make them later on,"[76] while seeming to listen to the workers' demands. By those means, the situation was diffused and complicated, forming a tangled skein behind which Machado's characteristic double-dealing could be seen. It had already proved successful during the December 1923 railroad strike; now, it was repeated on a larger scale. While government and railroad company officials and other opportunists joined forces against the Hermandad, Machado strove to get its leaders to trust him.

On April 11, 1926, after four months of negotiations, the Dirección Central of the Hermandad Ferroviaria decided to declare a strike. The movement affected Las Villas, Camagüey, and Oriente, but not the western provinces, whose delegations ceded to government pressure and stated that there was no cause for a strike. Even though limited to the eastern provinces, the strike was important enough to have repercussions in the New York sugar market. This alarmed the government officials so much that they ordered the repressive deployment of army forces in Camagüey. Even in those circumstances, the strikers were confused, for high-ranking government figures continued to give opinions and take measures that seemed favorable to them.[77]

At the beginning of May, the conflict spread, for the western railroad workers began a strike in solidarity. That step led President Machado, who had not seemed to be involved in the strike, to make a personal appearance. After meeting with the representatives of the Ferrocarriles Unidos workers and getting them to promise to go back to work, Machado said that he himself would intervene and seek a solution for the conflict. Some of the members of the Hermandad's Dirección Central didn't know any better; others acted in bad faith. As a result, they swallowed President Machado's protestations of "goodwill" and announced that the strike would soon be ended.[78]

With the solution of the conflict in his hands, Machado did not hesitate but signed a decree authorizing the use of army troops in the territory affected by the strike—"to keep the peace and protect lives and property." Taking advantage of that situation, the railroad company staged an act of provocation against the workers and sent strikebreakers to several centers, which led to disturbances. When the workers decided to continue the strike, brutal repression was unleashed against them. Under the decree Machado had signed, army forces occupied the railroad centers and attacked the Hermandad's main locals,[79] imprisoning many of the leaders. With their best leaders behind bars and still subjected to the violent repression, the railroad workers were informed of Machado's "solution": the congressional commission appointed to mediate in the conflict had gotten the company to agree to let the strikers go back to work. Naturally, no mention was ever made of the work agreement.

The main result of the "forty-five days' strike," however, did not lie in the movement's defeat. Right from the first negotiations on the work agreement through the tragic end of the strike, the company, the government, and the opportunists at their service had maneuvered to eliminate the honest members of the Hermandad Ferroviaria leadership. After the imprisonment of those leaders, the key posts of the Hermandad were filled with opportunists. Meeting on November 22, the new Dirección Central of the Hermandad decreed that the directive that had governed the April and May 1926 strike was no longer in effect. Shortly before, Oscar Díaz, the newly "elected" president, had told the press, "It is a source of pride to the present leaders of the Hermandad Ferroviaria of Cuba to have reestablished cordial relations with the companies and to be deserving of the confidence of the government of the republic, and we propose to continue in this constructive work, which will bring us the most pleasing success."[80]

With Varona murdered and the Hermandad handed over to traitorous yellow leaders, the railroad proletariat was helpless against the Machado dictatorship. Thus began one of the most critical and anguishing periods in its history.

16

The Crisis

The capitalist world crisis that began in 1929 had repercussions in the Cuban economy in particularly unfavorable circumstances. Ever since 1925, the world sugar market had displayed unmistakable symptoms of saturation. World production, which was more than 5 million tons over the prewar levels, appeared to exceed the effective demand of purchasers, so the price of sugar dropped from an average of 4 centavos a pound in 1924 to only 2.35 centavos a pound in 1925.

From then on, Cuba's sugar policy swung between restricting production, seeking stable prices, and having unlimited sugarcane harvests, in response to competing countries' wild promotion of their sugar exports. Under the mechanisms of free competition, the price of sugar remained low during the following years, averaging 2.18 centavos a pound in 1928. Hurt by five years of low prices and with its warehouses crammed full of sugar, Cuba had no defenses against the terrible effects of the world crisis.

In the situation created by the crisis, the price of sugar continued to plummet, even faster than before, until, in 1930, it was going for an average of only 1.23 centavos a pound. The ultraprotectionist Smoot-Hawley tariffs went into effect in the United States that summer, adding 2 cents a pound to the cost of Cuban sugar and effectively closing the doors of Cuba's main sugar market. In an effort to halt the disastrous trend toward lower prices, Cuba's sugar policy was adjusted to fit the Chadbourne Plan,[1] which called for a progressive cutback in production, seeking to stabilize prices by reducing the supply. The plan failed to produce the desired results, however, for prices continued to fall even though production was reduced. The result was catastrophic: the estimated value of Cuba's sugarcane harvest dropped from 129 million pesos in 1930 to 43 million in 1933.

Hit where it really hurt, Cuba's largely undiversified economy suffered the same fate as its sugar industry. The value of Cuba's exports, which had already dropped by 40 percent between 1924 and 1928, fell from 272 million pesos in 1929 to 80 million pesos in 1932. The drop in exports immediately reduced its import- ing capacity. In 1933, it imported only 42 million pesos' worth of goods, a ridicu- lous figure for a country that had to meet a large part of its needs through imports.[2] The drastic reduction in the exports and imports of a country such as Cuba, with an open economy, was a clear indication of the stagnation and generalized im- poverishment of its economic activities. In 1933, only 35 percent of the production potential of the sugar industry was used. A poll taken the next year estimated that 250,000 of Cuba's population of a little over 3 million were unemployed.

The economic recession accentuated the crisis of the neocolonial structure, which had been evident since the mid-1920s, in both the economic and political spheres. That process, accelerated by the people's struggles against the Machado tyranny, produced a revolutionary situation with the overthrow of Machado's government in August 1933.

Alarmed by the course of events, which endangered the entire system of impe- rialist domination in Cuba, the U.S. government implemented a policy aimed at rapidly stabilizing the situation on the island. In the economic sphere, it was expressed in two basic measures: the establishment of a system of sugar quotas and some reforms in commercial relations with the signing of a new treaty of reciprocity. Even though the sugar quotas assigned to Cuba were considerably lower than its traditional share of the U.S. sugar market, which Cuba had always supplied, the system guaranteed a stable volume of sales which was somewhat higher than in the most serious years of the crisis.

On that basis and with the later stabilization of the world sugar market, Cuba's production managed to return to an annual average of a little over 3 million tons in the 1935–40 period. That production recovery was accompanied by a slight increase in the price of sugar—it hovered around 1.5 centavos a pound, starting in 1934—but the average value of Cuba's five sugarcane harvests in the 1935–40 period was barely 50 percent of their average value in the five years prior to the crisis (1925–30). Thus, the recovery mechanisms that were applied failed to do more than achieve economic stability at low levels, which led to the permanent underutilization of Cuba's productive resources and sanctioned its economic stagnation.

The difficulties which the sugar sector experienced starting in 1925 were faith- fully recorded on the sensitive barometer of the railroads. The railroad com- panies' total income, which had averaged 51.6 million pesos a year in the 1921–26 period, dropped to an average of 42.3 million pesos a year in the 1926–31 period.[3] The reduction, though appreciable, was still far from creating a critical situation. However, it had various effects on rail service.

The first effect was a definitive halt to railroad expansion, which had been quite meager for some years already, because of the relative density of Cuba's railroad network.[4] The extension of Ferrocarril del Norte de Cuba's main line between Chambas and Santa Clara, a distance of 130 kilometers, which was completed in 1926, was the last important stretch of track laid in the neocolonial period. Once more, nearly automatically, paralysis of growth in the sugar sector led to the suspension of railroad construction.

Something similar occurred with the rolling stock, with practically no new cars purchased and none renovated after 1927, except for small purchases of self-powered gasoline coaches—gas-cars—for providing faster passenger service. Even though the prospects for any subsequent development of the railroad service seemed quite remote, the main companies' economic situation at the end of the 1920s could still be described as normal. Those companies had taken measures for dealing with the circumstances—the Tarafa Law and consolidation, for example—and the profits they had already made enabled them to meet their obligations.

The outlook changed completely in 1930, with the plummeting price of sugar and the Cuban government's policy of restricting production. The progressive decrease in the amount of freight to be carried and the unavoidable need to reduce rates in line with the drop in the price of the main products carried by the railroads caused the railroad companies' total income to drop off sharply. Between 1929 and 1931, at the outset of the crisis, the railroads' total annual income dropped from 37.5 million to 24 million pesos, and it continued to drop inexorably in the following years, as shown in Figure 16.1.

The drastic reduction in income was a serious blow for the railroad companies. Ferrocarriles Unidos's expenditures-to-income ratio rose from 77.1 percent in 1928–29 to 97.5 percent in 1930–31. Something similar, though to a lesser extent, occurred in the companies in the Ferrocarriles Consolidados group. The financial effects were felt immediately: in June 1930, the board of directors of Ferrocarriles Unidos announced the suspension of interest payments and of dividends on stocks and bonds,[5] and Ferrocarriles Consolidados and its subsidiaries followed suit two years later.

Seeking to counteract the drop in their income, the railroad companies implemented economy measures, laying off more than 40 percent of their personnel and reducing their track and rolling stock maintenance budgets to a point that was just a hairbreadth short of suicidal. But even those severe measures could not halt their sustained drop in income, which fell to its lowest point—12.7 million pesos—in 1932–33. (See Figure 16.1.)

"The railroads have had to share in the misfortunes of this country," the manager of Ferrocarriles Unidos concluded with typical British understatement in his report for 1930, when the disaster was just beginning.[6] Nothing could be fairer, but to what extent was this true? His words showed that the railroad crisis was only a sectoral reflection of the serious economic crisis with which the country was

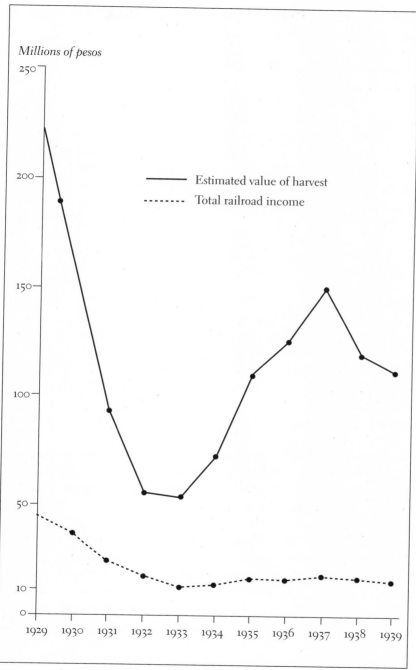

FIGURE 16.1. Sugar Harvest Value and Railroad Income, 1929–1939

TABLE 16.1. Comparative Analysis of Railroad Income, Value of Sugarcane Harvests, and Value of Trade, 1929–1939 (in millions of pesos and indexes [1929 = 100])

	Railroad Income		Value of Sugarcane Harvests		Value of Trade	
Year	Value	Index	Value	Index	Value	Index
1929	43.2	100	225.1	100	488.6	100
1930	37.5	86.8	156.1	69.3	329.8	67.6
1931	24.0	55.5	93.4	41.5	199.0	40.7
1932	17.3	40.0	55.6	24.7	131.6	26.8
1933	12.7	29.3	53.7	23.8	126.6	25.8
1934	13.7	31.6	73.1	32.4	181.1	36.7
1935	16.0	37.0	111.4	49.1	223.4	45.7
1936	15.7	36.3	125.4	55.7	258.0	57.5
1937	17.6	40.6	151.0	67.0	315.5	70.3
1938	16.2	37.4	120.2	53.4	248.6	55.1
1939	15.1	34.9	112.5	50.0	253.4	51.8

Sources: L. V. Abad, *Problemas de los transportes cubanos* (Havana: Editorial Mercantil Cubana, 1944), p. 60, and *Anuario Azucarero de Cuba* (195): 24, 93.

faced. Figure 16.1, which compares railroad income with the estimated value of the sugarcane harvests in the 1930s, largely bears this out.

However, a more detailed analysis shows that the two variables, which were closely linked through 1933, followed different paths in the 1934–39 period, for the estimated value of the sugarcane harvests recovered much more quickly than railroad income. This interesting phenomenon may be seen even more clearly in Table 16.1, which compares the indexes of railroad income, the estimated value of the sugarcane harvests, and the total value of Cuba's trade (imports and exports) in terms of the 1929 figures.

Table 16.1 shows that, during the 1929–33 period, when the crisis was most acute, railroad income followed the same trend of declining values as the sugarcane harvests and trade, though at a somewhat slower rate. A movement toward relative recovery began in 1934, and, by the following year, the values of the sugarcane harvests and trade were approaching 50 percent of their 1929 levels. In 1937, the year in which the greatest recovery was registered, they came close to 70 percent of those figures.

Railroad income, however, while demonstrating a slight tendency toward recovery, barely managed to attain 40 percent of its 1929 level, and that in the best year of that critical decade. That situation showed that railroad income was not determined exclusively by the main indicators of the country's economic activity but was also affected by other factors that, in those historic circumstances, exacerbated the railroad crisis, giving it a specific character within the general economic crisis in Cuba.

What were those factors? The financial reports of the railroad companies all coincide in one aspect: competition by automotive transportation. An analysis of railroad income broken down into its component parts corroborates that view because of the particularly serious contraction of income from the passenger service, which was unquestionably very sensitive to competition from automotive transportation.[7]

During those years, the movement of passengers by rail dropped from an average of 4.6 passengers per inhabitant in the 1921–28 period to an average of 1.5 in the 1930s—a very low figure, compared with the averages for countries whose dimensions and populations were similar to Cuba's, such as Ireland, whose average was 4.9 passengers per inhabitant; Denmark, 12.9; and Portugal, 4.3. Naturally, the depressive effects that competition from automotive transportation had on railroad income were not limited to passengers, for it also affected freight and, altogether, constituted a factor with considerable weight in accentuating the railroad crisis.

Although the presence of automotive vehicles in the Cuban transportation business had had an effect since the early 1920s, the new service appears to have become really competitive in the final years of that decade.[8] Ferrocarriles Unidos was the company hurt most by the new competitor, for there were some highways in its area of operations in the western part of the country early in the game.

In or around 1927, the Ferrocarriles Unidos management referred to the bitter struggle that was going on over the transportation of passengers in Havana's suburbs, where several bus companies had launched themselves into "throat-cutting competition." The British company admitted that the bus lines offered a regular and efficient service from Havana to practically all points along the routes served by their electric trains and, besides, offered its passengers virtually a door-to-door service at lower rates than the trains offered between its stations.[9]

This situation, which had affected only Havana Province up to the end of the 1920s, extended to nearly all the rest of the country when the Carretera Central (Central Highway) was built in the early 1930s. By 1934, some 1,535 buses, 8,802 trucks, and several thousand taxis were in circulation in Cuba, and their operations covered a large part of the services on which the railroads had held a monopoly up until some years before.[10]

In that same era, no fewer than ten bus companies operated along the Carretera Central, some of them with as many as forty buses. By means of internal

Coach constructed in Cuba on an imported chassis.

agreements and by offering low rates, they took passengers away from the railroad. For example, a traveler could go from Havana to Camagüey by bus for an average of 2.90 pesos, whereas a second-class ticket by rail over the same distance cost 9.20.[11] Something similar occurred with the transportation of general merchandise, especially express packages, for several trucking firms were in operation, offering low rates and special discounts for commercial travelers, trying to take freight transportation away from the railroad.

Of course, competition from road transportation was not an exclusively Cuban phenomenon. The invention and improvement of the internal combustion engine and rubber tires, plus the progressive development of networks of blacktop roads with optimal conditions for the circulation of vehicles, constituted a serious problem for railroad transportation in many countries.

However, everything seems to indicate that some specific factors considerably aggravated the problem in Cuba. Specifically, sources from the era coincided in holding the Cuban government largely to blame for the disastrous competition in the sphere of transportation.[12] Many felt that the government's transportation policy was, per se, the main factor aggravating the railroad crisis. The government's responsibility covered two main aspects: the policy followed in highway construction, and the rules governing the functioning of automotive transportation.

The former concerned the evident irrationality of the design of Cuba's highways. The Carretera Central itself is the best example of this. Constructed under a law that proposed to take the benefits of modern transportation to isolated areas, the Carretera Central was, in fact, planned and built to serve the interests of Machado's political hacks, whose only concern was to get the job done quickly and to milk it for all it was worth. The result was a highway laid out practically next to Ferrocarril Central's tracks, with the railroad in sight along a large part of the highway.[13] Because this absurd policy was repeated in the government's later highway construction, the network of highways in Cuba seems superimposed on the main railroad grid (see Map 16.1).

In spite of the importance of that mistaken road policy, the most criticized aspect of the government's activities in the transportation sector was the nearly complete lack of rules regulating the automotive transportation business.[14] The taxi, bus, and trucking companies operated in conditions of extreme liberality. In the absence of official lists, the carrier could set whatever rates he wanted for his service. Moreover, his fiscal obligations were reduced to an initial payment to obtain a license and then to a small, indirect tax on the price of gasoline, so his contribution to the cost of highway maintenance was minimal. Instead, the government maintained highways by drawing on other sources of funds.[15]

The situation thus created gave the automotive transportation sector an enormous advantage over the railroad companies, which had to use a large part of their capital and income for laying and maintaining their tracks. Add to this the relatively low cost of road vehicles in that era,[16] and you get a clear idea of how advantageous the carriers' position was in their competition against the railroads.

The ineptitude and venality of Cuba's neocolonial rulers therefore constituted an aggravating factor in the railroad crisis. However, it is also true that the eruption of automotive transportation as a business coincided historically in Cuba with the economic crisis, creating problems at that difficult time that other countries had confronted under more favorable circumstances.

We would be guilty of superficiality if we were to lay the seriousness of the competition existing in the sphere of land transportation entirely at the door of the government's mismanagement of the situation. A more detailed examination of the facts shows that the railroad crisis contained other factors, which, though less visible, were also important. Table 16.2 presents some of them and compares Cuba with countries and islands whose areas and populations were more or less similar to those of Cuba. Within the general picture, Cuba's situation draws attention, for its railroads were in last place in the group, in terms of both income

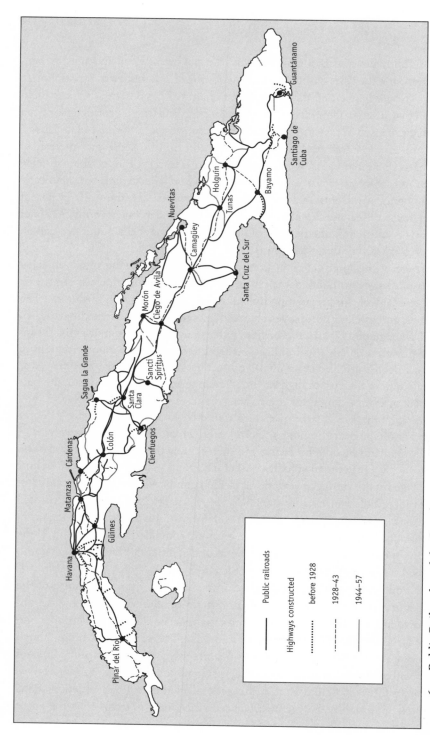

Public railroads

Highways constructed

...... before 1928

----- 1928–43

——— 1944–57

MAP 16.1. Public Railroads and the Development of the Highway System

Guantánamo

Santiago de
Cuba

Bayamo

Holguín

Tunas

Nuevitas

Camagüey

Santa Cruz del Sur

Morón

Ciego de Ávila

Sancti
Spíritus

Sagua la Grande

Santa
Clara

Cárdenas

Colón

Cienfuegos

Matanzas

Güines

Havana

Pinar del Río

TABLE 16.2. Income and Tonnage per Kilometer for Railroad Freight in
Several Countries, 1936–1938

Country	Income (in pesos)	Tonnage
Belgium	17.1	90
Hungary	7.9	99
Ireland	5.8	114
Java	5.5	84
Denmark	5.3	82
Cuba	3.2	47

Source: L. V. Abad, *Problemas de los transportes cubanos* (Havana: Editorial Mercantil
Cubana, 1944).

per kilometer and kilometers covered per ton of freight. It might be adduced that
some of the areas compared—Belgium, Hungary, and Denmark—are continental
nations whose railroads may benefit from external trade and the traffic generated
by the movement of merchandise between neighboring countries. Ireland and
Java, however, are islands similar in size to Cuba but rate much higher than Cuba
in both indicators.

Even though the situation is eloquent as a whole, it is worth centering our
analysis on the kilometers covered per ton, for this factor largely determines the
income per kilometer. As may be seen in Table 16.2, the number of kilometers
each ton of freight was carried by Cuban railroads was not only the lowest of the
group but was so much lower that it amounted to just under 50 percent of the
average for the five other areas. This fact is of singular importance, both because
of its effects on the railroads' income and because of its influence on the railroads'
competitive position vis-à-vis the other means of transportation.

The railroad rates were established on a kilometric scale that was inversely
proportional to the distance to be covered, taking into consideration the various
factors involved in the railroads' operating costs over different distances. On short
runs, the railroad service was necessarily expensive. And it was precisely in that
distance where automotive transportation revealed its greatest economic efficiency. This explains the Cuban railroads' specific competitive weakness.

Short-distance transportation was the result, first of all, of Cuba's geographic
characteristics as a long, narrow island with an abundance of natural ports. This
circumstance—which was an undeniable advantage from the point of view of its
global economy—put the railroads at a disadvantage. The railroads offset it with
the Tarafa Law, whose letter and spirit sought to impose artificial limits on the use
of the country's ports, a "solution" typical of Cuba's weak-kneed capitalism.

The national economy's essential characteristics, however, required that flow of merchandise which was unfavorable to the railroads' interests. The enormous importance of foreign trade, both for marketing the goods produced and for supplying articles for consumption, determined the prevalence of transversal traffic—from the interior of the country to the ports—which, because of the island's shape, meant relatively short trips. The lesser importance of interregional commercial ties meant that longitudinal traffic on the island—which, from all points of view, was most beneficial to the railroads—was limited.

The railroad crisis, therefore, had deep causes, whose roots stemmed from the country's weak, distorted economy. The country's lack of any great product diversification and the insufficiencies of the domestic market restricted the possibilities of railroad transportation, making it depend on a single industry, which, to top things off, was seasonal, as well. That attribute of sugar production imposed irrational norms on the railroad companies in the use of their equipment and meant that they were unable to tap many of their transportation possibilities.

Far from recent, those factors dated from the early days of Cuba's railroads, influencing their traditional operating model. But, under more favorable circumstances, when production was growing and sugar brought a good market price, that influence could be offset by the application of high rates and more intensive traffic. During the crisis, those negative factors weighed heavily, placing the railroad companies in a practically impossible situation.

Ferrocarriles Unidos de La Habana was one of the large companies in the country that felt the effects of the crisis most intensely. The old British company, which owned the most extensive network of tracks in Cuba—2,200 kilometers in all—had for many years been first in terms of total income. It lost that leading position to the U.S. companies in the eastern provinces, however, when they created Ferrocarriles Consolidados in 1924.

That significant displacement could not be considered the logical result of a proportional change between the large railroad companies in the country. In spite of the integration of the U.S. companies, Ferrocarriles Unidos continued to offer the most extensive railroad service in Cuba, and, if it didn't derive the greatest income from it, that was because of its low comparative income-yield capacity. In fact, Ferrocarriles Unidos had been losing ground ever since the early 1920s. Its average annual income in the 1925–30 period—19 million pesos—had been 2 million pesos less than the average for the 1920–25 period. Even though that drop did not endanger the company's financial stability, the management kept on expressing its apprehension concerning the business trend.[17] With such early symptoms of weakness, Ferrocarriles Unidos was ill prepared to withstand the reverses of the crisis.

During the first year of the crisis, the British company's earnings fell to 9,443,948 pesos, barely 50 percent of the average annual income it had obtained in the previous five-year period. By 1933, that figure was nearly halved again, amounting to only 4,745,541 pesos. A slight subsequent recovery placed the railroad's income between 1935 and 1940 at an average 6.2 million pesos a year, a little over 30 percent of its average prior to the crisis.

Compared with the general situation described in the preceding pages, Ferrocarriles Unidos's position was clearly unfavorable, for, at the worst of the crisis and in the later stabilization, the British company's income was lower than railroad income in general.[18] In spite of the drastic economy measures that Ferrocarriles Unidos's management took, the railroad ran at a loss in nine of the eleven years in the 1929–40 period. Since it was running in the red, the company had to suspend dividends, interest payments, and the payment of other obligations starting in 1930, which caused its debts to accumulate. By 1939, they amounted to over 40 million pesos.[19]

The fragility that Ferrocarriles Unidos, which had been considered a colossus in the transportation sector for decades, showed in the crisis was significant, even in an era in which many businesses were going on the rocks. The board of directors of Ferrocarriles Unidos claimed that the factors involved in the railroad crisis hurt the English company more than others. This appears to have been true, at least in one aspect: the competition of automotive transportation.

The British company and its subsidiary, Havana Central,[20] obtained a larger part of their income from passenger fares than did any other railroad on the island. Their income from that source had averaged 5.2 million pesos a year in the 1925–30 period, for they had carried around 12 million passengers a year. The rapid development of the network of blacktop roads, especially around Havana, and the construction of highways hurt Ferrocarriles Unidos's passenger service more and more. In 1939, it carried only 2,660,000 passengers. Logically, the railroad's income from its passenger service dropped quickly and steadily, as well; in 1939, it amounted to just a little over 700,000 pesos. Therefore, a third of the railroad's general loss of income between 1929 and 1939 was attributable to its loss of passenger income. The other two-thirds corresponded to the decline in the amount of freight carried—it dropped from 13.6 million tons in 1929 to 6.3 million tons ten years later.

Faced with the contraction of its sources of income, the board of Ferrocarriles Unidos came to the conclusion that its "only line of conduct would be to make drastic economies."[21] The policy of economies implemented by the British management affected all spheres of service, but it hit the railroad workers especially hard. The company's payroll, which had had 11,133 employees in 1928–29, was cut back to 6,934 in 1930–31 and continued to be reduced throughout the decade, winding up with only 5,591 workers in 1939.[22]

The cost-cutting measures were epitomized in expenditures for maintenance. In his address to the general stockholders' meeting that was held in 1932, Lord Ashfield, president of the Ferrocarriles Unidos noted that the usual maintenance regularly carried out during periods of high income had been postponed owing to the lamentable decline in income.[23] Expressed in as calming a way as possible, those words were but a pale reflection of what was really happening. A total of £880,659 sterling had been spent on maintenance work on tracks and rolling stock in 1927–28; in 1931–32, only £376,947 sterling was spent for the same purpose, an amount clearly inadequate for keeping the railroad operating in adequate conditions. Lord Ashfield tacitly admitted this when he warned that as soon as the circumstances changed, it would be necessary to resume maintenance expenditures on a more liberal scale.

However, the economy measures, which may have been originally drawn up as emergency measures, became the norm for the entire decade of the 1930s. By imposing such drastic reductions on its maintenance budgets, Ferrocarriles Unidos abandoned all possibilities not only of replacing its old equipment but also of maintaining the trains it was using in satisfactory condition. The result of that little-less-than-suicidal policy was the destruction of hundreds of cars, which were abandoned on sidings, and the deterioration of the track to levels that seriously endangered the safety of the service.[24]

In its obsessive cost-cutting campaign, the Ferrocarriles Unidos management applied a series of organizational measures that reduced the extent of its services. Thus, in 1931, it obtained official authorization to close thirty-one stations were considered "nonprofitable" and also to reduce the distance covered by its trains (by a total of 1,284,807 miles) by eliminating certain runs and modifying itineraries. But the company's aims in that regard were much more ambitious. The Ferrocarriles Unidos board wanted to completely eliminate its electric train service— originally provided by Havana Central, which had gone out of business—because it was running at a loss of around £45,000 sterling a year and was considered already obsolete, in view of the growing competition of automotive transportation.[25]

A spirit of withdrawal can be seen in Ferrocarriles Unidos's policy regarding the crisis, as reflected in the invariably defensive nature of the measures it adopted. Its attitude toward competing with automotive transportation was a clear example of this. At the end of the 1920s, the Unidos management made an effort to halt its flight of customers, first by introducing gasoline-powered coaches and then by making a general reduction in its rates. When those measures failed, Ferrocarriles Unidos seems to have become resigned to its progressive loss of income caused by competition from small road transportation companies.

Unidos's president, Lord Ashfield,[26] expressed the board's lack of combativeness in taking up the challenge thrown down by the road transportation carriers, just as Ferrocarriles Consolidados would do later on.[27] In view of its steady loss of customers, the Ferrocarriles Unidos management simply did what it could to oppose the rate-reduction measure, a decision that was also necessary because of the general depression of prices caused by the crisis. The tone of the annual reports which the Unidos board presented in that era conveys a conviction that there were no sure prospects for the recovery or subsequent development of the Cuban economy—much less, for the railroad sector.

The British point of view was based on the criterion that the Cuban railroads' future would be determined by the attitude the government took toward them. The government was the only agency that could protect the railroads against the stiff competition of automotive transportation, by establishing a system of coordinated rates among the various means of transportation. And that would be just a first step in the process of growing governmental responsibility for the railroads, which would perhaps wind up with subsidies.

The British board went all out, demanding that the government provide decisive assistance for the railroads. In addition to a series of direct appeals,[28] the company got the English party to the Anglo-Cuban Trade Treaty of 1937 to add an article requesting the Cuban government to take measures to alleviate the situation of Ferrocarriles Unidos.

The Ferrocarriles Unidos board was not unaware of the fact that, in spite of the size of its business, its position in the new economic situation was comparatively weak.[29] Since the company was the result of mergers and of the gradual absorption of the small railroads that had proliferated in the nineteenth century, its system of tracks was extremely complicated, overburdened with rambling branch lines that had been built originally to pull in freight for the small companies that were later swallowed up by the British monopoly. Moreover, many sections in the system were old and dangerous, so Ferrocarriles Unidos's trains had to reduce speed over them and often had to make detours. Meanwhile, its competitors could go shorter distances, with more rational schedules. Any radical change in this state of affairs would require an investment campaign, which the owners of the railroad had been hesitant to make even in the heyday of the business.

In addition to that unfavorable operational situation, there was the company's no less disastrous financial situation. Burdened with debts because of the Schröder bank's eagerness to engage in speculation, the railroad company had to confront financial responsibilities that demanded exceptionally favorable economic conditions if they were to be met in full. The suspension of dividends and interest payments caused by the crisis meant that the company's liabilities increased by nearly $5 million each year. By the end of the 1930s, the company's debts—by then amounting to nearly $40 million—were so out of proportion that nobody would have ventured to say how they could be paid.

From Schröder's point of view, it had already gotten as much out of Ferrocarriles Unidos as could be expected from a speculative investment. With its securities quoted at less than 1 percent of their face value, the railroad company had become an abomination in the world of business, and no foreseeable factors could reverse that situation. In view of those circumstances, the British board's strategy was fairly obvious: try to put up with the problem in the least onerous way and rely on the "good side" of the public nature of its business—that is, let others concern themselves over the progressive deterioration of a service that was absolutely necessary for the Cuban economy.

The adept board of the English company not only tried to reduce the railroad business's losses to a minimum but also came up with the idea of maintaining certain lines that, conveniently isolated from the ailing body of the great railroad company, were still able to yield a profit. Such was the case of Havana Terminal, the small "independent" company that operated Havana's railroad terminal and the tracks serving the docks.

Because of its privileged position and low operating costs, that company managed to stay in the black almost to the end of the crisis. Since Havana Terminal was an independent entity from the legal point of view and even a creditor of Ferrocarriles Unidos,[30] its operating results were unencumbered by the debts of the parent company.

The advantages of this system encouraged the English to extend its application to the port of Matanzas in 1937, when the Cuban government declared it a "free zone."[31] Since the tariff benefits made it pretty certain that Matanzas's port traffic would increase, it was decided to transfer the holdings of the old Matanzas Terminal—which was also controlled by Ferrocarriles Unidos—and some kilometers more of track that Unidos owned in the city to an entity created for the purpose: Ferrocarril Central de Matanzas.

The new company, whose main and only stockholders were A. G. Hunt, president of Ferrocarriles Unidos, and some other members of its board, operated so successfully that, in three years, it amassed a reserve of 1,717,502 pesos.[32] With the exploitation of these "tiny islands of prosperity," the main owners of Ferrocarriles Unidos ensured that they themselves would keep on making money, while reiterating to their stockholders and creditors that "the lamentable state of business" kept them from meeting their obligations.

The U.S. railroad companies in the eastern provinces were in a better position when the crisis hit. Having learned their lesson from the postwar deflation and with a realistic view of the country's economic possibilities, the U.S. businessmen carried out the consolidation as a maneuver for adjusting to less favorable circumstances. The creation of Ferrocarriles Consolidados did away with the earlier situation of competition and led to a regime of higher rates, which was also favored by the legal limitations placed on exporting sugar through private ports. Those factors made it possible for the companies in the Consolidados system to increase their income, even in the depressive situation which began to be manifested in 1925.[33]

When the crisis brought Cuba Railroad's and Ferrocarril del Norte de Cuba's combined income down from 18.3 million pesos in 1929 to 5.6 million in 1933, their accumulated reserves enabled them to meet most of their obligations up through 1932. Only the next year (1933), at the worst moment of the crisis, and under the Ley de Moratoria Hipotecaria (Mortgage Moratorium Law), which the Cuban government passed in April 1933,[34] did Ferrocarriles Consolidados and its subsidiaries suspend payment on their debts.

That line of conduct was not due to any particular sense of responsibility by the U.S. businessmen. It simply showed that their business wasn't doing as badly as the others. Even though the depressive trend reduced the income of Ferrocarriles Consolidados and its subsidiaries by nearly 70 percent, their severe cutbacks in spending enabled that group of companies to stay out of the red. As was only to be expected, after deducting the payment of taxes, insurance, and other obligations from its gross income, Ferrocarriles Consolidados declared net losses—amounting to 2 million pesos between 1932 and 1936—but more than one indication suggests that its real balance sheet was more encouraging than the figures presented in the company's public accounts.[35]

Naturally, although the companies in the Consolidados group survived the effects of the crisis better than others, they did not get off scot-free. Norte de Cuba, which was closely linked to sugar, saw its freight fall off alarmingly, from 3.5 million tons in 1929 to 1.6 million tons three years later, averaging 1.9 million tons a year in the 1935–40 period.

For Cuba Railroad, the crisis meant a 50 percent reduction in its volume of freight—with an even greater reduction in some years—and from 60 to 70 percent fewer passengers carried. The decrease in the passenger service stemmed, as in other cases, both from the drop in the people's purchasing power, which led them to curtail their traveling, and from the competition offered by automotive transportation, as a result of the opening of the Carretera Central.

Because of the conditions of transportation in the eastern provinces, the crisis had some specific characteristics in that region that should be mentioned. Faced with the catastrophic drop in the price of sugar, the estate owners and sugar companies made desperate efforts to cut their production costs. Transportation was a considerable item in the cost of sugar, and, as was only to be expected, the sugar producers did not delay in demanding that the railroad rates be lowered.

But, in the specific circumstances of the eastern provinces, the reduction in the cost of transporting sugar revived an old conflict: that of the private ports and landing stages.

During the crisis, some of the sugar companies sought to take advantage of the tax exemptions granted to some sugar mills and neighboring companies so they could use the private ports, both for shipping their products out and for saving themselves the cost of paying the public railroads. The three most outstanding cases of that kind of maneuver were in the area around Camagüey.

The first of them was related to the port of Palo Alto, an installation authorized for the exclusive use of the Stewart sugar mill but which began to be used by the Baraguá sugar mill and other neighboring sugar mills, as well.[36]

A similar situation was created with the port of Santa María, landing stage for the Vertientes sugar mill. General Sugar States, which owned the Vertientes, decided to use those shipping facilities for other sugar mills—the Pilar, Estrella, and Agramonte—which it owned in the same region.[37]

The third, perhaps best known, of these cases was that of the port of Chicola, near Morón. In 1932, the Machado administration authorized the Falla Gutiérrez sugar company, with which the regime had close ties,[38] to use that landing stage. The concession violated the Tarafa Law, but it meant a savings of 228,000 pesos a year for the Falla firm in transportation charges for the sugar from its Patria and Adelaida sugar mills—and, of course, a serious loss of income for Ferrocarril del Norte de Cuba, which had traditionally carried that freight to Puerto Tarafa.

Aware of the serious danger that an increase in shipping through private ports would mean for its interests, Ferrocarriles Consolidados resorted to all the mechanisms created under the Tarafa Law. The result was complicated lawsuits which dragged on for more than a decade. In that conflict of interests, both the railroad and the sugar companies mobilized the social forces that might be adversely affected by the thorny issue of the private ports—and, by doing so, added to the seriousness of the problem.

The railroad companies' victory in their struggle against the private ports was, in spite of everything, very relative. Only in the case of Palo Alto did the railroads score a clear victory, for the railroad crossing that made it possible for the non-authorized sugar mills to use the landing stage was closed. The case concerning the port of Santa María, which the railroads apparently won in 1938 with the promulgation of a decree that declared the landing stage illegal, was eventually lost when the Supreme Court ruled in favor of the sugar interests. The same thing happened in the lawsuit concerning the port of Chicola.

The companies in the Consolidados system were less affected than Ferrocarriles Unidos by the other factor in the crisis—competition by automotive transportation. Mainly involving the activities of private carriers along the Carretera

Central, automobile competition had the greatest effect on traffic on the Cuba Railroad Company's main line, between Santa Clara and Santiago de Cuba. Cuba Railroad's combined traffic with Ferrocarriles Unidos on the Ferrocarril Central route, which had brought it 2,200,823 pesos' income in fiscal year 1928–29, fell off so much that it brought in only 719,528 pesos in 1931–32,[39] the year after the Carretera Central was opened.

Since the network of highways in the eastern provinces was limited in practice to the Carretera Central, Ferrocarril del Norte de Cuba and important branches of Cuba Railroad remained untouched by competition. That situation was maintained at least until the latter half of the 1930s, when other highways began to be built in the eastern provinces.

Faced with the serious threat posed by the proliferation of highways in the area it served, Ferrocarriles Consolidados called on all the resources it could to frustrate the new highway projects. Drawing on the railroads' key importance for some of the cities in the region, such as Camagüey, Morón, and Ciego de Ávila, Ferrocarriles Consolidados pressured the municipal administrations and some labor organizations to try to get them to join the antihighway campaign.[40] In spite of all its efforts, however, the railroad company was not very successful. Highways were unquestionably spreading. Little by little, they also invaded the territory served by the railroad's secondary lines, enlarging the area affected by automotive transportation's competition.

While studying projects to challenge the competing automotive transportation companies on its own turf,[41] Ferrocarriles Consolidados joined forces with Ferrocarriles Unidos and other smaller companies to try to get the government to establish a system of rate controls for the various means of transportation. After some not very effective solutions were tried, such as the creation of a Comisión Nacional de Servicio Público (National Public Services Commission), for regulating the granting of licenses for using buses and trucks, the government finally decided to tackle the tough, extremely complex problem of competition in transportation and, in 1938, created the Comisión Nacional de Transportes (National Transportation Commission).[42]

The new agency replaced the old Comisión de Ferrocarriles, with the advantage that its powers extended to the entire sphere of transportation. In spite of the authority invested in it, however, the Comisión Nacional de Transporte dragged its feet in fulfilling one of the main purposes for which it had been created: that of coordinating the various means of transportation. It began drawing up a coordinated list of freight and express rates in 1938 but did not complete it until two years later, and it took yet another year before it went into effect permanently. By then, World War II had broken out, which added important modifications to the transportation problem.

The workers had to bear the brunt of the capitalist crisis; that axiom was borne out with undeniable rigor in the case of the railroad proletariat. In fact, the era of the crisis began for that sector of labor in distinctly disadvantageous conditions. After having given excellent proof of its combativeness and organizational ability during the early years of the 1920s, the railroad labor movement was tied hand and foot by the maneuvers of the Machado administration, the railroad companies, and opportunist elements acting within the proletarian groups.

The assassination of leaders of the stature of Enrique Varona and the expulsion and persecution of other honest leaders paved the way for the railroad labor organizations to fall into the hands of individuals who were willing to serve the interests of the owners and the government unconditionally. The service they performed was far from small. Supported by the internal splits of the railroad proletariat and by the weak class consciousness of some of the workers, the yellow leaders who took the top positions in the Hermandad Ferroviaria de Cuba and other organizations in the sector applied a policy that was contrary to the interests of the proletariat. Even though the formal aspects of labor union operation were carefully observed—for example, by holding discussions on collective work agreements with the companies—those formalities barely sufficed to disguise the real attitude of the new railroad workers' leaders.

Extremely circumspect in formulating even the most basic demands and always open to deals with the owners, the leaders of the Hermandad Ferroviaria did not improve the living conditions of their members in any way between 1926 and 1929.[43] To the contrary, the opportunist leaders went all out to promote trends among the railway workers that led to the formation of an aristocracy of labor and isolated that sector from the rest of the Cuban working class.

Nor did some of those leaders hesitate to include in their services the denunciation of those members of the railroad workers' collectives who engaged in any kind of political activism. Determined to make a career of representing the unions, the leaders of the Hermandad Ferroviaria contributed to the maneuvers that were creating government-sponsored labor unions, such as the Unión Federativa Obrera (Workers' Federative Union) and the Federación Cubana del Trabajo (Cuban Federation of Labor). Nor were they averse to engaging in the politicking of the traditional bourgeois parties that participated in Machado's "cooperativism."

Naturally, some railroad workers denounced the corrupt leaders of the Hermandad Ferroviaria. In the late 1920s, a group called Pro Unidad (For Unity) was formed among the Ferrocarriles Unidos workers. It consisted of a nucleus of activists linked to the nascent Partido Comunista de Cuba (Communist Party of Cuba).[44] That group denounced the maneuvers of the official leaders to the masses of workers and sought to politicize the workers, struggling not only against the leaders who served the companies' interests but also against the Machado dictatorship, whose growing use of repression made it the main force upholding the status quo.

The terrible consequences that the actions of the yellow leadership of the Hermandad Ferroviaria had for the railroad workers were shown particularly clearly starting in 1929, when the economic crisis began to have devastating effects on the railroad companies. Faced with the general contraction of their business, the managements of the railroad companies adopted a drastic policy of economies, based on laying off day and other laborers. In just a few months, thousands of railroad workers lost their jobs. In the 1929–32 period, Ferrocarriles Unidos and Ferrocarriles Consolidados, the two main companies, fired 8,115 workers, depriving them of even the minimum means of livelihood.[45]

It is amazing that a sector of the proletariat that, only a few years earlier, had rocked the country with tremendous strikes, meekly accepted those measures, which condemned thousands of its members to poverty, without a protest. The leaders of the Hermandad Ferroviaria not only did so but even turned the layoffs into a political tool against those workers who had expressed their opposition to the sellout attitude that prevailed in the railroad workers' organizations. Since the economy measures were mainly directed against the most advanced members of the proletariat, they further weakened class activities in the railroad collectives, which partly explains the low participation that sector had in the head-on battle the Cuban working class would wage against the Machado regime.

After courageously standing firm against the wave of repression that Machado unleashed starting in 1925 and in spite of the assassination or deportation of dozens of its best leaders, the Cuban working class had managed to reform its ranks and prepare for new battles. Rubén Martínez Villena, a poet and adviser to the Confederación Nacional Obrera de Cuba who had made a tremendous effort to preserve the organizational structures of the Cuban proletariat and deepen its political consciousness, and the young Partido Comunista played a decisive role in that process of resistance and reorganization.

On March 20, 1930, in response to a strike call issued by the Confederación Nacional, 200,000 workers walked off the job in Havana, Manzanillo, and other cities, showing Machado and his clique that the labor movement was still alive and ready to fight.[46] The railroad workers did not participate in the strike as a sector. Even though the members of the Pro Unidad group and other activists urged the railroad workers to join in, all they achieved were sporadic protests, because the leaders of the Hermandad Ferroviaria did everything they could to keep the strike from breaking out in the railroad centers. The president of Delegation 2 (Havana) of the Hermandad Ferroviaria expressed the cowardly attitude of the railroad "leaders" brazenly:

The Hermandad Ferroviaria de Cuba cannot have political tendencies of any kind. . . . The Hermandad Ferroviaria is on the side of the constituted government, of which Gerardo Machado is president, because it is with him that the Hermandad must solve a multitude of problems. . . . I know that there are persons alien to the railroad workers who are set on involving us in affairs that don't interest us directly, as they already tried to do on March 20 . . . but this [the Hermandad] is not a material that anyone can mold for tendentious purposes.[47]

While maintaining the opportunistic slant of their organizations, the leaders of the Hermandad Ferroviaria diverted the attention of the masses of workers to goals of secondary importance.

Even so, the corrupt railroad workers' leaders could not keep the masses of workers from becoming more radical, a logical result of the difficult economic situation prevailing at the time and of the broad movement against the Machado dictatorship that was taking shape in the country. The patient ideological work done by the Partido Comunista bore fruit in the railroad sector, not only by keeping the Pro Unidad group operating in Havana (even though most of its members had been fired) but also by founding the first Communist cells in the workshops in Camagüey, Morón, and other railroad centers in the interior of the country.[48]

In early 1933, the complicated Cuban political process became ripe for great advances with the upsurge of a revolutionary situation. The Machado dictatorship's unbridled repression and its manifest inability to handle the economic crisis had led a wide spectrum of sectors of Cuban society to struggle actively against it. The regime's base of support was reduced to its corrupt political apparatus—that is, to the repressive forces themselves and to the United States, which supported them. This last, decisive element of support also began to falter when Franklin Delano Roosevelt became president of the United States.

Convinced that Machado's situation had become untenable, the U.S. government began to work for a solution that would allow it to replace Machado without letting that risky movement lead to the collapse of the battered structures of imperialist rule. To carry out that delicate task, Benjamin Sumner Welles, an experienced diplomat, was named ambassador of the United States to Cuba. He immediately entered into negotiations with Machado's bourgeois opponents.

The situation on the island evolved more quickly than the mediator could handle, however. Washington's calculations were mistaken, especially as regards the belligerency of the Cuban working class. During 1932 and the early months of 1933, the Partido Comunista and the Confederación Nacional Obrera de Cuba had carried out a veritable feat by extending labor union organization to all work sectors, especially the sugar industry. The decisive economic importance of the sugar sector and the number and distribution of its units throughout the country made it a key sector in the workers' struggle against the Machado regime.

Strikes broke out in far-distant points on the island, stretching the government's repressive bodies thin and rapidly exhausting their operational capacity. A strike declared by the transportation workers in early August 1933 was the straw that broke the dictatorship's back. Begun as a local movement in Havana, the strike was taken up by one sector after another and, under the leadership of the Confederación Nacional, turned into a revolutionary general strike.

The ruling clique of the Hermandad Ferroviaria could not keep the railroad workers from participating in that decisive battle. In view of the growing wave of strikes, the railroad workers decided that the time had come to make the demands that had been put off for so long and to join in the final assault on the tyranny. As usual, the board of the Hermandad Ferroviaria opposed participating in the strike, but this time the masses ignored their "leaders," so the kingpins among them opted for lying low "until the danger has passed."[49]

Unable to control the powerful revolutionary movement and hearing that the army was withdrawing its support, Gerardo Machado decided to flee the country on August 23, 1933. It was a last-minute maneuver orchestrated by the U.S. government and its domestic allies to keep the crisis from leading to a real revolutionary triumph.

A compromise government was formed under the presidency of Carlos Manuel de Céspedes Jr., but the masses wisely repudiated it, realizing that that government would keep them from achieving their revolutionary goals. Therefore, even though the general strike was eased up after Machado's fall, a considerable number of small-scale conflicts remained active, benefiting from the complete collapse of the deposed dictator's repressive apparatus. The railroad sector was one of those centers of latent conflict, especially the units of Ferrocarriles Consolidados, whose workers refused to go back to work until the companies accepted their demands.

The collapse of the Machado regime made it possible to remove systematically the traitorous leaders from the various delegations of the Hermandad Ferroviaria and other railroad union organizations. The new leaderships were composed of workers who were linked to several anti-Machado organizations and who, though lacking true class consciousness in some cases, were unquestionably an improvement over the old leaders.

The workers' tenacious defense of the demands they had made during the August strike forced the railroad companies to accept most of them by the end of that month. They included an eight-hour day in all departments of the railroad and the suspension of the 15 percent wage reductions imposed as one of the economy measures implemented in April 1933.[50]

In view of the new situation, many of the workers who had been fired in the 1930–33 period, including some of the most advanced and radical ones in the sector, went back to work on the railroads. The reincorporation of those workers made a considerable contribution toward increasing the class consciousness of the railroad proletariat and helped to strengthen their organizations.

Some advances were made in this last regard, such as the founding of the Sindicato de Empleados de Oficina de la Industria Ferroviaria (Railroad Industry Office Workers' Union), in Camagüey, attached to the Confederación Nacional Obrera de Cuba and of a clearly revolutionary orientation, which brought in a sector that had traditionally remained apart from the workers' struggles. Naturally, there were setbacks, too: a group called Ferroviarios y Trabajadores Unidos (United Railroad and Other Workers)—better known as "the Spaniards' union"— was founded in Camagüey to defend the specific interests of the Spanish workers against the Work Nationalization Law.[51]

The last few months of 1933 saw feverish activity in the railroad collectives, for they were drawing up new work agreements and struggling to ensure that the advances they had won would be honored. Moreover, disputes broke out between the various unions in the railroad sector and especially between the supporters of different trends of thought in each organization. It seemed as if all of the contra-dictions and dissent that undermined the revolutionary movement in Cuba were present in their most acute forms in the railroad sector. Since the railroad unions lacked unity, the activities they undertook were weak and isolated. Some small-scale victories were achieved, but the crisis confronting the bourgeois regime in Cuba was more serious than the growing strength and organization of the labor unions.

On January 15, 1934, the provisional government headed by Grau San Martín fell. It had been weakened by internal contradictions and by fierce opposition from both the forces of the reaction and imperialism and from the Communist movement. During its four months in power, at the urging of Antonio Guiteras Holmes, secretary of the interior, the Grau-Guiteras government had approved a series of laws and measures that favored the people's aspirations. Betrayal by Colonel Fulgencio Batista, head of the army, had been the final blow, facilitating Carlos Mendieta's coming to power at the head of a coalition of bourgeois parties.

The Mendieta administration began a counteroffensive to do away with the revolutionary situation and strengthen the bases of the neocolonial system. Barely two weeks after taking power, Mendieta's government issued Legislative Decree

3, which, under the pretext of controlling the labor unions and the right to strike, introduced repressive articles against the workers' movement. The antilabor legislation was buttressed soon afterward with two new decrees, numbers 51 and 82, which established severe measures against those who violated the government's rules on strikes and outlawed workers' organizations that declared "unjustified" strikes.[52]

The new repressive legislation claimed its first victims in the railroad sector in March 1934, when a strike promoted by several organizations was declared illegal.[53] As a result, the Sindicato de Empleados de Oficina de la Industria Ferroviaria, the Dirección Central of the Hermandad Ferroviaria, Delegation 12 (Santiago de Cuba) of that organization, and some smaller organizations were outlawed. The organizations that were affected managed to be reestablished six months later, but under new leaders, for the leaders who had been in office at the time of the banning were prohibited from holding office for two years.

During the following months in 1934, strikes and protests continued to break out in various railroad centers, but most of them were defeated by the companies and the government's repressive apparatus, acting together.[54] In October 1934, the Morón Unión was added to the group of outlawed railroad organizations, accused of having declared an illegal strike. The militant Morón Unión, which represented the workers on Ferrocarril del Norte, had presented a series of forty-one demands, which the railroad's management turned down, alleging that the union was Communist-run. In view of the management's position, the leaders of the union had no alternative but to declare a work stoppage. When the government unleashed all of its repressive power against the union, the company took advantage of the situation to try to demoralize its workers and annulled the work agreement which it had agreed to the previous February.

The year 1934 ended with a negative balance for the Cuban labor movement. The railroad sector was no exception. With many of their organizations outlawed and some of their recent achievements wrested from them, the railroad workers had lost ground in their struggle. The asphyxiating repressive atmosphere in which the bourgeois counteroffensive enveloped the country placed the revolutionary forces in a very shaky position. As on other occasions, unity among those sectors was very precarious; there were differences over goals and tactics. Little by little, the idea of repeating the victorious August 1933 strike, that had put paid to the Machado dictatorship, took hold. A strike committee was set up in the University of Havana, in which the various revolutionary and other opposition organizations tried to coordinate their actions toward a general strike.

In early March, a teachers' strike sparked the larger strike movement. Even though the main leftist organizations—the Partido Comunista and Joven Cuba—

did not believe the conditions were ripe for guaranteeing the movement's success, the view of the university strike committee prevailed, and the paralysis of work activities spread.

In the railroad sector, the Havana delegation of the Hermandad Ferroviaria had the most outstanding participation in the strike movement. Headed by individuals close to the recently created Partido Revolucionario Cubano (Auténtico) (Cuban Revolutionary [Authentic] Party),[55] Delegation 2 had managed to escape the wave of outlawings decreed against the railroad labor organizations. Its leaders had spent most of 1934 engaged in peaceful but interminable negotiations with the management of Ferrocarriles Unidos concerning the signing of a new work agreement.

On March 10, as the strike spread, the leaders of Delegation 2 decided to join it. After obtaining the support of other delegations in the west, the strikers managed to halt the movement of trains from Pinar del Río to Las Villas, but they couldn't . maintain the strike. The army and police unleashed violent repression under Colonel Batista, and the absence of conditions offering even a minimum of safety to the strikers led many to cave in. Responding to the railroad management's imperious orders, many Unidos workers went back to work, and traffic began to return to normal on March 14.[56]

The strike did not reach very far into the territory controlled by Ferrocarriles Consolidados. Delegation 12 of the Hermandad Ferroviaria and the Morón Unión remained aloof from the movement, pointing out that they didn't have the conditions required for throwing themselves into a strike. In Camagüey, the Unión de Talleres and the Sindicato de Empleados de Oficina joined the strike on March 12, as did the Dirección Central of the Hermandad Ferroviaria, but this last organization simultaneously presented the company with a series of demands in an attempt to make it seem that its decision had an economic rather than a political base.

The railroad strike movement in Camagüey carried out only isolated actions. By March 13, the army chiefs in the province had managed to identify the main leaders and activists of the strike and ordered their arrest, and they also sent a blacklist of workers to the management of Ferrocarriles Consolidados so they would be fired immediately.[57] Sorely weakened by the arrest of its main leaders, the shaky strike movement speedily fell apart.

The failure of the March 1935 strike marked the ebb of the revolutionary movement. The fact that Rodrigo Rodríguez, long-time agent of the owners, who had been president of the Dirección Central of the Hermandad Ferroviaria during the worst days of the Machado dictatorship, resumed that post in June 1935 was eloquent proof of this. Thus, there was a return to the old days of yellow labor unionism, which was alien to the true interests of the working class.

Even so, it was impossible to split the masses completely. They continued to call for the release and reinstatement of the workers who had been fired during the strike, and they finally managed to achieve this. In Havana, the formation of the Renovación Ferroviaria (Railroad Renovation) group in 1937, heir to the militant traditions of the Pro Unidad group but with a wider scope, was a guarantee that the railroad proletariat's spirit of struggle would remain alive, looking to the future for new achievements.

17

Temporary Recovery

After the long depression in which Cuba had been submerged, the beginning of a new world war in 1939 awakened the vital reserves of production so they could be used, as in World War I, for Cuba's "great ally to the north." However, since the war also interrupted the island's trade with some of its European markets, its immediate economic effects were generally unfavorable. It created a deficit in Cuba's exports, which the United States's increased demand for sugar did not fill. Therefore, the total value of Cuba's exports was over 20 million pesos less than in the preceding year.

When the United States entered the war in December 1941, the big sugar speculators in that country, as in the previous war, assumed the remunerative role of intermediaries in selling sugar. Both sugar and some of its by-products had become strategic materials, not only because of their acknowledged importance as sources of energy but also because of their great value in the production of explosives, synthetic rubber, and other products. As a result, Cuba's "war effort" was to turn all of its sugar production over to the U.S. government, its "ally"—naturally, at "reasonable" prices.

In the negotiations that were held for that purpose in January 1942, Cuba's representatives pledged its sugarcane harvests up through 1947, with prices set at 2.65 centavos a pound for the first three years and 3.10, 4.12, and 4.96 centavos a pound for the sugar from the 1945, 1946, and 1947 harvests. The intergovernmental agreement was handled by the Instituto Cubano de Estabilización del Azúcar (Cuban Sugar Stabilization Institute) for Cuba and the Defense Supply Corporation for the United States. The war's direct consequences on the country's economy were seen immediately, with an increase of over 2.5 million metric tons in Cuba's sugar production between 1940 and 1947.[1]

Because of the war, Cuban industry recovered, and Cuba supplied a larger proportion of the sugar purchased by the United States. This time, however, the more complete control exercised over the prices to be paid for that product kept Cuba from benefiting—as it had during the "fat years" following World War I—from the world scarcity of the product. This time, the U.S. speculators intercepted the cash flow much more efficiently; as a result, Cuba received less, even though the world production of sugar had been reduced by 10 million tons, and the Philippines, one of the main suppliers of the U.S. market, had cut off its flow of sugar in that direction.

When sugar production increased, the railroads—which were closely linked to the production and shipping of that product—benefited. The dangers that submarine warfare brought to Cuba's coasts made it necessary to suspend coastal shipping and exports of sugar through most of the country's ports and, instead, send the sugar produced in the sugar mills in the large areas in the eastern part of the island to the western ports of Havana, Matanzas, and Cárdenas. The risks to maritime transportation were less from those ports—first, because of the shorter distance to the U.S. coast and, second, because the ships were sent in convoys, escorted by planes and warships.

This system meant that the sugar and molasses produced in sugar mills as far from Havana and Matanzas as the Santa Isabel, Céspedes, and Algodones, along Cuba Railroad's line, and the Carmita, Patria, Morón, and Stewart, along Norte de Cuba's tracks, were first sent to the city of Villa Clara and then hauled over Ferrocarriles Unidos's tracks to the western ports listed previously.

In general terms, that long-distance transportation resulted in an increase in the freight carried by Ferrocarriles Unidos and Ferrocarriles Consolidados. The practice had one drawback for Ferrocarriles Consolidados, however: even though the average distance over which each ton of freight was carried increased, creating supplementary traffic, the large port installations of Nuevitas and Nipe stopped operating at full capacity, the difference in traffic going to the old sugar ports in the west. However, other war needs arose that required Ferrocarriles Consolidados's services.

In mid-July 1942, the Department of Agriculture of the U.S. government chose the southeastern part of Cuba as a depot for storing the merchandise, which, coming from that country, would be sent to various places in the Caribbean, escorted by the U.S. naval forces stationed at Guantánamo Bay. The shipments received through the port of Havana were sent by rail to Santiago de Cuba, where they were loaded onto other ships to continue on their way, thus avoiding a great roundabout journey at sea, where the ships would have been open to attack by enemy submarines.[2]

The state of war was a determining influence on the amount of freight trans-

TABLE 17.1. Comparative Data for Passengers Carried by Ferrocarriles Unidos and Ferrocarriles Consolidados, 1940 and 1944

	1939–40	1943–44
FC Consolidados	2,199,144	4,635,600
FC Unidos	2,986,681	4,448,799

Source: Ferrocarriles Unidos y Ferrocarriles Consolidados, *Memorias* (1939–1940, 1943–1944).

ported. On Ferrocarriles Consolidados's lines, it rose from 5.7 million metric tons in 1940 to 9.5 million in 1944.[3] The same thing happened with Ferrocarriles Unidos, whose freight rose from 7.7 million metric tons in 1940 to 12.2 million in 1944.[4]

The special conditions caused by the war also brought about a drop in the competition that road transportation had offered the railroads, reducing its freight and passenger traffic. Hard hit by the war economies, the shortage of tires and spare parts, and the rationing of fuel, the bus and truck companies had to curtail their services. It is easy to suppose that, in that unfavorable situation, the growing demands for land transportation directly increased the railroads' business. This can be seen both in the volume of passengers and freight and in the increase in the average distance each metric ton of freight was carried. The figures presented in Tables 17.1 and 17.2 show this clearly.

However, the production and railroad traffic increases took place in a country that, as a neocolony, was trapped in the framework of restricted growth. Therefore, on this occasion, the war did not mean the opening of new productive zones or the construction or extension of the railroads. The productive material base that the country had was still more than large enough to meet the needs required by the war effort. The limits on the development of the sugar industry—and, therefore, on Cuba's railroads as well—had been established some decades earlier.

Starting in January 1944, the balance of forces in the world war had changed considerably. Hitler's Germany was being beaten back by the Soviet troops on the eastern front and was also losing ground before the combined forces of the western Allies. This situation almost completely ended the submarine war near Cuba's coasts, which made it possible to normalize sugar shipments. Ferrocarriles Consolidados began to use its own terminals for export operations again, reducing the traffic through the ports of Havana, Matanzas, and Cárdenas.[5]

The normalization of shipping did not mean an immediate readjustment of the railroads' income, however. This was so, first of all, because the countries that had been devastated by the war kept up the demand for sugar from the areas in production, while their old production centers recovered. Second, when the

TABLE 17.2. Volume and Distance of Freight Carried on Ferrocarriles Unidos

	1939–41	1943–44	Percentage Increase
Freight in Metric Tons	21,264,100	28,088,00	33.0
Metric Tons per Kilometer	604,093,000	1,284,959,000	112.0
Average Trip per Metric Ton/Kilometer	29	45	53.0

Source: Economic and Technical Mission to Cuba, *Report on Cuba* (Baltimore: Johns Hopkins University Press, 1951), p. 248.

restrictions placed on imports were lifted, the accumulation of hard currency that the favorable balance of payments had made possible facilitated an increase in imports—from 103.8 million pesos' worth in 1940 to 208.6 million pesos' worth in 1944 and to over 500 million pesos' worth in 1947–48.[6] Those import conditions also led to a tremendous increase in commercial activities inside the country.

The end of the war also meant the renewal and development of competition among the various branches of transportation. Automotive transportation operators were able to obtain equipment, tires, spare parts, and fuel again, which created conditions favorable for the growth of their business. Moreover, another important factor contributed to this: the inauguration of a new administration, headed by Dr. Ramón Grau San Martín.[7] This coincided with a great abundance of resources in the Hacienda (Treasury), thanks to which a vast plan of public works and urban renewal was begun. The execution of that plan, though beset by mismanagement and embezzlement, resulted in the country's highways being repaired and some new roads being built, which extended the system of land communication on the basis of automotive transportation. Coastal shipping was also resumed, and air transportation reached a level higher than in the prewar period. These factors tended to neutralize the railroad boom.

The inflation that was the natural result of the changes effected in world trade reached the vital activities of production and services, causing the prices of raw materials, fuel, and nearly all consumer and other articles to go up. Workers' demands came fast on the heels of inflation, increasing the cost of the work force. The railroads latched onto this as a pretext for demanding a hike in transportation rates. In response to those demands, the general freight rates were raised on a step-by-step basis, with each increase greater than the last.[8]

The higher rates and the great volume of freight and number of passengers carried brought funds flooding into the railroad companies' coffers. The income that the smaller companies—Hershey and Guantánamo and Western—obtained from their operations only doubled in the war and postwar years, because those railroads could not carry freight from diverse areas. But, in the case of Ferro-carriles Unidos and Ferrocarriles Consolidados, which controlled large railroad circuits, their income tripled or even quadrupled. Ferrocarriles Unidos's income rose from 6.3 million pesos in 1940 to 18.5 million in 1948, and Ferrocarriles Consolidados's, from 6.5 million pesos in 1940 to 24.7 million in 1948.[9]

The large companies' specific conditions were dissimilar, however, since Ferro-carriles Unidos was unable to keep on increasing its income at the same rate as Ferrocarriles Consolidados, nor could it manage to control the strong growth tendency in its operating expenses. It was impossible for Ferrocarriles Unidos to survive in the conditions in effect in 1948. In contrast, Ferrocarriles Consolidados's increases in expenses and operating income occurred more harmoniously, and its margins of gross profit in 1947 and 1948 even showed considerable growth.

The temporary effects that the war exercised on the economy of Ferrocarriles Unidos only served as a temporary palliative, prolonging its agony for a few years. Problems had been piling up for the company for many years, and, in the 1940s, it lacked the operating efficiency and financial capacity required for tackling them successfully. During those years, the exploiting company had milked the deteriorated western railroad and the still profitable Almacenes de Regla (Regla Warehouses) of practically the last pound sterling they could produce, leaving the aging system without any hope of attaining the operating efficiency it needed.

A large number of factors had led Ferrocarriles Unidos to such a disastrous state that its final liquidation seemed just around the corner. The first factor, of a general nature, affecting all economic activities in Cuba equally, was a result of the dependent, single-crop Cuban economy. The country's entire future was dependent on a single product and one main market, without any growth possibilities. Its ups and downs were determined by its sugar exports.

A second factor—a more specific one, since it affected the railroads in particular—was that of competition by highway transportation. This was expressed more sharply in the western region, where paved roads were more abundant and the towns were closer together. Because of this, it would not be very profitable for the railroad to increase the number of trains or try to take over the operation of trucking and bus companies, as Ferrocarriles Consolidados had done in Cama-güey and Oriente Provinces. Therefore, Ferrocarriles Unidos had few possibilities for challenging that kind of competition successfully.

Factors of a business and technological nature rounded out the far from encouraging picture for Ferrocarriles Unidos. The old English company, a manifestation of an imperialism that had been powerful in another age, had been fighting a rearguard action ever since World War II, and, rather than confronting the new situation with its old combativeness, its owners dithered between keeping it alive and liquidating the troublesome, not very profitable business. Their economic policy in Cuba during the past few years had consisted almost exclusively of quickly extracting what meager profits it produced.

Technological factors also conspired against the smooth functioning of Ferrocarriles Unidos, for the railroad's equipment dated from the company's founding. This mainly meant that its installations and equipment were technologically outdated, but this wasn't all. Ferrocarriles Unidos had incorporated a group of independent companies in its system. When they joined, they constituted a complex network, and, even though some duplicated branch lines were eliminated, the system continued to be difficult to operate, both because of lack of capacity at the sidings, with resultant long waits for trains, and because of the poor state of the tracks, which limited the trains' speed to sixty kilometers per hour. Other operational deficiencies stemmed from the inadequate use of equipment and the policy of economies followed with regard to repairs and renovations—which had been practically reduced to zero.[10]

Its financial situation was equally difficult. Many dividend payments were due on the company's stocks and bonds, having accumulated over the past fifteen years, and they had to be paid. And, to top things off, the Cuban government had undermined the mortgage securities of the bonds by exercising its sovereign right of eminent domain. In doing so, it took some of the company's urban land holdings, worth more than 8 million pesos, for urban renewal projects without having previously initiated the proceedings corresponding to those expropriations.

The same thing happened with the government's debt for services. It amounted to 5 million pesos in 1949 alone,[11] making for a total of 12.7 million pesos that the government owed the railroad. This particular situation led to continuous demands for payment, which the railroad company addressed to the Grau administration. The demands covered compensation not only for "property encroached upon" and the costs continually entailed for rebuilding the railroad yards, relaying lines, and the like but also for the government's responsibility in continually authorizing wage increases, which meant greater expense for the work force.

During a visit the British minister to Cuba paid on President Grau in Havana, the former pointed out, on behalf of the British Foreign Office, that Great Britain was Cuba's second most important trading partner and that the treatment given to English railroads in Cuba would certainly cause annoyance in London.[12]

Ferrocarriles Unidos's untenable situation came to a head in 1948. Up until then, the company's crisis had been quantitative, of a cumulative nature; from that year on, it changed qualitatively. According to the estate owners' publication, the company's income was 25 to 30 percent lower in 1948–49 than it had been in 1940–41, yet the monthly wages for its workers had increased by 195 percent, both because it had hired more workers and because workers in the sector were getting higher average wages.[13]

In February 1948, the government agreed to new demands by the workers and decreed a 5 percent wage increase. That action was the first in a series of events that created an emergency for Ferrocarriles Unidos. The owners claimed that they didn't have enough cash, so a demagogic railroad political hack suggested a formula by means of which the government should pay the wage increase out of the fiscal income that the company handed over to the public Hacienda. On July 1, 1948, that administrative irregularity became law, through Decree 2304. It stated the following:

> The Unidos and Expreso companies have alleged and demonstrated that the economic condition of their businesses doesn't permit them to defray the cost of the 5 percent increase that Resolution 7332 of the Ministerio del Trabajo [Ministry of Labor] prescribed on February 5, 1949. Therefore, it is ordered that the amount collected by the 2.75 percent tax on Unidos be used to set up a special account in the Tesorería General de la República [General Treasury of the Republic]. Those amounts will be turned over to the companies only to pay the 5 percent wage increase.[14]

When Decree 2304 went into effect, it closely linked the government, the company, and the workers—whose leaders tossed the sector's Caja de Jubilaciones y Pensiones (Retirement Fund) into the pot. That irregular procedure led to frequent overdrafts and spectacular transfers of funds, which meant that the workers did not always get paid on time.[15]

In spite of that irregular procedure, the company began to take its own economy measures in early 1949, firing workers—which, of course, triggered protests.[16] Carlos Prío Socarrás, former minister of labor (*trabajo*) and then president of the republic, had to solve the conflict.[17] For that purpose, he issued Decree 1122, of April 1, 1949, appointing engineer Sergio I. Clark, a former minister of communications (*comunicaciones*), as special comptroller of Ferrocarriles Unidos with limited powers. A few months later, the company began laying off a thousand workers and reduced wages by 20 percent, thus making the situation even more delicate.[18] The workers asked that the company be placed under government control.

The situation in the summer of 1949 made it necessary for the government to take a new step toward taking over Ferrocarriles Unidos—and Almacenes de Regla, the Compañía Internacional de Expresos (International Express Company), Ferrocarril Central de Matanzas (the old Ferrocarril de Dubrocq), and all the appurtenances and accessories of those entities in Cuban territory. The government takeover was carried out without delay on June 9, 1949, through Decree 1755,[19] thus initiating closer ties between the poor management prevailing in

Ferrocarriles Unidos and the corruption that was traditional in public administration in neocolonial Cuba.[20]

Ferrocarriles Consolidados de Cuba was in better shape than its western counterpart for successfully taking advantage of the possibilities the war provided for its sugar rear guard. Neither U.S. capital's financial capacity nor the company's operating links had suffered during the war. Together with this, Consolidados's superior technological and organizational conditions enabled that company to instill great dynamism in its mode of operations and profit from the conditions generated by the war and the postwar period.

Moreover, the Cuban government's differences with Ferrocarriles Consolidados were much less serious than the ones it had with Ferrocarriles Unidos. The Cuban government owed Ferrocarriles Consolidados only 1 million pesos in 1946, and the government's public works plan had not affected that company's property.[21]

More important, the Cuban government treated the differences it had with the U.S. company with more solicitude and care than it did the claims presented by the minister of His Brittanic Majesty[22] and, as a result, did not allow problems with it to accumulate. It also kept a lower ceiling on its debts to the U.S. company than on its debts to Ferrocarriles Unidos.

One of the aspects that showed Ferrocarriles Consolidados's vitality most clearly during the period in question was that of competition with automotive transportation. Ferrocarriles Consolidados's agents went out to drum up business for its services, and the company increased its radius of operations by purchasing transportation companies of various kinds, including everything from buses to coastal schooners. With them, it established combinations that were favorable to the railroad.[23] The company drew up its first project for getting a monopoly on road transportation in 1941. Its essence is set forth in the following passage:

> Our company's direct or indirect intervention in motorized highway
> transportation, far from being detrimental to the railroads—which now
> constitute and will continue to constitute the most important investment
> from our point of view—is sure to have a beneficial effect on the railroads
> themselves, including Unidos, since it will neutralize the uncontrolled
> competition which highway transportation has posed for us for so many
> years, forcing us to adopt special rates, which have considerably limited
> the income of several railroad transportation companies.[24]

By carrying out that project, it obtained the La Cubana and Flota Amarilla bus companies, which operated a total of fifty-two vehicles. With them, it founded the Omnibus Consolidados de Cuba, which ran between Santiago de Cuba and Havana, Palma Soriano and Bayamo, and Bayamo and Manzanillo.[25] The insolvency and chaos of most companies in the trucking sector led Ferrocarriles Consolidados to refrain from purchasing many of them. It limited itself to taking over the operation of the Wells-Fargo express company, reorganizing it as the Expresos de Cuba company, and combining railroad and highway cargo transportation.[26]

The most important expression of Ferrocarriles Consolidados's expansionist vitality was in the railroad sector itself, with the addition of the Guantánamo and Western to the group composed up until then of the Cuba Railroad Company and Norte de Cuba. The Guantánamo and Western was a small company that had only just managed to survive the bankruptcy of the Spanish and Cuban banks. It seems that a mortgage loan given it by the Cuban government had enabled the company to survive—but not its board of directors. Antonio San Miguel, a banker, had presided over the board from 1923 until his death in 1940; then Francisco Bartés, representing his interests, became chairman.

Guantánamo and Western operated in a very mountainous area, in the southern part of Oriente Province. Even though its tracks were not very long—147 kilometers—it offered some advantages, which made it a desirable prize. First of all, the area served by its short network did not have any highways, both because it was mountainous and because the governments in the republican period had not been interested in building any. Therefore, the railroad seemed to be permanently safe from competition.

Second, the Guantánamo and Western had stable foundations, for it had solid contracts for transporting the sugar produced by eight sugar mills—more than four million sacks of sugar, each weighing 325 pounds—and freighters put in frequently at its terminal of Boquerón, on the Bay of Guantánamo. In addition, during those years, a branch line had been built that linked the railroad with the U.S. naval base at Guantánamo, which guaranteed that it would have additional freight and passengers.[27]

For Ferrocarriles Consolidados, control of the Guantánamo and Western offered several advantages. Consolidados's manager, Gustavo Pellón Acosta, summed them up as follows. Control of Guantánamo's tracks and its terminal at Boquerón would make it possible to draw off part of the import business from Santiago de Cuba to Guantánamo, from whose docks it could be carried exclusively by rail to the interior of the country, without any danger of having that service challenged by automotive vehicles. Having a terminal farther to the east would make it possible to control a very extensive area and, at the same time, make more efficient use of those installations by linking them to a larger company than the Guantánamo and Western. Control of that railroad would ensure that it would not become dependent on one of the sugar companies in the region, with which it had very stable ties. And, finally, the railroad would serve as a starting point for what the manager of Consolidados called "the most practical and cheapest way of expanding eastward" toward areas not yet exploited by any system of land transportation whatsoever.[28]

The Guantánamo company had fifteen steam locomotives, twenty-seven passenger cars, and 450 freight cars. In the 1940s, it took no more than 2 million pesos a year to keep them up-to-date. The company had managed to weather the storms of the 1930s with few problems; only in fiscal year 1932–33 had it reported any losses.[29] The only unfavorable entry registered in its balance sheets was a result of its providing financial assistance for some sugar mills in the area, especially the Santa Cecilia—a total of 250,000 pesos which couldn't be collected.[30] With an authorized capital of 5.7 million pesos, the company's acknowledged liabilities amounted to only 3 million pesos' worth of bonds bearing 6 percent interest, held by the Irving Trust Company, of the United States.

The project for purchasing the Guantánamo and Western was presented to the Consolidados board meeting of November 5, 1948, which decided to approve the operation, using Ferrocarril del Norte de Cuba as the legal purchaser, since that company was registered as Cuban.[31] The total sales price was 3,740,000 pesos, 2,740,000 of which would be payment for the stock. Ferrocarriles Consolidados obtained 86 percent of the voting stock.[32] Two weeks later, the Guantánamo and Western became a subsidiary of Ferrocarriles Consolidados, with representatives of both companies having seats on the board of directors.[33]

The absorption of the Guantánamo and Western gave Ferrocarriles Consolidados the possibility of future expansion northward and eastward in Oriente Province. The operation was considered a first step toward purchasing the railroad operated by Guantánamo Sugar,[34] with which it would hold a monopoly on the railroads in that extensive region. It would be an advance toward the monopoly integration established twenty-five years earlier by the Tarafa Law.

The financial, organizational, and technological differences that were noted between Ferrocarriles Unidos and Ferrocarriles Consolidados were deeply accentuated during World War II and in the postwar period. To some extent, those differences were transmitted to the railroad workers, forcing them to confront regional problems that were specific to each company. However, aside from the problems of a more or less local nature, which the conditions of each system engendered, the railroad workers recognized goals that corresponded to the general interests of the sector. They were mainly related to two aspects: the search for the necessary unity of the railroad workers and the struggle to improve their living conditions. Some earlier efforts had been made to improve the difficult situation in which the workers had been submerged since 1935.

Up until around 1937, the Cuban labor movement was split, its unity destroyed by the violent repression to which it had been subjected during the March 1935 strike. Contacts between the cadres of the disbanded Confederación Nacional Obrera de Cuba, the Partido Comunista, and the railroad workers' movement were reestablished, but clandestinely. In those difficult circumstances, the labor organizations in the sector were able to regain their legal standing only if they were tied hand and foot by false "labor" leaders who served the interests of the owners. In some of them, such as the Morón Unión and the Unión de Talleres de Camagüey, the reorganization process was carried out on relatively more democratic bases, which meant that they had more progressive leaders.

The official activity of the restored labor organizations was languid and bore little fruit for the workers during the first few years. Most of the work agreements that were signed during that period confirmed situations that were disadvantageous for the railroad proletariat. However, a renovating trend had grown in Delegation 2—Havana—of the Hermandad Ferroviaria, through the organization initially called the Grupo Pro Unidad and, later, Renovación Ferroviaria. The basic work of the new organization was concentrated on creating a common front that would represent the true aspirations of the workers in the sector.

The changes that took place in the international arena were favorable to the work of Renovación Ferroviaria. The struggle against fascism caused a change in national policy, leading the country along a more democratic path. In line with that progressive trend, the Partido Comunista de Cuba was legalized in 1938 and was authorized to publish a newspaper. In 1939, the Confederación de Trabajadores de Cuba (Cuban Workers' Confederation) was founded, and an Asamblea Constituyente (Constitutional Assembly) was held in 1940 to give the country a constitution that was more in line with the times.

Renovación Ferroviaria campaigned among Havana's workers and succeeded in getting Ricardo Rodríguez elected president of the organization's Delegation 2 in 1938.[35] The fact that the railroad workers in the four western provinces were linked to a single organization,[36] the Hermandad Ferroviaria, helped the delegations in their railroad centers to coalesce around the strongest delegation, that of Havana, and follow its orientations, forming a bloc that acted independently of whatever guidelines the Dirección Central of the Hermandad might issue.

The struggle for unity in Camagüey and Oriente Provinces, however, came up against greater difficulties, because of the proliferation of organizations. The city of Camagüey, the most important railroad center in those provinces, had not only Delegation 1 of the Hermandad Ferroviaria but also its Dirección Central, the Unión de Talleres, the Asociación de Empleados de Oficinas, and Trabajadores Unidos de Cuba. The Morón Unión guided the workers on Norte de Cuba's lines, and five different delegations of the Hermandad Ferroviaria headed the workers' collectives in Oriente Province, sometimes following independent criteria. Meanwhile, the situation was particularly unfavorable for unity at the headquarters of the Hermandad Ferroviaria, because it suffered directly from the diversionist influence of Ferrocarriles Consolidados, which concentrated its efforts on splitting the workers into castes and creating a sense of collaboration between labor and capital.[37]

In the final years of the 1930s, the mechanisms favorable to unity in the railroad workers' movement were put to the test—both internally and, together with the rest of the proletariat, through two main problems that had to be faced: the sugar companies' violations of the Tarafa Law and the economy measures that the railroad companies decreed in 1939 and 1940.[38] Even though, in the second case, the struggle galvanized unity within the sector, the unity of the labor movement as a whole was threatened in the first case because lack of compliance with the Tarafa Law turned the workers of the railroad and sugar sectors against each other.

The confrontation between the sugar and railroad sectors stemmed from the already old contradiction between the interests of the sugar mill owners, especially in Camagüey and Oriente, and those of the railroad companies grouped in Ferrocarriles Consolidados. That contradiction was exacerbated by reiterated violations of the law by such sugar mills as the Patria, Adelaida, and Stewart, which not only exported sugar from other sugar mills but also, in the case of the first two, opened a new private port—Chicola—in direct contravention of the law in effect.

The fact that sugar was diverted to the private ports was beneficial to the sugar workers, up to a point, because it increased the volume of operations in those ports—and, therefore, the possibility of jobs and wages for workers linked to transportation and shipping operations. For the railroad sector, those diversions meant reduced income and, therefore, wage reductions as economy measures decreed by the companies.

Disputes between the railroad and sugar companies filled the Cuban court calendars. In seeking to increase the owners' profits, managers pushed the limits of the law farther and farther with each shipment of sugar through a private port. Dozens of files against shipments through Palo Alto, Guayabal, Santa María, and Chicola continually stirred up the railroad and dock workers against the sugar workers, citing Antilla's, Puerto Tarafa's, and Pastelillo's right to export. The refined tactic of using the workers to defend the interests of the owners was formulated by Gustavo A. Pellón, then comptroller general of Consolidados:

> One of the resources which I consider best in view of the circumstances is the mobilization of large nuclei of the classes which are adversely affected either directly or indirectly, getting them to engage in protests. This will counter and overwhelm that propaganda which, if it should grow stronger, might, through the repeal of the October 9, 1923, law, bring about the most complete bankruptcy of Consolidados's interests in Cuba.[39]

The bitter railroad-sugar struggle reached such a point that the unity of the labor movement was threatened during the Conferencia de Unificación Obrera (Labor Unity Conference), which was held in the city of Camagüey on December 18 and 19, 1938. The conflict between the workers led to arguments, and only the skill of labor leaders Justo Tamayo and Lázaro Peña managed to bring about a temporary solution of the problem, putting it on the agenda of the Congreso Obrero Nacional (National Workers' Congress) that was to be held in Havana in January 1939.[40] In spite of protests by representatives of the sugar and dock workers, the Congreso Obrero Nacional, which was finally held between January 23 and 28, 1939, passed a resolution respecting the Tarafa Law.

The railroad workers' continual struggle against the "economy" measures that the companies repeatedly imposed was of special importance in the struggle for their unity. Ever since the beginning of the 1930s, the railroad companies had systematically reduced wages and laid workers off. Even though this process had slowed in 1935, since it was felt that the payroll adjustments had been completed,[41] the two largest companies in the country—Unidos and Consolidados—announced new reductions in personnel and wages in 1939, based on the upsets that the situation in Europe was causing in Cuba's trade. The lowest-income—track, construction, and repair shop—workers were the hardest hit. Some were reduced to working only two days a week, and others were laid off entirely. In addition, wages were lowered.[42]

All the workers of Ferrocarriles Unidos mobilized around the leaders of Delegation 2, under the watchword "Economies, No!"[43] The company began to put its plans into effect quickly, while the railroad workers carried out their class activities publicly, using all possible means to make their position known. They even went so far in their demands as to request that Ferrocarriles Unidos be nationalized.[44] The support given to the movement by the recently created Confederación de Trabajadores de Cuba forced the government to intervene in the conflict. The economies could not be prevented, but limits were set for them. Thus, this first protest movement brought out the sector's possibilities for promoting the struggle for unity.

Unification, which was promoted during the following years, could not be achieved in organization until August 24, 1941, when the railroad workers' collectives in Camagüey and Oriente Provinces formed the Frente Unido de Colectividades Ferroviarias (United Front of Railroad Collectives). The Frente Unido's members worked for Ferrocarriles Consolidados and Guantánamo and Western—that is, they had been organized in the Dirección Central of the Hermandad Ferroviaria and its Delegations 1, 11, and 12; Camagüey's Unión de Talleres; the Morón Unión; the Asociación de Empleados de Oficina; the Sindicato Ferroviario; and Trabajadores Unidos de Cuba.[45]

The initial manifesto of the novel entity was filled with unquestionable class spirit and reflected the conditions in which the railroad workers struggled during World War II. Its main points denounced Nazi fascist Falangism and recognized the need to struggle against that system and its manifestations in Cuba; pointed out that the war meant greater profits for the companies but greater sacrifices for the workers, who could not obtain the wage increases they needed to meet the higher cost of living; and noted that, to increase their exploitation of the workers, the companies violated the legislation in effect and the work agreements that had already been approved.

To the aspects set forth in the manifesto of the organizations in the Frente Unido were added the specific demands of the various collectives: higher wages, to bring them in line with those of other workers; the rehiring of those who had been laid off in 1935 and who were still jobless; and the hiring of more personnel, to ease the work load of the workers and the degree of exploitation to which they were subjected and also to provide more jobs for the unemployed, of whom there were many in Cuba at the time.

Even though the organizations and collectives represented by the Frente Unido retained their organizational autonomy, their integration constituted a solid step forward for unity in the railroad sector. Thus, the workers in the two large circuits of railroad transportation were amalgamated in two main spheres: those in the west were grouped around Havana's Delegation 2, and those in Camagüey and Oriente were united for the first time in a common front.

The framework in which the Cuban labor movement developed in the 1940s, especially during the war and postwar years, was favorable for waging a united struggle that led to strikes in only some cases. The manifestations of the class struggle in the railroad sector were mainly directed toward improving the workers' living conditions in the midst of an inflationary situation that hammered on them constantly.

The constitution that was approved in 1940 led to the beginning of a new stage of legality, which gave the people's movement possibilities for promoting democracy in the country.

The war's effects on Cuba's economy were seen in an increase in national income which led to a greater demand for consumer goods. Since Cuba's industry could not produce all of the goods that war restrictions made it impossible to import, the prices of merchandise rose steadily, in spite of government-set price ceilings. As a natural result of the inflation, the labor movement centered its demands on higher wages, to keep the workers from having to bear the brunt of the crisis in supplies.

The movement for better living conditions for railroad workers began with Delegation 2 (Havana) in 1940, and some wage increases were obtained. In

September 1941, several demands were presented to the management of Ferrocarriles Unidos. Among other things, they called for a 26 percent wage increase and a minimum wage of 45 pesos a month, payment for holidays and days of national mourning, vacations with pay, and the payment of allowances for expenses and lost time. It also called for sanitation measures.[46] Several of those demands were granted by presidential decree in May 1942. They included wage increases ranging between 4.5 and 8 percent, vacations with pay, and half pay for sickness and for time lost due to rain.

The workers' triumph gave prestige to the procedure known as compulsory arbitration and conciliation, which the government established because of the pressure that the Confederación de Trabajadores de Cuba brought to bear, to solve conflicts between the workers and the owners without resorting to strikes for as long as the world war lasted.[47]

In 1943, the railroad labor movement achieved greater unity of action, as was demonstrated on April 3 of that year when a mass meeting was held in Havana's Central Park, showing the strength and organization of the railroad collectives. The demands made that day were granted by presidential decree on April 24. The main concessions were related to the establishment of a minimum wage of 50 pesos a month and wage increases of between 10 and 20 percent.[48] However, the decree benefited only the workers of the big companies, excluding those who worked for the smaller ones. As a result, mass movements continued, seeking to extend those benefits to all the railroad proletariat, and the workers in Delegations 10 and 11, corresponding to the easternmost railroads, went out on strike.[49] The situation created by the paralyzation of Ferrocarril de Guantánamo's trains led to direct intervention by the general secretary of the Confederación de Trabajadores de Cuba and railroad leader Ricardo Rodríguez, who managed to solve the conflict in favor of the workers.[50]

Struggles to raise the workers' standard of living continued, and they achieved new gains in 1944, when a minimum wage of 75 pesos a month was approved. Moreover, those benefits were extended to railroad workers throughout the country.[51]

New wage demands were presented to President Grau San Martín in May 1945. The workers asked for a 25 percent increase and a minimum wage of 90 pesos a month, plus the discussion of a new work agreement, the norming of jobs in all the companies, employers' contributions to the sector's Caja de Jubilaciones y Pensions (Pension Fund), and seniority pay.[52]

The government's lack of receptivity to the workers' demands led to an intensification of the struggle. Negotiations were finally held in August and resulted in a new decree that established a minimum wage of 85 pesos a month and wage increases of between 5 and 10 percent. In addition, it forced the companies to pay

TABLE 17.3. Minimum Wage Increases and General Wage Increases in the Railroad Sector, 1943–1946

Year	Increase (in percent)	Minimum Wage (in pesos)
1943	50	60
1944	40	75
1945	25	90
1946	30	110

Sources: ANC, Fondo Ferrocarriles, legajo 245, expedientes 1 and 11, and Hoy, January 5, 1944, p. 8.

a bonus for seniority.[53] During the months that followed publication of the decree, the railroad companies, hoping to pressure the government into approving new increases in railroad transportation rates, refused to comply with its terms.

During the Primer Congreso Nacional Ferroviario (First National Railroad Congress), the workers' response to the companies' attitude was to call a general work stoppage in September. The announced strike, which was effected on September 21, forced the companies to do what was stipulated. Other strikes aimed at pressuring the more recalcitrant companies to comply with the decree were held between January and August 1946, against the Guantánamo and Western and Ferrocarriles Unidos, in Havana.[54]

The steadily soaring cost of living led to new workers' demands soon after the former ones had been granted. In December 1946, the struggle was mainly aimed at obtaining a minimum wage of 110 pesos a month and a 30 percent general wage increase. The Grau administration, guided by the U.S. State Department, replied by engaging in systematic activities to divide the railroad workers' movement, but, even so, the movement managed to push its demands through to success in March 1947.[55]

In short, the minimum wages and increases that were attained between 1943 and 1946 meant a substantial increase in the railroad workers' income. As Table 17.3 shows, wages increased progressively during those years, but the effects of those increases were attenuated by the steady rise in the cost of living, which caused an inflationary spiral that was expressed very clearly in the class struggle.

The struggle against economies and the systematic work to raise the standard of living were unquestionably important factors in the attainment of a community of interests in the railroad workers' conglomerate and were responsible for the achievements in the sector. The unity attained, which was based on the organic integration of the collectives and associations of workers of this important means of transportation, was accompanied by the germs of division. Most of the members who had come from the Partido Revolucionario Cubano (Auténtico) were infected with it, as were some agitators and opportunists.[56] The sense of identification among those elements was based on militant anticommunism, and their work as a whole was systematically aimed at weakening the revolutionary labor movement and, sooner or later, at obtaining control not only of the workers' collectives but also of the highest organ of the proletariat: the Confederación de Trabajadores de Cuba (CTC).

Elements considered traitors to the labor movement stepped up their activities starting in 1942. In an interview granted to the organ of the Partido Comunista, railroad leader Ricardo Rodríguez stated this publicly:

> The elements of the Comisión Obrera [Labor Commission] of the PRC [Partido Revolucionario Cubano] do most of their work in this sector, particularly in Delegation 2, which is like the head that directs all railroad workers. . . . First they fought to obtain antiunity representation in the 3rd Congress of the CTC, and then they fought to win the elections in the delegations.[57]

The situation in Camagüey and Oriente was much more vulnerable to divisive attacks because of the many organizations there and because there was a strong reformist trend in the Dirección Central of the Hermandad Ferroviaria. There, the attacks were felt within the collectives that were most closely attached to the movement for unity in the sector, such as the Morón Unión, the Unión de Talleres, and the Asociación de Empleados de Oficina, the last two in Camagüey.

The Morón Unión was the first victim of those efforts. That came about in April 1943, when a group close to that trend called for the creation of a Delegation 17, claiming that the Morón Unión was run by Communists. Hermandad Ferroviaria President Carlos Zacarías Barrios,[58] representing its Dirección Central, supported the petition.

The delegations in Guantánamo and Santiago de Cuba had to deal with a specific situation that arose in May 1943 concerning the benefits that had been granted to workers in the big railroad companies, which had not yet been extended to those of Ferrocarril de Guantánamo. Contrary to the slogans of the 3rd Congress of the Confederación de Trabajadores de Cuba, which called for struggling without adversely affecting the war effort, they called a strike. For more than two weeks, the strike paralyzed sugar transportation. The promoters of the strike were egged on from Havana by Eusebio Mujal, a traitor to the labor movement.[59]

In 1944, an apparent truce in the divisive efforts began, because the Comisión Obrera Nacional of the Partido Revolucionario Cubano (Auténtico) joined the Cuban labor union—unquestionably, a tactical step to gain representation in the 4th Congress of the Confederación de Trabajadores de Cuba and, later, to partici-

Railroad workers' protest in Camagüey against fascism and the cost of living and in favor of a single railroad workers' union.

pate in preparations for the Primer Congreso Nacional de Trabajadores Ferroviarios (First National Congress of Railroad Workers). On May 20 of that year, Dr. Ramón Grau San Martín, president of the Partido Revolucionario Cubano, had won the election for president of the republic with a landslide victory, which offered the possibility of government support for the trend which the Comisión Obrera of that party continued to represent.

In mid-1945, preparations began for the Primer Congreso Nacional de Trabajadores Ferroviarios. Its general aims were a discussion of the problems that weighed most heavily on the railroad workers and especially the possibilities of uniting all workers in the sector in a single organization.

The congress was held September 13–15. All of the delegations of the Hermandad Ferroviaria and other railroad workers' organizations were represented. Even though it was a little late in coming, the congress did constitute a serious attempt to unite and strengthen the workers in the main means of transportation. Starting in its inaugural session, which was held in Havana's Campoamor Theater, the 299 delegates took up specific tasks that were of interest to the railroad proletariat.[60]

The main issues were related to norming wages on a nationwide basis; changing the pension law, requiring owners and workers to put in equal amounts and calling for government contributions; having labor represented on the Comisión Nacional de Transporte; maintaining high levels of employment and wages in the postwar period; creating a section in the Ministerio del Trabajo (Ministry of Labor) to rule on railroad workers' claims; and restructuring the Federación Nacional Hermandad Ferroviaria.[61]

The resolutions of greatest interest in the congress concerned issues that the work commissions had already taken up. They demanded that the workers who had been laid off by Ferrocarriles Consolidados be reinstated; denounced the massive layoffs of seasonal personnel and the companies' shutting down of services; and gave the recently elected Executive Committee thirty days to gather the data required for standardizing wages, in line with Article 62 of the constitution of the republic.

The congress also stated that Decree 2325, of August 1945, should be implemented; called for a minimum wage of 85 pesos a month for railroad workers and a 10 percent wage increase for all personnel;[62] demanded that seniority bonuses be paid to workers; called for a Departamento de Asuntos Sociales (Social Affairs Department) to be created in the Ministerio del Trabajo; demanded that each worker to be laid off for any reason whatsoever be given a month's wages for each year worked; called for the workers to be represented on the Comisión Nacional de Transportes; and asked that the pension law be modified to include contributions by the owners and the government.

The delegates to the congress also passed two resolutions of a political nature: a petition that diplomatic and trade relations be broken off with the regime in power in Spain and a greeting to the Pro República Española (Pro Republican Spain) and Sociedades Negras (Black Societies) conventions, which were being held in the capital.

The most important issue for the sector's unity was tackled successfully when it was resolved to create a national organization to direct the railroad workers in the class struggle. The main document containing the bylaws of the new labor organization stated that, "acting in line with the legislation in effect, the organizations representing the railroad workers hereby set up an agency called the Federación Nacional Hermandad Ferroviaria de Cuba [Railroad Brotherhood of Cuba National Federation] as the central entity representing and guiding all of them. This labor union is of a constructive nature, in accord with the democratic principles of the nation." The Federación Nacional's main office was established in Havana, so the railroad workers' headquarters was in effect moved to the capital of the republic.[63]

The railroad workers' organic unification in a national federation unquestionably constituted a great step forward, in contrast to the atomization and ideological deviations that characterized the sector—which, though one of the first to have been organized in the country, had suffered from disunity right from the start. The struggle to improve the workers' living conditions played a key role in that five-year process and continued to be important when the first congress in the sector was held. This took place in the midst of a struggle to achieve compliance with Decree 2325, which called for wage increases and a minimum wage for all railroad workers.

Complete integration was too much to hope for, however, not only because of the composition of the executive itself but also organically. The reformist elements' pressure, combined with the masses' demand that Ricardo Rodríguez be general secretary of the organization, led to the creation of three more posts: those of a president and two vice-presidents. This meant that power was less centralized, which the reaction made use of later on.

Toeing the line of the United States's cold war policy, the Grau administration began an offensive against the revolutionary labor movement, combining the dirtiest gangster tactics with political demagoguery. Internationally, the government signed military pacts and treaties with the United States and obediently voted as the U.S. government told it to in the United Nations. The key ingredient in all this was anticommunism as a government policy, which was applied at all institutional levels.

Partido Auténtico rule was continued by Carlos Prío Socarrás. Minister of Labor under Grau, he became president of the republic in 1948.

At first, the Grau administration had seemed to support the struggle for unity that was being waged within the labor movement. Using that unification current, the corrupt, reformist elements—who would later act as a Trojan horse, obedient to the owners and the dictates of Washington— gradually insinuated themselves in the movement. They then served as the base from which repression was unleashed against the organized labor movement when the V Congreso Obrero (5th Workers' Congress) was outlawed. Prestigious labor leaders were assassinated, and the organizations' locals and the Central Sindical (Labor Union Headquarters) were attacked.

The V Congreso Obrero was convened in February 1947, in the midst of the reactionary offensive that the government had unleashed. The government both used the traitors who infiltrated the movement and officially egged on the attacks. The president of the republic, in his metaphoric prose, had told the press, "The CTC cannot be in hands other than those of patriotic workers, because the CTC is the legitimate daughter of the first Auténtico administration. I never thought it would fall into the hands of those who upheld doctrines that introduced alienating customs in the country."[64]

The delegates of all nine hundred labor unions that sent delegates to the congress (there were a total of twelve hundred in the country at the time) sought unity for the labor movement. The railroad workers were no exception. The government, however, supported and promoted the holding of another workers' congress at nearly the same time as the one called by the Central Sindical. The Comisión Obrera of the Partido Revolucionario Cubano (Auténtico) and the so-called Comité Obrero Nacional Independiente (Independent National Workers' Committee) fell in with the government's plans and responded to its call. The congress representing the true interests of the workers was held on May 9,[65] and the anti-Communist one, on May 13.

That tragic period for the labor movement was reflected in the words of outstanding labor leader Lázaro Peña: "Think of all that unity will bring us: demands, rights, and respect. Think, comrades, that you are accompanying the divisionists and that division among the workers serves only the foreign imperialists and the owners who exploit us."[66]

The government's maneuver was completed with the nullification of the unifying congress that had been sponsored by the Communist leadership of the Confederación de Trabajadores de Cuba and with the removal of its legitimate leaders from the headquarters of that organization. In a second stage, it went on to the systematic, individual destruction of each of the collectives that remained faithful to the principles upheld by that body.

The methods used against the legitimate representatives of the railroad workers in no way differed from those employed against the other labor sectors. The leaders who were imposed carried out one part of the destructive work—that of waging campaigns to discredit the Communist leaders and making the workers who steadfastly opposed the government's maneuvers anathema.

The impostors then engaged in a second level of aggression, banning the workers' publications at the local level.[67] The campaign was then upped to a third level of intensity, because of the usurpers' inability to get the workers to recognize them as leaders[68] and the workers' refusal to turn over the locals, which belonged to the labor movement, to them. Force was then used to wrest from the workers what they were unwilling to give up voluntarily.

Attacks on the union locals took many forms, depending on how much resistance the workers put up, the extent of the divisive elements' political conspiracy, the size of the repressive apparatus of the state, and the personality of the participants in those acts of violence. Different procedures were used in each delegation of the Federación Nacional Hermandad Ferroviaria de Cuba.

Because Delegation 2, Havana, was considered a very important center and, for several years, had directed the railroad workers' movement in the west, the attack on its local is worth describing in detail. The individual whom Carlos Prío had appointed to head Delegation 2 was infamous among railroad workers as an informer and political hack.[69] Nearly all the railroad workers in Havana prepared to join their true leaders in defending their union and kept the usurping leaders from taking over for nearly a month. They also carried out protest demonstrations in various work places in Ferrocarriles Unidos. Because of the railroad proletariat's staunch attitude, the government resorted to attack as the only way to impose its will.

Roberto Alonso, head of Delegation 2's local, described the attack as follows:

> We were awakened at around 5:30 A.M. on the 7th of this month by heavy blows on the door of the local. It sounded as if many people outside were trying to force their way in. Even before we had decided what to do, we saw the pane of glass over the entry fall with a crash, and a sergeant of the national police pulled himself through the opening and into the local, revolver in hand. After severely reprimanding us for not having opened the door, the sergeant proceeded to remove the iron bar which held the door shut. Since he didn't have a key for opening the lock, he and some people outside—who turned out to be officers of the national police—forced it.[70]

The captain of the local police appeared, and Ricardo Rodríguez, the leader of Delegation 2, had a long argument with him. It ended with the police notifying the railroad leader that "from then on, the police would be in charge of the local and the union's property. We would all have to leave, by force if necessary, and not even a member of the Comité Ejecutivo of Delegation 2 of the Hermandad Ferroviaria de Cuba could go back in the local of that organization, much less use its belongings."[71]

Workers all over the country struggled against that state of affairs, mainly through the Comité de Reivindicaciones (Claims Committee) and the Comité de Lucha (Fight Committee) of the Federación Ferroviaria, which continued to seek unity and recognition of the workers' demands. Under the auspices of those organizations, the Segunda Conferencia Nacional Ferroviaria (Second National Railroad Conference) was held on May 13, 1948, promoted by the militant leader Ricardo Rodríguez.

The ousting of the pro-unity leaders from their positions in Cuba's labor unions placed the leadership of the proletariat in the hands of pro-owner elements. Their personal greed led to new splits which further weakened the workers' defense of their class interests.[72] Under those conditions, the II Congreso Ferroviario (2nd Railroad Congress) was held in Camagüey on December 17, 1947,[73] ushering in a period in which the owners could count on the complicity of the so-called leaders of the proletariat.

In the Shadow of the Bourgeois State

The fleeting respite that World War II gave the Cuban economy began to fizzle out in the late 1940s as the world economy returned to normal. A slight drop in the price of sugar in 1948 and 1949 was the first indication that the good years were drawing to an end. However, U.S. intervention in Korea brought about a new war, so the favorable market situation was prolonged for a few years more. The collapse finally came in 1953, when the price of sugar dropped to an average of slightly under 4 cents a pound.

In 1952, Cuba had scored a record for sugar production: a little over seven million tons. Therefore, it was forced to hold a considerable part of its sugar in warehouses and to establish a system of restrictions on future sugarcane harvests, in a new attempt to stabilize the world price of sugar. With no possibilities for expanding the production of its main product, Cuba returned to the difficult economic model it had had prior to the war, which condemned it to stagnation. It could not be otherwise. The 1940s had been favorable for Cuba, but no essential transformation had been made in its economic characteristics. Its single-crop economy, dependence on trade, and poor use of its natural and human resources—all of those factors which, combined, made for a permanent situation of crisis—had remained intact, weighing on the life of the country.

In contrast, the postwar world offered a panorama that was very different from that of the preceding decade. The defeat of fascism had led to the appearance of a bloc of socialist countries in Europe and Asia. In addition, the old colonial empires were quickly falling apart, with a growing number of new states breaking away from them. The two processes emphasized a crisis of the capitalist world system, which was seriously weakened by the war. The United States, the only capitalist power that emerged strengthened from the conflict, assumed the leadership of the system in crisis, exercising hegemony based on the economic clout of the dollar and threats of an atomic war.

In that "cold war" climate, international relations were characterized by an acute ideological confrontation. Economically, the experience of the world crisis of 1929 and the postwar demands for recovery favored greater interweaving of the capitalist economies in circumstances that were extremely favorable to U.S. economic dominion. Thus, a series of international economic agencies—some of which, such as the International Monetary Fund, the International Bank for Reconstruction and Development (World Bank), and the General Agreement on Tariffs and Trade, were attached to the United Nations—was created, through which U.S. interests implemented their decisions with the apparent endorsement of a world consensus.

This international atmosphere made itself felt in Cuba in diverse ways. Ever since 1946, the Auténtico governments had taken advantage of the "cold war" conditions to seize control of the labor movement. Under the slogans of saving the country from "foreign ideas" and the "Communist threat," a wave of repression was unleashed whose real aim was to cut short the independent development of the labor movement and wrest its most recent achievements from it.

The new currents of world capitalism, aimed at broadening governmental responsibility for and participation in the economy, were echoed in Cuba with the appearance of such agencies as the Banco Nacional de Cuba (National Bank of Cuba) and the Banco de Fomento Agrícola e Industrial (BANFAIC—Bank of Agricultural and Industrial Development). Their purpose was to regulate and stabilize the country's economy and to provide the government with financial tools for making the economy more dynamic. In the relaxed functioning of neocolonial policy, however, this instrument inspired in Keynesian ideas not only placed the nation's financial resources at the service of the domestic bourgeoisie and U.S. investors but also spread the defects of criollo politicking to the economy, opening up new sources of wealth to the ruling circles.

At the beginning of the 1950s, Cuba entered a new (and violent) upsurge of the national crisis. Faced with the uncertain prospects of the sugar market, the country displayed all of the fragility of its traditional single-crop economy. The ruling political force—the Partido Revolucionario Cubano (Auténtico), or Cuban Revolutionary (Authentic) Party—was incapable of contributing any real solutions for the nation's problems. It had made a bad name for itself in the exercise of power, having failed to satisfy even the most basic aspirations of the masses and also having failed to make U.S. capital and the criollo bourgeoisie very happy. These last began to view the political demagoguery of the Auténtico with disfavor, since it no longer served their interests.

The Cuban political process had virtually exhausted the reformist formulas that had governed its development since 1940. In those circumstances, the masses of the people hoped that, if the Partido del Pueblo Cubano (Ortodoxo), or Cuban

People's (Orthodox) Party, an organization containing the healthier elements of the reformist current, took power, it would provide possibilities for cleaning up Cuban politics. However, in the international situation then in force, that possibility involved a risk that was unacceptable to imperialism.

Therefore, the conditions for a military coup were created, and, on March 10, 1952, the coup took Fulgencio Batista to power. Batista's de facto government was the tool that the most reactionary circles used to confront the impending crisis. It was a "hard-line" government, without any electoral promises, which could apply the restrictive measures which were needed in the economy, create new ways for handing over the nation's resources, and—above all—unblinkingly deprive the proletariat of its hard won achievements.

However, by shutting down the "democratic" free play of factors in the economy, the Batista tyranny also marked the end of an era. The people's aspirations, which became ever more radical, now had to seek other channels of expression. The July 26, 1953, attack on the Moncada Garrison by a group of young people headed by Fidel Castro blazed a new path.

In mid-1949, in view of the evident symptoms of a contracting sugar market, the administration of Carlos Prío Socarrás had asked the World Bank for a loan of $200 million. In response to that request, the bank decided to send a mission to Cuba to study the economic situation and recommend a series of measures, which, following the usual practice of those financial institutions, would have to be applied by the government before any loan would be granted. Cuba was thus inducted in the complicated liturgy of financing from "international" agencies, a practice that would burden and shackle more than one Latin American country in the following decades.

The World Bank mission, headed by lawyer and historian Francis A. Truslow, president of the New York Curb Exchange, reached Cuba in August 1950 and spent three months in the country collecting information on various aspects of the Cuban economy. On returning to the United States, the Truslow mission drew up a voluminous and slightly improvised report replete with recommendations for solving Cuba's economic difficulties.[1] The report was completed in the summer of 1951, but the members of the mission felt that there was one matter of particular urgency and that they should present their views on it to the Cuban government immediately: the rehabilitation and reorganization of Cuba's public service railroads.[2]

The brief and disturbing synthesis of the railroad situation, which the mission presented in December 1950, constituted a sort of summing up of the prolonged crisis in Cuba's railroad sector. The picture described was only just short of distressing. The maintenance budgets approved by the public service railroads in the previous decade had not permitted either of the two systems to acquire modern or even relatively modern equipment. In the case of Ferrocarriles Unidos, its budget had not even allowed it to provide adequate maintenance for its tracks. The situation of Unidos was, unquestionably, the more chaotic of the two. More than 400,000 of the sleepers on its tracks had to be replaced urgently, and 16 percent of the spikes that held the track in place had been lost. The rails on more than fourteen hundred kilometers of track were thirty or more years old, and there was practically no gravel on vast sections of the line.

Even though the situation of Ferrocarriles Consolidados's tracks was more encouraging, both companies had very old rolling stock. The average age of the two companies' locomotives was between thirty and thirty-six years, and very few cars in circulation had put in less than twenty years of service.

In addition to the deplorable technical-operational situation, the Truslow mission pointed out that "Both railway systems are today overcapitalized in relation to present or reasonably foreseeable earning power or real asset."[3] Ferrocarriles Consolidados was far in arrears in paying dividends on its 30 million pesos' worth of preferred stock and also had to meet a consolidated debt amounting to more than 22 million pesos. The financial state of Ferrocarriles Unidos was even worse, for its debts and overdue dividend payments amounted to close to 100 million pesos.

What made that situation particularly serious, however, was the prospect that the railroad service would deteriorate yet again and more seriously while the companies were paying their debts. This would be caused not only by foreseeable limitations on the growth of the sugar industry, whose products accounted for 80 percent of the freight transported by the railroads, but also by the new upsurge in automotive transportation in the postwar years.

With its supplies of equipment, spare parts, and fuel reestablished at levels even higher than in the prewar period, automotive transportation was once more the railroads' most dangerous competitor. Between 1946 and 1950, the number of registered trucks increased by 93 percent, reaching a total of 29,638 vehicles. Moreover, the largest increases had been in trucks with the greatest carrying capacity. In 1948, it had been estimated that automotive vehicles carried 21 percent of all the freight transported in the country. That cargo included a high proportion of general merchandise, which brought the highest rates. In addition, trucks carried more general merchandise than the railroads did in absolute terms; it constituted less than 20 percent of the railroads' freight.[4]

It did not require much perspicacity to see that the public railroads were entering a relapse in their long crisis, one perhaps just as serious as the one experienced during the depression of the 1930s. Now, however, it would affect a railroad service with much more dilapidated, older equipment, whose operating conditions testified to prolonged deterioration. As a result, the railroad crisis could be quite serious for the Cuban economy as a whole.

The Truslow mission's report was fair in pointing out that it would be utopian to believe that Cuba could survive without its public railroads. Road transportation could not carry all the freight that had to be moved in the country and, even in that hypothetical case, would always be more expensive than and not as safe as the railroads, because of its greater dependence on external conditions, supplies of spare parts, and fuel. Therefore, it was absolutely necessary for the Cuban economy to maintain its railroad service at acceptable operating and efficiency levels.

In analyzing Cuba's railroad situation, the World Bank mission had observed details objectively, but it credulously ignored the key fact that the problems of Cuba's railroads were deeply rooted in the general crisis of the country's economic structure. Since it failed to address that key issue, the solutions it recommended could be little more than palliatives, to keep the "chronic illness" of the railroads from ending in death. Those recommendations clearly showed what interests lay behind the experts of the international financial institution.

The recommendations that the Truslow mission drew up for solving the railroad problem were divided in two large groups: one concerning matters of a general nature and the other, more detailed, group proposing a plan of specific action.

The general considerations, which were drafted in a restrained, technical style, weighed the "great alternatives" for solving the railroad crisis, pointing out the advantages and especially the disadvantages of nationalizing the service and the conditions that should be created to guarantee its efficient functioning in private hands.

Those conditions required "effective management," a euphemistic term used in referring to the railroads' "labor problem." In fact, the Cuban labor situation had become an obsession to the drafters of the report—so much so that they hammered away at it throughout their voluminous production. For the World Bank experts, the wage and legal advances won by the Cuban proletariat were far above what the country could afford and constituted the main obstacle to the mobilization of investment capital. In the specific case of the railroads, the mission considered that the companies were overburdened with more workers than they needed. Therefore, "effective management" meant making it possible to engage in massive layoffs so that, with fewer workers, the companies could introduce a work regime that would make their workers more productive.[5]

The aims behind the program of action were very precise; they sought a "solution" for the situation created by the government's intervention in Ferrocarriles Unidos. Therefore, the mission recommended:

1. That United and Consolidated should be combined into a new company and operated as a single railway system.
2. That individual sugar companies should acquire a substantial minority

interest and a minority participation in the control of the new railway company by purchase from it for cash of a class of its shares which will provide such a minority interest and participation.

3. That the government of Cuba give its full support to the reorganization and provide such reasonable assurances, with respect to payment of existing obligations, payment of new services, conditions of employment, conditions of competition with other forms of transportation, and other matters, as may be necessary to permit the new company to carry out an appropriate program of rehabilitation and to operate on a self-sustaining basis.[6]

The implications of such a program are easy to see. With the government taking over Ferrocarriles Unidos and its British owners withdrawing, the fusion of the two companies would, in fact, mean giving Ferrocarriles Consolidados control of the country's entire railroad service. In essence, implementation of the proposal would create a gigantic railroad monopoly under U.S. control. The World Bank's recommendations entirely coincided—by chance?—with Ferrocarriles Consolidados's interests. As we will see, that company had begun trying to absorb Unidos in 1949.

But that wasn't all. The takeover would offer the U.S. interests a tasty mouthful, but the report also asked the government to support the operation with a series of guarantees that would ensure the success of the business. In concluding its report, the mission recommended that the reorganized company—that is, the new monopoly—remain in contact with the World Bank "since it probably seems necessary or desirable at the appropriate moment for the reorganized company to seek a loan from the Bank to help its rehabilitation program."[7] The Cuban government could have no doubts about what "solution" the World Bank was willing to finance. Truslow's solution wasn't easy to apply, however, because extremely diverse, contradictory interests surrounded the complex situation that had been created around Ferrocarriles Unidos, and it took several years for the English company to emerge from the crisis.

Placed under limited government intervention in April 1949, Ferrocarriles Unidos de La Habana was subjected to complete government management in June of that year, when a presidential decree appointed a comptroller with full powers over the railroad company and all of its related businesses. The government intervention, carried out to stabilize the economic functioning of the railroad, in fact infected the railroad's management with some of the vices characteristic of the corrupt republican bureaucracy.

José Morell Romero, who was appointed comptroller plenipotentiary in June 1949, saw to it that his first actions were accompanied by tremendous fanfare in the press. A naive observer basing his opinions on newspaper articles might have thought that the wily President Prío Socarrás had appointed a magician to head up the railroad company. The report on the first month of government management declared that the railroad's income had risen by 5,000 pesos and pointed to an increase in purchases of Ferrocarriles Unidos stock on the stock exchange as an "encouraging symptom." The next month, income increased by 58,000 pesos. Shortly after the announced intervention, a "very advantageous" purchase of 1,347,000 pesos' worth of rolling stock in the United States was announced.[8] That was the first "serious" step toward the railroad's technical rehabilitation.

The publicity offensive began to get bogged down in November, however, when it was learned that comptroller Morell had urgently asked President Prío to pay 300,000 pesos on the government's debt to the railroad so it could meet its undeferrable expenses. It didn't take long to discover that, instead of reducing costs, Morell had added to them by spending 5,000 pesos a month on publicity; that most of the recently purchased rolling stock was obsolete; that the already unwieldy roster of railroad workers had had to be further enlarged to accommodate the appointments made by the comptroller; and that, even in the dicey economic situation of the business he was managing, the comptroller had given himself a very high monthly salary.[9]

Early in 1950, the government decided to replace discreetly the Ferrocarriles Unidos comptroller. Raúl Ramírez, the government's new representative, took a more cautious approach than his predecessor and limited himself to making abstract declarations of optimism.

When the accounts were drawn up at the end of the first year of government management, they showed that the company's operating deficit had quintupled. The questionable administrative virtues of public bureaucracy would not put Ferrocarriles Unidos's shaky finances back on a sound footing. From then on, the railroad company would limp along on the basis of periodic injections of government funds—which amounted to 1,317,000 pesos in the latter half of 1950 alone.[10]

Government intervention placed the English owners of Ferrocarriles Unidos in an ambiguous position because, although the company was still in existence and retained its legal liability, its officials had been removed from all administrative functions. Their first reaction to the intervention was irate: they presented various judicial complaints contending that the government's decision was unconstitutional.[11] However, the owners' lack of much insistence on those procedures gives the impression that it was nothing but grandstanding for the benefit of their stockholders, for the intervention lined the railroad up nicely for what the group that controlled the company really wanted: its liquidation.

Starting in 1949, R. G. Mills, president of Ferrocarriles Unidos, began traveling to Havana on a regular basis, keeping in close touch with high-ranking Cuban government officials concerning the future of the company. As the months went by without any signs of a governmental solution to Unidos's problem, the English-men began to become restive and decided to bring pressure to bear on President Prío. That pressure was partly diplomatic, exerted through the Foreign Office and the English ambassador in Havana, who paid frequent visits on the president and the minister of state (*estado*).

Supported by the concern of his government, the president of Ferrocarriles Unidos personally delivered a kind of ultimatum to Prío. It contained three alternatives for immediately solving the situation that had been created. The first of these entailed an immediate end to the government's intervention, leaving the company able to go about selling the business. In that case, it was considered indispensable that the government participate in the sale, since it was the only entity able to guarantee that the purchaser would have the means required for putting the business back on an even keel.

The second alternative was total nationalization, by means of which the gov-ernment would obtain full possession of the company's property and would pay it a satisfactory compensation. The third variant was partial nationalization, which would leave all of the company's holdings except the railroad in British hands. Those holdings consisted mainly of valuable urban real estate. Note that none of the three alternatives that the British presented implied their remaining in the railroad business, which shows their firm decision to withdraw from Cuba.[12]

Evasive as ever, President Prío took advantage of the World Bank mission's presence in Havana to suggest to the president of Ferrocarriles Unidos that he present his ideas to Mr. Truslow, to see if he would include them in a general plan that would provide a real solution for the railroad problem. Mills and Truslow had close and cordial relations, based on a community of interests, for the British aim of achieving a satisfactory sale of their property fit in perfectly with the U.S. interest of promoting a railroad monopoly under U.S. control.[13] Satisfied with that understanding, Mills returned to London, where he informed his stock-holders of his hopes that the plans proposed by the World Bank mission would favor the rapid solution of the railroad problem.[14]

On receiving the World Bank mission's proposals, the Prío administration fell all over itself praising the work and stated that it would give it a detailed study. However, it was careful not to take any concrete steps to approve its implementa-tion. The railroad program which the bank recommended was based on a general reorganization of the railroad system, which would mean the elimination of some and unification of other departments—repair shop, express, and others. It also called for the modernization of equipment and operating procedures. All these measures would result in large-scale layoffs.

To support a program of this nature on the eve of a general election would have been little short of suicidal for the Auténtico government, whose popularity was already waning. The serious implications of the mission's proposals wouldn't have gone unnoticed by the railroad workers, who had already expressed their opposition to attempts to apply them. If the government advanced in that direction, it would place the figureheads of the Auténtico unions, headed by Eusebio Mujal, in a critical situation. Installed in their leadership positions by means of government support and gangster-style procedures, they were having a hard enough time as it was, trying to "represent" the workers.

The government was fully aware of the serious poitical risks involved in a solution that would lead to a railroad monopoly controlled by Ferrocarriles Consolidados. Months before the Truslow recommendations were released, a U.S. lawyer called Conoley, representing an investment syndicate apparently headed by Ferrocarriles Consolidados, had presented a proposal for purchasing Unidos with the same monopoly aim. The government then began secret talks with the lawyer, but the Partido Socialista Popular (People's Socialist Party) denounced the maneuver, and the press had a heyday with it. That led to a mass meeting of the Unidos workers and forced the government to reverse its stand, withdrawing from the sales negotiations.

The principles of the workers' firm stand were set forth clearly by their most outstanding representatives: "We aren't opposed to progress . . ., but, in the conditions in which we find ourselves, in the conditions of capitalist production, and in this specific case—the planned monopoly for Ferrocarriles Unidos de La Habana—we are opposed to the scheme as long as there isn't any coherent plan for developing the national economy that will provide employment for the workers who are laid off."[15]

Even though the program that Truslow presented could not be applied immediately as a whole, Prío and his advisers considered some of its recommendations—particularly the one on giving the estate owners and sugar companies greater participation in the railroad business. The government interpreted the recommendation very loosely and began to maneuver to foist the problem of Ferrocarriles Unidos off on the sugar interests. They reacted strongly, rejecting the government's attempt, but Prío didn't hesitate to engage in blackmail, threatening the estate owners with a tax of 6 centavos on every sack of sugar to finance the government's purchase of the railroad. Forced to give way, the estate owners began to make concessions and agreed to stand surety for a loan that several Cuban banks would extend to Ferrocarriles Unidos in November 1951.[16]

At the same time, perhaps to gain time, the Asociación Nacional de Hacendados (National Association of Estate Owners) appointed a commission to study the situation of the railroad and determine the bases on which a company created by the sugar growers could take charge of it.[17]

All this fit in perfectly with the delaying tactics Prío adopted in view of the upcoming election, aimed at putting off a definitive decision on the railroad problem and handing that time bomb on to the administration that would succeed him in 1952. That maneuver also had a foreign aspect, for the government would have to face increasing pressure by the British, who were calling for a solution. For that purpose, Prío appointed a commission headed by Ernesto Dihigo, minister of state, to negotiate with the English. In their talks with the government commission, the British presented their sales conditions, setting a price of $14.5 million for all their property and also stating what payment procedures should be employed.[18]

In March 1952, the whole process of negotiations was cut short by the coup d'etat by means of which Fulgencio Batista's military dictatorship took power. At first, the de facto regime concentrated its efforts on consolidating its support among the various sectors of the ruling class by means of a series of promises and guarantees concerning its economic policy, a circumstance that freed the estate owners of government pressure so they could take charge of the railroad.

In May, Luis Chiappy, the comptroller whom the dictatorship appointed for Ferrocarriles Unidos, presented a new plan for solving that company's situation. As in the earlier attempts, this project considered a number of urgent measures, consisting of government payments to the railroad company to keep it functioning and a "definitive solution" that called for the government's purchasing the railroad and turning it into a joint enterprise, 51 percent of it owned by the government and the rest, by private stockholders. Even though the plan tried to offer some security to the workers, it was clear that its implementation would mean a wave of layoffs. In spite of that, it was supported by the railroad workers' "leaders," who had now become staunch supporters of the military dictatorship.

While the Chiappy Plan was the subject of furious arguments in labor circles, the government received several offers from private businessmen who wanted to buy the railroad, but it did not seem inclined to make a decision on the matter.[19]

In early 1953, journalist Raúl Cepero Bonilla published an article presenting the basic outlines of a new "solution" the government had drawn up. That plan, which had been devised by Joaquín Martínez Sáenz, the architect of Batista's economic policy, resurrected the old idea of a merger between Ferrocarriles Consolidados and Ferrocarriles Unidos. It was really nothing more than the old Truslow Plan dusted off, and the tyranny tried to apply its basic guidelines as far as they coincided with its possibilities and interests.

As the first step in that endeavor, the government would appoint Gustavo Pellón, president of Ferrocarriles Consolidados, as comptroller of Ferrocarriles Unidos. By doing so, it would create a management agreement between the two companies, leading to their merger three years later. As economic securities, the government would turn over 3 million pesos to Pellón as part payment of its debt to Ferrocarriles Unidos. It would grant tax exemptions to the railroads and would leave the new management free to close down services and lay off employees.

The workers strongly repudiated the plan. The more alert workers unmasked its real significance, not only for the railroad workers but for the nation's interests in general.[20] The serious resistance put up against the plan, plus the detailed and demanding conditions which Ferrocarriles Consolidados set forth for its implementation, resulted in its being shelved.[21] In those circumstances, a new purchase offer was tendered by a private businessman—Swiss millionaire Axel Wenner-Green, who added a picturesque note to the tragic situation of Ferrocarriles Unidos with his project for turning its railway network into a monorail system.[22]

The prolonged railroad crisis meant a steady drain on government funds in the form of subsidies and loans that would never be repaid, so the government decided to solve it. To do so, it adopted a plan very similar to the one outlined by Gustavo Gutiérrez, minister of the treasury in the regime, which proposed that the government purchase the railroad with a bond issue to finance the operation.

The "nationalizing" formula was established by Legislative Decree 980, of June 25, 1953, which also stipulated that, once the stock of Ferrocarriles Unidos de La Habana had been acquired, the railroad would be handed over to a joint venture, with both government and private capital. Even though the procedure was clearly defined, it took several months to put it in practice: the government encountered difficulties in placing the bonds for financing the operation on the local market, because the criollo bourgeoisie didn't easily accept the formula of a "mixed economy" enterprise.[23]

In view of the trouble it was having in placing the bonds, the government requested and obtained a $20 million loan from the Bank of America and the Hanover Bank, both of the United States.[24] With those funds, it paid the English owners $13 million, the last price set for their stock, retaining the rest for upgrading the railroad. After that, it set about reorganizing the railroad with the creation of Ferrocarriles Occidentales de Cuba, Sociedad Anónima, with an authorized capital of $30 million. Within that joint venture, the government held on to 17.5 million pesos' worth of stock—58 percent of the capital—and tried to get private businessmen to subscribe to the remaining 12.5 million pesos' worth.

That aspect of the plan was beset with difficulties. In particular, the estate owners, who should have purchased 5 million pesos' worth of stock, refused to have anything to do with the procedure, which they described as coercive.[25] In spite of the resistance, however, the stock that had been earmarked for private businessmen was finally purchased under the terms set by the government. Under the distribution achieved by the Batista regime, a considerable part of the railroad stock went to U.S. companies in Cuba, which was one more aspect showing the real nature of the "nationalization."

While the financial aspects of the railroad's reorganization were being worked out in high-level government and business circles, the management of the brand-new Ferrocarriles Occidentales didn't lose any time in beginning the "rehabilitation" of its service. The only thing was, the first rehabilitating measures consisted of firing several hundred workers, thus carrying out the sentence that had been hanging over them for the past five years.

After having benefited from the favorable situation created by World War II, Ferrocarriles Consolidados had three more good years, from 1949 through 1952. During the three fiscal years in that period, the two main companies in the Consolidados system, Cuba Railroad and Ferrocarril del Norte de Cuba, transferred net profits amounting to a total of 7,197,334 pesos to their surplus—and that didn't include the considerable income received from "products unrelated to the operation."[26]

Those circumstances enabled Ferrocarriles Consolidados to maintain far better operating conditions than Ferrocarriles Unidos, a situation that the Truslow mission noted in its report on Cuba's railroads. Even so, the World Bank technicians pointed out that Ferrocarriles Consolidados had excess capitalization in terms of present values and was subject to powerful arrears in its capital which implied a burden of liabilities that was "totally impracticable under present conditions."[27]

The financial maneuverings to which the companies in the Consolidados system had been subjected right from the moment of their constitution up to the consolidation effected in the 1920s had left a balance of an onerous debt. The total capitalization of Ferrocarriles Consolidados and its subsidiaries amounted to the astronomical sum of 89,275,000 pesos, of which no less than 30 million consisted of preferred stock with a fixed annual rate of interest of 6 percent—whose payments had been suspended since 1932.

In addition to this, there was a consolidated debt of approximately 25 million pesos. The accumulated interest and dividends due, which hadn't been paid for two decades, created a difficult situation for Ferrocarriles Consolidados and led its board of directors to decide to take advantage of the favorable situation at the beginning of the 1950s to put its finances back on a sound footing. For that purpose, the so-called Plan de Recapitalización (Recapitalization Plan) was put into effect in October 1951. It consisted of exchanging each of the 303,000 or so shares of preferred stock bearing 6 percent interest (mentioned earlier) for the following: a 100-peso bond, which would mature in the year 2001 and would pay 3 percent annual interest; a 29-peso joinder certificate; and a cash payment of 5.91 pesos.

With that maneuver, involving a relatively small immediate outlay, Ferrocarriles Consolidados freed itself of the financial burden of the unpaid dividends on its preferred stock, which had been accumulating since 1932; halved the interest rate; and set a new amortization period.[28]

Seeking similar aims as the Plan de Recapitalización, the board of directors of
Ferrocarriles Consolidados implemented a Plan de Reajuste de la Deuda Hipotecaria (Mortgage Debt Readjustment Plan), which went into effect in June 1952. It
was aimed at consolidating all of its mortgage debts, reducing the interest rate,
and extending the amortization period to 1970.[29]

Along with the regular mechanisms established by those financial reorganization plans, the Ferrocarriles Consolidados management implemented a policy of
periodically purchasing its subsidiaries' bonds as they were placed on the stock
exchange. Since the interest payments on those bonds were long overdue, they
were generally sold at prices far below their face value, which enabled the company to buy and cancel those debt certificates with an outlay that was only a
fraction of the amount required for their regular amortization. These stratagems
were essentially aimed at wiping out the small stockholders, so as to promote a
greater centralization of the company's capital. For the same purpose, the Ferrocarriles Consolidados management transferred certain services and income
from Cuba Railroad—a company with many small stockholders—to Ferrocarril
del Norte de Cuba, all of whose stock was held by Consolidados.

The financial recovery measures were of vital importance for Ferrocarriles
Consolidados's restoring the company's credit, which was an indispensable prerequisite for carrying out its plans for modernizing its equipment. The rolling
stock of the companies controlled by Consolidados—especially the locomotives,
which, on the average, were thirty years old—were too old to render efficient
service at a reasonable cost. The old steam locomotives, which had been repaired
and reconditioned over and over again, had already been totally depreciated and
could do only a mediocre and unsafe job—and that only on the basis of frequent,
costly maintenance.[30]

Encouraged by the economic conditions of the 1949–52 period, the board of
directors of Ferrocarriles Consolidados decided to implement a program of modernizing its equipment, a plan that would be known as "the dieselization plan,"
for it turned on replacing the steam locomotives with modern diesel-electric ones.
The program was inaugurated in 1951 when twelve 1,600-horsepower diesel-
electric locomotives that had been purchased from the American Locomotive
Company the previous year were placed in service. Their functioning was subjected to careful technical-economic controls, whose results would determine the
future course of the program. Between 1951 and 1953, Ferrocarriles Consolidados
purchased fourteen Budd motor coaches for its passenger service; 350 fifty-ton
boxcars; and nine more diesel locomotives, six of them similar to the ones purchased in 1950.

Convinced that the new equipment had had a beneficial effect on its operating
costs, the board of directors of Ferrocarriles Consolidados decided to purchase

Modernization of the Cuban railroads with the importation of German diesel engines in the 1950s.

fifty-one diesel-electric locomotives from the General Electric Company in 1954, with which it hoped to replace all of its antiquated steam locomotives. That 7-million-peso operation was carried out in an era in which Ferrocarriles Consolidados was once more hard hit by crisis, and it was possible only because GE extended credit for the deal. The purchase entirely exhausted Consolidados's mortgage and credit possibilities, so any more advances in its modernization program would be dependent on its obtaining financial backing from the Cuban government.[31]

The technical, organizational, and financial measures that the management of Ferrocarriles Consolidados took brought about interesting changes aimed at the "Cubanization" of the firm. Unlike Ferrocarriles Unidos, which had maintained an exclusively British management, Ferrocarriles Consolidados—ever since its beginnings with Van Horne and the Cuba Company—had upheld a policy of giving growing responsibility to Cuban officials in management. As a result, by the mid-1920s, after consolidation, nearly all the important posts in the eastern railroad system's management were held by Cubans—except that Domingo Galdós, an old official with a long record of service in Cuba Railroad, was executive vice-president. Thus, the handling of operational matters by Cuban officials was characteristic of Ferrocarriles Consolidados. And, when Galdós retired, he was succeeded by Gustavo Pellón, an official from Ferrocarril Norte de Cuba who, in the late 1940s, managed to attain considerable power in the railroad system's leadership.

The outstanding role that Cuban personnel played in management had not yet led to effective control of the business, however. Except for Tarafa's brief sojourn on the board of directors of Ferrocarriles Consolidados during the 1920s, the main stockholders and managers of the company were all U.S. citizens.

In the late 1940s, however, Cubans began to hold posts in other than strictly management spheres. In the spring of 1947, an investment group composed of sugar magnate Julio Lobo and his family, estate owner Esteban Cacicedo, and others began to make massive purchases of stock in the Cuba Company, and, by the middle of that year, controlled nearly half of the common and preferred stock in that firm. It seems that Lobo and his partners were not interested in management or in eventual control of a holding company. Rather, they wanted payment of the interest due on the stock acquired, for Lobo thought it might prove a saving, in view of the favorable situation with regard to sugar.

Payment of dividends on the stock, however, would mean mobilizing Cuba Railroad's operating funds to pay the debts of the Cuba Company, and F. Adair Monroe, president of the Cuba Company, refused to carry out an operation of that kind just to satisfy speculative interests. The confrontation led to a bitter struggle for control of the Cuba Company, in which the Lobo faction was finally defeated.[32]

To counter the attack, the managers of the Cuba Company had to engage in complex organizational and financial maneuvers, which involved allowing a group of important Cuban stockholders to enter the firm. One of those operations was the purchase of Guantánamo and Western—to which we referred in the preceding chapter—which left a large block of stock in the Cuba Company in the hands of the Bartés family.[33] As a result of those changes, the chairmanship of the executive committee of Ferrocarriles Consolidados was transferred to Cuba in 1948. Gustavo Pellón, who seems to have played a key role in the movements that led to Cuban investors' purchasing a large amount of stock in the Cuba Company, was named to fill that position.

The transfer of the railroad system's decision-making center to Cuba continued throughout the 1950s, first with the naming of Cubans to a majority of the seats on the board in 1953; then with the moving of board of directors meetings to Cuba in 1954; and, finally, with the dissolution of the Cuba Company in 1959 and the transfer of its stock to Ferrocarriles Consolidados and the Compañía Cuba, which were thus turned into independent entities.[34]

The reasons for that process can be understood in the light of historic circumstances. Ever since World War II, U.S. capital had been migrating to Cuba and leaving the less profitable sectors, such as the sugar industry, in favor of more remunerative investments in mining, foreign trade, and other branches.[35] Since the railroads were decidedly a low-profit sector, the Cuban stockholders' growing control of Ferrocarriles Consolidados may easily have been linked in some way to that migratory trend. Moreover, the railroads' growing dependence on the government favored their "Cubanization," since the mobilization of government funds to the railroads could be presented as assistance to a national concern that was confronting difficulties.

Certainly, there were plenty of difficulties. From 1952 on, Ferrocarriles Consolidados's economic situation again presented signs of crisis. After showing positive balances in its railroad operations for several years, Consolidados closed fiscal year 1952–53 with declared losses of 2,505,382 pesos, a situation that was repeated in subsequent years.[36] With problems characteristic of crisis, the old "economy" measures returned to the scene, this time presented under the solemn title of an "austerity plan." It became indispensable to cut maintenance costs; reduce or eliminate services; and, as the key savings procedure, cut back on wages.

Now, however, after the legislative victories the Cuban labor movement had won during the 1940s, wage "savings" could not be obtained by means of the easy administrative procedure that the company had used in the past, when it laid thousands of workers off during the depression of the 1930s. The mechanisms for firing workers were more complex now. Moreover, even though the company could count on the Batista regime's complicity, the regime had to observe some formalities with regard to Mujal's yellow labor union apparatus, which supported it. The Ferrocarriles Consolidados management, therefore, called in a firm of accountants to draw up a financial report to be presented to the government as a pretext for its authorizing the railroad to make "economies."[37]

Squeezed by the crisis, the railroad company desperately needed government assistance, and not only for solving its "labor problem." Consolidados needed financing to complete and extend its rehabilitation programs. It needed lower taxes to compensate to some extent for the contraction in its income. It needed higher rates, so its income would remain at an acceptable level in spite of the drop in the volume of freight it carried. It needed protection against the competition of automotive transportation. It needed many other forms of assistance, concessions, and favors, with which the government could help to keep it afloat.

The Batista dictatorship was not unwilling to play ball. The railroad received a conditional three-year tax exemption; was granted 500,000 pesos in credit securities on the Cuban treasury, to be deducted from the government's debt to the railroad; was exempted from customs duties and other taxes that would adversely affect "the dieselization plan"; and was authorized to make some rate increases. In addition, Ferrocarriles Consolidados obtained the promulgation of a legislative decree that banned the highway transportation of cattle, minerals, sugar, molasses, explosives, and fuel. It was a valuable safeguard against automotive competition.[38]

The collusion of the railroad monopoly and the neocolonial government, which boded nothing but ill for the workers, achieved its main goal when authorization was granted for making wage economies. Every study that was presented, like every plan that was proposed for putting the railroads back on a sound financial footing, contained justifications for the attempts to shift the brunt of the crisis onto the workers. In every case, the workers put up determined opposition to the measures, which led to a permanent state of conflict. Its climax was expressed in the insurrectional struggle.

During President Carlos Prío Socarrás's term in office (1948–52), the labor movement continued to suffer from the former Auténtico administration's attack on the labor organizations. The prevalence of corrupt, government-sponsored yellow unionism meant that the workers were represented more weakly, with their "leaders" concentrating on making deals with the owners and collaborating with the ruling party. In those circumstances, only the work of honest organizers in the work collectives kept the workers' struggle in defense of their rights alive.

The owners tried to push the labor situation back to the conditions that had prevailed in the years prior to the world war, cutting back on the number of workers, reducing wages, and casting off the bonds of the collective work agreements. In the railroad sector, that trend was particularly acute, for the large companies tried to make the workers bear the brunt of a crisis they hadn't caused.

Frequent conflicts broke out in the branches of Ferrocarriles Unidos, a company whose disastrous financial and operational situation had placed it under nearly complete government control. The reduction of personnel in Ferrocarriles Unidos, which began in 1947, was stepped up in September 1949, when eight hundred workers were laid off. At the same time, the railroad management announced the suspension of the wage increases it had granted in 1945 and 1946.[39] The vacancies created by laying those workers off were filled without respecting seniority, and the wage differences involved in those changes were not paid, in flagrant violation of the laws in effect.

As if emphasizing the magnitude of the abuse, while the company laid off old workers on the one hand, it increased the number of superfluous personnel on the other—to keep the promises it had made the government in exchange for governmental intervention and its commitments to the government-sponsored yellow union "leaders." Immersed in that atmosphere of arbitrary acts, the Unidos workers kept up their agitation, and frequent conflicts broke out.

The military coup of March 10, 1952, erased the already blurred outlines of legality, placing the labor movement clearly at a disadvantage for defending its achievements. After an extensive propaganda campaign, the dictatorship and the railroad companies engaged in joint efforts to cut the sector's wage fund immediately. The first important attack took place in the spring of 1953, when the union leaders in Ferrocarriles Unidos were informed of the details of the previously mentioned Chiappy Plan, which called for the imposition of obligatory retirement and layoffs with compensation.[40]

In spite of the workers' expressed opposition—which was channeled through "fight committees," outside the union organizations—the layoffs began in July, accompanied by the surprising measure of a general suspension of wage payments. The workers responded by walking off the job, to which the Batista dictatorship replied by appointing military supervisors to oversee the various branches of Unidos and by ordering that all workers who did not go back to work immediately would be fired. The executive of the Hermandad Ferroviaria, clearly demonstrating its complicity with the regime, ordered the suspension of the strike that the workers had begun spontaneously, promising at the same time that it would "do whatever is necessary to ensure that the reduction in personnel will be effected in numbers strictly limited to the needs of the companies."[41]

The strike was broken by repression. After that, the workers' protest took the form of a succession of disputes over each layoff or suspension of wage payments, to the extreme that work in Ferrocarriles Unidos was usually done at a snail's pace. In the environment of terror that the Batista tyranny created after the July 26, 1953, attack on the Moncada Garrison in Santiago de Cuba, a new, massive layoff of Unidos workers (decreed in August 1953) helped to create the conditions for implementing the project that would give rise to Ferrocarriles Occidentales de Cuba.

The railroad workers in the eastern provinces also suffered from "economy measures." In spite of its better financial situation, Ferrocarriles Consolidados did not entirely escape the effects of the depression that began in 1952, and, when its directors noted the drop in its income, they, too, decided to cut costs— especially wages.

As soon as the railroad workers became aware of the owners' intentions, they brought pressure to bear on their union leaders and got the Unión de Talleres de Camagüey, the Asociación de Empleados, and the Hermandad Ferroviaria in Camagüey to agree on a program of struggle against the projected "economies" in February 1953. The precaution proved wise. In a letter made public in April and May, the management of Ferrocarriles Consolidados announced wage reductions of between 8 and 11 percent, alleging diverse reasons for the action, including competition by automotive transportation and the fall in the price of sugar.[42]

The union "leaders" wanted the workers to be patient, but the more militant union organizers got the workers at the grass-roots level to decide to go out on strike if the company insisted on the wage cuts.

In view of predictions of a serious labor conflict, the management of Consolidados and the government decided to get a technical recommendation for justifying the economies and, at the same time, to wage an intensive campaign harping on the railroads' inability to make ends meet and to begin an "official" investigation into the company's economic situation.

Assuming that the barrage of publicity had had the effect desired, Batista surpassed himself by promulgating Decree 1155 of 1953, in which, after warning that it was "an aim of the government to maintain the level of wages and working conditions on the basis of and in line with business's real purposes and requirements and economic resources," he authorized the directors of Ferrocarriles Consolidados to make the company's wages proportional to the income it received.[43] The workers' vigorous response, however, led to the wage reductions' being postponed, for it was obvious that their application would generate a violent conflict, which the government wanted to stave off.

At the end of 1953, Batista decided to make his government legitimate, so he called for a general election, to be held in November 1954. Even though the outcome was taken for granted—Batista was the only candidate running for president—the dictatorship wanted to observe some formalities that would improve the regime's image abroad. That circumstance dictated a truce in its conflicts with labor, so the dictatorship engaged in a series of maneuvers to prevent any large-scale protests. While it left the wage readjustments pending, it offered economic assistance to Ferrocarriles Consolidados so the company could survive.

In November 1954, shortly after the electoral farce, the Consolidados management decided to begin hostilities. As its opening shot, it fired over a thousand workers. The company's aim was to reduce the payroll by 2.8 million pesos. To do so, it also announced a 20 percent wage cut for all workers.[44] The workers immediately protested by holding slow-down and sit-down strikes, which resulted in the suspension of a lot of trains in Guantánamo, Morón, and Camagüey.

In view of the seriousness of the situation, the Ministerio de Trabajo (Ministry of Labor) decreed a 15-day postponement of the "economy measures," to give the government time to present an appeal in the Tribunal de Cuentas (Office of the Controller of the Currency), the body that had to rule on the economic situation of Consolidados. The truce was accompanied by a new government loan to the company, but the company's managers weren't very willing to wait.

While stepping up their propaganda campaign about Ferrocarriles Consolidados's economic difficulties, its managers ordered company officials to ignore some of the aspects of the work agreement then in effect.[45] In January 1955, the company announced that it was withholding 40 percent of the workers' wages; suspending vacations with pay; and beginning pro rata payments for workers, to be in effect until the economic situation improved— all of which measures presumably were aimed at lighting a fire under the government.[46]

When they learned about the pro rata payments, the workers called a strike, which forced the government to maneuver once more, temporarily suspending the payment of discounted wages. Even though the government-sponsored yellow union "leaders" claimed that measure as a victory, they could not keep the strike from spreading to all the eastern provinces. Acts of sabotage were carried out as part of the strike movement, clearly showing that the workers' protest was beginning to reach the political sphere, in an open confrontation with the Batista dictatorship. The government did not hesitate to take repressive measures; it called out the troops to force the workers to go back to work, where some of them began a hunger strike.[47]

Impressed by the size of the protest, the government decreed another truce on February 8. This was to give all parties a hundred-day respite, during which it hoped the workers would calm down; it would negotiate with the union "leaders"; and the Tribunal de Cuentas would have time to hand down its ruling, on which the wage readjustment would be based. As on prior occasions, the cease-fire involved a government handout to Ferrocarriles Consolidados, this time amounting to 700,000 pesos.

When Batista took office as "constitutional president" in May 1955, he showed that the dictatorship hadn't changed at all. In the midst of the political crisis involved in that situation, the government issued Decree 1535, of June 7, 1955, which became famous as the "laudo ferroviario," or railroad finding. Taking the report of the Tribunal de Cuentas on the economic state of Consolidados as a base, the finding decreed solutions such as an annual 600,000-peso tax exemption for the railroads, with the money saved to be earmarked for the railroad retirement fund for three years, to facilitate the obligatory retirement of employees who had worked a certain number of years. The decree also allowed the company to reduce the workers' wages by 8 percent and recognized the company's right to cut back on the number of workers and to suspend service.[48]

Forty-eight hours after the finding was approved, the railroad workers went out on strike, paralyzing railroad service in the eastern half of the country. The head of the army issued instructions to the military districts affected by the conflict, ordering their forces to act energetically, considering every worker who didn't immediately go back to work to have been fired. The government-sponsored yellow union "leaders" found themselves trapped between the masses of strikers and the government's repressive apparatus. They had taken part in the discussions that had led to the finding, and now it was impossible for them to take an honorable stand at the side of the workers.

Faced with the government's repression, the displacements the company had begun, and the new talks suggested by the "leaders," the workers, fed up with being deceived, maintained their strike resolutely. While the trains that remained in circulation, guarded by the army, fell prey to acts of sabotage, public opinion was mobilized in favor of the railroad workers, and there were several expressions of solidarity with them.

Fidel Castro—who had just been released from prison, to which he had been sentenced for the attack on the Moncada Garrison—expressed the revolutionary movement's support for the rail workers when he told La Calle, "When the hacks who serve the vested interests write editorials supporting the foreign railroad company, we must speak out in favor of the workers. There is hunger for bread and hunger for freedom. We revolutionary combatants who are and will always be on the side of all good causes, with the poor of this world, express our support for them."[49]

The strikers' firmness made it necessary to consider modifying some of the articles of the finding and to reinterpret others. The government-appointed labor "leaders," terrified that they might be held responsible if they failed to control the strike, played a role in this. In the terms in which political struggle was waged in Cuba, strikes meant Communist and Ortodoxo opposition to the government.

The railroad workers' rebelliousness was negotiated by the government-sponsored yellow union and wound up in a no-strike pledge, which had to be submitted to the workers for their (signed) approval. The signatures were collected under threat by the repressive bodies, but the leaders of the Hermandad Ferroviaria didn't even wait for the signatures to be counted before they negotiated the agreement behind the backs of the masses. By virtue of that pledge, known as Acta Número XII (Memorandum Number 12), the strike movement was outlawed. That made it possible to apply the finding, both as regards the wage cuts and concerning the layoffs.[50] That last procedure was used selectively against the workers who upheld solid class positions and/or expressed their opposition to the Batista regime.

The dictatorship's escalation of repression, with continual acts of force in all aspects of the country's life, showed that all efforts or activities, whether conciliatory or not, that took place within the framework of the theoretical legality that prevailed at the time would be useless. Issues of a sectoral nature, therefore, were subordinated to the need to solve the key problem of Cuban life: how to overthrow the tyranny.

The Batista dictatorship had mobilized all its repressive means against the people's movement and was striving to shore up the neocolonial economy in the midst of the crisis. Faced with the drop in the price of sugar and with production restrictions, the government tried to make the country's economy more dynamic by mobilizing internal financial resources. This policy, called "compensatory spending," increased the government's role and influence in the economy to an extraordinary degree.

The Batista dictatorship was an extreme example of the process of degrading the bourgeois political models in Cuba, and it carried out its economic functions with scandalous irresponsibility. Government financial institutions proliferated, creating a veritable alphabet soup of entities in which it became very difficult to discern where public funds finally ended up.[51] They were squandered with a fine lack of concern on the construction of lavish projects; on financial "assistance" to powerful U.S. monopolies, such as Standard Oil and American Foreign Power; and on beefing up the repressive apparatus with technical aids. But, above all, funds were embezzled by the kingpins in the regime on a scale fantastic even to a country in which plundering the treasury was an old political tradition.

The railroads were not forgotten when it came to government handouts. We have already examined the procedures by means of which the government found a way out of the troublesome problem of Ferrocarriles Unidos. Ferrocarriles Occidentales de Cuba, the "joint venture" company that succeeded Unidos, was controlled directly by the main figures linked to the Batista regime,[52] which meant that a steady flow of government support was directed its way.

Even though it was privately owned, Ferrocarriles Consolidados was also on the receiving end of the government's munificence. The fact that the government had decreed and then repeatedly postponed Ferrocarriles Consolidados's "economy measures" had led it to assume direct responsibility both for the layoffs and wage reductions and for shoring up the company. With each postponement of the wage readjustments, the tyranny sent funds to Ferrocarriles Consolidados, either as loans or as payments on its debt for services.

Up to its neck in difficulties, the railroad company was unable to meet its payments for the diesel locomotives and other equipment it had purchased on credit in the early 1950s, but, once again, the government came to the private company's rescue. On December 22, 1955, it gave Ferrocarriles Consolidados a 700,000-peso loan ". . . to buttress the company's finances."[53] That loan was one of the first operations carried out by the Banco de Desarrollo Económico y Social (BANDES, or Socioeconomic Development Bank) since its founding in January of that same year. BANDES was the dictatorship's main tool for carrying out its program of assistance to private companies, pompously called the Plan de Desarrollo Económico y Social (Socioeconomic Development Plan). Consolidados was one of its main beneficiaries.

Less than a year after its first loan from BANDES, Ferrocarriles Consolidados once again called on the paragovernmental financial institution for help. This time, it asked for a giant, economy-sized handout, for it wanted to make a "serious effort" to recapture its lost passenger traffic, which required that the rolling stock for its passenger service be modernized and that the tracks be improved, so trains could go faster on them.[54]

BANDES approved the project without any great difficulty in November 1956, and a loan of 10 million pesos was granted for its financing. The bank used half of that money to purchase twenty-four self-propelled coaches and nineteen locomotives from the Fiat Company, of Italy, and leased them to Ferrocarriles Consolidados. That is, the equipment was paid for by the Cuban government, not the railroad.[55] The remaining 5 million pesos was made available to the railroad company for repairing its tracks.

That large-scale operation wasn't the last concession Ferrocarriles Consolidados got from the dictatorship's financial institution. Six months later, in April 1957, the railroad company asked BANDES for another loan— this time, 950,000 pesos for "working capital" for its subsidiaries, and it obtained three loans in a row (for a total of 3,090,000 pesos) the following year.[56] The Batista dictatorship had become the financial prop of Ferrocarriles Consolidados.

Adding up all of BANDES's loans to Ferrocarriles Consolidados and the 30 million-peso bond issue which that entity handled for Ferrocarriles Occidentales de Cuba, we see that the neocolonial government's assistance to the railroads during the Batista regime came to over 40 million pesos. Even though those funds made it possible to modernize the railroads somewhat, they contributed nothing toward solving their real problem. The funds were a palliative that made it possible to keep the railroads running, but they could not pull them out of their protracted crisis.

By mobilizing the nation's resources in aid of the railroad companies, the bourgeois government made the people pay for the consequences of a situation whose roots went back to the deformations of the neocolonial economic structure. Rather than seeking to provide permanent solutions, its job was to guarantee the continuity of the system in crisis. Thus, the financial resources that should have gone for economic development were used to shore up old, decaying companies. And the assistance given to the railroads was one of the more seemly uses the government made of public funds.[57] The policy of "compensatory spending" increased the public debt to unprecedented levels and produced continued and growing deficits in the country's balance of payments, quickly exhausting its fund of convertible currency. The Batista dictatorship not only subjected Cuba to a reign of terror but also led it straight to bankruptcy.

In 1956, the movement of opposition to the tyranny began to adopt more cohesive forms and a well-defined strategy of struggle. The creation of the Movimiento 26 de Julio (26th of July Movement) by Fidel Castro and the other survivors of the attack on the Moncada Garrison made it possible to channel the people's rebelliousness toward armed confrontation of the dictatorship. As the need for a new, more violent form of struggle was recognized, sectoral demands and actions that were bounded by a nonexistent legality became pointless.

With the battles waged against the 1955 finding, a whole stage of the railroad proletariat's struggle was left behind. The acts of sabotage and other actions of an insurrectional nature that had occurred during the strikes against the finding wound up as a constant expression of the rail workers' rebelliousness. Actions of this kind increased throughout 1956 as part of the preparations for the open war against the dictatorship.

At the beginning of December, Fidel Castro's promise to fight was kept with the landing of the expeditionaries of the *Granma*. In conjunction with that operation, the Movimiento 26 de Julio carried out a series of insurrectional actions in Oriente Province to provide cover for the expeditionaries on their arrival. A large group of railroad workers took an active part in implementing that plan. At about the time the landing was expected, twenty-eight acts of sabotage were carried out on Ferrocarriles Consolidados's lines, aimed at hindering the movement of the repressive forces.[58]

The railroad workers in Guantánamo, in particular, cooperated with the group that attacked the area around the Ermita sugar mill and cut off communication between that region and the rest of the province by derailing a train on the track between Guantánamo and San Luis. On December 2, the same day as the landing of the *Granma*, Delegation 11 of the Hermandad Ferroviaria (the Guantánamo and Western branch), supported by Delegation 10 (Santiago de Cuba), began a five-day strike in which the only thing the workers demanded was an end to the Batista tyranny.[59]

In spite of the initial setback dealt the expeditionaries of the *Granma*, the fact that a guerrilla nucleus headed by Fidel Castro had managed to establish itself in the eastern mountains raised the people's hopes, and the Sierra Maestra began to be identified as the political epicenter of Cuba. Meanwhile, underground fighters engaged in a veritable wave of acts of sabotage in the cities, which became both a battlefield against the tyranny and the effective rear guard of the nascent Ejército Rebelde (Rebel Army).

Batista's personal situation had become insecure at the time of the attack on the Palacio Presidencial (Presidential Palace).[60] Confrontation with the labor movement had to be avoided so as not to have too many complications. The threat of new railroad conflicts in the area Consolidados served triggered new flows of cash from BANDES to the company.[61] Barely two months later, Decree

1475 was announced. It canceled the 8 percent wage cuts decreed by the 1955 finding. Together with this, however, repression was applied indiscriminately against workers, students, and small farmers who were involved in the insurrection or who merely sympathized with it. As a result, that action couldn't possibly halt the revolutionary tide.

The railroad workers' insurrectional activities became quite important in the course of the revolutionary process. The railroad repair shops were turned into veritable arsenals. Molotov cocktails, packs of dynamite, and the like were part of the equipment of the underground cells in the Ciénaga repair shops. The huts that the track and maintenance workers used for storing their gear also hid those sought by the repressive forces and served as meeting places for the groups of conspirators. The repair shops in Guantánamo, though closely watched, provided technical support for the guerrilla struggle, especially after March 1958, when a new guerrilla front was opened in northern Oriente Province.[62]

On the fourth anniversary of the attack on the Moncada Garrison, acts of sabotage and agit-prop activities kept the tyranny's armed units busy in Havana and other cities. In Guantánamo and Camagüey, railroad workers observed the anniversary by halting work for fifteen minutes. And, on July 30, when revolutionary leader Frank País was assassinated, a huge strike was carried out in the Consolidados area in spite of betrayal and repressive measures.

That year, there were 226 acts of sabotage against Consolidados's track. The proximity of the guerrilla fronts to the company's installations and track created a crisis, especially in some parts of Oriente Province. In February 1958, writing to the chief of the naval post at Caimanera, the general manager of Ferrocarriles de Guantánamo noted that freight and passenger traffic had required increased vigilance because of the frequent attacks.[63]

Extending throughout nearly all of the nation's territory, the continual attacks on the railroads led the government and the companies to take more measures. First of all, they consisted of reinforcing the armed guards accompanying each train and of suspending those services that were most exposed to guerrilla activity.

As regards the first practice, the manager of Consolidados informed the president of that company in September 1958 that "the procedure of appointing armed guards for the trains has been disastrous in practice, because the surprise element and the fact that the train cannot leave the site of the ambush make it extremely unlikely that they will get out alive."[64]

As for the second, since it implied a reduction in personnel, the government-approved president of the Hermandad Ferroviaria dared to state, "As a supporter of the government, I oppose that measure, . . . since those workers [the ones who would be laid off] would be ready to join the ranks of the rebels."[65]

New economic difficulties stemming from the state of war in effect in Oriente

Province were now added to Ferrocarriles Consolidados's old ones. Continual acts of sabotage against the tracks, trains, and railroad stations not only meant interruptions in service and other losses but also resulted in loss of income, for the manifest lack of security in the service made customers reluctant to use the railroad. That situation led to closer ties between the railroad company and the Batista dictatorship. In May 1958, the minister of labor expressed the government's obligation to help the company remain functioning, a statement that was accompanied by a government handout of 500,000 pesos to the railroads "on account."[66]

Between March and April 1958, revolutionary activities reached a high level. The guerrillas spread beyond the area of the Sierra Maestra, and acts of sabotage by the underground movement were stepped up. All this was the prelude to a general strike that began on April 9. Even though the strike movement did not become large enough to topple the regime, it did demonstrate the Cuban workers' revolutionary militancy.

The railroad proletariat throughout the country took part in the movement. In Havana, where the strike took the form of acts of sabotage, the railroad repair shops in Ciénaga and Luyanó were centers of insurrectional activity. The strike as such had the greatest support in the Ferrocarriles Consolidados system, mainly in the Camagüey, Santiago de Cuba, and Guantánamo repair shops, where there was close contact with the guerrilla forces.[67]

The April strike was a valuable experience for the revolutionary movement, clarifying the role of the Ejército Rebelde as a strategic instrument of struggle against the tyranny and bringing out the need for a united workers' organization that would group the belligerent forces of the proletariat.[68] The creation of the Frente Obrero Nacional Unido (United National Workers' Front) was an extremely important step in this last regard. It strengthened the workers' solidarity and channeled their support for the rebel forces. At the same time, it used the workers' demands for mobilization purposes.[69]

After the failure of the April 9 strike, the tyranny unleashed a particularly virulent wave of repression against the revolutionary movement, even going so far as to take over some work places, either because of their strategic importance or because the insurrectional movement had attained considerable strength in them.[70] Ferrocarriles Consolidados was one of the companies subjected to this control, with a government supervisor in charge of keeping the railroad functioning efficiently.[71] That official coordinated his tasks with the corresponding military regiments, so as to guarantee protection for the trains and facilitate track repairs. (Several acts of sabotage against the tracks had been carried out during the strike.) At the same time, the supervisor asked for the "cooperation" of the armed bodies to solve whatever labor problems might arise on the railroads.[72]

TABLE 18.1. Comparison of Railroad Income, 1957–1958 (in pesos)

Company	1957	1958
Ferrocarriles Occidentales	13,666,108	14,490,110
Cuba Railroad	13,559,803	11,794,560
Ferrocarril del Norte de Cuba	5,558,124	5,401,328
Guantánamo and Western	2,531,462	2,008,866

Sources: Annual reports of the companies in 1957 and 1958.

An important part of the work of the supervisor who had been appointed on the railroads appears to have centered around mobilizing the company's resources so they could be used in the offensive that the tyranny unleashed against the Ejército Rebelde in May 1958. Enthusiastic over what he considered would be a sure victory for the Batista army, the supervisor hastened to inform his superiors that he had carried out his mission in full, since he had managed to normalize the movement of trains and no acts of sabotage against the railroad's property had been reported that month.[73]

The facts, however, were quite different: after the failure of the April strike, the insurrectional forces throughout the country had reorganized. In the Sierra Maestra, it was necessary to regroup the troops of the Ejército Rebelde to confront the huge offensive that the armed forces of the tyranny had unleashed against the revolutionary bastion. Even so, there were sixty-nine more acts of sabotage against Consolidados in June and July.

Acts of sabotage were carried out against the tracks, trains, and stations of both railroad systems during 1958, but most of the actions were directed against Ferrocarriles Consolidados, seriously affecting its freight and passenger operations. As may be seen in Table 18.1, the income of the companies in the Consolidados system fell considerably.

The government more than made up for the slightly less than 2.5-million-peso drop in Consolidados's income, for it paid 2.6 million pesos on account. With that money, the company paid off a part of its debt to BANDES and also paid wages for the period in question.[74] The government's constant handouts brought out the degree of Ferrocarriles Consolidados's dependence, while the use of those funds left a question mark hovering about the replacement of the company's president.[75] In October 1958, Consolidados pressed for yet another injection of cash from the government, which—facilitated by BANDES—was accompanied on that occasion by a nearly complete tax exemption.[76]

The defeat of the tyranny's army during its summer 1958 offensive marked a turning point in the revolutionary war. In a rapid counteroffensive, the rebel forces left their mountain redoubts and extended the theater of their operations throughout Oriente Province and to the central part of Cuba. With the expansion of the war and the revolutionary effervescence that was expressed in the cities in the latter part of 1958, the situation of the Batista regime became critical.

In September of that year, the general manager of Ferrocarriles Consolidados informed the head of the military district of Camagüey that the tracks were extremely vulnerable to insurrectional action and that train service was being paralyzed as a result. In view of the ineffective protection that the military forces in Las Villas and Oriente Provinces were providing for the railroads, the Consolidados official proposed that protection of the convoys and tracks be centralized under the Camagüey regiment, which would facilitate coordination with the company's administrative center.[77]

The consolidation of the guerrilla fronts in several areas of the country, especially in Las Villas, pushed the president of Consolidados to the brink of despair, since he could find no way in which the dictatorship could guarantee that the trains would keep running. In a letter addressed to the president of a Havana bank, the functionary described the situation in the first few days of December 1958 as follows: "The rise in the acts of sabotage, especially since the end of October, has physically paralyzed railroad transportation to such an extent that fifty-two bridges and culverts have been destroyed and more than seven kilometers of track bulldozed, which is equivalent to saying that more than 75 percent of our system cannot be used."[78]

When the sugarcane harvest of 1958–59 was about to begin, the government, together with the railroads, was forced to take measures to guarantee the most important productive activity in the country. The complicated links between the plantations, the sugar mills, the warehouses, and the ports, which the railroad provided, had been broken in several regions. Not only the appropriate materials but also the use of armed force was required to restore them. That knotty problem led to the idea of building an armored train that would serve as a mobile base from which repairs on the track and bridges in the areas where the guerrillas operated could be made quickly.

At the outset, the spectacular train was to have been built in Camagüey. However, in a meeting which the manager of Ferrocarriles Consolidados held with Colonels Leopoldo Pérez Coujil, chief of the military district of Camagüey, and Florentino Rosell, head of the army's Corps of Engineers, on December 11, the railroad company's representative noted that there were technical and economic drawbacks to having the work done there. He reiterated, however, that Consolidados was willing to provide all of the equipment necessary for building the train if it was decided to do the work in another city.[79] It seems that the railroad company's executives didn't want to let the cat out of the bag. Camagüey was too

An armored train, symbol of the last Batista military effort, derailed in Santa Clara by the troops of Column No. 8 of the Rebel Army under the command of Ernesto "Che" Guevara.

small a city in which to conceal the company's collaboration with the discredited dictatorship.

The head of the corps of engineers agreed to having the locomotive and cars sent to Havana to be adapted there, in the Ciénaga repair shops. The company also promised to assign two "politically sound" engineers to train technicians from the corps of engineers how to run the train. Moreover, Consolidados was to provide the materials and some crews to work with the soldiers repairing the track. This last promise was hard for the company to keep, because the tracks and maintenance workers were firmly opposed to doing any kind of work in collaboration with the army.[80]

While the rebel forces continued blowing up bridges and track and derailing trains,[81] the rolling stock for the military train was adapted in the Ciénaga repair shops. Many workers refused to take part in the task, and others gathered information and took photos to be sent through underground channels to the rebel command.

Workers in the railroad workshops in Morón support the nationalization efforts of the Cuban Revolutionary government.

The columns of the Ejército Rebelde began a general offensive in the second half of December, systematically attacking the tyranny's garrisons and other strongholds in towns and cities. The liberation of the towns progressed rapidly. On December 24, 1958, the rebel forces in Las Villas, under the command of Comandante Ernesto Che Guevara, entered their first provincial capital, Santa Clara. The battle of Santa Clara was of decisive importance for the dictatorship, because, if that strategic city fell into rebel hands, communication with the eastern half of the island would be cut off.

The staff (*Estado Mayor*) of the tyranny's army decided to send the armored train to Santa Clara at top speed. It left Ciénaga carrying logistic support and around 85 percent of the military personnel who were to have manned it. Thanks to that change of purpose, the armored train became the tyranny's last military effort. Shortly before the train's departure, the railroad workers in Ciénaga gathered together some civilian clothes, which they gave to the demoralized army recruits. This helped many of them to desert before the train reached its destination.[82] When the already notorious train reached Santa Clara, the rebels intercepted and derailed it.

The Ejército Rebelde's taking of Santa Clara on December 31 tipped the scales against the tyranny. A few hours after news of the battle's outcome reached Havana, the tyrant Batista and his closest collaborators fled the country. Thus, the derailing of the armored train became a symbol of the total defeat of the dictatorship. The crushing triumph of the armed struggle led to a popular insurrection. At the call of Fidel Castro, a general strike frustrated the last maneuver that the U.S. interests and elements of the Cuban bourgeoisie engaged in to try to install a "civilian-military" junta that would keep the revolutionary movement from coming to power.

With the triumph of the Revolution in January 1959, Cuba's railroads entered a new stage, characterized by a process of thoroughgoing transformations aimed at radically changing the socioeconomic structures in Cuba. The marked trend of government-supported railroad activity took on new meaning in that context, which was formalized in October 1960 with the nationalization of Ferrocarriles Consolidados and its subsidiaries. Since Ferrocarriles Occidentales had been a joint venture with majority government ownership right from the start, nationalization created the conditions required for the national system of public service railroads to consist of a single entity controlled by the revolutionary government. Cuba's railroads then entered on a new chapter that was entirely different from their long history.

Conclusion

The first railroads in Latin America were built not in any of the recently liberated republics but in one of the colonial survivals of the old Spanish empire: Cuba. Some of the colonial government's institutions, such as the Real Junta de Fomento (Royal Development Board), helped to make them a reality, but the government was not really responsible for that technological advance.

Railroads were introduced in Cuba at the initiative of the large Cuban sugarcane planters, who had increased their economic clout and political influence while the criollo groups in the rest of Latin America were fighting for their independence. The construction of railroads became a pressing necessity for those interests, whose power rested on an export economy based on sugar. The drop in the price of sugar on the world market forced the sugar producers to seek ways to lower production costs to guarantee the survival of their productive system. In the case of Cuba, that system was based on the barbaric exploitation of slave labor, which required continual renewal of the workers, and it became steadily more expensive when the slave trade was banned.

In or around 1830, the problem of land transportation was the bottleneck in the sugar cycle. For over three decades, the interests linked to that business had experimented with a wide range of solutions without coming up with any really economical ones. Road construction wasn't of the required quality, because the materials that were needed to build roads that would survive Cuba's subtropical climate and the characteristics and intensity of road traffic during the rainy season were not available on the island. That situation held back the sugarcane plantations' expansion toward the fertile land away from the coast, whose use would entail high transportation costs. River traffic had to be ruled out, because Cuba's rivers were not large enough and, in general, were navigable for only the first eight or ten kilometers upstream.

In view of the poor prospects offered by the traditional means of transportation, the railroads were a boon for Cuba's sugar producers. Therefore, it is hardly surprising that, barely a decade after railroads first demonstrated their commercial possibilities, the construction of a railroad was begun in Cuba, to link the rich

Güines Valley with the city of Havana. That first project was quickly followed by others, for the producers in various parts of the island, pressured by necessity, hastened to benefit from the manifest advantages of the new technology.

The identity of purposes that triggered that first wave of railroad projects in Cuba was responsible for the repetition of the same pattern in the design of the systems. Because of the long, narrow shape of the island, all of those tracks were laid out in a transversal, north-south direction, to link the inland productive areas with the nearest ports. Railroads were introduced in Cuba to take sugar to the ports, and, for a long time, that powerful motivation would overrule all other economic considerations. This explains why, in spite of the relatively rapid growth of the railroads, they didn't become a real system of inland communication until later on.

The slow and risky creation of a system of inland communication was a consequence of the nearly accidental linking of the regional networks, which were engaged in a process of autonomous expansion, not the result of an express desire to establish interregional communication. A system structured in that way was, naturally, quite irrational, plagued with frequent meandering. Not until later on, when the railroad companies began to compete with each other, were some shortcuts introduced, making the system more rational and its service more efficient.

The fact that only sugarcane growers and sugar producers were responsible for the railroads also determined their geographic distribution. While the western half of the island had an ever denser railroad network, there were practically no railroads in the eastern half until the end of the nineteenth century, save for a very limited number of isolated regions where sugarcane was being grown.

The case of Ferrocarril Central is an eloquent example of that situation. Surveys for the railroad were made in the mid-1800s, but nearly fifty years passed before any rails were actually laid, in spite of the obvious importance of a longitudinal, east-west railroad that would link all parts of the country. When the project was finally carried out, it was promoted by imperialist interests, which quickly understood that the strategic line was indispensable for opening up some of the richest regions in Cuba to the insatiable exploiting greed of their monopolies. Then, too, Ferrocarril Central was a sugarcane railroad, as shown, among other things, by the fact that the company which built it—the Cuba Company—lost no time in planting sugarcane and putting up sugar mills.

The other railroads built in the twentieth century (Norte de Cuba, Guantánamo and Western, and Hershey), each with its own specific characteristics, served the traditional purpose that had inspired the pioneers in this field: that of supporting exports. Frankly subordinated to the needs of sugar production, Cuba's railroads were constrained to a narrow and absorbent economic function—the exportation of sugar—and became an important link in the long chain that ran from the island's production centers to the capitalist world market.

Sugar also influenced the characteristics of railroad service. Throughout the period analyzed in this book, sugar, its raw material, and its by-products contributed four-fifths of the volume of freight transported by the railroads. The railroad companies concentrated on that kind of cargo, more or less (depending on the era and the company) ignoring passenger transportation. Rarely did Cuba's railroad passenger service achieve even median levels of the quality and efficiency typical of that service in the railroad systems of other countries. And Cuban railroads lost their passengers as technical development favored the appearance of other means of land transportation to take over that function.

At the time of the triumph of the Revolution, in 1959, the railroads carried barely 30 percent of the passengers who traveled from one town to another in the country, even though the level of development attained by railroad technology in the world allowed that kind of transportation to offer a more economical, faster, and more comfortable service than other means of land transportation.

Sugar was the lifeblood of Cuba's railroads, but it also constituted their misfortune. The seasonal nature of the sugar industry meant that the freight it generated or required was concentrated in one part of the year, the sugarcane harvest, during which railroad traffic reached a peak. That period was followed by long months of a slack period known as "the dead season."

That model required the railroads to have a great amount of rolling stock, which was exploited very little and was left standing on sidings and in railroad yards for several months a year, waiting for the next harvest. The lack of efficient exploitation of railroad equipment was aggravated by the one-sidedness in the movement of freight, since the flow of cargo from the productive areas toward the ports was much more voluminous than the return flow, which often resulted in cars going back empty. Those traffic characteristics meant high costs for the railroads, which the companies tried to counter by setting high rates.

Throughout nearly all of the nineteenth century, the railroad companies set the rates for their services unrestrictedly, governed only by supply and demand. The problems generated by competition between companies and the discounts granted to certain customers were the results of freely arrived at agreements between the companies or between the companies and their customers.

That laissez-faire paradise came up against its first limitations when the U.S. military government of Cuba dictated some railroad legislation in 1902. Motivated by vaster economic interests and overriding the loud protests of the railroad companies, the U.S. occupiers established a system of rates based on distance, such as the Spaniards had often attempted to impose by decree. From then on, matters concerning rates were settled by the Comisión de Ferrocarriles (Railroad Commission) and the government agencies that succeeded it in directing the transportation sector. Thus, the commission became a mediator between the interests of the railroad companies, which always advocated higher rates, and their customers, mainly the sugarcane estate owners.

In spite of the close links between sugar and railroad interests, they went through some periods of great tension. During the nineteenth century, because of the inefficiency of the colonial administration, the railroad companies had the upper hand and imposed their terms on the estate owners. The only thing that kept those terms from being even more onerous was the fact that the owners of the railroads were often estate owners as well.

In the twentieth century, while the railroad interests were strengthened by the growing process of monopolization that operated in the sector, the sugar interests also had a formidable weapon: private railroads. They had made their appearance in the last third of the nineteenth century and, at first, had been viewed benevolently and even supported by the public service railroads, which considered it preferable for the estate owners to have tiny railroad networks of their own for handling the troublesome and far from profitable work of hauling the sugarcane to the mills.

But, in the first few decades of the twentieth century, when the big U.S. sugar monopolies penetrated Cuba and created enormous land holdings, the private railroads acquired a new meaning. Instead of complementing the public service railroads, they began to edge them out. The sugar monopolies built enormous private railroad networks that enabled them not only to link their sugarcane plantations with their sugar mills but also to hook the mills up with private landing stages, which made it possible for them to export their products without using the public service railroads at all. Thus, the large sugar interests had a means of evading the railroads' attempts to make a larger profit from transporting sugar.

The contradictions between the two sectors turned into a serious national crisis in the early 1920s, but the battle was between foreign imperialist interests. The problem was solved by a law that sought to create an artificial balance between the railroad and sugar sectors, with manifest scorn for what might be considered the most rational way to use the country's resources.

The functional subordination of Cuba's railroads to the needs of the sugar-exporting economy considerably limited the favorable effect which that means of transportation might have had on the country's development. The introduction of the railroads brought about an appreciable reduction in transportation costs, which should have been used to strengthen Cuba's competitive position in the world sugar market. Because of the specific conditions of the traditional means of transportation in Cuba and the difficulties confronting their improvement, the railroad solution meant a considerable saving in resources for the island's economy. The use made of the resources thus saved, however, minimized the meaning and importance of that phenomenon.

Since sugar was the main beneficiary of the advantages offered by the railroads, the relative income-yield capacity of that sector increased even more and the sugar interests became the main recipients of the resources saved by the use of railroads. Thus, the railroads helped to promote reproduction on an extended scale in the sugar sector and, consequently, accentuated the Cuban economy's single-crop characteristics.

It is an indisputable fact that Cuba's sugar production could not have quintupled in three decades (between 1837 and 1867) without the railroads. The railroads facilitated capital; means for the physical expansion of the plantations; and the possibility of offsetting the increases in other cost factors, especially the higher cost of slaves. In the early days, a part of the savings provided by the railroads was used for purchasing men.

Since railroad technology never had an industrial base in Cuba, the railroads didn't exercise any action here which would stimulate other industrial sectors. Rather, the "multiplying effect" of investments in Cuban railroads had repercussions on foreign suppliers in the United States and Europe. The basically exporting function of Cuba's railroads—which could be seen, among other things, in where the lines were laid—limited the role which that means of transportation might have played in structuring a domestic market. Instead of promoting such a market, the railroads helped imported consumer and other goods to reach local markets in extremely advantageous competitive conditions, thus serving import trends. As may be seen, the railroads speeded the dynamics of the Cuban economy without making any changes in its ever more pronounced structural deformity.

The introduction of the railroads considerably matured the capitalist mode of production in Cuba. From the business point of view, the railroads contributed the most modern methods of business organization at the time and their corresponding management techniques, improving on the business efficiency of the sugarcane plantations. The development of society by means of stock was both a characteristic of and an indispensable element in the organization of the railroad companies. Therefore, their proliferation may be considered to have been an important contribution to the forms of capitalist organization in colonial Cuba.

Because of their continuing need for long-term loans, Cuba's railroads frequently had close relations with foreign banks. For short-term loans, however, they depended on domestic trade and Cuban banks. Even though the companies frequently called on their most powerful stockholders or on merchants who played the role of bankers, the size of the railroads' financial operations forced them to develop technical-financial adroitness in such practices.

Because of the close ties between the railroads and the sugar business, it isn't surprising that the railroads' main backers, in the early decades, came from the social class composed of the owners of sugar mills and sugar warehouses, the vast majority of whom were Cubans. However, starting in the middle of the nineteenth century, the railroads began to be controlled by groups of Spanish immigrants living in the colony—immigrants who, after having amassed enormous fortunes in trade and usury, extended their activities to sugar production and other sectors of the economy. Those groups, whose political definition was expressed by their militant defense of Spain's colonial interests, managed to get control of most of the railroad companies right after the Ten Years' War.

Although foreign (British) banks played an important role in financing the construction of the first railroad and in granting sizable loans for some later projects, they did not obtain direct or indirect control of any company in Cuba until the last third of the nineteenth century. In that era, when the island was being scourged by an economic crisis and some railroad companies found it impossible to make their mortgage payments, British capital, transformed into imperialist finance capital, used its position as creditor to obtain direct control of the companies in sore straits. Either through that procedure or by means of purchases and mergers, British capital managed to take over all of the railroad companies in the western half of Cuba, which it consolidated into a single monopoly in 1920.

Thus, a curious process of denationalization took place, by means of which Cuba's railroads, which had originally been Cuban-owned, passed into the hands of a foreign company. Even though the new British owners extended the tracks in some places and modernized the equipment, the English imperialist penetration was characterized by having taken place on the basis of control investments, which distinguished it from U.S. penetration, which, in the railroad sector, occurred through development investments.

U.S. imperialist capital penetrated Cuba's railroad sector under the protection of the U.S. army of occupation. Favored by that circumstance, U.S. capital managed to gobble up some small companies and, above all, make the largest railroad investment in the country: the construction of Ferrocarril Central.

Aware of the enormous importance of the old project, the U.S. interests didn't hesitate to transgress their own laws to build a railroad that, in addition to being of decisive importance for attaining political-military control of the country, provided access to some of its greatest wealth. Along with that basic investment, the U.S. interests built a regional railroad network in Guantánamo and had a key role in the company that built the country's main sugarcane railroad: Ferrocarril del Norte de Cuba.

U.S. investments, too, went through a centralizing process, creating an enormous monopoly that controlled nearly all of the railroads in the eastern provinces, plus the most important ports through which the island's sugar was exported. That monopoly enabled U.S. interests to exercise absolute control over the main elements of the infrastructure in the region where the largest U.S. sugar investments were made in Cuba. On the scale and within the organizational patterns of monopoly capital, U.S. railroad investments thus repeated the same functional model that had characterized Cuba's railroads since their origins.

Subordinated to the needs of sugar production, the railroads remained dependent on market fluctuations in the price of sugar. During the sugar boom, the railroad lines grew. Their expansion was halted each time the price dropped and was finally ended when the restrictive policy expressed in the agreements, legislation, and sugar tariffs imposed by U.S. interests set permanent bounds to the growth of sugar plantations. The last sugar mill in Cuba was built in 1925. The last important section of track laid in the neocolonial period was completed just two or three years later.

In the late 1920s, Cuba's railroads were submerged in a deep and prolonged crisis, a sectoral expression of the crisis that was threatening the very underpinnings of Cuban society and the economy. In the railroad crisis, two basic factors were intertwined. One, of a general nature, stemmed from the paralysis of growth in sugar production, which not only limited but also reduced railroad freight. The other, more specific, was caused by competition from automotive transportation. The development of that new mode of land transportation, which, to a greater or lesser extent, affected railroad traffic all over the world, had particularly negative effects in Cuba.

During the tyranny of Gerardo Machado, a public works program was launched in Cuba to build highways which, in most cases, paralleled the railroad tracks. At the same time, tariff advantages were granted for imports of the fuel used for automotive transportation. Succeeding administrations continued and stepped up that policy, with the logical result of increased competition in a branch of services with limited growth possibilities. The railroad companies, therefore, suffered from a double reduction in their sources of income, both from the limitation placed on the volume of cargo to be transported and from the loss of part of that already limited volume to their competitors in automotive transportation.

Those were the most obvious factors in the railroad crisis, but the irrational features implicit in the functional model of Cuba's railroads, which were firmly rooted in the country's economic structure, had just as negative an effect. Those were the root causes of the railroad crisis, which showed that, although that phenomenon could perhaps be alleviated—as it was by World War II—it could never be solved unless the basic problems from which the country suffered were solved as well. In the midst of economic stagnation, the large railroad companies demanded that the government help them bear their difficulties.

The relations between the government and the railroads in Cuba displayed a slow but sure closing of ranks. From the curious mixture of liberalism and prying inefficiency which were typical of Spanish colonial administration, the railroads passed to a regime of government control in the early years of the neocolonial period. The first neocolonial governments went a little farther in their relations with the railroad companies and introduced a system of subsidies for rail expansion, which was especially important for some branches of Cuba Railroad and, above all, for the construction of Ferrocarril del Norte de Cuba.

Not until the era of the crisis, however, did the railroads and the government begin to become truly interwoven. The first thing the railroad companies demanded of the government was the establishment of a regimen of coordinated rates for all means of transportation, to put an end to the unrestrained competition then in force. That measure could do little, though, in view of the seriousness of the railroads' crisis.

The railroads' situation continued to deteriorate, and, before the end of the 1940s, the neocolonial government had to take over one of the two large railroad companies in the country: Ferrocarriles Unidos de La Habana, which was on the brink of bankruptcy. Shortly afterward, the government's resources had to be mobilized in aid of the other—Ferrocarriles Consolidados de Cuba—which, though in better condition, was also experiencing serious economic difficulties in carrying out its operations.

In the general panorama of the crisis, the neocolonial government had to extend its functions to shore up its economic base. That growth in the role of the government, both at the national level and in the strictly railroad sphere—which was promoted and supported by imperialism and the bourgeoisie—was based not only on the country's economic difficulties but also on the level of development attained by the class struggle. This was particularly so in the railroad sector, where the companies, clamoring for government help, hoped that, in addition to providing economic support, the government would hold back the development of the railroad labor movement in its ongoing struggle to improve the workers' living conditions.

The historic significance of the railroads in Cuba cannot be fully understood without considering the role played by the railroad proletariat. In the labor problems of colonial Cuba, the introduction of the railroads meant the incorporation of a free work force—consisting of foreign workers, at first—in the ranks of the colony's incipient proletariat. Even though the railroads were not exempt from the social relations in effect in that era and used large contingents of Negro slaves and semienslaved Chinese laborers for the hardest work, it is very probable that there were very few slaves in the railroad sector when slavery was abolished in 1886.

In proletarian activities during the colonial period, railroad workers, along with the cigar makers, played a pioneering role. Its most important manifestations were the advanced organization of mutuality for the economic protection of workers and their families and the early use of one of the classical instruments of working-class struggle: strikes. The railroad workers' militancy and organizational skill resulted in their being the first to win two important gains: the creation of the first national sectoral labor organization and the promulgation of the first retirement law. In the 1916–26 period, rail workers staged some of the largest, most militant strikes in Cuban history, beginning an important tradition of struggle.

The railroad labor movement was not free of weaknesses, however. They stemmed from the marked differences between the various work categories in the sector, which led to the existence of large nuclei of workers with high wages who formed a sort of labor aristocracy of clearly reformist leanings. With the obvious support of the companies and the neocolonial government, those groups managed to take over the leadership of the labor organizations in the sector, on which they impressed a conservative, exclusivist approach.

Starting in 1937, however, the tenacious work done by members of the Communist Party in the railroad sector promoted a process of growing unity there and channeled the masses' militancy toward achieving an important series of social advances, won throughout the decade of the 1940s. When the railroad companies clamored for government help, they were trying to halt that trend.

That situation, of which the railroad sector was just one of many examples, led imperialism and the Cuban bourgeoisie to hand the reins of the neocolonial government over to Fulgencio Batista, a man whom they considered capable of unscrupulously pushing through whatever policy might be required for surviving the crisis. The worst example of the degradation of the neocolonial political forms, the Batista tyranny carried venality, administrative inefficiency, crime, and repressive brutality to extremes.

In view of the serious national crisis, sectoral problems, such as the railroad crisis, were subordinated to the country's main need: to do away with the neocolonial structures.

The revolutionary movement headed by Fidel Castro united the broad masses of the people, including the railroad workers, and led them to the decisive battle to seize power. Their January 1959 victory ushered in a new stage in history. Seeking to solve Cuba's problems, the triumphant Revolution initiated a process of thoroughgoing structural changes and radically transformed the social relations of production. That process and strategy of economic development opened up new possibilities for Cuba's railroads to achieve their full potential as protagonists in the new society.

Notes

Introduction

1. Geoffrey Blainey, *The Tyranny of Distance: How Distance Shaped Australia's History* (Melbourne: Sun Books, 1966).

Chapter 1

1. The result of the increased commerce is reflected in changes in the production and population of the island. Between 1778 and 1830 sugar exports increased from 9,676 to 104,971 metric tons. The number of inhabitants increased from 179,484 to 704,487. In the coffee sector production in 1792 was insignificant—about 92 metric tons—but in 1830 it reached 22,480 metric tons. See Manuel Moreno Fraginals, *El ingenio, complejo económico social cubano del azúcar* (Havana: Ciencias Sociales, 1978), 3: chart II; Francisco Pérez de la Riva, *El café* (Havana: J. Montero, 1944).

2. This resolution favored the oligarchy of the first seven towns established after the conquest since the cabildos then made use of their prerogative to distribute lands within their domain. The largest beneficiaries of these acts was the oligarchy in the city of Havana.

3. On the composition of the proprietors and other members of this first governing council of the chamber as well as other important aspects related to the development of the sugar industry until the middle of the nineteenth century, see Moreno Fraginals, *El ingenio*, 1:108.

4. Ibid., 3: chart II.

5. "Sobre los medios que convendría adoptar para la construcción de caminos necesarios" [Ways to construct needed roads], in *Memoria de Esteban La Faye*, in Fondo Junto de Fomento, legajo 115, expediente 4845.

6. Alejandro García, *El canal de occidente*, vol. 1, no. 1 (Havana: Centro de Información Científica y Técnica, 1972), pp. 4–7.

7. Gonzalo Menéndez Pidal, *Los caminos en la historia de España* (Madrid: Editorial Cultura Hispánica, 1951), pp. 123–37.

8. At the founding of the Real Consulado it was extended the right to levy a half percent tax on all exports. After 1818 there was also a road tax. Between 1794 and 1828 both sources accounted for 2, 438,444 pesos, equivalent to about 70,000 pesos per year. Given that the Real Consulado calculated a construction cost of 17,500 pesos per league, this sum was adequate for merely 4 or 5 leagues of new roads, without any allowance for maintenance.

9. The collection of tolls was characteristic of European road systems. In England and

the United States such roads were called turnpikes from the bars and turnstiles that had to be removed or turned before travelers, horses, and carriages could proceed.

10. Carta del Real Consulado a Pedro Diago, La Habana, June 9, 1800, in ANC, Fondo Junta de Fomento, legajo 115, expediente 4858.

11. Petición de la Condesa de Buenavista, Nicolás de Peñalver, Conde de Vallellano, Marqués de Casa Calvo y otros hacendados, al Real Consulado, en relación con la reparación del camino de Güines, en las inmediaciones de las lomas de Nazareno y La Corredora, in ANC, Fondo Junta de Fomento, legajo 116, expediente 4872.

12. When tolls were imposed on the Great North Road to Scotland in 1753, bands of armed folks damaged nearly a dozen gates made for the road. Eventually a permanent military force was deployed to protect the English turnpikes.

13. Carta de Blas Vidal a Pedro Diago, April 1801, in ANC, Fondo Junta de Fomento, legajo 115, expediente 4852.

14. Rafael M. de Quesada y Arango, *Informe expresivo de las causas que han motivado hasta ahora la construcción de caminos* (Havana: Imprenta del Gobierno y Capitanía General, 1832).

15. José Antonio Saco the well-known Cuban historian and polemicist was born in 1797, and was, at age twenty-three, professor of philosophy and law at the San Carlos Seminary. He was subsequently elected a deputy to the Spanish Cortes (Parliament). In 1829, he expressed his concern about Cuban roads in a *Memoria sobre caminos en la isla de Cuba*, which won a prize from the Sociedad Económica in 1830 and entitled him to membership. Rafael de Quesada y Arango, the author of the other report mentioned, was governor of Trinidad in 1816 and built a road paved with broken granite to the entrance of the port. Similar to Saco, Quesada defended the use of "Mc Adam" surfacing that combined proper drainage with a foundation of broken stones. He was appointed deputy in charge of construction when the Junta de Fomento was created in 1832 and made his report on that occasion.

16. N. Deerr, *The History of Sugar*, 2 vols. (London: Chapman & Hall, 1949–50), 1:492–94; Ramiro Cabrera, "La industria azucarera," in *El Libro de Cuba* (Havana, 1923), p. 713.

17. Julio Le Riverend, *Historia económica de Cuba* (Havana: Ciencias Sociales, 1971), p. 237. Average prices of slaves increased about 25 percent between 1814 and 1822. See Laird Bergad, Fe Iglesias García, and María Del Carmen Barcia, *The Cuban Slave Market, 1790–1880* (New York: Cambridge University Press, 1995), table 4.8, page 74.

18. *Informe de la deputación del Consulado de Matanzas a la Junta del Gobierno del Real Consulado*, March 28, 1828, in ANC, Fondo Junta de Fomento, legajo 117, expediente 4960.

19. Quesada y Arango, *Informe expresivo*, p. 32.

20. Although there was an overall increase between Havana and all ports throughout the island, the increase was most noticeable between Havana and Matanzas, and later Cárdenas. Steamships such as *El Pavo Real* (The Royal Swan) began to ply the route in 1834 with three weekly trips for passengers and cargo. An increasing number of schooners and brigs, Spanish as well as North American, traded with important sugar exporting firms such as Drake and Brothers and also took consignments from a number of ports to Havana. See *Diario de la Habana, Sección Económica*, 1830–38.

21. *Sobre la construcción de un camino a la villa de Güines*, in ANC, Fondo Junta de Fomento, legajo 117, expediente 4981.

Chapter 2

1. S. Lilley, *Hombres, máquinas e historia* (Madrid: Editorial Ciencia Nueva, 1967), p. 110.

2. M. Greenwood, *Railway Revolution* (London: Longman, 1963), pp. 46–47.

3. Charles Morazé, *El apogeo de la burguesía* (Barcelona: Editorial Labor, 1965), p. 234.

4. E. R. Johnson, *Principles of Railroad Transportation* (New York: Appleton, 1922), p. 22.

5. ANC, Fondo de Junta de Fomento, legajo 129, expediente 6374.

6. This long, detailed report reveals how closely the Cuban commissioners followed the result of railroad experiments. Beside a summary of the history of early railroad development, the report also contains precise technical information about Stephenson's locomotives, including the "Rocket." Ibid.

7. *Extracto de las memorias y acuerdos de la Junta de los Caminos de Hierro* (Havana: Imprenta Fraternal, 1831), p. 1.

8. Ibid., p. 2.

9. Sullivan was associated with Ross Winans of the Baltimore railroad enterprise, who had invented a new coach with a "great capacity." Also anticipating a new business opportunity was David F. Waymouth, who arrived shortly afterward but was not taken seriously by the Havana Commission.

10. *Extracto de las memorias y acuerdos de la Junta de Caminos de Hierro*, pp. 32–37.

11. Ibid., pp. 49–50.

12. ANC, Fondo Junta de Fomento, legajo 129, expediente 6374.

13. No satisfactory biography exists of the count of Villanueva. Born in Havana in 1782, Claudio Martínez de Pinillos, the count of Villanueva went to Spain at the age of twenty-three and saw service in the peninsular struggle against Napoleon and was promoted to colonel. In 1813 he served as an alternate delegate to the Cortes, and on his return to Havana the following year was appointed accountant general of Military Services and Customs for the island of Cuba. He was a close friend of Francisco de Arango y Parreño and substituted for him in the position of treasury intendant in 1825. He served in this post, with few leaves of absence, for twenty-five years. Martínez de Pinillos promoted technical education, and encouraged the modernization of the sugar industry. He also protected the illegal slave trade and supported a range of activities that benefited the Cuban sugar interests. In this sense he was a direct successor to Arango, although in the case of Martínez de Pinillos the support of the sugar interests did not extend to ideas of an emergent nationalism. His command of local finances enhanced his influence at Court in Madrid. This influence also gained from his close friendship with George Villiers, the British minister to Madrid, at a time when the Spanish Liberal cabinet needed British support against the Carlist insurgents. After 1841 his political influence gradually declined and in 1851 he was appointed an overseas counselor to the Court and moved to Madrid where he died two years later.

14. Violeta Serrano, *Crónicas del primer ferrocarril de Cuba* (Havana: Departamento de Orientación Revolucionaria, 1973), p. 19. This work contains detailed information on the first Cuban railroad.

15. ANC, Fondo Junta de Fomento, legajo 130, expediente 6375.

16. Serrano, *Crónicas*, pp. 24–25.

17. Ibid.

18. Ibid.

19. Eusebio Valdés Domínguez, in a series of articles published in the *Revista Económ-*

ica in April and May 1878, stated that there were two additional negotiations for the loan. One was negotiated by the count of Toreno, the Spanish government minister, with the banker, Ardoin, in Paris. The other was negotiated locally in Havana. Both seem dubious. It is quite clear that Valdés Domínguez confuses the Junta de Fomento negotiations with the 700 million reales loan contracted by the count of Toreno with Ardoin to support the Carlist Wars. See J. Vicens Vives, *Historia económica de España* (Barcelona: Vicens Vives, 1972), p. 653.

20. Serrano, *Crónicas*, pp. 24-25.

21. Ibid., p. 43.

22. Domingo del Monte, an outstanding literary promoter, made this complaint to his brother-in-law, José Luis Alfonso: "His Excellency Tacón-Bey would not allow the railroad to cross his beautiful gardens . . . especially given the contrast between his expensive and ostentatious construction project and the efficient and simple railway works so he used every subterfuge to undermine the plan." See Carta del Domingo del Monte a José Luis Alfonso, July 21, 1836, in *Correspondencía de Domingo del Monte*, 1: no. 4, in BNC, Departamento de Colección Cubana.

23. *Correspondencia reservada del capitán general don Miguel Tacón* (Havana: Biblioteca Nacional de Cuba, 1963), pp. 148-51.

24. ANC, Fondo Junta de Fomento, legajo 130, expediente 6390.

25. A. Cruger, *Informe general del ingeniero director del Ferrocarril del Júcaro* (Havana: Imprenta Oliva, 1841), p. 18.

26. The freedmen (*emancipados*) were Africans being introduced clandestinely for the slave trade in Cuba in open violation of the treaties signed between the Spanish and the English to end the trade. Captured by English ships off the Cuban coast, they were deposited in Havana under the custody of the Spanish authorities who then leased them for periods of five years with the proviso that, during that time, they would be taught useful skills that would facilitate their existence as completely free individuals. In practice, however, these contractees were horribly exploited, at times suffering conditions that were worse than slavery.

27. ANC, Fondo Junta de Fomento, legajo 130, expediente 6379.

28. Ibid., legajo 39, expediente 1745.

29. A. Cruger, *Informe presentado a la comisión directiva del camino de hierro a Güines* (Havana: Imprenta del Gobierno y Capitinía General, 1836), p. 10.

30. The first railroad in Spain—Barcelona to Mataró—began operation in 1848. Its sponsor, Miguel de Viada, made his fortune in the illegal slave trade to Cuba and was a member of Captain General Tacón's inner circle. Railroads were built in the rest of Latin America during the last half of the nineteenth century, beginning with one on the isthmus of Panama in 1850.

31. ANC, Fondo Junta de Fomento, legajo 179, expediente 8234.

32. Ramón de la Sagra, *Historia física, política y natural de la isla de Cuba* (Paris: Hachette, 1863), p. 192.

33. ANC, Fondo Junta de Fomento, legajo 164, expediente 7891.

34. Sagra, *Historia física*, p. 192.

35. ANC, Fondo Junta de Fomento, legajo 164, expediente 7891.

36. Jacinto Salas Quiroga, *Viajes: Isla de Cuba* (Madrid: Imprenta Boix, 1840), pp. 100-101.

37. ANC, Fondo Junta de Fomento, legajo 131, expediente 6412. The engines bought by

Cruger were built by the M. W. Baldwin Company of Philadelphia. Baldwin had entered the business by making the engine, "Old Ironsides" for the Pennsylvania Railroad. By the time Cruger approached the company, it had already made more than a hundred engines but it is quite likely that the two engines bought by Cruger represented the firm's first export sales and the first by any North American company. See John K. Brown, *The Baldwin Locomotive Works, 1831–1915* (Baltimore: Johns Hopkins University Press, 1995).

38. The engines made by Baldwin and Norris were bought by Dodd on December 11, 1838. See ANC, Fondo Junta de Fomento, legajo 131, expediente 6412.

39. Ibid.

40. E. Valdés Domínguez, "Primeros caminos de hierro en la isla de Cuba," *Revista Bimestre*, May 5, 1870, p. 270.

41. Carta de Domingo del Monte a José Luis Alfonso, December 2, 1839, in *Correspondencia de Domingo del Monte, 1837–1841*, 2: no. 37, in Departamento de Colección Cubana.

42. F. Xiqués, *Concesiones en ferrocarriles de servicio público en la Isla de Cuba* (Havana, 1902), pp. 17–23.

43. The corporation represented many of the well-known Spanish individuals resident in Cuba including Salvador Samá, Julián de Zulueta, Francisco Marty, Santiago Zuaznábar, and Joaquin de Aizpurúa, as well as some commercial enterprises such as Germán del Valle, Manzanedo y Abusqueta, and Fernández y Pozo.

Chapter 3

1. In 1828 a group of landowners obtained permission from Captain General Francisco Dionisio Vives to found a town along the Lagunillas coast. The early founders always saw the new town as a future commercial port.

2. C. Hellberg, *Historia estadística de Cárdenas* (Cárdenas: n.p. 1957), pp. 41–42.

3. Juan Montalvo O'Farrill was a scion of an old Havana oligarchic family. He studied and served in the Spanish army in the peninsula, attaining the rank of field marshall. He was also the prior of the Real Consulado.

4. ANC, Fondo Ferrocarriles (Ferrocarril de Cárdenas y Jaruco), legajo 7, expediente 2.

5. These compounds for the holding of runaway slaves constituted a source of manual labor for many purposes. Until a compound was built in Cárdenas, recaptured fugitive slaves from Lagunillas were sent to Havana.

6. Herminio Portell Vilá, *Historia de Cárdenas* (Havana: Talleres Gráficos Cuba Intelectual, 1928), p. 64. Portell Vilá was born in Cárdenas.

7. ANC, Fondo Ferrocarriles (Ferrocarril de Cárdenas y Jaruco), legajo 7, expediente 2

8. F. Xiqués, *Concesiones de Ferrocarriles de servicio público* (La Habana, 1902), pp. 7–10. ANC, Fondo Junta de Fomento, legajo 137, expediente 6670, p. 3.

9. Domingo del Monte Aponte (1804–53) was born in Maracaibo, Venezuela, and arrived in Cuba with his family at the age of six. His marriage to Rosa Aldama Alfonso tied him to one of the wealthiest families in Cuba. A patron of local culture, he was head of the literary and educational divisions of the Sociedad Económica. His outspoken views forced him to leave the island on two occasions, in 1844 and again in 1853.

10. ANC, Fondo Ferrocarriles (Ferrocarril de Cárdenas y Jaruco), legajo 7, expediente 2.

11. Xiqués, *Concesiones*, pp. 7–10.

12. *Actas de la Junta Directiva (Ferrocarril de Cárdenas y Jaruco)*, in ANC, Fondo Ferrocarriles, legajo 1, expediente 5.

13. These are the dates found in A. Torroadamé Bolado, *Iniciación a la historia del correo*, p. 248, and Gerardo Castellanos, *Panorama histórico* (Havana: n.p., 1935), p. 385.

14. Carta de M. de J. Carrera, January 10, 1839, in *Centón epistolario de Domingo del Monte*, vol. 4 (Havana: Imprenta del siglo XX, 1923), p. 10.

15. Carta de A. Gutiérrez, January 21, 1839, *Centón epistolario*.

16. Portell Vilá, *Historia de Cárdenas*, p. 80.

17. Xiqués, *Concesiones*, pp. 13–17.

18. *Informe de la Junta Directiva*, in ANC, Fondo Ferrocarriles (Ferrocarril de Cárdenas y Jaruco), legajo 1, expediente 7.

19. *Informe de A. Cruger a la Junta Directiva*, in ANC, Fondo Ferrocarriles, legajo 4, expediente 2.

20. L. García Chavez, *Historia de la jurisdicción de Cárdenas* (n.p., n.d.), pp. 242–43.

21. E. Carrerá, *Informe a la compañía fundadora de Ferrocarril de Sabanilla a Maroto* (Santiago de Cuba: Imprenta Martínez, 1855), pp. 49–51.

22. *Cuadro estadístico de la siempre fiel isla de Cuba al año de 1846* (Havana: Imprenta del Gobierno y Capitanía General, 1847), pp. 76–79.

23. Some examples are José M. Ximeno y Madan, founded in 1807; Alfonso, Madan and Company, founded in 1825; Torriente y Brother, 1828; Drake Brothers, 1829; and Fesser and Brother, 1834. Many of these firms had their headquarters in Havana. See J. M. Quintero, *Apuntes para la historia de la isla de Cuba con relación a la ciudad de Matanzas* (Matanzas: Imprenta del Ferrocarril, 1878), pp. 225–28.

24. Gonzalo Alfonso Soler was a councilor in Havana and owner of the sugar mills, San Gonzalo, and Majagua near Sabanilla. His sister, María Rosa, was married to the magnate Domingo Aldama.

25. Xiqués, *Concesiones*, pp. 11–12.

26. This represented the directorate in 1843. See Quintero, *Apuntes*, pp. 616–17.

27. Carta de Francisco de la O García, February 3, 1840, in *Centón epistolario*, 4:18.

28. Carta de José Luis Alfonso, September 15, 1841, in *Centón epistolario*, 5:42.

29. Cuba, Subsecretaria de Obras Públicas, *Memorias sobre los progresos en la isla de Cuba, 1839–1865* (Havana: Imprenta del Gobierno, 1866), p. 64. This is the only remaining engine from the first railroads in Cuba. Originally it was in the old railroad station in Matanzas, then it was subsequently moved to the main station in its present location.

30. AFC (Estación Terminal Habana), Documentación legal, entresuelo, anaquel 14, legajo 130.

31. ANC, Fondo Junta de Fomento, legajo 137, expediente 6670, p. 9.

32. On March 27, 1843, the slaves on Alcancía plantation in Cárdenas revolted and were joined by slaves from other estates as well as those working on the Cárdenas Railroad. On November 5, slaves from the Matanzas plantations including Triunvirato revolted. Both rebellions were put down with considerable loss of slave lives. See Ramiro Guerra, *Manual de historia de Cuba* (Havana: Edición del Consejo Nacional de Cultura, 1962), p. 437.

33. Carta de M. de J. Carrera, October 23, 1843, in *Centón epistolario*, 5:145.

34. Castellanos, *Panorama histórico*, pp. 389–90.

35. Xiqués, *Concesiones*, pp. 61–62.

36. Carta de Joaquin de Arrieta, October 23, 1842, in ANC, Fondo Intendencia de Hacienda, legajo 308, expediente 25.

37. According to A. Calvache, *Historia de la minería en Cuba* (Havana, 1944), pp. 47–53, the company was registered as La Consolidada.

38. ANC, Fondo Intendencia de Hacienda, legajo 308, expediente 25.

39. Ibid.

40. Cuba, Comisión de Ferrocarriles, *Memoria* (1903–4), p. 64.

41. ANC, Fondo Intendencia de Hacienda, legajo 308, expediente 25; J. Pezuela, *Diccionario geográfico, estadístico e histórico de la isla de Cuba* (Madrid: Imprenta Mellado, 1863–66), 2:354.

42. ANC, Fondo Gobierno Superior Civil, legajo 1009, expedientes 35 and 121; M. Torrente, *Bosquejo económico y político de la isla de Cuba* (Madrid: Imprenta de Barcini, 1853), 2:166; Pezuela, *Diccionario*, 2:354.

43. Gaspar Betancourt Cisneros (1803–66) was considered one of the most enlightened citizens of Puerto Príncipe. He was well known as a *costumbrista* genre writer under the pseudonym of El Lugareño. He tried to demonstrate that sugar could be produced without slaves by subdividing his plantation, Najasa, among white sharecroppers. His proannexationist politics led to his exile to the United States where he lived between 1846 and 1861.

44. Xiqués, *Concesiones*, pp. 4–7.

45. *Informe del ingeniero B. H. Wright a la Junta Directive del Ferrocarril de Puerto Príncipe a Nuevitas*, in *Memorias de la Sociedad Patriótica* (Havana, 1837), pp. 311–12.

46. A. Orozco y Arango wrote to Domingo del Monte on February 27, 1840, regarding his misgivings about the project. See *Centón epistolario*, 4:10.

47. *Escritura social y reglamento del Ferrocarril de Puerto Príncipe a Nuevitas*, in AHPC, Fondo Ferrocarriles, legajo 677.

48. Carta de Gaspar Betancourt Cisneros, January 14, 1842, in *Centón epistolario*, 4:73.

49. Carta de M. de J. Carrera, October 23, 1843, in *Centón epistolario*, 4:145.

50. Carta de Gaspar Betancourt Cisneros, January 14, 1842, in *Centón epistolario*, 4:94.

51. ANC, Fondo Junta de Fomento, legajo 137, expediente 6670, p. 14.

52. Torres Lasqueti in his *Colección de datos históricos, geográficos, y estadístcos de Puerto Príncipe y su Jurisdicción* (Havana: Imprenta El Retiro, 1888), p. 233, states that the last section of tracks was completed thanks to a loan of 500,000 pesos from A. Robertson. The Camagüey Railroad failed to be profitable and was shut down. In 1851 a group of wealthy individuals from Puerto Príncipe bought it.

53. E. Edo y Llop, *Memoria histórica de Cienfuegos y su jurisdicción* (Havana: Montero, 1943), pp. 65–70.

54. *Censo de la población de la isla de Cuba a fin del año de 1841* (Havana: Imprenta del Gobierno y Capitanía General, 1842), pp. 42–47.

55. J. Sagebién and Alejo H. Lanier, *Informe sobre el Ferrocarril de Cienfuegos y Villa Clara* (Havana: Imprenta del Gobierno y Capitanía General, 1848), p. 21.

56. Xiqués, *Concesiones*, pp. 56–60.

57. Edo y Llop, *Memoria histórica*, pp. 110–11.

58. Ibid.

59. ANC, Fondo Intendencia de Hacienda, legajo 308, expediente 32.

60. ANC, Fondo Tribunal de Comercio, legajo 174, expediente 617.

61. Edo y Llop, *Memoria histórica*, pp. 110–11.

62. This refers to Luis Juan Lorenzo D'Clouet, founder of Cienfuegos or Fernandina de Jagua.

63. Edo y Llop, *Memoria histórica*, p. 125.

64. ANC, Fondo Tribunal de Comercio, legajo 174, expediente 17.

65. AFC (ETH), Documentación legal, entresuelo, anaquel 4, legajo 32 (inventario).

66. Sagabién and Lanier, *Informé*, p. 11.

67. Ibid.

68. *Cuadro estadístico*, pp. 149–52.

69. *Memoria de la sociedad Patriótica, 1846*, 2nd ser., 2:221.

70. M. Martínez Escobar, *Historia de Remedios* (Havana: Montero, 1944), p. 298.

71. Manuel de J. Rojas was mayor of San Juan de los Remedios and colonel of the militia. He built Jimaguayabo sugar mill in Caibarién. Along with his son-in-law he was instrumental in moving the port of Remedios from Tesico to Caibarién where they possessed extensive property.

72. Ramón de la Sagra, *Cuba en 1860* (Paris: Hachette, 1863), p. 231.

73. Sugar prices declined from 49 shillings per quintal (some 11.4 cents per pound at the then exchange rate) to about 20 shillings (4.8 cents per pound) in 1852 on the London market. This decline resulted largely from an end to British protectionism, but it had worldwide effect. See N. Deerr, *The History of Sugar*, 2 vols. (London: Chapman and Hall, 1949–50), 2:531.

74. R. T. Ely, *Cuando reinaba su majestad el azúcar* (Buenos Aires: Editorial Sudamericana, 1963), pp. 144, 557.

75. The classic example of this system is that of France where all routes radiated from Paris to Tours, Lyons, Amiens, etc., in consonance with the requirements of their domestic market. See R. Barjot, *Les chemins de fer en France* (Paris: Didier, 1947).

76. Carta de José Luis Alfonso, December 23, 1844, in *Centón epistolario*, 6:144.

77. Ibid.

78. Cuba, Subsecretaría de Obras Públicas, *Memorias sobre el progreso de las obras públicas en la isla de Cuba, 1859–1865* (Havana: Imprenta del Gobierno, 1866), pp. 60–61.

79. These figures are derived from *Cuadro estadístico*.

80. Quintero, *Apuntes*, pp. 615–16.

81. Cuba, Subsecretaría de Obras Públicas, *Memorias*, pp. 62–64.

82. The commercial notices in the *Diario de la Marina* in Havana between 1838 and 1850 support this view.

83. These companies were Caminos de Hierro de La Habana, Ferrocarril de Cárdenas, Ferrocarril del Júcaro, Ferrocarril de Matanzas, Ferrocarril del Cobre, Ferrocarril de Puerto Príncipe a Nuevitas, Ferrocarril de Cienfuegos y Villa Clara, and a very small railroad, called "La Prueba," about a kilometer in length, that connected the town of Regla with Guanabacoa in the outskirts of Havana.

Chapter 4

1. N. Deerr, *The History of Sugar*, 2 vols. (London: Chapman and Hall, 1949–50), 2:531.

2. Juan Pérez de la Riva, "El Monto de la inmigración forzada," in *Revista de la Biblioteca José Martí* año 64 (1974), no. 1:108.

3. Between 1841 and 1845 sugar consumption increased in England from 17 to 34 pounds per capita and in the United States from 13⅛ pounds to 34. See R. T. Ely, *Cuando reinaba su majestad el azúcar* (Buenos Aires: Editorial Sudamericana, 1963), p. 427.

4. Ramón de la Sagra, *Cuba en 1860* (Paris: Hachette, 1863), p. 246.

5. It should also be noted that a new era of illegal slave trading began, and the "flexible" interpretation of its treaties allowed Spain to overlook the importation of some sixty thousand new African slaves between 1854 and 1859. See Pérez de la Riva, "El Monto," p. 108.

6. Deerr, *History of Sugar*, 2:531.

7. Sagra, *Cuba en 1860*, pp. 247–48.

8. G. García, "Papel de la crisis económica de 1857 en la economía cubana," in *Sobre la Guerra de los Diez Años* (Havana: Edición Revolucionaria, 1973), p. 163.

9. Sagra, *Cuba en 1860*, pp. 247–48.

10. From quite early the people of Trinidad engaged in illegal trade with many other cities throughout the Spanish Caribbean and with this experience broadened commercial contacts with the neighboring Caribbean islands of other European colonies. An important study by H. Venegas, "Apuntes sobre la decadencia trinitaria en el siglo XIX," *Islas*, no. 46 (September–December 1973): 214–23, offers abundant information and an adequate analysis on this process.

11. Ibid., p. 192.

12. ANC, Fondo Junta de Fomento, legajo 136, expediente 6655.

13. ANC, Fondo Intendencia de Hacienda, legajo 742, expediente 13. Arrieta is already familiar from a number of his previous enterprises. Manuel Pastor, who in his capacity as captain of the Corps of Engineers had participated in the studies on the first railroad, later became a very successful merchant. He benefited from his close friendship with governor Tacón for whom he carried out several lucrative urban contracts. Along with Antonio Parejo he was involved in the illegal slave trade, a business in which it was said he represented the queen mother, Maria Cristina. Later in association with Parejo he founded the San José warehouses in Havana. He served the crown in so many useful ways that he was granted the title count of Bagaez in 1852, a year before he died.

14. Sagra, *Cuba en 1860*, pp. 231, 237.

15. The possibility also exists that some wealthy people from Trinidad invested in regions of higher returns such as Cienfuegos and Sancti Spíritus. See Venegas, "Apuntes."

16. ANC, Fondo Junta de Fomento, legajo 137, expediente 6670.

17. Jacobo de la Pezuela, *Diccionario geográfico, estadístico e histórico de la isla de Cuba* (Madrid: Imprenta Mellado, 1863–66), 2:532.

18. Although Sancti Spíritus got permission to open a port at Tunas de Zaza in 1803, the town of Trinidad managed to obstruct the opening of the facility until 1835. See M. Martínez Moles, *Epítome de la historia de Sancti Spíritus* (Havana: Imprenta siglo XX, 1936), pp. 73–76.

19. Sagra, *Cuba en 1860*, p. 200. Lara came from an old Trinidad family but he had built the sugar mill Niña in Sancti Spírtus, and had married into the family of Valle, the local *cacique*. Together they worked on many business enterprises. See *Causa formada contra Roque de Lara, Modesto del Valle, and Fco. Antonio Marín, de Trinidad. por ser los autores de desembarcos de bozales in aquella zona* [Case against Roque de Lara, Modesto del Valle, and Francisco Antonio Marín for illegally landing African slaves in that region], in ANC, Fondo Miscelánea, legajo 3675, expediente A.

20. The sugar planters in this region built two small railroads drawn by animals, a five-kilometer track in Carahatas and another from Mallorquín to Las Pozas, a distance of three kilometers. See ANC, Fondo Junta de Fomento, legajo 161, expediente 7891.

21. *Cuadro estadístico de la siempre fiel isla de Cuba al año de 1846* (Havana: Imprenta del Gobierno y Capitanía General, 1847), pp. 149–52.

22. A. M. Alcover, *Historia de la villa de Sagua la Grande* (Sagua la Grande: Imprenta Unidas, 1905), p. 77.

23. By the middle of the nineteenth century the labor situation had become critical and

not only were large numbers of African *bozales* being imported again, but they were supplemented with "contracted" Chinese coolies, Yucatecan Indians, and Galician daily paid workers. Feijoo Sotomayor formed a company to import Galician laborers.

24. Alcover, *Sagua la Grande*, pp. 125–37.

25. The figures cited are 1841 and are taken from *Resumen del censo de la población de la isla de Cuba en 1841* (Havana: Imprenta del Gobierno, 1842), pp. 50–51. Export figures are taken from Sagra, *Cuba en 1860*, p. 231.

26. Pezuela, *Diccionario geográfico*, 2:214; L. Bou, *La cuestión de los bancos en la isla de Cuba* (Santiago de Cuba: Imprenta Espinal, 1867), p. 19.

27. F. Xiqués, *Concesiones en ferrocarriles de servicio público* (Havana, 1902), p. 78.

28. The following list reflects adequately the interest of the principal participants in the railroad:

Proprietor	Name of Sugar Estate
Antonio Vinent	Juninicú
Antonio Vinent	Sabanilla
M. del Castillo	San Rafael
M. del Castillo	Unión
Juan Boudet	Manacú
Juan Vaillant	Songo
Juan Vaillant	Yarayabo
Juan Kindelán	Palmarejo

29. According to an interesting note found by Professor Pérez de la Riva, the development of the Guantánamo plantation began with a grant of a thousand *caballerías* of land to a group of French immigrants from Haiti headed by Luis Bellegarde. Archives de Port de Toulon, 5th, III, no. 20.

30. In 1855 Guantánamo had twenty-five sugar mills, eleven of which used steam. See Pezuela, *Diccionario geográfico*, 2:496–511.

31. ANC, Fondo Consejo de Administración, legajo 25, expediente 2661.

32. ANC, Fondo Gobierno Superior Civil, legajo 1012, expediente 35164. Ely in his study makes numerous references to connections between Brook and Moses Taylor. Brook also had a small sugar mill, *Chivas*, in the jurisdiction of Santiago de Cuba.

33. The work was finished in December 1856. See Sagra, *Cuba en 1860*, p. 198.

34. E. Carrerá, *Informe a la compañía tundadora del Ferrocarril de Sabanilla a Maroto* (Santiago de Cuba Martínez, 1855), pp. 7–8.

35. The possibility of extending the line to Bayamo was explored by Pedro Griñan, one of the investors in the Santiago Railroad, who thought of a Bayamo-Enramadas railroad. Some years later two men from Bayamo, Francisco Vicente Aguilera and Vicente Collazo, revived the idea and drew up plans for a route but nothing came of the idea. See E. Bacardí, *Crónicas de Santiago de Cuba*, vol. 3 (Santiago de Cuba: Tipográfico Arroyo, 1925), p. 274.

36. Carrerá, *Informe*, pp. 18–33.

37. It was also agreed to pay an additional 300 pesos per mile to maintain the tracks during the first year. See *Escritura otorgada por la empresa a Robinson y Dalton sobre la construcción del camino, 1856*, in AFC (d.C.), Fondo Permanente, expediente 28, p. 1-A.

38. Xiqués, *Concesiones*, p. 78.

39. ANC, Fondo Gobierno Superior Civil, legajo 1017, expedientes 35277, 35279. Other sources set the capital at 1.2 million pesos. The largest stockholders were Griñán and Bon and Co. with 50,000 pesos each, followed by Vinent with 43,000.

40. Xiqués, *Concesiones*, pp. 116–19, states that the state support was a double-edged sword since by making the government the primary creditor, that inhibited others from investing in the venture.

41. Bacardi, *Santiago de Cuba*, 3:269–71, makes light of the festivities and provides a transcription of the poem composed for the occasion by Juan Napoles Fajardo, "El Cuculambé."

42. Ibid., 4:64.

43. *Actas de la Junta Directiva del Ferrocarril y Almacenes de Depósito de Santiago de Cuba* (1862–67), in AHPC, Fondo Ferrocarriles, pp. 24–25.

44. The Caney railroad grew up like a crippled sibling of the Santiago Railroad during the wild speculation of 1857. Its promoters, Joaquín Pagán, the marquis of the Delicias de Tempú, Juan Lacret, and others, wanted to build a small branch line connecting the town of Caney with the main line of the Santiago Railroad to facilitate the summer holiday travel of the elegant families of the town. The sponsors had difficulty raising the estimated 100,000 pesos. Although it opened in 1860, it failed to make money and closed in 1864.

45. In 1854 the Almacenes de Regla joined with a second company founded in 1850 to become an enterprise with capital of 1.5 million pesos. The storage capacity exceeded 500,000 crates. See J. G. Cantero, *Los ingenios* (Havana: L. Marquier, 1857).

46. *Escritura de la constitución de la segunda Compañía de Almacenes de Depósito del puerto de La Habana*, in AFC (ETH), Documentación legal, entresuelo, anaquel 11, legajo 30.

47. "El 6%," in *Compañía de Almacenes de Regla y Banco del Comercio*, Colección Facticia, II, BCOH.

48. Management attributed the situation to the high cost of salaries, contracts, and material. "The investment of funds before 1861 is amazing, because we have used one and half million feet of lumber, 800,000 bricks, and spent more than 50,000 pesos on picks, shovels, and other tools." *Memoria del ferrocarril de la Bahia de La Habana* (1861), p. 9.

49. To get the loan, the Banco de Comercio had to surrender its first-rights mortgage to Schröder and Company. In this and in other matters it seems that Fesser and his associates played hard and fast with both the bank and the company and made a number of business decisions that did not benefit either entity. See Banco de Comercio, *Antecedentes y contrato referentes a los negocios con el ferrocarril de la Bahia, El Correo Militar* (Havana, 1882).

50. ANC, Fondo Ferrocarriles (Ferrocarriles Unidos de La Habana), legajo 792, expediente 18.

51. In 1859 a company including the marquis of Esteva, Salvador Samá, Rodríguez Torices, and Eduardo Fesser bought the Coliseo Railroad for 1.3 million pesos. The new owners extended the track to Bemba where it connected with the Cárdenas Railroad and afterward they built a branch from Guanábana to Matanzas, freeing the Coliseo Railroad from the Matanzas Company with which it became serious rival. See ANC, Fondo Gobierno Superior Civil, legajo 1015, expediente 35229.

52. C. Rebello, *Estados relativos a la producción azucarera de la isla de Cuba* (Havana, 1860), pp. 8–9, 27–28, 32, 38, 73.

53. The Pedrosos were prominent investors in the Cárdenas and Júcaro Railroad—Luis

Pedroso was president of the company—and had bought a large number of shares in the Bahía Railroad.

54. Pezuela, *Diccionario geográfico*, 2:209–10.

55. Ships unloaded at Batabanó and the railroads took the freight to Havana. The principal freight line for the cabotage was the Empresa Navegación del Sur [Southern Shipping Lines] founded in 1843 by Joaquin Gómez and other rich Spanish merchants from Havana. See AFC (ETH) Documentación legal, entresuelo, anaquel 18, legajo 69.

56. Pezuela, *Diccionario geográfico*, 2:356.

57. Caminos de Hierro de La Habana, *Informe de la Junta Directiva a la general de accionistas* (Havana, 1858), p. 27. The refusal of the proposal of had negative effects on the Caminos de Hierro. In 1865 the directors reported that "the loss of merchandise hauled results mainly from the competition of the Ferrocarril del Oeste on our Guanajay line . . . and the effect can also be seen in the reduction of passengers, especially from San Antonio station."

58. *Memoria del Ferrocarril del Oeste* (1860), p. 27.

59. Ibid., pp. 9, 17.

60. Ibid., p. 15.

61. ANC, Fondo Gobierno Superior Civil, legajo 1015, expediente 35234.

62. M. Martínez Escobar, *Historia de Remedios* (Havana: Montero, 1944), p. 302.

63. Ibid.

64. Pezuela, *Diccionario geográfico*, 2:337–38.

65. Ferrocarril de Cárdenas, *Documentación de fusión*, in AFC (ETH), Documentación legal, entresuelo, anaquel, caja 1.

66. ANC, Gobierno Superior Civil, legajo 1007, expediente 35084.

67. This prolongation corresponded with the first section of the design for a longitudinal central railroad made by the officials of the Department of Public Works under the colonial government. Despite this history of official support, it was difficult to get the required permission to build this line. See AFC (ETH), Documentación legal, entresuelo, anaquel 29, legajo 10.

68. Xiqués, *Concesiones*, pp. 81–84, 97–100.

69. J. M. Quintero, *Apuntes para la historia de la isla de Cuba con relación a la ciudad de Matanzas* (Matanzas: Imprenta del Ferrocarril, 1878), pp. 225–28.

70. Caminos de Hierro de La Habana, *Memoria de la Junta Directiva a la general de accionistas* (Havana, 1869), p. 19.

Chapter 5

1. Conde de Armíldez de Toledo, *Noticias estadísticas de la isla de Cuba en 1862* (Havana: Imprenta del Gobierno y Capitán General, 1864); G. Tortella Casares, *Los orígines del capitalismo español* (Madrid: Tecnos, 1973), p. 194: H. Leyva y Aguilera, *La isla de Cuba y sus caminos de hierro* (Havana: Imprenta Mercantil, 1874), p. 17.

2. B. May and Company, *Almanaque mercantil de La Habana* (Havana, 1864). The times are calculated from schedules published by the following companies: Caminos de hierro de La Habana; Ferrocarril de Coliseo; and Empresa Unida de Cárdenas y Júcaro.

3. ANC, Fondo Junta de Fomento, legajo 136, expediente 6663.

4. The importance attached to the possibility of a central railroad will be examined in a later chapter.

5. Tortella Casares, *Los orígenes del capitalismo español*, p. 166.

6. Subdirección de Obras Públicas, *Memoria sobre el progreso de las obras públicas en Cuba, 1859–1865* (Havana: Imprenta del Gobierno y Capitanía General, 1866), p. 8.

7. The regulation of 1844 was contained in a decree that detailed the relations between the state and private companies. See Tortella, *Los orígines del capitalismo español*, pp. 167–68.

8. Ibid., pp. 50, 55, 168–69.

9. *Colección de reales órdenes y disposiciones de las autoridades superiores de la isla de Cuba* (Havana: Imprenta del Gobierno y Capitanía General, 1859), 5:18.

10. *Informe de la Junta Directiva de la Cia. de Caminos de Hierro de La Habana* (Havana, 1865), p. 13.

11. Ibid., p. 20.

12. *Informe de La Junta Directiva del Ferrocarril de la Bahia de La Havana* (Havana: Imprenta La Cubana, 1858), p. 6.

13. There were a few narrow-gauge railroads operating privately before 1865. Normally these connected sugar mills with their ports, or with public highways. Also some narrow-gauge railroads were authorized to connect warehouses with existing systems. See Subdirrección de Obras Públicas, *Memoria*.

14. The wider ratio of Spanish railroads differentiated them from the rest of the continent. It seems that the choice came from the need to use larger and heavier steam engines given the more mountainous peninsula. In Cuba, however, the wider tracks were used on a line that only traveled on the plains. See Tortella Casares, *Los orígines del capitalismo español*, p. 165.

15. Jacobo de la Pezuela, *Diccionario geográfico, estadístico e histórico de la isla de Cuba* (Madrid: Imprenta Mellado, 1863–66), 2:361.

16. In the nineteenth century it was the practice to name engines after historical figures or patrons of the companies, such as "El Lugareño" run by the Ferrocarril de Puerto Príncipe, the "Marquis of Marianao" by the railroad of the same name, and the "Marquis of Castell Florit" of the Matanzas Railroad, named in honor of general Domingo Dulce who had gratefully relieved the company of some tax burdens.

17. A. M. Jáudenes, *Memoria de las obras públicas en la isla de Cuba 1865–1866 á 1872–1873* (Havana: La Propaganda Literaria, 1882), p. 631.

18. *Reportes de combustibles de Caminos de Hierros de La Habana. Años de 1857 a 1866*, in ANC, Fondo Ferrocarriles (Caminos de Hierro Habana), legajo 23.

19. AFC (ETH), Ferrocarril de Cárdenas y Júcaro, anaquel 28, legajo 1.

20. R. H. Dana, *To Cuba and Back* (Boston: Tickner and Fields, 1859), p. 102.

21. Of the twenty-two jurisdictions of the western department, only Pinar del Río, San Cristóbal, Bahía Honda, and Santa María del Rosario did not have railroads, and only Bahía Honda was a major sugar producer. Of the seven jurisdictions of the eastern department, Guantánamo and Santiago de Cuba were the only significant sugar producers.

22. Dana, *To Cuba and Back*, pp. 108–9.

23. ANC, Fondo Junta de Fomento, legajo 137, expediente 6688.

24. M. Fernández de Castro, *Proyecto de Ferrocarril Central* (Havana, 1862), p. 10.

25. S. Hazard, *Cuba with Pen and Pencil* (Hartford, Conn.: Hartford Publishing Co., 1871).

26. Ferocarril de Cienfuegos y Villa Clara, *Memoria* (1863), p. 22.

27. Ferrocarril de la Bahía de La Habana, *Memoria* (1860), p. 8.

28. Leyva y Aguilera, *Cuba*, p. 17. Our calculation yields 4,782 pesos income per kilometer, which varies slightly from the 4,777 given by Leyva.

29. Bookkeeping entries at that time were extremely simple involving only two columns for income and expenditure.

30. The situation was further worsened by the presence of what were called "tardy shareholders," that is, those who, having ordered shares, refused to pay for them. This was especially prevalent in the later 1850s. The management of the Ferrocarril del Oeste referred these cases thus: "the shareholders who do not pay their obligations are a real nuisance to the company because there is no value in having 1,200 shareholders if only 600 or 700 pay. It is useless to have nominal capital of three million if it only amounts to two in real cash."

31. The German firm, J. Henry Schröder and Company, opened as a commercial bank in London in 1804, designed to provide credit for German importers and exporters, for which it also had branch in Hamburg. About the middle of the nineteenth century it turned to providing loans for railroads throughout Europe and the Americas. Its first recorded Cuban loan is to the Matanzas Railroad in 1853. During the second half of the nineteenth century Schröder expanded its operations throughout Latin America, with loans to Peru in 1870 and 1872, and to some Brazilian and Chilean cities. It lent to railroads in Mexico, Uruguay, Argentina, and Chile, becoming the largest private railroad owner in Chile, the Antofagasta and Bolivia Railroad, an important nitrate carrier. See P. H. Emden, *Money Powers of Europe* (London: Sampson, Low and Marston, n.d), pp. 128, 223, 381. Also, R. Roberts, *Schröders: Merchants and Bankers* (London: Macmillan, 1992), chap. 3.

32. Jacobo de la Pezuela, in his *Diccionario geográfico*, 2:359, estimates that the total capital for all Cuban railroads amounted to 58 million pesos fuertes.

33. Caminos de Hierro de La Habana, *Informe de la Junta Directiva a la general de accionistas* (Havana, 1860), pp. 21–22; Ferrocarril y Almacenes de Depósito de Santiago de Cuba, *Memoria* (1865), p. 12.

34. *Expediente para la concesión del Ferrocarril Central*, AFC (ETH), anaquel 29, pieza A.

35. ANC, Fondo Ferrocarriles (Ferrocarril de Matanzas), legajo 20, expedientes 9, 11.

36. The Alfonso and Aldama families were the principal shareholders of Caminos de Hierro as well as Crédito Territorial. As they were also the concessionaires of the Güines-Matanzas branch, when that was acquired by the Caminos de Hierro, the company owed them 1.7 million pesos.

37. Caminos de Hierro de La Habana, *Informe de la Junta Directiva a la general de accionistas* (Havana, 1863), p. 16.

38. Ibid. (1866), p.15.

39. Ibid. (1867), p. 14.

40. Subdirreción de Obras Públicas, p. 74.

41. Quoted by R. T. Ely, *Cuando reinaba su majestad el azúcar* (Buenos Aires: Editorial Sudamericana, 1963), p. 620.

42. "If an *ingenio* made 2,000 crates, the transportation of this would amount to between 7,000 and 8,000 pesos, but now the railroads have resulted in a savings of between 5,000 and 6,000 pesos." See José A. Saco, "La Supresion del tráfico de esclavos africanos en la isla de Cuba," in *Obras* (New York: Roe Lockwood, 1853).

43. *Libro manuscrito de testimonios de escrituras*, in AFC (ETH), anaquel 41, legajo 16, escritura 27.

44. M. Moreno Fraginals, *El ingenio complejo económico social cubano del azúcar* (Havana: Editorial de Biendas Socialos, 1978), 1:151.

45. C. Savage, *An Economic History of Transport* (London: Hutchinson, 1959), pp. 49–51.

46. This concept is taken from F. Voigt, *Economía de los sistemas de transporte* (Mexico: Fondo de Cultura Económico, 1964), pp. 47–49, where he presents the following definition: "The concept of 'economic restructuring force' of a system of transport connotes the capacity to change an economy either by modification or by innovation." In a limited sense this concept is based on the differential effect of the improvement of the means of transportation over the time of circulation of merchandise. See K. Marx, *El Capital* (Havana: Editorial Nacional, 1963), 2:235.

47. As will be seen later, the occupation of the area running between Calimete, Amarillas, and Yaguaramas by plantations took place in the decade of the 1870s, but the strict chronological precision is not important for this analysis.

48. The reference to the eastern part of Cuba includes the former eastern department plus the jurisdictions of Puerto Príncipe, Nuevitas, and Sancti Spíritus—in other words, everything to the east of Sancti Spíritus. The percentages are based on data taken from the censuses of 1827, 1846, and 1862. In 1862 the eastern region produced 6,753,302 arrobas of sugar with 5,225,000 of that coming from Santiago, Guantánamo, and Sancti Spíritus.

49. *Resumen del censo de población de la isla de Cuba a fin del año 1841* (Havana: Imprenta del Gobierno y Capitanía General, 1842).

50. See Laird W. Bergad, *Cuban Rural Society in the Nineteenth Century* (Princeton: Princeton University Press, 1990) chap. 7.

51. Herminio Portell Vilá, *Historia de Cárdenas* (Havana: Talleres Gráficos Cuba Intelectual, 1928), p. 95.

Chapter 6

1. The reference to the historical role of capital is drawn from a comment of Karl Marx in which he states: "If today, with good reason, we call the proprietors of American plantations capitalists, it is merely because they represent an anomaly in the world market based on free labor." Karl Marx, *Fundamentos de la crítica de la economía política* (Havana: Editorial de Ciencias Sociales, 1970), 1:394.

2. M. Moreno Fraginals, *El ingenio, complejo económico social cubano del azúcar* (Havana: Editorial Ciencias Sociales, 1978), 1:49.

3. The solution of this problem requires a double effort at both the theoretical and the empirical level. This lies beyond the scope of this work. An assumption is made here about the contradictory nature of this historical phenomenon as well as the patent absurdity of the concept of "slavist bourgeoisie." Any attempt to eliminate any of the contradictory elements of this phenomenon would do injustice to the historical reality and create an insuperable obstacle to any understanding of the historical role of this social class.

4. It would be exhaustive to offer a list of the cases here, but those interested might simply consult any of the annual Havana merchant guides from the first half of the nineteenth century where some of the most outstanding Creole landholders are registered as merchants. And the opposite case can be made by looking at C. Rebello, *Estados relativos a la producción azucarera de la isla de Cuba* (Havana: Imprenta del Gobierno, 1860), where a number of merchants are listed as owners of sugar mills. This situation did

not escape an acute observer such as David Turnbull, who noted that "In the larger cities of the island the role of merchant is often combined with that of landowner. . . . In Havana there are many Creole merchants who are estimated to be worth between £100,000 and £200,000 sterling." Quoted in R. T. Ely, *Comerciantes cubanos del siglo XIX* (Havana: Editorial Martí, 1961), p. 83.

5. This classification is more valid for the western department. In the east, where the plantation system was much less developed, the distinction was less clear.

6. The marriages were made not only within a narrow group but often within the same family to the extent that some members could have up to four identical family names. See the genealogies collected in Francisco Javier de Santa Cruz, *Historia de las grandes familias cubanas*, 7 vols. (Havana: Editorial Hércules, 1940–50).

7. Gonzalo Alfonso arrived in Havana from the Canary Islands in the 1770s; Aldama, a Basque, in the early nineteenth century. The Poeys, of French origin, arrived at the end of the eighteenth century, about the same time as James Drake arrived from England. The Escobedo family also came at the end of the eighteenth century from Saint Augustine, Florida. Jacobo de Villaurrutia came with his son-in-law, the Intendant (Alejandro) Ramírez, at the beginning of the nineteenth century. Pedro Diago (father) was born in La Coruña and arrived in Havana in 1792 as director of Maritime Insurance. Finally, Bernabé Martínez de Pinillos, father of the intendant, settled in Havana around 1775.

8. The cases of Aldama and Zulueta bring to mind the story of plutarchy. Domingo Aldama arrived in Havana at the beginning of the nineteenth century and started as a lowly employee in the textile warehouse called El Navio, owned by Don Gonzalo Alfonso. The clever young man soon won the favor of his boss and, what is more, the hand of his daughter, María Rosa, whom he married in 1815. An expert on local commerce, Aldama decided to invest his small savings in the slave trade, and within a short time had enough money to build his first sugar mill, Santa Rosa. He rapidly followed this with other sugar mills, all typically named after saints. By 1836 Domingo Aldama was included in a list compiled by the Junta de Fomento of the eighteen richest men in Cuba. Four years before, the young Julian Zulueta, a Basque like Aldama, arrived in Havana poorer than a "church mouse." After working like other young immigrants he received a timely inheritance that allowed him to establish a modest position in the Havana commercial world. In 1842 his marriage to Dolores Samá, Salvador Samá's niece, opened the doors of the palace to him and provided the opportunity to dedicate himself in a major way to the illegal slave trade. Within five years the enormous capital accumulated allowed Zulueta to build Alava, one of the biggest sugar mills of that time. Don Julian de Zulueta died in 1877, a millionaire and Spanish marquis.

9. R. T. Ely, *Cuando reinaba su majestad el azúcar* (Buenos Aires: Editorial Sudamericana, 1963), p. 640.

10. ANC, Fondo Junta de Fomento, legajo 129, expediente 6374.

11. Contemporaries were quite aware of the importance of the railroad in entrepreneurship. Indeed, Francisco Diago wrote to the North American merchant, Henry Coit, saying of the Júcaro railroad project: "So you see, little by little a spirit of enterprise is awakening among us." See Ely, *Cuando reinaba su majestad el azúcar*, p. 637.

12. *Centón epistolario de Domingo del Monte* (Havana: Imprenta del siglo XX, 1923–57), 4:137.

13. Ibid., 5:94.

14. *Memoria del Ferrocarril del Oeste* (1865), p.7.

15. Ferrocarril de Sabanilla, *Relación manuscrita de contratos*, in AFC (ETH), Documentación legal, entresuelo, anaquel 30, legajo 130.

16. A. Alvarez Pedroso, *Miguel de Aldama* (Havana: Imprenta Siglo XX, 1948), p. 14.

17. This has already been discussed in Chapter 2.

18. A. M. Alcover, *Historia de la villa de Sagua la Grande* (Sagua la Grande: Imprenta Unidas, 1905), pp. 117–20.

19. Wright defended his canals against the railroads, accusing them of a plot to monopolize transport. See H. U. Faulkner, *Historia económica de los Estados Unidos*, 2 vols. (Havana: Editorial de Ciencias Sociales, 1972), 1:321.

20. The many contractors included both Cuban born and foreign, with the foreigners given the more complex jobs such as the Vento Tunnel, contracted to a Mr. Pascoe, or the excavations in the Loma de Negrón, carried out by contractor Dennison. See "Apuntes para la historia de los caminos de hierro de la isla de Cuba," *Prensa de la Habana*, September 5, 1858, and successive numbers.

21. Ely, *Cuando reinaba su majestad el azúcar*, p. 644.

22. ANC, Fondo Junta de Fomento, legajo 179, expediente 8234.

23. A little before the start of work on the line in October 1835, the Junta de Fomento issued a loose flier in the daily press in Havana stating that it had decided to hire any slaves from anyone willing to rent such. See Violeta Serrano, *Crónicas del primer ferrocarril de Cuba* (Havana: Departamento de Orientación Revolucionaria, 1973), p. 33.

24. Work on the railroad was also used as a form of punishment for domestic slaves. One of the first measures adopted by the Caminos de Hierro de La Habana on taking over the Güines Railroad was to regulate the work of "Negroes sent by their masters as a form of punishment." ANC, Fondo Ferrocarriles (Camino de Hierro de La Habana), legajo 1, expediente 37.

25. To begin work, the Júcaro railroad bought eighty slaves and within a few years it owned some two hundred. See A. Cruger, *Informe general del ingeniero director del Ferrocarril de Júcaro* (Havana: Imprenta Oliva, 1841), p. 25.

26. It should not be forgotten that slaves were carried as company assets and therefore meticulously inventoried. Later in the century when slave gangs were smaller, it is possible to follow the fortunes of the runaways in the annual company reports. In the records of the Caminos de Hierro, Pablo appears as a runaway in 1872, and in 1876 is described as definitely lost. His companion, Andrés was not as fortunate, having been reported as recaptured in 1874. See Caminos de Hierro de La Habana, *Informes de la Junta Directiva* (1872–76).

27. Ferrocarril de Cárdenas, *Actas de la Junta Directiva* (1843), in ANC, Fondo Ferrocarriles, legajo 1, expediente 8.

28. Moreno Fraginals, *El ingenio*, 1:304.

29. Fondo Ferrocarriles, *Actas de la Junta Directiva del ferrocarril de Puerto Príncipe a Nuevitas*, book 1, p. 49-A, in AHPC.

30. ANC, Fondo Gobierno Superior Civil, legajo 1018, expediente 35297.

31. In this case the company reminded them that after only two years of work they each owed the company sixty-six pesos fuertes, which was due before the contract could be canceled. See *Actas de la Junta Directiva del Ferrocarril de Puerto Príncipe a Nuevitas*, book 2, pp. 5-A, 6, in AHPC.

32. Juan Pérez de la Riva, "Aspectos económicos del tráfico de culies chinos en Cuba, 1853–1874," *Universidad de La Habana*, no. 173 (May–June 1965), p. 97.

33. ANC, Fondo Ferrocarriles (Caminos de Hierro de La Habana), legajo 1, expediente 10.

34. Pérez de la Riva, "Aspectos económicos," p. 99.

35. Juan Pérez de la Riva, "Demografía de los culies chinos en Cuba, 1853–1874," *Revista de la Biblioteca Nacional José Martí*, año 57, no. 4 (1966), p. 8.

36. *Memoria del Ferrocarril del Oeste* (1959), p. 4. The other figures cited have been taken from the various annual reports of the different companies, except for the Coliseo Railroad figures, which are derived from AFC (ETH), Fondo Documentación legal, entresuelo, anaquel 11, legajo 32.

37. R. H. Dana, *To Cuba and Back* (Boston: Ticknor and Fields, 1859), p. 102.

38. "One of the ways of reducing expenditures has been firing all the wage-paid Negroes and replacing them with Asians in the running and repair operations." Ferrocarril de Cienfuegos y Villa Clara, *Informe de la Junta Directiva a la general de accionistas* (1861), p. 17.

39. Ferrocarril de Matanzas a Sabanilla, *Informe de la Junta Directiva a la general de accionistas correspondiente al año* (1862), p. 11.

40. *Memoria del Ferrocarril del Oeste* (1859), p. 4.

41. *Memoria del Ferrocarril de la Bahía de La Habana* (1867), p. 6.

42. Ibid.

43. ANC, Fondo Gobierno Superior Civil, legajo 1008, expediente 35103.

44. Empresa Unida del Ferrocarril de Cárdenas y Júcaro, *Informe de la Junta Directiva a la general de accionistas*, 1865, p. 5.

45. *Memoria de la Sociedad Anónima del Ferrocarril y Almacenes de Depósitos de Santiago de Cuba*, 1865, p. 8.

46. This is based on a variety of scattered sources and is not very precise. Daily wages in the early 1840s were around 10 pesos per month. By the mid 1850s they rose to about 15 to 17 pesos, and reached some 25 to 30 pesos in the boom year of 1857. In 1862 they stood at about 22 pesos per month. A French worker in an equivalent position gained—converting francs to pesos at the rate of 5.25 francs to the peso—about 14.3 pesos in 1856 and 19 pesos in 1862. See France, Ministère de Economie et Finances, *Annuaire statistique de la France* (Paris: Ministère de Economie et Finances, 1966), p. 422.

Chapter 7

1. Cuba, Secretaría de Obras Públicas, *Memoria sobre los ferrocarilles de la isla de Cuba en los años económicos de 1882–1883 hasta 1887–1898* (Havana: Imprenta Universal, 1902).

2. Railroad statistics for the era usually include two other small new companies: Ferrocarril de Placetas-Caibarién and Ferrocarriles de Viñales–San Cayetano, but those two "companies" arose as private service railroads, and their owners did not turn them into public companies until they had been operating as private lines for some time.

3. The Havana leadership was mainly composed of old reformists, some of whom, including Morales Lemus, Aldama, and Echevarría, also held important positions in several railroad companies.

4. In 1876, Captain General Jovellar continued to insist on this particular. See Ferrocarril de Puerto Príncipe a Nuevitas, *Actas de la Junta Directiva*, in AHPC, book 4, p. 594.

5. Ferrocarril de Cienfuegos y Villa Clara, *Memoria de la Junta Directiva a la general de accionistas* (1873), p. 4.

6. On more than one occasion, the Spanish military authorities recognized that "without the Nuevitas to Puerto Príncipe [railroad], it would be doubtful if we could have been in communication with the capital of the Central Department." See M. Martínez Campos, *Proyecto de Ferrocarril Central* (Madrid, 1880), p. 47.

7. ANC, Fondo Asuntos Políticos, legajo 60, expediente 52.

8. *Datos y noticias oficiales referentes a los bienes embargados* (Havana: Imprenta del Gobierno, 1870), pp. 25–27.

9. Ferrocarril de Cienfuegos y Villa Clara, *Memoria de la Junta Directiva a la general de accionistas* (1870), p. 9.

10. The financial reports of the various companies during the war years are literally filled with these expressions of fidelity to the cause of "national integrity." See, for example, the reports of Caminos de Hierro de la Habana, in which contributions and wages paid to the Volunteers appear regularly.

11. Compañía de Caminos de Hierro de la Habana, *Memoria de la Junta Directiva* (1875), p. 29.

12. *Revista Económica*, August 31, 1879, no. 97, p. 99.

13. See Ferrocarril de Trinidad, *Memoria de la Junta Directiva a la general de accionistas* (1872). In this financial report of the Trinidad railroad, the board of directors analyzed the cause for its liquidation.

14. Ferrocarril de Cienfuegos y Villa Clara, *Memoria de la Junta Directiva a la general de accionistas* (1870), p. 10.

15. Julio Le Riverend, *Historia económica de Cuba* (Havana: Edición Revolucionaria, 1971), pp. 459–60.

16. The monetary problems of this stage also caused difficulties for the researchers because some of the company accounts were in bills that had to be expressed in their gold equivalents to maintain coherence and make conversions possible. That conversion had to be made on the basis of the annual average for the quotations, a method that is far from precise, especially in the case of a seasonal economy such as Cuba's.

17. The first symptoms of the crisis were manifested in Vienna but its most serious outbreak was in New York, where the bankruptcy of Jay Cooke and Company led to the collapse of many banks and other businesses. That was the infamous "Black Friday" of September 19, 1873. From then on, the crisis hit nearly all the countries linked to the capitalist world market and left a trail of bankruptcies that did not end until 1876.

18. The prices have been calculated on the basis of the data given by N. Deerr, *The History of Sugar* (London: Chapman and Hall, 1949–50), 2:531.

19. Sugar production in 1881 was only 1,806,000 tons. See Deerr, *History of Sugar*, 2:490.

20. *Revista de Agricultura*, August 1, 1884, year V, no. 13, p. 576.

21. *Revista de Agricultura*, October 19, 1890, year X, no. 4, p. 491.

22. M. Moreno Fraginals, *El ingenio, complejo económico social cubano del azúcar* (Havana: Editorial de Ciencias Sociales, 1978), 3:76.

23. Raúl Cepero Bonilla, *Azúcar y abolición* (Havana: Editorial de Ciencias Sociales, 1971), p. 268.

24. M. Moreno Fraginals, "Desgarramiento azucarero e integración nacional," *Casa*, año 11, no. 62 (September–October 1970): 10–11. Even though Moreno Fraginals makes an acute analysis of the relations between slavery and technical development, the essential contradiction that this relationship embodies cannot be reduced to the slaves' inability to handle complex techniques. The contradiction is not between the slaves and the ma-

chines, but rather between slavery, with all its economic, social, and cultural assumptions, and industrial production, with its worldwide demands.

25. In 1873, by coincidence, the last attempt was made to introduce African slaves to Cuba. The long cycle of trade came to an end. The European powers, at the dawn of their imperialist expansion, began the division of Africa and the exploitation of its people in situ.

26. Cuba, Subsecretaría de Obras Públicas, *Memoria*.

27. In *El ingenio*, 1:141, Moreno Fraginals considered this to have been the case when he used this region for a statistical comparison of the areas planted in sugarcane in 1960 and 1959. The statistics, however, contain a fallacy, for while the total area under cultivation seems numerically to be the same, from the geographical point of view it is not the same since some areas that used to be cultivated in the past (for example, Cidra), have been abandoned in favor of new ones.

28. The remaining section (from Santo Domingo to Esperanza) was inaugurated in 1885. Until then one had to change trains three times to reach Santa Clara by rail. This involved considerable loss of time because of the round-about Santo Domingo–Cruces–Esperanza-Santa Clara route.

29. "This branch line was built to haul 50,000 boxes of sugar that the mills in that valley [Guamacaro] produced, but all of those farms began to decline . . . so much that, in this sugarcane harvest, only 3,583 boxes of sugar and 2,730 large casks were hauled." See *Informe de la empresa del Ferrocarril de la Bahía de La Habana* (1878), p. 9.

30. The construction of La Trocha began in 1869, but its complex work was carried out extremely slowly, so the line was not operational until 1870–71. La Trocha, as its name (narrow path) indicates, was a strip of cleared land from fifty to a thousand meters wide that crossed the island from Morón on the northern coast to Júcaro on the southern. A series of small forts and observation towers was built along the line, with patrols and flying detachments circulating constantly between them. The purpose of that spectacular fortified line was to keep the insurrection away from the central and western regions of Cuba, but it proved quite ineffective. In 1873 the Spanish command, dissatisfied with the number of men tied down by protecting the line, began work on a railroad line sixty kilometers long that facilitated movement of the troops and made it possible to reduce the size of the garrisons. At the end of the war, the railroad—which always retained its military nature—also offered some other services, but they were of little economic importance. During the War of Independence, La Trocha was brought back into service and was extended seven kilometers, to the landing at San Fernando, north of Morón. See A. Pirala, *Anales de la guerra de Cuba* (Madrid: González Rojas, Editores, 1895), 2:221–27.

31. The details of this process are examined in Chapter 9.

32. Cuba, Secretaría de Obras Públicas, *Memoria*, pp. 208, 243.

33. In the census of 1862, Viñales wasn't even listed as a hamlet in the secondary district of Consolación del Norte. Twenty-five years later it had been recognized as a municipality and, with its 11,550 inhabitants, was the fifth largest in Pinar del Río in terms of population.

34. ANC, Fondo Junta de Fomento, legajo 136, expediente 6633.

35. Fernández de Castro's plan was published that same year by the *Diario de la Marina*. Its route is shown on map 7.4, although the map corresponds to the official route of 1882, which introduced some changes to Fernández de Castro's initial plan.

36. One after another, the government turned down the requests presented by the marquis of Esteva, representing the group of railroad companies; Enrique Lavedán, on

behalf of the Sociedad de Crédito de España; Guillermo Knight; and others. See *Expediente para la concesión de Ferrocarril Central*, pieza 1, in AFC (ETH), anaquel 29, caja 10.

37. See Martínez Campos, *Proyecto del Ferrocarril Central*, p. 47. As a deputy to the Cortes, engineer Miguel Martínez Campos, brother of General Arsenio Martínez Campos, was another of the champions of the project.

38. L. de Tejada, *Memoria sobre el progreso de las obras públicas en la isla de Cuba* (Havana: Imprenta del Gobierno, 1887).

39. The offers included one that Enrique Lavedán made in 1879 that the Negociado de Obras Públicas of the Ministerio de Ultramar turned down, and another that señores Fremy and Filleul, of the Banque Romain in Paris, made in 1882. The latter deposited a million pesetas as a guarantee but failed to obtain favorable results. In 1884, three options were presented: one by Lavedán, José de Armas, and Alfonso Luckhaus, representing a European syndicate; another by Filleul, of the Banco Romano, this time associated with other interests; and the third by señores Correa and Rute, also representing European interests. In 1886, another offer was made, on behalf of the Frères Lille company, of Paris, also without positive results. See José Armas y Céspedes, "El ferrocarril Central," in L. Estévez Romero, *Desde el Zanjón hasta Baire* (Havana: Editorial de Ciencias Sociales, 1974), vol. 2: appendixes. The article originally appeared in *El Pais*, October 21, 1885.

40. Armas y Céspedes, "El Ferrocarril Central."

41. During the 1880s, Cuba's coasts were the scene of active traffic by coastal steamships, some of which belonged to small-scale individual owners, but most of them were owned by large companies, such as the one headed by Mamerto Pulido and Ramón Herrera's El Correo de la Antillas. The interests of those companies were closely linked with large transatlantic companies from Spain such as Transatlántica Española.

42. There is abundant information in this regard. In 1871, the administrator of Caminos de Hierro complained that he had been forced to introduce 30 to 70 percent reductions in the rates between Havana and Matanzas due to competition by the coastal shipping companies. ANC, Fondo Ferrocarriles (Ferrocarriles Unidos de La Habana), legajo 912, expediente 15.

43. *Expediente para la concesión del Ferrocarril Central*, pieza I, in AFC (ETH), anaquel 29, caja 10.

Chapter 8

1. The process began in the mid-1860s in Martinique with the founding of the D'Arboussier sugar mill, on the outskirts of Forte-de-France. It had a capacity for milling close to 125,000 tons of sugarcane each harvest. See G. Descamps, *La crisis azucarera y la isla de Cuba* (Havana: La Propaganda Literaria, 1885).

2. Conde Francisco Feliciano Ibáñez was another of the immigrants who were "ennobled" after achieving economic success in Cuba. He appears to have made his fortune in the 1860s and wound up as one of the most important estate owners on the island. As a sign of the times, Ibáñez in the last third of the century played the same role that Arango y Parreño and conde de Pozos Dulces, two of the Creole oligarchs, had played in their day. In addition to building sugar mills, he also pioneered in fertilizing sugarcane.

3. *Revista de Agricultura*, November 16, 1890, year X, no. 44. Those sugar mills included Apezteguía's Constancia, considered the largest of that period, with an estimated produc-

tion of 30,000 bocoyes (2,250 tons) of sugar, followed by Terry's Caracas, with 20,000 bocoyes.

4. José de la O García, "Centrales y colonias," *Revista de Agricultura*, February 16, 1890, year X, no. 7, p. 77.

5. Ferrocarril de Matanzas, *Libro de actas* (1880–84), p. 39, in ANC, Fondo Ferrocarriles.

6. Empresa Unida de los Ferrocarriles de Cárdenas y Júcaro, *Memoria de la Junta Directiva* (1882), p. 5.

7. The agreement between Caminos de Hierro de La Habana and Pascual Goicochea, owner of the Providencia sugar mill, in Güines, is a good example of this. The railroad company pledged both to provide the cars required for transporting the sugarcane and to do so at a set rate. In exchange, don Pascual Goicochea pledged to use the La Habana Railroad for sending all of the sugar, molasses, high wine, and other items produced by and consumed in the sugar mill.

8. Empresa Unida de los Ferrocarriles de Cárdenas y Júcaro, *Memoria de la Junta Directiva* (1885), p. 5. *Guía de los ferrocarriles de la isla de Cuba* (Havana, 1885), p. 10.

9. "El transporte de caña y los ferrocarriles," *Revista de Agricultura*, September 7, 1890, year X, no. 35, p. 414.

10. In their *Memoria* of 1894, the managers of Ferrocarriles Unidos de La Habana provided details about this operation: "Last year, we indicated the advisability of having the estate owners possess their own locomotives for service on the branch lines which link our lines with their sugar mills, and we explained the advantage that would accrue to them and to the railroads as a result. We have begun to implement that plan, and, this year, five locomotives have been acquired for the Toledo, Providencia, Margarita, Teresa, San Francisco de Paula, and Rosario sugar mills. The society has acquired these locomotives from the Rogers Locomotive Company, with the same terms of payment as for the railroads, with the railroads serving as intermediaries between the estate owners and the manufacturer." ANC, Fondo Ferrocarrilles (Ferrocarriles Unidos de La Habana), legajo 985, expediente 2, p. 30.

11. Cuba, Subdirección de Obras Públicas, *Memoria sobre el progreso de las obras públicas en la isla de Cuba* (1866), p. 73.

12. *Revista de Agricultura*, August 3, 1879, year I, no. 8, p. 211.

13. Ferrocarriles Unidos de La Habana was the result of the merger of Ferrocarril de la Bahía and Caminos de Hierro de La Habana in 1889. (The process that led to the formation of this company will be examined in Chapter 9.)

14. The following excerpt from a report by the managers of Ferrocarriles Unidos de La Habana summarizes the assistance given to the private railroads: "In addition to the service provided free of charge to the estate owners, with the railroads lending them credit and facilities for purchasing their own locomotives for use on their own branch lines with easy terms of payment, the railroads have undertaken several projects and work of other kinds, which [the estate owners] would otherwise have had to carry out at great difficulty and considerable cost. Thus, in our shops we have repaired several of the locomotives they owned; we have sold them four-wheeled cars that cannot be used by the railroads but which they can use on their farms or have built such cars for them; we have done repair work for them on their branch lines; we have built sidings for them for loading the sugarcane; we have sold them track materials, sleepers, and rails; and, as already stated, we have done all this without any direct benefit from the cost and price of the work." ANC, Fondo Ferrocarrilles (Ferrocarriles Unidos de La Habana), legajo 985, expediente 2, p. 56.

15. See Cuba, Secretaría de Obras Públicas, *Memoria sobre los ferrocarriles de la isla de Cuba* (Havana: Imprenta Universal, 1902), pp. 254–305.

16. José de la O García, "Centrales y colonias," p. 77.

17. W. H. Carlson. "Report of Special Commissioner of Railroads to Major General Leonard Wood," in Leonard Wood, *Civil Report of the Military Governor* (Havana, 1901). Because this report was made after the War of Independence, it may have left out some branch lines of sugar mills that were destroyed during the fighting and some others that were not legalized during the anarchic Spanish colonial administration.

18. In October 1868, the Junta Revolucionaria, which the uprising of Generals Prim and Serrano had formed in Spain in September of that same year, stated, "slavery is an outrage to human nature and an affront to the nation, which is the only one in the civilized world which still conserves it in all its integrity." See "Diario de la República Ibérica," Madrid, April 16, 1870, no. 113, reproduced in *La esclavitud de los negros y la prensa madrileña* (Madrid: Ed. Tipográfica de T. Tontanet, 1870), pp. 8–11.

19. "Ley de Vientres Libres," July 4, 1870, in Hortensia Pichardo, *Documentos para la historia de Cuba* (Havana: Editorial de Ciencias Sociales, 1971), 1:394.

20. Rebecca Scott, *Slave Emancipation in Cuba* (Princeton: Princeton University Press, 1985), table III.1.

21. *Revista Económica*, August 14, 1878, year II, no. 46, p. 66.

22. "Ley de Patronato," February 13, 1880, in Pichardo, *Documentos*, 1:423–28.

23. In this regard, the solution provided by Ferrocarril de Caibarién in its staff regulations was particularly inhuman. It consisted of locking up the slave and free day laborers separately at night. Both then and when it was time to go to work, a strict roll call was taken. Moreover, day laborers were allowed to go from one place to another on the line only when authorized to do so. See Ferrocarril de Caibarién a Sancti Spíritus, *Reglamento interior de guardaalmacenes* (Havana: Imprenta La Antilla, 1874), p. 5.

24. Ferrocarril de Cárdenas y Júcaro, *Memoria* (1883), p. 26.

25. Ibid., p. 7.

26. Ibid., (1884), p. 4.

27. *Revista de Agricultura*, May 1883, year IV, no. 5, p. 134; ibid., October 12, 1890, year X, no. 40, p. 469.

28. The sugar mill store was generally the only place on a Cuban plantation where workers could purchase the products they wanted to use and consume, using vouchers that would be debited against their wages. With that system, the workers were doubly exploited, both by being paid low wages and by having to pay high prices.

29. *Revista de Agricultura*, June 13, 1890, year X, no. 27, p. 313.

30. Ibid., November 22, 1891, year XI, no. 46, p. 565.

31. *Gaceta de los Ferrocarriles de la isla de Cuba*, January 14, 1896, p. 16.

32. Ibid., September 14, 1894, p. 417.

33. Ibid., July 7, 1895, p. 811.

34. Ibid., September 7, 1894, p. 472.

35. The case of León Lucumí, a former Negro slave belonging to Caminos de Hierro de La Habana, who had served it for more than fifty years, was a tragic example of the abandonment of a human being at the end of his life. Because of his exceptional situation, the company granted him a monthly allowance starting in 1890, but, as he took his time about dying, the company withdrew it in 1896. ANC, Fondo Ferrocarriles (Ferrocarriles Unidos de La Habana), legajo 573, expediente 1.

36. Ferrocarril de Sagua la Grande, *Memoria de la Junta Directiva* (Havana: Imprenta Howson y Heinen, 1885), p. 12.

37. ANC, Fondo Ferrocarriles (Ferrocarriles Unidos de La Habana), legajo 499, expediente 26, pp. 1–3.

38. ANC, Fondo Ferrocarriles (Ferrocarril de Matanzas), legajo 8, expediente 5.

39. *La Discusión*, June 7, 1892, p. 2.

40. *La Discusión* (June 24, 1892), p. 2. At the end of July, the promise still hadn't been kept, but the workers who had been fired had no recourse. All they could do was blame the company for an accident that occurred to some strikebreakers it had hired, because it had used unskilled workers.

41. The merger of Caminos de Hierro and Ferrocarril de la Bahía in 1889 led to the companies' adopting the new name of Ferrocarriles Unidos de La Habana. Therefore, in view of the name it adopted, the workers' society must have predated the merger. See *Gaceta de los Ferrocarriles de la isla de Cuba*, (October 28, 1894, p. 519. It is also known that a similar society, composed of the workers of Ferrocarril de Cárdenas y Júcaro, was functioning in 1887. See ibid., February 21, 1895, p. 780.

42. *La Discusión*, October 21, 1894, p. 2.

43. The representatives were Pedro Achot, for Ferrocarril de Cienfuegos; Pío Borinaga, Alejandro Muñoz, and Manuel Auside, for Ferrocarriles Unidos de La Habana; and Adolfo López, for Ferrocarril de Caibarién. See *Gaceta de los Ferrocarriles de la isla de Cuba*, November 14, 1894, p. 551. The society was legally constituted on February 10, 1895. See ibid., February 14, 1895, p. 745. The society thus created was the result of a campaign that José Feliú, editor of *Gaceta de los Ferrocarriles*, had been waging since 1893.

44. Luis Arrizurrieta García, operations inspector of Ferrocarriles Unidos de La Habana, was appointed president; Pedro A. Scott, bookkeeper of Banco del Comercio, vice-president; and Juan Francisco Gómez, verifications chief at Ferrocarriles Unidos de La Habana, and Carlos del Sol, chief foreman at Ferrocarril de Matanzas, to other posts. *La Discusión*, December 13, 1894, p. 3.

45. *Gaceta de los Ferrocarriles de la isla de Cuba*, March 28, 1895, p. 857.

46. Ibid., April 21, 1895, p. 903.

47. Ibid., March 21, 1895, p. 965.

48. Ibid., August 14, 1895, p. 1121.

49. Ibid.

50. Ibid.

51. Ibid., January 14, 1896, p. 13.

52. Ibid., January 21, 1896, p. 21.

53. Ibid., January 7, 1896, p. 1.

54. José Rivero Muñiz. *El movimiento obrero durante la primera intervención* (Las Villas: Universidad Central de Las Villas, 1961).

55. ANC, Fondo Ferrocarriles, legajo 795, expediente 53, p. 26.

56. *Gaceta de los Ferrocarriles de la isla de Cuba*, April 8, 1897, p. 73.

57. Ibid., June 1895, p. 1008.

58. Ferrocarril de Puerto Príncipe a Nuevitas, "Actas de la Junta Directiva," in AHPC, book 12, p. 139.

59. ANC, Fondo Ferrocarriles (Ferrocarriles Unidos de La Habana), legajo 425, expediente 22, pp. 5–6.

60. ANC, Fondo Ferrocarriles (Ferrocarriles Unidos de La Habana), legajo 23, expedi-

ente 3, p. 4. Examples of this include the following: "For the record in the case brought against fellow countryman Manuel Valido for helping the rebellion" in 1897 and against Juan García Lema, also a "fellow countryman," "in the case brought against that fellow countryman for propagating news favorable to the insurrection." See ANC, Fondo Ferrocarriles (Ferrocarriles Unidos de La Habana), legajo 499, expediente 42, pp. 55–56, 65–66, 69, 87, 88, plus other, related expedientes.

Chapter 9

1. It should be noted that some advances introduced in the sugar industry were also reflected directly in railroad transportation. This was so in the case of using jute sacks instead of the sugar containers known as *bocoyes* (large casks or barrels) and wooden boxes. The sugarcane estate owners began to use jute sacks in the mid-1870s; this reduced the weight and volume of cargoes on the return trip, when they were empty. Almost all of the sugar was transported in such sacks in 1894. Another innovation worthy of mention was the installation of tipping cranes at the intersections or centers where the sugarcane was received; that kind of crane, commonly called a transporter crane, became an efficient aid in the tenant farmer–railroad–estate owner trio starting in 1890.

2. Ferrocarril de la Bahía, *Actas de la Junta Directiva*, 3:132–33.

3. Caminos de Hierro de La Habana, *Informe de la Junta Directiva* (1887), p. 15, in ANC, Fondo Ferrocarriles (Banco de Comercio y Ferrocarril de la Bahía), legajo 8, expediente 5.

4. ANC, Fondo Ferrocarriles (Ferrocarril de Matanzas), legajo 8, expediente 5, 1892.

5. Ferrocarril de la Bahía de La Habana, *Informe de la Junta Directiva* (1886), pp. 21–22, in ANC, Fondo Ferrocarriles (Ferrocarriles Unidos).

6. ANC, Fondo Ferrocarriles (Ferrocarril de Matanzas), legajo 6, expediente 1, 1882.

7. Ferrocarril de Cárdenas y Júcaro, *Memoria* (1884–85), p. 8.

8. Caminos de Hierro de La Habana, *Informe de la Junta Directiva* (1884), p. 7.

9. Ferrocarril de Cárdenas y Júcaro, *Memoria* (1884–85), p. 3.

10. *Copia sellada de escritura pública* (1876), pp. 68–72, in AFC (ETH), anaquel 26, legajo 66.

11. In April 1868, a small group of stockholders of Caminos de Hierro de La Habana headed by Gonzalo Alfonso, José Morales Lemus, and José Manuel Mestre entered into an agreement with Francisco Fesser, Miguel A. Herrera, and Conde O'Reilly, representing Ferrocarril de la Bahía, for the merger of these companies. The merger was authorized by royal writ on August 22, 1869, but another group of stockholders of Caminos de Hierro, headed by Juan Poey, an estate owner, challenged its legality and obtained a decree issued by the regent of the kingdom on October 13, 1870, that invalidated the royal writ of the preceding year. The efforts that Fernando Vila made on behalf of Ferrocarril de la Bahía and that Antonio Cánovas del Castillo made on behalf of Caminos de Hierro de La Habana were unable to change the decision of the Supreme Court, which invalidated the merger. When the matter was once again submitted to the consideration of both stockholders' meetings, the merger was unanimously approved in the company that needed it the most—Bahía—while the stockholders of Caminos de Hierro, who considered it a monopoly takeover attempt by the Alfonso-Aldama family, turned it down. Caminos de Hierro de La Habana, *Informe de la Junta Directiva* (1867), p. 23, and *Estudio sobre la fusión de Caminos de Hierro de La Habana y el Ferrocarril de la Bahía*, p. 23. The latter work, signed by "a stockholder," must have been published by Juan Poey. Ferrocarril de la

436 · NOTES TO PAGES 174-76

Bahía de La Habana, *Actas* (1869), 3:2, 6, 18, in ANC, Fondo Ferrocarriles; Caminos de Hierro de La Habana, *Informe de la Junta Directiva* (1870), p. 11; and Ferrocarril de la Bahía, *Actas* (1870), 3:84, 85, 100, 104, 105, 107.

12. *Copia de escritura de cesión* (1886), in AFC (ETH), anaquel 9, expediente 13.

13. Politically, Ramón Argüelles Alonso was very closely linked to the Spanish government and, therefore, was a member of the Partido Unión Constitucional and a founding member of a body of urban militia (volunteers). He rounded out his "pedigree" as a reactionary and enemy of Cuba's freedom by being a member of the editorial board of the *Diario de la Marina*. His considerable fortune was built on his profits in the Argüelles y Hno. tobacco firm, founded in 1849. By making and foreclosing on loans to tobacco planters, he managed to take over vast amounts of land in Vuelta Abajo, Pinar del Río province. The firm's credit operations also enabled it to control blocks of stock in various railroad companies. At the time of his death in Spain in 1900, his holdings in Cuban railroads were worth more than 3 million pesos, the largest blocks being in Ferrocarriles Unidos de La Habana and Cárdenas y Júcaro—more than a million shares in each—and the rest, in the Matanzas, Cienfuegos, Sagua, and Caibarién companies. In recognition of his services to the crown, he was granted the title of marquis. The Cuban Central, *Escritura de fusión* (1899), in AFC (ETH); ANC, Fondo Ferrocarriles (Ferrocarriles Unidos de La Habana), legajo 703, expediente 2; Ferrocarril de Cárdenas y Júcaro, legajo 31; Ferrocarril de Matanzas a Jabanilla, *Libro de actas*; and *Libro de oro hispanoamericano de Cuba* (Havana, 1917), p. 246.

14. Caminos de Hierro de La Habana, *Informe de la Junta Directiva* (1878), p. 30; (1880), p. 15; and (1884), p. 24.

15. On that pretext, they obtained two loans from the Schröder bank: one in 1881 for 1,615,000 pesos and the other in 1885 for 1,725,000. Thus, during that critical period, Caminos de Hierro de La Habana assumed a foreign debt of more than 3 million pesos. See Almacenes de Regla, Banco del Comercio y Ferrocarril de la Bahía, Colección facticia (1880–90), 3:10, in BCUH.

16. Ibid., p. 38. Ferrocarril de la Bahía had to first go through a reorganization and rearrangement stage, overseen by a liquidation commission. *Escritura de traspaso del Ferrocarril de la Bahía* (1889), legajo 30, in AFC (ETH).

17. Almacenes de Regla, Banco del Comercio y Ferrocarril de la Bahía, Colección facticia, pp. 4, 39.

18. Efforts were made to purchase Ferrocarril de Marianao in November and December 1889, but the English firm that owned it at the time didn't accept the offered price of 200,000 pesos. ANC, Fondo Ferrocarriles (Ferrocarriles Unidos de La Habana), legajo 27, expediente H.

19. Ibid., legajo 107, expediente 14.

20. Ibid., legajo 91, expedientes 20, 21, 24.

21. Ferrocarril del Oeste, *Informe de la Junta Directiva*, 1882, pp. 4–5.

22. Ibid., pp. 3–4.

23. It should be pointed out that the company operating coastal schooners and steamships between Batabanó and the ports in Vuelta Abajo did a lot of damage to this railroad, for the ships carried nearly all of the region's tobacco.

24. Ferrocarril del Oeste, *Informe de la Junta Directiva* (1882), p. 21.

25. Ibid. (1884), pp. 4–5.

26. Ibid., p. 6.

27. Even though he had been born in Cuba (in Pinar del Río), he was rabidly pro-Spanish and a militant champion of foreign control over Cuba's wealth. He was a deputy to the Cortes from his native province and a senator of the kingdom for Burgos and Huesca. He began his career as a straw man for English and then for U.S. interests with the conveyance of this railroad to the British.

28. Ferrocarril del Oeste, *Informe de la Junta Directiva* (1891), pp. 6, 9.

29. Alberto Ximeno, *Origen y construcción de los ferrocarriles de Cuba* (Havana: Imprenta Rambla y Bouza, 1912), p. 14.

30. *La Discusión*, August 19, 1895, p. 2.

31. Ferrocarril de Cienfuegos, *Informes de la Junta Directiva* (1894–95), pp. 18, 25.

32. Ferrocarril de Matanzas, *Memoria* (1895), p. 26.

33. Ferrocarriles Unidos de La Habana, *Memoria* (1895), p. 26.

34. Ferrocarril de Cárdenas y Júcaro, *Memoria* (1895–96), p. 8.

35. ANC, Fondo Ferrocarriles (Ferrocarril de Matanzas), legajo 23, expediente 3, p. 2.

36. ANC, Fondo Ferrocarriles (Ferrocarril de Cárdenas y Júcaro), legajo 60, expediente 14.

37. ANC, Fondo Ferrocarriles (Ferrocarriles Unidos de La Habana), legajo 393, expediente 6.

38. Ibid., legajo 341, expediente 36.

39. Ibid., legajo 141, expediente 15.

40. Ibid., legajo 425, expediente 22, p. 9.

41. Ferrocarril de Matanzas, *Memoria* (1897), statement 11.

42. The Cárdenas company adopted a two-story model, one of ashlar stone masonry and the other of wood protected with iron rails, to make its bridges and stations impregnable. Ferrocarril de Cárdenas y Júcaro, *Memoria* (1895–96), p. 8.

43. Ferrocarril de Puerto Príncipe a Nuevitas, *Actas de la Junta Directiva*, book 12, p. 237, in AHPC.

44. Ferrocarriles Unidos de La Habana, *Memoria* (1895), p. 18.

45. ANC, Fondo Ferrocarriles, legajo 904, expediente 13-A, 1897–98.

46. ANC, Fondo Ferrocarriles (Ferrocarriles Unidos de La Habana), legajo 98, expediente 9.

47. ANC, Fondo Ferrocarriles, legajo 283, expediente 5.

48. Ferrocarril de Matanzas, *Informe de la Junta Directiva*, October 31, 1896, and ANC, Fondo Ferrocarriles, legajo 20, expediente 3, 1896.

49. This support was mentioned in Chapter 7. It consisted of 0.5 percent for every 10,000 pesos of capital and 1.5 percent taken from the workers' wages. ANC, Fondo Ferrocarriles (Ferrocarril de Matanzas), legajo 6, expediente 10, 1896.

50. ANC, Fondo Ferrocarriles (Ferrocarriles Unidos de La Habana), legajo 28, expediente 5, pp. 5, 6, and expediente 7, p. 143.

51. Tirso Mesa was one of the few Cuban millionaires of his time. He was the son of one of the founders of the city of Colón, Matanzas, and the owner of two sugar mills: La Vega, in Guareiras, and Santa Rita, in Unión de Reyes. In 1898, he owned 804 shares of stock in that company—worth 402,000 pesos—and was its largest individual stockholder. Ferrocarril de Matanzas, *Actas de la Junta de Accionistas*, in ANC, Fondo Ferrocarriles.

52. Aware that Ferrocarriles Unidos hadn't been using the lines of the San Luis Station halt since 1891, the managers of Ferrocarril de Matanzas, when faced with a shortage of their own railroad sidings, wrote Ferrocarriles Unidos as follows: "Since the railroad sidings

which this company owns in the city are completely filled by the rolling stock which it has brought in from the stations in rural areas—because, in view of current happenings, it fears that the cars would be destroyed if left there—I would be grateful if you would allow me to leave some rolling stock on the sidings in the San Luis Station yard belonging to those railroads." ANC, Fondo Ferrocarriles, legajo 115, expediente 12, p. 1.

53. William H. Carlson, "Report of Special Commissioner of Railroads to the Major General Leonard Wood," in Leonard Wood, *Civil Report of the Military Governor* (Havana, 1901), pp. 60–65.

54. Ferrocarril de Matanzas, *Memoria* (1897), p. 6.

55. Ibid., pp. 6, 8.

56. Ibid., p. 5. The Cárdenas Company was also able to pay a dividend of 3 percent in 1898. *Gaceta de los ferrocarriles de la isla de Cuba*, April 19, 1898, p. 62.

57. Ferrocarriles Unidos de La Habana, *Memoria* (1895), p. 19.

58. Of all the products stored in warehouses in those years, 75 percent in 1895 had been brought in by rail; the figure dropped to 23 percent in 1896. This indicates that what little sugar was produced, perhaps by sugar mills on the coast, had been brought to the Regla Warehouses by sea. ANC, Fondo Ferrocarriles (Ferrocarriles Unidos de La Habana), legajo 795, expediente 53, p. 17.

59. Ibid., legajo 405, expediente 5.

60. Ibid., legajo 795, expediente 53, p. 42.

61. Ibid., legajo 795, expediente 53, pp. 23, 37. One company—the Matanzas one—that wasn't the hardest hit with this traffic had performed 117,398 pesos' worth of services to the government in 1896 but collected only 77,816 pesos of that total, the rest of the services being considered to have been provided free of charge. ANC, Fondo Ferrocarriles (Ferrocarril de Matanzas), legajo 393, expediente 2, and legajo 23, expedientes 3, 14.

62. ANC, *Fondo Ferrocarriles (Ferrocarril de Matanzas)*, legajo 393, expediente 2, and legajo 23, expedientes 3, 14.

63. ANC, *Fondo Ferrocarriles (Ferrocarriles Unidos de La Habana)*, legajo 795, expediente 53, p. 7.

64. *Escritura convenio* (1896), in AFC (ETH), anaquel 11, legajo 30.

65. In *Origen y construcción de los ferrocarriles en Cuba*, p. 15, Alberto de Ximeno, longtime manager of Ferrocarriles Unidos, stated that the factors that made it impossible to pay the mortgage to Schröder included the "absorption of profits by the Banco." Apart from its property, that credit institution formally maintained a capital of 700,000 pesos. R. Argüelles continued to be its president even after the split. ANC, Fondo Ferrocarriles (Ferrocarriles Unidos de La Habana), legajo 795, expediente 54, pp. 7, 8.

66. Ferrocarriles Unidos de La Habana, *Escritura de constitución de los Ferrocarriles Unidos*, in AFC (ETH), anaquel 17, caja 68-A, expediente 64.

67. The plot of land known as Tallapiedra included an important section of Havana's harbor coastline; the plot known as Villanueva included the yard of the Villanueva Station. When the city grew and the wall surrounding it was knocked down, Villanueva was nearly in the center of the city. The former National Capitol, now the Academy of Sciences of Cuba, occupies the site.

68. *Escritura convenio*, in AFC (ETH), anaquel 11, legajo 67.

69. Ferrocarriles Unidos de La Habana, *Escritura de constitución de los Ferrocarriles Unidos*, in AFC (ETH), anaquel 17, caja 68-A, expediente 67.

70. Ibid.

71. In 1890, this company had merged with the narrow-gauge railroad that went to Placetas: the "Ferrocarril de Zaza."

72. *La Discusión*, November 21, 1890, p. 2.

73. Ferrocarril de Caibarién, *Escritura de fusión*, p. 70, in ANC, Fondo Ferrocarriles.

74. Ferrocarril de Cienfuegos y Villa Clara, *Memorias* (1897, 1898).

75. *Gaceta de los Ferrocarriles de la isla de Cuba*, November 28, 1898, p. 33.

76. Ibid., December 14, 1898.

77. ANC, Fondo Ferrocarriles (Cuban Central Railways), legajo 762, expediente 12. On page 26 of his work on Cuba's railroads, Ximeno gave somewhat different figures for the mortgage payments due: 3,395,000 for the principal mortgage at 4.5 percent and 967,000 for the old shares of the Cienfuegos and Caibarién Railroads.

78. Cuban Central Railways, *Escritura de fusión*, pp. 13, 71, in ANC, Fondo Ferrocarriles.

79. *Gaceta de los Ferrocarriles de la isla de Cuba*, May 28, 1899. The supervisory government approved the sale and merger of the companies in Las Villas shortly thereafter, on August 26, 1899. AFC (ETH), anaquel 12, legajo 38, expediente 17.

Chapter 10

1. V. I. Lenin, *Imperialism, the Highest Stage of Capitalism* (New York: International Publishers, 1939), p. 22.

2. Ibid., p. 42.

3. Rudolph Hilferding, *El capital financiero* (Madrid: Tecnos, 1963), p. 363.

4. Of a total of £2.7 billion sterling that England had invested abroad by the beginning of the twentieth century, £1.7 billion had been in the railroad sector. Ibid., p. 365.

5. Railroad promoters in the United States obtained state subsidies of from $16,000 to $42,000 per kilometer of track. Very favorable legislation, gifts of large tracts of land, free surveying, and the granting of state loans through direct purchases of railroad bonds were other factors in the extraordinary assistance the government gave those railroads. See H. Faulkner, *Historia económica de los Estados Unidos* (Havana: Editorial de Ciencias Sociales, Instituto Cubano del Libro, 1972), 2:543.

6. Faulkner. *Historia económica*, p. 638.

7. The joint resolution was the legal instrument by means of which the Congress of the United States, invoking as a pretext the Cubans' right to be free, empowered the U.S. president to use whatever resources might be necessary to intervene in Cuba's War of Independence and "pacify" the country.

8. "Tratado de Paz entre España y Estados Unidos de América," Paris, December 10, 1898, in Hortensia Pichardo, *Documentos para la historia de Cuba* (Havana: Editorial de Ciencias Sociales, 1971), 1:460.

9. Julio Le Riverend, *Historia económica de Cuba* (Havana: Edición Revolucionaria, 1972), chap. 33, p. 551.

10. "Special Report of Brigadier General Fitzhugh Lee," in John R. Brooke, *Civil Report of Major General John R. Brooke, U.S. Army, Military Governor, Island of Cuba* (Washington, D.C.: Government Printing Office, 1900), p. 1.

11. Reports of Brigadier General James H. Wilson, U.S.V., commanding the Department of Matanzas and Santa Clara for the calendar year of 1899, Matanzas, Cuba, 1899, p. 14.

12. "Special Report of Brigadier General Leonard Wood, U.S.V.," pp. 3–4, in Brooke, *Civil Report*, pp. 3–4.

13. Putnam's and Sons published this excerpted report in New York in 1899 under the title *Industrial Cuba*.

14. Gloria City was a small settlement of farmers from the United States to whom, soon after the turn of the century, the geophagous Cuban Land Company sold plots in the northern part of what was then Camagüey Province.

15. Robert Porter, *Industrial Cuba* (New York: Putnam's Sons, 1899), p. 413.

16. Ibid.

17. Ibid. The English consul in Havana also tried to interest British subjects in investing capital at that propitious moment, according to a report he published in the daily *La Discusión*, July 22, 1901, p. 2.

18. William H. Carlson, "Report of Special Commissioner of Railroads to the Major General Leonard Wood," in Leonard Wood, *Civil Report of the Military Governor* (Havana, 1901).

19. The budget of the government of the island paid for the construction of this railroad to keep the troops and supplies of the U.S. Army from using Havana's docks, which were supposedly infected with yellow fever. A few months later, the little use it had been given showed just how useless it was. "Report of the Quartermaster," in Wood, *Civil Report*, p. 9.

20. Cuba, Secretaría de Obras Públicas, *Memoria sobre los Ferrocarriles de la isla de Cuba en los años económicos de 1882–1883 hasta 1897–1898* (Havana: Imprenta y Papelería La Universal, 1902), p. 381.

21. Porter. *Industrial Cuba*, p. 413, and Carlson, "Report of Special Commissioner," pp. 273–75.

22. "Report of E. A. Moseley and M. S. Decker," in Leonard Wood, *Civil Report of the Military Governor* (Havana, 1902), 1:60.

23. We are referring to the enterprise promoted by William Van Horne. Because it is a topic of special importance, it will be studied in detail in Chapter 11.

24. Cuba, Secretaría de Obras Públicas. *Memoria*, part II, p. 359.

25. Ibid., (emphasis added).

26. Ibid., p. 352. This refers to Military Order 285, of June 29, 1900.

27. Ibid., pp. 364–65.

28. M. Sánchez Roca, *Leyes administrativas de la República de Cuba y su jurisprudencia* (Havana: Editorial Lex, 1942), 2:7.

29. Walter Vaughan, *The Life and Work of Sir William Van Horne* (New York: Century Company, 1920), pp. 288–89. Also Wood, *Civil Report* (1902), 1:165–66.

30. Leonard Wood, *Civil Report of the Military Governor* (Havana, 1901), 1:33.

31. Ibid., p. 34.

32. Ibid., pp. 80–91, and Pichardo, *Documentos*, 2:158–79.

33. José M. Gálvez, "La ley de Ferrocarriles," *El Economista*, February 14, 1903, p. 7.

34. Military Order 117 established higher rates but in hardly a fair way: increases of 50 percent for the Marianao, Unidos, Guantánamo, and Gibara Railroads; a 30 percent increase for Ferrocarril de Puerto Príncipe; and increases of only 20 percent for the Matanzas and Cárdenas lines. See "Report of E. A. Mosleley and M. S. Decker," pp. 107–8.

35. Ibid., 1:123. The U.S. companies' experience regarding rates was similar to that gained in Cuba. In the United States, the rulings of the Interstate Commerce Commission —on which the experts Moseley and Decker served—were not carried out, because the ICC was subordinate to the ordinary courts. The U.S. functionaries tried to reverse that situation in Cuba by placing the laws and rulings on railroads and the Comisión de

Ferrocarriles beyond the competence of the courts, to guarantee strict compliance with the established order and protection for the Cuba Company.

36. Sánchez Roca, *Leyes administrativas*, 2:5–7.

37. "Platt Amendment," in L. H. Jenks, *Our Cuban Colony: A Study in Sugar* (New York: Vanguard Press, 1928), pp. 78–79.

38. "Orden Militar número 34," in Pichardo, *Documentos*, 2:170–71.

Chapter 11

1. That's how President McKinley put it in his State of the Union message to Congress on December 5, 1899. See J. D. Richardson, ed., *A Compilation of Messages and Papers of the Presidents, 1789–1902* (Washington, D.C., 1896–1902), 10:152.

2. This refers to the jointly owned estates. When the estate was divided up among various heirs or ceded to several individuals, no physical division of the area was effected, but each beneficiary was assigned a proportion of the original value of the estate, calculated in pesos called "ownership pesos."

3. L. H. Jenks, *Our Cuban Colony: A Study in Sugar* (New York: Vanguard Press, 1928), p. 161.

4. Oscar Zanetti, Alejandro García, et al. *United Fruit Company: un caso del dominio imperialista en Cuba* (Havana: Editorial de Ciencias Sociales, 1976), pp. 63–66.

5. *Gaceta de los Ferrocarriles de la isla de Cuba*, February 1898, year VI, no. 3, p. 14.

6. Ibid., March 31, 1898, year VI, no. 6, p. 51.

7. Ibid., April 7, 1899, year VII, no. 6, p. 44. Ryan, Elkins, Widener, and Whitney controlled the Metropolitan Street Railway Company, which held a monopoly on New York's streetcars. The group was very important in this sector, and some of its members also controlled the streetcars in Philadelphia, Chicago, and other cities in the United States. Ryan and Widener had also joined forces in creating a tobacco trust, the American Tobacco Company. The syndicate which these individuals formed for controlling Havana's streetcars was called the American Indies Company.

8. In this book, we cannot go into the details of the confusing and contradictory "battle" for Havana's streetcars. It appears that the Farquhar-Harvey group won out after allying itself with Tiburcio Pérez Castañeda, who had represented the interests of a European syndicate up until then. However, the results would indicate that the various contenders made some sort of a deal, thanks to the "good offices" of the U.S. authorities in Cuba. More complete, though not entirely reliable, information in this regard may be found in C. A. Gauld, *The Last Titan: Percival Farquhar, American Entrepreneur in Latin America* (Stanford, Calif.: Stanford University Press, 1964), pp. 5–11.

9. See Chapter 7.

10. Robert P. Porter, *Industrial Cuba* (New York: Putnam's Sons, 1899), p. 30.

11. Alger thought the construction of the railroad would be the best means for resuscitating Cuba's economic life, since it would give the Cuban people work and teach them to be industrious. That paternalistic sentiment barely disguised his imperialistic intentions, for he added that he considered the railroad indispensable if complete peace were to be achieved in the Greater Antilles. See *Gaceta de los Ferrocarriles de la isla de Cuba*, 1898, year VI, no. 17, pp. 137–38.

12. Ibid., July 21, 1899, year VII, no. 13. More information, along with editorial commentary, may be found in the issues preceding and following the one cited.

13. Walter Vaughan, *The Life and Work of Sir William Van Horne* (New York: Century Company, 1920). This substantial "vanity" biography seems to have been the starting point for the Van Horne myth. See chapter 21 of that work in particular for the relations mentioned.

14. Ibid., p. 277.

15. General Dodge, who had fought in the Civil War, was one of the most prominent U.S. railroad men. Linked to the McKinley administration, he had headed a commission that looked into the conduct of the War Department during the hostilities with Spain and had upheld a position that was very favorable to Secretary Alger. See M. Leech, *In the Times of McKinley* (New York: Harper, 1959), pp. 315–20.

16. Vaughan, *The Life and Work*, p. 280.

17. Ibid., p. 282. Vaughan notes that Van Horne had some difficulty convincing Ryan.

18. See Chapter 9.

19. In June 1900, Van Horne and Samuel Thomas, director of the Cuba Company and of the Chase National Bank, jointly owned 670,000 pesos' worth of stock in Ferrocarril de Santiago de Cuba. In addition, in his own name, Sir William held another block of stock, worth $37,800. See W. H. Carlson, "Report of the Special Commissioner of Railroads," in Leonard Wood, *Civil Report of the Military Governor* (Havana, 1902).

20. Vaughan, *The Life and Work*, p. 285.

21. The job opportunities offered by the railroad's construction figured importantly in that propaganda. See *La Lucha*, August 7, 1900, p. 2.

22. The lawyers were Teodoro de Zaldo and Manuel de Jesús Manduley. The former was a member of a prominent family of Cuban bankers who, it seems, had formed ties with Farquhar while in the United States during the years of the War of Independence. Manduley had joined the Liberation Army at the end of the war. Later, he put out his shingle in Havana to handle legal matters for Governor Wood, Van Horne, the United Fruit Company, and other U.S. companies.

23. *La Discusión*, September 15, 1900, p. 1.

24. Ibid., December 20, 1900, p. 6.

25. Cited by H. Hagedorn in *Leonard Wood, a Biography* (New York: Harper, 1931), 1:330.

26. The list of licenses may be found in the reports that the secretary of public works presented to General Wood which are contained in the Civil Reports for 1901 and 1902.

27. Vaughan, *The Life and Work*, p. 292.

28. Hortensia Pichardo, *Documentos para la historia de Cuba* (Havana: Editorial de Ciencias Sociales, 1973), 2:118. This article ratified as valid all the actions of the U.S. military government in Cuba during the occupation of the island. It is significant that Cuba's Constitutional Convention's counterproposal to what would later be the Platt Amendment accepted Article 4 but made it abide by the stipulations of the Foraker Act. The U.S. government turned down the Cuban modification. This can be seen clearly by comparing the bases of the amendment, which Root formulated on February 7, 1901; the Cuban counterproposal of February 27; and the final version of the Platt Amendment, all of which appear in pp. 102–21 of the cited text.

29. J. Lacret Morlot, "Carta al Director," *La Lucha*, March 23, 1901, p. 2.

30. Vaughan, *The Life and Work*, p. 288.

31. Pichardo, *Documentos*, 2:156–79.

32. "Informe del cuartel maestre respecto a asuntos insulares," in Leonard Wood, *Civil*

Report. 1901 (Havana, 1902), 7:9–10. According to the copy of the contract contained in AFC (d.C.), the Cuba Company pledged only to construct a 25,000-peso dock in Júcaro.

33. *La Discusión*, March 7, 1902, p. 1.

34. Emilio Roig de Leuschsenring, *Historia de la Enmienda Platt* (Havana: Editorial de Ciencias Sociales, 1973), p. 165.

35. Cuba Railroad Company, *Certificado de constitución*, in AFC (d.C.), Departamento Legal.

36. That 60 percent of the preferred stock was distributed among the stockholders in the Cuba Company in the same proportion as their share of its stock. See ANC, Fondo Ferrocarriles, libros, and Cuba Railroad Company, *Minutes of the Stockholders' Meetings* (1902), 1:44–46.

37. This service was inaugurated on November 15, 1903. The trip using other means of transportation took nearly a week.

38. Fleming's company followed up this initial investment with the purchase of $4 million worth of stock in 1905.

39. Tomás Estrada Palma emphasized the fact that the railroad company hadn't received any kind of official assistance before, so the subsidy would show "our commitment to encourage and protect the big companies which invest millions in our country." See *El Economista*, November 19, 1904, no. 89, p. 78.

40. Cited by Vaughan, *The Life and Work*, p. 304. The lawyers were Manuel de Jesús Manduley, Antonio Berenguer and J. R. Betancourt. See AFC (d.C.), Fondo General de Paquetería, paquete I-936, expediente E. O. 129, "Development Costs."

41. A Scot like Fleming, Whigham was an engineer who had specialized in railroads and hydraulic work. At the time of his appointment, he was working in Egypt. Whigham's subsequent positions in the Cuba Company are a fair indicator of the British interests' influence in it.

42. The details of the route were largely determined by the company's interest in having the railroad cross its extensive Cabaniguán (Jobabo) estate, where it planned to build a sugar mill.

43. After its bankruptcy in 1873, Ferrocarril de Trinidad had passed into the hands of the state. When the Placetas branch was built, the Cuba Company acquired the old Ferrocarril de Trinidad, which ended at the port of Casilda.

44. On that occasion, he seems to have appealed to the senators and representatives from the areas the railroad would benefit—Fernández de Castro, from Bayamo, for example—for whom approval of a bill of this kind was of political interest. The text of the law is contained in the *Gaceta Oficial de la República de Cuba*, July 5, 1906, pp. 93–94.

45. The subsidy was finally adjusted to 5,000 pesos per kilometer. Gómez's administration gave the company a subsidy of 1,642,032 pesos in August 1910. *Questionnaires and Responses Relating to Cuba Railroad Company*, in AFC (d.C.), Fondo General de Paquetería, paquete 1941, expediente 2-A1.

46. The letter, cited by Vaughan, *The Life and Work*, pp. 286–87, stated, among other things, that "The country can only reach its highest prosperity and the greatest stability of government through the widest possible ownership of the lands by the people who cultivate them. In countries where the percentage of individuals holding real estate is greatest, conservatism prevails and insurrections are unknown."

47. Cuba Company, *Annual Report to the Stockholders* (1907).

48. The value of that urban land should not be underestimated. Years later, the Cuba

Railroad would state that those 5.5 million square meters of urban land were worth nearly 12 million pesos, a little more than all the capital that was invested in building the main line. Note that the original cost of the land was less than 400,000 pesos. *Recapitulation of Land Values*, in AFC (d.C.), Fondo General de Paquetería, paquete 1941, expediente I-A-1.

49. Cuba Company, *Annual Report to the Stockholders* (1907).

50. Map 11.2 shows the advance of sugar mill construction. The size of those holdings has been estimated on the basis of data in *Anuario Azucarero de Cuba* and Oscar Pino Santos, *El asalto a Cuba por la oligarquía financiera norteamericana* (Havana: Editorial Casa de las Américas, 1973), p. 160.

51. Cuba, Oficina Nacional de los censos demográfico y electoral, *Censo de población, vivienda y electoral*, January 28, 1953 (Havana, 1955), table 4.

52. A description of this situation and the differences between Oriente and Camagüey in this regard are presented in Juan Pérez de la Riva's "Los recursos humanos de Cuba al comenzar el siglo," in *Anuario de Estudios Cubanos* 1 (Havana: Editorial de Ciencias Sociales, 1975), p. 39.

53. Cuba Company, *Annual Report to the Stockholders* (1911–12).

54. See Chapter 4.

55. In 1900, Post promoted the consolidation of three New York refineries to create the National Sugar Refining Company. In addition to his Guantánamo holdings, he also had interests in the Cuban American Sugar Mills in Cuba. He was on the board of directors of Guantánamo Sugar, as was Gerald L. Hoyt, of the American Car and Foundry Company (which manufactured railroad equipment), who had also invested in the Havana Electric Company and the Cuba Company. There isn't much information about what happened to the Brooks, but this case is reminiscent of the Dumois family, which, at around that same time, facilitated United Fruit's penetration in the northern part of Oriente Province. Teodoro Brook very quickly ceased to hold any executive positions, and no more Brooks appeared among the members of the board of Guantánamo Sugar after 1929.

56. Jenks noted in *Our Cuban Colony*, p. 151, that the Knickerbocker Trust Company had planned to settle U.S. sugarcane growers in the region.

57. Northeastern Cuba Railroad Company, *Minutes of the Director's Meetings*, pp. 97–98, in ANC, Fondo Ferrocarriles, libros.

58. H. U. Faulkner, *Historia económica de los Estados Unidos* (Havana: Editorial de Ciencias Sociales, 1972), 2:558.

59. Northeastern Cuba Railroad Company, *Agreement of August 24, 1908*, in ANC, Fondo Ferrocarriles, libros.

60. Guantánamo and Western Railroad Company, *Libros de minutas de la Junta Directiva*, 1:136, in ANC, *Fondo Ferrocarriles, libros*.

Chapter 12

1. The list of stockholders at the beginning of the twentieth century is contained in W. H. Carlson's "Report of the Special Commissioner of Railroads," in Leonard Wood, *Civil Report of the Military Governor* (Havana (?), 1902), pp. 66–74.

2. See Chapter 9.

3. *Gaceta de los Ferrocarriles de la isla de Cuba*, May 14, 1899, pp. 57–58.

4. *La Lucha*, May 18, 1899, p. 2.

5. *Gaceta de los Ferrocarriles de la isla de Cuba*, May 28, 1899. During that same period,

the editor of the *Gaceta* and don Tiburcio Pérez Castañeda exchanged exaggerated eulogies, and the latter congratulated the former on "your campaign for the merger" of the three Las Villas railroad companies.

6. *La Lucha*, June 16, 1899, p. 1.

7. Ibid., October 30, 1899, p. 2.

8. *Gaceta de los Ferrocarriles de la isla de Cuba*, December 2, 1899, p. 166.

9. *La Discusión*, February 2, 1901, p. 1.

10. ANC, Fondo Ferrocarriles (Ferrocarriles Unidos), legajo 109, expediente 4.

11. In January 1902, shortly after it had been agreed to increase Cárdenas y Júcaro's capital to 10 million pesos, the treasurer and the cashier of the company were accused of having falsified some of the new shares that were issued. The affair was blown up by the same newspapers that had urged the sale of the railroad, which tried their utmost to implicate the president and the secretary of the Cárdenas Company in the supposed fraud so as to undermine the stockholders' confidence in the company. Finally, after some complicated judicial procedures, the accused were absolved, dissipating the atmosphere created around the hypothetical fraud.

12. A few months before occupying the presidency of the republic, Tomás Estrada Palma had stated that he favored a merger of all the railroads on the island. See *Gaceta de los Ferrocarriles de la isla de Cuba*, January 21, 1902, p. 6.

13. Schröder may have controlled even more shares, for Durham, Stokes and Company, a firm of British brokers, told one of its clients in June 1905 that the directors of Ferrocarriles Unidos had purchased more than a third of the stock of the Cárdenas Company. The figure given in the text was taken from Relación de accionistas de la Empres Unida de los Ferrocarriles de Cárdenas y Júcaro, in AFC (ETH), anaquel 11, legajo 31.

14. Ibid.

15. ANC, Fondo Ferrocarriles (Ferrocarriles Unidos), legajo 109, expediente 4.

16. This old firm, which began its operations with the slave trade and importing coolies in the nineteenth century, received a 3.3 percent commission on the amount of capital exchanged (272,112 Spanish pesos) for its services in the merger. Ibid., expediente 6.

17. *El Economista*, July 7, 1906, p. 592.

18. Cuba, Comisión de Ferrocarriles, *Memoria* (1901–2), pp. 283–87.

19. ANC, Fondo Ferrocarriles (Ferrocarriles Unidos), legajo 75, expediente 4.

20. In addition to claiming high indemnity (around $35,000) for the expropriated land, when laying its lines in the area the board of directors of Ferrocarriles Unidos tried to force Havana Central to build an expensive overpass and to knock down a considerable stretch of the wall of the neighboring Arsenal, which, alone, would cost 100,000 pesos. See ibid., legajo 703, expediente 7.

21. See Walter Vaughan, *The Life and Work of Sir William Van Horne* (New York: Century Company, 1920), pp. 312–14. After sharp contradictions, Van Horne managed to reach an agreement with Ferrocarriles Unidos in 1907, after which the relations between the two most important railroad companies in Cuba remained stable.

22. This process coincided in time with the one that led Frank Steinhart to take over Havana Electric, the parent company of Havana Central, which makes one think of a general withdrawal by the investment group that controlled the two companies. See L. H. Jenks, *Our Cuban Colony: A Study in Sugar* (New York: Vanguard Press, 1928), p. 170.

23. According to a circular that Ferrocarriles Unidos sent to the London Stock Exchange in the summer of 1907, that company controlled $4,112,500 worth of stock in Havana

Central—51 percent of the total issued—and $2.5 million worth of that company's mortgage bonds. In 1907, W. E. Ogilvie, a U.S. associate of the Schröder bank, began to head Havana Central. The other executive posts were filled by old officials of Ferrocarriles Unidos, such as Manuel L. Díaz, G. Morson, and H. Bellefuille. ANC, Fondo Ferrocarriles (Havana Central), legajo 6, expediente 1.

24. This refers to the land now occupied by the Academy of Sciences of Cuba, formerly the National Capitol.

25. ANC, Fondo Ferrocarriles (Ferrocarriles Unidos), legajo 703, expediente 4.

26. It shouldn't have been difficult for them to see President Gómez, for Ferrocarriles Unidos was one of the many companies that had contributed to his presidential campaign war chest. See A. Sanjenís, *Tiburón* (Havana: Lib. Hispanoamericana, 1915), p. 77.

27. Cited in *The Cuba Review* 8, no. 3 (February 1910): 21.

28. A. Pompeyo, *El tratado anglo-cubano* (Havana, 1905).

29. *The Cuba Review* 8, no. 3 (February 1910): 20.

30. Ibid. The arguments in favor of the strategic value of the Arsenal land noted that it had been used for the landing of U.S. troops in 1906, at the beginning of the second intervention by the United States in Cuba.

31. Constitución de la Havana Terminal Railroad Co., in AFC (ETH), anaquel 20, caja 98.

32. Hortensia Pichardo, *Documentos para la historia de Cuba* (Havana: Editorial de Ciencias Sociales, 1973), 2:341–44.

33. The assessing commission, composed of three experts and presided over by Joaquín Chalons, secretary of public works, assessed the Arsenal land at 2,732,900 pesos and the Villanueva land at 2,196,710 pesos. In spite of its port value, Arsenal's 14,000-square-meter strip of waterfront land was assessed at 50 pesos per square meter, while Villanueva's 11,000-square-meter strip of land along the Paseo del Prado was assessed at 65 pesos per square meter. The greatest difference in the transaction came from the fact that Arsenal's buildings were assessed at 1,029,104 pesos, while Villanueva's were assigned a value of 96,178. Informe de la Comisión del Canje al Presidente de la República, in AFC (ETH), anaquel 20, caja 98.

34. Escritura no. 70 de permuta, obligaciones y concesiones otorgada el 23 de diciembre de 1910 ante el licenciado Jesús María Barraqué, and Escritura no. 341 de cesión y transferencia de bienes efectuada ante Antonio González Solar, el 23 de diciembre de 1910, both in AFC (ETH), anaquel 20, caja 98.

35. This company had been founded on the basis of the diminutive Ferrocarril de Dubrocq, which Colonel José M. Tarafa built thanks to a concession by the Cuban government. Tarafa built the railroad and bought several plots of land. Later on, he joined some U.S. businessmen to establish Matanzas Terminal.

36. Cuba, Comisión de Ferrocarriles, *Memoria* (1902–3), pp. 116–18.

37. United Railways of Havana and Regla Warehouses Limited, *Annual Report* (1911–12), p. 16.

38. Cuban Central Railways Company Limited, "To the Preference Shareholders," in *Annual Report* (February 1914).

39. Oscar Pino Santos, *El asalto a Cuba por la oligarquía financiera norteamericana* (Havana: Editorial Casa de las América, 1973), pp. 33–42.

40. Ibid., p. 39.

41. Frequently, there was a year's delay between the operations and the changes in

capital, which can be explained by the fact that there was a lapse between the company's accounts in London and the time when the Havana office sent data to the Comisión de Ferrocarriles for publication in the *Memorias* from which they were taken.

42. The merger agreement with Ferrocarril de Cárdenas y Júcaro leads one to deduce that Ferrocarriles Unidos made a stock issue of £1 million sterling and a debenture issue of £1.2 million sterling, which amounted to a total of around $11 million, $2 million more than was needed for the exchange. See AFC (ETH), anaquel 11, legajo 31. To cover the absorption of Ferrocarril de Matanzas, it made a £608,500 sterling issue of 5 percent irredeemable debentures and a £912,750 sterling issue of ordinary stock, the total equivalent to around $7.5 million, at least $1.5 million more than was needed. ANC, Fondo Ferrocarriles (Ferrocarriles Unidos), legajo 109, expediente 6. Moreover, before the end of 1906, Ferrocarriles Unidos issued £730,000 sterling worth of preferred stock and £988,750 sterling worth more of debentures, this last to be placed on the French stock exchange by the Société Générale. Those additional issues were equivalent to nearly $9 million. See United Railways of Havana and Regla Warehouses Ltd., *Annual Report* (1905–6), p. 2.

43. Cited by Jenks, *Our Cuban Colony*, p. 127.

Chapter 13

1. Willet and Gray, *Sugar Statistics*, exhibit 4.

2. Ramiro Guerra, *Azúcar y población en las Antillas* (Havana: Editorial Lex, 1961).

3. L. H. Jenks, *Our Cuban Colony: A Study in Sugar* (New York: Vanguard Press, 1928).

4. Cuba, Secretaría de Agricultura, Industria y Comercio, *Memorias de las zafras azucareras* (1914–20).

5. "Cuba económica y financiera," *Anuario Azucarero de Cuba* (1959), p. 91.

6. For details on foreign trade in this period, see Oscar Zanetti, "El comercio exterior de la República neocolonial," in *Anuario de estudios cubanos*, vol. 1 (Havana: Editorial de Ciencias Sociales, 1975), pp. 47–126.

7. See ibid. cuadro 6.

8. Negotiations for establishing the ferry service between Ferrocarriles Unidos and the Florida East Coast Railroad began in 1913, shortly after the system of bridges that linked Key West to the peninsula of Florida was inaugurated. Finally authorized by the Secretaría de Hacienda in December 1914, the service was inaugurated the following year. The concessions that the Cuban state granted for that kind of operation were exceptionally liberal, for the railroad cars were allowed to be shipped loaded and to remain sealed without being subjected to any customs inspection until they reached their final destination. During its first decade in existence, the service was offered on a limited scale by a ferryboat that carried from twenty-five to thirty railroad cars at a time between Key West and Havana. Starting in 1929, the ferry service was increased with the opening of a new line between New Orleans and Havana, using ships that could carry up to a hundred railroad cars. The increase in the ferry and sea-train service would be a cause of frequent contradictions between the railroad and port sectors.

9. In or around 1927, the private railroads owned a total of more than 10,000 kilometers of track, around 6,400 of which belonged to the large U.S. sugar companies.

10. The documentation on these concessions may be seen in Jenks, *Our Cuban Colony*, pp. 326–34. The government gave Cuba Railroad the subsidy even though a Cuban had entered a bid whose terms were much more favorable to the interests of the state.

11. The first step in this regard was taken in 1913 when United Railways acquired 97 percent of the common stock of Cuban Central and 41.8 percent of its preferred stock. It began to exercise administrative control in 1914 by offering combined services and mutual discounts. It obtained complete administrative control in 1917 with the appointment of a single manager for Unidos and Cuban Central. The process of absorption wound up in 1920 when Schröder and Company used its control over Cuban Central to push through a merger with Ferrocarriles Unidos. See United Railways of Havana and Regla Warehouses, *Annual Report* (1913–17), and *Short Details of the Schemes of Amalgamation of the Cuban Central Ltd. and the Western Railways of Havana Ltd.*, October 19, 1920.

12. Even though this area was still cultivated, ownership of its small and antiquated sugar mills passed to the owners of medium-sized estates who were practically ruined by the beginning of the twentieth century. See Mirta Rodríguez and Carlos Fernández, *Historia de Santa Cruz del Norte* (unpublished thesis presented in the Department of Cuban History at the School of Philosophy and History of the University of Havana, n.d.).

13. Jenks, *Our Cuban Colony*, p. 210.

14. The Hershey Chocolate Corporation, a company with independent capital, was established in the Lebanon Valley in Pennsylvania early in the twentieth century. Several chocolate products and chewing gum were made there, using raw materials from Ceylon, Java, Trinidad, Mexico, and Cuba. See Hershey Chocolate Company, *The Story of Hershey* (Hershey City, Pa., 1920).

15. Ibid.

16. *Cuba Importadora e Industrial* (November 1937).

17. Ibid.

18. Cuba, Secretaría de Agricultura, Industria y Comercio, *Memorias de las zafras azucareras*, (1914–20).

19. Cuba, Comisión de Ferrocarriles, *Memoria* (1918–19), p. 366.

20. Ferrocarril de Hershey did everything possible to gain access to the capital, and it did reach Havana's coastline at several places, especially at Casa Blanca, on the eastern edge of the bay. However, the English refused to allow its trains to use Havana's Estación Central (main terminal), in spite of Hershey's many efforts starting in 1920. This was a serious disadvantage for the railroad's passenger service, for those who wanted to use the train had to cross the bay by ferry or other boat. ANC, Fondo Ferrocarriles (Ferrocarriles Unidos), legajo 855, expediente 5.

21. Cuba, Secretaría de Agricultura, Industria y Comercio, *Memoria de la zafra* (1927–28), and Cuba, Comisión de Ferrocarriles, *Memoria* (1927–28), p. 392.

22. The aim was to absorb all of the sugarcane plantations in the region northeast of Havana between that city and Matanzas. Only the fact that the owners of some small sugar mills, such as the Elena and the Puerto, refused to sell kept the industry's concentration in that area from becoming complete.

23. "Cuba económica y financiera," *Anuario Azucarero de Cuba* (1959), p. 91.

24. The U.S. supervisory government had leased those tracks first to the Cuba Company, which built the Ferrocarril Central, and then to other companies, finally leasing them in 1911 to Cuban Distilling, a company that exported molasses and alcohol.

25. *Heraldo de Cuba*, July 25, 1932, p. 1.

26. *El Mundo*, December 29, 1913, p. 26.

27. Horatio S. Rubens (1869–1941) was born in New York and studied law at Columbia University, later working in the law office of Elihu Root. His activities as legal adviser of the

Partido Revolucionario Cubano (Cuban Revolutionary Party) during the War of Independence gave him some prestige as a friend of the Cuban cause, a circumstance that Rubens made use of throughout his career. Early on, Tarafa established links with the Flora Sugar Company, and Rubens was associated with the astute colonel in most of his companies, always representing the U.S. interests in them. Linked to the National City Bank group and perhaps more directly with Percy Rockefeller, Rubens attained a top position in the Cuban railroad sector by being named president of Ferrocarriles Consolidados de Cuba in 1925.

28. Tarafa bought the land around the old Carmen, San Miguel de Azopardo, Luisiana, and Arratia sugar mills in Matanzas, a grand total of 12,150 hectares. ANC, Fondo Ferrocarriles (Ferrocarril Norte de Cuba), libros de actas, 1:13–17.

29. *Hispanic Notes and Monographs* (1919), p. 589.

30. *Memorándum de expropiación del Ferrocarril de Dubrocq*, in AFC (ETH), Documentación legal, entresuelo, anaquel 48, expediente 258.

31. *Escritura número 196 de traspaso de propiedad*, in AFC (ETH), Documentación legal, entresuelo, anaquel 38, legajo 123.

32. *Escritura de cesión de bienes inmuebles y derechos entre la Matanzas Rys. y la Matanzas Terminal Rr. Company*, in AFC (ETH), Documentación legal, entresuelo, anaquel 13, legajo 22. Matanzas Terminal was a subsidiary of Ferrocarriles Unidos.

33. Cuba, Comisión de Ferrocarriles, *Memoria* (1910–11), p. 347, and *Corporate History of the Cuba Northern and Predecessors Companies*, in AFC (d.C.), Fondo General de Paquetería, paquete 1941-0-119, expediente 2-AI, p. 190.

34. Cuba, Comisión de Ferrocarriles, *Memoria* (1910–11), p. 347, and *Corporate History of the Cuba Northern and Predecessors Companies*, in AFC (d.C.), Fondo General de Paquetería, paquete 1941-0-119, expediente 2-AI, p. 190.

35. *Libro de actas del Ferrocarril del Norte y del Sur*, in ANC, Fondo Ferrocarriles, folios 9, 10.

36. *El Mundo*, April 5, 1912, p. 4, and A. Berenguer y Sed, *Discurso contrario al proyecto de ley de subvención del Ferrocarril de Caibarién a Nuevitas* (Havana: La Moderna Poesía, 1912), p. 6.

37. *Escritura número 381*, in AFC (d.C.), Fondo Departamento de Ingresos.

38. *Libro de inscripción y transferencia de acciones*, in ANC, Fondo Ferrocarriles (Ferrocarril de la Costa Norte y del Sur).

39. Tarafa purchased Ferrocarril Nuevitas y Camagüey in 1914. It was still owned by the descendants of the original group of stockholders, especially the Betancourt family. *Escritura número 36 de compra-venta del Ferrocarril de Camagüey-Nuevitas*, in AFC (d.C.), Fondo Privado Administración, Documentación legal.

40. *Escritura número 36 de compra-venta del Ferrocarril de Camagüey-Nuevitas*, in AFC (d.C.), Fondo Privado Administración, Documentación legal.

41. *Escritura número 381 de compra-venta y cesión de derechos y acciones del Ferrocarril de la Costa Norte y del Sur*, in AFC (d.C.), Fondo Departamento de Ingresos.

42. *Corporate History of the Cuba Northern*, in AFC (d.C.), Fondo General de Paquetería, p. 33. Tarafa had controlled Ferrocarril de Morón previously by means of negotiations with the family that owned the two sugar mills.

43. *Escritura número 381 de compra-venta de derechos y acciones del Ferrocarril de la Costa Norte y del Sur*, in AFC (d.C.), Fondo Departamento de Ingresos.

44. Even though Tarafa maintained a controlling position in the company, U.S. participation was not limited to the financial aspect, for some prominent figures in U.S. big

business, such as William H. Woodin, president of American Car and Foundry, served on its board of directors. The National City Bank of New York served as trustee.

45. *Certificado de incorporación del Ferrocarril de la Costa Norte y del Sur*, in ANC, Fondo Ferrocarriles.

46. *Historical Data*, in AFC (d.C.), Fondo Permanente, expediente 100-30, 1944.

47. Ibid.

48. The public service sections of nearly all of those small companies were gradually absorbed by United Railways (Ferrocarriles Unidos).

49. Cuba, Comisión de Ferrocarriles. *Memorias* (1914–15), p. 16, and (1917–18), p. 11.

50. ANC, Fondo Ferrocarriles (Cuban Central), legajo 55, expediente 9, and *Gazeta Oficial de la República de Cuba*, Decree 196, February 18, 1916. A commission was appointed to examine the matter. Its members included the secretaries of the treasury and of justice, some bankers and senators, and railroad experts Luciano Ruiz and Tiburcio Pérez Castañeda.

51. ANC, Fondo Ferrocarriles (Ferrocarriles Unidos de La Habana), legajo 52, expediente 2.

52. Ibid., expediente 4.

53. Cuba, Comisión de Ferrocarriles, *Memorias* (1914–15), p. 16, and (1917–18), p. 11.

54. That high income allowed United Railways to remit between 2.5 and 3 million pesos to London each year. *Actas del Comité Local de la United Railways*, book 6, in AFC (ETH), Documentación legal, entresuelo.

55. It cost 3.50 pesos per person, first class, or 0.75 pesos per person, third class, to go by train from Havana to Madruga, a distance of approximately 60 kilometers. United Railways, *Informe del Administrador Robert M. Orr, 1914*, in ANC, Fondo Ferrocarriles (Unidos de La Habana), legajo 58.

56. In 1920, the operating ratios of some of those companies were as follows: Ferrocarril Norte de Cuba, 0.49; Ferrocarril Nuevitas y Camagüey, 0.64; Cuban Central, 0.66; Cuba Railroad, 0.72; United Railways, 0.72; Ferrocarril de Guantánamo, 0.77; Western Railways of Havana, 0.86; and Havana Central, 0.92.

Chapter 14

1. The difference in production between the sugar mills in the four western provinces and those in Camagüey and Oriente was quite considerable. In 1921, the western mills' annual averages were no more than 17,000 metric tons each, whereas those in the eastern part of the country achieved annual averages of between 27,000 and 30,000 metric tons. Cuba, Secretaría de Agricultura, Industria y Comercio, Sección de Estadísticas, *Memorias de las zafras azucareras* (1921).

2. L. H. Jenks, *Our Cuban Colony: A Study in Sugar* (New York: Vanguard, 1928), chap. 11, and Oscar Pino Santos, *El asalto a Cuba por la oligarquía financiera norteamericana* (Havana: Editorial Casa de las Américas, 1973), pp. 85–91. Both authors present a graphic description of this particular situation.

3. Jenks, *Our Cuban Colony*, chap. 11, and Pino Santos, *El asalto*, pp. 85–91.

4. Guantánamo and Western Railroad Company, *Annual Report and General Balance Sheet*, New York, March 21, 1921, report by R. Juvé, president of the company.

5. "Discurso de C. J. Cater Scott, esq., President," in United Railways of Havana and Regla Warehouses Limited, *Report of Proceedings at the Twenty-fifth Ordinary General Meeting*, London, February 10, 1922.

6. In his *Azúcar y población en las Antillas* (Havana: Editorial Lex, 1961), p. 289, Ramiro Guerra gave the following values for the 1919–23 sugarcane harvests:

Year	Value
1919	454,479,000 pesos
1920	1,005,451,000 pesos
1921	273,197,000 pesos
1922	255,009,000 pesos
1923	400,181,000 pesos

This shows that 1921 and 1922 were the only really critical years.

7. The Ports Law of 1890 classified the Cuban ports then in use. That classification could be changed only by law of Congress; therefore, the authorizations issued by the executive were a contravention of the law.

8. Cuba, Congreso, *Diario de Sesiones del Senado* 43, no. 18: 19.

9. Revisión de tarifas, in AHPC, Fondo Ferrocarriles, legajo 460.

10. León Primelles, *Crónica cubana* (1919–22) (Havana: Editorial Habanera, 1932), p. 410, and *Tarifas y aplicaciones*, in AHPC, Fondo Ferrocarriles, legajo A-32.

11. General Mario García Menocal was a staunch supporter of the U.S. companies, especially the Cuba Railroad Company. He was also closely linked to Cuban American Sugar, whose Chaparra and Delicias sugar mills were not dependent on the public service railroads. In 1925, it built the Santa Marta sugar mill on the Santa Cruz del Sur branch line belonging to Cuba Railroad.

12. Primelles, *Crónica Cubana*, p. 10.

13. Carta de H. C. Lakin a A. Gruber, June 29, 1921, in *Investigaciones especiales e informes* (1924), in AFC (d. C.), Fondo Permanente, legajo 100-17 (1943). At that time, Herbert C. Lakin was president of the Cuba Company and of its subsidiary Cuba Railroad Company. J. M. Gruber, a former vice-president of the Great Northern Railroad Company, of the United States, was then vice-president of the Cuba Railroad Company, in charge of its operations sector. "Jack" was General Archibald Jack, general manager of United Railways of Havana.

14. Carta de H. C. Lakin a A. Gruber, June 29, 1921.

15. Ibid.

16. Cuba Northern Railways Company, *Annual Report* (1921–22), p. 6; Carta de H. C. Lakin a J. M. Gruber, June 23, 1922, in *Investigaciones especiales e informes* (1924), in AFC (d. C.), Fondo Permanente, legajo 100-17 (1943); and Cuba Railroad Company, *Annual Report* (1921–22). By the end of 1920, a new issue of $6 million worth of fifty-year mortgage bonds bearing 7 percent interest and a Cuban government loan of 3 million pesos, granted under the Subsidies Law, had been added to the initial debt of $12.5 million. Carta de E. Azpeitía a J. M. Sundheimer, June 11, 1926, in *Bonos y certificados de hipotecas de los ferrocarriles del Norte de Cuba*, in AHPC, Fondo Ferrocarriles, legajo E-445.

17. Of all the companies operating in the country, Norte de Cuba had the lowest ratio of operating expenses to income. This was a competitive advantage.

18. Carta de H. C. Lakin a Domingo A. Galdós, November 30, 1921, in *Investigaciones especiales e informes* (1924), in AFC (d. C.), Fondo Permanente, legajo 100-17 (1943).

19. In his *El asalto a Cuba por la oligarquía financiera norteamericana*, Oscar Pino Santos reported that, in 1921 or 1922, the U.S. president had already advised Cuban Presi-

dent Alfredo Zayas and the U.S. sugar beet growers that the production of sugar might have to be cut back, but nothing definite came of it, because of the opposition put up by the U.S. sugar producers in Cuba. The issue was finally settled with the application of the Fordney McCumber tariff, which raised the duty on sugar imported by the United States.

20. This branch line was opened to traffic in April 1921. Its construction was made possible thanks to a loan facilitated by Edwin Atkins, president of the Punta Alegre Sugar Company, which owned the Florida sugar mill. Other sugar mills in the area included the Camagüey, Céspedes, Estrella, and Agramonte.

21. Minutes of the Director's Meetings, minutes 123, vol. 6, folios 163–72, in ANC, Fondo Ferrocarriles (Cuba Railroad Company).

22. Carta de J. M. Tarafa a A. Jack, June 22, 1921, in *Investigaciones especiales e informes* (1924), in AFC (d. C.), Fondo Permanente, legajo 100-17 (1943).

23. The contracts Norte de Cuba signed with the Vertientes and Agramonte sugar mills are typical of the ones it signed with the sugar mills linked to that bank. In line with the agreement, the railroad company made a large number of credit and rate concessions to offset the effects of the branch line that Cuba Railroad was building to Santa Cruz del Sur. AFC (d. C.), Fondo Permanente, legajo 100-17, folio 206.

24. Carta de H. C. Lakin a A. Gruber, June 15, 1922, in *Investigaciones especiales e informes* (1924), in AFC (d. C.), Fondo Permanente, legajo 100-17 (1943), folios 241–45.

25. Edward Stettinius, an agent of J. P. Morgan, proposed financing that consisted of a $13.5 million issue of bonds and other liabilities plus another issue of preferred stock for $5 million more at 8 percent to replace the securities that Norte de Cuba had in circulation. AFC (d. C.), Fondo Permanente, legajo 100-17, folios 238–40.

26. Ibid.

27. Carta de H. C. Lakin a J. M. Gruber, October 26, 1923, in *Investigaciones especiales e informes* (1924), in AFC (d. C.), Fondo Permanente, legajo 100-17 (1943), folios 234–40.

28. Carta de H. C. Lakin a A. Gruber, June 15, 1922, in *Investigaciones especiales e informes* (1924), in AFC (d. C.), Fondo Permanente, legajo 100-17 (1943), folios 241–45.

29. Ibid.

30. Ibid.

31. Pino Santos, *El asalto*, p. 128.

32. Ibid., p. 132.

33. *Heraldo de Cuba*, July 20, 1923, p. 9.

34. Tarafa owned the Cuba sugar mill in Matanzas and, therefore, used United Railways.

35. United Fruit boasted of its good relations with the Cuba Railroad Company and, therefore, hastened to clarify its position in the conflict, using Victor M. Cutter, vice-president of the tropical divisions of that banana and sugar company, for the purpose: "A rumor has been going around that we are trying to link our railroad with others and so deny your lines a large amount of cane and cargo and as a result many owners have been contacting [Central] 'Preston,' and we even heard that we intended to get rid of our properties. . . . You may be assured that whatever happens on the political front or to the future of our company, we will deal squarely with the Cuba Railroad Company. I wish to remind you that it was mainly through our help that Cuba Railroad bought Antilla and from the beginning, largely owing to our use of Cuba Railroad to expand our properties, the relations between our companies have been most cordial." See Carta de V. M. Cutter a W. F. Lynch, August 30, 1923, in *Investigaciones especiales e informes* (1924), in AFC (d. C.), Fondo Permanante, legajo 100-17 (1943).

36. *Heraldo de Cuba*, July 22, 1923, p. 9.

37. Ibid., July 24, 1923), p. 9.

38. The only recognized ports for handling imports and exports on the northern coast were those of Bahía Honda and Mariel, in Pinar del Río province; Matanzas; Havana; Cárdenas; Sagua la Grande; Caibarién; Puerto Tarafa and Pastelillo, on the Bay of Nuevitas; Puerto Padre, including Juan Claro Cay; Gibara; Antilla, on the Bay of Nipe; and Macabí, in Banes. The southern coast had the ports of Guantánamo, including Boquerón, Caimanera, and El Deseo; Santiago de Cuba; Manzanillo; Santa Cruz del Sur; Júcaro; Trinidad (Casilda); Tunas de Zaza; Cienfuegos; and Batabanó. On the Isle of Pines, the ports were Nueva Gerona and Los Indios. *Gaceta Oficial de la República de Cuba*, text of the law issued on October 9, 1923.

39. Cuba, Congreso, *Diario de Sesiones de la Cámara de Representantes* (1923), 40: no. 55, first legislature, folios 40–51, text of the Tarafa bill.

40. Root, Clark, Buckner, and Howland, and Sullivan and Cromwell, "Report of the Secretary of State of the United States," August 23, 1923, in *The Tarafa Bill* (New York: Evening Post Job Printing Office, 1923).

41. Carta de H. C. Lakin a A. Gruber, June 12, 1923, in AFC (d. C.), Fondo Permanente, legajo 100-17 (1943), folios 241–45.

42. Ibid.

43. The established procedure for the discussion of new business in the House of Representatives was as follows: any measure, resolution, or bill should be signed by from five to seven representatives. For it to be considered, it also required a favorable vote of two-thirds of those attending the session. If the proposal was considered, it became a "bill" and was sent to one or more committees for a thumbs-up or thumbs-down recommendation. If the bill got a favorable report, it was put on the agenda for discussion and voting, with copies of it sent to each representative. The Tarafa bill was presented by Representatives Santiago Rey, Carlos M. de la Cruz, Heliodoro Gil, Alberto Silva, and Angel Ravelo, who, in view of the importance and interest of the bill, asked that the previously mentioned requisites for its discussion be suspended. That position was approved by a vote of eighty-eight votes for and nine against, but the draft as such was voted down. See Cuba, Congreso, *Diario de Sesiones de la Cámara de Representantes*, 40:42–43, first legislature, sessions of August 9 and September 25, 1923.

44. Ibid., 40:40–51.

45. That kind of argument was the one Representative Carlos Manuel de la Cruz employed in his defense of the railroads. According to him, the monopolies could benefit only from the prices, "but the prices charged for the transportation of goods and persons are set not by the railroad companies but by the Comisión de Ferrocarriles." Ibid., 40:40–51.

46. Ibid.

47. Ibid., 40-2:34. Session of September 25, 1923.

48. The Movimiento de Veteranos y Patriotas (Movement of Veterans and Patriots) opposed the Tarafa Law in a manifesto addressed to the legislative power on August 30, 1923. See Hortensia Pichardo, *Documentos para la historia de Cuba* (Havana: Editorial de Ciencias Sociales, 1973), 2:159. The sugar interests immediately realized what a marvelous opportunity that political movement offered them for countering the publicity in favor of the Tarafa Law, and some of the sugar men involved in the movement, such as Antonio González de Mendoza, Raimundo Cabrera, Aurelio Portuondo, and Gonzalo Freyre de

Andrade, became spokesmen challenging it. See Asociación de Hasendados y Colonos de Cuba, *Impugnación al proyecto de ley de los Consolidados* (Havana, August 23, 1923).

49. *The Tarafa Bill*, p. 2.

50. Ibid., pp. 25–29.

51. *Heraldo de Cuba*, August 20, 1923, p. 12, and Cuba, *Congreso, Diario de Sesiones de la Cámara de Representantes*, 40-2:50–51.

52. The Senate passed it with a vote of fifteen for and four against. The House of Representatives also passed the reformed text, by a vote of ninety-two for and seven against.

53. All of these exceptions are contained in the text passed in September 1923. See *Gaceta Oficial de la República de Cuba*, October 9, 1923.

54. Ibid.

55. AFC (d. C.), *Fondo Permanente*, legajo 100-17 (1943), folios 241–45.

56. Ibid., folios 238–40.

57. *Cuba Importadora e Industrial* (November 1937), p. 50.

58. AFC (d.C.), Fondo Privado Administración, escritura 128.

59. Cuba Railroad Company, *Annual Report* (1926–27).

60. Ibid.

61. Vladimir Ilyich Lenin, *Imperialism: The Highest Stage of Capitalism* (New York: International Publishers, 1939).

62. The National City Bank financed the purchase of Ferrocarril de Tunas–Sancti Spíritus for 1,376,000 pesos, and the operation was concluded in 1926. Convenio, 1926, in AHPC, Fondo Ferrocarriles (Ferrocarril de Tunas-Sancti Spíritus).

63. AHPC, Fondo Ferrocarriles (Ferrocarril de Tunas–Sancti Spíritus), expediente C-225.

Chapter 15

1. ANC, Fondo Ferrocarriles (Ferrocarriles Unidos), legajo 703, expediente 1.

2. Rivero Muñiz. *El movimiento obrero durante la primera intervención* (Las Villas: Universidad Central de Las Villas, 1961), pp. 36–37.

3. Instituto de Historia del Movimiento Comunista y de la Revolución Socialista de Cuba, *El movimiento obrero cubano. Documentos y artículos* (Havana: Editorial de Ciencias Sociales, 1975), 1:177.

4. *La Discusión*, July 24, 1900, p. 2.

5. This movement is described in detail in *La Discusión*, September 3–29, 1900.

6. See Sergio Aguirre, "Algunas luchas sociales en Cuba republicana," *Eco de caminos* 1 (1974): 316–17.

7. Because of the depreciation of the Spanish currency in circulation, payment in U.S. currency was equivalent to a wage increase.

8. *La Discusión*, September 15, 1907, p. 12.

9. Even though this wasn't the only workers' organization in the sector, it was the most important one. Headed by José Alfonso, Obreros Unidos fell far short of representing all the workers of the western railroad companies, but its influence extended throughout the region.

10. *La Discusión*, October 4, 1907. The immigrants from Tiscornia, who were presumably Spaniards, didn't serve as strikebreakers. On learning of the contract for scabs from New York, the Strike Committee appealed to the government, pointing out that the immi-

gration law then in effect—Military Order 115—prohibited the contracting of workers outside the country, but the government didn't pay any attention to its protest.

11. The Comité Federativo had begun to set up assistance committees in other sectors. Moreover, the calling of a construction workers' strike enlarged the movement.

12. *La Discusión*, November 23, 1907, pp. 1, 12. Most of those arrested were freed two days later, but sixty of them, including the leaders, were tried, with bail set at 2,000 pesos each.

13. J. Rivero Muñiz, *El movimiento laboral cubano durante el período 1906–1911* (Las Villas: Dirección de Publicaciones, Universidad Central de Las Villas, 1962), p. 93.

14. *Constitución y Estatutos de la Liga Cubana de Empleados del Ferrocarril*, in AHPC, Fondo Gobierno Provincial, legajo 48, expediente 28.

15. *Actas de la Liga Cubana de Empleados del Ferrocarril*, in AHPC, Fondo Gobierno Provincial, legajo 48, expediente 28.

16. Carlos Loveira, *De los 26 a los 35* (Havana, 1918), p. 34. The minimum dues were one peso for those who earned less than fifty pesos a month.

17. According to Loveira, the company would have used the services of a Dominican agent provocateur who went by the rather odd name of X. Z. Anona Gómez. For its part, the Liga seems to have been subjected to harsh criticism by anarchistic elements. Ibid., pp. 31–36.

18. AHPC, Fondo Gobierno Provincial, legajo 48, expediente 28. Vice-President Bartolomé Cerda also resigned.

19. ANC, Fondo Ferrocarriles (Cuban Central), legajo 61, expediente 30.

20. After some deployment of military forces, Machado began negotiations with the parties to the conflict, getting the company to agree to take back the workers who had been laid off and getting the strikers to change their position. Afterward, the main leaders of the Liga Cubana, including Loveira, were unofficially told that their presence in town would be disruptive to the peace. Less than a month later, Cuban Central went back to its old tricks and fired seventeen workers. The inexperienced leaders who were left in charge of the Liga Cubana were lulled by politicians' promises and reacted slowly and unenergetically. That attitude disillusioned the Liga Cubana's members and proved the death blow for the organization.

21. Calculations are based on the price lists which *El Avisador Comercial* and other magazines and newspapers published regularly. The wholesale price of black beans, for example, rose from 5 centavos a pound in 1913 to 16.5 centavos a pound in 1920; in the same period, the price of potatoes rose from 3 centavos to 11.5 centavos a pound.

22. *El Mundo*, December 13, 1918, p. 1.

23. Those plans were shown in the Rules adopted by the Morón organization. See AHPC, Fondo Gobierno Provincial, legajo 46, expediente 12.

24. Interview of R. Alemar, Santiago de Cuba, June 21, 1974.

25. L. Primelles, *Crónica cubana* (Havana: Editorial Lex, 1955), 1:502.

26. ANC, Fondo Ferrocarriles (Cuban Central), legajo 347, expediente 13.

27. Interview of R. Victoria Jiménez, Camagüey, May 14, 1974.

28. The wage index was calculated on the basis of an analysis of the payrolls of Cuban Railroad and Ferrocarril del Norte de Cuba, deposited in the archives of the Camagüey division of Ferrocarriles de Cuba. Of course, this is a partial figure, but the figures for the other companies shouldn't have been very different.

29. *El Mundo*, February 18, 1921, p. 11.

30. The Marines set up a camp at La Zambrana, on the outskirts of Camagüey, when the

United States entered the war against Germany. When the conflict ended, the military contingent remained, "forgotten," in Camagüey, whose population had to put up with the excesses of the foreign troops until 1922.

31. R. F. Smith, *The United States and Cuba: Business and Diplomacy* (New Haven: Yale University Press, 1960), p. 104.

32. The agreement was based on the reinstatement of five of the twelve strikers who had been fired and the maintenance of the 1920 agreement until a new round of negotiations, to be held in July 1921. The company, which was reluctant to accept this solution, watched and waited for an opportunity to take reprisals—which arose when a new strike broke out during the July discussions. Herbert C. Lakin, president of Cuba Railroad, began mobilizing immediately with that end in view. On June 24, he wrote to A. Lombard, the company's lawyer, as follows: "This business [the possibility of a strike] ought to be of interest to General Crowder. If we are successful against the workers, the workers conditions in the eastern part of the island will stabilize rapidly. This would remove one of the preoccupations of the general." The means for establishing contact with Crowder, who had just engaged in his first actions as proconsul, were immediately forthcoming. Three days later, Lakin confessed to Asher Gruber, vice-president of the company in Camagüey, "I am beginning to think that it would be better for our workers to strike since this would allow us to find workers at lower wages." Lakin's hopes were dashed, however, for the July negotiations, in which the workers participated with extreme caution, didn't give him an opportunity to put his plans into practice. See Carta de H. C. Lakin a A. Lombard, June 24, 1921, and Carta de H. C. Lakin a A. Gruber, June 27, 1921, in AFC (d. C.), Fondo Permanente, expediente 100-17 (1943).

33. *El Mundo*, August 18, 1922, p. 1.

34. Its text is contained in the *Gaceta Oficial de la República de Cuba*, November 26, 1921.

35. *Nueva Luz*, September 21, 1922, p. 2.

36. *Heraldo de Cuba*, December 7, 1923, p. 1.

37. According to the correspondence between Lakin, president of Cuba Railroad, and Gruber, his vice-president in charge of operations, the company was considering making use of the differences between the leaders of the Hermandad and those of the Unión de Talleres to break the latter, who were more radical. Therefore, they were thinking of making some concessions to the Hermandad, for "It is quite possible that if the Hermandad returns to work, the Unión de Talleres might also return under a stipulation in the agreement still in place with the Talleres. I fully sympathize with your wish to get rid of the Unión de Talleres. If Loveira remains in Navana, it would be possible to pursue this objective, but if he goes to Camagüey I am less certain about this. Undoubtedly he believes in the Unión . . . but if we explain to him the characters of their leaders . . . providing a full account of the situation, you might have the possibility of working with a plan that, although it retains the Unión, guarantees us all the other things that we would like, and eliminates the objectionable elements of the Unión." See Carta de H. C. Lakin a A. Gruber, December 28, 1923, in AFC (d. C.), Fondo Permanente, expediente 100-17 (1943).

38. "El Governor [Zayas-Bazán] telegraphed General Machado requesting his intervention. At the same time the Hermandad telegraphed its representative, asking that he go see Machado, undoubtedly at the request of the governor." See Carta de H. C. Lakin a A. Gruber, December 30, 1923, in AFC (d. C.), Fondo Permanente, expediente 100-17 (1943).

39. Carta de H. C. Lakin a A. Gruber, January 1, 1924, in AFC (d. C.), Fondo Permanente, expediente 100-17 (1943).

40. "General Machado and Guitiérez have spent a great deal of time making sure that Adán and Arévalo accept their demands. . . . His impression is that both are extremely eager to end the strike. They personally are out money and give the impression that the Hermandad is also short of cash." See ibid. Of reformist leanings, Abelardo Adán was an important figure in the brotherhood of the Camagüeyan Railroad workers. Juan Arévalo, who was much better known, had become famous as a dock workers' leader in the previous decade but left that sector after being accused of "mismanagement" of union funds. Turned into a "professional" union organizer, Arévalo offered his "expert" services to the Camagüeyan Railroad workers, whom he represented in Havana during the strike.

41. Shortly before that, Alfredo Zayas had to calm a small tempest within his cabinet: some of the secretaries criticized him for having commissioned Machado, who wasn't in the government, to solve the conflict. For a while, that situation threatened Machado's position in Camagüey.

42. Academia de Ciencias de Cuba, *Indice histórico de Camagüey* (Havana: Instituto Cubano del Libro, 1970), p. 114.

43. The delegations were numbered consecutively as they were created.

44. Enrique Varona González had begun to work as an engineer for Ferrocarril del Norte de Cuba in 1920, after having gained experience as a stoker and engineer at the Patria sugar mill, in Morón. Born in Pinar del Río in 1888, Varona had worked for some time as a cigar maker; he probably began to become active in union activities and acquired his anarchosyndicalist convictions in that sector.

45. Its name was simply a translation of the U.S. Railroad Brotherhood. Its structure, too, was similar to that of the Brotherhood, except that the latter was based on craft unions.

46. *Heraldo de Cuba*, November 21, 1924, p. 3.

47. Archibald Jack, the manager, told the press that "I am not about to accept the dictates of the employees of other companies [referring to the Hermandad's Dirección Central] in matters of such great import." *El Mundo*, February 16, 1924, p. 1. It seems that the vinegary British general believed the rumors that were circulating at the time to the effect that Cuba Railroad looked kindly on the establishment of the Camagüey-based Hermandad at a time when, because of the railroad consolidation, that company was extending its sphere of action considerably.

48. The most important of the demands were recognition of the Hermandad as the sole representative of the workers; an eight-hour workday, with double pay for overtime; fourteen days of rest each year; application of the various wage adjustments made since 1921 to the wages then in effect; and review of the records of workers fired since 1922. *La Discusión*, March 27, 1924, p. 4.

49. In the agreement that was signed, the demands were visibly reduced. Thus, for example, the eight-hour workday was mentioned as established, but payment for overtime was left subject to the complicated mechanism of an adjustment committee, with nothing really decided in that regard. Likewise, no mention was made of days off or of the workers who had been fired. *La Lucha*, April 8, 1924, pp. 1, 4.

50. Arévalo and Castellanos began to shout the tidings of a great triumph and in their opportunistic enthusiasm forgot the mutual assistance pact signed with the Bahía Federación, which was still on strike. *La Discusión*, April 29, 1924, p. 2.

51. The motives for confrontation included Jack's attempt to fire a group of workers for not working on May Day and an attempt to fire the Matanzas railroad workers who, in solidarity with the Armour and Company workers who were out on strike, refused to handle merchandise from that company. *Heraldo de Cuba*, May 3, 1924, p. 3, and *El Mundo*, May 22, 1924, p. 1.

52. The Cámara de Comercio, Industria y Navegación (Chamber of Commerce, Industry, and Navigation); the Asociación de Comerciantes de La Habana (Havana Traders' Association); and the American Chamber of Commerce were other organizations that expressed their solidarity with Archibald Jack. *Heraldo de Cuba*, June 4, 1924, p. 9.

53. The attacker, a young worker named Emilio Marichal, stated that "I did it because of my family's neediness and poverty. . . . I went out of the house to get something to eat or, if I couldn't, to teach a lesson to the man I thought responsible for my family's hunger." *El Mundo*, June 10, 1924, p. 1.

54. The organizations that declared their support for the strikers included the Morón Unión, Havana's Federación Obrera, and the Bahía Federación, which had not supported them previously because of the Hermandad leaders' sellout attitude during the dock workers' strike in April.

55. Among other advantages, the company obtained a "reinterpretation" of the April work agreement by President Zayas, which considerably reduced the extent of some of its bases. *El Mundo*, June 20, 1924, p. 1.

56. The Arteaga Law, which had been promulgated on June 24, 1909, prohibited the use of scrip and tokens for paying workers. The sugar companies had systematically ignored it. See Hortensia Pichardo, *Documentos para la historia de Cuba* (Havana: Editorial de Ciencias Sociales, 1973), 2:328.

57. Interview of N. Carranza, Havana, May 7, 1974.

58. *El Mundo*, October 24, 1924, p. 24.

59. Reproduced by *El Machete*, organ of the Partido Comunista Mexicano (Mexican Communist Party). See Raquel Tibol, *Julio Antonio Mella en El Machete* (Mexico City, 1968), p. 21.

60. *Heraldo de Cuba*, October 29, 1924, pp. 6, 11.

61. Ibid., November 7, 1924, p. 8.

62. *El Mundo*, December 2, 1924, p. 24.

63. *La Discusión*, December 9, 1924, p. 1.

64. Among others, Rogerio Zayas-Bazán, governor of Camagüey, had to take a hand. He went to see the governor of Havana and convinced him that Delegation 2 didn't have the power to remove Arévalo. *Heraldo de Cuba*, November 18, 1924.

65. To make his retirement more enjoyable, Cuba Railroad gave him a post as inspector in the company. See Tibol, *Julio Antinio Mella*, p. 29.

66. Fabio Grobart, "El movimiento obrero cubano de 1925 a 1933," *Santiago* no. 5 (December 1971): 24.

67. Ever since he had been secretary of the interior in José Miguel Gómez's cabinet, Machado had shown that he took a hard line with labor, for he was responsible for the deportation of a large number of union organizers of Spanish origin. Even though Machado's actions are well enough known not to require further documentation here, we are including Lakin's description of the tyrant, which he sent to Asher Gruber at the time of the December 1923 strike, because we consider it important: "You ought to know who General Machado is. You probably know that he is the candidate picked by the Liberal Party, but

above everything he is an important businessman. When we built Central Jatibonico he was one of our suppliers of wood, and a sugarcane *colono* [small farmer]. He has mediated some of the most important strikes in Cuba. He owns Central Carmita and, as you know, ships much cane on our lines. He is the personal representative in Cuba of the new subsidiary of General Electric, which has purchased plants in Santa Clara, Cienfuegos, and other cities. He is a very special friend of our good friends over at the Royal Bank of Canada and he sees labor problems from a businessman's point of view, but he knows the Cuban psychology and has extensive political experience so he is the most competent man I know to control the workers." Carta de H. C. Lakin a A. Gruber, December 30, 1923, in AFC (d. C.), Fondo Permanente, expediente 100-17 (1943).

68. During his visit to the United States as president-elect, Machado took pains to offer guarantees to U.S. businessmen concerning his labor policy. At a luncheon given by E. D. Babst, of American Sugar Refining, Machado declared, "One of the problems I'd like to talk about this afternoon is that of strikes. As soon as I take office, I plan to send a message to Congress asking for the passage of a law under which whatever difficulties may arise between capital and labor may be solved by means of arbitration." *Luchas obreras contra Machado* (Havana: Editorial de Ciencias Sociales, 1973), p. 53.

69. Strict compliance with railroad legislation meant that trains would run at less than their customary speeds, because that legislation stipulated a series of obligatory stops—which generally were ignored. This caused losses for the company because it slowed the movement of trains.

70. "Declaraciones de Otero Bosch y Juan Arévalo," *Heraldo de Cuba*, March 2, 1925, p. 3.

71. *Informe oficial del Ferrocarril de Cuba*, in AHPC, Fondo Ferrocarriles, legajo 2, expediente F-7a.

72. Carta de M. Cibrán a D. Galdós, August 20, 1925, in AFC (d. C.), Fondo General de Paquetería, paquete "Labor Negotiations."

73. Interview of N. Carranza, Havana, May 7, 1974.

74. Academia de Ciencias de Cuba, *Indice histórico de Camagüey*, p. 114.

75. Carta de R. Zayas-Bazán a A. Pérez, December 15, 1925, in AFC (d. C.), Fondo General de Paquetería, paquete "Labor Negotiations."

76. Carta confidencial de M. Cibrán a D. Galdós, September 9, 1925, in AFC (d. C.), Fondo General de Paquetería.

77. The Comisión de Ferrocarriles, composed of the secretaries of communications, public works, and agriculture, tried to get Cuba Railroad to present a set of work regulations governing its employees, but the company ignored the request. *El Mundo*, May 6, 1925, p. 1.

78. *El Mundo*, May 13, 1926, p. 12.

79. In Santiago de Cuba, Lieutenant Larrubia, the military supervisor, sent the cavalry into the meeting hall of the Hermandad's local delegation, destroying it. Interview of R. Alemar, Santiago de Cuba, June 21, 1974.

80. Carta de Oscar Díaz al periódico *La Prensa*, Camagüey, November 11, 1926, in AHPC, Fondo Ferrocarriles, legajo 2, expediente 7-A.

Chapter 16

1. The stabilization plan was presented by T. L. Chadbourne, a New York lawyer employed by some powerful U.S. sugar monopolies that operated in Cuba. The plan consisted

of reducing the volume of Cuba's sugar exports to the United States by 2.8 million tons and signing an international agreement that would set export quotas for the main sugar-producing countries. See Oscar Pino Santos, *El asalto a Cuba por la oligarquía financiera norteamericana* (Havana: Editorial Casa de las Américas, 1973), pp. 185–89.

2. Oscar Zanetti, "El comercio exterior de la República neocolonial," in *Anuario de Estudios Cubanos*, vol. 1 (Havana: Editorial de Ciencias Sociales, 1975), 47–126.

3. L. V. Abad, *Problemas de los transportes cubanos* (Havana: Editorial Mercantil Cubana, 1944), p. 60.

4. At that time, Cuba had more than 13,000 kilometers of public and private railroad track, for the high proportion of 12.2 kilometers of track for every 100 square kilometers of territory.

5. United Railways of Havana and Regla Warehouses Ltd., *Annual Report*. 1929–1930, pp. 7–8.

6. Ibid., p. 19.

7. In the 1935–40 period, the passenger service brought in only 27 percent as much income as it had averaged in the years prior to the crisis. Freight in the same period brought in 37 percent as much as the precrisis average.

8. During the 1920s, Cuba imported 43.1 million pesos' worth of automotive vehicles of all kinds.

9. United Railways of Havana and Regla Warehouses Ltd., *Annual Report* (1927–28), p. 10.

10. Foreign Policy Association, *Problemas de la nueva Cuba* (New York, 1935), p. 480.

11. AHPC, Fondo Ferrocarriles, legajo "Competencia por carretera," expediente 2.

12. Luis V. Abad, the author of several studies on transportation in the 1935–45 period, pointed out, "Cuba has been the only country whose rulers have acted in fact, if not de jure, as if the railroads were no longer useful or necessary." L. V. Abad, *Los servicios de transporte terrestre y la función del Estado* (Havana: Caraza y Compañía, 1937), p. 23.

13. Only in the stretches between Havana and Ceiba Mocha (84 kilometers long), Guayos and Jatibonico (43 kilometers), and Las Tunas and Bayamo (138 kilometers) was the Carretera Central at any appreciable distance from Cuba's main railroad.

14. "In Cuba any person may establish a road transport service simply by getting permission from the authorities." *Discurso de lord Ashfield ante la 34 Junta general de accionistas*, in ANC, Fondo Ferrocarriles (Ferrocarriles Unidos), legajo 803, expediente 14.

15. It was considered that, of every hundred pesos invested in the automotive transportation service, seventy-six went for highway construction and only twenty-four for the cost of vehicles. However, the fee that carriers had to pay barely covered a third of the cost of building the highways. Abad, *Los servicios*, p. 41.

16. A bus or truck generally didn't cost more than 500 pesos. Of that amount, it was only necessary to pay 200 pesos down—100 for the chassis and the other 100 for the body. The rest could be paid in installments.

17. Financial normality should not be interpreted as a prosperous economic situation. The drop in income to 17 million pesos in 1926–28 was greeted with great lamentations by the board of Ferrocarriles Unidos, which went so far as to confess that its reserve for special maintenance costs had been exhausted. However, from the financial point of view, the company was still able to meet its heavy obligations. United Railways of Havana and Regla Warehouses Ltd., *Annual Report* (1927–28), pp. 4–5.

18. This refers to its average annual income in the 1925-30 period.

19. The exact figure in June 1939 was £8,238,131 sterling. United Railways of Havana and Regla Warehouses Ltd., *Annual Report* (1938-39), p. 4.

20. Passenger transportation provided 50 percent of Havana Central's income. That electric railroad company merged completely with Ferrocarriles Unidos in 1928, after the Machado administration's measures forced it to sell its power plants to the American and Foreign Power monopoly, of the United States. In that transaction, Ferrocarriles Unidos obtained 81,000 shares of preferred stock in the electric consortium.

21. *Discurso de lord Ashfield en la 34 Junta general de accionistas,* in ANC, Fondo Ferrocarriles (Ferrocarriles Unidos), legajo 803, expediente 14.

22. Cuba, Comisión Nacional de Transportes, *Memorias* (1939-1948), pp. 666-67, and United Railways of Havana, *Payroll Statistics.* The number of employees does not include high-ranking officials.

23. ANC, Fondo Ferrocarriles (Ferrocarriles Unidos), legajo 803, expediente 14.

24. That deterioration made it necessary to gradually reduce the speed of the trains, which in some cases reached the point that it was slower than had been normal in the nineteenth century.

25. The company began to move in that direction in 1936 but came up against serious opposition in the government agencies that would have to authorize the closing of those services. In 1939, it seems that the government's attitude was somewhat more flexible, for it allowed the Havana-Marianao line to go out of service. United Railways of Havana and Regla Warehouses Ltd., *Annual Report* (1936-37), p. 17.

26. Ashfield, who had been president of Ferrocarriles Unidos for more than a decade, resigned in 1933 to become president of the London Passenger Transport Board. An important figure in the business world, Ashfield was also a director of Imperial Chemical Industries, Amalgamated Anthracite, and half a dozen other companies.

27. In his report for 1930, the president of the company had dismissed that possibility, saying that "It is impossible to foresee any lasting benefit to our company from passenger service." ANC, Fondo Ferrocarriles (Ferrocarriles Unidos), legajo 803, expediente 14. When Lord Ashfield resigned (at the worst moment of the crisis), he was succeeded by Arthur G. Hunt, an official with considerable experience in Ferrocarril de Antofagasta a Bolivia, which the Schröder bank also controlled. Rather than changing the company's conservative policy, he reaffirmed it.

28. They included a memorandum that the company presented to the government on February 5, 1936, in which, among other things, it requested authorization to cancel a series of services and asked that the government pay what it owed to the railroad.

29. L. Simpson, manager of Ferrocarriles Unidos, had admitted this during a meeting with Domingo Galdós, vice-president of Ferrocarriles Consolidados. Carta de D. Galdós a H. Rubens, September 4, 1931, in AHPC, Fondo Ferrocarriles, legajo K-43 (1931-32).

30. Havana Terminal was one of the few creditors which Ferrocarriles Unidos was punctilious about paying.

31. In 1937, the Cuban government granted a series of special tariff exemptions to the port of Matanzas in order to revive activity there.

32. AFC (ETH), Fondo Documentación Legal, anaquel 26, legajo 36, and ANC, Fondo Ferrocarriles (Ferrocarriles Unidos), legajo 176, expediente 2.

33. The annual income of the companies which were subsidiaries of Ferrocarriles Con-

solidados de Cuba in the 1925–30 period averaged 21.5 million pesos; their annual average had been 19.8 million pesos in the preceding five-year period, when they operated as independent companies. Cuba, Comisión de Ferrocarriles, *Memorias* (1919–20 through 1928–29).

34. The mortgage moratorium began on April 3, 1933, and was successively extended until 1940, when a transitory provision of the constitution established formulas for liquidating debts. In line with the moratorium, mortgage foreclosures were suspended, and companies were authorized to postpone payment of their mortgage debts without incurring any criminal liability. The Cuba Company made intelligent use of those legal remedies to further centralize its control of the stock of Ferrocarriles Consolidados and its subsidiaries.

35. *Moody's Manual of Investments* (New York: Moody's Investors Services, 1938), p. 54.

36. The trains used the Quesada crossing. The company had been given limited access to that railroad junction in 1917. AHPC, Fondo Ferrocarriles, expediente N-769.

37. The case of the private port of Santa María is interesting, because the National City Bank had interests in Cuba Railroad, and Percy Rockefeller, one of its directors, was also a director of the railroad company. Since the bank was one of the railroad company's creditors, as well, the railroad accused it of having "created or helped to create the economic penury which has made it impossible for the railroads to continue servicing their mortgage bonds." *Subpuerto de Santa María*, in AHPC, Fondo Ferrocarriles (Ferrocarriles Consolidados), expediente 24.

38. The Fallas had made hefty contributions to Machado's war chest in the 1925 election, and Viriato Gutiérrez, a member of the family, was the author of the regime's "economic policy."

39. *Competencia al Ferrocarril de Cuba en el tráfico de carga*, in AFC (d. C.), Fondo General de Paquetería, contaduría, expediente 803.

40. The Camagüey-Nuevitas highway was a typical example of those situations. That project was promoted by the Sánchez family, which owned the Senado sugar mill. The Senado would benefit directly from the highway if it ran alongside the tracks. Ferrocarriles Consolidados wanted the highway to be built farther to the east, through San Miguel, which would avoid any competition. The railroad company exerted all its influence, but all it achieved was to postpone the highway project. The road was finally built paralleling the tracks.

41. In the mid-1930s, the Ferrocarriles Consolidados management began taking steps to create a bus service that would be dependent on the railroad. As a result of those efforts, the Consolidados Sociedad Anónima bus company was created, which went into operation in the 1940s.

42. The Comisión Nacional de Transportes was supposed to deal with a wide range of problems related to that activity and to coordinate the relations between the government, the companies, and the users.

43. That line of conduct frequently plunged the yellow leaders into ridiculous situations. Oscar Díaz, president of the Hermandad Ferroviaria, wrote Machado in May 1927, noting that the most recent agreement his organization had signed with Ferrocarriles Consolidados—an agreement that the Hermandad Ferroviaria had accepted at Machado's behest—stated that the tracks and projects workers would have a nine-hour workday, though the workers in that department in Ferrocarriles Unidos had had an eight-hour workday for the last three years. See *Luchas obreras contra Machado* (Havana: Editorial de Ciencias Sociales, 1973), pp. 141–42.

44. Ricardo Rodríguez, who had been a railroad workers' leader in the western delegations for a long time, was one of the most active members of this group.

45. Between 1928 and 1938, the number of employees of the six main railroad companies was cut back from 20,470 to 10,353. See Cuba, Comisión Nacional de Transportes, *Memorias* (1939–48, pp. 666–67). The data for 1931 were taken from *Sueldos y jornales*, in AHPC, Fondo Ferrocarriles, expediente N-457.

46. Fabio Grobart, "El movimiento obrero cubano de 1925 a 1933," *Santiago* (December 1971), no. 60.

47. *Declaraciones de Antonio González*, in AHPC, Fondo Ferrocarriles, legajo 1, expediente I-349.

48. The first Communist organization in the Camagüey shops was founded in 1932. Members included Manuel García Hagrenot, Sebastián Tornavaca, Manuel Gaona, and Alberto Olivera. Interview of Tornavaca and Olivera, Camagüey, May 15, 1974.

49. Ibid.

50. The companies were stubbornly opposed to ending the wage cuts, but Decree 1763, of September 20, 1933, forced them to do so. The decree was issued by the Grau-Guiteras government, which had taken power just two weeks earlier. *Informe anual* (1933–34), in AFC (d. C.), Fondo Permanente, expediente 100-12 (1934).

51. The bylaws of that new organization clearly set forth its goals: "Chapter I, Article III. To achieve its purposes, the Sindicato will use all methods of working-class struggle, working to achieve the mediate and final interests of the proletariat." AHPC, Fondo Gobierno Provincial, Registro de Asociaciones, legajo 63, expediente 16. The Ferroviarios y Trabajadores Unidos group was created after the provisional Grau-Guiteras government issued a law on November 8, 1933, which, among other things, stipulated that 50 percent of the jobs in each workplace should be reserved for Cuban workers.

52. Though presented in a slightly distorted way, the details of this legislation are contained in Foreign Policy Association, *Problemas de la nueva Cuba*, pp. 220–28.

53. The strike was called in protest against the arbitrary firing of engineer Valdés Roig, a member of the Sindicato de Empleados de Oficina, who, while making an inspection at Puerto Tarafa, discovered and denounced some fraudulent activities carried out by the management of Ferrocarriles Consolidados.

54. Although deprived of their legal standing, some of the organizations against which Decrees 3 and 82 had been applied continued to carry out some activities, working under the disadvantage that the companies refused to recognize them. For example, the Dirección Central of the Hermandad called a slowdown strike in August 1934. The movement was repressed violently, and its main leaders were fired.

55. Reformists who had been linked to the provisional government of Grau San Martín founded the Partido Revolucionario Cubano (Auténtico) shortly after that government's fall in January 1934. Grau himself was its main leader.

56. *Huelga general de marzo*, in AFC (d. C.), Fondo Permanente, expediente 105 (1935).

57. AHPC, Fondo Ferrocarriles, legajo 105, expediente 131–07.

Chapter 17

1. Arnaldo Silva, *Cuba y el mercado azucarero mundial* (Havana: Editorial de Ciencias Sociales, 1975), cuadro 17, and *Anuario azucarero de Cuba* (1959), p. 91. The favorable effects of the war continued in the following years. The following table sums this up.

Year	Sugarcane Harvest (in metric tons)	FOB Price (in centavos)	Total Value (in millions of pesos)
1940	2.7	1.53	110.1
1941	2.4	1.86	127.8
1942	3.3	2.69	255.9
1943	2.8	2.69	179.3
1944	4.1	2.69	330.5
1945	3.4	3.11	265.0
1946	3.9	4.37	417.7
1947	5.6	4.97	617.1
1948	5.8	4.39	632.9
1949	5.1	4.55	534.8

Source: *Anuario azucarero de Cuba* (1959), p. 91.

2. Ferrocarril del Norte de Cuba, *Libro de actas*, 3: folios 503–4, in ANC, Fondo Ferrocarriles, and Cuba Railroad Company, *Director's Meetings*, vols. 90–91.

3. Ferrocarriles Consolidados de Cuba, *Memoria anual* (1940, 1944–45).

4. United Railways of Havana, *Annual Report* (1940, 1944–45).

5. The figures for Cárdenas and Havana show this clearly. Between July and December 1944, they received and shipped out 675,573 sacks of sugar from the sugar mills in the eastern part of the country. The next year, they didn't handle any sugar from that area. AFC (d. C.), Fondo General de Paquetería (Ferrocarriles Consolidados), expediente 101 of 1945, paquete 3, and Ferrocarriles Consolidados de Cuba, *Carta anual* (1947), p. 60, in AFC (d. C.).

6. Oscar Zanetti, "El comercio exterior de Cuba," in *Anuario de estudios cubanos* (Havana: Editorial de Ciencias Sociales, 1973).

7. Ramón Grau San Martín, professor of physiology at the University of Havana, was part of the movement opposing the Gerardo Machado administration (1925–33). As such, he became a political figure and was nominated and elected president of the republic in late 1933. The reaction and U.S. imperialism sniped at his administration, which Antonio Guiteras Holmes, his secretary of the interior, filled with revolutionary dynamism, and Grau was deposed just four months after taking office. His prestige was increased by his deposition, and he won a landslide victory in the 1944 election, defeating Carlos Saladrigas. His new administration (1944–48) was characterized by gangsterism, embezzlement, and the initiation of a systematic policy of splitting the labor movement.

8. The March 3, 1947, rate is an example of this. It constituted a 20 percent increase on an already granted 20 percent increase. Resolution 1181, of June 25, 1947, also authorized Ferrocarriles Consolidados to increase its shipping rates at its Puerto Tarafa, Antilla, and Pastelillo terminals. According to the company itself, the increase amounted to 159 percent. Carta de Alfredo Lombard, July 23, 1947, in AFC (d. C.), Fondo General de Paquetería, paquete 38, expediente TA-321-7. We suppose that a coordinated freight rates system—which took the rates in all branches of transportation into account—had been in effect in Cuba since 1941. Between 1942 and 1944, however, nearly all freight was carried by rail. Therefore, problems related to the application of coordinated rates did not become an issue again until 1945.

9. United Railways of Havana, *Annual Report*, 1940, 1948), and Ferrocarriles Consolidados de Cuba, *Memoria anual* (1940, 1948).

10. L. V. Abad, *Problemas de los transportes cubanos* (Havana: Editorial Mercantil Cubana, 1944).

11. Carta del presidente de los Ferrocarriles Unidos, F. G. Mills, a E. Dihigo, presidente de la Comisión gubernamental para los ferrocarriles, January 2, 1952, in AFC (d. C.), Fondo Permanente, expediente 100–28, and "El problema ferroviario," *Cuba Económica y Financiera* (January 1951), p. 16.

12. United Railways of Havana, *Annual Report* (1947–48), pp. 14–15.

13. *Cuba Económica y Financiera* (January 1951), p. 16.

14. ANC, *Fondo Ferrocarriles* (Ferrocarriles Unidos), legajo 172, expediente 2.

15. Ibid.

16. *Cuba Económica y Financiera* (April 1949), p. 47.

17. A participant in the struggles against the Machado tyranny, he had the dubious distinction of beginning to break up the labor movement as minister of labor in the Ramón Grau San Martín administration and of continuing the job as president (1948–52). He was deposed by Fulgencio Batista on March 10, 1952.

18. "En Cuba" section, *Bohemia*, June 12, 1949, pp. 78–82.

19. "Decreto 1755," *Gaceta Oficial de la República de Cuba*, June 9, 1949.

20. Carta del presidente de los Ferrocarriles Unidos, F. G. Mills, a E. Dihigo, presidente de la Comisión gubernamental para los ferrocarriles, January 2, 1952, in AFC (d. C.), Fondo Permanente, expediente 100–28, and "El problema ferroviario," *Cuba Económica y Financiera* (January 1951), p. 16.

21. Carta de A. Lombard al Ministro de Comunicaciones, July 1946, in AFC (d. C.), Fondo Administración, expediente 110, paquete 513.

22. In 1944, U.S. Ambassador S. Braden informed Ferrocarriles Consolidados that a list of U.S. company claims against the Cuban government was being drawn up in the U.S. Embassy, to be presented through diplomatic channels. Ferrocarriles Consolidados, *Libro de actas*, 3:267, in ANC, Fondo Ferrocarriles.

23. Ferrocarriles Consolidados de Cuba, *Memoria anual* (1944–45), p. 5.

24. Alejandro Herrera Arango, *Proyecto*, October 13, 1941, in AFC (d. C.), Fondo Paquetería (1942), expediente 319, p. 69. Unidos didn't look kindly on Consolidados's activity regarding highway transportation, as it considered it to be an "invasion" of the Carretera Central, which would prolong the old competition. This caused friction between the two companies. AFC (d. C.), Fondo Administración, paquete C-17, expediente 17.

25. Ferrocarriles Consolidados de Cuba, *Memoria anual* (1943–44), pp. 470–71. In 1945, it acquired four more companies: La Universal, Aliados del Cristo, Los Angeles, and Melero. *Compra de ómnibus en 1948*, in AFC (d. C.), Fondo Ingresos (Ferrocarriles Consolidados de Cuba).

26. *Compra de ómnibus en 1948*, in AFC (d. C.), Fondo Ingresos (Ferrocarriles Consolidados de Cuba), p. 93.

27. Ferrocarriles Consolidados, *Memoria anual* (1945–46), p. 47.

28. G. Pellón, *Informe general sobre el Ferrocarril de Guantánamo y Western*, Camagüey, November 8, 1948, p. 1, in AFC (d. C.), Archivo Legal.

29. Guantánamo and Western, *Libro de actas de la Junta Directiva y de accionistas* (1946–50), 9:4, in ANC, Fondo Ferrocarriles, and *Annual Report* (1948).

30. Since 1927, Guantánamo and Western had suffered from a reduction in the number

of sugar mills in the area it served. The Confluente, Santa María, and Monona closed down, as did the Santa Cecilia later on, but this last was started up again in 1934. Guantánamo and Western provided financial assistance for rehabilitating that sugar mill, thus increasing its interests in that production unit. The bill for the Santa Cecilia was declared a bad debt and was later transferred to the railroad company's books as a deficit, which benefited the sugar company—and, thus, the interests of Francisco Bartés, president of Guantánamo and Western, who was one of its main stockholders. Guantánamo and Western, *Annual Report* (1944–45).

31. Ferrocarriles Consolidados, *Libro de actas*, libro 53, folios 482, 515–19, in ANC, Fondo Ferrocarriles.

32. Ibid.

33. The members of the *junta de directores* (board of directors) were Gustavo A. Pellón and Alfredo Lombard, of Consolidados, and Francisco Bartés, Mario Bartés, and Pedro Figueredo, of Guantánamo and Western. Ferrocarril del Norte de Cuba, *Libro de actas*, 4:36, in ANC, Fondo Ferrocarriles.

34. G. Pellón, *Informe general sobre el Ferrocarril de Guantánamo y Western*, Camagüey, November 8, 1948, p. 1, in AFC (d. C.), Archivo Legal.

35. Railroad leader Ricardo Rodríguez, who was a member of the Partido Comunista, worked tirelessly in the Pro Unidad group and Renovación Ferroviaria. His prestige in Havana's railroad sector led to his becoming president of Delegation 2 in January 1939. In the first national congress of the Confederación de Trabajadores, he was elected vice-secretario general (deputy general secretary).

36. In the western part of the country, there was only one organization other than the Hermandad: the Matanzas Terminal union, which also supported unity.

37. Ferrocarriles Consolidados applauded fraternization between the company and the Hermandad Ferroviaria. It also created categories of workers grouped in such things as the Legión de Honor Ferroviaria (Railroad Legion of Honor), Columna de Plata (Silver Column), and Botón de Oro (Gold Button). Interview of Ernesto Agüero, Camagüey, May 19, 1974.

38. The movement for reinstating those fired during the March 1935 strike played an important role in the struggle for unity. Interview of Sebastián Tornavaca, Camagüey, May 15, 1974.

39. Carta del contador general de los Ferrocarriles Consolidados, Gustavo A. Pellón, al presidente de dicha empresa, Domingo Galdós, in AHPC, Fondo Ferrocarriles, legajo 27, expediente 282-E.

40. Ibid., and *Hoy*, December 20, 1938. Lázaro Peña was one of the most outstanding leaders of the Cuban labor movement. He was general secretary of the Confederación de Trabajadores de Cuba from its founding, in 1939, to 1947, and then again after the triumph of the Revolution until his death.

41. As seen in the previous chapter, the railroad companies' payrolls were very high in 1928–29. To survive the crisis, they applied a policy of laying off workers and cutting wages, to reduce those expenditures to the absolute minimum required to keep the trains operating. By 1938–39, Ferrocarriles Unidos had laid off more than five thousand workers. ANC, Fondo Ferrocarriles (Ferrocarriles Unidos), legajo 784, expediente 4.

42. Ibid. The company claimed that its action was based on a reduction of service as part of its economies. During that year, the Havana-Rincón-Güines service was closed down.

43. Ibid. The workers refuted the owners' economy claims, pointing out that forty-eight English employees received a total of 226,084 pesos a year—that is, an average of 392.50 pesos each a month—which was incomparably more than the highest monthly wage paid to a Cuban worker.

44. Ibid.

45. The elected leaders were Rogelio García, of the Pro Unidad group, and Sebastián Tornavaca and Calixto Agüero, of the Partido Comunista.

46. ANC, Fondo Ferrocarriles (Ferrocarriles Unidos), legajo 214, expediente 4.

47. Ibid.

48. ANC, Fondo Ferrocarriles (Ferrocarriles Unidos), legajo 245, expediente 1.

49. AFC (d. C.), Fondo General de Paquetería (Guantánamo and Western), expediente 105.

50. Ibid.

51. *Hoy*, July 7, 1944, pp. 7–8.

52. ANC, Fondo Ferrocarriles (Ferrocarriles Unidos), legajo 172, expediente 3.

53. Ibid.

54. AFC (d. C.), Fondo General de Paquetería (Guantánamo and Western), expediente 105.

55. Ibid.

56. Two anti-Communist agents who later played an important role in the Cuban labor movement came from these groups: Eusebio Mujal and Francisco Aguirre.

57. *Hoy*, December 20, 1942.

58. In 1943, Barrios went so far as to suggest that the Hermandad Ferroviaria break off from the Confederación de Trabajadores de Cuba if it didn't support it in its conflict with the leader of Delegation 2. The essence of the conflict turned on their class positions. Barrios, disagreeing with Rodríguez, tried to make the wage increases dependent on higher transportation rates. Barrios was an agent of the owners whom some workers considered a traitor to his class. *Delegación No. 2*, p. 19.

59. Interview of Communist leader Ricardo Rodríguez, Havana, May 8, 1974.

60. The inaugural ceremony was held in the Campoamor Theater, but the work sessions took place in the local of Delegation 2, in the Luyanó part of Havana. The speakers in the inaugural ceremony were Ricardo Rodríguez, deputy general secretary of the Confederación de Trabajadores de Cuba and leader of Delegation 2; Arturo Agüero Vives, president of the Dirección Central of the Hermandad Ferroviaria; Dr. Azcárate, minister of labor; Lázaro Peña, general secretary of the Confederación de Trabajadores de Cuba; and Dr. Ramón Grau San Martín, president of the republic.

61. *Hoy*, September 14, 1945, p. 8.

62. Ibid.

63. *Estatutos de la Federación Nacional de la Hermandad Ferroviaria*, private papers of José Soltura, Morón, Camagüey.

64. *Hoy*, July 10, 1947, p. 3.

65. The elected slate, headed by Lázaro Peña, included railroad workers Ricardo Rodríguez, deputy general secretary; Rogelio García Hagnenot, deputy organizing secretary; Teolindo Jurjo, deputy secretary of culture; Francisco Malpica, secretary of legal matters; and José Miguel Espino, secretary of social security.

66. Evelio Tellería, *Los congresos obreros en Cuba* (Havana: Editorial de Ciencias Sociales, 1973), pp. 361–64.

67. For example, Delegation 5, of Cruces, was prohibited from selling the newspaper *Hoy*, organ of Cuban Communists. *Hoy*, October 3, 1947.

68. Workers expressed their contempt for the government-approved union—which they called the "CTK," because of its fraudulent milking of Clause K in the Ministry of Education's budget—by dropping out of their unions in spite of threatened reprisals by union "leaders."

69. This was Oscar Amable, who came from the Comité Obrero Nacional Independiente (Independent National Workers' Committee). Its members were followers of Angel Cofiño, of the electricians' union; Angel Rubiera, of the telephone workers' union; and Ignacio González Tellechea, of the maritime workers' union.

70. *Hoy*, October 8, 1947, p. 2.

71. Ibid.

72. The main groups were the Comité Obrero Nacional Independiente, or CONI (Independent National Worker's Committee) and the Comisión Obrera Nacional (National Workers' Commission) of the Partido Revolucionario Cubano (Auténtico), headed by Eusebio Mujal. Another group from the Auténtico party, Acción Revolucionaria Guiteras (Guiteras Revolutionary Action), had some elements in the heart of the labor movement.

73. Oscar Amable chaired the inaugural session. Arturo Agüero Vives, former president of the Hermandad Ferroviaria, was elected chairman of the congress. *Hoy*, December 28, 1947, p. 3.

Chapter 18

1. The World Bank published the report in a voluminous 1,050-page volume called *Report on Cuba* (Baltimore: Johns Hopkins Press, 1951). The Banco Nacional de Cuba reproduced it in Spanish later.

2. Economic and Technical Mission to Cuba, *Report on Cuba* (Baltimore: Johns Hopkins Press, 1951), p. 29.

3. Ibid., p. 252.

4. Automotive vehicles transported an estimated 9.5 million metric tons of freight, while the railroads carried only 5.3 million metric tons of general merchandise.

5. Economic and Technical Mission to Cuba, *Report on Cuba*, pp. 259, 261.

6. Ibid., pp. 262–63.

7. Ibid., p. 263.

8. The rolling stock that was purchased consisted of seventeen passenger cars; three mixed cars; eight self-propelled cars; and some other, less important, equipment. ANC, Fondo Ferrocarriles (Ferrocarriles Unidos), legajo 165, expediente 6.

9. *Bohemia*, November 13, 1949, pp. 80–81.

10. ANC, Fondo Ferrocarriles (Ferrocarriles Unidos), legajo 165, expediente 6.

11. Ibid.

12. Carta de R. G. Mills a Carlos Prío, August 21, 1950, in AFC (d. C.), Fondo General de Paquetería, paquete 26, expediente AG 222–6.

13. Truslow died on July 8, 1951. The president of Ferrocarriles Unidos commented at the time that "We are maintaining close cooperation with Mr. Truslow and this cooperation is maintained even after the report had been finished. During his brief time with our business, he [Truslow] was a very good friend of this company." United Railways of Havana and

Regla Warehouses, Ltd., *Proceedings of the Fifty-Third Annual General Meeting of the Company* (1950).

14. United Railways of Havana and Regla Warehouses, Ltd. *Annual Report, 1950. Statement by the Chairman R. G. Mills accompanying the Director's Report*, pp. 10–11.

15. Francisco Dorado, "La crisis de los Ferrocarriles Unidos," *Fundamentos*, año 8, no. 135 (June 1953): 541.

16. The owners of a group of sugar mills served by Ferrocarriles Unidos pledged that, if the railroad didn't make its loan payments on time, they would pay the banks instead of the railroad the amounts they owed the railroad in freight charges. ANC, Fondo Ferrocarriles (Ferrocarriles Unidos), legajo 198, expediente 7.

17. The commission appointed by the Asociación de Hacendados met with government officials and officials of the British company. As a result of its efforts, it drafted a memorandum setting forth the conditions under which the estate owners would be willing to take charge of the railroad. They included the construction of several branch lines, authorization to lay off fifteen hundred workers, and the government's payment of its debt to the railroad. Memorándum, February 22, 1952, in AFC (d. C.), Fondo Permanente, expediente 100–28 (1953).

18. Memorándum de R. G. Mills a E. Dihigo, January 16, 1952, in AFC (d. C.), Fondo Permanente, expediente 100–28 (1953). The price of $14.5 million had been set a year earlier, in a memorandum addressed to Primer Ministro Manuel A. de Varona.

19. The purchase offers included one tendered by the shipping company that operated the ferry service between Florida and Havana and another presented by estate owner Marcelino García Beltrán, who stipulated that he would pay for the railroad with 300,000 tons of sugar. ANC, Fondo Ferrocarriles (Ferrocarriles Unidos), legajo 165, expediente 2.

20. Francisco Dorado, "La crisis de los Ferrocarriles Unidos," p. 543.

21. In 1953, Ferrocarriles Consolidados didn't have the favorable situation it had had in earlier years, which led its management to demand unfair conditions for implementing the plan. Memorándum de G. Pellón y J. de Cubas al Ministro de Comunicaciones y Transporte, in AFC (d. C.), Fondo Permanente, expediente 100–28 (1953).

22. Though curious in its technical aspects, the Swiss millionaire's project was by no means farfetched. Brought to Cuba by lawyer Guillermo Belt, former Cuban ambassador in Washington, Wenner-Green wanted to take advantage of the circumstances to use the capital he had lying idle in the United States and Great Britain.

23. Raúl Cepero Bonilla, "Motivos económicos," *Prensa Libre*, January 5, 1954, p. 2.

24. The funds for amortizing this loan would be obtained by means of a series of temporary taxes, which would be imposed both on sugar exports and on imports and other merchandise. Thus, the Batista regime shifted the burden of the operation onto both the bourgeoisie and the people as a whole.

25. This led to a public debate between the executive of the Asociación de Hacendados and Fidel Barreto, recently appointed vice-president of Ferrocarriles Occidentales. Since Barreto—a businessman who was very closely linked to the tyranny—was also vice-president of the Asociación de Hacendados, the polemic was very virulent. *Carteles*, April 4 and 11, 1954, year XXXV, nos. 14, 15.

26. Those "products unrelated to the operation" came from renting equipment and land and engaging in other business. In 1950 alone, the company reported 700,000 pesos in income from such sources. Memorándum, April 3, 1959, in AFC (d. C.), Departamento de Tesorería, paquete 43, expediente 506–3.

27. Carta de F. A. Truslow a José Bosch, ministro de Hacienda, October 5, 1950, in AFC (d. C.), Fondo Privado Administración, paquete 19.

28. Carcas, Estébanez, y Barreneche, *Informe sobre la costeabilidad de los Ferrocarriles Consolidados*, in AFC (d. C.), Fondo Contaduría. That recapitalization plan was linked to the project for dissolving Ferrocarril del Norte de Cuba and placing its stock under the direct control of Consolidados, so as to apply the same procedure to Cuba Railroad and Guantánamo and Western later on, which would bring about the complete modification and reduction of the system's capital stock.

29. That plan was based on a temporary provision of the constitution of 1940, which permitted companies to make agreements with their mortgage creditors—bondholders—concerning the amortization of their debts. In line with that provision, the company had, since 1940, drawn up amortization formulas for the mortgage loans of Cuba Railroad and Ferrocarril del Norte de Cuba, which were given their definitive shape in this readjustment plan of 1952.

30. Most of those locomotives had been purchased during the years of the sugar boom caused by World War I. Even though many of them had been reconditioned to burn oil, their maintenance and operation required high expenditures. That situation and the no less deplorable state of the tracks caused frequent accidents. In fiscal year 1949–50 alone, there were 432 train accidents, 256 of which were attributed to the poor state of that means of transportation.

31. Under "the dieselization plan," Ferrocarriles Consolidados purchased a total of 82 locomotives, 16 passenger motor coaches, 350 boxcars, and 60 gondolas, all of which required an investment of 15,355,878 pesos. With that new equipment, its main locomotive needs were met, but not those for rehabilitating its freight and passenger services, as the rolling stock acquired for that purpose was insufficient. *Carta anual* (1954–55), pp. 75–76, in AFC (d. C.), Fondo Permanente, legajo 1 (1955).

32. J. C. Santamarina, "The Cuba Company and Cuban Development, 1900–1959" (Ph.D. dissertation, Ohio State University, 1995), pp. 157–67.

33. The Cuba Company's balance sheet for 1953 showed that (through a group of eight Panamanian companies) the Bartés family owned 234,655 shares of common stock and 20,090 shares of preferred, representing 36 percent and 80 percent, respectively, of the total. University of Maryland at College Park, McKeldin Library, *Cuba Company Records*, series 3, box 140. Something similar seems to have occurred with the Compañía Cubana, the Cuba Company's subsidiary that operated its sugar mills, in which Cuban stockholders also entered. The most important of them was Amado Aréchaga, a large-scale sugarcane grower who provided 20 percent of the sugarcane ground at the Jatibonico sugar mill.

34. The details of that process are contained in Santamarina, "The Cuba Company," pp. 166–71.

35. See Oscar Pino Santos, *El asalto a Cuba por la oligarquía financiera norteamericana* (Havana: Editorial Casa de las Américas, 1973), pp. 197–98.

36. The declared losses between 1952 and 1956 amounted to a total of 6,862,174 pesos. *Estado de productos de explotación*, in AFC (d. C.), Fondo Privado de Administración, paquete 24, expediente AG-228.

37. This study was carried out under Decree 1501, which Batista issued in June 1953. It appointed a ministerial commission for studying the situation of the railroads.

38. AFC (d. C.), Fondo Privado de Administración, paquete 47-A, expediente 506–3.

39. *Hoy*, December 18, 1949, p. 6.

40. The plan was based on a decree that modified Article 23 of the railroad retirement law. The modification established an increase in the contributions to the Caja del Retiro (Retirement Fund) and a reduction in retirement rights, increasing (from ten to fifteen) the years of service required to qualify for a pension. The Chiappy Plan also stated that workers who were laid off and weren't entitled to a pension would be paid 50 percent of their wages as compensation during the first six months after they were fired.

41. "Declaraciones de los dirigentes Oscar Amable y Javier Bolaños, presidentes de la Delegación 2 y de la Federación de la Hermandad Ferroviaria, respectivamente," Hoy, July 17, 1953, pp. 1, 8.

42. Hoy, April 9, 1953, p. 3, and Carta circular de los Ferrocarriles Consolidados a todo el personal, in AFC (d. C.), Fondo Privado de Administración, paquete 3-A, expediente AG-102.

43. "Decreto-ley 1155," Gaceta Oficial de la República de Cuba, November 11, 1953, no. 87.

44. Carta de Gustavo Pellón a J. Villarnovo, October 13, 1954, in AFC (d. C.), Fondo Privado de Administración, paquete 4, expediente 2-202.

45. The violations mainly concerned failure to fill the vacancies caused by retirement. Carta de G. Pellón a J. Villarnovo, December 2, 1954, in AFC (d. C.), Fondo Privado de Administración, paquete 3, expediente A-G-102.

46. This cannot be explained in any other way, since, when the first measures were announced, the delivery of cash to the company had practically been approved. When the last measure was announced, the loan had already been granted, although payment probably had not yet been made. Carta circular de los Ferrocarriles Consolidados a todo el personal, in AFC (d. C.), Fondo Privado de Administración, paquete 3, expediente AG-102.

47. Informe de A. Quintana, oficial de estaciones, al presidente de Ferrocarriles Consolidados, in AFC (d. C.), Fondo Permanente, expediente 105 (1955). Railroad strikes.

48. "Decreto 1535," Gaceta Oficial de la República de Cuba, August 6, 1955.

49. La Calle, June 15, 1955, pp. 1, 6.

50. "Acta Número XII" contained some statements concerning certain interpretive aspects of the finding, but it was mainly a pledge renouncing strike tactics.

51. They included the Banco del Comercio Exterior de Cuba (BANCESCU, or Foreign Trade Bank of Cuba); the Fomento de Hipotecas Aseguradas (FHA, or Promotion of Insured Mortgages); the Banco de Desarrollo Económico y Social (BANDES, or Socioeconomic Development Bank); and such other sonorous and abstract abbreviations as CEMPLUC, CENCAN, CENOP, and ONDI.

52. The board of directors was composed of Joaquín Martínez Sáenz, president of the Banco Nacional; Emeterio Santovenia, for BANFAIC; and Gustavo Gutiérrez, ministro de hacienda (minister of the treasury). Even though Marino López Blanco was elected chairman of the first board, Martínez Sáenz became chairman for six years starting in 1955.

53. Libro de actas del Ferrocarril del Norte de Cuba, 4: folio 533, in ANC, Fondo Ferrocarriles.

54. In 1957, the Corporación Nacional de Transportes (National Transportation Corporation) reported that 15.83 percent of the Cuban railroads' income came from their passenger services. Between 1951–52 and 1954–55, the number of passengers carried by Ferrocarriles Consolidados dropped by 2.5 million. Carta anual de 1954–1955, in AFC (d. C.), Fondo Contaduría, paquete 51.

55. *Acta de la Junta Directiva de los Ferrocarriles Consolidados*, in AFC (d. C.), Fondo Privado de Administración, paquete 1, expediente AG-100.

56. Ibid.

57. For an analysis of the Batista dictatorship's squandering and embezzlement of public funds, see Oscar Pino Santos, "El 10 de marzo o el vandalismo y la irresponsabilidad financiera en el poder," *Bohemia*, January 25, 1959, year LVIII, no. 3, p. 148.

58. *Daños ocasionados a edificios, apeaderos, puentes, etcétera, con motivo de actos insurreccionales*, in AFC (d. C.), Fondo Permanente, expediente especial.

59. Interview of Octavio Louit, Havana, January 1978.

60. A group of young members of the Directorio Revolucionario (Revolutionary Directorate) attacked the Palacio Presidencial on March 13, 1957. Although well planned, the action failed to achieve its purpose of executing Batista. Immediately after the attack, the tyrant moved his residence to Camp Columbia, a military stronghold.

61. That 959,000-peso loan was given to avoid new conflicts over withheld wages and wage cuts, which the company kept bringing up for discussion.

62. The martyrs in the struggle against the dictatorship included members of the railroad proletariat. Mario Aróstegui was the first railway man to be assassinated, followed by José Ramírez Casamayor and other old railway leaders and by young rail workers who belonged to the Movimiento 26 de Julio. Aróstegui was tortured and killed by members of the Servicio de Inteligencia Militar (Military Intelligence Service), who left his body on the Bayamo-Manzanillo highway. Ramírez Casamayor was assassinated at the entrance to the Ciénaga repair shops.

63. Carta del administrador general del Ferrocarril de Guantánamo al teniente de Navío Heriberto Izquierdo, jefe del puesto naval de Caimanera, in AFC (d. C.), Fondo Permanente, expediente 105 (1958).

64. Carta de A. M. Figueredo a F. Bartés, September 29, 1958, in AFC (d. C.), Fondo Privado de Administración, paquete 4, expediente AG-105, p. 73.

65. *Expediente relativo a modificaciones en el servicio de viajeros*, in AFC (d. C.), Fondo Permanente, expediente 105 (1958).

66. Of that amount, 100,000 pesos went for wages and 300,000 pesos, for repairs. The rest was used to create a corps for the armed defense of the trains. See Carta de Pío Elizalde a A. Pérez, March 19, 1958, in AFC (d. C.), Fondo Privado de Administración, Personal.

67. Interview of Alvaro Vázquez Galego, Camagüey, May 16, 1974; Manuel García, *Apuntes de las luchas obreras en el sector ferroviario*, mimeographed material, p. 18; and interview of Ignacio Filiberto Ruíz, Havana, May 13, 1974.

68. Ernesto Che Guevara, "Una reunión decisiva," in *Pasajes de la guerra revolucionaria* (Havana: Editorial Arte y Literatura, 1975). The Frente Obrero Nacional Unido (United National Workers' Front), a labor organization supporting the insurrectional movement, had been created at the beginning of 1958, but its mechanisms had been no more than sketchily drawn up, so information about and preparations for the strike were not extensive enough.

69. See FONU, *Proclama a los trabajadores ferroviarios* (November 1958), in AFC (d. C.), Fondo Privado de Administración, legajo 1, expediente AG-102, p. 8.

70. In Camagüey, the military chief of the garrison threatened to take over the government-sponsored labor organizations because the delegates in some departments, who were supposed to be pledged in some way to the government, had not gone to work on April 9, thus contributing to the work stoppage. *Declaraciones del coronel V. Dueñas, jefe*

del regimiento 2 Ignacio Agramonte, in AFC (d. C.), Fondo Privado de Administración, Personal, legajo 1, expediente 71.

71. Sergio Parra Pérez, the supervisor, was appointed on April 11, 1958. AFC (d. C.), Fondo Privado de Administración, legajo 8, expediente AG-102.

72. S. Parra Pérez, *Comunicación a los jefes militares de Camagüey,* in AFC (d. C.), Fondo Privado de Administración, Personal, expediente 102, p. 7.

73. Carta de S. Parra Pérez a Gonzalo Güel, ministro de Estado, May 6, 1958, in AFC (d. C.), Fondo Privado de Administración, legajo 1, expediente AG-102.

74. *Gaceta Oficial de la República de Cuba,* August 14, 1958, p. 12.

75. In 1957, Pellón was surprisingly replaced as president of Ferrocarriles Consolidados. His successor was Francisco Bartés, the main Cuban stockholder in the company. At the time, it was rumored that Pellón's removal was related to his role in the Fiat deal.

76. Acta de la Junta de directores del Ferrocarril del Norte de Cuba, October 27, 1958, in AFC (d. C.), Fondo Privado de Administración, legajo 1, expediente AG-100, p. 1.

77. Carta de A. Figueredo a F. Bartés, September 9, 1958, in AFC (d. C.), Fondo Privado de Administración, Personal, expediente AG-105, p. 73.

78. Carta de F. Bartés a A. Rangel, presidente del Trust Company of Cuba, December 3, 1958, in AFC (d. C.), Fondo Privado de Administración, paquete 5, expediente 506-3.

79. Carta de A. Figueredo a F. Bartés, December 11, 1958, in AFC (d. C.), Fondo Privado de Administración, Personal, paquete 73, expediente AG-105.

80. Ibid.

81. On December 23, 1958, only 386 of Consolidados's 2,310 kilometers of track could be used. *Daños ocasionados a edificios.*

82. Carta de S. Parra Pérez.

Sources

Archival Material

Archivo Histórico Provincial de Camagüey (AHPC), Camagüey
    Ferrocarriles Gobierno Provincial
Archivo Nacional de Cuba (ANC), Havana
    Consejo de Administración
    Ferrocarriles
    Gobierno Superior Civil
    Intendencia de Hacienda
    Miscelánea
    Real Consulado y Junta de Fomento
Archivos de los Ferrocarriles de Cuba. División Camagüey (AFC, d.C.), Camagüey
    Departamento de Contabilidad
    Departamento legal
    General de Paquetería
    Permanente
    Privado de Administración
    Tesorería
Archivos de los Ferrocarriles de Cuba. Estación Terminal Habana (AFC, ETH), Havana
    Documentación Legal
Biblioteca Central de la Universidad de La Habana (BCUH): Almacenes de Regla,
    Banco de comercio y Ferrocarril de la Bahía. Colección facticia, 1880–90.
Biblioteca Nacional de Cuba (BNC): Colección Cubana, Havana
    Correspondencia de José Luis Alfonso
    Correspondencia de Domingo del Monte

Printed Primary Sources

Asociación de Hacendados y Colonos de Cuba. *Impugnación del proyecto de ley de consolidación de los ferrocarriles*. Havana, August 23, 1923.

Biblioteca Nacional de Cuba. *Correspondencia reservada del capitán general don Miguel Tacón*. Havana, 1963.

Centro de Estadísticas. *Noticia estadísticas de la isla de Cuba en 1862*. Havana: Imprenta del Gobierno y Capitanía General, 1864.

Cuadro estadístico de la siempre fiel isla de Cuba al año de 1846. Havana: Imprenta del Gobierno y Capitanía General, 1847.

Cuba. Comisión de Ferrocarriles. *Memorias*. 1901–37.

Cuba. Comisión Nacional de Transportes. *Memorias*. 1939–48.

Cuba. Congreso. *Diario de Sesiones del Senado*.

Cuba. Junta de Fomento. Documentos relativos a la enagenación del camino de hierro de la Habana a Güines. Havana: Imprenta del Gobierno y Capitanía General, 1839.

Cuba. Junta de Fomento. *Informe presentado por el excelentísimo presidente de la Junta . . . sobre el proyecto de dirigir al surgidero de Guanímar un ramal de camino de hierro*. Havana: Imprenta del Gobierno y Capitanía General, 1839.

Cuba. Military Governor John Brooke. *Civil Report*. Havana, 1899.

Cuba. Military Governor Leonard Wood. *Civil Report of the Military Governor, 1901*. Havana, 1902.

Cuba. Military Governor Leonard Wood. *Civil Report of the Military Governor, 1902*. Havana, 1903.

Cuba. Oficina Nacional de los censos demográfico y electoral. *Censo de la población, vivienda y electoral. 28 de enero de 1953*. Havana, 1955.

Cuba. Secretaría de Agricultura, Industria y Comercio. *Memorias de las zafras azucareras, 1907–1930*.

Cuba. Secretaría de Obras Públicas. *Memorias sobre los ferrocarriles de la isla de Cuba en los años económicos de 1882–1883 hasta 1897–1898*. Havana: Imprenta Universal, 1902.

Cuba. Subdirección de Obras Públicas. *Memoria sobre el progreso de las obras públicas en la isla de Cuba desde 1869 hasta 1875*. Havana: Imprenta del Gobierno y Capitanía General, 1876.

Cuba. Tribunal de Cuentas. *Informe sobre la costeabilidad y situación financiera de las empresas que integran el sistema de Consolidados de Cuba*. Havana, 1955.

Cuban Communist Party. *Informe del Comité Central del partido Comunista de Cuba al primer Congreso presentado por el compañero Fidel Castro Ruz, Primer Secretario del PCC*. Havana: DOR, 1975.

Cuban Communist Party. *Tesis y resoluciones del Primer Congreso del Partido Comunista de Cuba*. Havana: DOR, 1976.

Instituto de Historia del Movimiento Comunista y de la Revolución Socialista de Cuba. *El movimiento obrero cubano. Documentos y artículos*. 2 vols. Havana: Editorial de Ciencias Sociales, 1975, 1977.

Jáudenes, A. M. *Memoria sobre las obras públicas en la isla de Cuba, 1865–1873*. Havana: La Propaganda Literaria, 1882.

Pichardo, Hortensia. *Documentos para la historia de Cuba*. Havana: Editorial de Ciencias Sociales, 1971, 1973.

United States of America. *Informe del censo de Cuba*. Washington, D.C., 1900.

Company Annual Reports

Banco de Comercio, Almacenes de Regla y Ferrocarril de la Bahía

Banco de Comercio, Almacenes de Regla y Ferrocarriles Unidos de La Habana

Compañia de Caminos de Hierro de La Habana

Compañia de Ferrocarril de Júcaro

Compañia del Ferrocarril de Trinidad

Compañia del Ferrocarril y Almacenes de Depósito de Santiago de Cuba

Cuba Company

Cuba Railroad Company
Cuban Central Railways of Havana Limited
Cuban Northern Railways Company
Empressa Unida de las Ferrocarriles de Cárdenas y Júcaro
Empressa Unida de las Ferrocarriles de Matanzas a Sabanilla
Ferrocarril de Cárdenas y Júcaro
Ferrocarril de Cienfuegos y Villa Clara S.A.
Ferrocarril de la Bahía de la Habana
Ferrocarril de Marianao
Ferrocarril de Sagua La Grande
Ferrocarril del Norte de Cuba
Ferrocarril del Oeste
Ferrocarril y Almacenes de Depósitos de Santiago de Cuba
Ferrocarriles Consolidados de Cuba
Ferrocarriles Occidentales de Cuba
Guantánamo and Western Railroad Company
United Railways of Havana and Regla Warehouses Limited
Western Railways of Havana Limited

Books and Articles

Abad, L. V. de. *Los ferrocarriles de Cuba*. Havana: Imprenta La Habanera, 1940.
——. *Problemas de los transportes cubanos*. Havana: Editorial Mercantil Cubana, 1944.
——. *Los servicios de transporte terrestre y la función del Estado*. Havana: Caraza y Compañia, 1937.
Academia de Ciencias de Cuba. *Indice histórico Camagüey*. Havana: Instituto del Libro, 1970.
Aguirre, S. *Eco de caminos*. Havana: Editorial de Ciencias Sociales, 1974.
Alcover, A. M. *Historia de la villa de Sagua la Grande*. Sagua la Grande: Imprenta Unidas, 1905.
Alvarez Pedroso, A. *Miguel de Aldama*. Havana: Imprenta Siglo XX, 1948.
Barjot, Robert. *Les chemins de fer en France*. Paris: Didier, 1947.
Berenguer y Sed, A. *Discurso contrario al proyecto de ley de subvención del Ferrocarril de Caibarién a Nuevitas*. Havana: La Moderna Poesía, 1912.
Betancourt Cisneros, Gaspar. *Ferrocarril de Puerto Príncipe a Nuevitas*. Havana: El Faro Industrial, 1844.
Bou, L. *La cuestión de los bancos en la isla de Cuba*. Santiago de Cuba: Emprenta Espinal, 1867.
Brooke, John R. *Civil Report of Major General John R. Brooke, U.S. Army, Military Governor, Island of Cuba*. Washington, D.C.: Government Printing Office, 1900.
Brown, John K. *The Baldwin Locomotive Works, 1831–1915*. Baltimore: Johns Hopkins University Press, 1995.
Calcagno, F. *Diccionario biográfico cubano*. New York, 1878.
Carrerá, E. *Informe a la compañía fundadora de Ferrocarril de Sabanilla y Maroto*. Santiago de Cuba: Imprenta Martínez, 1855.
Carrerá y Heredia, M. *Informe general presentado a la Junta Directora del Ferrocarril de la Sabanilla*. Matanzas: Imprenta del Gobierno, 1846.

Centón epistolario de Domingo del Monte. Havana: Imprenta del siglo XX, 1923.
Cepero Bonilla, Raúl. *Azúcar y abolición*. Havana: Editorial de Ciencias Sociales, 1971.
Coatsworth, John H. *El impacto económico de los ferrocarriles en el porfiriato*. Mexico, 1976.
Corbitt, C. *El primer ferrocarril construido en Cuba*. Havana, 1937.
Cruger, A. *Informe general del ingeniero director del ferrocarril del Júcaro*. Havana: Imprenta Oliva, 1841.
———. *Informe presentado a la comisión directiva del camino de hierro a Güines*. Havana: Imprenta del Gobierno y Capitanía General, 1836.
Dana, R. H. *To Cuba and Back*. Boston: Tickner and Fields, 1859.
Datos y noticias oficiales referentes a los bienes embargados. Havana: Imprenta del Gobierno y Capitanía General, 1870.
Deerr, N. *The History of Sugar*. 2 vols. London: Chapman and Hall, 1949–50.
Deschamps, G. *La crisis azucarera y la isla de Cuba*. Havana: La Propaganda Literaria, 1885.
Donovan, F. *Railroads of America*. Wisconsin: Kalmbach Publishing Company, 1949.
Economic and Technical Mission to Cuba. *Report on Cuba*. Baltimore: Johns Hopkins Press, 1951.
Edo y Llop, E. *Memoria histórica de Cienfuegos y su jurisdicción*. Havana: Montero, 1943.
Ely, R. T. *Comerciantes cubanos del siglo xix*. Havana: Editorial Martí, 1961.
———. *Cuando reinaba su majestad el azúcar*. Buenos Aires: Editorial Sudamericana, 1963.
Emden, P. H. *Money Powers of Europe*. London: Sampson, Low and Marston, n.d.
Estévez, Romero L. *Desde el Zanjón hasta Baire*. Havana: Editorial de Ciencias Sociales, 1974.
Fernández de Castro, M. *Proyecto de Ferrocarril Central*. Havana, 1862.
Fogel, R. W. *Railroads and American Economic Growth*. Baltimore: Johns Hopkins, 1964.
Foreign Policy Association. *Problemas de la nueva Cuba*. New York, 1935.
García, A. *El canal de occidente*. Havana: Centro de Información Científica-téchnica, 1972.
García, G. "Papel de la crisis económica de 1857 en la economía cubana." In *Sobre la Guerra de los Diez Años*. Havana: Edición Revolucionaria, 1963.
García, M. *Apuntes de las luchas obreras en el sector ferroviaria*. n.p., n.d.
Grobart, Fabio. "El movimiento obrero cubano de 1925 a 1933." *Santiago*, no. 5 (Dec. 1971): 24.
Guerra, R. *Azúcar y población en las Antillas*. Havana: Editorial Lex, 1961.
Hazard, S. *Cuba with Pen and Pencil*. Hartford, Conn.: Hartford Publishing Co., 1871.
Hellberg, C. *Historia estadística de Cárdenas*. Cárdenas, 1957.
History of the Baldwin Locomotive Works, 1831–1923. Philadelphia: Bingham, 1923.
Humboldt, A. *Ensayo político sobre la isla de Cuba*. Havana: Office of the City Historian, 1959.
Jenks, L. H. *Our Cuban Colony: A Study in Sugar*. New York: Vanguard Press, 1928.
Johnson, E. R. *Principles of Railroad Transportation*. New York: Appleton, 1922.
Josephson, M. *The Robber Barons: The Great American Capitalists, 1861–1901*. New York: Harcourt, Brace, 1934.
Kirkland, E. C. *Men, Cities and Transportation*. Cambridge, Mass.: Harvard University Press, 1948.

Leech, M. *In the Times of McKinley.* New York: Harper, 1959.
Lenin, V. I. *El desarrollo del capitalismo en Rusia.* Moscow: Editorial Progreso, 1976.
——. *Imperialism: The Highest Stage of Capitalism.* New York: International Publishers, 1939.
Le Riverend, J. *Historia económica de Cuba.* Havana: Edición Revolucionaria, 1971.
——. *La Habana: biografía de una provincia.* Havana: Academia de la Historia, 1959.
Leyva y Aguilera, H. *La isla de Cuba y sus caminos de hierro.* Havana: Imprenta Mercantil, 1874.
Lilley, S. *Hombres, máquinas e historia.* Madrid: Editorial Ciencia Nueva, 1967.
Locklin, P. *Economics of Transportation.* Chicago: Richard D. Irving, 1951.
López Goicochea, F., and J. Parés. *Legislación del transporte.* Havana, 1954.
Loveira, C. *De los 26 a los 35.* Havana, 1918.
Luchas obreras contra Machado. Havana: Editorial Ciencias Sociales, 1973.
Martínez Campos, M. *Proyecto del Ferrocarril Central.* Madrid, 1880.
Martínez Escobar, M. *Historia de Remedios.* Havana: Montero, 1944.
Martínez Moles, T. *Epítome de la historia de Sancti Spíritus.* Havana: Imprenta Siglo XX, 1936.
Marx, C. *El Capital.* Havana: Editorial Nacional, 1963.
——. *Fundamentos de la crítica de la economía política.* Havana: Editorial de Ciencias Sociales, 1970.
Marx, C., and F. Engels. *Obras escogidas.* 2 vols. Moscow: Lenguas Extranjeras, 1955.
May, B., and Company. *Almanaque mercantil de La Habana.* Havana, 1864.
Menéndez Pidal, R. *Los caminos de la historia de España.* Madrid: Editorial Cultura Hispánica, 1951.
Menshikov, S. *Millionarios y mánagers.* Moscow: Editorial Progreso, n.d.
Moody, John. *The Railroad Builders.* New Haven: Yale University Press, 1919.
Morazé, C. *El apogeo de la burguesía.* Barcelona: Editorial Labor, 1965.
Moreno Fraginals, M. *El ingenio, complejo económico social cubano del azúcar.* 3 vols. Havana: Ciencias Sociales, 1978.
Overton, R. *Gulf to the Rockies.* Austin: University of Texas Press, 1951.
Pérez, H. *Economía política del capitalismo.* Havana: Editorial Orbe, 1976.
Pérez de la Riva, Francisco. *El café.* Havana: J. Montero, 1944.
Pérez de la Riva, Juan. *El barracón.* Havana: Editorial Ciencias Sociales, 1975.
——. "El monto de la inmigración forzada." *Revista de la Biblioteca Jose Martí,* año 64, no. 1 (January–April, 1974).
——. "Los recursos humanos de Cuba al comenzar el siglo." In *Anuario de Estudios Cubanos* 1. Havana: Editorial de Ciencias Sociales, 1975.
Pezuela, J. *Diccionario geográfico, estadístico e histórico de la isla de Cuba.* 5 vols. Madrid: Imprenta Mellado, 1863–66.
Pino Santos, O. *El asalto a Cuba por la oligarquía financiera norteamericana.* Havana: Editorial Casa de las Américas, 1973.
Pirala, A. *Anales de la guerra de Cuba.* Madrid: González Rojas, Editores, 1895.
Pompeyo, A. *El tratado anglo-cubano.* Havana, 1905.
Portell Vilá, Herminio. *Historia de Cárdenas.* Havana: Talleres Gráficos Cuba Intelectual, 1928.
Porter, R. P. *Industrial Cuba.* New York: Putnam's Sons, 1899.

Primeles, L. *Crónica cubana*. Havana: Editorial Habanera, 1932.

Quesada y Arango, R. de *Informe expresivo de las causas que han motivado hasta ahora la construcción de caminos*. Havana: Imprenta del Gobierno y Capitanía General, 1832.

Quintero, J. M. *Apuntes para la historia de la isla de Cuba con relación a la ciudad de Matanzas*. Matanzas: Imprenta del Ferrocarril, 1878.

Rebello, Carlos. *Estados relativos a la producción azucarera de la isla de Cuba*. Havana: Imprenta del Gobierno, 1860.

Rivero Muñiz, J. *El movimiento laboral cubano duranto el periodo 1906–1911*. Las Villos: Universidad Central, 1962.

———. *El movimiento obrero durante la primera intervención*. Las Villas: Universidad Central de Las Villas, 1961.

Robbins, M. *The Railway Age*. London: Penguin Books, 1962.

Robinson, A. G. *Cuba and the Intervention*. New York: Longman's, 1905.

Roig de Leuchsenring, E. *Historia de la Enmienda Platt*. Havana: Editorial de Ciencias Sociales, 1973.

Sagebién, J., and A. H. Lanier. *Informe sobre el Ferrocarril de Cienfuegos & Villa Clara*. Havana: Imprenta del Gobierno y Capitanía General, 1848.

Sagra, Ramon de la. *Historia física, política, y natural de la isla de Cuba (Suplemento: Cuba en 1860)*. Paris: Hachette, 1863.

Salas Quiroga, J. *Viajes. Isla de Cuba*. Madrid: Imprenta Boix, 1840.

Santa Cruz, F. J. *Historia de familias cubanas*. Havana: Editorial Hércules, 1940–50.

Savage, C. *An Economic History of Transport*. London: Hutchinson, 1959.

Serrano, V. *Crónicas del primer ferrocarril de Cuba*. Havana: Departamento de Orientación Revolucionaria, 1973.

Silva, A. *Cuba y el mercado azucarero mundial*. Havana: Editorial de Ciencias Sociales, 1975.

Smith, R. F. *The United States and Cuba: Diplomacy and Business*. New Haven: Yale University Press, 1960.

The Tarafa Bill. New York: Evening Post Printing, 1923.

Torrente, M. *Bosquejo económico-político de la isla de Cuba*. Havana: Imprenta de Barcini, 1853.

Tortella Casares, G. *Los orígines del capitalismo español*. Madrid: Tecnos, 1973.

United Fruit Company: Un caso de dominio imperialista en Cuba. Havana: Ciencias Sociales, 1976.

Vaughan, W. *The Life and Work of Sir William Van Horne*. New York: Century Company, 1920.

Venegas, H. "Apuntes sobre la decadencia trinitaria en el siglo XIX." *Islas*, no. 46 (September–December 1973): 214–23.

Voigt, F. *Economía de los sistemas de transporte*. Mexico: Fondo de Cultura Económica, 1964.

Wood, Leonard. *Civil Report of the Military Governor*. Havana: n.p., 1901–3.

Ximeno, A. *Origen y construcción de los ferrocarriles de Cuba*. Havana: Imprenta Rambla y Bouza, 1912.

Zanetti, O. "El comercio exterior de la República neocolonial." In *Anuario de estudios cubanos*, vol. 1. (Havana: Editorial de Ciencias Sociales, 1975), 47–126.

Zaragoza, J. *Las insurreciones en Cuba*. Madrid: Imprenta M. Hernández, 1872.

Journals (Havana)

Anuario Azucarero de Cuba
Anuario de Estudios Cubanos
El Avisador Comercial
Bohemia
Boletín Ferroviario
Carteles
Casa
Cuba Económica y Financiera
Cuba Importadora e Industrial
Cuba Review
Delegación
Eco de Caminos
El Economista
Fundamentos
Gaceta de los Ferrocarriles de la isla de Cuba
Gaceta oficial de la República de Cuba
Moody's Manual of Investments
Revista Bimestre Cubana
Revista de Agricultura
Revista de Ferrocarriles
Revista Económica

Newspapers (Havana)

El Camagüeyano
Diario de la Marina
La Discusión
Heraldo de Cuba
Hoy
La Lucha
El Mundo
La Noche
Nueva Luz
Prensa de La Habana
Prensa Libre
Revolución

Interviews

Agüero, Ernesto. Camagüey, May 19, 1974.
Alemar, Ramón. Santiago de Cuba, June 21, 1974.
Carranza, Norberto. Havana, May 7, 1974.
Escobar, Rafael. Camagüey, May 15, 1974.
García, José. Morón, May 22, 1974.

Goñi, Angel. Morón, May 23, 1974.
Louit, Octavio. Havana, January 6, 1978.
Olivera, Alberto. Camagüey, May 15, 1974.
Roríguez, Ricardo. Havana, May 8, 1974.
Ruiz, Ignacio Filiberto. Havana, May 13, 1974.
Soltura, José. Morón, May 21, 1974.
Tornavaca, Sebastián. Camagüey, May 15, 1974.
Torres, Antonio. Havana, April 5, 1974.
Tur, Manuel. Havana, April 5, 1974.
Vázquez Galego, Alvaro. Camagüey, May 16, 1974.
Victoria, Rafael. Camagüey, May 17, 1974.

Index

Association of Estate Owners. *See* Asociación
Nacional de Hacendados
Atlantic, 20
Atrevido, 138
Australia sugar mill, 138
Austria, 20, 91, 134
Auténtico government, 377, 378
Ayllón, Cecilio, 108

Bahía, 148, 110, 167
Bahía Honda, 5, 158
Bainoa, 261
Baldwin, M., 32
Baldwin Locomotive Company of Philadel-
phia, 116
Baltimore & Ohio Railroad, 20
Banagüises, 42, 55, 76, 98, 103, 188, 189
Banco de Comercio, 69, 70–71, 73, 96–97,
174–75, 183
Banco de Cuba, 68, 96
Banco de Fomento Agrícola e Industrial, 371
Banco Español de la Isla de Cuba, 96
Banco Nacional de Cuba, 371
BANDES (Banco de Desarrollo Económico
y Social), 391, 392, 393, 396
Banés, 5, 302
Bank of America, 380
Baracoa, 292
Baragua, 33, 285, 291
Barrio, José, 151
Barrios, Carlos Zacarías, 364
Bartes, Francisco, 362, 384
Basque contract laborers, 72
Batabanó, 2, 5, 11, 12, 22, 33, 34, 50, 53, 72, 80,
86, 102, 127, 161, 187, 250
Batista, Fulgencio, 372, 379–80, 385, 387–95,
397, 399, 409
Bavaria, 20
Bayamo, 67, 141, 355; heights of, 33, 53, 98
Bayona, Casa, 3
Bay Steamship Company. *See* Compañía de
Vapores de la Bahía
Beattie sugar mills, 289
Bejucal, 28, 31, 34, 56
Bejucal-Madruga-Coliseo mills, 6
Belgium, 20, 35, 58, 91, 167, 331
Bemba (Jovellanos), 7, 40–41, 44, 45, 55, 76,
88, 103, 119
Bemba-Colon-Macagua Line, 76
Beola and Company, 67, 140
Bermeja, 102

Berwind, J. E., 294
Betancourt, Pedro, 55
Betancourt, Tomas Pío, 48
Bolondrón, 55, 75, 102
Boniato, 68
Bonilla, Raúl Cepero, 379
Boquerón, 356
Bosch, Andrés Otero, 310, 311
Boston, 87; sugar mill, 270
Botanical Garden, 26, 35, 37
Boudet, Francisco, 67
Bourbon mercantilism, 106
Brady, Anthony, 216
Braithwaite locomotives, 31
Bramosio, Antonio Fernández, 129
Brazil, 58
Bridgewater canal, 10
British North American colonies, 1
Brook, Thomas, 66, 67, 140
Brunet, Casa, 61
Brussels, 20
Bucarely, Antonio M. (governor), 11
Budweis, 20
Buenaventura, 22, 33
Bull, H. W., 294
Bustamante Piélago, Antonio G., 174, 189

Caballero de Rodas, Antonio, 128, 138
Cabañas, 5
Cabello, Felix, 73
Cacicedo, Esteban, 384
Cagigal, 37
Caguaguas, 139
Caibarién, 5, 52, 158, 263, 265, 269, 310
Caimanera, 67, 394
Caja de Jubilaciones, 307, 308, 354, 362
Calabazar, 139
Calero, Marcelino, 21, 22
Calimete, 137
Calvo, Nicolás, 3, 10, 106
Camagüey, 5, 47–49, 88, 128, 139, 169, 182,
198, 222, 227, 231, 265–67, 270, 274–75, 279,
282–85, 290, 301–15; uprising in, 127, 128;
province of, 205, 210, 211, 229, 258, 263,
269, 273, 286, 328, 338, 339, 342, 346, 358,
359, 360, 361, 369; city, 314–20, 328, 344,
364, 388, 395, 397
Camino Real de Cuba, 141
Caminos de Hierro de la Habana, 53, 72, 73,
77, 80, 86–97; company of, 38, 77, 97, 102,
112